NORTH AMERICA'S MARITIME MUSEUMS:

An Annotated Guide

Hartley Edward Howe

Dedicated to the memory of
Robert Howe Baker, 1927-1983,
who loved the historic small craft of America
and devoted much of his life to their discovery,
restoration, and preservation.

NORTH AMERICA'S MARITIME MUSEUMS:
An Annotated Guide

Copyright © 1987 by Hartley Edward Howe

Library of Congress Cataloging in Publication Data
Howe, Hartley Edward.
   North America's Maritime Museums
   1. Navigation—United States—History. I. Title.
VK23.H68 1985   387.5'0973   83-1442
ISBN 0-8160-1001-3

Composition by Facts On File/Maxwell Photographics
Jacket and Interior Design by Oksana Kushnir

10 9 8 7 6 5 4 3 2 1

CONTENTS

INTRODUCTION

In its chapter on the materials of history, *The Harvard Guide to American History* notes that "In addition to the written sources of history, there exists a variety of nondocumentary sources of information and understanding in the form of three-dimensional survivals from the past—both man-made and natural. To view Ford's Theater or drive through the Donner Pass, to examine a flintlock musket or the Spirit of St. Louis, to observe the tools and processes related to spinning and weaving yields a wealth of facts and impressions, available in no other way, about the events, people, and ideas of the past."

The *Harvard Guide* might equally well have used as its examples "to stand on the quarterdeck of Old Ironsides, to savor the narrow streets and ancient buildings that survive from New York's seaport district of sailing ship days, or to examine a whaleship and whaleboats with their gear, a sperm-oil press and the casks, of the whaling industry." For no three-dimensional survivors of the past will yield richer and more vivid facts and impressions than those related to our maritime and naval history. Nor is their interest limited to history-writing scholars. Often strikingly beautiful, their past in many cases studded with dramatic incidents, ships and artifacts have broad appeal to everyone interested in our maritime heritage.

Today there are more such three-dimensional survivors of our maritime past preserved and accessible than ever before. As a result of dedicated enthusiasts and a striking growth in public interest in recent decades, not only maritime museums but ships of the past, both sail and steam, can be visited on every coast and many inland lakes and rivers of the United States and Canada.

This multiplication of sites has not been matched by the availability of information about them, however. The would-be visitor may have real difficulty in learning about a good many of them—or in some cases even in becoming aware that they exist. Some of the most interesting sites are little known outside their immediate area, and not always there. To plan visits to such places requires poking through a raft of hard-to-find local and state guidebooks, writing tourist agencies, and in the end often depending on luck or guess-directions from a local gas-station attendant.

The purpose of this guide is to remedy the confusion by telling what ships and museums can be visited—and where. The guide is inclusive rather than selective, designed for the average traveler rather than the student with sharply focused historical queries. The entries are not concerned with critical analyses or collection inventories, rather they try to tell enough about each place so the traveler can decide whether he or she would like to visit it.

The guide also includes brief sections on the early maritime history of various regions, lakes, rivers, and ports. Necessarily highly compressed, these background notes give a taste of the riches of the past and will, one hopes, lead the reader to explore further. As veteran travelers know, the pleasures of visiting new places are enhanced in direct proportion to what they have learned about those places.

Early in the preparation of the guide the decision was made to broaden its coverage to include Canada. The decision proved a most happy one; not only did it permit the inclusion of a number of ships and oustanding museums, but Canada's maritime and naval past offer a fresh perspective that often provides an interesting counterpoint to the American one.

As the preparation of the guide got fully under way it quickly became apparent that there were far more places of maritime interest in the United States and Canada than originally thought. "New" ships and museums kept turning up, from sources that included obscure press references, travelers' reports, and suggestions made by staff members of other museums. The result is a guide with 261 entries, more than double the number envisioned at the outset. With such numbers involved, and sites scattered over a continent, the original plan of visiting each place could not be carried out in any reasonable time span. Nevertheless, the great majority of the entries are based on the writer's personal visits, including practically all the reports on ships and museums on the ocean coasts of the two nations and a great many of those on the inland lakes. The remainder are described on the basis of their own information materials, backed up in many cases by telephone interviews with staff.

A brief summary will give an idea of the variety and interest of the entries. Ten or so tall-masted merchant sailing ships and barks and roughly about the same number of coastal and fishing schooners are on display in harbors from Lunenberg to Honolulu. Commercial steam is largely represented by lake steamers and river tugs, plus a huge transatlantic luxury liner and a Liberty ship, both berthed on the Pacific Coast. There are also a number of specialized government vessels such as survey ships, ice breakers, and lightships.

Early naval vessels are scarce: two famous frigates of the newly created United States Navy and one steam warship, all from the late 19th and early 20th centuries, are all that survive afloat. However, a whole fleet of more recent U.S. Navy ships (larger in number than many of the world's navies today) is on display in ocean harbors and inland lakes and river ports. Almost all World War II veterans, ranging from submarines to battleships, have been saved from the scrap heap and many have become war memorials. Together these ships provide a unique record of a climactic era of naval warfare.

There is another group of vessels of great interest on exhibition: some 16 modern recreations of historic ships of the 16th to the 19th centuries. If these recreations cannot claim to be three-dimensional survivors from the past, in the same sense as original vessels that have been preserved, nevertheless these reincarnations embody such scholarly research in their design and construction that they are of immense help in visualizing long-vanished ships and their roles in maritime history. Many were built in connection with anniversary celebrations of the European exploration and early settlement of North America. All are seaworthy vessels, and some have been sailed across the Atlantic like their namesakes of long ago.

There are also a number of replicas of 19th-century canal boats, boats that were important in the western expansion of America. None of the original craft survive.

Spectacular though they are, the ships are nevertheless only a part, and the smaller part, of the three-dimensional witnesses of the maritime past. Far greater in number and often equal in interest are the artifacts, the objects and relics of every kind that have been preserved in museums across the United States and Canada. Ranging from the salvaged remains of entire small vessels to the personal effects of long-gone sea captains, from harpoons to ship models, these collections are of inestimable historical value and of broad popular appeal. The traveler will find them not only in North America's handful of large and famous maritime museums but in many smaller institutions too, where they are often more sharply focused on a port or region. Some of the most interesting exhibits are in the little-publicized maritime galleries of general museums. The maritime artifacts in the cherished collections of small local historical societies often have a special personal flavor that gives the visitor a unique sense of closeness to mariners and ships of the past. The traveler will also come upon interesting collections in such unexpected places as public libraries, art galleries, and great universities.

Some museums with important maritime exhibits are among the oldest in the country, but many were founded in recent decades and a number in just the past few years—another reflection of the burgeoning public interest in the maritime past.

Visiting a large portion of this diverse and geographically scattered group of ships and museums for the preparation of this guide was a demanding experience for the writer in terms of time and travel, but a vastly enriching experience in terms of seeing, enjoying, and learning. It is not only the ships and museums that are teachers either. As the traveler quickly finds, each coast, each port, has it own distinctive geography and history, beauty, and flavor to be discovered and savored.

At the same time, visiting a variety of diverse ports the traveler comes to recognize certain recurring events, problems, and experiences that help to provide a better understanding of our maritime past. Hinterlands were (and are) all-important to a port, it seems; the essential ingredient being not a fine deep-sheltered harbor but a hinterland that produced cargoes or customers. Witness San Pedro. Again, the fact that 19th-century ports from New Orleans to Newburyport found shipping hindered by bars of silt across the entrance channel perhaps gives a clue to a not so obvious interaction between farmland erosion and maritime enterprise. Some broad trends are hammered home. Almost everywhere the traveler finds that once flourishing shipyards saw their markets slip away when they failed to adapt, first to a shift in demand from wooden hulls to those of iron and steel, then from sail to steam. Even more universally the traveler finds that in roughly the same period after the Civil War, American ports saw their harbors increasingly taken over by foreign vessels as the number of American flag ships in world commerce dwindled.

Above all, increasing familiarity with the maritime

past of many coasts and ports makes one fact more than ever clear: in the great age of sail, ship and sailor were constantly at risk. The account of many a master mariner or famous ship closes abruptly with the words "lost at sea." With perverse pride, scarcely a section of the East Coast from Cape Breton to Cape Fear was not known to its residents as the "graveyard of the Atlantic." The rock-bound coast of the Pacific Northwest had a fearsome—and justified— reputation. The wild autumn gales that sweep the Great Lakes took a toll of hundreds of ships and thousands of lives. The disasters of whalers and the banks fishermen are legendary to this day. We enjoy the rich heritage of our maritime past; we must not forget the grim price that was paid by many of those who created it.

A word on the structure of the book is in order. The guide is organized entirely on a geographical basis. Three major divisions, the Atlantic Coast, the Pacific Coast and the great heartland of North America, are in turn divided as far as possible into regions that share common maritime backgrounds. Within regions, the guide reflects the pattern of the sections of the coast, bays, lakes, and rivers, following where possible the likely routes of the automobile traveler. Necessarily to some extent arbitrary, the sequence is clearly laid out in the table of contents. The index permits the reader to locate entries alphabetically and plan his own sequence.

Every effort has been made to incorporate up-to-date and accurate information about admission charges and the times and seasons that ships and museums are open to visitors. Readers should be aware, however, that such information is subject to change, not only from year to year but within a season. Travelers would be well advised to telephone ahead to check for possible changes, particularly in spring and fall when schedules tend to be uncertain.

Inevitably, this guide could never have been written without the help and cooperation of many people. To name them all would be impossible, but particular thanks must be given to the generous museum staff, both professional and volunteer, who opened their cherished museums at times or seasons when they were usually closed to visitors, often driving from a distance and on extremely short notice to do so.

A special note of thanks is due to Wilmot Ragsdale who drew on his recollections as a Time/Life correspondent in World War II to tell readers what it was like when a German shell hit the battleship *Texas* off Cherbourg.

The permissions received to use a number of quotations from published works are very much appreciated. Specific acknowledgments and credits are listed elsewhere but the writer would like to give particular thanks to J. Bryan III for permission to quote from his book *Aircraft Carrier*, a vivid firsthand account of the carrier *Yorktown* in action in the Paific. Mr. Bryan's fine book, which is happily still in print, deserves to be read in its entirety. This is true also of William Sclater's *Haida*, which gives an exciting account of the battle record of the famous Canadian destroyer.

Credits and acknowledgments for the photographs that illustrate this guide will also be found elsewhere in these pages. I am grateful to the many museums and ships that sent in pictures for consideration.

My list of acknowledgments would not be complete without grateful recognition of the cheerful patience and wise counsel of Dr. Eleanora Schoenebaum, Editorial Director of Facts On File Publications. As the guide doubled in size while deadline after deadline slipped quietly overboard, she never revealed dismay but continued to provide the positive support that did a great deal to bring the book to a successful conclusion.

And a very special note of gratitude is due the hands-on editor, Ms. Ellen Meltzer, who dealt valiantly and successfully with the innumerable details of preparation for publication.

And, finally, my warm thanks to Mrs. Eunice Healey whose concern for the proper presentation of the copy often led her to put aside other obligations to decipher, type, and retype battered drafts with skill and accuracy.

PART ONE

WHERE IT ALL BEGAN: ATLANTIC AND GULF COASTS

I.
NEW ENGLAND
(AND ITS STEPCHILD LONG ISLAND)

The Hub of the (Yankee) Universe: Boston
North of Boston to the Piscataqua
Where the Piscataqua Meets the Sea
Way Down East
South of Boston and Into the Old Colony
The Old Colony II: Cape Cod
The Old Colony III: The Whaling Towns
Narragansett Bay
Along the Connecticut Shore
The Island Like a Great Whale

There's no better place to start the search for America's maritime heritage than in New England, for here much of that heritage was born. Driven by harsh economic necessity, New Englanders turned to the sea to lift them above bare survival on hardscrabble farms. To the shipyards that soon lined New England rivers came timbers from New England's great forests; out of the yards came everything from fishing smacks to great ships known around the world.

New England fishing fleets fed landsmen in faraway islands and distant continents. New England whaleships lit the western world with spermaceti candles. New England trading ships found new markets from Nootka Sound to the Spice Islands. New England merchants built sparely beautiful houses on profits earned in Canton and Mauritius, in Sumatra and Jamaica. And from along the great harbors and tiny coves that line New England's rugged coasts came men who lived—and often died—afloat in the most dangerous and demanding of professions.

In New England, there is no better place to start than Boston—if not exactly the Hub of the Universe as its inhabitants once boasted, at least the hub of maritime New England. Where but in Boston does a carved fish, the Sacred Cod symbolizing dependence on the sea, hang in the state legislative chambers?

The Hub of the (Yankee) Universe: Boston

Coming into Boston by air, it is easy to see what made the city a great port. To be sure, the growing city has nibbled away at rivers and inlets over the centuries, blurring the aboriginal edges as islands and marshlands turn into runways and office buildings. Nevertheless, the main outlines remain: a great outer harbor, sheltered from the Atlantic by a handful of rocky islets, an inner harbor with many indentations and four entering rivers, and 4,000 acres of sheltered anchorage. The Puritan immigrants who settled here in 1630 moved with determination and intelligence to make the most of these assets—and succeeded. In seven decades Bostonians turned the wilderness into the third largest port in the burgeoning British empire, exceeded only by the ancient cities of London and Bristol in the mother country.

From the beginning, the history of Boston long continued to be intertwined with ships and the sea. By the Revolution, the shipyards of Boston and smaller towns of New England were launching two-thirds of all the vessels built in the American colonies—and nearly one-third of all English-owned ships were American built. Boston waters drank the tea dumped to dramatize the Colonial grievances that led to the Revolution. The closure of Boston Harbor was Britain's way of punishing the unruly Americans. Here in Boston was built, and is today preserved, the most famous and beloved vessel of the United States Navy. Here was based the seaborne trade around the Horn to the Pacific Northwest, so much so that the Northwest Indians who sold their furs to American ships came to call all Americans, wherever they came from, "Boston men."

Here in Boston were financed, designed, built, and owned the most famous and successful of the great clipper ships. And here the movement for sailors' rights against the tyranny of the quarterdeck was born and fostered by an undergraduate who dropped out of Harvard to go to sea.

Once the premier port of North America, Boston has long since been outstripped by rivals down the coast, closer to the interior of the nation that provides cargoes for exports and markets for imports. The city's appreciation of her maritime heritage remains strong, however, and there is much to see.

Any tour of Boston's maritime heritage properly begins with a look at Old Ironsides, now berthed in the waters where she was launched almost two centuries ago.

"Ay, tear her tattered ensign down! Long has it waved on high, And many an eye has danced to see That banner in the sky;" declared generations of American schoolchildren. "Beneath it rung the battle shout, And burst the cannon's roar;" they went on, "—The meteor of the ocean air Shall sweep the clouds no more."

Oliver Wendell Holmes was stirred to write "Old Ironsides" by the announcement in 1830 that the frigate *Constitution* was condemned to be broken up as unseaworthy. Thanks in large part to public response to his poem, the meteor of the ocean air still sweeps the sky: Old Ironsides was saved and rebuilt in 1833. After a number of subsequent rebuildings she is still afloat in Boston Harbor not far from where she was launched in 1797.

The tall frigate—her masts are as high as a 20-story building—is a striking sight as she towers over the Boston Navy Yard in Charlestown, across the Charles River from old Boston. But the visitor will get much more out of his ship tour if he first visits the USS Constitution Museum, lodged in a handsome old granite yard building opposite the dock. Besides artifacts relating to the ship, the museum is outstanding for imaginative displays explaining how the *Constitution* was built, sailed, and fought.

Near the museum entrance, full-scale mock-ups of shipwrights at work on the *Constitution*'s frames make clear how the ribs and planking of a late 18th-century wooden ship were put together. A reconstruction of the berth deck shows how the crew slept in hammocks slung from the overhead deckbeams. A seven-foot model of the frigate with all sails set, gives an easily grasped overall view that helps visitors understand what will later be seen on the ship herself.

A grim reminder of the harsh discipline felt necessary to keep the ship in fighting trim is a reproduction of the log of punishments administered while *Constitution* was on the Mediterranean station. Several unfortunates, courtmartialed for drunkenness or fighting, received three or four dozen lashes with the cat-o'nine-tails. One unhappy man, convicted of treasonous correspondence with the British, was flogged through the fleet; no note indicates whether he lived through it. Nearby is posted, without comment, the Navy Regulations of the time; 12 lashes were the maximum theoretically allowed.

Highlights of the displays, many of particular interest to young people but not to be missed by anyone, include:

- a slide film of the problems faced by the ship's surgeons during the cruise in which *Constitution* fought the *Java*;

Figure 1
The frigate *Constitution*, the oldest U.S. Navy ship in commission, takes her annual "turnaround" cruise down Boston Harbor and back to her berth at the old Navy Yard. Launched in 1797, Old Ironsides is probably the best known and most loved of America's historic ships

- a complete fighting top, removed from the *Constitution* during renovation, into which the visitor can clamber and exercise his imagination;
- a large sail on its yardarm; halyards attached so the visitor can hoist it up a section of mast;
- a major wall display, identifying by name five actual members of the ship's company—a surgeon's mate, the sailing master, a Marine sergeant, an able-bodied seaman, and a ship's boy—and explaining what each one did during a day at sea;
- an ingenious video quiz in which the visitor can put himself in the place of the commodore aboard the *Constitution*, commanding a squadron of several ships during a transatlantic passage to the Mediterranean. Typical problems—a storm scatters the squadron, supplies run low, and so forth—are flashed on the screen. The visitor can choose from several suggested responses, then press a button to learn whether he made the right decision.

USS *Constitution* Museum is at the Charlestown Navy Yard. Open all year. January through March, 10 a.m. to 4 p.m.; April 1 to Labor Day, 9 a.m. to 5 p.m. Admission: $2.00; seniors, $1.50; children 6 to 16, $1.00. Library open to researchers by appointment. USS *Constitution* Museum, Charlestown Navy Yard, P.O. Box 1812, Boston, Massachusetts 02129. Telephone (617) 426-1812.

Still a commissioned ship of the United States Navy, the *Constitution* is manned by Naval personnel. Although over the years the old frigate has been rebuilt so many times that only 10 percent of her timbers are original, the work has been done with such care and fidelity that a visit aboard is a journey back in time to the first years of the Navy of the young republic.

The *Constitution* won her fame during the War of 1812 when she successively defeated in battle three British frigates and a sloop of war. She was an unusual ship from the beginning. Larger and more heavily armed than the standard frigate of her day, she was designed on the same principle as the pocket battleship of World War II—able to outgun any vessel of her size, and to outrun any vessel large enough to defeat her. During the battle with HMS *Guerriere*, the British cannon balls bounced from her sides and ever since she has been *Old Ironsides*.

The visitor senses this when he steps aboard the ship; his first impression is likely to be the *Constitution's* solidity and size. More than 200 feet long on deck, she carried a crew of 450 men. Her three principal anchors weigh almost three tons apiece, and her bulwarks are higher than a man's head. The visitor tours the ship with a group, guided by a crewman from today's Navy. Here an earlier visit to the museum pays off; while the guides do an excellent job, of necessity they cannot give the detailed background provided by the museum exhibits. Some little things to watch for during the tour:

- the individual names given the 24-pounders on her gun deck—"Victory or DEATH," "Liberty Forever," "Jumping Billy";
- the ship's wheel, taken from the British frigate *Java* after she was defeated in battle;
- the grog tub—the U.S. Navy didn't go dry until just before World War I.

USS *Constitution*, at dockside, Boston Naval Shipyard. Open every day all year, from 9:30 a.m. to 3:30 p.m. Admission: free. The frigate is in active commission in the United States Navy. Telephone (617) 242-5670.

After his visit to the Navy of 1800, the visitor may want to stroll down the dock to take a look at the Navy of World War II. In striking contrast to the *Constitution* is the USS *Cassin Young*, tied up on the opposite side of the pier. The *Young* is a destroyer escort, roughly the equivalent of a frigate in the modern Navy. The ship is currently deactivated and displayed by the National Park Service.

Visitors should not leave without taking a look around the Navy yard itself. Founded in 1800, for a century and three-quarters the yard built, repaired, overhauled, and converted naval vessels. Over the years, more than 200 naval vessels went down the ways, starting with the USS *Suffolk County*, an LST, in 1956.

Although no longer an active naval base, the yard retains many of the beautiful old buildings of granite and brick built during the nineteenth century. Particularly striking is the commandant's house, on the hillside overlooking the yard. Once the quarters of such authentic naval heroes as Isaac Hull and William Bainbridge, the three-story brick house has an unusual double bowfront. According to a recent history of the yard, "Local terminology for the double bowfront house has for years been an unflattering

anatomical reference. The story has grown that the original architect . . . was so annoyed with the lack of interest displayed by the Commodore that the architect spurted, 'Well, then, what design would you have me make it?' 'My arse,' replied the Commandant." Apparently, so the story goes, the architect complied.

Charlestown is, of course, the site of the Battle of Bunker Hill and the Navy Yard is at the foot of the hill bearing the Bunker Hill monument. The battlefield itself has long since been built over but most travelers will want to visit the 220-foot granite obelisk that marks the American battle line.

Now back across the river to old Boston proper. To encourage visits to the city's waterfront area, a "Harbor Walk" has been devised, described as "a walk through Boston's maritime history," in a booklet available at many places downtown. Besides visiting the New England Aquarium, historic Fanueil Hall, and the Children's Museum, the walk begins and ends at places of considerable maritime interest.

Starting point is the Old State House at the head of State Street, the "Great Street" leading down to the waterfront. Within the Old State House is the small but choice Museum of the Bostonian Society. Much of it is taken up with historical antiquities—fine furniture, silver, portraits—related to the social, political, and cultural life of Boston from the 17th to the late 19th centuries. On the second floor, however, is the marine gallery with a fine collection of ship models and nautical prints and paintings, largely 19th century.

Among the most interesting is a large model of the side-wheeler *Portland*; the ill-fated coastal steamer wrecked in 1898 on the overnight run from Boston to Portland. One hundred seventy-six lives were lost in a fierce storm known forever after as the "Portland Gale." Other models include the medium clipper *Great Admiral*, 1862, and the 1848 tea clipper *Living Age*. A fine example of the woodcarver's art is a great figurehead, which once stood outside the carver's shop to advertise his trade. There are nice collections of scrimshaw and ships' documents.

The Old State House, erected in 1713, is itself of great interest. The gilded lion and unicorn of the royal arms of England on the gable end are a reminder that this little building once housed not only Boston's town hall and the colony's legislature but the Royal governor. Look out the big windows at the east end of the building and you'll see the spot where confrontation between a mob and British soldiers led to the Boston Massacre. Don't be alarmed by an occasional rumble from the depths below: All is not antiquity here; down below is a station of the Boston subway system.

Bostonian Society Old State House Museum, in the heart of downtown Boston. Open all year, except major holidays. April through October; daily, 9:30 a.m. to 5 p.m.; Sunday; 11 a.m. to 5 p.m. Admission: $1.25; seniors and students, 75 cents; children, 50 cents. Gift shop, books and publications. The Bostonian Society, 206 Washington Street, Boston, Massachusetts 02109. Telephone (617) 242-5655.

Now to the other end of Harbor Walk.

The Boston Tea Party, in which the Sons of Freedom threw overboard British tea as a protest against a hated import tax, was "the catalyst that set off the revolt of the colonies," according to a historian. The Tea Party took place at Griffin's Wharf, now buried under landfill by the expanding city. A tablet was erected in downtown Boston near Atlantic Avenue and Pearl Street to commemorate the event, but a more imaginative memorial is afloat in Boston Harbor itself. At the nearby Congress Street Bridge the brig *Beaver II*, representing one of the Tea Party ships, is tied up alongside a floating museum that tells the story.

Beaver is a converted 82-foot Danish fishing vessel, built of oak. Under the supervision of the late William A. Baker, who designed *Mayflower II*, she was refashioned and rerigged as a typical Colonial brig of the late 18th century, loaded with a cargo of tea, and sailed across the Atlantic in the track of her namesake in time for the Bicentennial.

Young people will be particularly interested in a reenactment of the Tea Party, which takes place every hour or so during the summer months. "Patriots disguised as Indians" rush aboard *Beaver II*, hoist tea chests out of the hold, and hurl them into the harbor. In between there are a few "tea packets" left on deck and the visitor is invited to "make a personal protest" by throwing one overboard (thriftily tied to a line so that it can be hoisted out and used again by the next protester).

The little museum alongside the brig should not be overlooked. A series of visually interesting and well-arranged displays clearly explains the issues that led up to the Tea Party, and its effect on the growing discontent in America. A diorama of Boston in 1773 shows the route taken by the "Indians" from the Green Dragon Inn, where they met, to the ships at Griffin's Wharf. Contemporary documents are shown in facsimile, among them a copy of the East India Company's bill of lading listing the tea cargo that was aboard the three ships in 1773. (Incidentally, a little-known fact that the museum displays make clear is that the tea ships were owned and commanded by Americans from Nantucket.) The museum is enhanced by a number of nice models, including the privateer *Fair American* and a planked model of the Newburyport brig *Topaz*.

An imaginative touch is a little questionnaire in the museum's folder describing the original Tea Party. The visitor is invited to check how much he agrees with such statements as "A crowd of marching men is a threat to peace," and "A clever speaker can turn Bostonians into a mob almost at will." By adding up his score, the respondent can get an analysis of his political inclinations had he been a colonist in the 1770s, with accompanying advice and comment ranging from "Better get out of town or get tarred and feathered!" to "You're a signer of the Declaration of Independence!" The visitor may be surprised at where his answers place him in the political spectrum of 1773.

Brig *Beaver II* and Tea Party Museum Gift shop. Open every day except Thanksgiving, Christmas, New Year's: 9 a.m. to dusk. Admission: $2.75; children 5 to 15, $1.75. Boston Tea Party Ship and Museum, Congress Street Bridge, Boston, Massachusetts 02210. Telephone (617) 338-1773.

The Massachusetts Institute of Technology (MIT) in Cambridge, just across the Charles River, is an interesting but relatively little known museum and center of maritime research. Now a part of MIT's Department of Ocean Engineering, the Francis Russell Hart Nautical Museum is particularly concerned with the history of ship design and construction.

Ship models on display cover many centuries of maritime development, from a Norse round ship of the type probably used by Leif Ericsson and a 12th-century Korean war vessel, to a 1968 steel trawler. Particularly fine is a built-up model of the frigate USS *President*, showing details of her hull construction.

Models of vessels important in the evolution of steamships include Fulton's historic North River steamer called *Clermont*, (commonly known simply as the *Clermont*), and the British paddle steamer *Sirius*, which in 1837 became the first vessel to steam all the way across the Atlantic, thanks to the use of fresh water condensers. The 1874 steam yacht *Turbina* was the first vessel propelled by steam turbines, while the USS *Jupiter*, a Navy collier, was converted to the USS *Langley*, the Navy's first aircraft carrier. Another model shows the 11,000-ton SS *Narrangansett*, which was twice the size of any previous oil tanker when she was built in 1903. Her two masts with leg-of-mutton sails and staysails reflect the past, but her unusual size marked the beginning of a trend that has culminated in the million-ton supertankers of today.

The museum's office and research center are now in a separate building at 265 Massachusetts Avenue, a short distance from the main MIT complex. Here, in banks of file drawers, hung on walls, and stacked in boxes, are ship plans, working drawings, prints,

Figure 2
Brig *Beaver II* crossing Atlantic in nor'easter, repeating 1778 passage of original *Beaver*, the
Boston Tea Party ship.

paintings, photographs, and documents. Still more is stowed away elsewhere for lack of space, to be brought out for special exhibits or loaned to other museums. Among special treasures are half models, whaling paintings and prints, 10,000 Herreshoff working drawings, thousands of yacht photographs, and a portion of the famous Stebbins photographs of Boston Harbor.

Here is enough to keep the enthusiastic amateur and the serious scholar of maritime history alike busy for several lifetimes. The Research Center is open to visitors by appointment: phone ahead to make sure that someone will be on hand.

Francis Russell Hart Memorial Museum. Display area on first floor of Building 5, to the right of the MIT entrance at 55 Massachusetts Avenue, Cambridge. After 5 p.m. and on weekends or holidays, enter at 77 Massachusetts Avenue. First floor model exhibits open every day from 9 a.m. to 10 p.m. Research files and special collections open for researchers by appointment. Admission: free. MIT Museum, 265 Massachusetts Avenue, Cambridge, Massachusetts 02139. Telephone (617) 253-5942.

North Boston to the Piscataqua

A straight line from Boston north to where New Hampshire meets Maine at the Piscataqua River is less than 60 miles. The distance along the rugged coastline is longer, thanks to Cape Ann. Yet in this tiny segment of the Atlantic coast of the United States are five historic ports, famous names in the maritime history of colonial America and the young republic: Marblehead, Salem, Gloucester, Newburyport, all in Massachusetts, and Portsmouth in New Hampshire. Only Gloucester, with its great fishing industry, remains an important port today, but all cherish relics of their maritime heritage.

Salem, of course, had a brief but glorious reign as

queen of the East India trade; not so brief but that its merchants had time to build some of the most beautiful houses in America, still surviving in the midst of the industrial city of today. Marblehead was the premier fishing port of Colonial Massachusetts but was overtaken by her rival Gloucester in the 19th century and today is known primarily as a yachting center. Gloucester remains a great fishing port, having successfully managed the shift from the famous schooners to today's motor trawlers.

North of Cape Ann the coast drops down to low marshy meadows, protected by sandy Plum Island, to where another famous Yankee maritime city, Newburyport, sits at the mouth of the Merrimack River. According to geologists, the Merrimack is probably the Ancient River of New England that over thousands of years carved out the huge valley of Boston Harbor. The river and its valley were buried by the great glacier; when the glacier eventually retreated, a tongue of ice blocked the outflow of the river through its old valley. A lake was formed and the river gradually silted up until it found a new outlet, the present mouth of the Merrimack, 40-odd miles north of Boston. As a result, Boston lacks the great river that would have given it the same access inland that the Hudson gives New York—and the mouth of the Merrimack lacks the deep broad harbor that would have made a major port out of Newburyport.

The low shoreline continues north of the Merrimack across the 16-mile seacoast of New Hampshire all the way to Cape Elizabeth in southern Maine. The Piscataqua River forms much of the boundary between New Hampshire and Maine, and at its mouth is another historic port, Portsmouth, once the terminus of lively river traffic up into New Hampshire, later the site of a famous Navy yard.

Our first stop north of Boston, however, will be inland, at the little exurban town of Andover.

The Addison Gallery in Andover, Massachusetts, is the home of a small but distinguished collection of American paintings, drawings, photographs, and sculpture. As part of a famous secondary school, Phillips Academy, the Gallery is a central element in the school's concern with the teaching of art and its dedication to seeing that students obtain a well-rounded cultural education.

Surprisingly, this non-maritime institution is also the home of a fine collection of ship models—and not run-of-the-bench models, but little ships with some unusual characteristics that make them of special interest. For one thing, rather than being assembled over many years from a wide range of sources like most collections, these ships were built to order in a relatively short time by a handful of top model makers, giving them a unity of construction and approach

rarely found. At the same time, to make it easier to recognize how ships changed and grew over the centuries, all the models were built exactly to the same scale: one-quarter inch to one foot of the original. This enables the visitor to compare the ships in size and shape, as if the originals were being floated side by side.

Great attention was paid to historical accuracy; in some cases two years of research preceded actual construction. The records of the original shipwrights were consulted and, where possible, eyewitness evidence was obtained from men who actually sailed in the ships being modeled. This could not be done today, and was already difficult when the collection was gathered in the early decades of the 20th century. All the larger models and the majority of the smaller ones are built up plank by plank from keel to deck, like the originals, rather than being carved from a single piece of wood. The detail is magnificent, although unfortunately much of it could only be fully appreciated by taking a model out of the case and examining it closely.

Far from being chosen at random, the miniature vessels represent different eras of merchant and naval ships, ranging from Columbus's *Santa Maria* to the Gloucester fishing schooner *Columbia*, built in 1923. Here are some of the highlights of individual models:

- As the wonderfully complete caption in the case points out, the model of the *Dreadnaught* incorporates such fascinating deck details as the passengers' latrine, the casks for meat, sugar, and water, and the pigpen, which looks like just another deckhouse until you look closely and see the bars on the window to keep the pig from getting out. According to notes in the catalog, inside the ship there are mahogany seats and brass cuspidors in the smoking rooms and the bunks in the luxury cabins are made up with red flannel blankets. Unhappily, the visitor has to take these ultimate refinements on faith.
- In the model of Fulton's *Clermont*, the steam engine actually works and can get up a head of steam. Notice the pile of logs just aft the funnel ready to be chucked into the firebox.
- The full-rigged model of the ship *Thatcher Magoun* is the gift of the grandson of the shipowner, for whom the ship was named. In the case with the model is the original ship's log.
- The model of the *Lottie Warren* was given by the daughter of a man who sailed in her on a voyage carrying 1,300 pounds of New England ice to Calcutta.
- The model of the *Corsair*, J.P. Morgan's yacht, was the gift of Junius Morgan, J.P.'s son. The yacht, incidentally, was turned over to the Navy in World War I and won two chevrons for its

service. In the model, a real course is laid out on the miniature charts, which are ready on the bridge.

- A model of *Young America*, a clipper ship, was given by the daughter of a man who sailed in her on a voyage from New York around Cape Horn to San Francisco with a cargo of railroad iron.
- The *Ann McKim* was one of the earliest large vessels built to the lines of the Baltimore clippers, and her specifications were obtained from the grandson of one of the Baltimore builders. The figurehead on the model bears such realistic details as the stylish ringlets of the 1830s.

How did this wonderful collection arrive at a school? The treasurer of Phillips Academy believed that it was important to impress upon the students' minds the beauty of the sailing ship and its contribution to the growth and prosperity of America. A further note in the collection's catalog points out an additional reason why a gallery dedicated to American art should have ship models in its collection. "To an age which thinks of art almost exclusively in terms of easel painting . . . the inclusion of a ship model collection in an art gallery may seem somewhat strange. But the Addison collection . . . was designed to represent an older and perhaps broader understanding of art as an expression of skill as well as talent, of beauty in the fashioning of functional objects, as well as in the fashioning of personal vision; in short, as an expression of the artisan as well as the artist. This concept is older than American art, of course, but it is especially that of a culture in whose beginnings practical purpose and austere beauty were often closely linked. The American concern with ships was more than a matter of growth and prosperity; for the building of successful and beautiful ships—and by extension the preservation of their spirit and beauty in models—is an architectural activity. And is not architecture, even marine-architecture, the 'mother of the arts'?"

The **Addison Gallery of American Art**, part of Phillips Academy in Andover, Massachusetts, is in a Classic Revival building on Chapel Avenue in the academy grounds. Open September through July, Tuesday-Saturday; winter, 10 a.m. to 5 p.m.; Sundays, 2:30 to 5 p.m. Closed national holidays and entire month of August. Admission: free. Addison Gallery of American Art, Phillips Academy, Andover, Massachusetts 01810. Telephone (617) 475-7515.

Now back to the coast, to one of the most historic of American ports:

"A Salem boy in those days was born to the music of windlass chanty and caulker's maul; he drew in a taste for the sea with his mother's milk; wharves and shipyards were his playground; he shipped as boy on a coaster in his early teens, saw Demerara and St. Petersburg before he set foot in Boston; and if he had the right stuff in him, commanded an East-Indiaman before he was twenty-five."

So wrote maritime historian Samuel Eliot Morison about the Salem of the last decade of the 18th century. The port, located on the shore of Massachusetts Bay at the base of Cape Ann, was then the sixth city in the United States and the formidable rival of Boston, 20 miles to the southwest. In the remarkable half-century that followed, the little fishing port of Colonial days flowered into the world famous center of America's East India trade. Pepper, spices, coffee, tin, Indian cottons, poured into the new republic in Salem bottoms, often to be re-exported for a further profit. So dominant was the city in the trade, that in 1833 the wealthiest merchant in Quallah Battoo in the East Indies is said to have believed that Salem was an independent country, rich and important.

To this remarkable port its shipmasters brought home strange and beautiful objects from many parts of the world, particularly Asia. When the East India Marine Society—membership limited to Salem captains who had navigated near or beyond either the Cape of Good Hope or Cape Horn—was formed in 1799, the members included among its purposes, "to form a museum of natural and artificial curiosities." Today their collection, vastly augmented over the years, forms the heart of the magnificent Peabody Museum in Salem.

Like those of many another fine museum, the Peabody's maritime exhibits consist primarily of ship models, paintings, prints, and artifacts. Perfectly true—and most misleading: the Peabody is unique, as much like the average museum as Tiffany's is like the average jewelry store. The Peabody maritime collection as a whole is unmatched for quality, beauty, and both historical and intrinsic interest.

An example: The frigate *Constitution* has probably been modeled more often than any other ship; nearly every sizable collection has at least one Old Ironsides. The Peabody has a *Constitution* model too, a fine big one, beautifully made and absolutely unique. In the display case is a faded letter from Captain Isaac Hull, USN, presenting the model to the East India Marine Society a few months after *Constitution* under his command defeated the *Guerriere*. A museum note explains that the model, floating in a miniature sea of its own, was moored in the center of the banquet table at the Marine Society's dinner honoring Captain Hull and, at the climax of the evening all the brass cannons of the frigate were fired. The broadside not only ended the dinner with a bang, but damaged the rigging of the little ship. Also in the case is a receipt of $12 paid to British prisoners of war for making her shipshape again.

Some of the other treasures:

- A model of the twin-screw steamer *Midas* shows the vessel that in 1844 became first American steamer to enter Chinese ports. No ordinary model, it was made at the time by none other than her famous captain and part owner, the master mariner and shipowner, Robert B. Forbes. (*Midas* is in the steamship gallery.)
- A 40-foot panorama shows an entire whaling voyage in successive scenes. A true primitive, it was painted by a crewman.
- A model of a Merrimack River gundalow was made in 1862 by a river skipper who used his own boat as a model. Nearby, two 30-foot sweeps used on gundalows hang from the ceilings.
- Look particularly for the reconstructed cabin of *Cleopatra's Barge*, America's first ocean-going yacht, built in 1816 for Salem shipping magnate George Crowninshield, Jr. (Easily missed—look for the little door in one corner of East India Hall.) The accompanying collection of Crowninshield portraits and memorabilia includes not only a model of the yacht but her original silk boat flag and most of her cabin furniture. Incidentally, the faces of three Crowninshields—George, his brother, and a cousin—provide fascinating contrasts in Yankee physiognomy.
- One of the earliest known American ship models, a 1750 sloop, has been left unrestored to show the original work.
- The huge—some twelve feet long—model of the Salem ship *Friendship* of 1797 was made on board by the ship's carpenter during an 1803 passage to Sumatra. Built for the captain's son, who was along for the voyage, the model was fitted with guns cast by Indonesian smiths.
- A special exhibit is devoted to one of Salem's most distinguished sons, Nathaniel Bowditch, the sea captain who revolutionized the art of navigation with his treatise *The American Practical Navigator*. The centerpiece is the original Gilbert Stuart portrait of the navigator.
- A 10-foot mural of Crowninshield's Wharf, with Salem ships alongside, was painted in 1806.

The evolution of New England fishing vessels, is portrayed in a series of models, from early heel-tappers (reportedly so-called because their crews spent the stormy winter season making shoes) through the clipper schooners, the later knockabouts, and on to an early steam mackerel seiner. A largely forgotten type of coastal workhorse is the Quincy stone sloop, represented by a big model of the *Star Light*. A contemporary model of a Yankee privateer was made by a ship's carpenter. The collection of steamship models is dominated by a twentieth century note—an enormous (21-foot) model of the *Queen Mary*—but the most interesting steamship paintings are of 19th-century paddlewheelers. A particularly handsome painting shows an American mail steamer leaving Liverpool with Jenny Lind standing on the paddlebox waving goodbye to her British admirers who have come out in harbor craft to see her off.

The museum has been greatly expanded in recent years, but the most striking building remains the oldest, the granite East India Marine Hall, built in 1824. On the walls of the high-ceilinged banquet hall is a beautiful collection of brightly painted ships' figureheads—highlanders, Indian maidens, classical warriors—folk sculpture at its highest level.

Maritime history is only one of the four curatorial departments of the Peabody Museum; the exhibits of ethnology, natural history, and the new department of Asian Export Art have a fascination of their own. Again, many of the most interesting exhibits were brought back to Salem by her shipmasters. The China Trade displays include furniture, paintings, and a beautiful collection of Chinese porcelain, recently expanded when the Peabody Museum absorbed the China Trade Museum in Milton, Massachusetts. The Asian Export Art collection is now believed to be the largest in the world and the Peabody is building a new wing to house it. Small craft, carvings, and weapons, make a fascinating array in the Pacific islands collections. And there is a small but very attractive collection of plants, birds, mammals, and fishes of New England.

The Peabody Museum of Salem is the oldest continuously operating museum in the U.S.; on Liberty Street between Charter Street and the Essex Street Mall. Parking meters on street; parking garage on next block of Liberty Street. Library, photo files, large book and art shop. Open all year except Thanksgiving, Christmas, and New Year's: Monday-Saturday, 10 a.m. to 5 p.m.; Sundays and holidays, 1 to 5 p.m. Admission: $3.00; seniors and students, $2.00; children 6 to 16, $1.50. The Peabody Museum of Salem, East India Square, Salem, Massachusetts 01970. Telephone (offices) (617) 745-1876; (information) (617) 745-9500.

The Peabody Museum is, of course, only one of Salem's treasures, not the least of which is the old waterfront where once her ships arrived almost daily from the far corners of the world.

Salem's old waterfront is centered around the 1819 Custom House facing the Derby Wharf, which stretches half a mile out into the harbor; the area has

Figure 3
Original paneling and most of the original furniture of the saloon of *Cleopatra's Barge*, first
private American yacht, have been reassembled at The Peabody Museum of Salem.

been made a National Historic Site. In the Custom
House itself, the most interesting exhibit is the
Surveyor's Office where Nathaniel Hawthorne
worked when he held the post. Across the hall are the
counters and desks of the public office where ship
captains came to sign their papers; in the fireproof
vault behind it, beautifully paneled, a slide show tells
the story of Salem's years of maritime glory.

The elegant brick Derby House, home of Salem's
most successful merchant, is the other major building
on the Historic Site. Built in 1762, with late 18th and
early 19th-century furnishings, it is open for group
tours, which are given several times a day. This is true
of other buildings on the Site, including the bonded
warehouse in the back of the Custom House building
and the little Scale House nearby.

Salem Maritime National Historic Site is on the waterfront,
along Derby Street. Open all year except for Christmas, 8:30

a.m. to 5 p.m. daily. Reservations are required for the Derby
House tour. Admission: free. Operated by the National
Park Service. Salem Maritime National Historic Site, Salem,
Massachusetts 01790. Telephone (617) 744-4323.

Although today an industrial city, Salem's
treasures do not end on the waterfront. Salem
merchants and shipowners spent their money on
beautiful houses. Chestnut Street, lined with early
19th-century mansions, many by famous architect
Samuel McIntyre, has been called the finest street,
architecturally, in America. Salem's Essex Institute
owns a number of houses open to visitors. In the Institute's own building, down the street from the
Peabody Museum, is a major collection of books,
manuscripts, furniture, and furnishings. And of
course Salem's 17th-century House of the Seven
Gables is on everyone's list.

Now on northward up the coast.

Jutting out into the the Atlantic just northeast of Salem is granite-bound Cape Ann, surrounded by dangerous ledges but with such a good harbor on its south side that it has made Gloucester one of the most famous of American ports. The road along the coast from Salem to Gloucester is a scenic route that passes through the little town of Manchester, once a fishing village but now for more than a century a fashionable summer resort for prosperous Bostonians.

Just before the edge of Gloucester, a side road on the right leads down to Rafe's Chasm, the nearest point on the shore to the "reef of Norman's Woe." Local historians tell us that the *Hesperus* was really wrecked somewhere else, but that Longfellow so liked the name that he moved the tragedy to Norman's Woe. Don't feel cheated; on this coast there were more than enough wrecks to go around.

As the visitor drives into Gloucester from the west, he comes to a great bronze statue, *The Gloucester Fisherman*, on the shore, two or three times life-size. The young fisherman grips the wheel of his schooner, peering ahead to where Banks trawlers are coming up harbor past the reef of Norman's Woe. "They that go down to the sea in ships 1623-1923" is the only legend: Nothing more is needed; here is a very special part of America's maritime heritage.

And a very dangerous one. Each August, flowers are placed at the feet of the bronze fisherman; more flowers dropped into the sea float out on the ebb while the names of Gloucestermen lost at sea in the past year are read aloud. In three and a half centuries of fishing, most of it on the fish-rich Grand Banks and Georges Banks, Gloucester has lost more than 10,000 men—washed off bowsprits, lost in a fog in their dories, gone down with their vessels in a gale. Banks fishing has always been the most dangerous of the seaman's trades, more so than merchant service, more dangerous even than whale hunting.

Gloucester has always been a fishing town. The first settlers in the early 17th-century were rough fishermen, a very different breed from the pious Puritans. In Colonial times, Gloucester and Marblehead together landed more than 60 percent of New England's catch. Although Gloucester fishing declined for a while after the Revolution, the port eventually absorbed the fisheries of the smaller Cape Ann towns and became the nation's principal fishing port. The trade changed over the years as salting down the catch gave way to carrying live fish back to port in salt-water tanks, and later still to packing the catch in ice. The design of Gloucester's famous schooners also changed from time to time as owners experimented with new types, sometimes with disastrous results: A clipper model popular for its speed in bringing fish to market proved all too ready to capsize with all hands.

With the coming of the internal-combustion engine, the last all-sail schooner was launched in 1905. In a few decades sail disappeared entirely; today, the steel-hulled Gloucester fleet is diesel powered.

The story of Gloucester's maritime heritage that has made it the most famous fishing port in America is told in two museums, both interesting and complementary in approach. The Gloucester Fishermen's Museum is described by its director as primarily a teaching museum, set up to explain the skills, gear, and tools of Cape Ann's fishermen and shipwrights. The Museum of Cape Ann History beautifully displays models, paintings, and folk artifacts that are not only significant to Gloucester's past but of great aesthetic and visual interest in themselves.

The Gloucester Fishermen's Museum is housed on the lowest floor of a brick store building in downtown Gloucester. Crammed so full of exhibits that at first glance it seems overstuffed, the museum is actually carefully arranged to tell a coherent story. Successively, the displays describe dory fishing, tub trawling, the evolution of Gloucester schooners, wooden shipbuilding in nearby Essex, and the characteristics of various species of North Atlantic

Figure 4
A hands-on exhibit at the Gloucester Fishermen's Museum helps a young visitor recall the great days of the banks fishing schooners.

fish. There are also artifacts dredged up from the sea, whale skeletons, recipes for enjoying fish at its finest, and a whole section is devoted to a whale-study display.

Retired fishermen are on hand to talk about the exhibits and a high point is their explanation of how all the various pieces of dory gear were used. The line tub, lantern, nippers, mittens, hooks and hook benders, gaffs, clubs, and knives are all demonstrated, dispelling any notion that the dory fishermen simply dropped a line overboard and hauled in the fish. At the push of a button the taped voices of veterans of the age of sail tell of life aboard the banks fishing schooners.

The museum emphasizes a hands-on, learn-by-doing approach, particularly in the shipbuilding section. "Help us shape the mast" says the little sign, and there at hand is a 100-year-old shipwright's tool and a piece of timber. "Try caulking these seams" says the legend next to a mallet, caulking iron, and strips of caulking laid out beside an open seam between two planks, ready to be worked on. The exhibits are particularly fascinating for young people, but few visitors, regardless of age, can resist the temptation to pick up a tool and at least take a whack at it.

Two unusual exhibits are plaster working models from the studio of Leonard Craske, the sculptor of *The Gloucester Fisherman*. One is a companion work to *The Fisherman*: *The Fisherman's Wife*, her child in her arms as she peers out to sea. The other is a bas-relief commemorating a famous Gloucester dory fisherman who was separated from his schooner in a fog and rowed for several days through winter seas to port, his hands frozen to the oars. Neither sculpture was ever erected, but even in miniature they are pretty impressive.

Gloucester Fishermen's Museum. Entrance on the west side of Porter Street, between Rogers and Main. A modest sign marks a small door leading into lowest floor of a brick store building. Open all year except major holidays: Monday-Friday, 12:30 p.m. to 4 p.m.; Saturday, 10 a.m. to 4 p.m.; Sunday, 12:30 p.m. to 4 p.m. Admission: $2; children, $1; families, $5.50. Gloucester Fishermen's Museum, Box 159, Gloucester, Massachusetts 01930. Telephone (617) 283-1940.

The Cape Ann Historical Association is a block from Main Street in Gloucester. The original building is the 1804 house of a merchant sea captain. The beautifully organized museum features American decorative arts and furnishings, but includes a notable maritime section in a handsome new wing. The marine paintings are particularly fine, with what is said to be the nation's largest collection of the work of Fitz Hugh Lane, Gloucester born and bred and recognized as one of America's foremost 19th-century artists. Most of his paintings and drawings are concerned with ships or harbor scenes.

The museum also has an unusual collection of large models of fishing schooners, made for the Gloucester exhibit at the 1893 Columbian Exposition in Chicago. The seven schooners, built with loving accuracy by men familiar with the original vessels, are each fitted with the deck gear for a different type of fishing. With them are earlier models of a heel-tapper, a Chebacco boat, and a pinkie—all distinctive types developed on Cape Ann and predecessors of the famous Gloucester schooners.

A remarkable piece of maritime folk art is a three-dimensional model of a lifesaving crew rescuing wrecked seamen with a lifeline and breeches buoy. Found in a Gloucester attic, the simply carved and painted figures, each some six inches tall, are tremendously appealing. Another fascinating example of Gloucester folk art is a wooden model of the Gloucester waterfront. The tiny houses, simply painted, show the city "as it looked before 1830," according to the man who made it from memory 50 years later.

Museum of Cape Ann History. Library and photo archives. Open all year except the month of February. Tuesday-Saturday, 10 a.m. to 5 p.m. Admission: $2.00; seniors and students, $1.00. Sponsored by Cape Ann Historical Association, 27 Pleasant Street, Gloucester, Massachusetts 01930. Telephone (617) 283-0455.

While on Cape Ann, the visitor should drive out to the tip of the rocky peninsula. There, north of the little village of Rockport, look out to the open Atlantic as the grey combers roll in across the ledges to smash against the cliff base. Due east are the Salvages, which inspired a poem by T.S. Eliot, who sailed these waters as a boy.

Driving north to Newburyport, take Route 133, which carries you to the little coastal town of Essex on the north side of Cape Ann. Never an important port, Essex has a distinction all its own. Here for some 300 years Essex yards have built wooden ships on the banks of the little tidal river. The famous Story Yard still carries on the tradition; the memory of past centuries when there were many yards is preserved in the small Essex Shipbuilding Museum in an old white building, next to where the first settlers are buried on the hill. The museum, manned entirely by volunteers, is closed in the winter; in season visitors will find shipwrights' tools, artifacts, and other relics of the trade.

Continuing north, the traveler comes to Newburyport at the south bank of the Merrimack River at its mouth. A handsome old town, Newburyport is now largely industrial but with many fine old houses, mostly late 18th and early 19th century.

Long the trading center of the lower Merrimack valley, which stretches far up into New Hampshire, the town was once a considerable port. On the eve of the Revolution and for many years afterward about six out of every ten adult males of Newburyport earned their living in a sea-related trade. If not mariners, they were shipwrights, sailmakers, shopkeepers whose shelves were stocked with locally imported goods, rum distillers whose vats were fed with West Indian sugar, merchants, mastmakers, caulkers, and a variety of others.

This was despite the fact that the entrance to the Merrimack River, which provides Newburyport's harbor, was far from easy; a bar built up across the mouth that at low tide blocked the entrance to ships of any size. With only seven feet of water, the swells broke right across the mouth and Newburyport had to set up an elaborate system of day and night signals to warn approaching ships when it was unsafe to enter.

Although the town suffered in the Revolution and old fortunes disappeared, the first decades of the 19th century found it at the height of its maritime prosperity. The little city's property values quadrupled from 1793 to 1807, its wealthy merchants supporting parks, schools, and libraries, and Newburyport rum was nationally famous.

Historians have traced a trading sequence typical of those that built the port. In 1807, an 80-ton sloop took fish, lumber, provisions, and beef to Martinique, and returned with molasses, sugar, and coffee. A bigger Newburyport ship took the sugar and coffee, plus pepper, to Amsterdam, and loaded for the return voyage with Holland gin, nails, paints, paper, and cloth. At the end five thousand dollars' worth of the homely products of forests and fields had been exchanged for manufactures valued at eighty thousand dollars.

The embargo and the subsequent War of 1812 put a lid on the growth of Newburyport's shipping, but a steady flow of commerce continued. The fine new Custom House built in 1836 was an important center of the port for decades before the Civil War and it is highly fitting that it should now be the center of efforts to preserve the city's maritime heritage.

At the Custom House Maritime Museum in Newburyport, are fine ship models, pictures, and artifacts related to the marine activities of the lower Merrimack Valley. The handsome granite Custom House building, designed by the architect of the Washington Monument, went through hard times until rescued by the museum. When Newburyport's foreign trade dwindled to nothing in the early 20th century, the building was sold by the Federal government and passed through various vicissitudes as a hay storeroom, a shoe factory, and a junk shop.

Most appropriately, one room has been recreated as the office of a 19th-century collector of customs, with furnishings of the period, including a high clerk's desk and a sturdy safe, not to mention some Caldwell rum casks, presumably dropped off by an appreciative merchant.

An entire wall is covered by a huge framed sheet of tiny portraits of Newburyport shipmasters from 1792 to 1887. The earliest are cut-out silhouettes, followed successively by drawings, daguerreotypes, and finally photographs.

Newburyport claims to be the birthplace of the United States Coast Guard, since here was built and launched the *Massachusetts*, first vessel of the U.S. Revenue Cutter Service, the Coast Guard's original ancestor. A fine model of the *Massachusetts* is in a room on the lower level devoted to the Coast Guard, along with more recent cutters and other artifacts and pictures related to the service.

In another gallery, a ship model illustrates how maritime matters gripped the imagination of Newburyporters in humdrum shoreside jobs. The model of the ship *Titania*, plain and simple but nicely made, was built by a Newburyport bank clerk in 1856. Beside the model is displayed the maker's account of his pride and joy when his employers allowed him to display his handiwork in the bank. A contemporary newspaper account of how much the little ship was admired by the bank's customers completes the story.

One gallery of the museum is devoted to objects Newburyporters brought back from overseas. Most interesting are a number of large and intricately carved models of Asiatic and Mediterranean craft, among them a zebec, a Chinese junk, and an East Indian vessel. Reflecting the area's eminence as an early 19th-century center of wooden ship construction, are a number of fine half models dating back to 1831, which were used by shipbuilders in planning their vessels. Photographs preserve a record of the last square-rigger built in Massachusetts, the ship *Mary L. Cushing*, launched at Newburyport in 1883. The museum's new "Timber and Tide" exhibit tells the story of area shipbuilding with tools, ship carvings, models, and pictures.

A particularly interesting photograph shows the schooner *Polly*, built in nearby Amesbury in 1805 and believed, when the photograph was taken in 1900, to be the oldest privateer extant at that time. (One can't help wondering how many *younger* privateers there were around 1900.) A curiosity: a pair of beautifully embroidered seabags. Were they sewn by loving hands when Johnny went to sea? Or did Johnny decorate them himself when off watch?

The museum is not entirely limited to maritime exhibits. One gallery is devoted to fine colonial and

Federal furniture and paintings. Another contains the library of novelist John P. Marquand, Newburyport-born into a seagoing family that had lived in the town for many generations.

Custom House Maritime Museum of Newburyport is in the 1836 Custom House. Open December 21 to March 15, Monday-Friday, 10 a.m. to 4:15 p.m.; balance of the year, open Monday-Saturday, 10 a.m. to 4:15 p.m., Sunday 1 p.m. to 4 p.m. Admission: $1.50; seniors, $1.00; children 5 to 16, 75 cents. Sponsored by Newburyport Maritime Society, P.O. Box 306, Newburyport, Massachusetts 01950. Telephone (617) 462-8681.

Now north along the coast to another fine old rivermouth city: Portsmouth on the Piscataqua.

Where the Piscataqua Meets the Sea

The Piscataqua (the accent is on the "cat") is not one of the mighty rivers of America—at least in size. After all, while the river forms the boundary between New Hampshire and Maine for its entire length, it is just 12 miles from the point where the Piscataqua is formed by the junction of the Cochecheco and Salmon Falls rivers to where it swirls out into the Atlantic past Fort Point.

But geography, economics, and history combined to make this little stretch of water (most of it a saltwater estuary with a seven-knot tide) a center of maritime and riverine activity from the early settlement of this part of New England well into the 19th century—a heritage that is today remembered and cherished.

Short though it is, the Piscataqua drains a river basin of about 1,000 square miles, veined by seven navigable rivers and hundreds of smaller streams. Here inland were two of the four original towns that for many decades composed the entire colony of New Hampshire. To pay for scanty supplies of tools and manufactures, they sent downstream the products of forests and fields to Portsmouth, the third of the original towns, on the coast at the river mouth. From one of the finest harbors on the New England coast, Portsmouth ships carried the products of New Hampshire to Europe and the West Indies.

In the very earliest days, furs were the principal exports but soon lumber, barrel staves, and most particularly masts and spars from the great New Hampshire forests were being shipped out. New Hampshire masts were so fine that in Colonial times they were often reserved for the King's tall ships. Getting these products from up-country down to Portsmouth led to a busy carrying trade that produced a distinctive regional type of riverboat, shallow flatbottom scows known locally as gundalows; at first simple craft that were rowed and poled, they became increasingly sophisticated, with elaborate sailing rigs. For centuries these gundalows were built along the Piscataqua and its tributaries. When the Industrial Revolution reached the villages upriver, the gundalows carried up bricks and granite to build the mills, wood and coal to fuel them, cotton to feed the looms, and then brought the finished products back down river to market. The last working gundalow was built as recently as 1886.

Founded only three years after the Plymouth Colony, Portsmouth long made its living from the sea, a busy center of shipbuilding and ship owning and the transfer point between river gundalows and bluewater ships. Fifty years after the first settlers arrived, New Hampshire was shipping 20,000 tons of boards and staves every year, much of it, together with fish, to the West Indies, Spain, and Portugal. At the same time, masts and spars went off to England where they were in great demand. To carry these cargoes, ships of two-hundred to three-hundred tons were built on the banks of the Piscataqua by local shipwrights.

During the American Revolution, Portsmouth shipwrights built three fine frigates for the Continental Navy: the *Raleigh*, the *America*, and the *Ranger*. The last was the first warship to fly the American flag. The frigates, alas, were snapped up by the overwhelming strength of the Royal Navy. Probably more damage was done to British interests by Portsmouth privateers; the little port sent to sea 100 or more small vessels, armed with eight to ten guns apiece and manned perhaps by a total of some 3,000 adventurous young men eager to make their fortunes from prize money—and, incidentally, help win a war.

In 1800, one of the original shipyards of the United States Navy was established at Portsmouth and over the years many famous warships were built there. In the 20th century the Portsmouth Navy Yard (actually across the river in Kittery, Maine) came to specialize more and more in submarines. Today, the Navy Yard facilities are mainly devoted to repair and maintenance.

Portsmouth's deep-water shipping began to decline after the War of 1812. Merchants preferred to route their vessels to the big ports where there were better markets for import cargoes and Boston and New York began to soak up the shipping of the smaller New England ports. Nevertheless, many vessels continued to be owned in Portsmouth, even though they may not have brought their cargoes home there.

Merchant shipbuilding on the Piscataqua reached its peak in the first half of the 19th century. Then it dwindled as ship owners turned first from wood to iron and then to steel, and from sail to steam. The Portsmouth shipyards, like many others, failed to keep up with changing trends.

Today, only the Portsmouth Navy Yard maintains the bustling activities of the maritime past. But their maritime heritage, on the river and on the high seas, is cherished by local people who are determined that it shall not be forgotten. Today, a gundalow once again braves the Piscataqua's tides. In the cloistered reading rooms of the Portsmouth Athenaeum, ancient ship models, pictures, documents, and artifacts gathered by generations of Portsmouth shipmasters are on display. And across the river in Kittery, the story of the Navy's long association with the area is told in the Kittery Historical and Naval Museum.

Portsmouth might have been a rough, tough seaport at the beginning in the 19th century, but its merchants and shipmasters were pretty literate people and they had long had a library in the town. When the books were lost in a fire that swept the city, the community set to work to provide a substitute. In 1818, the Portsmouth Athenaeum was opened as a subscription library in which a member took up shares and received the right to use the reading room, which was installed in a building on Market Square taken over from the defunct Marine Fire Insurance Company. Eventually the Athenaeum inherited the artifacts and treasures of the Portsmouth Mariners Association when that once vigorous organization dwindled away with the decline of blue-water shipping in Portsmouth harbor.

Still in this same 1805 building, the Athenaeum has served as a library, a reading room and social club, an art gallery, and a museum. Today, it is as a remarkable little museum that it is most interesting to the maritime-minded. Inside its walls, the visitor can easily imagine himself back in the early 19th century: the rooms stacked to their high ceilings with ancient books, winding stairs leading up to a fine two-story reading room surrounded by a book-lined balcony, and everywhere marine artifacts, paintings, and models, modestly displayed, that have accumulated over the years.

Two of these treasured relics are exceptionally remarkable. One is believed to be the oldest authenticated ship model in the country, a contemporary built-up model of HMS *America*, 44, the third warship launched in Portsmouth, way back in 1749. Complete with the beautifully carved bow and stern of a mid-18th-century frigate, this is the kind of model hull shipbuilders made to show their work to the British Admiralty.

Equally striking is a primitive painting of the ship *Elizabeth* of 1756; it carries the legend "draft drawn to proportion." According to the Athenaeum's catalog, this is the earliest scale drawing of a ship in the United States. Other interesting exhibits in the Athenaeum include:

- half models of sailing vessels built in Portsmouth, used by the builders as part of the creation of a new design;
- a half model of the USS *Sassacus*, a double-ended Civil War gunboat, built in Portsmouth in 1863; vessels of this type are rare in model form;
- a scale model of a whaleboat on a wooden base painted to show reefs and waves—a most unusual piece of primitive realism;
- a painting of the clipper ship *Typhoon*, a gift to the Athenaeum from the family of the ship's captain;
- two watercolors of the 1810 wreck of the Portsmouth vessel *Eudora*: These belonged to the insurance company that originally owned the Athenaeum building;
- a white bone model of the French ship-of-the-line *Clovis*, carved by French prisoners of war in England and brought home to Portsmouth by a local sea captain and presented to the Athenaeum;
- a U.S. Navy boarding pike in a rack on the wall: few specimens are to be seen today of this weapon from the days of hand-to-hand naval combat.

Portsmouth Athenaeum is in a 1805 brick building on Market Square in the center of Portsmouth, N.H. Open to public Thursday, 1 p.m. to 4 p.m. only. Admission free. Portsmouth Athenaeum, 9 Market Square, Box 848, Portsmouth, New Hampshire 03801. Telephone (603) 431-2538.

There has been a lot of publicity in recent years about running vehicles on alcohol. In northern New England alcohol propulsion isn't all that new. The gundalows that once were laboriously poled up the Piscataqua and its tributaries carrying heavy cargoes from Portsmouth sometimes seem to have come close to being fueled by alcohol, fed not into an internal combustion engine to be sure, but into the sturdy men who handled the poles and sweeps that took these clumsy vessels up the turbulent rivers.

In *Piscataqua Gundalow*, Richard Winslow's fine account of the river craft, the author reports that "going up the Long Beach" on the Piscataqua the men would shout "barn door" when they saw a barn on a distant hillside; this was the signal for a dram of rum "the better to stem a strong current." At the Horse Races, the rapids where the river swings around Bloody Point, another dram was called for. Gundalows continuing up the tributary Oyster River relied on a third dram to help them navigate past Half Tide Run at the mouth of the stream. "All were happy at arriving at Durham Land," Winslow writes.

Take a look at the beautiful recreated gundalow *Edward H. Adams* at her berth on the Portsmouth river front and imagine yourself poling her—loaded with bricks or granite blocks—up the river on a sultry afternoon when the wind drops, so you get no advantage from the big sail. Perhaps a dram will seem like a pretty good idea.

The *Adams* represents the gundalow in its ultimate sophisticated form, her lines taken from a whittled model of the *Fannie M.*, launched in 1886 and the last gundalow in commercial service on the Piscataqua. The new gundalow is named after the skipper, designer, and builder of the *Fannie M.*, Captain Edward H. Adams.

The earliest gundalows were built in Colonial times, often in a farmer's back pasture, to take farm produce down river to market. They were simply open barges, 20 to 30 feet long, no sails, rudder, decks, or cabins; with clumsy square bows and sterns, and pretty much dependent upon the tides to take them up and down the river, poling and rowing with sweeps to take them through the hard parts. In contrast, the beautiful *Adams* is seventy feet long with a spoon bow, round stem, lee boards, a little cabin, her rudder controlled by a helm. Most important of all, she has the rig that made the latter gundalows far easier to handle than the primitive designs of earlier years. Lateen-rigged, she carries her huge triangular sail, 1,000 square feet, on a 70-foot-long yard, swiveled onto a stump mast only 15 to 20 feet high. This distinctive rig makes it possible to drop the spar and sail quickly to get under a bridge, leaving only the stump mast sticking up, and then quickly raise them when the vessel shoots out the other side.

The *Adams* was not only designed but built following Piscataqua traditions. Her knees are Maine hackmatack, natural crooks of 110 degrees. Her bottom is planked with four-inch white oak on eight-inch timbers, while the side planking is white pine. She is fastened in the old way, not with spikes or nails but with 18-inch wooden pegs called trunnels (originally spelled tree-nails), made of hard locust wood—as hard as iron, an old-timer would tell you.

Even the launching of the *Adams* was traditional. The gundalow had been built in a meadow close to the Piscataqua in the middle of Portsmouth. The big heavy hull was hauled to the river's edge by eight oxen, collected with some difficulty from various parts of New Hampshire and Maine.

Today, the gundalow is based at a dock in the Piscataqua in the heart of the Strawbery Banke, the historic waterfront neighborhood in the heart of Portsmouth. Visitors should be sure to look at the little Sheafe Museum in the old river warehouse next door to the gundalow dock. The warehouse, the last survivor of many that once lined the bank, was built during the American Revolution and has the typical overhanging second story that made it easier to load and unload cargoes. The museum focuses on the carvings of Captain Edward Adams himself, the man for whom the new gundalow was named, and displays a series of his models showing the evolution of Piscataqua gundalows from simple open poling scows to relatively sophisticated sailing vessels. Other Adams carvings include models of schooners and carved birds and animals of the area. His work is primitive in feeling but highly skilled in craftsmanship.

Gundalows lend themselves to stories and many are told about the old-timers. One concerns Pulpit Rock, a massive piece of granite on the river bank above Portsmouth. River men believed that everyone should take his hat off to Pulpit Rock as he passed; otherwise, bad luck would follow him. As a local poet put it:

> Now we're past the Pulpit pressing:
> Lift your hat, and bend your head,
> To the Parson for his blessing.
> Stationed in the rocky bank
> From his Pulpit, as we near him.
> Through the pine-trees, whispers he
> Solemn words, would we but hear him.

Governor Sullivan of New Hampshire, a sturdy individualist who had led the Revolution in the colony, ran into tradition when he was a gundalow passenger down the Piscataqua. The Governor was damned that he'd take his hat off to a rock, but the boatmen had their own way of meeting the situation. "Governor," one of them said as they approached Pulpit Rock, "seems like that seagull has shown no respect for your fine hat." The governor snatched his hat off to look at the plumes and before he got it on again the gundalow had passed Pulpit Rock with all heads bared.

The gundalows disappeared from the Piscataqua when the railroads and, later, trucks replaced river traffic as basic transportation. But with the *Captain Adams* there to remind them, the memory of these distinctive river sloops will be kept warm by a beautiful work of craftsmanship. In the old days, they say, a builder didn't need any plans drawn on paper when he started a gundalow: "He'd just spit here and he'd spit there, and then he'd build the boat in between." Well, the *Adams* was not built in the old-fashioned way to that extent; it took great research to supply what the old-timer knew from tradition and experience. But the level of workmanship is high, perhaps higher than in the originals. The *Adams* will long be a part of the maritime heritage of the Piscataqua and its tributary rivers.

Replica Gundalow *Captain Edward H. Adams* is berthed on shore of the Piscataqua River in Portsmouth, N.H. From Memorial Bridge in center of Portsmouth, follow Strawbery Banke signs; dock is opposite Strawbery Banke ticket office. *Adams* can be viewed when at berth but often away cruising nearby waters, so best to query ahead. Wharves are in midst of Portsmouth historic Strawbery Banke district; many old houses on display. Open May 1 to June 20, Saturday and Sunday, 10 a.m. to 4 p.m.; June 21 to Labor Day, daily 10 a.m. to 4 p.m.; September, Saturdays and Sundays, 10 a.m. to 4 p.m. Balance of the year by appointment. Suggested contribution: $1.00, children 12 to 18, 50 cents. Piscataqua Gundalow Project, P.O. Box 1303, Portsmouth, New Hampshire 03810.

Now we'll cross the Piscataqua to Kittery—technically in Maine, but very much a part of the Portsmouth scene.

The naval heritage of the towns at the mouth of the Piscataqua River goes back almost 300 years. In the 1690s, two fine ships were built for the Royal Navy: HMS *Falkland*, and HMS *America* (renamed the *Boston*), a 44-gun ship. New Hampshire's forests produced tall pines so sought after for masts that the Crown preempted the best specimens for the Royal Navy by having them marked with the King's broad arrow; this was so resented locally that there was a "mast-tree riot" in nearby Exeter in 1734.

During the American Revolution, the 32-gun frigate *Raleigh* and ship-sloop *Ranger* were built for the Continental Navy on an island in the Piscataqua River. Construction for *Ranger* was superintended by Lieutenant John Paul Jones, and the house where he boarded while awaiting completion of his ship still stands in Portsmouth and is open to visitors.

With this background, Portsmouth was naturally chosen as the site for construction of one of the six frigates, authorized in 1794, that marked the real beginnings of the United States Navy. The Navy rented a private shipyard and built the ship itself. The USS *Congress*, 38, a sister ship to the *Constellation*, put to sea on her shake-down cruise in December 1799. When shortly afterward the Navy established its own yards, Portsmouth was one of the six places selected. Seavey's Island in the Piscataqua was purchased; although actually across the state line in Kittery, Maine, it became the Portsmouth Navy Yard. Known today as the Portsmouth Naval Shipyard, it is claimed to be the first government installation of its kind in America.

The Portsmouth Yard launched its first ship, the 74-gun ship-of-the-line *Washington*, in 1815. Since then it has turned out a long succession of naval vessels. When the U.S. Navy began building its own submarines in 1914, the first one, the L-8, was laid down at Portsmouth. From then on, the Portsmouth yard became a specialist in submarine construction. By the outbreak of World War II, 38 undersea craft had been built on the Piscataqua; after Pearl Harbor, the Navy Yard went into high gear and by 1945 had turned out 75 submarines. In the postwar era, Portsmouth was the first naval shipyard to build a nuclear-powered submarine. The Yard's crowning achievement was the development and construction of the experimental submarine *Albacore*, designed to operate entirely under water. The lessons learned from *Albacore* became the design basis of today's high-speed underwater fleet.

In recent years the Portsmouth Naval Shipyard has concentrated on repairing and maintaining, rather than building, submarines. Still in active commission, the Yard is not open to visitors, but its history and achievements are a principal focus of the Kittery Historical and Naval Museum, just a short distance away, next to the Kittery Town Hall.

The major exhibits at the museum are ship models, many of them portraying vessels built at the nearby Naval Shipyard. Particularly notable is a huge waterline model of the Continental sloop of war *Ranger*. There is also a very large full model of the USS *Kearsarge*, launched here in 1861, which hunted down and sank the Confederate commerce raider *Alabama* during the Civil War. And to bring the collection down to more recent times are models of the destroyer *John Paul Jones*, a 1920 four-stacker that served in World War II, and the submarines *Charr* and *Scorpion*. A collection of fine, and unusual, half models includes the 60-gun steam frigate *Franklin*, the biggest ship in the U.S. Navy when launched here in 1864, and the USS *Agamenticus*, a turreted ironclad also launched locally the same year.

Two exhibits will particularly interest visitors familiar with the magnificent golden eagle, from the bow of the USS *Lancaster*, now at the Mariners

Museum at Newport News, Virginia. Here is a fine big half model of the *Lancaster* herself. And also on display are wood carvings by the man who carved the Lancaster's eagle, John Haley Bellamy of Kittery Point.

The collection also includes a variety of naval weapons, artifacts, scrimshaw, and prints. A huge double steering wheel from a U.S. steam frigate of the post-Civil War era is particularly notable.

Kittery Historical and Naval Museum. Open all year. Monday-Friday, 9 a.m. to 4 p.m.; Saturday and Sunday, Memorial Day weekend to Labor Day weekend, 10 a.m. to 4 p.m. Admission: $1.00; children 7 to 15, 50 cents; families, $2.50. Sponsored by nonprofit preservation society. Kittery Historical and Naval Museum, P.O. Box 453, Kittery, Maine 03904. Telephone (207) 439-3080.

Way Down East

Although a seagull winging over the arc of the Maine coast from New Hampshire to the Canadian border would cover only some 220 miles, the state of Maine nevertheless has 2,500 miles of shoreline. Rocky capes and points drip down from the mainland into the Atlantic like icicles, while bays and sounds are littered with more than 400 islands each over 1,100 acres in area, plus innumerable smaller ones.

Maine owes this wealth of seacoast to the retreat of the great Ice Age glacier, from which the run-off carved deep river valleys in the land it left exposed. As the melting ice raised the sea level, the valleys were drowned and became tidal bays and rivers. The hills between became the capes and islands.

These shores have a 400-year tradition of maritime activities. European fishermen were on this coast long before permanent settlement, sun-drying their catch at shore camps before carrying it back at the end of the season. In Colonial times, much of Maine was disputed ground between France and Britain, each destroying the other's settlements. With the 19th century, however, maritime Maine came into its own. As timber supplies dwindled and labor costs rose in southern New England, Maine became the major shipbuilding area, not only of the region but of the nation. By the 1850s, Maine was turning out more than one-third of all the ships built in the United States. But the Down Easters were distinctive: not the high-speed, low-capacity, high-cost clipper ships, but substantial and efficient general-cargo carriers.

Some of these Maine-built ships carried Maine's own products—typically, fish, lumber, stone, and lime—to other American ports or overseas. Return cargoes were usually molasses, cotton, or manufactured goods. Many of these ships were sold away, however, or if owned in Maine, carried freight between distant ports. By 1860, for example, the Waldoboro customs district ranked as the fifth largest in the United States in tonnage of ships owned—only New York, Boston, Philadelphia, and Baltimore were larger—but was far down the list of ports ranked by volume of commerce.

Often Maine men went with the ships as mates and masters, even though they rarely saw their native ports. Some little Maine coastal towns boasted scores of sea captains who kept their homes where they were born and raised while shipping out of New York or Boston, only returning as full-time residents after they had retired.

The jagged coastline made land travel from town to town difficult; it was usually easier to go by sea. Packet ships carried passengers until they were superseded by a host of side-wheel steamers, while schooners carried general merchandise and bulk cargoes well into the 20th century.

As American-flag shipping on the high seas dwindled after the Civil War, the nation's maritime traditions were kept alive by ships, master mariners, and shipbuilding Down East. Maine yards built wooden square-riggers for ocean freighters and multi-masted schooners for carrying bulk cargoes along the coast. Today, fishing, lobstering, small-craft construction, and recreational boating are the state's principal maritime activities. But the memory—and the relics—of Maine's blue-water past are being preserved in a fleet of fine museums, large and small, from the Piscataqua River to the Bay of Fundy.

Before we head way down east we'll pay a visit to York, the next small town up the Maine coast from Kittery. There the visitor will find a rare survivor of the shore facilities that once lined every New England harbor: The John Hancock Warehouse and Wharf on the York River, built somewhere around 1750, served also as a custom house and store, and as a center of the town of York's seaborne mercantile activities.

York, originally several small villages clustered around the river, has been involved with the sea from the earliest settlement, which occurred only four years after Plymouth Colony. By 1634, the townspeople had built a wharf for the coastal vessels that came to trade for their furs, fish, and grain. By 1670, they were building their own brigs, brigantines, schooners.

York River was lined with warehouses and wharves by the mid-18th century, and the harbor was home port for 20 coasters and some half dozen fishermen. While most York vessels traded along the Colonies from Nova Scotia to Georgia, some voyaged to the West Indies, carrying fish, lumber, and provisions, and bringing back rum, sugar, and molasses. The West Indian traders usually made two voyages a year, in December and March, thus avoiding the dreaded seasons of fevers and hurricanes. The rest of the year they went on coastal voyages—or stayed home and worked their farms.

During the American Revolution when peaceful trading was cut off many York ships and men became privateers; at one point no fewer than 34 captured York seamen were held in one British prison. The postwar years saw the peak of the little port's maritime activities—building and operating ships for the West Indies trade. An observer reported 13 vessels in the harbor at one time in 1788. Here, as elsewhere in New England, however, local shipping was badly hurt by the Embargo and later by the War of 1812 and never really recovered. By 1875, only a few coasters were left in the almost empty river and the wharves and warehouses were disappearing.

The exception, of course, is the John Hancock Warehouse and Wharf, now carefully preserved by the Old York Historical Society. Once the Warehouse was the United States Custom House for the York District, established after the Revolution, the place where captains returning from abroad entered their cargoes. The Collector of the Port was usually a local merchant or sea captain; from 1793 to 1804, for example, he was a former privateer captain.

Over the years the warehouse passed through many hands. John Hancock, the Boston tycoon and one-time President of the Continental Congress, held a half interest in the building for several years in the 1790s, although he is not known to have visited it.

Today, the warehouse is used by the Old York Historical Society to house a small museum that deals particularly with York's maritime past. The simple two-story wooden building with its wharf is a masterpiece of New England understatement. The exhibits include gundalow-related artifacts and a model

of the last gundalow in the area, the famous *Fannie M.*, long active on the Piscataqua and nearby rivers. Also on display is a reconstruction of a bateau, the flat-bottomed workboat of Colonial times. The second floor of the warehouse museum is devoted to a special exhibit on "Life and Industry on the York River."

From time to time, the Warehouse wharf is occupied by the reconstructed gundalow *Capt. Edward H. Adams* when the Portsmouth-based replica makes one of its cruises along the coast.

The Warehouse is only one of a number of interesting buildings preserved by the Old York Historical Society. Although the others do not have any particular maritime connection, other than being in an ancient port town, they are well worth visiting for anyone interested in America's past. Among them are the Old Gaol, the oldest public building in the one-time English Colonies, and one of the oldest surviving 18th-century schoolhouses. The Society's unusually fine collections of early furniture, textiles, and ceramics are displayed in period settings in six 18th-century buildings.

John Hancock Warehouse and Wharf are on the bank of the York River in York, Maine. From I-95, the Maine Turnpike, take the York exit to Route 1. Follow Route 1 south for a quarter mile to traffic light. There turn left onto York Street (Route 1-A) to York Village. Turn right (west) on Lindsay Road past the old cemetery; follow to two-story gray building on river. Eighteenth-century warehouse is now museum. Open daily, mid-June through September, 10 a.m. to 5 p.m. Admission to all seven York Historical Society buildings: $4.00; children 6 to 10, $2.00; under 6, free. Buy tickets at Jeffards Tavern just off York Street on Lindsay Street. Sponsored by Old York Historical Society, Box 312, York, Maine 03909. Telephone (207) 363-4974.

Now we'll take a long cruise Down East to a college with a fine little museum that honors a pair of famous seagoing graduates.

Remember when every kid wanted to be an Arctic explorer wearing a fur hood and shouting "Mush" to his faithful sledge dogs? Much of the romance of Arctic exploration seems to have drained away as millionaires fly to picnics at the North Pole and Eskimos buy computers to help invest their oil royalties. But when explorers traveled by ship and dog team, the courage, the danger, the ever-dramatic struggle of man against nature made the expeditions genuinely exciting. Ships trapped in ice, men pushing ahead on foot across the floes, native hunters attacking whales in their frail skin boats—all these are a part of our maritime heritage.

In the historic Maine town of Brunswick, northeast of Portland, this heritage can be savored anew at a little museum on the campus of Bowdoin

College, dedicated to two distinguished alumni: Robert E. Peary, class of 1877, and Donald B. MacMillan, class of 1898. Peary was, of course, leader of the little party that in 1908-09 became the first to reach the North Pole. On this expedition MacMillan made his tenderfoot trip north, the beginning of his own half century of Arctic exploration.

Almost-lifesized photomurals of the two explorers in Arctic furs dominate the entrance to the museum, which is in Hubbard Hall at the south end of the Bowdoin campus. Handsomely displayed in three large, well-lit galleries are artifacts, models, paintings, photographs, photomurals, and personal mementos of their expeditions, including the ships they sailed in, and gear, native carvings and hunting weapons, and some examples of Arctic wildlife (stuffed, of course) brought back by their expeditions.

In the first gallery, an unexpected note is the poetry Peary wrote as a Bowdoin undergraduate. Photographs and artifacts of his various early expeditions are on display as well as some of the instruments he used and the honors and decorations he received in later years.

In a second gallery the focus is on the polar-expedition itself. The equipment includes one of the sledges taken to the pole, and models of Peary's ship, the three-masted auxiliary steamer *Roosevelt*, designed with curved, egg-shaped sides so that the pressure of ice squeezed the ship upward instead of crushing it in. There are also models of Donald MacMillan's famous schooner *Bowdoin*, in which he made 26 voyages to the Arctic, and a diorama showing the vessel at Refuge Harbor, North Greenland.

Of special interest is a three-dimensional display demonstrating how Peary had to lie on his back on the ice to determine by sextant his position at the North Pole, where the sun traveled almost parallel to the horizon.

The exhibit of Inuit artifacts in the third gallery, largely collected by MacMillan, includes small, grotesque spiritual figures carved from walrus ivory, and knives, lamps, and bowls of stone. Fur clothing worn by the explorers is displayed as well as a beautiful costume from South Greenland designed for a woman. A full-sized kayak hangs from the ceiling while the construction of Eskimo kayaks and also uniaks (open boats) is shown in models.

Peary-MacMillan Arctic Museum is at the south end of the campus of Bowdoin College in Brunswick, Maine. Open all year: Tuesday-Friday, 10 a.m. to 4 p.m.; Saturday, 10 a.m. to 5 p.m.; Sunday, 2 to 5 p.m. Closed Mondays and holidays. Open evening hours in summer. Admission: free. Peary-MacMillan Arctic Museum, Bowdoin College, Brunswick, Maine 04011. Telephone (207) 725-8731, X275.

At this point, travelers with a special interest in lake steamers may want to leave the coast for a trip inland to Moosehead Lake where loving hands have given a fine old vessel a new lease on life.

The staunch and comfortable steamers of this line afford an agreeable change from the hot and dusty railroads to the cool breezes of this magnificent lake, the scenic beauties of which are unsurpassed. The fleet is commanded by experienced and reliable captains whose enthusiastic funds of forest and lake lore are at the service of patrons seeking information.

Coburn Steamship Company, 1911

The Coburn Line's modest boast referred to a flotilla of sprightly little steamboats with such names as *Twilight, Reindeer, Louisa, Comet, Katahdin,* whose experienced and reliable captains presumably regaled passengers with the lore of the Maine wilderness while steaming up and down Moosehead Lake.

Moosehead has been a center of Maine's wilderness recreation area for a century and a half and it was just a century and a half ago, in 1836, that steamboating began on the lake with a little 40-h.p. woodburner. The early boats were used largely as tugs and to carry lumbermen's supplies, but as Moosehead grew as a recreation area the steamboats became essentially passenger carriers. Thirty-five miles long, ranging from one mile to 20 in width, the lake not only attracted hunters and fishermen who built camps along its 350 miles of shoreline, but summer vacationers—such as Whittier who wrote a poem to a pine tree after a Moosehead visit—who came to relax in the resort hotels. Sportsmen, vacationers, or lumbermen, they all had to take a steamboat ride; the highway ended at the village of Greenville at the foot of the lake.

At one point Moosehead was such a popular resort that there was through sleeping-car rail service from New York City. Competition among the rival steamships was intense until the turn of the century; by then the Coburn company had swallowed up its rivals and established a tight little monopoly.

Eventually technological change penetrated the depth of the Maine woods and roads were built for automobiles to bring in the hunters and vacationers. The last regular passenger service ended in the late 1930s; after that the surviving steamers were owned by a big paper company and used for rafting logs and carrying supplies. The *Katahdin*, launched in 1911, was the last steamboat on the lake—and she was taken out of service in 1976.

So much for Moosehead steamboating—or so it seemed. But as it has turned out, *Katahdin* is once again carrying passengers out of Greenville to admire what has been described as "the greatest of New England lakes."

Her rebirth is yet another example of how the deep-rooted love of watercraft has resulted in determined and successful efforts to keep them on the American scene. Steamboat enthusiasts persuaded the *Kate*'s last owners to give them the boat, which had been left to quietly rot away. With the help of public donations plus preservation grants, the 75-year-old ship has been rebuilt, repowered, and relaunched on a new career. The project has taken several years: the *Katahdin* has a wooden superstructure on a steel hull and her upper decks and interior woodwork were badly rotted and had to be replaced.

Technically, *Katahdin* is no longer a steamboat; the cost of restoring and operating her ancient steam engine proved prohibitive so it has been replaced with an 8-cylinder diesel. But as *M.V. Katahdin* she carries up to 150 passengers on cruises up the lake several days a week during the summer and fall. She no longer calls at shore points along the lake: the docks at the little lake settlements have rotted away, and the magnificent Mt. Kineo House to which she once took guests halfway up the lake has also vanished. Once a week, however, *Katahdin* cruises to where rugged Mt. Kineo itself remains as beautiful as ever.

Between trips, the 120-foot *Katahdin* can be visited without charge. The restoration work has been carefully and nicely done and is still continuing to put back in place original features that were removed at various times during her 64-year career on the lake. But with her paneled lounge and working pilot house with its great wheel, *Katahdin* is already an interesting little vessel—worthy of the beautiful lake on which she rides. Next to the ticket office at the *Katahdin*'s landing is a small museum with models, photographs, and memorabilia of the Moosehead Lake steamers.

The Moosehead Marine Museum and its *M.V. Katahdin* are at Greenville, Maine, at the southern end of Moosehead Lake. Dock is in center of town. 1911 steamer *Katahdin*, now restored as diesel, carries passengers on day trips up lake, may be viewed when at dock. Season: July 1 to October 15. Museum, and vessel when docked, open every day, 8 a.m. to 6 p.m. Lake cruises: July 1 through Labor Day; two-hour cruises to Sugar Island, Wednesday through Saturday 10 a.m., 2 p.m.; 6-hour cruise to Mt. Kineo, Sundays only, 9 a.m. After Labor Day to October 15; two-and-half hour cruises, Wednesday through Friday, 2 p.m., one-and-half hour cruises, Saturday, Sunday, 10 a.m., 1 p.m., 3 p.m. Hot dogs, hamburgers, sandwiches, etc. available. No charge for ship visit or Museum. Cruise tickets: 6-hour cruises, $15.00; seniors, $13.50; children over 5, $7.50. Other cruises: $7.50; seniors, $6.00; children, $3.75. Moosehead Marine Museum, Box 1151, Greenville, Maine 04441. Telephone: (207) 695-2716.

Now back to the coast and the most famous of Maine's shipbuilding centers, Bath, on the west bank of the Kennebec River a few miles above its mouth. A port for more than three centuries, Bath is today the home of the last big commercial shipbuilding company left in Maine, the Bath Iron Works.

The first vessel built by English-speaking people in the New World, the *Virginia of Sagadahoc* was laid down in 1607 about 10 miles south of Bath, where the Kennebec reaches the sea. The settlers who built her lost heart after suffering through a Maine winter and sailed for home, but the tradition of shipbuilding they began survives to the present.

Besides low-cost timber from logs driven down to it down the Androscoggin and Kennebec rivers and skilled craftsmen willing to accept low wages, Bath benefited from a river bank with a natural slope to the water. It was just right for building ways. From 1850 to 1860 Bath yards launched 232 vessels, and the city became second only to Boston among New England ports in total tonnage built. Bath-built square-riggers, for example, replaced ships abandoned in San Francisco Bay when their crews deserted to join the gold rush.

In the post-Civil War era, Bath built the famous "down-easters," described by experts as "the highest development of the wooden square-rigger." The town's leading shipowners, the Sewell family, were also shipbuilders, and from 1823 to 1923 their yards turned out 105 ships for their own use, beside many more built for others. Like many Bath shipbuilders and shipowners they built a fine mansion and today the 30-room Sewell family house is one of the exhibition centers of the Maine Maritime Museum, dedicated to preserving the maritime traditions —particularly shipbuilding and coastal steamers —of the Maine coast in general and Bath in particular. With two sites, 15,000 objects—including many ship models, paintings, tools, and instruments—a whole wooden shipyard, and a large collection of small craft, the museum is a major institution.

The Sewell House, built in 1844 when Bath was reaching the height of its prosperity, contains many fine, full-captioned ship models, artifacts, and paintings, as well as portraits and memorabilia of the Sewell family. Of particular interest are displays explaining hand-line fishing from dories, the traditional method of New England fishermen, now no longer practiced. An unusual model portrays the USS *Saranac*, a side-wheeler built in 1848 when the Navy was slowly converting to steam. A large diorama of a Bath ropewalk provides a glimpse of an often overlooked maritime support industry.

One gallery at Sewell House will be welcomed by small-fry, often frustrated by "hands-off" instructions.

In the "Please Touch Me" room they are encouraged to ring the ship's bell, turn the steering wheel, and generally pretend they are aboard ship. For grown-ups, the most interesting Sewell gallery is the collection in the basement, sponsored by the Bath Iron Works. Founded in Bath nearly a century ago, the Iron Works in its first five years built two gunboats and an armored ram for the United States Navy; today, after surviving periods of hard times, the yards are turning out guided-missile frigates. The Bath Iron Works galleries display many models and photographs of cargo ships, yachts, and naval vessels built at the yard. Models of particular interest include the 1890 gunboat *Machias*, the first U.S. Navy vessel entirely constructed at the yard, and J.P. Morgan's famous steam yacht *Corsair*, also built in Bath. Miniature mock-ups used to plan the machinery space in naval vessels give insight into the problems of ship designers.

The Maine Museum's other major site is at the south end of Bath, a couple of miles down Washington Street. The Percy and Small Shipyard is described as the only surviving shipyard in America to have constructed large wooden sailing vessels. Here 44 vessels—four-, five-, and six-masted schooners—went down the ways from 1896 to 1920. For the past decade the museum has been restoring the yard, not merely as a relic of the past but as an activity center where the traditional skills of the wooden shipbuilders are demonstrated and preserved.

Eventually Percy and Small will once again be a full working shipyard; in the meantime it already houses some extremely interesting exhibits. Outstanding is a display of original small craft, each an example of a historically important type, drawn from the museum's large collection. Here the visitor will find a lumberman's bateau, a Swampscott dory, a Hampton boat, a schooner's gig. Each type is explained to the visitor by a placard headed "Things to Notice" providing the equivalent of a guided tour through the history of American small craft.

In another yard building, a loft is devoted to explaining how wooden ships were built, from the initial design to the final rigging and fitting out. One unusual artifact preserved here is a woodcarver's pattern for a larger-than-life figurehead: a silhouette cut out of a flat board.

Now under reconstruction at the yard is the steam tug *Seguin*, launched in 1884 and in active service until 1969, which once towed sailing ships up and down the Kennebec. Other working small craft at the yard include a pinkie, a Tancook whaler, and ketches and sloops.

Many of these small craft were built or rebuilt at the museum's Apprenticeshop, also located in the yard. At the Apprenticeshop "no tuition is expected and no wages are returned," the museum points out, as students learn the boatbuilder's skills by constructing traditional Maine coastal craft, most of which are eventually sold. The Apprenticeshop building also houses a two-floor exhibit on Maine lobstering that includes lobsterboats and both historical and current lobstering gear, dioramas, and a mock-up of a lobster cannery. An audiovisual show relates a day in the life of a Maine lobster fisherman.

A major exhibit at the Percy and Small yard is one of the few surviving banks fishing schooners, the *Sherman Zwicker*. When you come upon her alongside her dock in the Kennebec River she looks enormous. For a fishing schooner, she is—the second largest ever built, 142 feet from stem to stern. That's only 12 feet shorter than the famous clipper ship *Rainbow*.

Although only a little more than 40 years old, the *Zwicker* is already part of history, survivor of a vanished breed. She is one of the last banks fishermen built as schooners; today they are all designed for power only. Actually the *Zwicker* is very much a transitional vessel. Although a sister ship of *Bluenose*, the Canadian schooner famous for speed under sail, *Zwicker* depended primarily upon her 12-cylinder diesel engines. She never carried topmasts, and the sails on her stubby main and foremasts were used primarily to steady her when hove to or moving slowly along the fishing grounds; her engines took her to and from the banks.

The *Zwicker* is also one of the last North American vessels built for dory fishing. The 12 dories stacked on deck were put overside at the fishing grounds, each manned by two fishermen tending mile-and-a-half-long fishing lines with a hook every few feet. Today, American and Canadian banks fishermen, whether longlines or trawlers, fish directly from their motor vessel—far safer and faster.

The *Sherman Zwicker* was built in Lunenberg, Nova Scotia, where the Zwicker family has owned fishing vessels since the 18th century. She was retired from active fishing in 1968. With a rebuilt stern the *Zwicker* is still seaworthy but because she was not built in the United States she is not allowed to carry passengers.

Except for her big 320-hp diesel engine, the *Zwicker* has the traditional layout of Gloucester fishing schooners. In the bow, the visitor finds the big fo'c'sle where most of the crew bunked; the older men and the skipper lived in the main cabin aft. Although she carried 28 men all told, there are only 25 bunks; with men always on watch, some bunks were shared. Below decks between the fo'c'sle and the cabin, the bins where the salted fish were carried are now used for an exhibit on dory fishing.

Because the dorymen came and went at all hours when the fishing was good, there were not only four

Figure 5
In the Apprenticeshop at the Maine Maritime Museum in Bath, young people learn to build the
traditional types of wooden small craft, preserving a great tradition.

regular meals a day but snacks always available in an open locker. The provision list for a cruise, posted on a forward bulkhead, makes impressive reading.

The Maine Maritime Museum: at two locations in Bath. Driving from east or west, turn off Route 1 at Washington Street, just west of the Bath end of the bridge over the Kennebec River. North on Washington is the Sewall House at No. 963, on right. South from Route 1 on Washington Street is the Percy and Small Shipyard, at No. 263, on left. Summer boat rides on river available. All sites open Memorial Day weekend to October 15th, every day, 10 a.m. to 5 p.m. For the remainder of the year, Monday-Saturday, 10 a.m. to 3 p.m.; Sundays and holidays, 1 p.m. to 4 p.m. Some exhibits may be closed; check in advance by telephone. Admission: $4.00; children 6 to 15, $2.00; family rates valid for 2 days, $12.50. Reduced rates in the winter season. Maine Maritime Museum, Bath, Maine 04530. Telephone (207) 443-6311.

Little museums, manned by volunteers, have a fascination all their own; a couple of peninsulas further east down the coast is one with special interest for the small-boat sailor.

Friendship, a long-established fishing port, is only one of many similar villages along the Maine coast, but its name is widely recognized—thanks to the skill of its boatbuilders. Like Gloucester, Friendship has given its name to a widely known and easily recognized type of small vessel, the Friendship sloop, developed here to meet the special needs of local offshore fishermen. After nearly disappearing as fishermen abandoned sail for power boats, the Friendships are enjoying a new lease of life as small yachts, due in no small part to the characterization of them by the expert Howard Chapelle as "eminently suitable for deep-water cruising and racing; they are undoubtedly superior to some of the much-touted foreign types . . ."

What is a Friendship sloop? A book published by the Friendship Sloop Society, *Enduring Friendships*, gives an ambiguous triple answer: "A Friendship Sloop is a gaff-rigged sloop with a fisherman look about her. A Friendship Sloop is a beautiful fusion of form and function. A Friendship Sloop is a state of mind composed of independence, tradition, resourcefulness, and a most fortuitous combination of geography and language in the name Friendship."

Lyrical definitions aside, most New England boat people have learned to recognize a Friendship as a small sloop—usually 30 feet or less in length—with a beautiful clipper bow, a long bowsprit, a rather short mast with a gaff-rigged mainsail, and a deep hull and fixed keel. Chapelle pointed out that the sloops were built for fishermen who worked offshore winter and summer, in all kinds of weather. In winter they had to beat their way back to port, heavily laden, often against savage north-westers. For this their sloops had to be stiff and weatherly, achieved by making them deep in proportion to their length. But the sloops also had to carry a lot of sail in order to sail well in light summer winds. And all year round, Friendship fishermen had to get their catch to market as quickly as possible, which meant the little sloops had to have fine lines.

To preserve the Friendship Sloop heritage, local people have set up the Friendship Museum in a little brick building, formerly a one-room schoolhouse. Here are a variety of pictures and records, shipbuilders' tools, and models. At the opposite end of the museum spectrum from the huge seaports, the little collection is well worth visiting for what it tells about the authentic achievements of the little towns who played so large a role in our maritime heritage.

Incidentally, a great gathering of Friendship sloops occurs each summer when the annual Friendship Sloop Regatta and Races are held the last week in July.

Friendship Museum: at corner of Route 220 and Martin Point Road, about half mile west of principal village street. Models, artifacts, pictures, primarily related to Friendship sloops. Open July 1 to Labor Day; Monday-Saturday, noon to 4 p.m.; Sunday, 2 to 4 p.m. Donations welcome. Sponsored by the Friendship Sloop Society. Friendship Museum, Friendship, Maine 04547. No telephone at the Museum.

By water, the passage from Friendship to Rockland requires a long trip out to sea around the peninsula and islands that mark the western edge of Penobscot Bay, but by land it is only a few miles. Rockland's harbor, on the southwest shore of the Bay, was once bustling with coasting schooners loading with lime and stone from nearby quarries. Today the town is largely industrial and the harbor is used primarily by fishermen, yachtsmen, and the ferry steamers to islands in Penobscot Bay. However, Rockland's small but interesting Shore Village Museum recalls the maritime past of the area, with particular focus on the lighthouses and other navigational aids that keep these dangerous coasts safe—or at least safer—for the sailor.

The moving spirit behind the maritime exhibits of the Shore Village Museum, which is entirely the work of volunteers, is a retired warrant officer, formerly in command of the Rockland Coast Guard station. The nucleus of the collection came from coastal lighthouses, artifacts that he saved from the scrapheap when automatic lights and signals took over.

The prize exhibit is an enormous Fresnel lens, originally in the lighthouse on Petit Manan Island. A 10-foot tower of beautifully cut glass, the lens is a magnificent example of the art of the French optical glassmaker. A somewhat smaller—still, about six feet high—but equally beautiful lens has the opening for the lamp-trimmer removed so that a visitor, even a substantial adult, can climb inside to see how the lens serrations bend light. Technology's impact on navigational aids is dramatically demonstrated by displays of the tiny electric bulbs and acetate lenses that have replaced the big lamps and huge Fresnel lenses of the past.

An unusual aspect of the museum is that visitors are encouraged to touch and even manipulate exhibits—a hands-on approach that is particularly delightful for children. Press a button and a lighthouse foghorn belches a deep-sea squawk, push another and a great light glares out. Turn the ship's wheel mounted in one corner and the gauge that once stood beside it on the bridge moves to show the angle of the rudder. Pull down the handle of the engine room telegraph and jingling bells signal to change the throttle setting.

The Coast Guard exhibits share the museum building with the Shore Village Historical Society, whose upstairs gallery includes a number of handsome ship models, among them one of the *Marie Celeste*, the famous mystery ship found on a calm sea abandoned by her crew. Shipwrights' tools are displayed next to a photomural of Rockland in the 19th century, its shipyards crowded with vessels in various stages of construction.

Non-maritime galleries of the museum contain Civil War uniforms and artifacts and a fine collection of handsomely costumed dolls. A wooden plow dramatically illustrates the problems of 18th-century farmers, struggling to till Maine's rocky soil.

Incidentally, Rockland is also the home of one of the finest regional art museums in the nation, the Farnsworth Museum, endowed by a lifelong Rockland resident.

Shore Village Museum in Rockland, Maine on the west shore of Penobscot Bay, in Grand Army Hall on Limerock Street. Three blocks south of Park Street (Route 1). Open July to October 15, 10 a.m. to 4 p.m. Other times by appointment, call: Ken Black (207) 236-3206 or Robert Davis (207) 596-6527. Donations welcome. Shore Village Museum, 104 Limerick Street, Rockland, Maine 04841. Telephone (207) 594-4950.

Most Maine coastal towns had a shipyard and townspeople who went to sea. Some became known for a specialty: Bath for big cargo carriers, for example. Although Searsport, with eight yards, built many ships in the years before the Civil War, the town eventually became better known for a different maritime specialty: master mariners. In 1860, when the little town on the northwest shore of Penobscot Bay had 1,700 inhabitants, 150 of them were captains of full-rigged ships. In the 1870s, some 10 percent of all the deep-sea shipmasters in the American merchant marine are estimated to have come from this one little town on Penobscot Bay. By 1889, there were still 77 captains—and 33 of them commanded Cape Horners.

These shipmasters brought home to their families and friends not only a rich harvest of exotic gifts but also fine pictures of their ships, painted to order in foreign ports by artists specializing in portraits of visiting vessels. The Penobscot Marine Museum displays a notable collection of these ship portraits, both oils and watercolors, as well as other marine paintings, mostly from the 19th century. In fact it was to preserve these paintings, along with the other maritime artifacts and documents in local homes, that the museum was founded nearly half a century ago. The Searsport shipyards had dwindled away much earlier when shipowners demanded larger vessels than could be floated in the town's shallow harbor, and master mariners skilled in sail together with their ships had practically disappeared from the high seas. At that time in Searsport, however, the ships and the captains were relatively recent memories. Indeed some of the masters still survived in retirement. Pictures and artifacts were still in possession of the original families, not yet bought up by antique dealers for dispersal to collectors across the country as was happening in many places. The moving spirits in starting the museum were Lincoln Colcord, a journalist and writer with a unique maritime heritage, born at sea in a bark commanded by his father, and Searsport native Clifford Nickels Carver, a one-time assistant on the National Council of Defense.

Today the Nickels-Colcord-Duncan House is one of the seven buildings of the Penobscot Marine Museum complex, all on their original sites. As its name implies, the museum is concerned with far more than Searsport itself. Penobscot Bay, that many-islanded body of water that splits southern Maine up the middle, has seen major maritime activities from colonial days. A diorama in one gallery, converted from a barn, vividly explains an important segment of Penobscot maritime history: the attempted amphibious attack on a British fort in 1779 that ended in the complete destruction of the American fleet.

Many of the paintings are gathered together in the Captain Merithew House, an 1816 brick dwelling a little way up the street. In addition to many fine ship portraits, two rooms are devoted to the fine 19th-century oils of Thomas and James Butterworth; their work ranges from miniature ship portraits to large paintings of ship-to-ship combats in the War of 1812. Two whole walls are covered with daguerreotypes and photographs of hundreds of Searsport sea captains, sometimes several generations of the same family—a panorama of Yankee faces. Nearby, is a striking special display of "Working Boats of the World," comprising many models gathered from all over the globe.

The Merithew House also contains one of the few museum exhibits anywhere related to modern whaling: a model of the SS *Ulysses*, converted from a tanker to a whaler factory ship in 1937. There is also a striking oil painting of the whale factory ship *Pango* with her high-powered chaser boats out hunting down whales.

For many visitors, the most interesting exhibit will be found in the old Town Hall, the original museum building, across from the church at the top of the hill. Here a carefully arranged show, "Challenge of the Down Easters," uses drawings, charts, photographs, and models, with ample explanatory text, to demonstrate how and why sailing ship design changed in the 19th century. From the North Atlantic packets through the much publicized but short-lived clipper era to the big, highly efficient wooden windjammers built in Maine after the Civil War, the exhibit shows how ships evolved to meet the needs of commerce. The impact of economics on ship design, often overlooked, is here made clear.

A half model of the kettle-bottomed bark *Saone* built in 1846, shows how her tumblehome reduced her taxes and port charges, partly based on the dimensions of her deck, while retaining large carrying capacity in the bulging hull below. The high economic efficiency of the Down Easters is made clear by a chart comparing the 2,006-ton clipper *Challenge* with the 2,076-ton Down Easter *Benjamin Packard*, built in 1883. The *Challenge*, with a 230-foot mainmast, required a crew of 64. The *Packard*, of approximately the same carrying capacity, had a 159-foot mainmast and could be handled with a crew just half the size—32 men.

The Town Hall building also contains some striking wall-sized photomurals, enlarged from early photographs. One of the most interesting, entitled "Captain's Saloon," shows the captain's wife seated in the ship's cabin as in her front parlor at home ashore, with the children playing on the floor.

A number of the museum's many models are unusual enough to deserve special notes. In the barn gallery, is an enormous—some seven feet long—model of a derrick barge, used for offshore oil drilling. Another, in the Captain Merithew House, is a tiny model, only a few inches in length, of an armored steam warship of the mid-19th century, possibly, judging from her flag, from the Austro-Hungarian Navy. And in the Town Hall is a fine big model of the ship *El Capitan*, built in Bath in 1871, which had a lifetime berth in the federal court in Portland. There it was used by counsel and witnesses as an exhibit to demonstrate the circumstances of incidents that led to lawsuits, such as collisions at sea.

Penobscot Marine Museum is a cluster of seven buildings on first block of Church street off the Searsport main street. Open Memorial Day weekend through October 15th; Monday-Saturday, 9:30 a.m. to 5 p.m.; Sunday, 1 to 5 p.m. Admission $2.00; children 7 to 15, 75 cents. Penobscot Marine Museum, Church Street, Searsport, Maine 04974. Telephone (207) 548-2529.

Now, across to the east shore of Penobscot Bay and the much fought-over town of Castine.

A sleek yawl tacks up into the harbor. In the distance, small white wings race in the Bagaduce River. In open-air wharf restaurants voracious visitors tear boiled lobsters limb from limb. A summer day in Castine, Maine.

Hard to imagine, but for almost two centuries this quiet harbor off Penobscot Bay repeatedly saw hostile fighting ships stand in with shotted cannon run out ready for action. This scenario took place here perhaps more often than in any other port in New England. In the 17th century, the invaders came to seize or sometimes just to loot the fur trading post on the point. The post was profitable—it is said to have made Baron de Castin a rich man—and well worth stripping. At the same time it was on disputed territory, so when the English held the post, French ships captured it; when the French were the fur traders, English ships came to seize them. Still other attacks came from Flemish pirates, or New England traders, or Dutch frigates.

In the 18th century, Castine harbor saw naval action on a far larger scale. During the American Revolution, British forces occupied the little town and its harbor as an advanced naval base for operations against New England ships and ports. To seize Castine, Massachusetts sent militia in a fleet of transports escorted by Continental Navy warships. The expedition ended in total disaster; a superior Royal Navy squadron came up Penobscot Bay behind the American task force and cut it off. Every American ship was captured or destroyed. (The action is portrayed in a big diorama at the Penobscot Marine Museum across the bay at Searsport.)

In the early 19th century, fighting ships came again to Castine harbor. During the War of 1812, a British naval squadron seized the village and port, once again as an advanced base for the blockade of the New England coast. The Royal Navy held the town until the end of the war, providing cover for a highly illegal and highly profitable contraband trade between Yankees and Maritimers.

Since then, Castine has been at peace. During the 19th century, the town became a prosperous port and shipbuilding center. At one point it was the second wealthiest town per capita in the United States. Castine merchants traded to the West Indies and Europe; sometimes there were several hundred ships in the harbor. The yards had turned out 121 vessels by 1887. In the later decades of the century, however, commerce dwindled and Castine changed from a bustling port to a summer resort.

Today, Castine, Maine, is helped in remembering its maritime past by the fact that it is the home of the Maine Maritime Academy, which trains young people to be officers in the merchant marine. The town, and the academy, is also the home of an outstanding maritime collection, concerned with one special aspect of Castine's seagoing past: its steamboat heritage. Once little steamboats swarmed in Maine coastal waters. With many villages on points extending out into Penobscot Bay, travel from one coastal town to another was usually easier by water than by roundabout land routes. With the coming of steam, the bay was crisscrossed by small steamboats carrying freight and passengers from one town to the next. Larger steamers connected the major ports with Portland, Boston, and even New York.

The golden age of Penobscot Bay steamboating is the focus of the fine ship models and prints in the Allie Ryan Maritime Collection, now housed in Quick Hall on the grounds of the Maine Maritime Academy. A branch of the Maine State Museum, the collection includes hundreds of paintings, lithographs, photographs, and other materials.

For many visitors, the steamboat models will be the highlight of the collection. The little ships, which portray a variety of Maine coastal steamers, are simple, straightforward representations, rather than the elaborately finished productions of professional model builders. Many were made by men who knew the coastal steamers at firsthand; many of the original vessels served Penobscot Bay. Two very large models portray the SS *J.T. Morse* and SS *Penobscot*; while at the other extreme is a tiny recreation of the SS *Vinalhaven* of 1892.

Other models include various sailing craft—full-rigged ships, schooners, barks—and builders' half models. A particularly fine example of the latter shows the lines of the USS *Algona*, 1860.

The many prints include naval scenes from the Civil War to the early 20th century, and there is a large and wide-ranging collection of steamship pictures. One gallery has been devoted to prints and paintings of shipwrecks. Among the photographs are particularly interesting shots of steam tugs towing schooners up the Penobscot.

As is often the case, this fine collection came into being as the result of the enthusiastic interest of one man. Allie Ryan was born and raised on the Maine coast when steamboats and schooners were still the most common and reliable means of transportation. As he observed the gradual decline of the salt-water carriers in the face of highway transportation, Ryan realized that he was witnessing the end of an era and started collecting memorabilia of coastal shipping. Ryan originally concentrated mainly on pictures, but as people of the region learned of his interest they brought him an increasing number of artifacts and ship models and his collection broadened in scope.

Allie Ryan Maritime Collection is housed on the campus of the Maine Maritime Academy in Castine. Best to call ahead for hours. Admission: free. Maine State Museum is responsible for care and maintenance. Allie Ryan Maritime Collection, Quick Hall, Maine Maritime Academy, Castine, Maine 04421. Telephone (207) 326-4311, x 485.

Maine is fringed with hundreds of rocky islands. Here's one that is preserving relics of its maritime past—and present—in its own little museum.

Nowhere are maritime traditions stronger than in the state of Maine, and nowhere in Maine are they stronger than among the hardy people who live on the rocky islands that fringe the coast. Like their ancestors for centuries past, the island fishermen and lobstermen brave the swirling tidal currents, blinding fogs, greedy reefs, to wrestle their living from the sea. Unlike their ancestors, today they tend their pots and their nets from powerboats, but they still cherish the memory of the old-timers who did the job with sail and oar.

In this spirit, Little Cranberry Island off the Maine coast, has a small museum full of the flavor of a sea-drenched past. Little Cranberry Island is a short distance off the shore of Mount Desert Island and is reached by the mailboat from Northwest Harbor. Sometimes the mail gropes through fog (radar-aided, these days). Sometimes, on a bright day, the little launch chugs through a wonderful panorama of spruce-covered islands and granite ledges. In either case, a visit to Little Cranberry Island and its museum makes a fine mini-expedition into maritime Maine.

The Islesford Historical Museum (Islesford is the town) is a pleasant, small building dedicated to preserving the documents and artifacts relating to the history of the Cranberry Islands. Since the islanders made their living from the sea, primarily lobstering and fishing, there is necessarily a pervasive maritime flavor to the exhibits. There is also a local one; practically all the displays are either made by or owned by local people.

In addition to ships' logs, records, and other documents, the maritime exhibits are basically models and artifacts. The miniature vessels and small craft are particularly interesting because they were mostly made by islanders who knew the original vessels. The makers were not necessarily skilled craftsmen; some models are a little rough and might be called primitive, but they are convincingly authentic.

Here are some highlights to look for:

- several models of schooners and fishing boats made by local people and given to the museum;
- the log of a schooner owned locally;
- paintings of the island;
- a sea chest that washed ashore in the 1870s from some unknown source—probably flotsam from a wreck along the coast: Inside the cover sails a painted ship;
- miniature lobstering display—pots, lobster boats, and gear, scaled to Lilliputian fishermen;
- maps, charts, and photographs all relating to the island, its boats, and people.

Non-maritime exhibits include furniture, tools, household equipment, needlework, and so forth. The museum, which was started by local people, is now under the guidance and control of the National Park Service and is technically part of the Acadia National Park. Headquarters of the park are in Bar Harbor on nearby Mount Desert Island.

Islesford Historical Museum is on Little Cranberry Island, reached by 20-minute motorboat trip from Northeast Harbor on Mount Desert Island, Maine. From U.S. Route 1, turn south at Ellsworth on Route 3. After crossing Mount Desert Narrows bridge, keep right at Y on Route 198 to Northeast harbor. Boats leave from town dock, five daily, 8:30 a.m. to 8 p.m. in summer; reduced schedule other seasons. Phone (207) 244-3575 for departure times. Museum is three-minute walk from boat landing on Little Cranberry. Open late June to Labor Day, daily 9:30 a.m. to 4 p.m. Call to confirm hours. Donations welcome. Operated by National Park Service as part of Acadia National Park; information, Superintendent Acadia National Park, Bar Harbor, Maine 04609. Telephone (207) 288-3338. Islesford Historical Museum, Islesford, Little Cranberry Island, Maine. (No telephone at museum.) Restaurant on island.

Now—way, *way* down east, almost to the Canadian border.

History brushed the quiet village of Machiasport, Maine, in June 1775, when a British armed schooner demanded two schooner loads of lumber to build barracks for British troops in Boston. Aroused by news of Lexington and Concord, townspeople had already raised a liberty pole; now they not only refused the lumber but recruited an attack commando armed with muskets and pitchforks. Led by fiery Jeremiah O'Brien and his five brothers, the Americans seized a lumber schooner, put her alongside the King's ship, and took her by boarding. O'Brien's name has been kept alive by the U.S. Navy as the name of a series of naval vessels.

This little battle and the subsequent retaliatory attack by a Royal Navy task force are the major theme of the exhibits of the Machiasport Historical Society, lodged in the spare, Federal-style Gates house, built about 1807. There are models of the schooners involved—the Colonial coaster *Unity* and HMS *Margaretta*—and paintings of the battle. Other exhibits of pictures and artifacts concern Machiasport and Machias Bay marine activities, particularly the extensive shipment of lumber southward on coastal schooners, as well as the many shipmasters who lived in the town.

The remains of Fort O'Brien, earthworks originally thrown up as defense against British attacks, can be seen at the point where the narrow Machias River enters the broad Machias Bay.

Machiasport Historical Society Museum, on a hillside overlooking Machias River. Driving from east or west, just west of center of Machias turn south on Route 92. Museum is about 4 miles south in white house on left of road. Library. Open June to October, Monday-Friday. Admission: free. Machiasport Historical Society, Gates House, Route 92, Machiasport, Maine 04655. Telephone (207) 255-8461.

We've reached the Canadian border: the interesting museums that lie beyond in the Atlantic Provinces will be found elsewhere in this guide. At this point, let's return to Boston and start out again—southward this time to the museum-rich towns of the Old Colony.

South of Boston and Into the Old Colony

The breaking waves dashed high/On a stern and rockbound coast" was how English poet Felicia Hemans visualized the landing of the Pilgrims from 3,000 miles away. Of course, she was dead wrong: Plymouth Rock was a lonely boulder on a sandy beach. In fact, most of the Massachusetts coast south of Boston is sand and boulders, dumped by the retreating Ice Age glacier. Sand hills a few miles inland blocked drainage eastward into Massachusetts Bay, so no large rivers carved out good harbors. Barrier beaches provided sheltered waters but such harbors were too shallow for great ships. Cape Cod, wrote Samuel Eliot Morison, has been the "greatest nursery of seamen in North America, but its offspring have had to sail from other ports than their own."

Yet the Old Colony, the land of the Pilgrims, has its own rich maritime heritage. From the earliest settlements, fishing has been a major source of income and so remains today. In Colonial times, busy shipyards lined the little rivers, turning out a steady stream of small ships that traded to the West Indies and to Europe. And for the past century, people who sail purely for pleasure have happily made use of

rivers and harbors grown too small for merchant shipping.

The same glacier dumped its terminal and recessional moraines to form Nantucket, Martha's Vineyard, and the Elizabeth Islands off the south shore of Cape Cod. The American whaling industry was born on Nantucket but gradually shifted to New Bedford, just off Cape Cod, when the bar built up across the mouth of the island's only harbor. New Bedford's whale ships, many with Vineyard mates and harpooners, prowled the world's oceans from the icefields to the South Seas, dominating a rich industry.

Further west, the glacier scoured out Narragansett Bay but left it filled with islands. The largest, Aquidneck or Rhode Island, was blessed with a noble deep-water harbor, where Newport blossomed to become the fifth largest port of colonial America.

The visitor will find this rich and varied heritage lovingly cherished in museums large and small—and all worth visiting. Let's start in the little town of Sharon.

Not every maritime museum is set on a hillside overlooking the ocean. The Kendall Whaling Museum, for example, is in the midst of a pine forest, in Sharon, Massachusetts, southwest of Boston and many leagues from salt water. Yet its collection of artworks, artifacts, documents, and publications pertaining to whaling and seal hunting is not only one of the largest in the nation but one of the broadest in scope.

Kendall exhibits cover the rise and decline of American whaling and illuminate the activities of Dutch, English, Native American, and Japanese whalemen. Equally distinctive is the museum's coverage of modern whaling—and also of the contemporary efforts to end all hunting of some species to save them from extinction.

The museum's Dutch Gallery has fine 17th- and 18th-century paintings of Dutch whalers at work, as well as a unique 17th-century model of a whaleship—a Dutch "fluyt"—proper reminders that whale hunting was not invented this side of the Atlantic. The considerable part that whaling played in Dutch maritime life is reflected in a set of Delft tiles decorated in blue with whaling scenes. Even more striking is a set of a dozen handsome Delft platters (circa 1760) that tell "The story of the Greenland Whale Fishery."

Traditional American whaling is well covered with fine paintings, artifacts, instruments, and ship models. The scrimshaw collection, according to the museum, is the largest in the world. The changes in whaling techniques with improved technology, an aspect not often recorded by marine painters, is shown in a painting entitled "Shooting a Sperm Whale with a Shoulder Gun." And there's an odd little touch of realism in one exhibit: a small piece of genuine whale blubber that looks remarkably like a chunk of salt pork.

Particularly interesting are photographs and artifacts relating to the schooner *John R. Manta*, including one of her whaleboats complete with gear. Rare photographs picture the whalemen in action. A model shows the schooner herself, one of the last of the New Bedford whalers, which eventually was converted to carrying passengers between New Bedford and the Atlantic Islands—a trade in which she went missing with all hands.

The Japanese have been for centuries, and still are, active whale hunters. In the Japanese Gallery of the Kendall is a wonderfully detailed model of a traditional Japanese whaleboat, about as different from the Nantucket type as can be imagined. Here also are displayed 18th- and 19th-century Japanese scrolls vividly portraying whale hunting in old Japan.

Native Americans—coastal Indians and particularly Eskimos—were avid whale hunters. Here again the Kendall collections explore a little-known area, with a gallery devoted to the Arctic hunting of whales and seals. On display is an original Alaskan Eskimo kayak used by the whale hunter. The Arctic and Antarctic have been rich hunting grounds for Americans and Europeans both, and the gallery includes a particularly interesting diorama of the steam bark *Vanguard* believed made by one of her crew about 1900. *Vanguard* was a Newfoundland sealer, and her hunters are shown fanned out across the ice, clubbing seals.

In the 20th century, of course, whale hunting has become mechanized with fast catcher boats that chase down and kill whales, then take the carcasses back to a nearby factory ship for processing. The Kendall is one of the few collections that has followed whaling into this modern phase, with paintings and a diorama of a modern factory boat surrounded by its smaller catchers killing whales. The terrible efficiency of modern whale-killing technology has driven some species close to extinction and led to demands that all whaling be forbidden. The Kendall Whaling Museum has followed the whaling story to its contemporary—and perhaps final—phase, collecting artifacts and documents chronicling the "Save the Whale" movement.

The Kendall welcomes the general public, but it also describes itself as "historically a preservation institution dedicated to advanced research," making a special point of assisting scholars in the use of its facilities. The museum's manuscript collection includes some 800 whaling logs, business papers, letters, and account books. Each fall the museum holds an annual whaling symposium for interdisciplinary exchanges of recent research about whales and whaling in the biological and social sciences, and in archaeology. The public is cordially invited; information can be obtained from the director.

The away-from-the-sea location of the Kendall Whaling Museum results from the fact that its fine whaling collection has as its nucleus the artworks, artifacts, documents, and publications gathered over 40 years by Sharon industrialists, Henry and Evelyn Kendall. Mr. Kendall set up the museum to house his collection in 1956.

"From humankind's enduring relationship with whales and with the sea," says the museum's brochure, "arise lessons in humanity, humility and scholarship which wait in every corner to be explored."

Kendall Whaling Museum is about a mile north of the center of Sharon, Massachusetts. Watch for small museum sign pointing north from Sharon's main street. Library. Facilities available for scholarly inquiry. Educational programs, speakers. Open Tuesday-Friday, 1 to 5 p.m.; Saturday, 10 a.m. to 5 p.m., other times by appointment. Admission: $2.00; seniors and students, $1.50; children 5 to 16, $1.00. Small gift shop and bookstore. Kendall Whaling Museum, 27 Everett Street, P.O. Box 297, Sharon, Massachusetts 02067. Telephone (617) 784-5642.

Figure 6
The Dutch Whaling Gallery in the Kendall Whaling Museum in Sharon, Massachusetts, reminds the visitor that Yankees were not the first to hunt whales on the high seas. This action-filled oil painting by the 17th century artist Ludolf Backhuysen, in the Kendall collection, shows Dutch whaling in the Arctic.

Now out to the coast.

About a mile south we could see, rising above the rocks, the masts of the British brig which the *St. John* had endeavored to follow, which had slipped her cables and, by good luck, run into the mouth of Cohasset Harbor. A little further along the shore we saw a man's clothes on a rock; further, a woman's scarf, a gown, a straw bonnet, the brig's caboose, and one of her masts high and dry, broken into several pieces. In another rocky cove, several rods from the water, and behind rocks twenty feet high, lay a part of one side of the vessel, still hanging together. It was, perhaps, forty feet long, by fourteen feet wide. I was even more surprised at the power of the waves, exhibited on this shattered fragment, than I had been at the sight of the smaller fragments before. The largest

timbers and iron braces were broken superfluously, and I saw that no material could withstand the power of the waves; that iron must go to pieces in such a case, and an iron vessel would be cracked up like an eggshell on the rocks.

Henry David Thoreau, *Cape Cod*, Chapter 1

So Thoreau reported on his visit to the village of Cohasset in October, 1849, two days after the wreck of the brig *St. John*, of Galway, Ireland. Thoreau was on his way to Cape Cod; Cohasset is on the shore of Massachusetts Bay, just south of the entrance to Boston harbor. Cohasset's oceanfront is rimmed with rocks, the entrance to the little harbor is narrow and obscure; in a gale the *St. John*, carrying Irish immigrants to Boston, had gone on the Grampus Rock a mile offshore, with a tremendous loss of life. The wreck was one of a number that led to the building of the famous Minot Light on an offshore ledge. (The first lighthouse was destroyed by a storm the year after it was erected; the present 114-foot granite tower was built in 1860. Now unattended, the light still flashes 1-4-3, said locally to stand for "I love you.")

Cohasset's maritime past was already more than two centuries old at the time of Thoreau's visit; Captain John Smith looked in there in 1614. Cohasset townspeople were active fishermen and shipbuilders until 100 years ago. Today, Cohasset has been swallowed into Boston's exurbia but it has not forgotten its maritime past. In the center of "downtown," the local historical society has established the Cohasset Maritime Museum. The simple wooden building, built around 1790, was once a ship chandlery. (Next door, separated by a beautiful little garden, is the Cohasset Historical Society's general museum.)

Among the Cohasset Maritime Museum's exhibits is a fine big model of a full-rigged ship. Here, also, are the high desks where Cohasset merchants once kept their accounts of ships and cargo, and the sea chests where the men before the mast kept their few possessions. Shipwrights' tools recall long decades, roughly from 1708 to 1880, when Cohasset's shipyards turned out small sailing vessels.

Other exhibits include marine artifacts and whaling harpoons, as well as a collection of prints and paintings of maritime subjects.

Cohasset Maritime Museum is in the center of town at 18 Elm Street, where Elm meets Main Street. Open June through September, Tuesday-Sunday, 1:30 to 4:30 p.m. Admission: 75 cents; children 6 to 12, 25 cents. Owned by the Cohasset Historical Society. Cohasset Maritime Museum, P.O. Box 324, Cohasset, Massachusetts 02025. Telephone (617) 383-6930.

Heading south from Cohasset we quickly enter the "Old Colony"—the original Plymouth Colony, independent of the Massachusetts Bay Colony until late in the 17th century. Before long we reach Duxbury, one of the first towns settled by the Pilgrims as they spread out from Plymouth itself.

Duxbury Harbor is today a quiet place devoted to yachtsmen and their small craft. Once, however, it was a very considerable shipbuilding and shipping center. To be sure, the harbor—which opens into the north end of Plymouth Bay—was too shallow for the largest vessels of the 19th century, but nevertheless deep enough to float ships that went all over the world at the height of the great American shipping boom in the first half of that century. There had been shipyards in Duxbury since 1720.

Prosperity came after the War of 1812; in 1830, Duxbury, Plymouth, and Scituate, three adjoining towns, were home ports for some 27,000 tons of oceangoing vessels. This didn't even count local small craft. Probably some 135 deep-sea ships called these little villages home. Over the years almost 650 vessels were launched in Duxbury; in the 1830s no less than 20 shipyards were there.

A number of maritime notables came from Duxbury including the famous Captain Amasa Delano, author of *Delano's Voyages*, 1817, which was used for its sailing directions covering most of the world. Another native son was Captain Gamaliel Bradford, noted for his successful defense against four French privateers who attempted to capture his ship in 1800. But overshadowing all others were shipbuilders and shipowners Ezra Weston, and his son, Ezra Weston II, both of whom were called "King Caesar" because of their tremendous economic power. In the early 19th century, the younger Ezra Weston was described by Lloyds of London as owning the largest such enterprise in America. Weston operations were vertically integrated. In the Weston shipyard timber from the Weston forest built the Weston ships that carried Weston goods imported from Europe to be unloaded on Weston wharfs. The ships' hardware was turned out by the Weston forge, the sailcloth came from the Weston cotton mill, and the sails were cut and sewn in the Weston sail loft. Provisions such as meat and produce came from the Weston farm.

Over the years, the Weston fleet numbered close to 100 vessels. Their largest was the 881-ton *Hope*, launched in 1841.

In 1808, Ezra Weston II built a handsome mansion on Powder Point at the north end of Duxbury harbor. The house is still there on King Caesar Road, and is now owned and exhibited to the public by the Duxbury Rural and Historical Society. Besides being beautifully and authentically furnished, the house contains a small historical museum where shipbuilders' tools and various objects of maritime interest make up the bulk of the exhibits. Ship models include a large model of the famous American sloop of war *Kearsarge*, and half models from the Duxbury Sailors' Snug Harbor. Other exhibits include a four-foot ship's weathervane that was mounted on the Duxbury Liberty Pole in 1835; for years it pointed out which way the wind was blowing, then, in the terrible Portland gale of November 1898, it was blown down itself. On the walls is a list of the Weston ships built between 1794 and 1841.

Scattered through the house are several ship watercolors by Anton Roux, the famous Marseilles artist who painted ships of many nations as they visited his home port. One of the Roux pictures at the King

Caesar House shows the Duxbury brig *Argus* drifting onto the rocks at the entrance to Marseilles harbor.

There is a whole room full of small photographs and drawings of Duxbury ships. An exhibit of instruments, pictures, prints, and artifacts concerns the French trans-Atlantic cable, which comes ashore at Duxbury.

For many people, the most interesting exhibit—perhaps because it is the most personal—is a beautiful table. One of the many pieces of fine furniture in the house, the table has a remarkable association: The men rescued from HMS *Rodney*, wrecked nearby in 1793, ate their dinner at it when they were brought ashore and fed as the guests of King Caesar himself.

King Caesar House, fine mansion of shipbuilding and shipowning magnate, is on Powder Point in Duxbury, Massachusetts. Open mid-June through Labor Day, Tuesday-Sunday, 1 to 4 p.m. Admission: $1.00; youth, 50 cents children, 25 cents. Owned and maintained by Duxbury Rural and Historical Society, Inc., King Caesar House, King Caesar Road, Powder Point, Duxbury, Massachusetts 02332. Telephone (617) 934-2378.

Now to the next town, New England's most famous settlement, Plymouth, on Massachusetts Bay, where the Pilgrims landed in 1620 and founded Plymouth Colony, known as the "Old Colony" long after it had merged with Massachusetts. Today supported by manufacturing and tourism, Plymouth both preserves and recreates its unique maritime heritage.

Plymouth Bay was nicknamed "Thievish Harbor" by some early voyagers along the coast who claimed that a local Indian had stolen a harpoon there. The Pilgrim settlers were happy enough to land there in 1620, however, after a scouting party had determined that the water was deep enough for the *Mayflower*. There they built a rough village next to a little brook running down the hillside into the harbor. The bay is large and well-sheltered behind two barrier beaches extending out into the ocean like the claws of a crab, but over the years it became too shallow for anything much bigger than a fishing boat or coasting schooner.

Aside from its historical significance as the first permanent English settlement in New England and the second in North America, Plymouth today holds special appeal for anyone interested in ships of the past. Carefully preserved in a museum are the skeletal remains of one of the few survivors of the ships of nearly four centuries ago. Equally interesting, and more visually exciting, is one of the finest reproductions of a 17th-century vessel in this country: *Mayflower II*, designed and built with the greatest scholarly care to make it as authentic as possible.

Drive down the narrow Plymouth streets to the waterfront and your heart lifts at the sight of the gaily painted ship towering over her dock off Water Street. *Mayflower II* may be only a recreation, but she has been so beautifully designed and built that for a time the visitor is back in the early 17th century.

The first glance tells us this is unlike any ship we have ever seen before. The Pilgrims sailed only a few years after Queen Elizabeth's death. *Mayflower II's* poop climbing high above her narrow stern, her beaked bow and boxlike forecastle all make it clear that this is an Elizabethan ship, a younger sister of the armed merchantmen who went out to fight the Armada.

But more than her exotic appearance sets *Mayflower II* apart. Whimsy played no part in her design, the result of long and scholarly research. And she is no mock-up, no cosmeticized barge, but a true ship, built from the keel up in an English shipyard in close accordance with the shipwrights' methods of Elizabethan times. *Mayflower II* is also quite seaworthy, as she proved in 1957 when, like the original *Mayflower*, she sailed westward across the Atlantic to Plymouth, "weathering a fifty-knot gale with ease," as her designer noted with proper pride.

Mayflower II's authentic design and construction did not happen by chance. Her designer, William A. Baker, the distinguished naval architect and scholar of the history of ships, devoted his spare hours to research for six years. No plans of the original *Mayflower* survive (it's doubtful any ever existed) so Baker set out to plan a typical merchant ship of her day. Among his guides were the meager comments in the *Journal* of William Bradford, who crossed in the *Mayflower* in 1620. From her tonnage, her dimensions were deduced, and the probable hull lines and rig for a ship of these dimensions were calculated from contemporary shipbuilding treatises.

How the designer did this has been well described by Baker himself in his book *The New Mayflower*. The visitor, however, does not need to know how the design was arrived at in order to appreciate the result. Here are some suggestions of what to watch for:

- First her shape, starting with the sturdy beak that juts out below her bowsprit. This is a survival of the ram used by medieval vessels to attach each other. Another such survival is the curiously boxlike forecastle set on the forward deck, left over from the days when the forecastle was literally a little wooden castle, crowded with archers and men at arms. In ships of the Middle Ages, the forecastle was so high that it created windage that made a vessel hard to handle, so by the *Mayflower's* time it had been considerably cut down.

- The high poop at the *Mayflower*'s stern was to some extent a similar survival of a fighting castle, but it also served as a command center and provided cabin space for the captain and important passengers.
- The striking narrowing of the stern as the cabins pile up was for a very practical reason: to keep the vessel from being made top-heavy by too much weight high in the air.
- The square yard under the bowsprit carried the spritsail; the handling of this canvas can be envisioned by thinking of the bowsprit as another mast, leaning so far forward that it's closer to horizontal than vertical. The spritsail yard was hauled out on the bowsprit just as the regular yards were hoisted up the masts. A great improvement in rig that came into use in the 15th century, the spritsail exacted leverage at the extreme forward end of the ship, making her far easier to steer. (Spritsails were eventually superseded by jibs and staysails that did the same job more effectively.)
- The sail on the mizzen, the mast nearest the stern, is also unfamiliar to modern eyes. Triangular with its yard carried at a sharp angle to the mast, so that one end was close to the deck, the other high in the air, this was a lateen sail. It both made it easier to steer the ship, and also improved a vessel's ability to beat the windward. The lateen was hard to shift when tacking; eventually it was superseded by a gaff-rigged fore-and-aft sail, the spanker.

Now climb the gangplank and drink in what it was like to be a Pilgrim, a landsman packed into a small ship with more than 100 people crossing the stormy Atlantic in the late autumn. Aboard *Mayflower II* you will find "seamen," in the rough sailors' garb of 350 years ago, stationed at strategic points, ready to explain what you're looking at and answer questions. But keep a particularly sharp lookout for some features that you will find on few other ships you visit:

- Take a good look at the whipstaff, the long pole sticking up through the deck in the little room—called the steerage—just forward of the great cabin in the stern. The lower end of this pole projects through the deck into the cabin below where it is fastened to the ship's tiller. By moving the whipstaff right or left, while at the same time pushing down on it, the steerman could make the end of the huge tiller move in the opposite direction. This vertical lever provided mechanical advantage that made steering far easier. The whipstaff was another fairly recent improvement in ship design in the

Mayflower's time. Steering was still awkward, nevertheless; the *Mayflower*'s helmsman had to squint through a small half hatch above his head to catch a glimpse of the sails. When the watch officer on the open deck above wanted a change of course he had to shout down through the hatch. (For safety reasons a modern steering wheel was installed for the voyage of the *Mayflower II* across the Atlantic.)
- You'll find the binnacle just in front of the helmsman, just where it is placed today. *Mayflower*'s binnacle was pretty primitive, however, as you'll see. A small wooden cabinet holds the compasses, candles to see them by at night, and sandglasses, turned every half hour to keep track of the time.
- In the next little room forward of the steerage, take a good look at the ship's capstan—or at least the upper portion. The lower end of it extends down onto the deck below, so that two crews, one on each deck, could man the capstan bars at the same time. The capstan was used to hoist the yards and topmasts into place and to lift cargo out of the hold.
- The galley in the forecastle. Stoves hadn't been invented yet, so the galley was a seagoing version of the brick hearth, built right on the forecastle deck, that was used in homes ashore.

When you visit the lower deck, stop a minute and imagine what it was like in the original *Mayflower* that autumn of 1620. This space, the 'tween decks', was perhaps 75 feet long but broken up by the masts, pillars, the ship's pumps, and a knocked-down shallop carried for use in inshore exploration. Here, most of the Pilgrim party—50 men, 20 women and 34 children—lived for 66 days at sea. Ventilation came only from the small hatchway overhead, and even this had to be tightly closed in bad weather. Many passengers were undoubtedly seasick. Sanitary facilities consisted of buckets.

Yet in a voyage of over two months, only one *Mayflower* passenger died—a remarkable record, particularly compared with the terrible losses among passengers crammed into the immigrant ships a couple of centuries later.

A good ship, worthy of her passengers.

Mayflower II is docked off Water Street on the waterfront of Plymouth, Massachusetts. Open April through November, Monday-Friday, 9 a.m. to 5 p.m. Call for admission prices. Sponsored by nonprofit Plimoth Plantation, Box 1620, Plymouth, Massachusetts 02360. Telephone (617) 746-1622.

On Plymouth's Main Street, up the hill from *Mayflower II*, is Pilgrim Hall, a solid granite building

Figure 7
These timbers are battered but historic: the remains of *Sparrow-Hawk*, wrecked on Cape Cod in 1626 and visited by Pilgrims. They are preserved in Pilgrim Hall Museum, Plymouth, Massachusetts.

housing what is said to be the oldest public museum in the United States. Here are documents, artifacts, and pictures relating to the early days of the Plymouth Colony, including two enormous 19th-century paintings of the Pilgrims that have been reproduced on thousands of schoolroom walls. Most interesting, however, is Pilgrim Hall's "Seventeenth Century Ship Room," where rest the remains of a genuine 17th-century vessel, believed to be *Sparrow-Hawk*, wrecked on Cape Cod in 1626 while carrying settlers to Virginia. In the mid-19th century the remains came up out of the marsh mud, and were identified by local tradition and a passage in Bradford's *History* that told of the loss of a vessel in that vicinity. After various vicissitudes, including exhibition on Boston Common and in Barnum's circus, the wreck ended up in Pilgrim Hall.

After the magnificent *Mayflower II*, *Sparrow-Hawk* may seem anticlimactic: She was only about 40 feet long overall and nine feet deep. All that remains are the lower portions of her ribs, with keel and keelson and some planking. The bow is missing entirely. Nevertheless, she possesses one attribute denied to *Mayflower II*: She is an original. Enough remains to give valuable details of the shipbuilding methods of the early 17th century, information used in designing *Mayflower II*. At the same time, these battered timbers were in all probability boarded by the Pilgrim party, headed by Governor Bradford himself, that went to the rescue of the shipwrecked survivors.

A model of the *Sparrow-Hawk*, based on her remains and what is known about early 17th-century vessels of that size, is also in the ship room. Other exhibits include pictures and charts and there is a model of the *Mayflower*, slightly different in appearance from the full-sized *Mayflower II*. The model was felt by naval architect Baker to be based on vessels of a somewhat later period than the original *Mayflower*.

Sparrow-Hawk, Seventeenth Century Ship Room, Pilgrim Hall. At the corner of Main and Chilton Streets, Plymouth. Open all year except Christmas and New Year's Day. Daily from 9:30 a.m. to 4:30 p.m. Admission: $2.50; seniors, $2.00; children 6 to 15, 50 cents. Sponsored by nonprofit Pilgrim Society, 75 Court Street, Plymouth, Massachusetts 02360. Telephone (617) 746-1620.

Now down to that long spit of sand sticking out into the Atlantic into which the Plymouth colony quickly expanded.

The Old Colony II: Cape Cod

Cape Cod is the bared and bended arm of Massachusetts: the shoulder is at Buzzard's Bay; the elbow, or crazy bone, at Cape Mallebarre; the wrist at Truro; and the sandy fist at Provincetown,—behind which the State stands on her guard, with her back to the Green Mountains, and her feet planted on the floor of the ocean, like an athlete protecting her Bay,—boxing with northeast storms, and ever and anon, heaving up her Atlantic adversary from the lap of the earth,—ready to thrust forward her other fist, which keeps guard the while upon her breast at Cape Ann.

Henry David Thoreau, *Cape Cod*, Chapter 1

To appreciate the accuracy of Thoreau's anatomization of Cape Cod, it should be read with a map of the Cape at hand. Cape Mallebarre is the name on old charts for the sandy point, now known as Monomoy, sticking down from the southeast corner of the Cape at Chatham; the other place names are unchanged, although Buzzards Bay refers both to a town and the bay it's named after. Unchanged, also, is the essential shape of the Cape itself despite almost 150 more years of battering by the Atlantic adversary since Thoreau wrote.

Cape Cod itself was given its name by old Cap'n Ben Gosnold, who explored much of this coast in the *Concord*. On May 15, 1602, he recorded: "Near this cape we came to anchor in fifteen fathoms, where we took great store of codfish, for which we altered the name to Cape Cod."

Eighteen years later the Pilgrims first landed at the outer end of the Cape and thanked God for setting their feet once more "on ye firm and stable earth, their proper element." They went on to Plymouth, but people from that colony soon moved down onto the Cape, settling one town after another until they reached the very tip, which became Provincetown. From the beginning, the settlers made their livings as much from the sea as from their sandy fields: fishing, gathering clams and oysters, harpooning whales off their beaches, building small vessels along the little tidal rivers, to trade along the coast or, from the north side, to carry their catch and produce across Massachusetts Bay to Boston. During the Revolution the Cape Codders also did a little privateering in open boats, rowing out on dark nights to pick off British vessels passing through Vineyard Sound on their way to New York. When a blockade cut off the import of salt, essential for curing fish and preserving meat, enterprising Cape people started making their own salt from sea water. At one time the shore was lined with salt works: 136 of them between Sandwich and Provincetown in 1800.

Cape Cod living was frugal, but substantial—provided you liked fish: fish for breakfast, fish for supper, and quite possibly fish for noonday dinner in between. Every now and then, some town would have a windfall when a richly laden ship would come ashore. Often told is the story of the Wellfleet minister who happened to look out the church window from his lofty pulpit and saw a vessel driving onto the beach. He immediately stopped his sermon and, in the words of Samuel Eliot Morison, "descended the pulpit stairs, and with a shout of 'Start fair!' led his congregation pell-mell out the meeting house door." There is a tradition that wrecks were encouraged by decoying vessels ashore with false lights—a lantern hung on a cow say, so that it bobbed up and down as she meandered along the beach, appearing from a distance like the light of a wave-tossed ship.

The first half of the 19th century saw Cape Cod's maritime activities at their peak: The Cape towns, says Morison, increased their seaborne tonnage six-fold between 1815 and 1850. Fishermen, coasters, and small trading vessels made up the bulk of the Cape fleet. As Morison noted, Cape Cod's harbors were too small and shallow for the big square-riggers that came to dominate world trade. Nevertheless, the Cape was a cradle of famous shipmasters, who made their name in the ships of New York or Boston.

In the latter half of the 19th century, Cape Cod's maritime activities dwindled, smart investors turned to cranberry bogs, but inshore fishing, shellfishing, and lobstering remained. They still do, even though the Cape has become flooded every summer with such swarms of summer visitors that it sometimes seems it must sink beneath their weight.

Let Mr. Thoreau close, as he opened, these brief comments on Cape Cod, still from the perspective of the 1840s:

> The time must come when this coast will be a place of resort for those New-Englanders who really wish to visit the sea-side. At present it is wholly unknown to the fashionable world, and probably it will never be agreeable to them. If it is merely a ten-pin alley, or a circular railway, or an ocean of mint-julep, that the visitor is in search of,—if he thinks more of the wine than the brine, as I suspect some do at Newport,—I trust that for a long time he will be disappointed here. But this shore will never be more attractive than it is now. Such beaches as are fashionable are here made and unmade in a day, I may almost say, by the sea shifting its sands. Lynn and Nantasket! this bare and bended arm it is that makes the bay in which they lie so snugly. What are springs and waterfalls? Here is the spring of springs, the waterfall of waterfalls. A storm in the fall or winter is the time to visit it; a light-house or a fisherman's hut the true hotel. A man may stand there and put all America behind him.

Thoreau's prophecy has more than been fulfilled; not just New Englanders but it seems half of America has made Cape Cod its seaside resort and the Cape has not wholly escaped the 1980s equivalent of 10-pin alleys and circular railways. Happily, Cape Codders and many of their visitors have joined to preserve the maritime memories, traditions, and relics of this bare and bended arm intruding into the sea.

Let's travel down the Cape and take a look, starting with two museums on the Buzzards Bay side.

Fine ship models, beautiful pictures, the gear of daily life at sea, restored windjammers—all these help us to visualize our maritime heritage. But sometimes a door to the past can be opened by something as prosaic as a tiny slip of paper. For example, the insurance company's certificate that the visitor can see at the museum of the Falmouth Historical Society at Falmouth Center on Cape Cod.

The certificate, along with $100, was presented to mariner Silas Jones of the whaleship *Awoshonks* as recognition and reward for his saving the vessel after it was attacked by natives in the South Seas. When the *Awoshonks* called at a group of islands, natives came aboard the ship, apparently to trade with the captain and crew. Suddenly, the visitors picked up the sharp whale-cutting spades and attacked all the crew

members and officers on deck. Jones was below. Observing what was happening on deck he deliberately exploded a powder keg, which blew off part of the deck of the ship, killing a number of the attackers and scaring off the rest. Jones, apparently the only surviving member of the ship's company who was able to navigate, then sailed the *Awoshonks* to safety in Hawaii.

Falmouth today is a quiet little Cape Cod town principally concerned with the summer tourist traffic that is its livelihood, but Silas Jones' certificate is evidence that it was once a very different kind of place. With one shore on Buzzards Bay and the other on Vineyard Sound, Falmouth was a lively maritime center, sending ships and seamen to remote parts of the world. Their memory, and the Jones certificate, are preserved in the pleasant little museum of the Falmouth Historical Society in two fine old houses facing on the triangular green in Falmouth Center.

Although most of the museum is concerned with furniture, silver, and other non-maritime aspects of Falmouth's history, there are a number of exhibits of maritime interest. Among them are:

- sailors' valentines;
- a sea captain's medicine chest;
- ship prints;
- various oil portraits of Falmouth sea captains;
- whaling harpoons and other tools of the trade.

The society suffered a grievous loss some years ago when the museum was broken into and a major part of a notable collection of scrimshaw was stolen, but the surviving exhibits are well worth a visit by lovers of maritime Cape Cod.

Falmouth Historical Society's Museums are in two fine old houses side by side on the north side of the Village Green at Falmouth Center, on Cape Cod. Open Monday-Friday, June 15 to September 15, 2 to 5 p.m. Admission: $1.00; children, 50 cents. Falmouth Historical Society, P.O. Box 174, Falmouth, Massachusetts 02541. Telephone (617) 548-4857.

Now to another little museum in the town of Falmouth, at the village of Woods Hole, at the southwest angle of Cape Cod, Thoreau's "shoulder."

Fishermen and watermen in many small coastal towns developed distinctive small craft adapted to local needs. Some of these proved useful beyond their home ports and gave their names to generic types, such as the Friendship sloop. Others were known only in their immediate neighborhoods and today these are highly endangered species, which require lovers of small craft to recognize their unique qualities, track down surviving examples, and see to their preservation.

Extinction was almost the fate of one such handsome little vessel, the small catboat known in Woods Hole on Cape Cod as the "*spritser*" (probably a corruption of "spritsail"). Spritsers had open cockpits and were smaller than the usual Cape Cod catboats; both characteristics were developed to make them handier with oars in the tricky, eddying tides that rush through Woods Hole, the narrow passage between the mainland and islands just offshore. Most spritsers were kept in an eel-pond, sheltered but with a low highway bridge over the narrow entrance. The spritsail rig was combined with a hinged mast that could be folded down to pass under the bridge.

Happily, a handful have survived. Three are in the Mystic Seaport small craft collection; one was found locally and has been restored to first-class condition. Now, in the summer time, when the Woods Hole Historical Society Museum is open, the little spritser rides the lawn beside the museum building, on the hill above the ferry landing.

Within the museum, the society's displays include drawings and photographs of small craft as well as artifacts and memorabilia of the area. The museum is easy to find. Everyone who goes to Woods Hole to take the ferry to Martha's Vineyard passes its modest building.

Woods Hole is, of course, famous as the home of the Marine Biological Laboratory, one of the world's great centers for the study of ocean life. Here, also, are the Woods Hole Oceanographic Institute and the Fisheries Research Station, which are devoted to other aspects of the marine world. Yachtsmen remember Woods Hole for the famous passage between Buzzards Bay and Vinyard Sound, where the tides roar through at speeds to make the novice pale.

Woods Hole Historical Society, Bradley House Museum, white wooden building next to public library opposite entrance to Martha's Vineyard ferry docks. Open June and September, Wednesday and Saturday, 1 to 3 p.m. July and August, Tuesday-Saturday, 11 a.m. to 4 p.m. Admission: 50 cents. Woods Hole Historical Society, Bradley House Museum, Woods Hole, Massachusetts 02540. Telephone (617) 548-7270.

Now back to the north shore of the cape, the Massachusetts Bay side.

Drive east through the little village that is the center of the Cape Cod town and county of Barnstable, past the somber granite courthouse, up Cobb's Hill, and you will come to a fine local history museum where the Barnstable Historical Society displays its collection, augmented by loans from friends.

Lodged in the old redbrick custom house, the Donald G. Trayser Memorial Museum is full of the spirit of the old Cape Cod before it sagged under the weight of summer visitors. The visitor can easily imagine Joseph Lincoln puttering around, gathering ideas for his turn-of-the-century novels about the Cape.

As a true Cape establishment, the museum has a strong and completely authentic maritime component in its collection, concentrated on the first floor and in the little carriage house adjacent. Ship models, paintings, photographs, ships' records, the tools of the shipwrights and sailmakers, nautical instruments, and artifacts tell the story of the day when Cape Codders lived by the sea and sometimes died by it.

Particularly notable is the museum's small but choice collection of ship models, all with a slightly rough finish, suggesting that each miniature vessel was the labor of someone familiar with the original ship rather than a model built under contract by a professional craftsman. Among the models are:

- a so-called working model of the steamer *George S. Homer*, five feet long, its master a Cape Cod man from East Dennis—notice that in the *Homer's* day steamers carried auxiliary sails in case the engine broke down;
- a small model of the ship *Belle of the West*, built in East Dennis on Cape Cod in 1853, and as the caption succinctly reads: "Foundered 1868;"
- the sloop *Mail*, 1837, which carried the United States mails and passengers back and forth between Barnstable and Boston in the days when the land trip meant a long, roundabout dusty journey by jolting stagecoach on rough roads around the rim of Massachusetts Bay. According to Cape Cod historian Henry C. Kittredge, *Mail* was built to beat the fast schooner-packet of rival Yarmouth on the Boston run: *Mail* won the first race by a scant length.

Among the handsome furniture exhibits is a merchant's desk with a high open file for books and papers. Lying on the desk is the day-by-day journal of a Barnstable man; the visitor may read how the journal keeper started each day with an entry noting the wind direction, clouds or fog, and the condition of the sea: calm, stormy, or otherwise. Even those who lived ashore in Barnstable lived by the weather and the sea.

In the carriage house next door, is a big photo sequence from the early 20th century showing the operation of the fishtraps by which many Cape Cod fishermen earned their living in the shallow waters of Massachusetts Bay.

Besides furniture, the non-maritime exhibits include dolls, toys, clothing, and so forth. Of particular interest is a display of very simple, very beautiful table silver made by a local silversmith right in Barnstable Village.

The building itself is an interesting one. High and square atop its hill, it was the customs house for the Cape Cod district. Built in 1856, it was said to be the first fire-proof building on Cape Cod. The original heating system was most unusual: The interior cast-iron pillars are hollow and run down into the basement where a stove at the foot of each column sent warm air up through it to heat the building.

The Donald G. Trayser Memorial Museum is lodged in the one-time custom house, 1856, atop Cobb's Hill on Route 6A, just east of the center of Barnstable Village on the north shore of Cape Cod. From Route 6, main east-west Cape Cod highway, turn north at Barnstable sign to 6A, then east. Redbrick museum is on right just beyond Hyannis Road traffic light. Staffed by volunteers. Open July 1 to September 15, Tuesday-Saturday, 1:30 to 4:30 p.m. Admission: 50 cents; under 12, 25 cents. Sponsored by Barnstable Historical Society and Association. Donald G. Trayser Memorial Museum, Barnstable, Massachusetts 02630. Telephone (617) 362-2092.

Now, way down Cape to the very tip.

Few parts of the Atlantic Coast have been so littered with wrecks as the ocean-face of Cape Cod. There the U.S. Life-saving Service—and earlier, the volunteers of the Massachusetts Humane Society—fought a continuing battle to save the men whose vessels were driven ashore as they sought to beat out around the dreaded Cape in the face of winter gales. Today, lifesaving stations are no more; their function has been replaced by Coast Guard rescue cutters and helicopters. Indeed, in these days few wrecks occur on the Cape, although a freighter went ashore there as recently as the spring of 1984.

However, at least one lifesaving station still survives. To be sure, the Chatham Old Harbor Station is no longer in its original position down at the southeast corner of the Cape. That site has been eroded away by wind and water; in order to save the building, the National Park Service has moved the station to Race Point Beach on the very northern end of the Cape.

According to a 1902 account, the Old Harbor Station at its original Chatham site had then been in commission "less than five years during which timekeeper Doane and his crew have rescued 21 persons in their surfboat and taken 13 shipwrecked sailors ashore in the breeches buoy."

A station at Race Point had been established much earlier: in 1873. In the 15 years before 1902 there had been 92 wrecks nearby and more than 600 persons, including two women, were taken ashore. Thirty-seven were rescued by breeches buoy, the rest by surf boat, which meant launching a boat from an open beach through heavy seas, rowing through the surf, maneuvering alongside a stranded vessel, and holding the boat there for the shipwrecked crew to jump aboard.

According to the 1902 account, "The coast at Race Point is very treacherous, and has been the scene of many wrecks. The tides run past the point with great velocity, and vessels are frequently swept to destruction on the sunken wrecks which lie along the coast there.

The surfmen of the station go over a patrol westward of two and one-half miles, and eastward about one and three-quarters miles."

The visitor to Race Point on a summer day must use his imagination to visualize the winter gales; he'll probably find the ocean gently embracing a broad beach crowded with summer visitors.

The original Race Point Station no longer exists, but Chatham Old Harbor Station has been relocated a few hundred yards from the site. A two-story shingled structure, it has been extensively restored and the large boat room devoted to exhibits. Here is displayed a large Race Point surfboat, the standard lifesaving craft, about 24 feet long, and double-ended with watertight compartments at bow and stern. A strip of cork around the gunwale served as a fender alongside a wreck and also helped to keep the boat afloat if swamped in the surf. The boat seated five to six oarsmen; rescued persons sat in the bottom while they were brought back through the surf.

Other exhibits include a large dory and, of more particular interest, a hand-drawn beach cart that the lifesaving crew rushed along the shore loaded with equipment to a point opposite a wreck. All the lifesaving gear is there, including the Lyle gun with its projectile which was used to hurl the lifeline—far further than a person could throw it—until it caught on the rigging of a vessel stranded out beyond the surf line. Here, also, is the breeches buoy that was run out on the lifeline and hauled back and forth, each time bringing a rescued person ashore.

A traditional "wreck pole" has been set up at the station and used in the summer time to demonstrate how the breeches buoy was used. In the old days, of course, a lifesaving crew held actual practice sessions with the wreck pole taking the place of the mast of the wrecked vessel.

Old Harbor Lifesaving Station is now on the north-facing beach at Race Point, just outside Provincetown on the tip of Cape Cod. Approaching from up-Cape on Route 6, turn right at the only traffic light; sign says Race Point and Provincetown Airport. Province Lands Visitors Center, atop high dune, well-marked. Bookstore. Road continues past airport to Race Point Beach (fine, wide beach, cold water). Parking, small fee, next to National Park Rangers Station in former Coast Guard building. Path to lifesaving station east behind boardwalk. Open summer months. Admission: free. Administered by Cape Cod National Seashore of the National Park Service. Mailing address: Cape Cod National Seashore, South Wellfleet, Massachusetts 02663. Telephone (617) 487-2100 or 487-1256.

Now, back to the south shore of the Cape to take to the sea for a visit to those famous islands: Nantucket and Martha's Vineyard. The Nantucket boats leave from Hyannis.

The Old Colony III: The Whaling Towns

And thus have these naked Nantucketers, these sea hermits, issuing from their ant hill in the sea, overrun and conquered the watery world like so many Alexanders; parcelling out among them the Atlantic, Pacific, and Indian oceans . . . two thirds of this terraqueous globe are the Nantucketer's. For the sea is his; he owns it, as Emperors own empires; other seamen having but a right of way through it. Merchant ships are but extension bridges; armed ones but floating forts; like pirates and privateers, though following the sea as highwaymen the road, they but plunder other ships, other fragments of the land themselves, without seeking to draw their living from the bottomless deep itself. The Nantucketer, he alone resides and riots on the sea; he alone, in Bible language, goes down to it in ships; to and fro ploughing it as his own special plantation. *There* is his home; *there* lies his business, which a Noah's flood would not interrupt, though it overwhelmed all the millions in China. He lives on the sea, as prairie cocks in the prairie; he hides among the waves, he climbs them as chamois hunters climb the Alps. For years he knows not the land; so that when he comes to it at last it smells like another world, more strangely than the moon would to an Earthman. With the landless gull, that at sunset folds her wings and is rocked to sleep between billows; so at nightfall, the Nantucketer, out of sight of land, furls his sails, and lays him to his rest, while under his very pillow rush herds of walruses and whales.

Herman Melville, *Moby Dick*, Chapter 14

Melville's celebration of the salt-water empire of the Nantucketers was published in 1851, just 10 years after he shipped before the mast in a whaleship. In those 10 years something had happened to Nantucket and its whaling empire on the seven seas. The year 1843 saw Nantucket at the peak of its population and its prosperity. The little island, 25 miles off the Cape Cod coast, for a century the world's greatest whaling port, was home to 88 whaleships and the village boasted the largest output of refined whale oil and spermaceti candles of any American community. But that year was the peak; from then on Nantucket whaling was all downhill.

A major problem was the sandbar that kept forming across the mouth of Nantucket Harbor, making it more and more difficult for whaleships to get in and out, particularly as these vessels grew bigger and deeper. At the same time, national financial panics made it more difficult for whaleship owners to raise capital, while fires devastated Nantucket village and consumed local resources. Now the whaling industry was shifting its base to New Bedford on the mainland, once almost a Nantucket colony, now a victorious rival. New Bedford could handle the largest whaleships, while its railroad connections made it possible to ship whale oil and bundles of whalebone directly to the markets of Boston and New York. Nantucket suffered the final blow when its whaleships, along with those of other whaling ports, were ravaged by Confederate raiders during the Civil War.

The last Nantucket whaleship put to sea in 1870. Ironically, the economic collapse of the mid-19th century is what makes Nantucket so attractive to visitors today. Coming into the dock on the ferry steamer you see stretching up the hillside what historian Samuel Eliot Morison described as "the one unspoiled seaport town of New England, a town in which every house built before 1840—and few were not—was sired out of the sea."

For Nantucket owes the preservation of its wonderful old houses not to any early surge of archaeological interest among its inhabitants but to hard times. Where the prosperous New England towns on the mainland tore down their colonial houses to replace them with factories or the latest Victorian mansions, Nantucket was so poor that it had to make do with the beautiful simple houses of the past. In the latter part of the 19th century, the saying was common among Nantucketers that their island had "just three exports after the whaling ended. These were fish, cranberries, and schoolteachers."

Actually, what kept the island alive and its houses from falling into their cellar holes, was the new and profitable trade of taking in summer boarders. At the same time, the events that led to the survival of the houses "sired out of the sea" has also meant the survival of many relics of Nantucket's maritime past. Two fine museums close to the steamer landing preserve many of these relics to tell the story of the maritime traditions of the island. Visitors should also plan to drop into the Nantucket Athenaeum, a few blocks away.

As you step off the boat and head up the street from Steamboat Wharf, almost the first building you come to on the right is the center of the preservation of Nantucket's whaling tradition. The famous Nantucket Whaling Museum, at the head of Steamboat Wharf on Broad Street, is housed in a building which is itself an important part of Nantucket's whaling and maritime heritage, a one-time "candle house," a factory for the manufacture of whale-oil candles. Built in 1847, it was associated with many of the Nantucket whaling families who provided the captains, merchants, and manufacturers of the island.

The building has been expertly converted to a museum by the Nantucket Historical Association but it retains an important relic of its days as a candle factory: the only remaining spermaceti press in existence, which the visitor will find in Sanderson Hall, the largest museum gallery. By pressing down on the enormous lever, clear strained sperm oil, guaranteed not to congeal in the coldest weather, was squeezed out of blocks of congealed crude whale oil, called "black cake." The pure pressings made the finest lubricating oil, while the solid matter left after all the liquid was squeezed out was used for spermaceti candles.

But before he gets to the famous press the visitor has a lot to see. For many, the greatest prize in a great collection is probably what is believed to be the oldest surviving whaleship model. The little vessel was made in 1765 by a 14-year-old Nantucket boy, William Meador, presumably with the help of other family members. In the lower gallery is another unique exhibit, a large wooden model of Nantucket's "camels," an ingenious—and expensive—attempt to overcome the problem of the bar blocking the harbor mouth. These enormous wooden pontoons were floated out, filled with water, and sunk on either side of an entering ship; then pumped out, an action that lifted the ship so it could clear the bar and be towed into the harbor. In effect, a floating drydock: a desperate but unsuccessful attempt to halt the decline of Nantucket whaling.

Here are other highlights of the museum, starting at the entrance:

- Notice the desk from a Nantucket shipowner's office. Beside it a huge armchair presented to an equally huge whaleship captain after his ship took a sperm whale that yielded a record-breaking 162 barrels of oil.

- To the left of the entrance, a diorama shows a Nantucket harbor from a wharf stacked with whale-oil barrels. Here also is a watercolor of the whaleship *Hero* of 1820, an unfortunate vessel that was captured by pirates and her captain killed, but which was later recaptured by the crew.

- In the lower gallery are five craftsmen's shops, mock-ups fitted with the original tools and equipment of the various maritime crafts that serviced the whaleships. Here are a cooper shop, a ship-smith shop, a sail loft, a rigging loft, and a whaleboat shop. (Note that the whaleboat frame is only half scale, necessary to make it fit the space. The visitor will find a full-sized whaleboat with all its equipment on the entrance-level floor of the museum.)

- On the ground floor of the new museum wing, the visitor finds a beautifully detailed scale model of the whaleship *Essex*, which was sunk by a whale that rammed it head-on in 1819. This incident was the basis of Melville's *Moby Dick*, in which Captain Ahab's ship is rammed and sunk by the very whale he is relentlessly pursuing.

- Along the wall in this section is an enormous map of a Nantucket whaleship voyage around the world in 1846, which makes clear the location of the principal whaling grounds. Nearby is the big Fresnel lens of the old Sankaty Light at the east end of Nantucket Island.

- Here also is the Hussey Collection of whaling tools and weapons—harpoons, lances, spades, knives, and so forth. Along the walls are portraits of whaling masters from Nantucket, men who risked their lives to make the fortunes of the island shipowners and merchants.

- Along the ramp to the first floor is the complete skeleton of a 43-foot finback whale that washed ashore in Nantucket some 20 years ago. It is beautifully displayed so that the entire structure is clear; the accompanying photographs show the whale on the beach.

- On the entrance level of the museum, in addition to the whaleboat, is a model of the whaling bark *Morning Star* of 1853. An accompanying diagram of the deck layout identifies the various hatches, the galley deck house, boats, winches, and so forth; it's a valuable aid to learning the parts of the whaleship. Nearby is a beautiful

Figure 8
Huge wall chart, right, in Nantucket Whaling Museum plots the track of the ship *Nantucket* on a round-the-world whaling voyage in 1846. At left is the Fresnel lens from the old Sankaty light at the east end of Nantucket Island.
(Photo courtesy of Nantucket Historical Society.)

whalebone model of a mid-19th century whaleship, with such nice details as the yards for double topsails and with the staging on which crewmen stood to cut up dead whales, ordinarily carried folded flat against the ship's side, shown extended ready for a whale brought alongside.
• Upstairs on the second floor, in a little room over the entrance is an extensive and remarkably fine scrimshaw collection centered around an enormous piece of bone that shows three ships with their boats attacking whales. Another fine example of the sailor's pictorial art shows the battle between the *Monitor* and the *Merrimac*.

The core of the museum's exhibits was gathered by a summer resident, Edward F. Sanderson, who was guided by expert advice and well-supplied with funds. Starting in the 1920s, when there were still many whaling artifacts and memorabilia available on the island, Sanderson collected tools, implements, gear, models, scrimshaw and craft work, paintings and prints, books and documents, and eventually he gave these to the Nantucket Historical Association. The exhibits were arranged and installed by a retired whaleman, the son of one of Nantucket's most successful captains, who made certain that they were authentic and described with complete accuracy.

The Nantucket Whaling Museum is lodged in a large brick building at the head of Steamboat Wharf where the mainland steamers dock. Open May 28 to October 12: daily, 10 a.m. to 5 p.m. October 13 to December 31 and April 1 to May 27: Saturday and Sunday only, same times. Closed Christmas Day. Admission: $2.50; ages 5 to 14, $1.00. A museum of the Nantucket Historical Association, Box 1016, Union Street, Nantucket, Massachusetts 02554. Nantucket Whaling Museum, Broad Street, Nantucket, Massachusetts 02554. Telephone (617) 228-1899.

Although frequently overshadowed by whaling in the public mind, there were, of course, other aspects to Nantucket's maritime past. These, as well as non-maritime history, are cherished in another museum, the Peter Foulger Memorial, in its new building cheek by jowl to the Nantucket Whaling Museum. ("Foulger," incidentally, is the old spelling of the familiar Nantucket name of Folger.)

Although Nantucket never was a major port except for whalers, her ships and shipmasters, especially the latter, played an active role in 19th-century American maritime and naval affairs. Later, Nantucket became a center for yachting and pleasure boating. Fishing—and more recently scalloping—are important island sea trades. All these activities are reflected in the Peter Foulger Museum collections.

The museum exhibits include maritime artifacts, ship models, and paintings, as well as such non-maritime displays as furniture and china. A very fine model portrays the clipper *Houqua*, which was commanded by a Nantucket shipmaster who, incidentally, disappeared with his ship on a voyage from Japan to New York in 1864. Another model is of the ship *St. Nicholas*, also commanded by a Nanucket man and famous for the rescue of the crew of a sinking English bark off Cape Horn.

On the floor of the museum is the little catboat *Mincie*, a fine specimen of local pleasure craft. Another exhibit of special interest is a Starbuck sea chest. Starbuck, like Foulger, is one of these enduring Nantucket names. The Starbuck who owned this chest was Albert W., who somewhere around 1825 drew a picture of the ship *Agnes* on the inside cover of the chest.

Also of special interest is a small portrait of Captain Abraham Boston, the first black shipmaster in Nantucket. In 1822, Boston sailed on a whaling voyage to the South Atlantic in the schooner *Industry* with an all-black crew. A touching remembrance of the perils of the sea is a small memorial drawing to Stephen G. Coffin—yet another famous Nantucket name—who was killed by a fall from aloft in the early 19th century.

Of course, as an island Nantucket has always been dependent upon good waterborne communications to the mainland. Many of the maritime exhibits of the Peter Foulger Museum are concerned with the steamers that have connected Nantucket to Cape Cod over the decades. Pictures, paintings, and photographs show how these vessels have grown and changed over the years. Wrecks on the island and on the dangerous shoals that stretch far out into the Atlantic south of its shores have an exhibit of their own.

The greater part of the museum is devoted to works of art and domestic community-related exhibits of furniture, china, toys, glassware, silver, paintings, and costumes. But on Nantucket even these frequently have a strong maritime flavor. A fine example is a wonderful collection of Liverpool-ware pitchers—easy to imagine holding a concoction of rum and hot water on a cold winter's night. Each pitcher is decorated with a picture of a Nantucket ship and we learn that the pitchers were often made to order for the shipmaster to bring home.

Even as humble a domestic object as a woven basket has a sea flavor on Nantucket. A whole exhibit in the Foulger is devoted to what are called "lightship baskets." It seems that the crews of lightships found time hanging heavy on their hands and many men learned how to weave baskets. The baskets were distributed all over the island and eventually became famous and much sought after by collectors. Today, Nantucket Lightship baskets are a highly prized remembrance of times past.

Peter Foulger Museum is next to the Whaling Museum on Broad Street. Research library. Open daily, May 29 to October 12; 10 a.m. to 5 p.m. Open on limited basis spring and fall. Admission: $1.50; ages 5 to 14, 50 cents. A museum of Nantucket Historical Association, Box 1016, Union Street, Nantucket, Massachusetts 02554. Peter Foulger Memorial Museum, Broad Street, Nantucket, Massachusetts 02554. Telephone (617) 228-1894.

It is a miracle that the vessel is still on her station. We are all well but have had a very hard winter. Gale after gale has tossed us about but the vessel has been true to her moorings.

Years will not recall to mind such a winter as this at the South Shoal. The boat has been completely covered with snow and ice. It has been a winter that will never be forgotten by me, or those with me. It has been full of heart-rending scenes. I have seen men call for help when it was impossible to render it and assistance asked for which I have given. And there have been vessels, the crews of which have probably been washed overboard, leaving their barque to drift by our vessel. The ice has been twelve inches thick for two days. There is no water in sight. I expect every moment to have to let our boat go to keep the vessel and ice from coming over us. Worse than all, I have seen bodies go by, and on life preservers, too.

From boyhood I have been on the ocean but never before saw sights so sad as this winter have presented. In the gales that we have had, I have thought it impossible to keep this vessel here, but we have been protected by a higher power than that of man.
Inquirer and Mirror, Nantucket, February 13, 1857. Letter from the captain of the Nantucket Lightship.

Few lightship stations on the North American coast are as exposed as that which marks the cruel Nantucket Shoal stretching 40 miles southeastward of Nantucket Island. The scene of many wrecks, the shoals were marked by a lightship for generations, warning vessels to stay outside. The Nantucket light is the first seen by vessels approaching North America from Europe or the south. The shoals were the last in the United States to be marked by a manned lightship; it has now been replaced, like all the others, by an automatic buoy.

The retired lightship, *Nantucket*, was until recently on exhibition at Straight Wharf. Away from the island during the summer of 1986, she is expected to return, although when and where is uncertain. In the expectation that she will once again be on exhibition at Nantucket, a report on this interesting vessel is included here.

The largest lightship ever built, 149 feet long, the *Nantucket* was the next to last lightship on Nantucket Shoals, where she served almost 40 years. *Nantucket* is one of the most interesting of the several lightships that have been preserved at various places along our coast. The bridge, deckhouse, radio room, lower deck, crews' quarters, mess hall, wardroom, and recreation room are almost entirely open to visitors, and you can look down through gratings to the engine room. Full descriptive placards in each room not only explain what you are looking at but provide background and anecdotal information. The quotation from the Nantucket newspaper that opens this section, for example, is taken from a poster in the pilothouse.

Here are some things to watch for:

- The pilothouse is completely equipped with wheel, engine-room telegraph, binnacle, and radar.
- The chart in the pilothouse shows the various locations of the lightship since its establishment in the mid-1850s. Notice the tip of Nantucket Shoals stretching southward out into the Atlantic.
- The huge windlasses below decks in the bow used to control the two great anchors, each weighing 7,000 pounds and each held by 1,000 feet of heavy chain. Note the anecdote, posted in the pilothouse, of the captain's account of almost drifting onto the shoal when the anchor

chain broke while steam was down. Later on, incidentally, the lightship was converted to diesel engines so that they were always ready for use.
- The picture gallery in the port passageway shows the various lightships that have been stationed on Nantucket Shoals since 1854. Other photographs show wrecks on or near Nantucket, including photos of the *Andrea Doria* and the *Stockholm* after the collision in which the Doria was sunk.

Service aboard a lightship anchored in rough seas day after day, month after month, year around, despite occasional periods ashore, was both monotonous and dangerous. The predecessor to the lightship on display, for example, was lost with all hands in 1934, run down by an enormous transatlantic liner that was homing on the lightship's radio beacon.

An idea of what it was like to be on a stationary light vessel can be obtained from the doggerel, posted in the radio room, that some operator wrote to while away his time. An excerpt:

On that lonely lightship job
Much dreaded by every gob
Who's sent to serve his country on the foam
Surely all a fellow's thoughts
Get where they hadn't ought
And he gets to wishing he was safely back home.

For its roll, roll, roll
With the sea a mountain high all around
She lunges and you fall
She is never still at all
And oh, you wish you were on the ground.

The replacement for the retired *Nantucket* on display took over the station in 1975. This replacement vessel eventually became the last lightship on active duty as one by one all the others were replaced by automatic buoys. Now she too is gone.

For information about the lightship's return to Nantucket, check with the Nantucket Historical Association, (617) 228-1894.

For sunbaked visitors seeking relief from the tourist-crowded streets of Nantucket village, a refuge is the big white Greek Revival building that houses the Nantucket Athenaeum. Basically a library and reading room, the Athenaeum like everything else on Nantucket has a strong maritime flavor.

On top of the eight-foot bookcases, for example, are three ship models. More easily seen are other models in glass cases: the whaleship *Charles W. Morgan* and the bark *Benjamin F. Packard*, a famous Bath-built vessel.

The Athenaeum also houses a small but interesting collection of scrimshaw; the central piece is a 30-

inch section of whalebone, inscribed with a picture of a whaleboat attacking a whale, with three ships in the background—a fine example of not-so-primitive art. The Athenaeum also has several fine oil paintings of ships, including portraits of the clipper *Surprise* and Captain Nat Palmer's famous vessel, the *Samuel Russell*.

Now to the other island, Martha's Vineyard, to the west of Nantucket and much closer to the Cape Cod shore.

> Next was Tashtego, an unmixed Indian from Gay Head, the most westerly promontory of Martha's Vineyard, where there still exists the last remnant of a village of red men, which has long supplied the neighboring island of Nantucket with many of her most daring harpooners. . . . no longer snuffing in the trail of the wild beasts of the woodland, Tashtego now hunted in the wake of the great whales of the sea; the unerring harpoon of the son fitly replacing the infallible arrow of the sires.
>
> Herman Melville, *Moby Dick*, Chapter 27.

Tashtego was one of two Gay Head Indians aboard Melville's mythical whaleship *Pequod* and "the third mate was Flask, a native of Tisbury, in Martha's Vineyard. A short, stout, ruddy young fellow, very pugnacious concerning whales . . . ." While Martha's Vineyard, a triangular island some five miles off the southwest corner of Cape Cod, never had a very large whaling fleet of its own, in real life, as in Melville's novel, the island supplied many skilled whalemen, both Indians and Yankees, to neighboring Nantucket and New Bedford. According to local historians, for example, the small settlement of Chilmark on the southwest corner of the Vineyard, from which only one whaling vessel ever sailed was nevertheless home port for some 150 whaling masters and scores of mates, while nearly every family included at least one whaleman.

Martha's Vineyard has been for a century largely a summer resort with activities afloat limited to fishing and yachting, but many aspect of the island's maritime traditions are the themes of exhibits in the small but interesting and well-arranged Francis Foster Museum of the Dukes County Historical Society, on one of the oldest streets of Edgartown, the oldest settlement on the island. Models, paintings, and artifacts tell the island's story. A sailor-made model of the whaleship *John Coggeshall* is simply finished but with a feeling of authenticity often lacking in the smoother work of professional modelers. Each tiny whaleboat is equipped with oars, harpoons, and lances.

Steam whalers are less often pictured than their sail-only predecessors; the museum has a primitive oil painting of the steam whaler *Belvedere* wintering in the ice off Alaska. Illustrated logs of whalers and other ships on display have a fascination of their own, as we look at a slice of the past through the eyes of a long-vanished mariner.

In the shed behind the museum is a Nomans Land double-ender, a wet smack with a well for carrying live fish to market. There is also a full-size whaleboat, but it never went on a voyage; it is preserved because in it Captain Isaac Norton won every whaleboat rowing race in the harbor for 30 years. (The boat was built for racing, a local sport.)

Also in the shed is a most unusual artifact, a battered old wooden door from a fishing shack on Chappaquiddick, on which local residents scribbled notes about the harbor: for example, "March 1885—Harbor frozen over." Recorded are a couple of decades of storms and freezes. Nearby is the big nameplate of the luxury steamer *City of Columbus*, wrecked on the Devil's Bridge off Gay Head in January 1884. In the museum itself is the New York *Daily Graphic*'s picture story of the wreck. The steamer was bound from Boston to Savannah, and took the inside route through the treacherous waters of Vineyard Sound; the loss of life, luridly illustrated by the tabloid's steel engravings, was heavy.

As on any island, the ships that tie the Vineyard to the mainland have always played an important role in daily life. Besides fine paintings of several of the 19th-century ferry steamers, the museum has a nice collection of tiny models of ferries from 1891 to the present. Other models include a large one of the coastal schooner *Mary Anne*, sailor-made, rough but nice, while out in the shed is a remarkable piece of folk art: a five-foot wooden model of a turn-of-the-century battleship, very crude but very detailed.

In the yard of the museum there is a reproduction of a whaleship's tryworks, as well as a little tower containing the beautiful Fresnel lens of the Gay Head Lighthouse, saved by the society when the light was replaced by an automatic beam in 1952. Also in the yard is the Historical Society's cherished Thomas Cooke House, built in 1765. Beside island tools, toys, portraits, costumes, furniture, and artifacts, the house contains the Vineyard's earliest Customs Office.

Dukes County Historical Society Museum (Francis Foster Museum), Cooke & School Streets, Edgartown, on Martha's Vineyard. Library. Open all year; June 15 to September 18, Tuesday-Saturday, 10 a.m. to 4:30 p.m.; September 19 to June 14, Thursday and Friday, 1 to 4 p.m.; Saturday 10 a.m. to 4 p.m. Admission: $2.00; children, 50 cents. Sponsored by Dukes County Historical Society, Cooke and School Streets, Edgartown, Massachusetts 02539. Telephone (617) 627-4441.

In Vineyard Haven is a tiny museum right next to where the Woods Hole boats dock, in one end of the

Seaman's Bethel Chapel. On display are a variety of small artifacts, paintings, and photographs. The most interesting is a primitive painting of an American steam warship, probably an armored cruiser of the Great While Fleet. Among the artifacts is a life belt from the *Titanic*, left at the chapel by a seaman who served on the *Carpathia* when she went to the rescue of the survivors.

The Bethel was founded in 1893 as a "Reading Room for sailors, as a shelter for sick and destitute sailors, and for such similar purpose as the [Boston Seaman's Friend] Society may choose." The Vineyard Haven harbor was often filled with coasting schooners waiting for favorable weather, and the Bethel aimed to provide a respectable place for sailors to spend their time ashore, as well as for religious services. The Bethel chaplain was frequently called on to care for shipwrecked sailors. Eventually the Bethel had its own cemetery lot for the final resting place of men who died at sea or were found cast up on the shore.

Seaman's Bethel Chapel and Museum is at Ferry Wharf, Union and Water Streets, Vineyard Haven. Open June through August, daily 10 a.m. to 4 p.m.; September, October, April, and May: Thursday-Sunday, 10 a.m. to 4 p.m.; November through March: Friday-Sunday, 10 a.m. to 4 p.m. Admission: $1.00; children free. Seamen's Bethel Chapel and Museum, P.O. Box 1821, Vineyard Haven, Massachusetts 02568. Telephone (617) 693-9317.

Now back to the mainland and New Bedford, the famous home port of the great whaling fleet in which many Vineyarders sailed.

Along the way, alongside the traffic circle near the west end of the Bourne Bridge is a big tug. New York Central Steam Tug *Number 16* was hauled to the site, bedded in a sea of gravel, and put on display next to a restaurant.

> . . . nowhere in all America will you find more patrician-like houses; parks and gardens more opulent, than in New Bedford. Whence came they/ how planted upon this once scraggy scoria of a country?
>
> Go and gaze upon the iron emblematical harpoons round yonder lofty mansion, and your question will be answered. Yes; all these brave houses and flowery gardens came from the Atlantic, Pacific, and Indian Oceans. One and all they were harpooned and dragged up hither from the bottom of the sea.
>
> Herman Melville, *Moby Dick*, Chapter VI

Melville wrote some 130 years ago; the last New Bedford whaler was wrecked in 1924, and the city now lives on industry and fishing but some of the lofty mansions of the shipowners remain. Drive down County Street to see the survivors, even if no "iron emblematical harpoons" are to be found round them. (Local historians believe that they existed only in Melville's symbol-drenched imagination; recently the Whaling Museum installed a harpoon fence to bring reality into line with art.)

A high price in human lives was paid for the whale oil that built these mansions.

Slip in the door of the Seaman's Bethel, in New Bedford, the simple wooden chapel on Johnny Cake Hill, above the waterfront. Here Ishmael, the narrator of *Moby Dick*, heard a whaleman's sermon before setting out on his fateful voyage; the Bethel looks much the same today. The best preparation for a visit is to read chapters seven through nine of Melville's masterpiece. Although the bowsprit pulpit, which figures prominently in Ishmael's account, is a recent addition, all else is as it was. The marble tablets on the walls still mourn the death of young whalemen in far places, lately supplemented with the names of local fishermen lost at sea, making the Bethel a pantheon for New Bedford's missing sons.

Seaman's Bethel is at 15 Johnny Cake Hill. Open May 1 to Columbus Day, Monday-Saturday, 10 a.m. to 5 p.m.; Sunday, 1 to 5 p.m. Admission: free. Seamen's Bethel, New Bedford, Massachusetts 02790. Telephone (617) 992-3295.

The Whaling Museum of the Old Dartmouth Historical Society, in New Bedford, is a mecca for everyone interested in the most far-flung and combative of America's maritime activities. Unique is the half-size replica of the whaling bark *Lagoda*, complete in every detail above the waterline. Half size she may be, but *Lagoda* towers impressively over the visitor who comes upon her riding out the years in the great hall of the museum. Children are particularly enthralled: Ship, masts, spars, sails, rigging, boats, gear, all to the smallest detail are meticulously matched to the half-size crewman who can roam her decks, stand at the wheel, peer ahead from her bow (but not climb the rigging). For everyone, the *Lagoda* provides an opportunity to examine at leisure the complexities of a square-rigged three-master and her whaling gear.

The replica and her hall were given to the museum by the daughter of the 19th-century owner of the original *Lagoda*, a capitalist farsighted enough to enhance his whaling fortune by shifting his investments at the right moment to the booming textile industry.

Alongside the replica *Lagoda* are original whaleboats—full size, of course—one with its working gear. They are worth some study, for these highly efficient small craft were the real secret of the success of the American whaling fleet. Along the walls of the hall are photographic displays of the various laborious steps required to turn a dead whale into barrels of oil and bundles of whalebone. On another wall are racks of harpoons and lances—one of them twisted into a corkscrew by an angry whale. Of particular interest are the harpoon guns that eventually replaced hand-hurled weapons, one of the technological advances that eventually brought the race of whales to the brink of extinction.

Visitors should be sure to climb the stairs to the balcony that rims the hall, where they will find some of the shore establishments that supported the whaling fleet. Furnished with original tools and furniture are recreations of a sail loft, a cooper shop, and a rigging loft. In the shipowner's office, the morning paper lies open on the desk where that worthy dropped it as he stepped out a moment before you entered.

Nearby is another prize of the museum: two 60-foot sections of the *Panorama of a Whaling Voyage*, an enormous 15-foot by quarter-mile canvas painted in 1848 for commercial exhibition. Primitive in technique, the work was carried out with great spirit and vigor by local artists intimately familiar with the subject matter.

Figure 9
Half-size whaling bark *Lagoda*, largest ship model in the world, is just the right size for half-size crew members to explore at Old Dartmouth Historical Society Whaling Museum in New Bedford, Massachusetts.

The museum's gallery of paintings is dominated by the work of two New Bedford masters: the 19th-century William Bradford, and Clifford Ashley who went to sea in a whaleship early in this century. Very different in style, their paintings share a fascination with New Bedford and its whaling fleet. Other prints and paintings portray not only whaling and other marine scenes, but the city's shipowners and their families.

A recent and highly-prized acquisition of the museum is a watercolor of the whaleship *Manhattan* painted by an unknown Japanese artist when the vessel visited Japan in 1845. At that time, Western ships were barred from Japan's ports and the *Manhattan* was admitted only to land shipwrecked Japanese fishermen picked up at sea. Obviously the painter was unfamiliar with square-rigged vessels and his painting offers a fascinating insight into a different cultural perspective.

On a lower floor of the museum is an interesting collection of ship models. Included are not only whaleships and clippers but also coasters, fishermen, and other small vessels. Particularly notable are large and beautifully carved Admiralty models of British, French, and Spanish three-deckers.

Whaling Museum of the Old Dartmouth Historical Society, open Monday-Saturday, 9 a.m. to 5 p.m.; Sunday, 1 p.m. to 5 p.m. Admission: $2.50; seniors, $2.00; children 6 to 14, $1.50. Whaling Museum of the Old Dartmouth Historical Society, 18 Johnny Cake Hill, New Bedford, Massachusetts 02790. Telephone (617) 997-0046. Arrangements can be made to use the library, which contains over 1,000 logbooks and 15,000 books and pamphlets on whaling.

Within easy walking distance of the Whaling Museum, the New Bedford Free Public Library contains whaling paintings and a fine collection of almost 500 logbooks covering three centuries. Among them are 11 logs of the whaleship *Charles W. Morgan*, as well as the log of the ship *Junior*, which records a famous mutiny. Besides many hundreds of books on whaling, the library possesses a 38-foot scroll picturing Japanese whaling. An index of crew members who shipped out in New Bedford vessels contains a quarter of a million names.

New Bedford Free Public Library is at 613 Pleasant Street, New Bedford. Most whaling materials are kept in the Whaling room, which will be opened to visitors who apply at the Genealogy room. Open Monday-Saturday, 9 a.m. to 5 p.m. Telephone (617) 999-6291.

At the foot of the hill below the Whaling Museum, the lightship *New Bedford* (open to visitors during the summer months) has been docked in honorable retirement (her post at the entrance to New Bedford Harbor is now marked by an automatic light). The *New Bedford* has been well maintained but has been largely stripped of her equipment and is sparsely furnished in the living spaces. Little explanatory information is provided for the visitor. There is, however, a small museum in a forward compartment with lifesaving gear. The engine room, reached down a steep companionway, is the most complete and interesting section of the ship. It contains the generator for the ship's electric beacon in addition to her electric propulsion machinery and heating boilers.

The admissions office is in a large geodetic dome, which also houses a 36-foot Coast Guard rescue boat, a self-righting type that could carry 20 survivors to safety from a wreck. Such sturdy boats were in use from the 1920s well into the 1970s but now all have been retired, their rescue assignment taken over by amphibious craft and helicopters.

Lightship *New Bedford*, now retired, is tied up on the New Bedford waterfront at the foot of Johnny Cake Hill. Parking on adjacent State Pier. Open during July and August; 10 a.m. to 5 p.m. Admission: 50 cents; children over 6, 25 cents. Owned by city of New Bedford. Lightship New Bedford, Waterfront Park, State Pier, New Bedford, Massachusetts 02740. Telephone (617) 992-3749.

Many visitors will be interested in strolling further along the waterfront of one of the nation's great fishing ports—the greatest in the nation, measured by the value of its annual catch. New Bedford men and vessels still harvest the ocean waters. If their crop is now fish and scallops rather than whale oil and baleen, their trawlers and draggers nevertheless make the docks colorful and interesting. Incidentally, like whalemen before them, the fishermen work for a "lay," a share of the profits of a trip, rather than for fixed wages.

Now a few miles westward to another New England industrial city with a very different maritime heritage.

Narragansett Bay

On the Old Fall River Line
On the Old Fall River Line
I fell for Susie's line of talk
And Susie fell for mine;
Then we fell in with a parson,
And he tied us tight as twine . . .

Fall River, a child of the Industrial Revolution, was never an important seaport despite its location on an arm of Narragansett Bay, but it boasts a couple of unique distinctions. One is this more-or-less maritime ditty that became part of the national culture. The other, of course, is the remarkable steamship line that the song is about—the Fall River Line.

In Colonial times, Fall River was open farmland; Newport, 20 miles down Narragansett Bay to the southward, right on the Atlantic Ocean, was a major port. Later on, Providence, a larger city to the westward, offered more facilities for steamships. But geography gave Fall River a maritime heritage just the same. For much of the 19th century and well into the 20th, the preferred mode of passenger travel was by coastal steamer. Before a canal was opened through the narrow neck of Cape Cod, however, a voyage by sea between Boston and New York meant going well out to sea to get around Cape Cod—not only roundabout, but slow and sometimes dangerous.

Here's where the sheltered location of Fall River, well to the west of Cape Cod and only 50 miles from Boston, offered a tremendous advantage. Trains could carry Boston passengers to the Fall River steamer dock in an hour and a half. Across the dock they boarded a fine coastal steamer that took them in comfort to New York overnight, almost all the way in the sheltered waters of Narragansett Bay and Long Island Sound.

The Fall River Line began operation in 1847 and ran until 1937, when the railroad, the automobile, and the depression combined to put it out of business. The line's safety record was remarkable; in an era when steamboat accidents were all too common, the Fall River Line lost only one passenger in an accident.

Today the memory of the Old Fall River Line is preserved in the Marine Museum at Fall River, established in a redbrick one-time factory building a few hundred yards from the old steamboat pier on the banks of the Taunton River. The museum is crammed with prints, photographs, posters, and memorabilia of the Fall River Line, from the first steamship, the *Bay State* of 1847, to the mighty *Commonwealth*. The latter was the largest passenger ship ever operated on Long Island Sound and the biggest and proudest of the four vessels in service when the line quietly died in 1937.

Particularly striking is a huge model of the steamer *Priscilla*, another of the four finalists, and the

Figure 10
S.S. *Puritan*, one of the popular overnight passenger carriers between New York and New England, is kept fresh by this fine big model in the Marine Museum at Fall River, Massachusetts.

largest sidewheeler afloat when she was launched in 1894, accommodating 1,500 passengers, plus a crew of 200. Some idea of what this involved is given by the provision list of the *Priscilla*, which is prominently displayed; for a single overnight trip, the shopping list starts with a ton of meat and 500 loaves of bread.

The museum exhibits are by no means limited to the Fall River Line; its many fine models include owners' models of 20th-century freight and passenger liners, tankers, and refrigerator ships. Other interesting models include Donald McKay's historic *Great Republic*, a steam trawler of the 1880s, the Winnepesaukee lake steamer *Washington*, and a four-masted coal schooner of the turn of the century.

A recent addition to the exhibits is a magnificent, very large model of the ill-fated transatlantic liner *Titanic*, sunk with great loss of life following collision with an iceberg on her maiden voyage in 1912. About 28 feet long and finished with painstaking detail, the model was built for use in a motion picture of the disaster and is strikingly realistic. A survivor of the *Titanic* who now lives in a neighboring town has made a tape

recording of her childhood recollections of that dreadful night, which can be played by visitors.

But the Fall River Line is the focus of the collection, as it should be. Incidentally, lest you think the 19th century was sloppily sentimental, here's how the song ends:

> Then we fell in with a parson,
> And he tied us tight as twine.
> But I wish, O Lord,
> I fell overboard,
> On the Old Fall River Line.

The Fall River Marine Museum is best reached from I-195 by following the signs to Battleship Cove (see below). Open all year: Monday-Saturday, 9 a.m. to 5 p.m.; Sundays and holidays, 10 a.m. to 5 p.m. Admission: $2.00; 12 and under $1.00. Gift shop. The Marine Museum at Fall River, Inc., 70 Water Street, P.O. Box 1147, Fall River, Massachusetts 02722. Telephone (617) 674-3533.

The Marine Museum is not the only place that the nation's maritime heritage is preserved in Fall River: A block away in Battleship Cove is the USS Massachusetts Memorial. The mighty World War II battleship *Massachusetts* is the flagship of a small squadron of retired naval vessels in Fall River; in the next berths are also the destroyer *Joseph P. Kennedy, Jr.*, and the attack submarine *Lionfish*. Ashore under cover is a PT boat, said to be the last operational craft of its type from World War II.

The *Massachusetts*—"Big Mamie" to her crew—displaces 45,000 tons fully loaded. She was the first American battleship to fire her 16-inch guns in World War II combat. Starting with the invasion of North Africa, she took part in 35 major engagements, and was the last battleship to fire her big guns when she bombarded the Japanese island of Honshu just before the end of war. The visitor can wander at will through her upper decks; no tour lectures are provided, but a taped commentary is available that explains the various elements of the ship.

Although not the largest American battleship, the *Massachusetts*, with her vast decks and heavily armored barbettes under 16-inch batteries, gives a tremendous sense of power. Visitors can go inside one of her five-inch gun turrets, climb up into the bridge and conning tower, inspect the combat information centers, clamber down into the depths of the ship. Impressive in their own way, and a little easier to comprehend, are the immense galley and supply areas. The ship fed her 2,300-man complement right around the clock; the galley was never closed. The crew and officers quarters, and the various service shops—laundry, cobbler, and so forth— are all open to inspection.

The battleship is a memorial to the service men and women from Massachusetts who died in World

War II. The memorial room, with its 13,000 names individually inscribed on wall tablets, is a sobering reminder that the price of admiralty is blood.

Other special areas aboard the ship include an aircraft exhibit center, showing models of United States, Allied, German and Japanese combat planes of World War II and earlier, and a special PT boat display.

The destroyer *Joseph P. Kennedy, Jr.*, was named for the oldest of President Kennedy's brothers, a U.S. Navy aviator killed in World War II. Launched in 1945, the destroyer was considerably changed during her years of active service. As a specialized ASW (Antisubmarine Warfare) destroyer, she had had some of her original guns replaced by launchers for antisubmarine missiles and a helicopter landing deck topsides. Reflecting important changes in the technology of naval warfare, these alterations add considerably to the vessel's interest.

The destroyer's upper decks are open for the visitor to wander through, including the bridge and combat information center. A special memorial to "Kennedys and the Sea," tells about Joseph P. Kennedy, Jr., who was killed while testing a pilot-less plane.

The *Kennedy* served in both the Korean and Vietnam Wars. She also took part in the blockade of Cuba in 1962, when she turned back a Soviet freighter. A section with appropriate displays is set apart as a memorial to the Armed Force's casualties in those wars.

The other vessel in the Fall River flotilla is the submarine *Lionfish*. Launched too late for World War II service, she was the flagship of the naval force taking part in the nuclear tests on Bikini Atoll in 1946. Here again the visitor can clamber at will through her cramped spaces, including the torpedo rooms, control room, and maneuvering room, the heart of the ship. The result is a good general impression of what it was like to serve on a submarine.

Ashore on the dock is PT boat 796, preserved from the elements in her own little exhibition hall and said to be the only one of her kind on display in the world. The visitor can walk around the 78-foot wooden craft, commissioned in 1945, but not go aboard. Surrounding her are related artifacts, including an impressive display of the mammoth gasoline engines—12-cylinder Packards—that gave these tiny craft their great speed and maneuverability. (There is also a special PT display aboard the *Massachusetts*.)

USS Massachusetts Memorial is at Battleship Cove, next to State Pier on Fall River riverfront, under The Braga Bridge and two blocks north of Fall River Marine Museum. Open all year, except Thanksgiving and Christmas: June 30 to Labor Day, 9 a.m. to 7 p.m.; otherwise 9 a.m. to 5:30 p.m. Admission: $5.00; children 6 to 13, $2.75; children 2 to 5, 75 cents. Gift shop. Sponsored by nonprofit USS Massachusetts Memorial Committee, Inc., Battleship Cove, Fall River, Massachusetts 02721. Telephone (617) 678-1100.

Now a short drive south onto the island of Rhode Island brings the visitor to Newport, once one of the busiest American ports and still a place of great maritime interest.

A handsome old city strategically located on the southern tip of the island of Rhode Island where the 200 square miles of sheltered waters of Narragansett Bay reach the open Atlantic, Newport has for almost 350 years been concerned with ships and the sea. Over the centuries, however, this concern has been focused at various times on three sharply different areas. In the Colonial era and the early years of the Republic, it was the home port of blue-water merchant ships. In the years after the Civil War and through World War II, Newport became a Navy town. And from the late 19th century to the present, Newport has been the most prestigious center of American yachting.

Colonial Newport was one of America's largest and most active ports, ranking with Boston and New York. The city's merchants built ships and sent them on trading voyages to Europe, the West Indies, Africa, and the southern Colonies. Not a few Rhode Island fortunes were made in the African slave trade, although the human cargoes were usually not brought home but rather sold in distant Southern or West Indian ports. In the many wars with France, Newporters turned enthusiastically to privateering.

Throughout the Colonial era, British trade restrictions were frequently ignored. In a violent precurser to the American Revolution, sturdy Rhode Islanders—smugglers or free-traders, as you will—attacked British warships, too zealously trying to enforce the King's laws in Narragansett Bay. In the most serious of these incidents, HMS *Gaspee*, which had run aground after a chase, was captured and set afire.

During the Revolution, Rhode Islanders in general were active at sea, providing ships for the Continental Navy and outfitting many privateers. However, Newport was occupied for several years by British troops and its shipping suffered heavy losses from which the town never fully recovered. Many fine Colonial and Revolutionary period houses have survived along the narrow streets of the old downtown area and a vast restoration and preservation project, launched by a generous donor, seems likely to maintain the antique flavor of the town.

While Newport had always been Navy minded, its close relations with the service developed after the Civil War, during which the Naval Academy was temporarily moved to the city from Annapolis. Attempts to keep it in Newport permanently failed, but in the eighties the city became the home of the Naval War College, Torpedo Station, and Training Station. Newport was always a favorite port of the North Atlantic Squadron and after the turn of the century was the principal anchorage of the North Atlantic Fleet.

Today, following the concentration of Navy activities in the Chesapeake after World War II, the city has less of a Navy flavor, particularly since urban renewal along the waterfront has replaced the sailors' bars and tattoo parlors with boutique shops and fancy restaurants. The Navy's educational facilities remain, however, and Newport is the home of many retired naval officers, attracted by its pleasant climate and social activities.

The third maritime interest of Newport, and the most active one today, is yachting. In the latter half of the 19th century, as the city became the favorite summering place of New York high society, millionaires' yachts began to frequent the harbor. Eventually, Newport became the established base for the defense of the America's Cup and the many elimination trials that preceded the international race itself—most of which of course have now been moved to Australia. The annual visit of the cruising squadron of the New York Yacht Club remains a highlight of the summer season and in recent years Newport's yachting activities have been further augmented by the annual Classic Yacht Regatta and various in-the-water boat shows. Fun afloat remains a serious concern.

The Naval War College, established at Newport in 1884, was the first of its kind in the world, a landmark in the modernization of the United States Navy. Now a museum has been installed in two floors of the original War College building on Coaster's Island. This small but burgeoning institution concentrates on two principal themes: the art and science of naval warfare and the history of the U.S. Navy in Narragansett Bay.

The exhibits are attractive and well-arranged. Full-hull models include HMS *Gaspee*, the British warship that was attacked and burned by angry Rhode Islanders in Narragansett Bay, foreshadowing the Revolution to come. Another is the Continental sloop *Providence*, bought and armed by the rebellious colony as the start of a navy designed to drive the British from the Bay. Special exhibits, changed from time to time, focus on such Navy-related subjects as the famous Perry brothers, and the naval prints of Currier and Ives. Maps and documents tell the story of naval activity in the bay while photographs record the U.S. Navy's long use of Newport as a major base and the site of its various educational and training centers.

A most ambitious project under way is to use dioramas, maps, ship models, graphics, to portray the history of naval warfare from the victory of the Greek fleet over the Persians at Salamis in 480 B.C. up to modern times.

In nearby Mahan Hall is the War College's Historical Collection, a depository for primary source materials on naval warfare and the archives of the college. These are open for scholarly research, but arrangements for access should be made in advance by telephone or letter.

The Naval War College Museum is in Founders Hall of the Naval War College, atop a hill on Coasters Harbor Island, Newport, just north of Newport-Jamestown bridge. Open all year, Monday-Friday, excluding holidays, 10 a.m. to 4 p.m. Also, June through September: Saturdays, noon to 4 p.m.; June through August: Sundays, noon to 4 p.m. No admission charge. Naval War College, Newport, Rhode Island 02840. Telephone (401) 841-4052.

A marina in Newport at the foot of the War College hill is the home base of a modern reproduction of the Continental Sloop *Providence*. In winter she is snugged down, however, and from May to October she is usually off on a visit somewhere along the coast.

The original *Providence* started her career as the Rhode Island sloop *Katy* in the West Indies trade. In 1775 she was commissioned in the Rhode Island Navy and her capture of the *Diana*, a tender to the British frigate *Rose*, is said to be the first sea fight of the Revolution. Sold to the new Continental Navy and renamed *Providence*, she was John Paul Jones' first command, and during her three years of cruises took 40 prizes, including a Royal Navy brig.

The new *Providence* was commissioned in 1976 as part of the bicentennial celebration. She closely resembles the original in appearance as reconstructed from various models and a contemporary painting. There are two significant differences, however: the new *Providence* has a fiberglass hull, rather than being framed and planked of oak like her namesake, and she carries the equipment that makes her a Coast Guard-certified passenger carrier. The average visitor would have to look hard to see these differences, however, and the diesel engine that permits her to overcome adverse wind or tide is of course completely out of sight.

In any case, the *Providence* is impressive, reminding us once again that the best of plans or the most vivid of pictures cannot match the impact of a full-scale ship, recreated or not. Her square topsail above the big gaff-rigged fore-and-aft mainsail sets her apart at once from any contemporary vessel. Her broad beam, great freeboard, and high bulwarks convey a sense of capacity and strength. Clearly she is much more of a high-seas ship than would be a modern yacht of the same length.

When she is at her Newport base, *Providence* is ordinarily closed to visitors except by special arrangement. The best way to insure seeing her is to obtain a copy of her cruising schedule—practically continuous from May and through October—and plan to visit her at one of her ports of call along the coast. Since her visits are handled by local sponsors, the hours and admission charges, if any, vary from place to place. In addition to her scheduled cruises, *Providence* is available for private charters and special cruises: all these activities help to defray her operating expenses. The sloop also takes part in the American Sail Training program, cruising with young people along the coast manned by professionals, volunteers, and trainees.

Continental Sloop *Providence* is berthed at marina near entrance to Naval War College, Newport, Rhode Island, but can be visited only by special arrangements. Most of May-October season spent cruising and visiting ports along Atlantic coast; local sponsors set visiting hours and any admission charges. Information as to places and dates of visits may be obtained from non-profit Seaport '76 Foundation, Box 76, Newport, Rhode Island 02740. Telephone (401) 846-1776.

Now for a look at another important strand of Newport's maritime past—and present.

The days when Newport was a bustling commercial port are long gone, but the town remains perhaps the most famous center of American yachting—a maritime tradition that is reported and preserved in the Museum of Yachting at Fort Adams on the south side of Newport harbor. This young and interesting museum is believed to be the only one in the country entirely devoted to this important element in our maritime activities. Launched with wide support from Americans who find their recreation afloat, the Yachting Museum seeks "to provide the continuity necessary for an understanding of the place of yachting in our social, economic, and artistic history."

In keeping with this ambitious goal, the first gallery to be opened in the museum's new home, a spacious building in the Fort (which has now become a state park) focuses on "The Mansions and the Yachts." Here photographs, models, and memorabilia tell the story of the magnificent yachts afloat and the palatial "cottages" ashore of the Morgans, Astors, Vanderbilts, and their fellow millionaires who summered in Newport in its high-society heyday. A second gallery is devoted to display of the museum's growing collection of such small craft as the Newport catboat and the famous one-design racing sloops. More galleries are in preparation, including a Hall of Offshore Racing, an

America's Cup gallery, and a special room for rotating displays of the work of great yacht designers.

The Museum already owns a number of interesting yachts, among them a wooden "A" scow, an Alden-built Sekonnet, and a turn-of-the-century steam launch. In prospect is the acquisition of larger craft, which will be displayed in the water at the museum's pier.

Each Labor Day weekend the museum sponsors a three-day Classic Boat Regatta for boats 35 feet or more in length built before 1955. In the winter months there are films, seminars, and discussion meetings on yachting-related topics.

The Museum of Yachting at Newport, Rhode Island, is in a large brick and timber building at Fort Adams State Park, overlooking the harbor and Narragansett Bay; yacht basin adjoins. Fort is on Ocean Drive, just beyond Hammersmith Farm. Parking. Exhibits open June 15 to October 31: Tuesday-Sunday: 10 a.m. to 5 p.m.; other times by appointment. Admission $2.00; children under 12, free. Museum of Yachting, P.O. Box 129, Newport, Rhode Island 02840. Telephone (401) 847-1018.

The surviving palaces of the millionaires who made Newport the summer capital of American Society are not to be missed—and at least one of them has a maritime association.

The Vanderbilt Memorial Room in the fantastic Marble House on Newport's elegant Bellevue Avenue is of interest primarily for the glimpse it provides of yacht racing at the fanciest level. The room itself has no direct association with Harold Vanderbilt, the highly successful racing yachtsman, having been a guest room when he lived in the house as a child. However, it was dedicated to hold Vanderbilt's trophies and yachting memorabilia after his widow left them to the Newport Preservation Society in 1978.

In the Memorial Room, which can be viewed only as part of a guided tour of the whole house, a whole wall glitters with the silver trophies that Mr. Vanderbilt won during his lifelong career as a yachtsman. A handsome oil painting of Harold Vanderbilt shows him at the helm of *Ranger*, in which he successfully defended the America's Cup, in 1937, for the third time, having previously done so in *Enterprise*, 1930, and *Rainbow*, 1934. Below the painting is the wheel itself. In addition to an oil of Vanderbilt's beautiful *Intrepid*, there is a fine portrait of the founder of the family fortune, Harold's great-grandfather, Commodore Cornelius Vanderbilt. The Commodore, born a Staten Island farm boy, started on the road to fortune in the early 19th century by buying a perriauger (a river sloop) and ferrying freight and passengers between Staten Island and Manhattan. Young Cornelius was a real professional seaman; he is credited with using his sloop ferry to rescue people from a vessel overturned by a harbor squall.

A visitor might wish that there was more of the salty old Commodore in the $11 million palace built by his grandson. Nevertheless, the Marble House is well worth seeing quite aside from its rather modest maritime interest. Here, at the end of the 19th century, conspicuous consumption reached its extravagant extreme with gold-encrusted ballroom, grand staircase reminiscent of New York's Grand Central Station, and halls hung with priceless tapestries. The house is a landmark in American social history the like of which we are unlikely to see again.

The Vanderbilt Memorial Room, in the Marble House on Bellevue Avenue, Newport, Rhode Island. Open daily April 1 to October 31: 10 a.m. to 5 p.m.; November 1 to March 31: Saturday and Sunday, 10 a.m. to 4 p.m. Admission: $4.50; children 6 to 11, $2.00. Small gift counter. Sponsored by the nonprofit Preservation Society of Newport County, 118 Mill Street, Newport, Rhode Island 02840. Telephone (401) 847-1000.

Back up Narragansett Bay now, to the venerable Town of Bristol—and memories of a famous family of yacht designers.

Yachting trivia quiz. Q.: Name two things that the following have in common: *Vigilant, Defender, Columbia, Reliance, Resolute.*

A. (1): As might be deduced from their names, all were yachts—no ordinary yachts either, but successful defenders of the America's Cup. (2) What may be forgotten is that all five, all the defenders from 1893 through 1920, were designed and built by one man: Nathanael Greene Herreshoff, the "Wizard of Bristol."

Bristol, of course, was Bristol, Rhode Island, the small port on a point at the head of Narragansett Bay. In Colonial days, Bristol merchants grew rich trading to the West Indies, Europe, and Africa. In the War of 1812, one of several Bristol privateers captured British property worth some one million pounds sterling, but the port's merchant shipping practically ceased. After the war, many Bristol merchantmen were converted to whaleships; as many as 19 were at one time based in the port. By by the mid-century this maritime trade also declined and, like many New England ports, Bristol became a milltown.

But Bristol did not completely lose its ties to the sea. Among the new plants was the waterfront firm started by John Herreshoff, a blind graduate of MIT, to build boats and engines. John and his more widely known younger brother Nathanael, were both enthusiastic yachtsmen and eventually the two became partners in the Herreshoff Manufacturing Company. For a time the firm concentrated on steam yachts,

engines, and boilers, but eventually under Nathanael's—Nat's—leadership turned to racing yachts with outstanding success.

Cap'n Nat designed and built boats for 70 years. In the words of Bill Robinson, longtime editor of *Yachting Magazine*, "Of all the men who have worked in the field of yacht design, Nathanael Greene Herreshoff has had the widest and most lasting influence." The five great America's Cup Defenders were only one segment of his achievements. Consider that Nat and the Herreshoff firm are also credited with the following:

- building the first torpedo boats for the U.S., British, French, and Russian Navies;
- improving wooden boat construction methods with such weight-saving techniques as screw-fastened double planking over steel frames, and the placing and stressing of small frames;
- being the first to use hollow steel spars;
- being one of the first to see the possibilities of catamarans as racing craft (and Nat built one that beat the sandbaggers);
- developing crosscut sails, which gave his racing boats another advantage in addition to their fine lines;
- developing flat sterns on powered craft to prevent "squatting."

Cap'n Nat was also responsible for many refinements in fittings and rigging. He turned out everything from the famous little Herreshoff Twelves or Bullseyes, to the enormous 149-foot *Reliance*, the biggest America's Cup Defender ever built. Such famous classes as the New York 30s, 40s, and 50s were Herreshoff designs. When he was 23, Nat designed and built *Shadow*, which later became famous for defeating a hitherto unbeatable English cutter. When he was 87, Nat designed the beautiful yawl *Belisarius* of 1935, his last boat.

Two of Nathanael Herreshoff's sons, Sidney and Francis, became distinguished yacht designers in their own right. Francis was particularly remembered for his ocean cruisers, including not only such famous craft as *Ticonderoga*, but special types such as *Rozinante* and *Meadowlark*. Today the Herreshoff building yard has disappeared from the Bristol waterfront, but some of the other buildings are used by Nat's grandson Halsey, himself a successful yacht designer.

In one of them, Halsey Herreshoff has installed a small museum to preserve and display some of the work of the earlier generations. The collection is small but select, a treasure trove of the work of America's first family of yacht designers.

As visitors have noted, the little museum still retains much of the feeling of a boatshop. Among the small craft on the floor are:

- the 20-foot catboat *Sprite*, built by Nat, John, and Charles Herreshoff when they were still boys in 1857-60. Lent by the Henry Ford Museum in Dearborn;
- Cap'n Nat's dinghy, the tender for *Water Lily*;
- the 16-foot centerboard catboat *Cygnet*;
- the *Two-Forty*, a beautiful 30-foot launch, all gleaming bright work.

The walls are lined with drawings, photographs, and memorabilia of the Herreshoffs and their boats, including a whole wall on the vessels built for the U.S. Navy, such as the torpedo boat *Cushing*. Many America's Cup Defenders are shown in drawings and photographs. Among the artifacts is a Herreshoff steam launch engine of 1893, in which firebox, boiler, and engine proper are combined in a single compact power plant; a reminder that both Nat and his brother John (J.B.) were mechanical engineers and worked on improving marine engine design.

Members of the Herreshoff family frequently staff the museum themselves, and if the visitor is fortunate he may find one of the senior ladies. Their firsthand recollections, readily shared with visitors, provide unique insights into one of America's great yacht designer families—recollections that no printed page or museum placard can match.

Herreshoff Marine Museum is in a Herreshoff Manufacturing Company building in Bristol, Rhode Island; turn east off Route 114 (Hope Street) onto Burnside Street. Admission: free. Open May through October, Wednesdays and Saturdays, 1 to 4 p.m.; other times by appointment. Herreshoff Marine Museum, 18 Burnside Street, Bristol, Rhode Island 02809. Telephone (401) 253-5000.

A final Trivia quiz: Q.: What boat won the Classic Yacht Regatta in Newport in 1982?

A.: *Trivia*, sailed by Halsey Herreshoff, designed and built by his grandfather Nat Herreshoff for Harold Vanderbilt in 1902.

Now to the northwest corner of Narragansett Bay where the third of Rhode Island's venerable ports, Providence, has become a sprawling industrial city. Founded on a little point where two streams came together to form the Providence River, Providence built its first wharf in 1680. As a port the town grew slowly, then flourished during the late 18th century with the trade in slaves, rum, and molasses, and in privateering. After the American Revolution the city outstripped Newport as the major maritime center of the region, its merchants building great houses on College Hill, overlooking the little tidal river where their ships lay along the docks.

Today, the fine houses on the hill are almost the only reminder of the city's maritime heritage. Much of the Providence River has been put underground, and the city's economy depends on industry, services, and state offices. Nevertheless, tucked away in the Providence Public Library are collections of ship models, maritime documents, and artifacts well worth investigating.

Providence Public Library's Alfred S. Brownell collection of small models of Atlantic Coast fishing vessels, which is in the lobby on the second floor, is outstanding. The models, most of them made by Mr. Brownell himself, range from a Colonial fishing schooner to a Chesapeake Bay skipjack of the 1930s. Included are such notable types as a New Haven sharpie, a Tancook whaler, and an Eastport pinkie. Brownell, who began model-making as a hobby and after retirement devoted all his time to it, was clearly a highly skilled craftsman. Visitors interested in comparing the different types should note that they range in scale from 3/4 inch down to 5/16th of an inch to the foot, so that the models do not demonstrate the relative sizes of the originals.

The models are only the most visible part of the Brownell collection. Stowed away in the Special Collections Room off the model gallery, are 800 pieces related to ship-model building and naval architecture, including many technical drawings and photographs. Here also is the Nicholson collection of almost 600 whaling logs and journals, ranging in date from 1785 to 1922, which can be read on microfilm. Among the most interesting are a log written entirely in verse, which includes a report of the rescue of two survivors from the *Essex*, sunk by a whale, and an account of the wild and bloody voyage of the whaleship *Sharon* in 1842.

Scrimshaw in the Special Collections Room includes a beautifully detailed model of a whaleboat, built up in ivory plank by plank, and completely equipped with its whaling gear. Also in ivory is a six-inch model of a ship, completely rigged.

Alfred S. Brownell Collection of Atlantic Coast Fishing Craft Models and Paul C. Nicholson Logbook Collection. Second floor of Providence Public Library, in downtown Providence a block west of the common. Brownell Model Collection and Library open all year, Monday, Tuesday, and Thursday, 9:30 a.m. to 9 p.m.; Friday and Saturday, 9:30 a.m. to 5:30 p.m. Closed holidays. Nicholson Collection open all year, Monday, Tuesday, Thursday, and Friday, 9:30 a.m. to 1 p.m., 2 to 5 p.m. Closed weekends and holidays, and during curator's absence: best to phone ahead. Admission: free. Providence Public Library, 150 Empire Street, Providence, Rhode Island 02903-3283. Telephone (401) 521-7722.

Along the Connecticut Shore

In the late Colonial era, historians tell us, Connecticut was compared to "a cask of good liquor, tapped at both ends, at one of which Boston draws, and New York at the other." But the lack of a world-famous port of its own did not keep Connecticut from taking advantage of its 125 miles of coastline.

Among America's saltwater states, Connecticut is unique: the state's entire coastline faces sheltered waters—Long Island Sound—rather than open ocean. With a number of relatively deep-water ports and rivers that tapped the inland farms and forests, Connecticut settlers started early to build ships and load them with lumber, livestock, and tobacco for markets in other colonies and the West Indies.

During both the Revolution and the War of 1812, Connecticut men and ships were enthusiastic privateers, drawing down upon her little ports vengeful raids from British squadrons. In the peaceful years that followed, coastal shipping boomed, while Connecticut yards built ships for New York owners and Connecticut master mariners commanded them.

Some Connecticut mariners voyaged far afield indeed. Stonington, Mystic, New London, and New Haven all sent seal hunters and whalers to distant waters. New Haven sealers became so active off the coasts of Chile and Peru that a stretch of deserted coast where they dried their skins ashore became known as "New Haven Green." Connecticut seamen early found that in the South Seas they faced unfamiliar perils in addition to the usual storms and uncharted reefs. In one 1829 voyage, a Stonington ship put a landing party ashore in the Fiji Islands to gather sea cucumbers, a delicacy esteemed in China. Fourteen crewmen were captured by cannibals—13 were eaten, one escaped.

The long, protected passage of Long Island Sound came into its own with the arrival of steam. Steamboat lines sprouted like mushrooms, carrying passengers and freight along the coast to and from New York and up the rivers into the interior of the state.

The great age of sailing ships and their master mariners has long vanished from Connecticut as elsewhere, and the last steamboat has made its final run. Today submarines and yachts dominate the maritime scene.

The principal shipbuilding activity in Connecticut is the enormous submarine yards at Groton. Just up the Thames River from the private building yards is the U.S. Navy's center of submarine activity on the Atlantic coast, where underwater craft are based and maintained and their crews trained. And all along the shore yachts are built and sailed, filling every little harbor with a forest of masts.

Few states are more conscious than Connecticut of its own—and the nation's—maritime heritage. As we travel westward along the shore we will find museums large and small, ships old and new, each with much to tell us about aspects of our past. First stop is Stonington, a little port that has seen a lot of history.

One of the more innovative naval weapons in World War II was an enlarged version of the familiar Fourth of July rocket—filled with deadly explosives. Mounted in massive banks on landing craft, these rockets were fired in tremendous salvos to smother shore defenses.

Actually, as Stonington, Connecticut, could tell you, naval rocket attacks on shore targets began at least as far back as the War of 1812. British task forces raiding various American ports along the Atlantic coast fired barrages of what were called Congreve rockets. In August, 1814, the defenders of Stonington beat off one such attack. Today, the curious will find an example of the fearsome Congreve rocket, salvaged after the battle, preserved in the Old Lighthouse Museum at the tip of Stonington Point.

The lighthouse is a small octagonal tower rising out of a granite cottage that now houses the museum, which is sponsored by the Stonington Historical Society. The collection of artifacts, photographs, paintings, and memorabilia related to Stonington focuses particularly on the long maritime background of the town. Stonington was not only once a prosperous trading port but, among other marine activities, had a whaling fleet of its own. Stonington ships traveled all over the world. Two of its 19th-century captains in particular, Edmund Fanning and Nathaniel B. Palmer, became famous, not only as expert master mariners, but also as the discoverers of new lands. Fanning was 18 when he discovered the Fanning Islands in the Pacific. The museum has a striking filigree dish made of tortoiseshell that he brought home from some faraway port. Captain Palmer was just three years older when he took the 44-ton sloop *Hero* so far south in pursuit of seals that he discovered—it is claimed—the Antarctic continent. A fine portrait of Palmer, who was later known both for his fast passages in clipper ships and his contributions to ship design, is a prized exhibit of the museum.

Among the other treasures that the visitor will find here is the beautifully carved and painted wooden tailboard of the whaleship *Mary & Susan*, a local vessel.

A number of fine ship models include a particularly handsome primitive model of the steamboat *Rhode Island* of the Stonington Line. This line, which ran between Stonington and New York City, was at one time the principal link between eastern Connecticut and the great metropolis.

Other exhibits include a half model of the schooner *Nereus* of 1826; a model of a whaleboat painstakingly carved out of whalebone by some patient hand in the long hours between whale sightings; and many fine prints of steamers and ships that called Stonington their home port. There are also a number of fine early-19th century portraits of Stonington worthies, some quite sophisticated.

No visitor should leave the museum without making the short climb up into the lighthouse, which rises from the entry to the museum itself.

Old Lighthouse Museum is at the very south end of Water Street, on the tip of point extending into harbor of Stonington, Connecticut. From I-95 (Connecticut Turnpike) take Borough of Stonington exit south. Squat stone lighthouse rises from keeper's cottage, where exhibits are displayed. Open May through October, Tuesday-Sunday, 11 a.m. to 4:30 p.m. Admission: $1.00; children, 50 cents. The museum of the Stonington Historical Society, P.O. Box 103, Stonington, Connecticut 06378. Telephone (203) 535-1440.

Now a little further west along the shore to Stonington's ancient rival, Mystic—and one of the biggest and finest maritime museums in North America.

In the 19th century the little Long Island Sound port of Mystic was best known for its whalers and its shipyards—particularly the latter. Along the banks of the Mystic River were built such well-known vessels as the Civil War ironclad *Galena*, sometimes described as the first armored warship, and the medium clipper *Andrew Jackson*, which tied *Flying Cloud*'s record 89-day passage from New York around the Horn to California.

Today the town thrives on summer vacationers and visitors, particularly the sea-minded: Mystic is famous as the home of one of the world's great museums: Mystic Seaport. Other museums have exhibits in certain interest areas that equal, even in a few instances surpass, those of Mystic. None, however, surpasses the Seaport in its broad coverage of the many aspects of maritime history, in the sustained high interest level of its exhibits, or in the care that has gone into their selection, preparation, and maintenance. A traveler with time to visit only one maritime museum in the United States might very well choose the Mystic Seaport, dedicated to preserving the "materials, artifacts, vessels, and skills relating to maritime history in order to enhance man's knowledge and understanding of the sea's influence on American life."

And the visitor should allow at least a full day to wander unhurriedly through its treasures. As the Mystic Seaport itself declares with no false modesty, it has "the most significant collection of historic ships and water craft in the world." Add to ships the 20 exhibition galleries, the 50 historic buildings, and the huge Preservation Shop, bigger than many a commercial boatyard, and a day is none too much. Better make it two days.

The queen of the Seaport's flotilla of ships afloat is the venerable whaleship, *Charles W. Morgan*. Built in New Bedford in 1841, the *Morgan* served as an active whaleship for 80 years before being retired and put on public exhibition in South Dartmouth, Massachusetts, a few miles from her birthplace. Eventually she came to the Seaport where she has been recently undergoing major repairs to her 140-year-old hull. Now the *Morgan* is back at her regular berth at Chubb's Wharf. The distinctive features of a whaleship are all to be found on this historic *Morgan*. Some things to notice when you go aboard:

- Her many boats. The actual attack on a whale was made by her whaleboats, each manned by a mate and five men. The average whaleship carried six boats, a couple of them spares to replace those smashed by whales.
- Her fo'c'sle, where her crew of 30-odd lived literally on top of each other for two, three, even four years. It's easy to see why smart captains ordered the point cut off each man's knife at the start of a voyage.
- Between the mainmast and the foremast are the great tryworks: huge kettles over bricked-in fire boxes. Here the oil was boiled out of strips of whole blubber to be stowed away in great cakes. Whaleships were the first factory ships.

At the very outset of her career, the *Morgan*'s launching was delayed by a strike of New Bedford shipwrights demanding a 10-hour work day instead of "sun-up to sun-down." (They won 10-1/2 hours.) Once afloat, the ship made 36 consecutive voyages. Almost continuously at sea, she survived hurricanes and typhoons, fire at sea, ice packs. In 1850, the *Morgan*, becalmed in the Kingsmill Islands, was attacked by natives; the crew beat them off with lances and cutting spades while the ship barely escaped drifting onto a reef. In 1864, the captain's teenage son fell overboard and drowned; the next year the same captain took his brand-new baby son on a two-year cruise. In 1870, *Morgan* rescued the crew of a blazing cargo carrier; eleven years later she herself was set afire by a mutinous crewman but the flames were extinguished. In 1889, one of her boat crews was towed away by a whale and lost the ship in the darkness; eventually the crew landed in Siberia. Three years later the ship rescued some Russian political prisoners, who had escaped Siberia in a makeshift boat. In 1906 and the following year the *Morgan* rode out hurricanes. And during World War I, she sailed within 10 feet of a floating mine. Some record!

Mystic's other full-rigged ship is the *Joseph Conrad*, a beautiful little vessel that was launched in 1882 as the Danish training ship *Georg Stage*. During the 52 years she spent in this service she never left the Baltic and the North Sea and was laid up every winter to avoid the ice. The ship went on to sail the seven seas, however, when she was purchased by the noted Alan Villiers for a venture of his own: a voyage round the world as an international schoolship. He renamed her the *Joseph Conrad* and in 1934 took her around both Capes, finding her he reported later, weatherly and able. *Conrad* made the run from Tahiti to New York in 105 days, despite the fact that, because of her small size, Villiers had to heave to several times while running for the Horn for fear of driving her under.

Subsequently, the *Conrad* served as an English floating school and a millionaire's yacht before finding her snug harbor at Mystic.

The third of the larger vessels at the Seaport is the Gloucester fishing schooner *L.A. Dunton*. Actually she is longer than either of the full-rigged ships—10 feet more than *Morgan*, 20 feet more than *Conrad*. She is also the newest, having been built in 1921 by the famous Story Yard in Essex, Massachusetts. She served for many years as a dory fisherman, then was sold and became a carrier.

Each of the smaller vessels afloat at the Seaport's long wharf has a special interest of her own: *Sabino*, a little 1908 steamboat that takes visitors on cruises in the river, is one of the last surviving coal-fired steamboats. The schooner *Regina M.* has a pinkie's pointed deck projecting from her stern. The *Emma C. Berry* is an alongshore fishing smack. *Nellie* is an oyster sloop. The *Orca* is a little double-ended fishing boat from Noman's Land, a small island off Martha's Vineyard where there is no harbor; fishermen had to pull their boats up onto the beach. *Annie* is a sandbagger, an extreme type of 1880s racing sloop, so tender that in order to keep her from capsizing her ballast had to be carried in sandbags and shifted to the windward side each time she tacked. *Estella A.* is a fine specimen of a Friendship sloop, despite the fact that she was built on Long Island rather than Maine.

All the exhibition galleries are interesting, but two in particular should not be missed: the handsome redbrick Stillman House and the small craft exhibit.

"New England and the Sea" is the theme of an exhibit in the Stillman building that coordinates ship models, artifacts, prints, and paintings. Arranged chronologically and tied together by excellent explanatory captions, they tell the story of the region's maritime history. The 19th-century section is particularly informative, covering some 10 aspects of maritime life in the last century, from fishing and whaling to shipbuilding and foreign trade.

Stillman's second floor is given over to scrimshaw and fine ship models, including a very large and handsome model of the steam yacht *Arrow*, beautifully made to show the details of its construction. For the model maker, and those interested in learning about model-making, the third floor is the most interesting of all. Here a carefully conceived and constructed series of models leads the viewer step-by-step through major aspects of the model maker's craft. Style, building methods, and choice of materials are all illustrated with examples of various approaches. On one side of the gallery is the workshop of the museum's own model maker; partitioned off but with big windows through which the visitor can watch the model maker at work.

The small craft exhibit, on show in a long building that was once a factory, contains beautifully restored and preserved examples of all the major types of small boats. Here the visitor will find serried ranks of dories, Whitehalls, Hampton boats, and so forth, each as gleamingly perfect as the day she came out of the builder's shop.

The small buildings that line the little waterfront street within the Seaport are all authentically ancient structures and were moved to Mystic when threatened with destruction at their original sites. In them have been installed shops of many of the maritime trades that would have been found along the streets of a coastal town, including a cooperage, a mast-hoop shop, a ship smith, and a ship carver. One of the most interesting is a major portion of an old rope walk, complete with tracks along which roll the simple machines that twist multiple strands to make manilla lines.

Nearby is a large sail loft, with its stove suspended from the rafters in order to keep the floor clear to lay out and cut the canvas for ships' sails. Two floors below is a ship chandlery, while next door is a lifesaving station completely equipped, moved to the Seaport from Block Island. Within are surfboat and its beach wagon, Lyle gun and breeches buoy, and a complete outfit of gear—lamps, anchor, lines, and so on, with the beach cart they were carried on.

An enormous diorama of old Mystic in the mid-19th century is so large it has a building of its own. Modeled on a scale of 3/32nd of an inch to a foot, the 50-foot model shows the old town at the time that clipper ships were being built on the river bank where the Seaport is now.

In a display area at one end of the Boat Shop, small models demonstrate successive stages in the construction of a Whitehall pulling boat. In the shop itself, visitors can watch small craft being constructed and can even take courses to learn to do it themselves. Those with sufficient self-confidence to go ahead on their own can buy detailed plans for building various types of small craft developed at the shop.

The ships and shops are by no means all of the Seaport's facilities. A recent acquisition is a fine collection of the yachting photographs made by New York's famous Rosenfeld family of photographers. The museum has its own research library of 40,000 volumes and 400,000 manuscripts. The Seaport's Planetarium has regular visitors' programs and special classes in astronomy and navigation. An intern program helps young people develop curatorial skills, while in a joint program with Williams College some students become skilled boatbuilders while others study marine sciences. Mystic Seaport's Munson Institute offers both undergraduate and graduate courses on maritime topics. A publishing division has an extensive program, both of books for the general reader and of specialized monographs.

With these far-ranging exhibits and activities, the Seaport is one of the few, perhaps the only, exclusively maritime museum to rank in size and scope with the giants of the museum world. With an annual operating budget of some six million dollars, Mystic is probably in the top 10 percent of America's multifarious museums. Half a million people a year visit the Seaport and 18,000 belong to the membership association that helps to support the museum both with dollars and many hours of volunteer work.

A big operation—in dollars, in scope, and, happily, in interest for the visitor.

Mystic Seaport Museum is on the east bank of the Mystic River, a short way above where it flows into Long Island Sound. Planetarium, library, restaurants, large gift, book, and souvenir shops. Extensive, varied educational programs. Special events. Open all year every day except Christmas. May through November, 9 a.m. to 5 p.m.; grounds open in summer until 10 p.m.; December through April, 9 a.m. to 4 p.m. Admission: $9.00; children 5 to 15, $4.50. Mystic Seaport Museum, Inc., Mystic, Connecticut 06355. Telephone (203) 572-0711.

Now westward along the shore to an old maritime town on the east bank of the Thames River: Groton, Connecticut.

Coming off the interstate the traveler is immediately made aware that this is a town where submarines have a special significance as he is suddenly confronted by a conning tower surfacing through a sea of grass. The U.S.S. *Flasher*—at least a portion of her superstructure—has returned close to where she was born beside the Thames River. Once *Flasher* was the deadliest submarine flying the American flag, credited with sinking 24 enemy ships totalling more than 100,000 tons. Now she reminds us of the price of victory at sea: "Dedicated to our Shipmates on Eternal Patrol" reads the inscription on the Submarine Memorial.

Erected by the U.S. Submarine Veterans Association of World War II in memory of the 3,505 men lost in American submarines in that war, the simple memorial in the little park on Thames Street records the names of 52 United States submarines and the dates when they were lost—from "Sealion SS195, December 10, 1941," to "Bullhead SS332, August 24, 1945," 10 days after Japan formally announced its surrender.

There could be no more appropriate spot for the monument than Groton, for no town in America, or the world, has closer associations with the submarine service. Upriver from the memorial is the Navy's huge submarine base. A little way down toward the harbor

Figure 11
The steamboat *Sabino*, the historic 1841 whaleship *Charles W. Morgan* (center), and the beautiful square-rigger *Joseph Conrad* (right) comprise a most unusual trio of rarely seen ships of the past on the waterfront of the Mystic Seaport, the nation's largest maritime museum, at Mystic, Connecticut.

mouth is the enormous building-yard of the Electric Boat Company, now a division of General Dynamics, which has been building undersea craft for the Navy for many years. And next to the huge yard, another submarine is now on duty as a memorial. But unlike *Flasher*, *Croaker* survives as a whole vessel afloat in the river, a memorial that shows the visitor a little bit of what it was like to fight a war underwater.

In April, 1944, *Croaker* pulled away from the Electric Boat Company dock, headed for six combat patrols in World War II; she would account for a cruiser, four tankers, two freighters, two escort craft, a minesweeper, and an ammunition ship. Now after a postwar career as a training ship, the *Croaker* has been acquired by a nonprofit foundation and is on public display.

Although without her deck guns and some of her equipment, enough remains to give the visitor on a guided tour a clear picture of her operation.

USS Croaker, alongside dock in Thames River at Fort Griswold Moorings, south end of Thames Street, Groton. Open daily all year. April 14 to October 15, 9 a.m. to 5 p.m.; October 16 to April 13, 9 a.m. to 3 p.m. Admission: $3.00; senior citizens, $2.00; children 5 to 11, $1.50. Sponsored by Submarine Memorial Association, Inc., 359 Thames Street, Groton, Connecticut 06340. Telephone (203) 448-1616.

On to the U.S. Navy's base at the northern end of Groton.

On January 1, 1955, the newly commissioned USS *Nautilus*, a 4,000-ton submarine, steamed down the Thames River from the Naval Submarine Base at Groton, Connecticut, off on her shakedown cruise. "UNDERWAY UNDER NUCLEAR POWER," her captain reported.

A historic message. From that moment, submarine design and tactics would never be the same again—with major impact on the whole theory of naval warfare. As the world's first atomic-powered submarine, *Nautilus* pinpointed a critical change in the history of sea power. Which is why today *Nautilus* is back at Groton at the submarine base in honored retirement as a truly historic ship despite a career that never saw combat.

The significance of *Nautilus* and her atomic-powered engine is made clear by a brief look at traditional submarine technology. *Croaker* and *Flasher* and their comrades and enemies of World War II evolved in a straight line from the primitive craft of John Holland and Simon Lake half a century before. Many times bigger, more powerful, more far ranging, they were nevertheless basically similar: surface vessels capable of diving and cruising underwater. On the surface they were propelled by diesels, but these air-gulping engines would have quickly used up the oxygen in a submerged submarine. Underwater, therefore, traditional submarines had to be driven by electric motors powered by storage batteries, which after a few hours' use had to be recharged on the surface. Limited submersed time also sharply, if indirectly, limited the underwater speed of traditional submarines underwater; their hulls, designed for stable, efficient operation, on the ocean's surface, where they spent most of their cruise, performed very poorly when submerged.

Nautilus wasted no time in demonstrating that a nuclear-powered submarine had no such limitations. On her shakedown, she cruised the entire 1,300 miles from Connecticut to Puerto Rico without surfacing. This was only the beginning of her record-shattering cruises. At one point, she traveled 150,000 miles before her atomic power plant needed to be refueled. She cruised deep in the Arctic Ocean beneath the polar ice pack. And in August 1958, *Nautilus* made the first transpolar passage from the Pacific to the Atlantic Ocean, traveling underwater from Pearl Harbor in Hawaii to Portland, England, via the North Pole. Today, nuclear-powered submarines are considered to be able to operate submerged for practically unlimited periods of time. Nuclear power has also made it possible to design hulls for maximum underwater efficiency, making them far faster and more maneuverable submerged than ever before.

Now *Nautilus*, her atomic engines removed, is being gradually prepared for public exhibition at the Submarine Force Museum, a few miles up the Thames River from the Electric Boat Company where she was built. As of mid-April 1986, the *Nautilus* is on display at her dock beside the museum's striking new exhibition buildings. The first portion open to visitors is the forward spaces, including the attack center, wardroom, chief petty officer and crew spaces, the commanding officer's tiny stateroom, gallery, and forward torpedo room.

Ashore, the Submarine Force Museum's new buildings are just outside the main entrance to the Naval Submarine Base, making unnecessary the base passes previously required of museum visitors. *Nautilus* and the museum neatly complement each other. The vessel tells the story of the comparatively recent historic developments that have changed the whole nature of the submarine and underseas warfare. The museum is concerned with the background and history of submarines, "the collection and display of historical information, artifacts and memorabilia on the development of the submarine in the U.S. and foreign countries" is the way the museum's goal is officially described. Some high spots:

• A wall of models depicts the development of American submarines, all built to the same scale so that the relative size of the originals is easy to see. The vessels range from the 53-foot USS *Holland* of 1900 to the USS *Los Angeles*, SSN 688, the first attack submarine of its class, and USS *Ohio*, SSN726, the first Trident submarine.

- A cut-away half-size model shows the innards of the *American Turtle*, the submarine built by David Bushnell during the American Revolution.
- An enormous nine-foot model of submarine *Torsk* is controlled by sonar.
- A model of the *Alligator* shows a little known Union Navy submarine, built in 1862 for use on the James River in the Civil War.
- Several actual mini-submarines of World War II include two Japanese two-man craft and a German "seehund," which was carried by truck along the coast to the point where it was launched for a torpedo attack on Allied craft offshore. Particularly interesting is an Italian Maiale (pig), a two-man submarine designed to carry scuba divers into enemy harbors. Three of these tiny Special Assault Craft entered a British naval base in Egypt in 1941 and sank two battleships, a destroyer, and a tanker—one of the most remarkable naval feats of World War II.
- A special feature of the museum is a fine collection of drawings, photographs, and papers relating to the work of Simon Lake, one of the great American pioneers of submarine design. Included, for example, are drawings of underwater craft he designed for the Russian government before World War I. The museum also displays Lake's experimental submarine *Explorer*. Completed in 1932, the 22-foot craft had wheels for traveling along the ocean floor.

The museum's new building includes an authentic reconstruction of a submarine control room and a working periscope. Two mini-theaters show films on the *Nautilus*, and the development of the U.S. submarine force. The library at the museum includes thousands of volumes, films, and photographs relating to underwater craft.

The Submarine Force Museum is located on the shore of the Thames River, just outside the main gate of the Naval Submarine Base in Groton, Connecticut. Open mid-April to September 30, 9 a.m. to 5 p.m., Wednesday through Monday; October 1 through April 14, Wednesday through Monday, 9 a.m. to 3:30 p.m. Museum closed the first week of January, the first two weeks of April and October, and Thanksgiving, Christmas, and New Year's. Admission: free. Nautilus Memorial and Submarine Force Library and Museum, Box 571, Naval Submarine Base, New London, Groton, Connecticut 06349-5000. Telephone (203) 449-3174 or 3290.

Now across the Thames River to New London. This ancient town on Long Island Sound has one of the deepest harbors on the Atlantic Coast. In the 19th century it was the home port of a very considerable whaling fleet, now remembered in a pleasant small museum. More recently it has been the home of the United States Coast Guard Academy.

Motorists racing westward across the high bridge that spans the Thames at New London can sometimes catch a glimpse of a square-rigged vessel far below them. She's the *Eagle*, at her berth where the campus of the U.S. Coast Guard Academy comes down the hill to the Thames River; the Coast Guard is the last of the three federally sponsored seagoing academies to train prospective officers in sail.

The *Eagle* is a working ship, open to visitors only at certain times of year, but the Academy has its own museum exhibiting a fine collection of Coast Guard-related ship models, pictures, and artifacts. In a wing of the Academy Library, at the far northwest corner of the campus, the museum fills one enormous square room, crammed with ship models, pictures, documents, a lifeboat, model aircraft, portraits, memorabilia, and assorted artifacts. They are clearly displayed, labeled, and lit, but not in any obvious sequence.

The Coast Guard, as such, was formed by the amalgamation of three long-existing organizations: the Revenue Cutter Service, the Life-Saving Service, and the Lighthouse Service. The museum covers all three. The cutters went on duty in 1790 as the Revenue Marine, charged not only with patroling against smugglers and slavers, but with saving lives and salvaging ships at sea. Not surprisingly, its ships and activities form the major part of the museum exhibits.

From the outset, the Revenue Marine vessels were remarkably fine: fast, to catch smugglers and pirates; seaworthy, to stay out in all kinds of weather. Almost all were schooners, although regardless of size or rig all of the Revenue Marine vessels were called "cutters." The museum has many fine cutter models, ranging from the little *Massachusetts* of 1791, to the big, powerful motorships of recent years. Included are models or pictures of such famous vessels as the *Harriet Lane* and the Bering Sea patrol ship *Bear*. Although most models of a given period are grouped together, the groups are scattered around the museum; it takes a little searching to follow their development in historical sequence.

Paintings vividly recall some of the service's historic rescue operations, such as the relief of whaleships trapped in the Arctic ice, and wartime activities that included the World War II landing on the Normandy coast.

The Life-Saving Service, which became part of the Coast Guard in 1915, was preceded and inspired by the volunteer activities of the Massachusetts Humane Society. At the west end of the museum is one of the Society's surfboats, dating from 1870, mounted on the simple carriage on which it was dragged to the shore point nearest a wreck. Alongside is the two-wheeled beach cart that carried gear, and the little cannon that could hurl a lifeline to a wrecked vessel hundreds of yards off shore.

According to the staff, the exhibits include only about one-third of the museum's possessions; the balance is in storage because of lack of space to display it. What is shown, however, is a fascinating report on the Coast Guard's historic role in the nation's maritime activities.

United States Coast Guard Museum, on the United States Coast Guard Academy campus on the west bank of the Thames River. Open all year, Monday-Friday; 7:30 a.m. to 4 p.m.; April through October; weekends 10 a.m. to 5 p.m. Admission: free. US Coast Guard Museum, Waesche Hall, New London, Connecticut 06320-4195. Telephone (203) 444-8510.

Now a look at New London's major maritime heritage: whaling. It is easy to forget that Nantucket and New Bedford weren't the only New England ports with important whaling fleets of their own. But in New London, for example, whaling began around 1819 and by the mid-1840s the port at the mouth of Connecticut's Thames River boasted a fleet of 81 whale ships employing no less than 2,500 men.

This was the peak of whaling out of New London as elsewhere. The loss of markets with the coming of kerosene lamps, and the loss of ships, first in the Civil War and later in the Arctic ice, eventually killed the fishery: The last whaleship cruised out of New London around 1908. The memories of New London's distinctive maritime past have been preserved in the city, however, by the little Tale of the Whale Museum, which is housed in a rebuilt Greek Revival house on the hill overlooking New London harbor.

Perhaps the pride of the collection is a fully-equipped whaleboat, with all its gear, from the famous whaler *Charles W. Morgan*. Here, also, is the medicine chest from the whaler *Colgate*, which was one of the last whalers to sail from New London, although it was built way back in 1860. An important part of the museum collection consists of photographs of New London ships, ship captains, agents, and owners. Shipwrights' tools form another exhibit. Other interesting displays include scrimshaw, products made from whale oil, and

the figurehead of the ship *Flora*. The jawbone of a 65-foot fin whale is a striking artifact and gives dramatic evidence of the size of these creatures.

Like many small museums, the Tale of the Whale is the fruit of the energy and enthusiasm of one man, in this case the founder and director, Dr. Carl H. Wies. His personal collection of whaling artifacts and memorabilia form the nucleus of the exhibits. They are augmented by the whaling collection of the New London County Historical Association, on loan, and maritime artifacts gathered by the Jibboom Club of New London, an exclusive society to which no one could belong except old salts who had sailed vessels overseas.

Children will be particularly interested in a slide show that Dr. Wies has prepared on whaling, which is especially geared to a young audience.

The museum is small but the artifacts are well displayed and carefully described.

Tale of the Whale Museum is on the second floor of a restored Greek revival row house on the hill overlooking the harbor of New London. Reference library. Open Tuesday-Sunday, 1 to 4 p.m. Closed various holidays; best to check. Admission: $1.00; children, 50 cents. Tale of the Whale Museum, 3 Whale Oil Row/115 Huntington Street, New London, Connecticut 06320. Telephone (203) 442-8191.

Further west on Long Island Sound, in Essex, Connecticut, the tree-lined main street winds eastward between handsome old houses down the hill to the west bank of Connecticut River. There the village inn, built in Independence Year, overlooks the steamboat landing and its dockhouse, now the museum. The epitome of a peaceful country village, a visitor might think, the kind of place where nothing has ever happened and people are glad of it.

No such thing—as a few minutes in the Connecticut River Foundation Museum on the wharf quickly reveals. Here you'll find a working replica of the world's first operative submarine, invented by a local youth nearby and tested in the river. On the wall, a painting of this very spot one not-so-quiet night in April 1814 is lurid with red coats and the glare of burning ships. Those stern shipmasters, whose pictures are assembled in a corner, commanded the finest ships of their time—and came home to build the proud houses up the street. The archaic hand tools over there were used in a score of clanging shipyards along the river banks. And the steamship models show vessels that once pulled in to the dock outside the window and kept the river churning with busy traffic.

In short, Essex and the lower Connecticut River valley around it has a fascinating maritime tradition—and the museum is dedicated to its preservation. Opened relatively recently, the museum already has a

Figure 12
Working replica of David Bushnell's *American Turtle*, historic submarine used in American Revolution, is displayed at Connecticut River Foundation Museum at Essex, Connecticut, following successful dive in river.

small but rather choice collection of artifacts and exhibits that tell the story of the four major maritime themes: the invention of the submarine, the many yards building wooden sailing ships, the Essex shipmasters who commanded the top ships of New York, and the steamboats that made the river a major commercial artery.

The Connecticut River Foundation Museum's full-sized replica of David Bushnell's *American Turtle*, which inaugurated submarine warfare during the American Revolution, is unique. Two enthusiasts in the area, a journalist and a boatbuilder, joined forces to reproduce the original as closely as possible, following exactly what is known of Bushnell's design and using the same materials and building techniques. Confident in their craftsmanship, they followed

Bushnell a giant step further and in August, 1975, took the new *Turtle* down for a dive in the Connecticut River. Spectators held their breath as the new *Turtle*, looking like a huge oak cask, disappeared beneath the surface. It came up.

In the American Revolution, Essex and nearby Saybrook, then one town and already an important maritime area, made a considerable contribution in ships and men to Continental Navy activities afloat. Among the models in the museum are fine miniatures of the frigate *Oliver Cromwell*, built for the Connecticut Navy in 1776 before there was a national sea force. Another, large, model of the noted North Atlantic packet *Dreadnaught* of the Red Cross Line is said to have been made by her master, Captain Samuel Samuels, who commanded her for 10 years during which she crossed the Atlantic 70 or 80 times, establishing a reputation for uniformly fast passages.

The 1814 raid on Essex and Saybrook, during which some 28 vessels were burned in the river, was a British attempt to wipe out a nest of American privateers locally built and manned. The museum has a musket and other relics related to the raid and the local militia's response. The events leading up to the War of 1812 are brought vividly to life by seamen's papers of a few years earlier. These certify that the possessor is an American citizen, a necessary precaution since British vessels were stopping American ships and carrying off any sailors they claimed were British subjects.

Steamboating was a major activity on the Connecticut River well into the 20th century, both local traffic and long distance lines running out into Long Island Sound with freight and passengers. One nice model is of the sidewheeler *City of Hartford*, which served on the New York run from 1852 to one foggy day in 1886, when she ran onto a rock in the East River. There are also a model of one of her successors, the propellor steamer *Hartford*, and photographs of a number of river steamers, including the S.S. *Middletown* making her last stop at the Essex wharf in 1931.

Connecticut River Museum, Essex, Connecticut. Turn off Route 9 at Exit 3, then follow signs east to Main Street, continue east to end at Connecticut River; Museum is in a large white wooden building on the dock at the left. Open April 1 to December 31, Tuesday-Sunday, 10 a.m. to 5 p.m. Admission: $1.50; seniors, $1.00; children under 16, 50 cents. Sponsored by nonprofit Connecticut River Foundation at Steamboat Dock, P.O. Box 261, Essex, Connecticut 06426. Telephone (203) 767-8269.

Still further westward, now, along the Connecticut shore to Bridgeport.

At first glance, the 18th-century British frigate berthed at Bridgeport seems pretty incongruous. Actually it's quite appropriate, particularly in the case of HMS *Rose*. The original of this replica of a 24-gun frigate spent much of her active career in the New England and New York waters as part of the British effort to force the rebellious American colonies to return to their allegiance to King George.

The original *Rose* was built in Yorkshire in 1756, served in the French wars in Europe and the West Indies, and eventually was sent to the North American colonies on the eve of the American Revolution. Here she was assigned to Narragansett Bay to take over the hated customs-enforcement duties of the HMS *Gaspee*, which had been burned by rebellious Colonists. HMS *Rose* did her job with such effectiveness that eventually the Rhode Islanders armed a little navy to drive her

off, but the British frigate left for a refit before a battle took place.

Some pieces of the original *Rose*, which was dredged from the bottom of the Savannah River, where she was eventually sunk during the Revolution to block the channel, have been incorporated into her replica. Built in Nova Scotia in 1969, "to show people what a Revolutionary warship looks like," the new frigate was constructed from the plans of the original vessel, although for practical reasons steel masts and steel and synthetic rigging have been substituted for wood and hemp. The replica's distinctive ochre paint is believed to be the color of British frigates of her time.

Visitors will be struck by the frigate's gundeck, so low that a walkway has been cut down the center so that visitors can walk through without bending into a crouch. According to the designers, this reflected the low stature of 18th-century seamen.

The great cabin in the stern is impressive. In the original *Rose* this cabin was mentioned in a report the captain made to his superiors in July, 1776. After her refit, the *Rose* had been sent to New York, where she was ordered up the Hudson to cut off the flow of supplies down the river to Washington's army in Manhattan. The Americans had built batteries along the Hudson, and the *Rose* came under fire, as her captain reported afterward:

> . . . we have met with no damage coming up except a 12-pound shot in our foremast. Another shot came into the cabin and seated itself in a chair; one through our pinnace, which carried away three capstan bars, two oars, and went through the captain's cot. We had two men a little hurt by the blowing up of a powder horn . . . . As soon as we passed the last battery, as we supposed, the captain ordered a bowl of punch and a bottle of claret; but whilst we were refreshing ourselves we were accosted by the last shot, which I mentioned, to have gone through the captain's cot.

Currently, *Rose* has been undergoing major repair to bring her back to first-class condition. Though a considerable portion of her starboard side is being replaced, she remains open to visitors. Thus, there is an opportunity to view portions of her hull structure not ordinarily visible. When her refit is completed she will once more be able to put to sea and visit other ports.

HMS *Rose*, replica of 18th-century British frigate, is now berthed in Black Rock Harbor on the waterfront at Bridgeport, Connecticut. Open Memorial Day weekend through Labor Day, Tuesday-Sunday, 10 a.m. to dark. Balance of year, by appointment only. Admission: $2.00. HMS *Rose* Foundation, Captain's Cove Seaport, Bostwick Avenue, Bridgeport, Connecticut 06605. Telephone (203) 335-1433.

The Island Like a Great Whale

A continuation of the Ice Age glacier's terminal moraine that created Cape Cod and the offshore islands, Long Island is shaped like a great whale, with its split tail to the east stretching for 125 miles parallel to the Connecticut coast. Along its south shore are barrier beaches, separated from the mainland by broad shallow bays, the natural home of shellfish. Between the flukes of the tail and at places along the north shore are harbors deep enough for the blue-water ships of a century ago.

Eastern and central Long Island were settled in early Colonial times by Connecticut Yankees from across the sound (the western end was still Dutch). When the islanders found whales playing off the shore, they launched pulling boats from the open beaches and rowed out to hunt them down (according to one controversial theory, a skill learned from the local Indians). In the little deep-water ports of the island this activity led eventually to the development of whaleships and ocean whaling as well as to a modest shipping industry. Most of the Long Islanders' maritime activities, however, particularly in the last century, have been inshore fishing and shell-fishing in the bays and harbors—once the source of the famous Blue Point oysters, now, alas, no more.

Long Island can be reached at its western end by bridges or by a tunnel from New York City, via a ferry from Bridgeport to Port Jefferson about half way along its length, or via another ferry between New London and Orient Point at the eastern tip of the north fluke. The traveler from the east can choose between riding the ferries, which charge high fares for automobiles, or driving a couple of hundred extra miles via New York City. The ferries are more fun, but experienced travelers should be aware that in the summer they are so crowded that last-minute arrivals on the dock are unlikely to get aboard.

Travelers disembarking at Orient Point to visit Sag Harbor and Amagansett on the southern fluke, again have a choice between making a long detour by road around the head of Peconic Bay or heading directly southward by ferries on and off Shelter Island. Again, the ferries are recommended as the more interesting route.

The Long Island museums that follow are listed in their approximate east to west sequence. Travelers starting from New York City may find it more convenient to reverse the order.

To all appearances a New England village, despite its New York state post office address, Sag Harbor is the most widely known of the Long Island deep-water whaling ports. Whaling and merchant shipping began there in Colonial times and in 1790 the little port had more square-rigged ships in foreign commerce than New York City itself. At the height of its prosperity in 1844-45, 63 whaleships called Sag Harbor home and it is estimated that over the years Sag Harbor ships and seamen earned $25 to $35 million dollars. James Fenimore Cooper, who was once the agent for a whaling company there and held shares in the whaling bark *Union*, used his Sag Harbor background in several of his books.

The Sag Harbor Whaling and Historical Museum is in a large Greek revival building on Main Street, near the corner of Garden Street, built in 1845 by a whaling magnate. Do not be confused by "Masonic Temple" in large letters across the pediment, the museum occupies the entire first floor. A whaleboat in the front yard is the more significant marker.

The entrance to the museum is framed by the jaws of a right whale, but despite its name, the Whaling Museum is a good deal more than that; a traditional historical society museum, it houses all kinds of relics and artifacts from Sag Harbor and eastern Long Island. The whaling artifacts, largely concentrated in a couple of rooms, are interesting, however—the kind of collection that's fun to poke around in.

Here, for example, is the record of a significant advance in the weapons of the whale hunter, an early example of the technological changes that led eventually to over-fishing and the near extermination of some whale species. This rocket missile was developed by Captain Thomas Welcome Roys of Sag Harbor, a veteran whaling captain, the first to take his whaleship into the Bering Straits. On display are a model and patent papers of the Roys-Lilliendahl Whaling Rocket, invented in 1856. The rocket made it possible to shoot the harpoon into the whale, rather than depend on the strength of the harpooner's arm.

Several ship models show whaling vessels of historical interest, including one of the *Excel*, which in an 1857-59 voyage brought back whalebone worth $30,000, no doubt a boon to corset manufacturers. Another is of the bark *Wanderer*, the last working whaleship; she was driven ashore and lost on Cuttyhunk Island in the 1920s. A real sailor's model is that of a man-of-war made by a crewman aboard the Sag Harbor whaler *Phenix* in the 1830s.

The museum's collection of prints includes the famous Garnery/Marten series of whaling aquatints, praised by Melville in *Moby Dick*. Papers of Sag Harbor ships, beginning with an early specimen signed by President George Washington, are of special interest, as is the collection of ships' logs.

A unique exhibit is a series of photographs of a

Figure 13
Sag Harbor Whaling and Historical Museum; Sag Harbor, Long Island, New York.

whale that was pursued and killed off Amagansett as recently as 1907. The whale was gravely wounded by a harpoon hand-hurled from the whaleboat, then finished off by a bomb exploded inside it. As shown in the photographs, the whale was hauled up on the beach and cut up. The skeleton ended up in the American Museum of Natural History in New York City, where it was prepared for display by famed naturalist Roy Chapman Andrews. The replica whaleboat on the lawn was the type used in this kind of off-the-shore whale hunt after earlier service on a whaleship.

Interesting as the museum is, the real star of Sag Harbor is the village itself. As in New Bedford, the whaling captains and shipowners put their money into fine houses. Unlike New Bedford, Sag Harbor never grew into an industrial city but remained a compact village around its harbor, so that today the visitor is likely to find more of the "feel" of a 19th-century whaling port than in its more widely known rival on Buzzards Bay.

The visitor should be sure to buy a copy of a fine little booklet entitled "A Tour of Historic Sag Harbor," by Nancy Boyd Willey, and use it to guide him on a walk around the village. Besides many interesting houses, the tour will lead him to two places of particular maritime interest. The Presbyterian Church, built on Madison Street in 1844, was known as the Whalers' Church. Although it lost its remarkable steeple in the 1938 hurricane, it remains a beautiful and historic building. In the Oakland cemetery at Suffolk Street and Jermain Avenue, is the Broken Mast Monument. A marble memorial to six young Sag Harbor shipmasters killed by whales, it depicts a splintered mast rising over a bas-relief of men clinging to an upturned whaleboat in a roiled sea. Sag Harbor's prosperity, we are reminded, came at no small price.

Sag Harbor Whaling Museum is on Main Street, at corner of Garden Street, across from public library. Small gift shop. Open May 15 to September 30, 10 a.m. to 5 p.m.; Sundays, 1 p.m. to 5 p.m. Admission: $1.00; senior citizens, 75 cents; children, 50 cents. Sag Harbor Whaling and Historical Museum, P.O. Box 1327A, Sag Harbor, Long Island, New York 11963. Telephone (516) 725-0770.

Now to the ancient fishing/whaling village of Amagansett, on the south shore of the island, facing the Atlantic.

Set among sand dunes, where summer places of affluent urbanites now intermingle with ancient cottages, Amagansett has no harbor and faces directly on open ocean, being eastward of the barrier beaches that protect most of the south shore of Long Island. Yet its maritime traditions date back to the earliest settlement in the mid-17th century.

Here, as in early Nantucket, whaling was carried on in boats launched from the beach. With the help of the Montauk Indians, the newcomers rowed out through the surf, speared the whales, and dragged the carcasses ashore to be cut up and rendered for oil. Fishing was the other main source of income of the villagers. The exhibits in the East Hampton Marine Museum, which is installed in a modern building down a side road toward the sea, center on whaling and fishing.

That the local tradition is shore-based whaling is made clear in the ground floor gallery where a well-preserved beach-launched whaleboat is displayed. Equally out of the ordinary is a big, heavy two-wheeled beach cart that was hitched to a horse to carry nets or other heavy fishing gear down onto the beach. Other small pulling boats on display include a round-bottomed "striker boat" used to set heavy purse seines—round nets laid around a school of fish in order to trap them in a bag at one end. The purse seines were used in the menhaden fisheries.

On the museum's third floor, dioramas and three-dimensional models explain the five basic commercial fishing techniques. Half models show the standard rigs of various types of draggers, while lobstering has its own exhibits of equipment and models. A whole wall is covered with photographs of area fishermen past and present, including two Indians, descendants of the original sea hunters of Montauk.

East Hampton is one of the few museums, perhaps the only one, to have a display on aquaculture fish farming. Models make clear how fish are raised in tanks rather than hunted in the sea, a technology that someday may supersede fishing, just as cattle raising has superseded hunting.

On the bottom floor of the museum is a cannon from HMS *Culloden*, wrecked on the eastern shore of nearby Fort Pond Bay on January 29, 1781. *Culloden*, a ship of the line, was part of the British fleet on its way to intercept the French fleet off Newport. The gun, salvaged from Block Island Sound with other artifacts, has been mounted in a realistic mock-up of the gun station and port of an 18th-century battleship.

One unusual attraction at the museum deserves to be copied elsewhere: a 25-foot "trawler" sailing a sea of sand in the backyard. Designed for small-fry who are bored with looking at exhibits, this useful vessel has a wheelhouse with steering wheel and a mast with a boom rigged with a pulley so the young fishermen can hoist small fish boxes into or out of the tiny hold. In the bow is a snug fo'c'sle with mini bunks just the right size for three-foot mariners.

Also in the museum gardens are the hull of a 25-foot Great South Bay catboat, and a "sink box"; the latter was anchored in the midst of a marsh by professional wildfowl hunters, and there sunk until just the gunwall was above water in order to make it as inconspicuous as possible.

East Hampton Town Marine Museum is at eastern edge of Amagansett village. Watch for museum sign and turn right off Route 27; watch for second sign at Bluff Road, turn right again; museum is white three-storied building on left. Open July and August, Tuesday-Sunday, 10:30 a.m. to 5 p.m.; June and September, Saturday and Sunday, 10:30 a.m. to 5 p.m.; balance of the year by appointment only. Admission: $2.00; seniors, $1.75; children, $1.00. East Hampton Historical Society, Town Marine Museum, Box 858, Bluff Road, Amagansett, New York 11930. Telephone (516) 267-6544.

Westward of Amagansett, Great South Bay stretches for 30 miles between the south shore of Long Island and the barrier beaches that parallel the coast, two to five miles offshore. From the bay's shallow waters, only six feet deep, and once warm, clean, and just salty enough, oystermen formerly tonged and dredged millions of gallons of the famous Blue Points, whose size, plumpness, and flavor set gourmet mouths watering.

Now, alas, the industry is no more, done in by a combination of increased salinity, caused by breaks in the outer beaches, pollution, attacks by natural predators, and overfishing. The memory of the great days of oystering, as well as other maritime activities in the Great South Bay, are kept fresh in the Suffolk Marine Museum in West Sayville. The museum, a cluster of buildings down on the edge of the bay, is in a county park, a former private estate.

The oystering sector of the museum centers in the William Rudolph Oyster House, moved here from its original location and set down at the edge of the water. Typical of many such buildings once scattered along the bay shores, it was used to cull, open, and pack the oysters for shipment. The long, well-lit opening bench is still in place, but now the building also houses oyster dredges, a reconstruction of an oyster shipper's office, a panoramic display explaining the different types of oystering, and photographs of bay oystermen at work.

William Rudolph was the son of Dutch immigrants, part of a whole group of neighbors who

Figure 14
Historic 1888 schooner *Priscilla* is berthed on the Great South Bay waterfront of the Suffolk Marine Museum at West Sayville on New York's Long Island. The main museum building is in the background; at right is the Oyster House, once a busy shipping center for famous local oysters, now moved to museum grounds.

(Mitch Carucci photo, courtesy of Suffolk Marine Museum.)

crossed the Atlantic together in the 1850s and settled along the bay to become oystermen and fishermen. A photograph of one family on its arrival in the mid-century shows them still wearing the traditional dress of their native village—picturesque costumes to American eyes, everyday work clothes to the newcomers.

At the dock next to the oyster house are two oyster boats. The 36-foot sloop *Modesty* is the last commercial sailing vessel built on Long Island, taking to the water in 1923. The 34-foot schooner *Priscilla*, 60 feet overall, was built in 1888 in the nearby town of Patchogue. In the summer, the two boats cruise the bay, but one of them is always on exhibition alongside the dock. Both these handsome little craft were restored by volunteers and the museum has now added a regular restoration boat shop to its facilities; it is lodged in a transplanted building that still carries its original sign: "Frank E. Penney, Boatbuilder."

Yachting has been the other major marine activity on Great South Bay, and around the turn of the century the area was famous for its racing catboats, broad-beamed with centerboards. Tremendously fast in light airs and smooth water, the type evolved from the working catboats used by oystermen but with the lines and rigs modified for speed at the expense of working usefulness and handiness. The hulls of a dozen of these rather exotic craft, very different from the husky working catboats of Cape Cod, are on display in two open-sided pavilions on the museum grounds.

In the main building of the museum, converted from the estate garage, is a fine collection of half models of sharpies and catboats designed and built locally. Among other models is a particularly interesting one of the 1897 steam yacht *Preston*. In the Lifesaving room are the beach cart, pulled by hand through the sand to carry lifesaving gear to the scene of a wreck;

and a breeches buoy, the little carrying device that was hauled out along a line to a wreck to bring people ashore. Most interesting and unusual are two thick volumes that list chronologically and alphabetically the names of the scores of vessels lost over the years in the area, wrecks that are shown dramatically in a series of accompanying photographs.

Suffolk Marine Museum, on Montauk Highway in West Sayville. Turn is south off 27A; principal sign reads "Suffolk County Park." Drive through golf links, past clubhouse, to shore. Research library. Gift shop. Open all year, Monday-Saturday, 10 a.m. to 3 p.m.; Sunday, noon to 4 p.m. Admission: 75 cents; children, 50 cents. Sponsored by nonprofit Suffolk Marine Museum, Box 144, Montauk Highway, West Sayville, New York 11796. Telephone (516) 567-1733.

Whaling on western Long Island was long confined to smaller chaser boats launched off the beaches of the south shore. In 1836, however, a group of businessmen in Cold Spring Harbor on the island's north shore saw the profits in high-seas whale hunting. Starting from scratch, their little company built a fleet of nine whaleships, all second hand, and operated them until the hard times of the Civil War.

At first glance, Cold Spring Harbor would seem an odd place to base a seagoing fleet; open ocean is 50 miles away to the west and twice that distance to the east. Since most whaling voyages took three years or more, however, a few extra days made little difference. The first captains, like their ships, came from older whaling ports, but in time local men worked their way up to become master mariners. The quarter-century of Cold Spring Harbor whaling was long enough to leave many local families with personal traditions and artifacts of worldwide whale hunting, and led eventually to the establishment of a museum to preserve them for posterity.

The original nucleus of the exhibits was the donation of a fine local collection, but the museum was really launched by the gift of a fully fitted whaleboat from the American Museum of Natural History in New York. The gift was arranged by the museum's famed ornithologist, Dr. Robert Cushman Murphy; and the boat came from the whaling brig *Daisy* in which Dr. Murphy himself had gone on a South Atlantic whaling voyage as a young man, pulling an oar in that very boat. Today the whaleboat is a prized exhibit at the museum, shown with all its gear exceptionally well-labeled with name and function.

Dr. Murphy is also responsible for the remarkable whaling film that can be viewed at the museum on request. On his 1912 trip the young scientist shot footage of traditional whale hunting, using whaleboats and harpoons. Almost 50 years later he went back to the South Atlantic and filmed scenes of modern whaling, in which two whales are killed by explosive shells fired from a high-powered chaser vessel. The result is a graphic and fascinating report on how technology has changed whaling. Together with Dr. Murphy's filmed commentary on the danger of exterminating the species, it makes a compelling argument for ending 20th-century whale hunting.

The museum's principal permanent exhibit, "Mark Well the Whale!—Long Island Whaling," starts with the Indians of the shore tribes: a diorama shows them towing in a dead whale to be cut up on the beach. Artifacts include an Indian stone lamp that burned whale oil. Other exhibits report on the shore-based whaling of European settlers who launched boats from south shore beaches.

A big model of the whaleship *Charles W. Morgan*, scaled an inch to the foot, dominates the deep-sea whaling section. With the tools and hunting weapons of the 19th-century whalemen on display are some of the end products, such as whale-oil candles. A very unusual and most interesting exhibit deals with the roles of minority groups in the whaling industry. As readers of *Moby Dick* will remember, blacks and Indians were among the whalemen.

The final, Cold Spring Harbor, section centers on the local whalers, with special emphasis on Arctic whaling, using pictures, artifacts, charts, and memorabilia of the port and its ships.

The museum's collections include 600 pieces of scrimshaw carved by whalemen. Its 3,000 manuscripts comprise 95 percent of the surviving material from the Cold Spring Harbor Whaling fleet, including logs, personal journals, and business correspondence.

Cold Spring Harbor Whaling Museum is housed in a modest building at the eastern end of Main Street. Open Saturday, Sunday and national holidays all year and daily, Memorial Day to Labor Day. Hours, 11 a.m. to 5 p.m. Admission: $1.50; seniors, children, 75 cents. Sponsored by nonprofit Whaling Museum Society, Inc., Main Street, P.O. Box 25, Cold Spring Harbor, New York 11724. Telephone (516) 367-3418.

Now to the greatest of American ports.

II
THE PORT OF NEW YORK
AND ITS INLAND EMPIRE

Around New York
The Lordly Hudson
Down Along the Erie Canal
Champlain: Lake of Battles

Around New York

In 1626, the little Dutch settlement at the mouth of the Hudson River sent off to the homeland the first shipload of exports of which we know the manifest: beaver, otter, mink, and wildcat pelts, plus logs, made up the cargo of the *Arms of Amsterdam* (*Wapen van Amsterdam* in the original Dutch). The port of New York was launched on its course toward becoming one of the greatest maritime cities in the world.

Geography has been New York's major asset from the beginning. Eight large bays and four river mouths give access to 771 miles of protected waterfront, 578 miles of them within New York City itself. On the west, the Hudson provides a navigable waterway far into the hinterland—a waterway extended many times farther in the early 19th century when the Erie Canal linked the river to the Great Lakes. On the other side of Manhattan, the East River offers sheltered anchorages and access to Long Island Sound, a 125-mile sheltered waterway. And on the south, the Atlantic comes up the harbor to lap the city's doorstep, ready to carry a ship around the world.

New York has always been among the first ports of North America, although it long lagged behind its rival, Boston. New York's Colonial merchants thrived on a triangular trade—provisions to the West Indies, sugar to England, British manufactures back to New York—but there was always a strong undercurrent of less orthodox activities. The slave trade was, of course, legal and very profitable. During the endless wars with France, privateering filled many a sailor's pockets, and when peace came it was all too easy for some to slide over into piracy. Smuggling was a major industry. At the beginning of the 18th century, historians estimate, about one-third of New York's trade was in violation of British laws, though winked at by Colonial officials and courts.

During the third quarter of the 18th century the number of New York-owned ships increased sevenfold. Although the port was occupied by British troops during most of the Revolution, shipping boomed again with peacetime. By the turn of the century, New York's exports were worth eight times as much as they had been only a decade before, and in the next few years the port finally raced past its New England rival. In 1840, one of every three ships flying the American flag in foreign trade was owned in New York, making the city second only to London among the ports of the entire world.

Three developments helped New York thrive. The construction of the Erie Canal channeled the rich commerce of the Middle West through the port. The establishment of transatlantic packet lines, ships that sailed on a regular schedule every month whether fully loaded or not, promoted trade with Britain—and brought immigrants into New York harbor. And the cruise of Fulton's steam-powered *Clermont* up the Hudson, in 1807, started a new wave of maritime activity that made New York the center of a network of coastal and inland steamboat lines that brought the city further wealth.

American shipping never recovered from the Civil War, but the port of New York continued to grow and prosper as the harbor became crowded with ships flying foreign flags: British, French, German. In the century-long reign of the great transatlantic liners, it was the sailings of Cunard, White Star, the French Line, Hamburg-American, that drew the glamour passengers and the publicity.

Today, New York remains one of the great ports of the world, although its preeminence on the North Atlantic coast is threatened by Baltimore. Not only do the city's maritime traditions remain strong, but there is growing appreciation among New Yorkers of the need to cherish and preserve the heritage of the past. The visitor will find the result is ships and museums that are a joy to explore.

The New-York Historical Society—that hyphen is itself a bit of history—has been around for a long time. Since 1804 the organization has been gathering the odd, the beautiful, and the significant that tell the story of New York City. The visitor will find on display at the society's massive headquarters on Central Park West a fascinating collection of Americana including artifacts and paintings relating to the maritime heritage of the city and the nation.

The ship models, largely concentrated in the History of Transportation galleries in the basement, are interesting, although the visitor is sometimes frustrated by a scarcity of labels or background information and the mixing together of different types and periods. One model is a vessel particularly identified with New York City: The side-wheeler *Mary Powell* ran on the Hudson from 1861 to 1923 and won the affection of travelers for not only never losing a passenger but all the while maintaining perfect schedules. Another ship represented by a model was also long remembered by New Yorkers, although for a very different reason: the Black Ball packet *Albion* driven ashore on the Irish coast in 1822 with only seven survivors. Yet another model, the steam frigate *Hartford*, shows the ship in which Farragut damned the torpedoes at Mobile Bay during the Civil War.

Upper galleries of the Historical Society display other objects of maritime interest. Notable among them are aquatints of sea battles in the War of 1812, paintings of Colonial shipmasters with their vessels portrayed sailing across the background, and a fine model of a Dutch yacht, shaped remarkably like a wooden shoe. A lighthearted note is struck by a sunny painting entitled *Fishing Party in a Catboat*. The ladies, in 1871 versions of sports outfits, are obviously enjoying themselves while the gents are happily sailing the boat or hauling in fish—all except one poor fellow who clearly wishes he'd stayed ashore.

Frequently there is a strong maritime element in the society's special but temporary exhibits. A beautifully presented show on the birth of Nieuw Amsterdam, for example, included ship models, early views of the harbor filled with ships, and portraits of shipping magnates and master mariners. It is always worth checking to see what special shows will be in the Historical Society's galleries at the time of any given visit.

New-York Historical Society faces Central Park. Open all year. Monday-Friday, 11 a.m. to 5 p.m.; Saturday, 10 a.m. to 5 p.m.; Sunday, 1 to 5 p.m. Admission: $2.00; seniors, $1.50; children under 12, $1.00. Library. Gift shop. Sponsored by New-York Historical Society, 170 Central Park West, New York, New York 10024. Telephone (212) 873-3400.

Across Central Park from the New-York Historical Society is a larger museum with much the same focus. The Museum of the City of New York is on Fifth Avenue at 103d Street, at the upper end of what is sometimes called "Museum Mile."

The five floors of the museum are filled with fascinating displays, including John D. Rockefeller's bedroom and a theater collection, but for maritime-minded visitors the place to start is at the north end of the first floor hall. Here are lined up models of three important ships in New York's earliest history.

The *Dauphine*, a 100-ton, three-masted carrack, borrowed from the French Navy, brought explorer Giovanni da Verrazano into New York Bay one beautiful spring day in April 1524: "A very pleasant place," he called it.

Alongside is a fine built-up model of the famous *Half Moon—Halve Maen* in the original Dutch—in which Henry Hudson paid his visit in 1609; well-known, of course, partly because Hudson's name became attached to the great river up which he explored some 140 miles.

The third model is of a vessel little known to most of us, the *Onrust*, Dutch for "restless." This little sloop, about 44 feet long and 16 tons burden, was the first vessel built in the area by Europeans, having been constructed in 1614 on Manhattan Island to replace a vessel burned while riding at anchor. The shipwrights were Dutch fur traders, not settlers, but *Onrust* has been hailed as the forerunner of New York's one-time great shipbuilding industry.

More about the earliest maritime activities around New York can be found in the Dutch gallery, adjacent to the models. Here, for example, is a model of a Dutch "schrache," a small coasting vessel, ketch-rigged. Most of the maritime exhibits of the museum, however, are in the Port of New York gallery, at the south end of the second floor.

The gallery is dominated by two enormous figures. At the entrance looms Robert Fulton, cast in metal, twice life-size—appropriately enough, since Fulton's little steam up the Hudson in 1807 probably did more to change New York port, and every other port, than the activities of any other single individual. Within the gallery towers Andrew Jackson, carved in wood, no mariner but here a historic figurehead from the frigate *Constitution*. The President was stealthily beheaded one night by an angry anti-Jackson ship captain while the frigate was at the Boston Navy Yard in 1833. Eventually, Andrew was replaced by a less politically controversial figurehead.

The visits of both Verrazano and Hudson are the subjects of dioramas in the gallery, while a third diorama shows 19th-century South Street along the East River when it was the heart of New York's waterfront. The main focus of the gallery, however, is its collection of ship models. Among the most interesting and unusual are models of the small harbor and river craft that were taken for granted in their time and forgotten after they were outdated. Here are the 1820 hay sloop *Mary L.*; the sailing ferry *Independent* of 1784; and one of the vessels that eventually replaced sail for harbor crossings, the side-wheeler *Brooklyn*, typical of the ferries that criss-crossed the harbor well into the 1920s. Two Hudson River sloops, the workhorses of local transport, are particularly interesting; one, the little 76-ton *Experiment*, left the sheltered river waters to make the second voyage ever from the port of New York to China. Her round trip to Whampoa took about 16 months.

Models of other vessels include the famous *Savannah*, the first ship with steam power to cross the Atlantic (she sailed most of the way), and the famous clipper ship *Challenge*. It was on the *Challenge*'s maiden voyage to San Francisco that Captain Waterman and his officers either murdered several crew members or bravely put down a vicious mutiny, according to which version you choose to believe.

Naval vessels in the model collection range from French and British frigates of the 18th and early 19th centuries to the famous USS *Monitor*, built in Brooklyn, and the 1910 battleship *North Dakota*. Yachting is represented by two prime specimens: the *Sappho*, which successfully defended the America's Cup in 1871, and the schooner *Atlantic*, winner of a famous transatlantic race in 1905. There are a number of handsome owner's models of 20th-century steamships, and not to be overlooked is a model of a

liner that was never built, a super-streamlined vessel designed by Norman Bel Geddes, better known for his imaginative stage-set designs for plays and operas.

Two other things to look for: the fine collection of steamship prints gathered by Andrew Fletcher, a famous New York builder of ship engines; and a curious but handsome piece of 19th-century cabin furniture used at sea by a Navy captain, a small oval table that unfolds to form a desk and chair. Just the thing for a studio apartment.

Museum of the City of New York is at Fifth Avenue at 103d Street, facing Central Park. Gift shop. Open all year, Tuesday-Saturday, 10 a.m. to 5 p.m.; Sunday and holidays, 1 to 5 p.m. Free admission. Sponsored by the City of New York. Museum of the City of New York, 1220 Fifth Avenue, New York, New York 10029. Telephone (212) 534-1672.

Now down to lower Manhattan, the teeming waterfront district of 150 years ago . . . .

In Colonial New York the East River side of Manhattan was preferred for wharves over the rocky Hudson River shore, more exposed to winter storms and ice. In the great days of 19th-century sail, ships from all over the world tied up at the East River docks, their bowsprits stretching out into busy South Street, which ran along the waterfront. Here was the maritime heart of the city, crowded with merchants' countinghouses, warehouses, shipping offices, ship chandlers, provisioners—and sailors' bars, dance halls, hotels, whorehouses.

By the mid-20th century, shipping activities had moved elsewhere in the port leaving South Street and its docks a down-at-the-heel backwater of Manhattan. Today, however, the masts of tall ships once again loom high over the waterfront—a tiny handful, to be sure, compared to 150 years ago, but enough to remind us of the great role the area once played in American maritime history. For here has been established one of the nation's outstanding maritime museums, the South Street Seaport.

Actually, the South Street Seaport is unique among America's maritime museums. The seaport's preservation and ultimate restoration of two major full-rigged ships plus a small squadron of other vessels will in itself be a striking achievement. But as its name implies, the South Street Seaport has an even larger objective—the preservation of at least a portion of the waterfront milieu of a great port, perhaps as important to our maritime heritage as the ships themselves. Projects of this size take a long time to mature; the Seaport has not yet been able to carry out all its ambitious plans. What has already been achieved, however, is remarkable, not only in the sheer magnitude and broad scope of the Seaport's activities—these might be expected in a great metropolis—but in the successful combination of historic preservation ashore and afloat into an integrated whole.

The vessels currently open to visitors at the Seaport are berthed in the East River at Piers 15 and 16 on South Street, opposite Fulton Street and Burling Slip (John Street). Here the visitor will find the huge four-masted bark *Peking*, and the *Ambrose*, the lightship that once marked the entrance to New York Harbor. Visitors can also watch the restoration of the full-rigged ship *Wavertree*, already well-advanced. Also at the piers but not currently open to visitors are the Gloucester fishing schooner *Lettie G. Howard*, which is undergoing major repairs, the ferryboat *Major General William H. Hart*, awaiting restoration, and the 19th-century work schooner *Pioneer*, which carries passengers on short cruises around New York Harbor. The Seaport also has a new harbor excursion boat, the *Andrew Fletcher*, a modern replica of the sidewheel steamers of a century ago.

Peking is a remarkable vessel, the ultimate windjammer, a type developed by German shipowners in the early years of the 20th century in a last desperate effort to keep sailing ships competitive with the tramp steamers that were fast taking over ocean freight carrying. To compete, a sailing ship had to carry as much cargo as possible as fast as possible with as small a crew as possible—and at the same time as safely as possible. The *Peking* and her even larger sisters of the Hamburg-based Flying P Line met these requirements admirably and the line survived until World War II. You can see why as you tour *Peking*. Here are some things to note:

- *Peking*'s carrying capacity is obvious as she towers over her dock. Her steel hull has a gross tonnage of 3,100; she could carry a huge cargo of Chilean nitrates, the cargo for which she was designed.

- *Peking*'s four-masted bark rig—square sails on three masts and fore and aft on the small jigger mast nearest the stern—was designed to combine driving power with maneuverability. As ships grew bigger and longer in order to increase cargo capacity—(*Peking*'s hull is 347 feet long) more sails were needed to drive them. But if the masts and yards of the traditional three masted square-rigger were made proportionately larger, they set up dangerous stresses. Designers solved the problem by adding a fourth mast, and they found that using fore-and-aft rig on this mast improved balance and made the ship more manageable.

With four masts, including a mainmast as tall as a 17-story building, and carrying more than an acre of canvas under full sail, *Peking* had a top speed of 16.5 knots (19 miles an hour) and a voyage-long average rate that matched that of most tramp steamers of her time. Alan Villiers has listed *Peking* voyages from the English Channel to Valparaiso, which involved beating around Cape Horn against the prevailing westerlies: 1912, 70 days; 1913, 74 days; 1914, 79 days; and 1923, 67 days.

- You'll see that despite her size, *Peking* has quarters for only 4 officers and 28 men. With a rig designed to minimize the need to handle the sails and barrel winches to give mechanical advantage in hauling on lines, that's all she needed. A clipper ship less than half her size would have had twice the crew.

- The winches, set in the center of the ship abaft the masts, also greatly increased the safety of handling lines in heavy weather. Villiers, in his fine book, *The Way of a Ship*, explains that in a conventional square rigger most of the braces—the lines controlling sails and yards—ran down to the sides of the ship where the men hauling on them had nothing to hang on to. Thus exposed they could be thrown around the deck as the ship rolled in heavy weather or even washed overboard should a big sea come aboard. The central location of the winches not only kept the men away from the sides but placed them near gear that they could grab for a handhold.

- The big amidships deck house, which makes *Peking* look like a steamship with masts, also increased the crew's safety. As Villiers points out, the raised house kept the men working amidships above most of the water that came aboard. At the same time it broke the sweep of waves across the deck. Within the house were reasonably dry quarters for the crew, the galley, and the sailmaker's and carpenter's shops.

Villiers emphasizes that these and other safety features, such as protective netting hung along the exposed main deck in bad weather, did much to raise crew morale. He has high praise for these huge, immensely strong steel ships of the last days of sail. Because they could be driven hard in gale-force winds without going under or being dismasted, these last of the windjammers could make fast passages carrying heavy cargoes half way around the world.

Built in 1911, the *Peking* was in her prime before World War I. Back into service as a bulk carrier after the war, she eventually became a floating school for boys in England and had her rig cut down and school facilities added. Putting her back into her original condition since she arrived in New York in 1975 has been a long slow job, not yet fully completed, although the officers' staterooms and the fo'c'sle have been recreated.

The technological advances in the use of windpower that she demonstrates have given *Peking* added interest in recent years. Should the day come when the high cost of fossil fuels once more makes it cheaper to use the wind to move bulk cargoes at sea, something like the *Peking* may be the starting point for a new age of sail.

The *Ambrose* is a fine specimen of lightship, a type of vessel that has vanished from our coasts. The last lightship, the vessel at Nantucket Shoals, has recently been replaced by an automatic buoy. The *Ambrose*'s original function of marking the Ambrose Channel into New York Harbor was earlier taken over by a Texas tower. *Ambrose* was the first lightship on the station after the channel was dredged in 1907, and in 1921 she received the world's first successful radio beacon, a tremendous improvement in navigational aids.

Although lightships never cruised the high seas, the service had its own dangers; some vessels were run down in fogs, others sank with all hands during hurricanes. Visitors can clamber around the *Ambrose*, and admire the immensely powerful lights above her twin masts. Be sure to visit the anchor windlass room. Anchor size was even more important to a lightship than to most vessels, since she had to be held exactly in her appointed place; if her anchors dragged in a gale a lightship was not only worthless as a reference point for incoming ships but actually dangerous, since her light would give a false position.

The *Wavertree*, the Seaport's full-rigged ship, provides an opportunity to see a major restoration project in full swing. Built in Southampton in 1885, *Wavertree* had an active quarter century at sea, her later years spent picking up general cargoes wherever she could find them. In 1910 she lost her masts in a gale off Cape Horn and became a floating warehouse in the Straits of Magellan. Eventually *Wavertree* was towed north to Buenos Aires to spend 20 dismal years as a sand barge. Her stout iron hull survived, however—she is the largest iron sailing ship left afloat—and in 1970 the ship was towed north again, this time all the way to New York for eventual restoration. *Wavertree*'s decks and most of the masts have already been replaced; now the work centers on the completion of her rerigging and recreating the living quarters of officers and crew. Visitors can take a "behind the scenes" group tour with a guide who points out and explains the restoration work being done.

At the head of Seaport's piers, a couple of one-time cargo containers have been converted into a little building that houses the Seaport's Crafts Center, where ship-model building, wood carving, and other maritime crafts are demonstrated. Across South Street, however, is the Seaport's other major project, the preservation and rehabilitation of a portion of New York's historic maritime neighborhood. In its own way, the shoreside restoration is as striking as the great ships.

According to the Seaport's president, the museum from its foundation, in 1967, was a unique concept: "to document and to evoke a rich and varied history in the streets and buildings on the waterfront, and aboard the ships." Two entire city blocks, buildings constructed from the late 18th to the mid-19th century, have now been preserved and restored. Built for shopkeepers and merchants who often lived, worked, and kept their merchandise in the same structure, many used over the years by maritime-related trades and services, most of these buildings have considerable architectural and historical interest. The Seaport sees them as providing a "museum without walls" in which the visitor will "experience" the history of South Street and its environs, stimulated not only by the buildings—and the ships—but by exhibitions, lectures, educational programs, and a rich program of events.

The visitor will find the Seaport's admission and information office in the Titanic Memorial Tower on the corner of Fulton Street, two blocks west of South Street and the piers and ships. The tower was once atop the Seamen's Church Institute on South Street and was saved when the building was torn down some years ago. Just across Water Street is the Seaport's Museum Gallery, which displays changing exhibitions on maritime New York. Upstairs is the Herman Melville Library, open by appointment for research in maritime history. Adjacent in 1835 row buildings are the Visitors Center, a marine book and chart store, and a stationers and working print shop.

On other sides of the block are the Seaport offices and a small theater where a multi-media presentation tells the story of the South Street Seaport. On the far side of Seaport's other block, just to the south, is the Museum Program Center, facing John Street, in a building that once was the counting house of New York's leading China-Trade merchants.

Architecturally, the centerpiece of the Seaport's preservation area is the beautiful Schermerhorn Row, at 2-20 Fulton Street, built on newly filled land for a ship chandler in 1812. In a major portion of the row the Seaport plans eventually to establish its permanent museum, which will become the focal point of the shoreside exhibits. One end of the Row was once the

Figure 15
The once-towering masts of the ships at the New York City's South Street Seaport now seem tiny
compared to the skyscrapers pressing in behind them. Recreated steamboat is in foreground,
lightship at right, the two square riggers in the center.

Seamen's Hotel, and about half of this will be restored, using original materials found in the space. Other of the Seaport's ambitious future plans include an educational center and a children's center dedicated to P.T. Barnum, whose own museum was not far away.

Close to the Seaport are the famous Fulton Fish Market and also two modern buildings now filled with a variety of shops and restaurants: the Pavilion on Pier 17, behind the Fish Market, and the Fulton Market Building, facing South Street.

South Street Seaport Museum: on the East River in lower Manhattan, south of the Brooklyn Bridge. Ships at piers off South Street, opposite John and Fulton Streets. Gallery, Model Shop, Library, on Water Street between Fulton and Beekman Streets. Museum activities include educational tours of ships and adjacent historic district, lectures, workshops, classes. Bookstore. Galleries, piers, and ships, open all year except Thanksgiving, Christmas, and New Year's; galleries, piers, open 11 a.m. to 5 p.m.; ships in summer, 10 a.m. to 6 p.m.; in winter, shorter hours; check by telephone. Admission to ships: $4.00; students, $2.00.

South Street Seaport Museum, 207 Fulton Street, New York, New York 10038. Telephone (212) 669-9424.

A note in passing. For many years the collection of the Seamen's Church Institute in lower Manhattan was one of New York City's little-publicized maritime treasures. For more than a century and a half, the Institute has been one of the few social agencies working to make a better life for Jack ashore. And over the decades the Institute's sailor guests, friends, and residents have shown their appreciation by giving the organization every kind of maritime artifact —knotwork displays, pictures, documents, memorabilia, and, above all, many, many ship models. These were informally displayed in the library and corridors of the various successive Institute headquarters, most recently located in a 23-story building on State Street, facing Battery Park and New York Harbor.

But the port of New York has changed. The docks that once ringed lower Manhattan are gradually disappearing; the survivors stand empty or have been turned to non-marine uses. Today, ships dock in Brooklyn or on the New Jersey side of New York Harbor. And the seamen who find their way to Manhattan are no longer looking for the clean, safe, inexpensive places to live that the Seamen's Church Institute buildings so long offered them.

Adapting to these changes, the Institute has sold its State Street building, auctioned off a portion of its huge maritime collection, lent many exhibits to other museums, and placed the remainder in temporary storage. A new, smaller building is planned for Manhattan; it will be largely offices, but with exhibition space for the cream of the collection.

This will be at some time in the future, but New Yorkers and visitors interested in America's maritime heritage should keep track of the plans. The collection of the Seamen's Church Institute is a distinguished one, including unusual period ship models, wreck artifacts, and memorabilia of Joseph Conrad, who was a great friend and supporter of the Institute. Informa-

tion about when the collection will again be on view will be available, as plans progress, from the information officer at the Seamen's Church Institute's temporary offices at 50 Broadway; telephone (212) 269-2710.

Back to midtown and the Hudson River.

She is by no means the largest of the Navy's aircraft carriers, yet as *Intrepid* sits there at a Hudson River pier she looms over the Manhattan waterfront like an enormous whale beached in a tiny cove. A whale of great strength and massive solidity—almost indestructibility.

If any warship has a right to appear indestructible it is *Intrepid*. During World War II she took five direct hits—four kamikazes on her decks and a torpedo in her innards—and lived to be called the most-hit ship of the war. The big carrier was very much part of the action at Okinawa and Leyte Gulf, and her planes were credited with destroying 650 enemy aircraft and sinking or damaging 289 enemy ships. Later she served three tours of combat duty off Vietnam.

Now this combat veteran, with 40-odd years

Figure 16
Visitors crowd the retired aircraft carrier *Intrepid*, now a museum ship berthed at a Hudson River pier in New York City. That's a Grumman F-11 hung above the deck, one of many naval aircraft displayed on the ship.

under her belt, 30 of them on active service, has left the high seas to become a floating museum, telling the story of the Navy fliers who turned the tide of Pacific battle in World War II. School children wander wide-eyed where pilots once raced to their planes, or climb into seats where once desperate gunners tried to hold their sights on a diving suicide plane. The hangers once crammed with aircraft are now devoted to multimedia presentations, movies of space flights, and a snack bar.

Not that the *Intrepid* has been stripped of airplanes; 19 are still aboard, including such famous types as Skyhawks, Avengers, and Tiger Cats. They are, of course, specimens on display, not fighting machines waiting to be scrambled. When the ship is not too crowded, Walter Mittys can strap themselves into the seat of a fighter, pull down the hatch, grab the stick, and take off into the wild blue yonder of their fantasies.

Fantasies aside, there is no better way to get an impressionistic picture of the Navy's air war in the Pacific than a tour of *Intrepid*. A recorded commentary can be rented to lead you through the ship. Four so-called halls have been installed on the hangar deck; they are devoted respectively to naval aircraft, the *Intrepid* herself with dioramas of naval actions, the early days of aviation with examples of pioneer aircraft, and space technology—the *Intrepid* picked up space capsules after two flights. On the 900-foot flight deck above, aircraft are in position for launching. Films and multimedia presentations are used throughout; describing a day in the life of a carrier, for example, or filling in visitors on the Apollo program, or recounting the history of the ship.

This new career is in a very real sense a rebirth for the old carrier. *Intrepid* was laid up in 1973 and was quietly rusting away when a nonprofit foundation persuaded the Navy to donate the ship for exhibition. There is still a lot of work to be done; the mess halls and crew's quarters, for example, will eventually be on display, but there is already much to see.

The *Intrepid* is preserved as a relic of the past, but carriers are still very much a part of the nation's defense program. Perhaps she's also a harbinger of the future.

USS *Intrepid*, a World War II aircraft carrier, is berthed at Pier 86 in the Hudson River, opposite 46th Street. Open Wednesday-Sunday, 10 a.m. to 5 p.m.; the last tickets go on sale at 4 p.m. Admission: $4.00; children under 12, $2.50. Call for special holiday hours. Sponsored by nonprofit Intrepid Museum Foundation, 46th Street and 12th Avenue, New York, New York 10036. Telephone (212) 245-0072.

Now, across the Hudson, over the hill, and a little way into New Jersey to the Hackensack River.

Unlike USS *Intrepid*, so big, complicated, and many-faceted that more than one visit may be needed to comprehend it all, USS *Ling* is small, single-purposed, and easy to take in. Although as a submarine *Ling* has equally complex technology, it is so beautifully explained that the visitor comes away with a clear picture of how it is possible to carry out elaborate attack maneuvers underwater.

And as any submariner will tell you, underwater warfare is today as important as air warfare in our national defense.

The *Ling*—SS297—is berthed in the little Hackensack River that meanders through the Jersey flats, a little more than half an hour from midtown Manhattan. The boat (all submarines are "boats," not "ships," regardless of size) is an attack submarine, designed to be fast enough and with sufficient range to accompany a surface task force. Actually, *Ling* herself never saw combat: Launched in 1945, she went on only one Atlantic patrol before the war ended. After years in the reserve fleet and as a training vessel, she has now been taken over by a nonprofit group as a memorial "to perpetuate the memory of our shipmates who gave their lives in the pursuit of their duties while serving their country."

The sponsors have done a fine job of restoring and maintaining their vessel. Most former naval vessels on display have been at least partially cannibalized before passing into private hands, and practically all arrive in poor condition; the Navy naturally prefers to use its limited funds on the active fleet. The *Ling* has been refitted with almost all the appropriate gear and is painted and kept up in true Bristol fashion.

What is really outstanding about a visit to the *Ling* is the guided tour that is offered. Visitors must go through the vessel in a group with a guide, but there should be no grumbling about undue regimentation. The guide's explanation of how the submarine operated and the function of each piece of equipment is unusually clear and complete, with sufficient homely metaphors to keep it from being overwhelmingly technical. The tour takes about 45 minutes, but the spiel transforms what might be merely a jumble of wheels, levers, dials, and steel compartments into a picture of a highly organized fighting machine.

To supplement what you hear, invest in the modestly priced diagram/brochure available. Again, this is an outstanding piece of exposition, and fills in the background of both *Ling* and her class of submarines.

USS *Ling*, 1945 attack submarine, is berthed in the Hackensack River at Borg Park. Visitors must take guided tour, leaving approximately every 45 minutes, excellent commentary. Gift shop. Open daily February through

November, 10 a.m. to 5 p.m.; December and January. Thursday-Sunday, 10 a.m. to 5 p.m. Admission: $2.50; children 5 to 11, $1.50. Sponsored by nonprofit Submarine Memorial Association, P.O. Box 395, Hackensack, New Jersey. Telephone (201) 487-9493.

The *Ling*, although now outmoded by nuclear submarines, nevertheless represents relatively advanced technology. For a look at a historic underwater craft from the very beginnings of modern submarine design, we only have to travel a few miles further west in New Jersey to Paterson and its museum.

History, including maritime history, is full of paradoxes and events that turned out very different from what was expected or intended. Consider the case of the modern submarine and John P. Holland:

- The man who perfected the most deadly weapon in the history of naval warfare was no naval officer, engineer, or scientist, but a slight, bespectacled parochial-school teacher who left the Irish Christian Brothers because the austerities of the order were beyond his physical endurance.
- His research was not supported by a great engineering firm or armaments maker but by a little group of Irish exiles and sympathizers, digging into their own pockets, hoping for a weapon to use against the British Navy in their struggle for an independent Ireland.
- The research they financed on a shoestring ultimately succeeded but never was the slightest use to the political cause of the people who paid for it.
- Nevertheless, the weapon, the modern submarine, almost caused Britain's defeat in two world wars—but by an enemy totally unconcerned with Irish independence.

Irish-born John P. Holland, the central figure in this highly significant chapter in the history of naval technology, grew up in a Gaelic-speaking family and had to learn English as a second language. He emigrated to America in his early 30s and became a science teacher in St. John's Parochial School in Paterson, New Jersey. A young man whose wide interests included music and astronomy, he had been trained by the Christian Brothers in mathematics, mechanics, and drafting. From boyhood, Holland had been deeply interested in such then exotic subjects as machines designed to fly through the air or cruise under water. Now, in Paterson, he stayed in his classroom after school hours and with an engineer friend drew plans for a submarine on his blackboard.

In 1876, Holland built a model submarine, driven by clockwork and with rudder and diving planes, and used it to persuade the American Fenian Brotherhood, would-be Irish revolutionaries, to finance the construction of a submersible large enough to carry a man. An ironworks in New York City built the craft to his plans; at 14-1/2 feet long, 3 feet broad, and 2-1/2 feet high, plus a small turret, it was perhaps the smallest submarine ever built. Holland had originally planned to drive it by foot treadles, but he learned of a newly invented engine that ran on petroleum and had one installed—leaving barely enough room for the operator. This was to be Holland himself, who was going to risk his neck by taking the machine underwater.

In May 1878, Holland had his little submarine loaded onto a wagon and carried down to the bank of the Passaic River. While onlookers watched from a nearby bridge, making such skeptical comments as "I see the professor has built a coffin for himself," the two-and-a-half-ton craft was pushed into the river at the end of a towline.

It floated. And then slowly sank by the stern.

The leaks—due to faulty rivets—were repaired. The trim was adjusted by shifting ballast. The new engine refused to run on gasoline, so Holland hooked it up with a waterproof line to the steam boiler of an accompanying launch—a jury rig that permitted testing.

On June 6, 1878, representatives of the Fenian Brotherhood came to Paterson to see what they'd gotten for their $5,000. Holland squeezed himself into the operator's seat between twin drive shafts, connected the steam hose, closed the turret, flooded two ballast tanks, pushed the diving plane levers—and dived 12 feet below the surface of the river. The diving planes reversed, she returned to the surface, and Holland emerged smiling. The Fenians, impressed, agreed to finance a larger boat. The modern, power-driven diving submersible had arrived.

John Holland's contributions, demonstrated in the little *Holland I* and in later experimental craft, were positive buoyancy; low, fixed center of gravity for stability; and great progress toward "porpoising," driving the submarine underwater by diving planes.

Holland gave up teaching to work full-time on perfecting his invention. He took the machinery out of little *Holland I* and sank the hull in the Passaic River. Local scavengers, trying to raise it by a block and tackle from a bridge in order to sell it for scrap metal, tore away the turret. Because of damage to the bridge, city authorities stopped would-be scavengers and the remains of the hull went back to the river bottom.

There in the Passaic River the remains of historic *Holland I* sat for nearly half a century. Finally it was

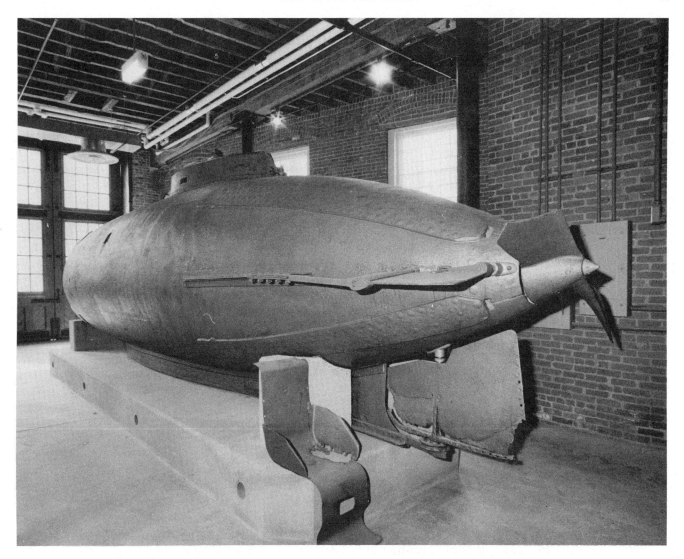

Figure 17
This so-called "Fenian Ram" was John P. Holland's second experimental submarine. A major step in Holland's development of the modern submarine, she was eventually sunk. Now, exterior restored, the underwater craft is on display in the Paterson Museum in Paterson, New Jersey.

fished up by people who understood its historic significance and ultimately given a home in the Paterson Museum.

And there what is left of *Holland I* may be seen today, in a big redbrick museum building that was formerly a mill. The lower half of *Holland I*, all that survived the crude attempt to salvage it, looks rather like a 14-foot iron bathtub, but it is one of the few significant artifacts of naval technology to be preserved. The remains give a clear idea of the small size of the historic craft: The visitor can easily imagine slender Holland squeezing himself into a space 28 by 36 inches between the turning drive shafts.

Holland I is one of the only two pioneer Holland

submarines to survive, even in part. The other one, *Holland II*, is also in the Paterson Museum, exhibited a few feet away from its tiny predecessor. Called by the press the "Fenian Ram," *Holland II* is far larger: a huge (35-foot) iron cigar, 8 feet deep, with an entrance hatch at the top. Operated by three men, it was powered by an internal-combustion engine, vented underwater. The armament was unique: a gun that fired 6-inch projectiles propelled by compressed air, plus a ram nose intended to smash into the hull of a vessel underwater.

In 1881, Holland tested *Holland II* and ran it several hundred feet underwater in the Morris Canal Basin. The underwater air cannon was less successful:

The projectiles rose from the depths and soared through the air but did not hold a fixed course.

Holland II was eventually seized by the inventor's Fenian supporters following a disagreement, became the subject of lawsuits, was stored in sheds, exhibited at fund-raisers, brought to a Paterson park, and finally also came to rest in the Paterson Museum. The exterior, of riveted iron plates, with rudder, propeller, and two diving planes, has been restored; the interior, said to contain the original internal-combustion engine and gear, has not been restored and is not viewable.

After *Holland II* passed to other hands, John Holland found other backers, interested the U.S. Navy, and kept on building experimental submarines. By 1900, he had spent more hours submerged than anyone in history. With the acceptance of *Holland VI* by the Navy in 1901, Holland's submarines became a recognized arm of 20th-century navies. In the world war that started 13 years later, the German U-boat campaign almost cut off supplies from the British Isles, destroying millions of tons of Allied shipping with heavy loss of life.

Holland I and **Holland II**, historic submarines, are on display at Paterson Museum, in former mill building at Spruce Street end of Market Street, near Passaic River in Paterson, New Jersey. Parking. Open all year; Monday-Friday, 10 a.m. to 4:30 p.m.; Saturday-Sunday, 12:30 to 4:30 p.m. Donation: $1.00; children, free. The Paterson Museum, Thomas Rogers Building, 2 Market Street, Paterson, New Jersey 07501. Telephone (201) 881-3874.

Now, back to New York City—and out the other side to a most interesting maritime museum in an eastern suburb, on Long Island.

There are many museums largely devoted to America's merchant shipping. They tend to focus, however, on either the age of sail or the flamboyant side-wheel steamers of our rivers and coasts. Yet these picturesque, sometimes romantic, vessels are only a part of our maritime heritage. Although American steamships have never been able to recapture the dominant place in world shipping held by their windjammer predecessors, they have their own interesting history.

In time of peace American blue-water ships struggle to survive; in war they have proved invaluable and their numbers multiply with astonishing speed. Even today a substantial number of steamships and motor ships continue to ply the seven seas under the Stars and Stripes. In recent decades, many of the officers of these ships have been graduates of the United States Merchant Marine Academy, the fifth and probably least known of the national service academies.

Most appropriately, therefore, the American Merchant Marine Museum, the only museum in the country dedicated solely to the United States Merchant Marine "from the age of steam to the nuclear age," is on the Academy's campus at King's Point, Long Island, just east of New York City.

The American Merchant Marine Museum is lodged in a former Gold Coast mansion overlooking Long Island Sound. The wheel of *Constitution*, taken from the ship after the battle with *Guerriere*, is proudly displayed at the entrance, and the ship models and artifacts cover a considerable span, from the 18th century to the present day. The museum collection, however, heavily emphasizes American merchant shipping since World War I. At the core of the collection are many modern ship paintings and a fleet of beautiful owners' models of freight and passenger steamships of such American flag lines as Grace, Moore-McCormack, and American Export.

The evolution of the federally subsidized freighters of World War II and after, is illustrated by fine builders' models of Liberty ships, Victory ships, C-1s, C-2s, tankers, container ships, and so forth, as well as the P-2 liner *President Wilson*. Of special interest is a 6-foot model of the *Savannah*, the only American merchant ship powered by a nuclear reactor, which is cut away to show its power plant. The flagship of the museum's merchant fleet is an 18-foot model of the SS *Washington*, beautifully detailed down to the instruments on the bridge and said to be worth $400,000.

The great American ship designers of the 20th century have received little museum attention, even though they have produced some strikingly fast and handsome vessels, such as the *Washington*. The American Merchant Marine Museum has a special exhibit devoted to the work of William Francis Gibbs, who designed the SS *United States* of the U.S. Lines. The *United States* was the last ship to hold the Atlantic Blue Ribbon for the fastest crossing between Britain and the United States. The museum displays the glittering three-foot Atlantic Trophy, its gilt inlaid with enameled portraits of some of the famous ships that have held the transatlantic record.

In 1982, a National Maritime Hall of Fame was established in the museum. Each year a selection committee chooses four great ships and four equally outstanding persons to be commemorated by a portrait and an inscription in a special gallery. Aimed at making "Americans from all walks of life better aware of the merchant marine," the awards are divided among four principal geographic areas. The first ships chosen were: deep sea, SS *Savannah*, 1819; coastal, SS *Priscilla*, 1893, of the Fall River Line; inland waterways, SS *Clermont* 1807; and Great Lakes, SS *Walk-in-the-Water*, 1818.

Not all of the museum is devoted to famous ships and famous men; a pleasantly offbeat note is struck by a newly opened gallery displaying five or six hundred cups and saucers, each with the insignia of a vessel or shipping line. The collection was made by a couple of Panama Canal pilots, who levied a toll of china from each ship they took through the canal. Actually, the collection is something more than a curiosity; in their own odd way the cups provide a non-documentary check list of the ships and shipping lines that used the canal.

American Merchant Marine Museum, on the shore of Long Island Sound at the United States Merchant Marine Academy, King's Point, Long Island. Open all year, except July. Saturday and Sunday, 1 to 4:30 p.m. Monday-Friday by appointment. Admission: free. American Merchant Marine Museum, U.S. Merchant Marine Academy, King's Point, New York 11024. Telephone (516) 482-8200, ext. 304.

Now, across the sound.

Ship model enthusiasts, particularly those interested in the classic transatlantic liners of the recent past, will find them on the north shore of Long Island Sound at the New York State Maritime College. There, on Throgg's Neck, which narrows the entrance of Long Island Sound into the East River, the Maritime College has taken over old Fort Schuyler. The College has no formal museum, but a number of ship models and a few maritime artifacts are in the library and the nearby corridors and classrooms—all within the fort itself, which is today only one of the many buildings of the college.

Preserved in the college library are relics and models of the full-rigged New York State training ships *St. Mary's* and *Newport*, much beloved by old-time master mariners who learned their profession in them. Here also is a fine model of the clipper ship *Lightning*, alongside a fragment of the original vessel, dredged up from the bottom of Melbourne harbor where she burned in 1869.

In the corridors of the fort are large, detailed owner models of mid-20th-century liners, including a number of the big German ships on the North Atlantic run, such as the famous *Bremen*. A 12-footer of the destroyer escort *Epperson* is the largest of several naval models in the collection.

Stop for a moment at the angle in the fort corridor where photographs of the 37 graduates of the College killed in World War II are mounted on the wall. Nearby are photographs of other graduates who have died in the course of duty: lost at sea, killed in shipboard accidents or collisions, or who died while serving in Vietnam.

Any visitor to the New York State Maritime College should take time to look over Fort Schuyler itself. Its granite ramparts were originally built to

Figure 18
This glittering Hales trophy, awarded to the liner making the fastest time across the North Atlantic, is now preserved at the American Merchant Marine Museum at King's Point, Long Island, New York.

defend the eastern water approaches to New York City. The fort is an impressive multi-sided granite structure, whose massive walls protected the cannon that commanded the channel. The guns are long gone; now college classrooms and offices are lodged within the casemates, but the visitor can peer out across the sound and imagine it filled with the coastal windjammers and bustling side-wheelers of 150 years ago.

New York State Maritime College, Fort Schuyler. Open all year except New Year's Day, Thanksgiving, and Christmas. Monday-Friday; 8:30 a.m. to 4:30 p.m. No admission charge. Maritime College of the State of New York, Fort Schuyler, Throggs Neck, The Bronx, New York 10465. Telephone (212) 409-7200

To the very edge of the city now.

New York City is not only a megalopolis; the city is also a collection of villages, self-contained neighborhoods each concerned with its own affairs. In the 19th century, the Manhattan waterfront section around South Street was such a neighborhood, and its memory at least is being preserved. Far away at the other end of the city, another neighborhood with strong maritime traditions is very much alive and flourishing: City Island.

Linked to the mainland by a single bridge, City Island juts into Long Island Sound just on the Bronx side of the Westchester line. Once Indians fished and clammed there, and it has been a community of boatmen from the earliest colonial settlement; "clamdigger" is an appellation treasured by old time City Islanders.

With a deep, sheltered harbor, the island became a yachting center in the 19th century, both for yacht building and as the home port of the floating palaces of millionaires. The famous Lawley and Nevins yacht yards that once flourished here are no more, but there is still an active boatbuilding industry; the twelve-meter *Independence*, *Enterprise*, and *Courageous* were all City Island-built.

Members of the City Island Historical Society work to preserve the records of the past and present marine activities of their community, and their little museum, staffed by volunteers and lodged in an old school building, has a nautical gallery. Although there are models of Cup Defenders, the exhibits are mostly pictorial: paintings of the island's building yards and yacht clubs, construction and launching photographs of City Island-built Cup Defenders, photos of Sir Thomas Lipton, and so forth. A collection from the famous Nevins yard includes memorabilia of Henry B. Nevins and his trophy-winning yacht *Polly*.

The museum is modest, but City Island itself is very much a part of New York City's maritime traditions; together they are well worth a visit. Once across the bridge, the visitor finds himself in a village where every other building seems to be a yacht club, a building yard, a boating supply store, a yacht broker—or a seafood restaurant. A few blocks in either direction off the single main street brings you to the waterfront and in the summer the waters are thickly clustered with moored yachts.

City Islanders are as marine-minded as their island. Mrs. Emily Rosenfeld, for example, who retired not long ago as head of the historical society, is the daughter of a yacht captain ("he had a crew of 53 men"), and is the daughter-in-law and wife of yacht photographers of the famous Rosenfeld family. Now in her mid-70s, she recalls with pleasure going out to photograph ships and yachts and coming back to develop the prints and rush them to the *New York Times* for the Sunday sports section. She was born on the island, next to the school where the museum is now installed, and married the boy down the street. That's the way things have always been on City Island.

City Island Historical Nautical Museum is located on City Island in the extreme northeast corner of the Bronx, between Eastchester Bay and Pelham Bay. Museum is at No. 190 Fordham Street, an old redbrick building, formerly a school. Open Sundays, from 2 to 4 p.m. Admission by donation. Sponsored by nonprofit City Island Historical Society, 412 Minneford Avenue, City Island, The Bronx, New York 10164. Telephone (212) 885-1211.

The Lordly Hudson

North America is a land of great rivers: the Hudson is arguably the most noble and the most beautiful of all. Sweeping southward for more than 300 miles from its birth at Lake Tear-in-the-Clouds past mountains, cliffs, meadows, forests to broad New York Bay, the Hudson has for centuries been compared with the Rhine, the most picturesque of European rivers. Significantly, alone of American rivers the Hudson has produced a distinctive school of landscape artists.

But the Hudson has far more than beauty. No other river can match its role in American history: military, political, economic, and, not least, maritime. Here was the very birthplace, in terms of commercial success, of the steamboats that turned rivers into the highways that opened the West. Linked by canal to the Great Lakes, the Hudson is itself a key section of the greatest of those highways. Looking in the opposite direction, to seaward, the little towns along the Hudson sent their ships downriver and out to sea to ports all over the world. And, of course, on the island at the Hudson's mouth is one of the world's greatest ports.

The Hudson's chief tributary, the Mohawk River, which flows in from the westward, long provided access to the center of New York State. The Hudson itself is navigable by large ocean vessels all the way to Albany. Thanks to human activity, the river is also connected by canals northward to Lake Champlain and eventually to the St. Lawrence, the great river of eastern Canada.

The Hudson flows through a deep gorge which was carved by the waters of the Great Lakes ages ago when ice sheets blocked the St. Lawrence: Much of the river bottom today is below sea level. In fact, the Hudson River canyon continues far out to sea across the Continental Shelf. The Hudson is really an estuary or fjord, tidal for 150 miles inland, which makes navigation easy.

Verrazano, in his ship the *Dauphin*, visited the bay at the mouth of the Hudson in 1524, but the river itself was little explored for almost a century. An Englishman in the service of the Netherlands, Henry Hudson, really discovered what the river had to offer. Hudson gave the river his name when in 1609 his ship, the *Half Moon*, sailed far upstream and his boat crews traveled even further upriver, to the head of navigation north of Albany.

Hudson was looking for the fabled Northwest Passage to the Orient through the barrier of North America. He never found it, of course, but the Dutch quickly followed up his exploration by planting settlements on the river. The importance of the Hudson was recognized from the very beginning. The two centers of the New Netherlands, established simultaneously in 1624, were almost at the opposite ends of the navigable Hudson: New Amsterdam on Manhattan Island where the Hudson met the sea; Fort Orange (Albany) 110 miles north, just below the mouth of the Mohawk River. From the beginning through most of the 19th century the Hudson was the principal highway of the region, whether it was New Netherlands or New York, colony or state.

The Dutch settlers traveled their river in bluff-bowed river sloops. The great patroon families whose estates lined the upper Hudson kept their personal sloops at their own wharfs. In the early days, Fort Orange at the upper end was primarily a trading post where furs, lumber, and provisions were sent downriver on sloops to Manhattan to be transferred to oceangoing vessels for export overseas. Manufactured and trade goods were taken back upriver on the return passage. By the end of the Colonial period, Albany had more than 30 market sloops, each able to carry four or five hundred barrels of flour and each making a dozen round trips a year down the river to New York City and back.

During the American Revolution the great strategic importance of the Hudson was obvious. In an attempt to prevent the British forces from coming up the river from New York and splitting the rebellious colonies in half, a chain was put across the Hudson at Anthony's Nose, near where Washington maintained his headquarters at Newburgh for much of the war. Expeditions of British troops came up the river, escorted by frigates, and broke the chain, but they never succeeded in wholly controlling the river.

In the early 19th century, Hudson saw the first economically successful steamboat, Robert Fulton's *Clermont on the North River*, to give her original long name. There had been other steamboats before her, but because of Fulton's alliance with powerful New York financial and political interests he received a monopoly for steamboating on the Hudson River and became the first steamship magnate of the new country.

This did not mean the end of sail on the river; sloop traffic continued to multiply. But the steamboats kept on becoming bigger and faster. Soon they were racing each other for the enjoyment of passengers, for it was a great drawing card to say that you beat every other boat on the river. Inevitably, as engineers held down the safety valves while stokers sent flames roaring around the boilers, steamboats were lost. Some caught fire, some blew up; so many lives were lost that at one point cautious passengers preferred to ride in barges towed behind a steamboat so they would be safely away from the dangerous boilers if they blew up.

Meanwhile, a new maritime trade came to the river. Right after the Revolution, some Nantucketers sought a less exposed home port for their whaleships and bought land at Claverack Landing on the upper Hudson. Here, Nantucket seamen and their families—plus others from Martha's Vineyard and New Bedford—founded the town of Hudson in 1784. They brought house frames with them and in a couple of years there was a Hudson River town that was home port for 25 whaleships. By 1830, the river towns of Poughkeepsie and Newburgh were also sending whaleships to sea, and four Hudson River companies owned some 30 vessels.

Although a financial panic and low prices for whale oil eventually led to the disappearance of the Hudson whaling companies, some of the whaleships were converted to merchant ships trading to Africa and South America. In *The Hudson*, a wonderful book about the river, Carl Carmer has told of some of the adventures of Hudson River mariners in the far corners of the world. The ship *Oswego*, for example, was wrecked on the coast of Africa on her homeward voyage; the crew was enslaved by Arabs until they were finally ransomed. In 1821, the schooner *Combine* of Catskill was stripped by pirates in the Yucatan Passage. The schooner *Colonel Crockett* of Newburgh, trading to the African Coast, was wrecked on those shores in

1840; after many misadventures only one survivor came back to his Hudson River home. In 1846, the whaleship *Lawrence* of Poughkeepsie was wrecked off Japan and the survivors were imprisoned by the Japanese in a wooden cage. (This was eight years before Japan was forced to accept Western visitors by an American naval squadron.)

As significant in the Hudson's maritime history as Fulton's *Clermont*, was the opening of the Erie Canal in 1825. At one stroke, as the Hudson became the road between the sea and the whole upper Midwest, New York City became America's greatest port; from New York the rising tide of immigrants could make most of the long journey to the virgin lands by water, and when their farms were established, their crops could be carried back to the coast—and New York City—by water.

In later decades, railroads diminished the economic significance of the Hudson and its canal connections westward; later, truck-crowded highways took away much of the remaining freight, but the river is still an important waterway. And the Hudson is today, despite the industrialization of the northeastern United States, arguably the most beautiful of America's rivers.

One reason for this is the determination of the people who love the river to keep the Hudson beautiful. That is the mission of the sloop *Clearwater*, a true daughter and defender of the great river.

In 1786, the *Experiment* of Albany became the first American vessel to make a direct voyage from the United States to China. A historic achievement for any ship—but doubly so for *Experiment*. For the sturdy little vessel was actually not a ship at all, in fact she wasn't an oceangoing vessel of any kind but a river boat, a Hudson River sloop. This doughty example of the one-masters that normally confined their passages to the 110 miles between Albany and New York, was manned by eight men and two boys. She sailed with her hold crammed with ginseng, the herb treasured in China, along with furs, rum, snuff and varnish. Two and a half years later, after being given up for lost, *Experiment* returned to New York harbor with a cargo of tea, silks, satins, and Chinese porcelains. She then went back into the Albany-New York passenger service.

Which gives an idea of the quality of the Hudson River sloops and the men who sailed them. Developed in colonial days, the sloops were for more than two centuries the principal means of travel for the people of the Hudson Valley up and down their noble river. Originally bluff-bowed Dutch craft, as time went on they became sharper and faster as they were improved and refined. Their skippers—the Dutchmen were the best—knew all the tricks of the river. They learned from their fathers where the currents and back eddies were, where the wind shifted, how best to take advantage of the tides. When wind and tide were against them they simply anchored and waited for better times.

Eventually, the sloops became both fast and beautiful, one of the most successful of American small craft. They weren't so small at that—some of them were more than 100 feet long. As river steamboats took away the package-freight business, the later sloops were left with bulk cargoes, such as cattle, bricks, and quarry stone. As late as 1860 there were still 200 sloops sailing the Hudson.

Many decades have passed since one of the original Hudson River sloops was seen on the river. In recent years, however, a fine full-scale replica has been built, the *Clearwater*, her construction and operation inspired in large part by folk singer Pete Seeger. *Clearwater* sails the Hudson with a double purpose. In part she calls attention to this beautiful and characteristically American type of vessel, a significant and relatively little-known part of our maritime heritage. *Clearwater*'s larger mission, however, is to rally support for keeping the Hudson River clean—or, at least, making it cleaner—by ending the pollution that has threatened to destroy fishing in its waters and bathing along its banks.

Based in Poughkeepsie, about midway in the river, *Clearwater* in season sails the Hudson and pays visits to neighboring Long Island Sound, New York Harbor, and the little ports along the Jersey shore. Wherever she goes she is a center of attention. One hundred and six feet overall, *Clearwater* carries more than 4,300 square feet of sail and her boom is 66 feet long. Unlike her predecessors, she has a diesel engine and Coast Guard-required safety equipment so that she can carry passengers.

The public gets a chance to sail on the sloop when she takes part in various waterfront festivals. These are advertised and also announced in the newsletter of sponsoring organizations. Groups can engage the *Clearwater* for special cruises, and instructive or educational programs can be carried out during the cruise if desired. Sails are scheduled about two months in advance and are said to be booked well ahead. For information on the *Clearwater*'s seasonal schedule, would-be travelers should get in touch with the organization's headquarters early in the preceding spring.

Hudson River Sloop *Clearwater* is based at Poughkeepsie, New York about 65 miles north of New York city, 60 miles south of Albany, via Route 9 (Albany Post Road) or Taconic State Parkway. Sloop can be engaged for special cruises. Hudson River Sloop Clearwater, Inc., 112 Market Street, Poughkeepsie, New York 12601. Telephone (914) 454-7673.

Now, a marvelous—and famous—ship model collection just a few miles up the Albany Post Road from Poughkeepsie.

No president has been more deeply interested in the nation's maritime heritage than Franklin Delano Roosevelt, perhaps to be expected in a man whose mother was a Delano, a member of a great New England maritime family of shipmasters, shipowners, and shipping agents. As a very small child, Roosevelt's mother went around Cape Horn on a windjammer and never forgot the experience. In her son's case, his interest in the sea found expression not only in a career that included service as Assistant Secretary of the Navy and, as President, rebuilding the United States Navy just before World War II, but in his private life. Roosevelt enjoyed living with ship models and naval prints and paintings, and gathered what eventually became one of the outstanding maritime collections of his time.

After FDR's death, much of his collection was dispersed. However, when a new wing was built onto the Franklin Roosevelt Library at Hyde Park, New York, representative examples of his maritime collection were gathered together and can now be seen there.

Called "America on the Seas," the collection is displayed in cases rimming the little basement auditorium of the Eleanor Roosevelt Wing of the library. Before you enter, be sure to read the informative and amusing note at the entrance, which describes FDR as a collector and tells how he went about gathering his ship models, prints, and other naval and maritime memorabilia.

The exhibits are arranged by topics, roughly in chronological sequence, starting with the Continental Navy and running through to the steam auxiliary sloops of war built just before the Civil War. Each display centers on one or more of FDR's beautiful models, usually made about the same time as the ship portrayed. In the background are maritime and naval prints. Most unusual are the series of original documents and manuscripts relating to maritime activities. In the first display case, for example, which

Figure 19
Naval prints from F.D.R.'s collection are an important part of the maritime collections at the Franklin D. Roosevelt Library and Museum at Hyde Park, New York.

starts with the Continental Navy, is a holograph record of the passage by the Continental Congress of an act establishing a committee to manage the naval affairs of the rebellious colonies, the first step toward establishment of a Navy Department and, of course, of the Navy itself. The various displays cover such significant periods and topics as the War of 1812, the Barbary pirates, whaling, the great clipper ships, and the China tea trade.

The remarkably fine models that illuminate each period are not the only FDR ship models in the Library. Upstairs, in the original museum and library, are very handsome large models that were given to President Roosevelt by various nations. These are beautiful examples of outstanding European sailing ships but perhaps lack the American interest of those found in the "America on the Seas" collection down below.

Before leaving, the visitor should be sure to take a look at the office that FDR established in the library during his presidency so that he could work there while taking a brief break at Hyde Park. There, he was surrounded by some of his favorite marine paintings and small models; today they give us a revealing picture of a man and his interests.

The Franklin D. Roosevelt Library and Museum is on the Roosevelt family estate on the east bank of the Hudson River, just south of the village of Hyde Park, about eight miles north of Poughkeepsie on the Albany Post Road. Extensive research facilities. Open every day except Thanksgiving, Christmas, and New Year's, 9 a.m. to 5 p.m. Admission includes Roosevelt home and nearby Vanderbilt mansion: $1.50; seniors and youth, free. Operated by the National Archives and Records Service. The Franklin D. Roosevelt Library, Albany Post Road, Hyde Park, New York 12538. Telephone (914) 229-8114 or 229-8115.

Now, across the river, and a half-hour's run up the West Shore to a young museum with an ambitious program.

Rondout Creek, a mini river that runs into the Hudson from the westward at the south end of the river town of Kingston, has seen plenty of action over the centuries. The Dutch had a fur-trading post there before there was a house on Manhattan Island. In Colonial times it was twice attacked by Indians. During the American Revolution, the temporary government of rebellious New York met in the Kingston courthouse in 1777 and adopted the first constitution of New York State—and by no coincidence a British task force came up the Hudson and landed at Rondout Creek to burn Kingston to the ground.

Slightly over 150 years ago, Rondout Creek became the eastern terminus of the Delaware and Hudson Canal, which linked the two great rivers with a 107-mile waterway and brought anthracite coal east from Pennsylvania. During much of the 19th century, Rondout/Kingston was the busiest port on the Hudson. Eventually, however, railroads killed the D. & H. Canal, and automobiles and trucks killed the river traffic. By mid-20th century, the banks of Rondout Creek were lined with the rotting hulks of barges, river boats, and wharfs gradually falling away into the water.

Now, however, there is new life at the mouth of Rondout Creek. This historic mid-section of the Hudson River Valley has begun to remember with pride its maritime past. In 1980, the Hudson River Maritime Center, was established, a new and vigorous museum, set up to "preserve the vast disappearing heritage of the Hudson River and its environs," not only by preserving the artifacts of the past but also by encouraging new riverine activities in the present.

The center, which is largely manned by volunteers, has three major elements. A large building right on the bulkhead at the edge of Rondout Creek, houses its exhibits and boatbuilding and rigging shop. The museum gallery is currently a block away up the hill at 41 Broadway in the Rondout Historic District. Finally, there are various vessels in and out of the water on the grounds beside the museum building, a part of the program still in developmental stage.

Focusing on Hudson River steamboating, the main collection includes a fine group of waterline models, most of them apparently contemporary with the ships portrayed. Of special interest is a model of the famous *Mary Powell* of 1861, said to have been the best-loved ship on the Hudson River. The *Powell* left Kingston every morning for New York City and arrived back at nine in the evening; in the many decades that she was on the river she never lost a passenger and was always on time. Also on display is a working model of the type of steam engine used to drive side-wheel steamers, showing how the drive shaft was connected to the paddle wheels. The history and development of Hudson River steamboating is graphically portrayed in excellent wall displays using drawings, prints, paintings, and photographs.

On the floor of the museum is a Hudson River shad skiff, an interesting type of pulling boat about 20 feet long. The shad fishery was long an important source of income for Hudson River watermen, and is said to be gradually coming back as the river is cleaned up. In the east end of the Center's building is a large boat shop and rigging loft with a visitors' gallery where the work can be observed; the shop's facilities are available to individuals to work on their boats. There is also a sailing school at the center's landing.

In the museum's gallery on Broadway another collection of models on permanent display is

Figure 20
A classic Eleo launch of 1898 glides past the recently restored Rondout lighthouse, both symbolic of the activities of the Hudson River Maritime Center at Kingston, New York.

comprised of miniature Hudson River tugboats made by a veteran tugboat skipper. However, the gallery is primarily a showcase for changing displays of paintings and photographs dealing with Hudson River subjects. The building itself is part of the historic restoration of the riverfront section at Kingston.

The center's principal vessel is at present the 72-foot steam tug *Matilda*, which is cradled in the big yard west of the main museum. Built in 1899, she had a long and active career in the St. Lawrence River. Plans call for her engine to be operated electrically or by compressed air so that it can be observed in motion. Visitors are likely to find scattered about the yard such interesting small craft as a centerboard sloop, canoes, and pulling boats.

The Hudson River has a long and proud maritime heritage. There is every evidence that as the Center gathers momentum much of that heritage will be recalled for visitors to the mid-Hudson River Valley.

The Center already has an extensive summer-long program of activities, lectures, boat rides, and rendezvous for antique boats.

Hudson River Maritime Center is currently located in two buildings in the Rondout historic district of Kingston, New York, on west bank of Hudson. Open mid-May to October 31; Wednesday-Sunday, noon to 5 p.m. Admission: $1.00; children, 50 cents. Hudson River Maritime Center, One Rondout Landing, Kingston, New York 12401. Telephone (914) 338-0071.

Hudson River traffic was fed from two directions. From the north, Lake Champlain, a river, and canals, made a continuous waterway to Canada's mighty St. Lawrence river. And, from the west, the famous Erie Canal was even more important in providing a connection to the Great Lakes. There are interesting museums along both waterways: let's look at the Erie Canal first.

Down Along the Erie Canal

'Tis Done! The monarch of the briny tide
Whose giant arm encircles earth
To virgin Erie is allied
A bright-eyed nymph of mountain birth

Today the Sire of Ocean takes
A sylvan maiden to his arms
The goddess of the crystal lakes
In all her native charms

She comes attended by a sparkling train;
The Naiads of the West her nuptuals grace
She meets the sceptred father of the main
And in his heaving bosom hides her virgin face

A broadside distributed in October 1825,
quoted by Carl Carmer in The Hudson.

So, according to Hudson River historian Carl Carmer, the opening of the Erie Canal was hailed in a broadside distributed to a crowd of New York City celebrants. It was some celebration, a worthy prelude to New York's ticker-tape parades of a later century. The Erie Canal parade began at the Battery in the forenoon and lasted until late in the day; it was followed by a tremendous fireworks display (including 350 rockets! 1,500 fireballs!) in the evening.

These festivities were only the climax of a 10-day celebration that stretched 500-odd miles across New York State as a procession of canalboats brought Governor DeWitt Clinton and other dignitaries the length of the canal from Buffalo to Albany, then down the Hudson to New York City. (River steamers towed the canalboats on the Hudson.) Cannon boomed, bands played, militias deployed, orators orated, toasts were drunk and drunk again, and everywhere crowds along the way burst into storms of cheers. The climax came when Governor Clinton poured a keg of Lake Erie water into the Atlantic Ocean off Sandy Hook, symbolizing the union of the Goddess of the Crystal Lakes with the Monarch of the Briny Tide.

The crowds had a lot to cheer for. The Erie Canal was a great engineering project by any reckoning; for one state of a small new nation barely recovered from a damaging war it was a fantastic achievement. A ditch 40 feet wide sloping inward to 28 feet at the bottom and four feet deep, the canal had 83 locks which raised and lowered canalboats a total of 675 feet in the 363 miles between Buffalo and Albany. When the Erie Canal project got under way in 1817 there were no native-born civil engineers in the United States; in fact, there were almost none of any nationality. The Erie was surveyed, planned, built, and largely superintended by a couple of country lawyers. Laborers, working for 80 cents a day, dug the whole length with picks, shovels, horse-drawn scrapers, sharp plows to cut tree roots, and endless sweat.

The resulting channel was carried on aqueducts over valleys and streams (a 1,100-foot aqueduct over the Mohawk River) while more than 300 highway bridges were built to span the canal. In *Moby Dick* Herman Melville described the result in one noble nonstop declamatory sentence: "For three hundred and sixty miles, gentlemen, through the entire breadth of the state of New York; through numerous populous cities and most thriving villages; through long, dismal, uninhabited swamps, and affluent, cultivated fields, unrivaled for fertility; by billiard room and bar-room; through the holy-of-holies of great forests; on Roman arches over Indian rivers; through sun and shade; by happy hearts or broken; through all the wide contracting scenery of those noble Mohawk counties; and especially, by rows of snow-white chapels, whose spires stand almost like milestones, flows one continual stream of Venetially corrupt and often lawless life..."

We'll let Melville expand his sardonic comment on the "often lawless life" on the canal a bit further on. But first note that the Erie was not only an engineering feat that gave a great boost to national pride, but a highly successful waterway that altered the economic and political development of the United States.

The spring after the Erie opened, 50 canalboats a day were starting from Albany for the long haul west. Twenty years later, there were some 4,200 boats on the canal, valued at one million dollars. Sixty-two of them were the elite "packet boats" that raced across the state—not so elite but that the passengers were packed in like sardines, sleeping on tiers of shelves. The big flow of passenger traffic, however, was comprised of immigrants who carried all their possessions on the slower "line boats" headed for the promised land, the fertile wilderness of the upper Midwest. By the 1830s and 40s, the Erie canalboats were carrying as many as 2,000 passengers a week. Before too long they were sending back cargoes of grain, meat, provisions, and lumber to be added to the output of the upstate New York farms for the canalboats to carry on their return trips east to Albany. The canal reduced the freight rate from Buffalo to New York from $100 to $6 a ton.

The immediate result was the firm establishment of New York City as the biggest, busiest port in the United States. The harbor was filled with ships bringing immigrants and European imports to be transshipped via the Hudson River, the Erie Canal, and the Great Lakes to the new Midwestern territories.

At the same time, the canal brought to the East cargoes to be loaded for Europe, trade that had formerly gone down the Mississippi to New Orleans or down the St. Lawrence to Montreal. Buffalo at the western end on Lake Erie was equally prosperous, ballooning from a small village to one of the largest of the Great Lakes ports.

The Erie Canal cost $8 million. By 1830, the tolls were bringing in more than a million dollars a year. By 1847, this had climbed to more than $3,600,000 a year.

Impressed by the success of the Erie, other states built canals. Pennsylvania built a combined canal-rail route across the state. Canals connected the Delaware and Hudson rivers, Lake Erie with the Ohio, Lake Michigan with the Illinois and Mississippi rivers. None was as successful as the Erie Canal; several were dismal financial failures; for one thing, the new railroads, some of which were originally built merely to operate in winter when the canals froze up, gradually stole their traffic. Even the Erie gradually lost business to the rail lines, although in the early 20th century it was to some extent revitalized by its conversion into the large, modern New York State Barge Canal which still operates along roughly the same route.

In its heyday, the Erie Canal employed some 25,000 men, women, and boys as drivers, boatsteerers, and cooks. The canal people had a reputation as a wild, tough bunch. Back to Melville:

> Freely depicted in his own vocation, gentlemen, the Canaller would make a fine dramatic hero, so abundantly and picturesquely wicked he is. Like Mark Antony, for days and days along his green-turfed, flowery Nile, he indolently floats, openly toying with his red-cheeked Cleopatra, ripening his apricot thigh upon the sunny deck. The brigandish guise which the Canaller so proudly sports; his slouched and gaily-ribboned hat betoken his grand features. A terror to the smiling innocence of the villages through which he floats; his swart visage and bold swagger are not unshunned in cities. Once a vagabond on his own canal, I have received good turns from one of these Canallers; I thank him heartily; would fain be not ungrateful; but it is often one of the prime redeeming qualities of your man of violence, that at times he has as stiff an arm to back a poor stranger in a strait, as to plunder a wealthy one. In sum, gentlemen, what the wildness of this canal life is, is emphatically evinced by this; that our wild whale-fishery contains so many of its finished graduates, and that scarce any race of mankind, except Sydney men, are so much distrusted by our whaling captains. Nor does it at all diminish the curiousness of this matter, that to many thousands of our rural boys and young men born along its line, the probationary life of the Grand Canal furnishes the sole transition between quietly reaping in a Christian cornfield, and recklessly ploughing the waters of the most barbaric seas.

The Canallers rather gloried in their reputation. A favorite song ran:

> Oh the Erie was a-rising'
> The gin was a-gittin' low
> And I scarcely think
> We'll git a drink
> Till we git to Buffalo.

The cooks were reputed as tough as the mule drivers. Consider the sad case of Sal, immortalized in another bit of doggerel:

> Drop a tear for big-foot Sal
> The best damn cook on the Erie Canal
> She aimed for heaven but she went to hell—
> Fifteen years on the Erie Canal.
> The missioner said she died in sin.
> Hennery said it was too much gin;
> There wasn't no bar where she hadn't been
> From Albany to Buffalo.

Sal may not have been "a bright eyed nymph of mountain birth," but she too was an integral part of the Erie Canal scene—and of its legends and traditions.

Today, the Erie Canal is recognized as having played an important part in the nation's history, even as a good portion of the remaining stretches of the original canal are used for recreation: In 1984, nearly 100,000 pleasure boats were locked through the 36 surviving canal locks, and tour boats cruise the Erie's waters. (The New York State Department of Commerce reports that information about two, three, and four-day canal cruises, departing Albany, Syracuse, and Buffalo, can be obtained from Mid-Lakes Navigation Company, Box 61, Skaneateles, New York 13152. Telephone (315) 685-5722.)

One section of the Erie where the heritage of the great canal is being particularly recognized and preserved is the 35-mile stretch that survives between Rome and Syracuse, New York. Not only is the old canal itself available here for canoeing in the summer, skating in the winter, and hiking or bicycling along the towpath, but three canal museums and an interpretation center tell the story of the Erie's history and significance.

Let's start at the east end of this section of the Erie, at Rome, New York.

The site of Rome in New York's Mohawk Valley was an important point in the Native American water transportation network long before Europeans arrived. Here, the upper reaches of the Mohawk River, which flows into the Hudson, run close to Wood Creek, which runs into Lake Ontario. A portage of only a mile made it possible to canoe between the Great Lakes and the Atlantic Ocean. First the British, then the Americans built a fort at this strategic point. The successful American defense here of Fort Stanwix during the Revolution helped defeat Burgoyne's invasion, a victory that later led to naming the little settlement Rome in tribute to the "Heroic defense of the Republic made here."

The Mohawk-Wood Creek portage was replaced by a small canal in 1797, but it was another and much grander canal project that turned Rome into a bustling town. The construction of the Erie Canal began here in 1817 and Rome soon became a prosperous station on the great water highway to the west.

Rome developed into a manufacturing center, but with this historic association with the Erie, it is most appropriate that the city itself sponsors the nearby Erie Canal Village. Located on a restored three-mile stretch of the old canal on Rome's outskirts, the village is composed of early 19th-century buildings, which have been moved to the site for restoration and preservation.

Two of the village's exhibits are particularly related to the Canal: The Erie Canal Museum displays an animated model showing the operation of an Erie Canal lock and a replica of the passenger cabin of a canal packet boat. There are also models of the canal, tools used in its excavation, and various canal-related artifacts and pictures.

The *Independence*, a full-size replica of an Erie Canal packet boat (the express passenger carrier of the boom days on the Erie) was built on the spot of native oak. Drawn by two mules along a three-mile reconstructed section of the Erie, the *Independence* gives visitors a chance to get at least a taste of what canal travel was like.

Other buildings at the Canal Village include a stagecoach stop, meeting house, tavern, carriage museum, and various residences.

Erie Canal Village is on state Routes 46 and 49 on the outskirts of Rome, New York. Crafts demonstrations. Open every day, first week in May to October 31, 9:30 a.m. to 5:30 p.m. Admission: $3.00; seniors and children, $2.00. Owned by City of Rome. Erie Canal Village, Rome, New York 13440. Telephone (315) 336-6000.

The little upstate New York town of Canastota, about six miles from Oneida, is built right on the Erie Canal, with a row of 19th-century buildings facing the towpath where it runs through the center of the town. Some of these have been lost through fire, but the survivors are gradually being restored and opened to visitors. Among the handsome old houses in the town is an 1820 mansion built by Nathan S. Roberts, a self-taught engineer, who surveyed, located, designed, and built a large section of the Erie Canal at its western end. (Privately owned, the house is not open to visitors.)

One of the buildings on the canal is the small Canastota Canal Town Museum, devoted to local history. Here in the Erie Canal Room a small collection of canal relics is preserved and displayed. Beside pictures of the Erie in its prime, there are models of both the fast packet boats, the express passenger carriers of the canal, and the slower line boats that carried both people and freight. Original canalboat artifacts include such equipment as the horns used to alert the lockkeepers, various lanterns, and the bilge pump—essential for keeping a leaky craft afloat.

Canastota Canal Town Museum faces a surviving portion of the Erie Canal at 122 Canal Street. Canastota, a small village, is reached by exit 34 from the New York State Thruway. Museum's Erie Canal Room contains pictures, models, maps, and original canalboat equipment. Open all year, Monday-Friday, 9 a.m. to 4 p.m. Admission: free. Canastota Canal Town Museum, P.O. Box 51, Canastota, New York 13032. Telephone (315) 697-3451.

Again, we'll head westward to an old canal town that's become a substantial city.

Many places along the Erie Canal prospered, but few more so than Syracuse, almost exactly midway between Albany and Buffalo. The original settlers had braved swampy ground in order to make salt from natural salt springs nearby. Transporting the bulk product to market was expensive and the salt manufacturers were ardent advocates of the canal project. Their judgment was good; when the Erie arrived at Syracuse, freight rates dropped sharply, and salt production boomed. Syracuse became a major port on the Erie Canal and eventually one of the major manufacturing cities in upstate New York.

The city's importance as a canal port was further enhanced in 1828 when the Oswego Canal was built connecting the Erie Canal at Syracuse with Lake Ontario. Here, at the junction of the two canals, a "weighlock" was built in 1850 to weigh canalboats and their cargoes in order to figure the canal tolls, based on tonnage. The lock and its scales were sheltered by a handsome brick Greek revival building.

After almost a century, the Erie was superseded by the New York State Barge Canal, designed for use by barges drawn by tugs instead of mules and following a somewhat different route to take advantage of natural lakes and rivers. The section of the Erie Canal that ran through the middle of Syracuse was filled in and became Erie Avenue. Despite its architectural distinction and historical significance, the Weighlock Building was at that point abandoned for demolition, but was then saved by a determined campaign by preservation groups.

Now on the National Register of Historic Places, the Weighlock Building today houses the Erie Canal Museum, which is dedicated to the collection, preservation and interpretation of America's canal history. With a special focus on the canal of which the

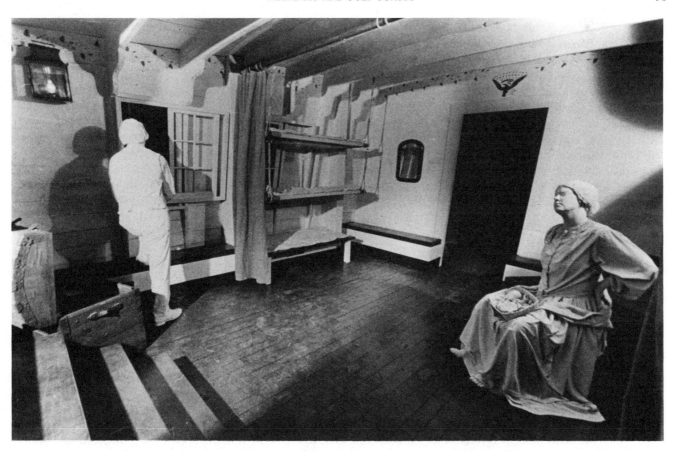

Figure 21
This period recreation of the forward cabin aboard the canalboat *Frank Buchanan Thomson* at the Erie Canal Museum, Syracuse, New York, features canvas and rope bunks. The forward cabin housed the most precious cargo transported on the Erie Canal—European immigrants coming to America to swell the populations of its cities and to people the wilderness beyond the Appalachian Mountains.

weighlock was once an integral part, the museum's exhibits include tools, artifacts, models, photographs, and an extensive collection of documents on canal history and technology.

The weighlock itself, however, is the core of the museum's exhibits. A full-scale recreation of an 80-foot "line" canalboat, complete above the waterline, has been built within the lock. The line boats were the standard passenger/freight carriers on the Erie, and visitors can see the crew's quarters, cargo hold, and passengers' cabin authentically reproduced.

Outside the weighlock, at the gate where the canalboats entered, the bow section of a "laker" type canalboat has been reconstructed. This shows how the off-duty mule team was carried on the boat, eating and resting between six-hour shifts. (By using two teams alternately the canalboat could keep moving 24 hours a day.)

On the same floor of the museum as the weighlock is the "Hands on" gallery, which should have a special appeal to younger visitors. Here, they can steer a canalboat, weigh a cargo, learn how a bilge pump

works—even build a weighlock out of blocks. An animated model demonstrates how canal locks work, raising and lowering boats.

Next door in the orientation theater a 14-minute audiovisual show explores the impact of the Erie Canal on American history. What would have happened differently if the canal had never been built? A fascinating question with some controversial answers.

Also on this floor is the restored office of the weighmaster, the official responsible for the whole toll-taking operation until canal tolls were finally abolished in the 1880s because of cut-rate railroad competition.

Upstairs a Special Exhibition Gallery is used for rotating exhibits built around such themes as the Erie Canal and the Civil War. These are usually changed a couple of times a year.

The museum has another facility at DeWitt, five minutes or so away at the outskirts of Syracuse, at the western end of the 35-mile surviving segment of the Erie Canal, here part of the Old Erie Canal State Park.

At DeWitt, the museum's Canal Center interpretation building exhibits focus on the history and significance of the Erie. Displays include small craft used on the canal, explanatory descriptions of various structures found along its banks, maps of the region, and graphic exhibits portraying life on the Erie. Admission to the Canal Center is included in admission to the museum.

Erie Canal Museum is in the 1850 Weighlock Canal Building in the center of downtown Syracuse, New York. Extensive library on canal topics. Open all year, Tuesday-Sunday, 10 a.m. to 5 p.m. Suggested donation: $1.00. A

chartered nonprofit educational institution. The Erie Canal Museum, Weighlock Building, 318 Erie Boulevard East, Syracuse, New York 13202. Telephone (315) 471-0593.

The Canal Center at DeWitt is open the same hours as the museum, but only from May 1 to November 1. Admission is included in entrance fee for museum. Visitors should ask at the museum for directions for driving to the Canal Center, which is at the Cedar Bay Picnic Area in state park.

Now we'll take a look at the Hudson River's northern connection, up Lake Champlain.

Champlain: Lake of Battles

In July, 1609, Samuel de Champlain and some 20 other Frenchmen accompanied a war party of Indians from the St. Lawrence valley in a raid on the Mohawks, their fierce enemies to the southward. Their allies had led the Frenchmen up a river flowing into the St. Lawrence from the south, above Quebec; at rapids the Frenchmen had left their two heavy shallops and taken to Indian canoes. Seventy-five miles up the river (later named the Richelieu) they came to its head, a beautiful long lake stretching away to the south through a wild forest with mountains looming to the west.

Now as the flotilla of 24 canoes paddled up the lake they came upon a fortified Mohawk camp on the west shore. The Canadian Indians were far outnumbered, but they landed and produced their secret weapon: Champlain in armor and plumed helmet, carrying his heavy arquebus, and its slow match burning, and loaded with four bullets, ready to be fired. The Mohawks had never seen firearms and their chiefs came striding confidently forward. Champlain fired and his single shot killed two chiefs and mortally wounded a third, one of the more remarkable feats of marksmanship in history. The terrified Mohawks fled. Champlain gave the lake his own name, which it retains to this day.

So at the very beginnings of European settlement the newcomers were led to the north-south invasion route long followed by the war parties of the ever-warring tribes of the Hudson and St. Lawrence valleys. The Europeans were not slow in making use of it. In the course of the following two centuries Lake Champlain not only became a highway for large invading armies but itself became the scene of battles where

seapower—naval power—once again changed the course of history.

Geography inevitably gave Lake Champlain its role. Most of the undefined border between French Canada on the St. Lawrence and the English colonies in New York and New England was pathless wilderness, difficult terrain even for small raiding parties, impassible for forces of any size. But through the middle of this barrier was a low valley running north and south, providing an all-water highway almost the entire way from the Hudson to the St. Lawrence. From the southern tip of Lake Champlain it is only 20 miles to the Hudson River below its fall line (actually there is only a half-mile-wide, 20-foot-high watershed between the tributaries of Lake Champlain and the Hudson). The narrow southern extrusion of Lake Champlain is paralleled a few miles to the westward by 35-mile-long Lake George, which eventually empties into Champlain through a short, rapids-filled passage at Ticonderoga (which made this isthmus a strategic point to be controlled by a fort).

Lake Champlain itself covers 490 square miles, the fourth largest fresh-water lake in the United States. From half a mile to 14 miles in width, the lake runs 125 miles north and south along the eastern edge of the Adirondack Mountains. At the northern end Champlain's waters drain into the Richelieu River, which in turn empties into the St. Lawrence.

The rivalry of Britain and France, intensified in their colonies in America, led to four wars between them, beginning in the late 17th century. At first the Champlain invasion route was largely used by small parties of frontiersmen, often accompanied by allied Indians, moving to attack the exposed settlements of the other nation: French raiders destroyed

Schenectady and even ravaged the outskirts of Albany, for example, while English attacks to the northward hit settlements close to Montreal. By the mid-18th century, however, the wars were fought on a much larger scale.

Earlier, in an interlude of peace, the French had seen the strategic value of controlling the lake route and built a fort at Crown Point where Lake Champlain is so narrow that its entire passage was within range of cannon on the shore. The fort was supplied by lake craft. Now in the 1750s came the climactic struggle. To block further French moves southward, the English built Fort William Henry at the south end of Lake George, and started a small naval building program: constructing and arming small lake vessels to control the lake. In the winter of 1757, however, French troops skated and sledged up the lake on the ice to where the English armed sloops were frozen in and set the vessels afire, along with a half-built vessel on the shore. With British naval power out of the way, French General Montcalm moved 5,000 troops up the lake in 250 batteaux, large open boats that were the workboats of French Canada. The French besieged, captured, and destroyed Fort William Henry, but the next year the British launched a counter invasion down Lake George with an even larger armada: no less than 900 batteaux, 135 whaleboats, a large number of flatboats transporting field artillery, and even two "floating castles"—scows mounted with cannon to bombard the shore should the landing be opposed. "A spectator watching them from the shore," wrote historian Frances Parkman, "says that when the fleet was three miles on its way, the surface of the lake at that distance was completely hidden from sight."

Objective of the offensive was the fort that the French had recently built at Ticonderoga; but despite the impressive armada brought against it the fort held out. The British tried again the next year and this time the French garrison blew up the fort and retreated by boat down Lake Champlain. Four French armed vessels still commanded the lake, however, and British General Amherst delayed his pursuit many weeks until the Royal Navy captain on his staff built a small British squadron that could win control of the lakes. When the warships were ready, the British moved down the lake; but although the French armed sloops made no resistance, it was now October, storms made Lake Champlain too rough for the safe movement of troops by water, and the final push north to capture Montreal was delayed until the next year.

This was not the last time that naval power played a major role in campaigns on the invasion route. Early in the American Revolution, in 1776, Benedict Arnold's little Continental flotilla on Lake Champlain, although defeated, forced a British invasion to be postponed a year, and the delay may well have played a part in General Burgoyne's ultimate defeat.

And yet again, in the War of 1812, when another British invasion threatened in 1814, a U.S. Navy squadron controlled Lake Champlain and the British army halted to await the building of a fleet. This time, however, the Americans won the decisive naval battle and kept control of the lake; the British army was not merely delayed but forced to retreat to Canada. Naval power had once again proved the decisive factor.

After 1814 the Lake Champlain invasion route became a trade route. Soon after the war, canals were built between the Hudson River and the southern tip of Lake Champlain and around the rapids on the Richelieu River in Canada, providing an uninterrupted inland waterway between major cities in the United States and Canada. This river/canal/lake/river/canal route continues in use to this day, although now perhaps more appreciated by yachtsmen than commercial shippers.

In recent years a number of the ships from Lake Champlain's war-filled past have been discovered sunk in the lake, and some of them have been raised. Arnold's 1776 gundalow *Philadelphia*, the only surviving warship of the Continental Navy, is on display in Washington, while the remains of the United States Navy's 1814 schooner *Ticonderoga* are exhibited at the Skenesborough Museum in Whitehall, New York. Even earlier vessels have been located by underwater archaeologists who are studying them without attempting to raise them from the lake bottom. Among the finds are the *Boscawen* and the *Duke of Cumberland*, built at Ticonderoga in 1759 as part of the British squadron constructed to win control of Lake Champlain from the French. The *Boscawen* was a 70-foot gaff-rigged sloop that carried 16 small cannon and 110 soldiers. She is believed to have been stripped and left to rot away at her moorings after the French and Indian War ended with the British conquest of Canada.

Naval artifacts recovered from the lake, as well as a big diorama of the Lake Champlain naval battles in the Revolution and the War of 1812, are on display at the Clinton County Historical Society's little museum at Plattsburgh, New York. A Lake Champlain vessel of a much later era has been preserved ashore at Shelburne, Vermont. After a long career as a passenger/freight carrier on the lake, the S.S. *Ticonderoga* is on exhibition at the Shelburne Museum, on the east side of the lake.

Incidentally, both Lake George and Lake Champlain are noted for the beauty of their scenery—an extra dividend of pleasure for the traveler exploring this important segment of America's Maritime heritage.

We'll start our Champlain tour at the southern end.

At first glance the little town of Whitehall seems to be deep in the heart of the New York countryside, a land of big cowbarns set on rolling meadows. Which makes it all the more startling to be greeted with signs proudly proclaiming Whitehall "The Birthplace of the American Navy." Local historians can make a pretty good case, too, as against competing claims; their story involves a little known bit of American history.

First, let it be said that Whitehall really is—or at least was—a little port on Lake Champlain, at the extreme southern end, on the long narrow extension of the lake. Here at the very head of the lake but with easy access to the main body, the village of Skenesborough was settled in the 18th century. Local magnates, including the prominent Skene family, owned small sloops and schooners for lake travel.

In May, 1775, only a few days after Concord and Lexington, Ethan Allen and Benedict Arnold were in joint command of an American militia force planning to capture Fort Ticonderoga from its tiny British garrison. A vessel was needed to carry the Americans across Lake Champlain from Vermont to Ticonderoga on the west shore. At the same time it was necessary to seize control of the lake from the British, who had a 70-ton sloop and bateaux—large open boats that could be sailed or rowed—at St. John on the Richelieu River, a few miles down from where it runs out of the north end of Lake Champlain.

Step One was to send 30 Green Mountain Boys to capture the schooner *Katherine* at Skenesborough, owned by Loyalist/Tory Philip Skene (which is presumably why Skenesborough became Whitehall). The rebels renamed the Skene sloop *Liberty* and Benedict Arnold sailed her north down the lake to carry out Step Two.

This was a surprise attack on the British fort at St. John. ("Saint-Jean sur Richelieu" on today's maps of the Province of Quebec). The fort, a sloop, and a number of bateaux were captured, leaving no watercraft for British use on the lake. The captured sloop became the *Enterprise*, and along with *Liberty* and others formed a small American squadron that patrolled Lake Champlain during the summer of 1775. On June 14th, the Continental Congress declared that all men under arms were to be part of the Continental Forces. The payroll of *Enterprise*—some 155 for May 3 to July 12 and listing the entire roster as seamen or marines—is considered the oldest payroll of the American Navy.

The capture of the Skenes' *Katherine*, and her transformation into the Continental schooner of war *Liberty* were more of symbolic than military importance. The next year, however, Skenesborough played a major role in events leading to a turning point in the struggle for American independence. In the spring and summer of 1776 hundreds of carpenters, smiths, riggers, sailmakers, soldiers, seamen, gathered in this tiny frontier village and in a few weeks built from scratch, equipped, armed, and manned eleven small fighting ships. The eight 53-foot gundalows and three 72-foot row galleys became an integral part of Benedict Arnold's little American flotilla whose control of Lake Champlain held up the threatened British invasion from Canada that might have crushed the Revolution then and there.

The Royal Navy, with far superior resources, rushed to build a stronger squadron at the north end of the lake, but it was October before the British ships were ready to challenge the Americans. Arnold fought a delaying action at the Battle of Valcour Island, then retreated up the lake. All his ships were sunk or captured, but by then it was so late in the fall with autumn gales and winter blizzards soon to come that the British postponed the invasion until the following year. The delay gave the Americans time to gather resources and troops for the defensive campaign of 1777 that led to Burgoyne's surrender at Saratoga.

The building of Arnold's flotilla is the subject of a major exhibit at the Skenesborough Museum in Whitehall. A large—roughly 10 by 20 feet—and beautifully detailed diorama gives a birds-eye view of the galleys and gundalows at various stages of completion on the seven shipways while the sloops and schooner of the squadron are at anchor out in the lake. Houses, warehouses, work buildings, blockhouse, along the lake give the feeling of what Skenesborough must have been like that frenzied summer of 1776.

The diorama is the work of a talented local craftsman, who also made the fine big model of the USS *Saratoga* in a nearby case. The *Saratoga* was Commodore Thomas Macdonough's flagship in the other major naval action on Lake Champlain, the battle in Plattsburgh Bay in 1814 in which the American squadron was victorious, blocking another threatened British invasion from Canada.

Among other Navy exhibits to be looked for in the Museum are a big model of the Continental gundalow *Philadelphia*, built at Skenesborough and sunk at Valcour Island, and artifacts from the Revolutionary period, largely recovered from the lake, including cannon balls and tools.

The most interesting and important naval exhibit at the Skenesborough Museum is on the museum grounds beside the Champlain Canal—the remains of the USS *Ticonderoga*, a 125-foot schooner mounting 17 guns, that was one of the major vessels in Commodore Thomas Macdonough's squadron at the Battle of Lake Champlain in 1814. After the war, a number of his vessels were tied up near Whitehall (ex-Skenesborough) where they gradually rotted away and sank at their moorings. *Ticonderoga* was raised in 1959 (further damaged in the process) and is now protected by an open-sided shed. Still in place are her keel, portions of 55 frames, most of the sternpost, and the base of the stem. Fragments though they are, the pieces are all original and largely in their original relationship to each other. (In contrast, the beautifully preserved USS *Constitution*, afloat in Boston harbor, can boast only about 10 per cent of her original timbers.)

The Museum also has exhibits related to the modern American navy. Models of World War II fighting ships include the destroyers *Bainbridge* and *Sherman* and the carrier *Saratoga*. A room is devoted to naval memorabilia collected by Secretary of the Navy William Franke, who served in the Eisenhower cabinet, including many interesting models of naval aircraft.

A second Skenesborough Museum focus is on the Champlain Canal, which connects the Hudson River and Lake Champlain. The canal runs past the back door of the museum, housed in what was once the Canal Headquarters building, and the northernmost lock, Number 12, is only a short distance away. For many decades the canal brought business and bustle to little Whitehall. Eventually, first railroads and then trucks stole much of the canal's cargoes, but today, more than 160 years after it was built, the canal is still operating—largely for pleasure craft and barges carrying petroleum products to towns on the lake.

Another fine diorama in the museum portrays Whitehall during the hey-day of the Canal in the 19th century, showing the lock and canal boats moving through the town. There are also many photographs of the canal and its traffic in the busy years, but of special interest are several models of canal boats. Locally made, these are primitive and rough, but with a great feeling of authenticity: these must have been carved by people who worked on canalboats—or at least lived on the banks and watched them go by every day.

Even more primitive—but equally authentic in feeling—are rough models of Lake Champlain steamers, including the passenger carrier *Mohican*, the tug *Defender*, the ferry *Chateaugay*, and big *Ticonderoga* (the original of which is now on display at the Shelburne Museum, down the lake near Burlington).

Incidental note: the main museum gallery has a play boat for kids to "sail" while their parents are looking at the exhibits. Good idea.

Skenesborough Museum is in Whitehall, New York. In Whitehall look for Museum sign on left just past railroad bridge after leaving downtown eastbound on Route 4. Museum building short distance on right next to red D.&H. caboose, on bank of Champlain Canal. Bookstore/gift shop. Open last week in June through Labor Day, daily, 10 a.m. to 5 p.m. Admission: $1.00; students, 50 cents. Sponsored by Historical Society of Whitehall. Skenesborough Museum, Skenesborough Drive, Whitehall, New York 12887. Telephone (518) 499-0716.

Now we'll head up along the eastern shore of the lake to visit a vessel from a different era.

Of all the waters of America, only the Hudson saw a steamboat before Lake Champlain. In 1808, the year after Fulton's *Clermont*, the sidewheeler *Vermont* was built in Burlington and the next year she made her maiden voyage on the lake, from Burlington to Whitehall, 150 miles, in 24 hours.

In 1823 the Champlain Canal opened between Lake Champlain and the Hudson River, linking the lake directly to New York City and producing a shipping boom on the lake. Three years later the Lake Champlain Transportation Company was chartered and by 1846 it had swallowed all its rivals and had four steamers in regular service between St. John on the Richelieu River at the north end of the lake and Whitehall at the south.

That was the peak of Lake Champlain steamboating. In 1849 the railroads arrived at the lake towns, and waterborne traffic began a long decline that left the steamboats carrying little more than summer visitors and package freight from one little town to the next along the lakeshore. Nevertheless they hung on gamely and in the 1930s the Lake Champlain Transportation Company was still operating, by then the oldest active commercial steamship company in the world.

Among the survivors afloat was Champlain Transportation's luxury sidewheeler *Ticonderoga*, built on the Hudson and assembled at Shelburne, Vermont, in 1906. She continued the tradition of American steamboating with a grand staircase, beautiful paneling, etched glass ports, gold-stenciled ceilings. *Ti* had overnight accommodations and until the 1930s ran on a regular schedule up and down the lake.

Eventually, the automobile and improved roads provided easy, high-speed travel with which the surviving lake steamboats could not compete—not even the handsome *Ticonderoga*. In 1950 her owners were prepared to scrap her and she was kept in service only by public contributions. The Shelburne Museum, near Burlington, owned and operated her for several years but the difficulty of maintaining her aging hull and steam engines, together with a lack of operating personnel, forced her lay-up. The decision was made to haul her out for preservation in a permanent berth ashore.

Figure 22
To preserve her, the steamboat *Ticonderoga* was laboriously dragged two miles across the Vermont countryside from Lake Champlain to a new home on the grounds of the Shelburne Museum, where she is now on display.

The site chosen was two miles from the lake shore on the grounds of the Shelburne Museum. The *Ticonderoga* is 220 feet long and weighs some 900 tons. For two months in the winter of 1954-55 she was, as the museum summarizes it, "hauled across frozen swamps, through the Vermont woods and meadows and across roads and railroad rights of way to the museum grounds."

And there she sits today—high and dry but all there, just over a little hill from busy Route 7. Not merely preserved but restored with loving care with the exuberant decorations of her youth, *Ticonderoga* has been placed on the Register of National Historic Landmarks. Every year many thousands visit her to see the last survivor of a great breed.

S.S. *Ticonderoga*, veteran Lake Champlain steamer, is in dry berth at Shelburne Museum on Route 7, Shelburne, Vermont, 7 miles south of Burlington. 220-foot sidewheeler is on display from mid-May to late October, 9 a.m. to 5 p.m. Art, book, gift shop. Admission to entire museum complex: $9.00; 6 to 18, $3.50; under 6, $3.00. Nonprofit. Shelburne Museum and Heritage Park, Shelburne, Vermont 05482. Telephone (802) 985-3346.

Now north and west across the lake to the west shore.

In 1814, the defeat of Napoleon enabled the British government to transfer veteran regiments from Europe to North America to take the offensive against the United States. As in the Revolution, an invasion was to be launched from Canada, aimed southward along the traditional invasion route of Lake Champlain. Also repeating the past, the advance of the large British army depended upon the Royal Navy's winning and holding naval control of the waters of the lake.

The American troops gathered at Plattsburgh were far inferior in numbers and experience to the war-hardened British regiments moving south toward them along the west shore of Lake Champlain. On the waters of the lake, however, the situation was very different. Both the British and the Americans had been building fleets of small warships to contest control of the lake; by early September the American squadron, commanded by energetic young Commodore Thomas Macdonough, was momentarily ahead and held the lake. The British, however, were completing a new vessel, the ship *Confiance*, carrying 37 guns, including 27 24-pounders, potentially the strongest vessel on the lake, although finished so late that she was sent out to battle the second week in September while ship carpenters were still working on board.

With the two squadrons roughly equal, Macdonough anchored his ships in a defensive line across Plattsburgh Bay and forced the British ships to attack him. In the hotly fought battle that followed, with heavy losses on both sides, the British squadron was roundly defeated and surrendered. The British invasion army retreated to Canada, and British hopes for territorial gains in the final peace treaty with the United States were thwarted.

The battle of Lake Champlain was fought only a few miles north of the area on the lake where the naval battle of Valcour Island had taken place 48 years earlier. A clear idea of the relative position of the two battles to each other and to Lake Champlain's islands and west shore can be obtained on a big diorama in the Clinton County Historical Museum in Plattsburgh. A taped commentary coordinated with overhead lights that illuminate first one battle, then the other, explains the movements of the opposing squadrons in each engagement.

The diorama is the central exhibit in the Lake Champlain Gallery of the Museum, housed on the third floor of Plattsburgh City Hall. Other exhibits in the gallery related to Macdonough's victory include many prints, maps, portraits and a complete set of china decorated with battle scenes.

The museum is in general devoted to local history, but there are a number of naval artifacts on display that have been found in the lake over the years. Among them is a gun mount from the American ship *Royal Savage*, lost in the Valcour Island battle, and a swivel gun dating from the earlier Colonial period when French and British forces contested for control of the lake. In the center of the City Hall lobby on the floor below is a 12-pound brass cannon from the French sloop *Musquelongy*, jettisoned when she was run aground to avoid capture by a superior British force during the French and Indian War. The British recovered the sloop but never found the cannon, which lay undisturbed until three teen-agers came across it in 1968.

The Clinton County Historical Museum is on the third floor of City Hall, Plattsburgh, New York. Small gift/book shop. Open year round; Monday-Friday, 1 to 4 p.m.; also by appointment. Admission: 50 cents; students and children, 25 cents. Sponsored by Clinton County Historical Association, P.O. Box 332, Plattsburgh, New York 12901. Telephone (518) 561-0340.

Before leaving the area, many visitors may want to drive west from Lake Champlain to Blue Mountain Lake, in the heart of the Adirondacks, where there is a museum with interesting small craft of the region.

New York is the third most populous state in the nation, but the upper right hand corner of its roughly triangular shape is almost empty. Here, where Canada's great Laurentian Shield extends south of the St. Lawrence River, are the Adirondacks, a huge wilderness area. Squeezed between Lake Champlain and Lake Ontario are 42 mountains interspersed with 2,800 lakes and ponds, 1,200 miles of rivers, and 30,000 miles of brooks and streams.

In Colonial days, war parties ranged between the St. Lawrence and the Mohawk rivers. Later the Adirondacks were largely left to hunters and trappers; the great westward push of settlements passed them by as unsuitable for farming. Eventually, lumbermen moved in and started methodically to mow down the virgin forest.

And then, in the mid-19th century, the Adirondacks were discovered by well-to-do city folks; here was a glamorous and romantic wilderness, remote but not too remote, where the hunting and fishing were great and there were by now no pesky redskins to worry about. The native woodsmen transformed themselves into Adirondack guides and saw to it that city dudes could rough it in comfort and go home with satisfying trophies and great fish stories that were actually true. (Eventually the lumbering was slowed to a halt as much of the area became a vast state park.)

With a string of lakes stretching 150 miles through the heart of the Adirondacks, boats and canoes played a large part in carrying the sportsmen into the wilderness. New types of wooden small craft were developed to meet the demand; they were easier for the hardworking guides to row or paddle, light enough to be portaged without backaches, and more comfortable for the dudes. The Adirondack guide boats and canoes became nationally known.

Today, a fine collection of these magnificent boats has been gathered at the Adirondack Museum at Blue Mountain Lake, in the heart of what is now the six-million-acre Adirondack Park. One of the 20 buildings of the regional museum is devoted to displaying 70 of the 200-odd boats in the collection. Particularly notable are 30 of the famous Rushton wooden canoes, designed and built by John Henry Rushton in the last two decades of the 19th century. The Rushtons were designed to be rowed rather than paddled.

The museum also has on display, out of the water, the sloop *Water Witch*; built around 1900, one of the Idem class designed for the St. Regis Lakes in the

northern Adirondacks. A special boat pond floats the little steamboat *Osprey*, whose service on Adirondack lakes spanned the years from 1882 to 1929, along with the 1925 excursion launch *Mountaineer*.

Many other aspects of the Adirondacks are, of course, covered in the museum, which has been described as the finest regional museum in the United States.

The Adirondack Museum is at Blue Mountain Lake in the heart of Adirondack Park in northeastern New York state. Library. Bookshop. Open June 15 to October 15, every day; 10 a.m. to 6 p.m. Admission: $6.00; children 7-15, $3.75. Adirondack Museum, Blue Mountain Lake, New York 12812. Telephone (518) 352-7311.

III
THE ROAD TO CANADA

Along the St. Lawrence

On the 10th of August, 1535, Master Pilot Jacques Cartier of St. Malo, captain by command of King Francis of France of three small exploration ships, took his little flotilla into a bay on the north shore of the wide gulf west of Newfoundland. August 10 is the feast day of St. Lawrence the Martyr, and Cartier named the harbor "La Baye sanct Laurins." Then he sailed on southwestward into the mouth of an enormous river, which he explored for hundreds of miles up to the fall line. Cartier called his discovery "La Grande Riviere," but his reports were misread and the river and the great gulf it enters went into the geographies as the St. Lawrence River and the Gulf of St. Lawrence—"le fleuve Saint-Laurent" and "le golfe du Saint-Laurent" to the people who live along their shores.

Cartier's La Grande Riviere was certainly appropriately named: the St. Lawrence is one of the grandest rivers of North America. The Indians told Cartier that the St. Lawrence was "the road to Canada" and while by "Canada" they apparently meant only their native village where Quebec now is, the description is equally appropriate for the whole vast region of today's Canada. From the river's source at the eastern end of Lake Ontario to the point where it enters the gulf is 750 miles, making the St. Lawrence the longest North American river flowing eastward toward the Atlantic. But the water highway into the heart of the continent is three times as long: Lake Ontario is the easternmost of the Great Lakes, the chain of inland seas stretching 1,500 miles further westward. From the canoes of the French fur traders to the big ocean freighters that pass through the St. Lawrence Seaway today, this 2,300-mile water route has been the key element in the European exploration and economic development of eastern and central Canada.

Not that the St. Lawrence in its natural state was an easy road to follow. Jacques Cartier and his crewmen, the first Europeans to push up the river, left their two larger ships by the great rock of Quebec and continued upriver in his pinnace, towing the ships' boats. The ebb current was strong against him, in places the channel narrowed sharply, and the river grew shallower. Finally, Cartier had to anchor his pinnace; he went on in the longboats, eventually reaching the island where Montreal now stands. Climbing the height he named Mount Royal, the explorer looked up river and saw that his boats could proceed no further. Tumbling rapids blocked the river, which was passable only by light canoes.

Cartier also encountered the other, more enduring handicap to maritime activity on the St. Lawrence: the climate. The explorer wintered aboard his ships at Quebec. The vessels froze in hard and fast, as the St. Lawrence and its tributaries turned to solid ice. For five months a year the road to Canada was closed.

In the years that followed Cartier's voyages, fishermen from Europe, already swarming around Newfoundland, moved into the Gulf of St. Lawrence and the lower river. They were summer visitors only, however, drying their codfish ashore for the voyage back across the Atlantic in the fall and carrying on an increasingly profitable fur trade with local Indians. For more than 60 years France, torn by internal dissension, made no move to follow up Cartier's exploration of the St. Lawrence. Eventually, however, Samuel de Champlain and others with a royal monopoly of the fur trade saw the value of a permanent trading post on the St. Lawrence, closer to the major source of pelts than an earlier settlement in Acadia (Nova Scotia). Champlain unfurled the French flag at Quebec on July 3, 1608, the birthday not only of Quebec but of Canada itself.

At Quebec, beside a towering rocky cliff, a little river flowed in from the north and provided one of the few anchorages out of the main sweep of the St. Lawrence. Champlain chose the site because it was the center of a network of waterways, was easily made defensible, and was close to abundant fisheries. He chose well: Quebec remained the major city and port of Canada for more than two centuries.

Montreal, the rival and ultimately the successor of Quebec as the principal port on the St. Lawrence, was not founded until 1642. The settlement, 160 miles upriver, was originally a wilderness mission but quickly became a military outpost and the vital center of the fur trade with the western Indians. Montreal was at the head of navigation, just below the first of many rapids that made the rest of the St. Lawrence passible only by canoe. (Actually, because of the danger of Iroquois attacks, the fur traders from the west took a roundabout route via the Ottawa River, which flows into the St. Lawrence a short distance above Montreal.)

Both Montreal and Quebec were transfer points. Cargoes brought across the Atlantic in seagoing vessels were unloaded at Quebec. Those for places further up the St. Lawrence were reloaded onto shallops and bateaux to be carried—if necessary, poled—over the shallows up river. At Montreal, goods intended for western trading posts or missions were transferred again, to flotillas of canoes, while Montreal's exports—mostly furs—went down the St. Lawrence in the river craft to be loaded on ships for Europe at Quebec.

Despite this dependence on transatlantic shipping, New France was not maritime minded like neighboring New England. The rich fisheries in the gulf of St. Lawrence were dominated by summer fishermen from Europe. The settlers of New France, relatively few in number, were peasants or discharged soldiers rather than seamen or shipwrights, and they concentrated first on clearing enough land to grow crops to live on. Rather than going to sea, the most adventurous young men of New France were lured into the wilderness by the ever-growing fur trade with the Indians. The merchants of Quebec and Montreal made their profits by dealing in pelts, not by trading voyages to Europe or the West Indies. Bateaux and small sailing craft were built for trading and fishing on the St. Lawrence, but when Canadian merchants wanted larger vessels they tended to buy them from their shipbuilding neighbors and rivals—and sometimes enemies—in New England.

There were other possible reasons for the lack of maritime activity: the limited ice-free season on the St. Lawrence, for one thing. Francis Parkman, noted historian of New France and a rugged New England individualist, blamed the rigidly paternalistic economic system of Louis XIV for smothering local in-itiative. In any case, the French government was unsuccessful in repeated attempts to encourage the Quebecers to build ships with the vast supplies of timber at their doorstep. Private shipyards on the St. Lawrence were government subsidized—and failed. Royal shipyards were established—and proved shortlived. The practical problems were manifold. Most of a ship's fittings (sails, ironwork, cordage) had to be shipped from France and were expensive. The scarcity of skilled craftsmen meant that seamen and shipwrights had to be brought from France to teach the Canadians, and the local high cost of living made labor expensive. By 1730 only some 100 or so vessels had been built at Quebec. Subsequently Royal yards in Canada turned out 10 ships for the French Navy, including the 700-ton, 45-gun *Caribou*, which was launched in 1744, but they had proved more costly than ships built in France. By the time French rule in Canada ended in 1763 the Royal shipyards had already been closed and private shipbuilding on the St. Lawrence was at a low ebb.

Throughout its existence, sea power was essential to the survival of New France. The sea lanes across the Atlantic to France were the lifeline of the colony, albeit a tenuous one in wartime as British fleets dominated the North Atlantic and enemy privateers cruised along the shipping lanes to snap up unwary French merchantmen. And the St. Lawrence itself was a gateway not only for settlement and commerce, but for hostile invasion. Several times British or Colonial fleets sailed up the St. Lawrence to attack Quebec, capturing it at least once in the early days. Ultimately Canada was lost to France when the Royal Navy in 1759 carried General Wolfe's army up the St. Lawrence to Quebec and a British victory on the Plains of Abraham.

A few years after the British conquest of Canada another war brought fleets and armies back to the St. Lawrence. The British colonies to the southward rebelled and for years Canada was primarily a military and naval base. With peace, however, the population grew. There was an influx of American loyalists seeking new homes, followed by a growing number of emigrants from Britain, and Canadian maritime activity picked up.

Montreal's importance as the entry point to the Great Lakes increased with the settlement of lands along the north shores of Lake Erie and Lake Ontario. More furs than ever came down to Montreal from farther west, as enterprising entrepreneurs challenged the monopoly of the Hudson's Bay Company. Whichever way they were going, all through cargoes and passengers had to transfer at Montreal, the junction point. The river craft used between Montreal and Quebec grew bigger with far greater carrying capacity, but they had that stretch of river practically to themselves for very few deep-sea ships came all the way up the river. The channel was shallow and difficult for sailing vessels that had to depend on a favorable wind to push them against the strong downriver current: just below Montreal this current sometimes reached six knots. While cargo-carrying riverboats could be sweated through by sheer muscle power as crewmen strained at the oars or pushed poles against the bottom, the few ships that came up usually had to be towed up the final stretch to Montreal by huge teams—as many as 40 oxen—on the riverbank. Not surprisingly, in 1813, for instance, only nine small sailing ships came up to Montreal from the sea.

Meanwhile, Quebec retained its place as the most important port and commercial center on the St. Lawrence, the port of entry for ocean ships to what had become Britain's major North American colony. With growing prosperity, local shipbuilding revived, on a small scale at first to meet demand for coastal and rivercraft. In 1797 there were half a dozen small yards, and from this modest beginning the industry took off, flourishing for half a century until at its height in the early 1850s half the workmen in Quebec were building ships. Quebec shipbuilding went hand in hand with a booming export trade in Canadian timber; both were fueled by Britain's needs in an era of wars, colonial expansion, and growing world trade. Quebec yards did not build ships for local owners but loaded them with timber and sent them off to Britain where ship and cargo were sold profitably: Quebec-built ships could be found all over the world, but they worked for British shipowners. Production grew steadily, both in numbers and sizes of ships. In 1825, the output was a record 69 ships. Gold-rush year, 1849, saw the launch of 14 ships between 900 and 1,400 tons register, many of them to go into the California run. With British demand spurred by the Crimean War, 80 ships were built in 1853, a good number of more than 1,000 tons. By this time, 5,000 men were working in 26 shipyards in Quebec and the nearby river towns. When the 1,800-ton *Ocean Monarch* was laid down the following year she sold for a high price while still only half built.

As it turned out, *Ocean Monarch* was the climax of Quebec shipbuilding. The British market was saturated, and ships suddenly became a drag on the market. Renewed demand for bottoms during the American Civil War revived the industry for only a few years. The 1,200-ton ship *Cosmo*, was described by Lloyd's surveyor as the finest ship ever built in Quebec, but she was the industry's swan song. Quebec yards turned out their last square-rigger in 1893, the 430-ton barkentine *White Wings*. The day of the wooden ship, Quebec's specialty, was passing. Progressive shipowners now wanted hulls of iron or steel because of their sharply reduced maintenance costs. Indeed the Age of Sail itself was drawing to a close as more

fuel-efficient engines enabled steamships to capture an ever-larger share of the world's ocean cargoes.

And to compound the decline in Quebec's maritime activities, the city had by now lost its place as the major port on the St. Lawrence—overtaken by its upriver rival.

Montreal's spurt to first place came as a result of changes in maritime technology, and because enterprising and alert Montreal businessmen recognized these changes and moved quickly to take advantage of them. Only two years after Fulton's *Clermont*, brewer John Molson financed the little paddle steamer *Accommodation*, her wooden hull built in Montreal, her 6-hp engine imported (like Fulton's) from England. She made the trip from Montreal to Quebec in 36 hours running time and became the first of a long line of river steamers that transformed travel on the St. Lawrence.

But for Montreal, the coming of steamships meant a lot more than merely fast, regular service between St. Lawrence river ports. At first, the little steamboats were too low-powered to tow ships upstream against the current. In 1823, however, the *Hercules* was fitted with a 100-hp steam engine and became the first tug in the river; Montreal at once became accessible to blue-water sailing ships. At the same time the city took to the new technology: Montreal foundries began to produce the iron fittings for steamboats and before long were making the steam engines themselves so that they no longer had to be imported. When in 1833 the SS *Royal William* became the second ship in history to cross the Atlantic principally under steam power, her hull had been built in Quebec but her two 90-hp engines were products of Montreal.

Now that Montreal was becoming a world port, the government took steps to improve accessibility from both east and west. In the 1820s, canals were built around the rapids on the St. Lawrence between the city and Lake Ontario and around Niagara Falls between Lake Ontario and Lake Erie. Together with later ones built around the rapids on the St. Mary's River connecting Lake Superior to Lake Huron these canals, which were repeatedly deepened and enlarged, created a viable all-water route the entire distance between Montreal and the furthest reaches of the Great Lakes. Eventually, a flood of wheat began to pour down through the lakes from the newly settled Canadian prairies, making Montreal one of the world's great grain ports. At roughly the same time, other canals opened a direct water route between Montreal and New York City via Lake Champlain and the Richelieu and Hudson rivers.

Nonetheless Montreal's port development would have stagnated without equally important improvements in the St. Lawrence River between

Montreal and Quebec. Although sailing ships could now be towed to the port, shallows, reefs, and narrow winding channels continued to make navigation difficult and kept ship insurance rates high. As the oceangoing ships coming to Montreal steadily grew larger and drew more water, the natural channel became increasingly a barrier. Beginning in the mid-19th century, the government repeatedly dredged the channel to keep pace with the growth of ships.

Meanwhile, Montreal had become a port of entry in its own right. In 1853 regular steamship service had been established directly between Montreal and Europe. And by the 1860s, as iron hulls continued to take over from wood, and steamships from windjammers, Montreal had replaced Quebec as the major port on the St. Lawrence. The port continued to grow. In the 40 years after 1898 the tonnage of ships entering Montreal increased six-fold.

There is more to the maritime heritage of the St. Lawrence than the long rivalry between Quebec and Montreal for ocean shipping, of course. Until the coming of automobiles and trucks, the river remained the principal highway between the river towns. Steamboat lines established passenger and freight service along the St. Lawrence early on. And downriver from Quebec, where the little harbors dried out at low tide, a special type of schooner used for fishing and coastal transport was developed with a flat bottom so it could squat on the river mud. Some of these downriver villages, in the heart of French-speaking Canada, became famous for the many Canadian seamen and shipmasters who called them home.

In 1959, not only the St. Lawrence valley but the whole Gulf/River/Great Lakes complex underwent a sea change with the opening of the St. Lawrence Seaway. This gigantic engineering project, long proposed and debated and finally carried out jointly by Canada and the United States, broadened and deepened the waterways between Quebec and Lake Erie so that all but the largest seagoing ships could proceed directly to the furthest point in Lake Superior.

On the upper St. Lawrence above Montreal, the old canals around rapids were replaced by new deep, broad waterways with bigger locks. Together with deepening the river channel to the seaway's minimum depth of 27 feet, the canals made it possible for 28,000-ton vessels, 730 feet long, to proceed upriver to Lake Ontario. A similar expansion of the Welland Canal between Lakes Erie and Ontario completed the all-deep-water route to the west. Now the ice-free season has been extended by installing air pumps so that bubbles retard the freeze-up of the lock gates. Canadian Coast Guard icebreakers keep a channel open through the ice as long as possible.

The seaway stimulated the flow of world commerce to the Great Lakes via the St. Lawrence, but it was not an unmixed blessing for the port of Montreal. Hitherto, bulk cargoes, such as grain, had been carried east to Montreal on small lake vessels (or rail) and there transshipped to ocean freighters. Now the ocean shipping can bypass Montreal and proceed directly to Great Lakes ports.

Considerable portions of Canada's maritime/riverine heritage are preserved, reconstructed, and interpreted on the banks of the St. Lawrence. Montreal's museum on St. Helen's Island (named for his teenaged wife by Champlain) covers maritime as well as other aspects of the early days of Canada's major port. In Quebec, a handsome full-scale reconstruction enables the visitor to visualize the 16th-century ships that brought Jacques Cartier to the St. Lawrence, while an interpretation center on the waterfront recounts the history of the port. And down the St. Lawrence in a tiny village on the south bank is a fine maritime museum with a special emphasis on the achievements of French-speaking Canada and Canadians.

A British hero as the victor of Waterloo, the Duke of Wellington entered British political life and became Master General of the Ordnance. One of his major concerns was strengthening the defenses of the far-flung British Empire. Relations between Britain and the United States were still strained in the years after the War of 1812, and Wellington ordered the construction of a major fort on St. Helen's Island in the St. Lawrence River at Montreal. Built from 1820 to 25 as the citadel of Montreal, the fort contained an armory, storehouses, powder magazines, and barracks, constructed with heavy walls of local red stone, guarded by its location in the rushing river.

After a long career that never saw a battle, the old fort with its massive buildings eventually became a part of a city park and the home of the Montreal Military and Maritime Museum, which became the St. Helen's Island Museum, with broadened interests, only very recently to be renamed again as the David M. Stewart Museum, honoring a founder and generous benefactor. (Local guides may still use St. Helen's Island name.)

The maritime exhibits in the museum are largely integrated into a series of displays covering chronologically the discovery, exploration, first settlements, and colonial eras of the St. Lawrence region in general, with special focus on Montreal. Instruments, ship models, artifacts, pictures, are included.

Of very special interest are two ship models. One of these is a fine large model of La Grande Hermine, Jacques Cartier's flagship during the last two of his three historic voyages to North America early in the

16th century. On his second voyage, 1535-36, Cartier became the first European to discover the mouth of the St. Lawrence River and ascend it as far as Hochelaga, the Indian town where Montreal now stands. Not only is the model very nicely done—and believed by experts to be a scholarly recreation of a vessel for which no plans survive—but in the original case with it is an original piece of Cartier's smaller vessel, *La Petite Hermine*, which the explorer was forced to abandon at Quebec because scurvy had killed so many of his crewmen that he did not have enough to man it.

Pieces of *La Petite Hermine* were recovered at Quebec in the mid-19th century and divided between Canada and France. Unfortunately the Montreal museum of the period burned and Canada's share of the artifacts was lost. The relic now displayed—which looks like a fragment of one of the frames—was recently sent back from France as a gift of friendship.

Incidentally, the museum displays a nice model of Cartier's country house at Limoilon, close to St. Malo, his home port in Brittany. The house still exists and is a museum affiliated with the Stewart Museum.

The other unusual ship model is an enormous, very fine model of a French warship some two centuries later: *Le Jupiter*, 70 guns, dating from 1740. Some 10 feet long, beautifully detailed, she is built to a scale of 7 to 144. The complete accuracy of every detail is assured by the fact that the mini-Jupiter was used for the instruction of French ship designers, shipwrights, dockyard workers, in the naval shipyards of the period.

A display of original 18th-century navigating instruments includes a back-staff and cross-staff, the simple ancestors of sextants and octants. Among the naval artifacts are relics from the fleet of British Admiral Havenden Walker, who lost three ships with all hands during a great storm in the Gulf of St. Lawrence in 1711.

The historical gallery also displays weapons, armor, costumes, and pictures from the days of French Canada. A huge diorama of Montreal as it appeared as a walled city in the mid-18th century is especially striking. Of special interest are porringer and spoon carried by Pere Marquette on his historic canoe trip to the upper Mississippi River.

Other surviving portions of the Old Fort are open to visitors, and in summer drill teams in the uniforms of 18th-century French and Scottish Highland regiments carry out maneuvers on the parade ground. The fort is set in a beautiful wooded park with two restaurants and many walks and picnic grounds.

David M. Stewart Museum, formerly St. Helen's Island Museum, is lodged in the one-time Arsenal (1822) in the Old Fort on St. Helen's Island in the St. Lawrence River at Montreal. Two restaurants. Bookstore/gift shop. Open daily Labor Day to Memorial Day, 10 a.m. to 5 p.m.; balance of the year, Tuesday-Sunday, 10 a.m. to 5 p.m. Closed Christmas and New Year's Day. Admission: $3.00; children, $2.00. Donald M. Stewart Museum, Old Fort, St. Helen's Island, P.O. Box 1024, Station "A", Montreal, Quebec H3C 2W9. Telephone (514) 861-6701 or 861-6738.

Among the early European explorers of North America, Jacques Cartier stands in the first rank for his personal qualities, professional skills, and above all, the importance of his discoveries. Between 1535 and 1542 Cartier made three voyages to the New World for King Francis of France. His objectives were much the same as those of other early explorers of North America: to find a sea passage through the continent to China, and to locate precious minerals such as the gold and silver the Spanish had found in Mexico. He did not succeed, but in his search Cartier explored the east coast of Canada and discovered one of the great rivers of North America, the St. Lawrence, the entrance to the 2,000-mile water highway from the Atlantic Ocean to the heart of North America. The names Canada and St. Lawrence, incidentally, first appeared in his narrative.

Later studies showed the accuracy of his description of these regions, which laid a basis for French claims to northern North America. Traveling in tiny ships in unknown waters, now known to be full of hidden dangers, Cartier never lost a ship or a man at sea (the only casualties among his crews came from devastating illness while wintering ashore). Samuel Eliot Morison, the most maritime minded of historians, summed up his view of Cartier: "among the most expert seamen and careful explorers in the era of discovery."

In the first voyage, Cartier pushed through the Straits of Belle Isle, between Newfoundland and Labrador, sailed completely around the fish-rich Gulf of St. Lawrence, and discovered a huge river entering the Gulf from the southwest. In his second expedition he took his three ships up this river, the St. Lawrence, to the great rock where the city of Quebec now stands. There Cartier left the two larger vessels and proceeded further up river in his pinnace, towing the ships' two longboats. As the river shallowed, he moored the pinnace and went on in the longboats to Hochelaga, a great Indian town on the site of Montreal. His further progress blocked by rapids, Cartier returned down the St. Lawrence to his ships moored at the mouth of the St. Charles River. By now it was well into October, too late in the season to risk the run out past Labrador to the Atlantic and France, so the little expedition wintered there.

It was a rugged winter—six feet of ice in the river from November to April, four feet of snow on the shore, four inches of ice coating the interior of the ships. Scurvy broke out and killed almost a quarter of the crew but was halted when the Indians showed the Frenchmen how to make a brew of arborvitae bark and needles that was an anti-scorbutic. In the late spring, after the ice was out of the river, they sailed back home, carrying with them the kidnapped chief of the local Indians—the one major blot on Cartier's character in modern eyes.

Cartier's principal ship on his last two voyages (the third one was an unsuccessful attempt to plant a settlement on the St. Lawrence above Quebec) was *La Grande Hermine*—"the great weasel," more elegantly, "ermine"—named for the animal that appeared on the heraldic arms of Anne of Brittany, the queen of Louis XII. A French naval vessel lent Cartier by the King, she was eventually given the explorer as a reward for his services. Today there is once again a *Grande Hermine* at Quebec, a recreation of the original—not an exact replica, for no plans exist, but a vessel of the approximate size and type based on 16th-century pictures and records.

The new *Grande Hermine* floats in a little pond in Cartier-Brébeuf Park, approximately at the spot where Cartier and his party wintered in their three ships in 1535-36. (The original river at the point where the ships were moored is no longer there, having been piped underground.) Designed by a French expert on 16th-century ships, she was built by traditional methods at a yard across the St. Lawrence from Quebec. After display at Expo '67 in Montreal, she was towed back down the St. Lawrence and trucked the short distance overland from the river to her permanent berth in the little lake in the park. (Although sails have been made for her, *Hermine* has never used them.)

The new *La Grande Hermine* won the critical approval of historian S.E. Morison as "in my opinion, correct." Slightly under 80 feet long, she is a three-masted ship, square-rigged on main and foremast and with a lateen yard on the mizzen. The original vessel was considerably earlier in date than any of the various exploration/early settlement vessels of which recreated versions have recently been built for exhibition in North America. The high, narrow poop, square-box forecastle, and pointed beakhead projecting under the bowsprit of the Quebec ship all reflect the antiquity of her design.

Somewhat battered in appearance—probably appropriately so—the *Grande Hermine* has nevertheless been carefully designed and finished. she is open, in season, from stem to stern, and there is much to see. Here are some things to watch for:

- In the cramped cabins for the master and the officers in the high poop a distinctive feature is the "Breton berths"—built against the side of the ship with sliding panels completely cutting them off from the cabins. Found in old Breton farmhouses, these closed berths provided warmth (and presumably a modicum of temporary privacy—a rare commodity in these little ships.)
- The whipstaff—a tall vertical lever—in the poop controlled the tiller on the deck below (steering wheels had not yet been invented). Notice the little port in the steerage bulkhead facing the helmsman, enabling him to hear the orders of the watch officer on the deck above and at the same time catch a glimpse of how the sails set.
- The great tiller on the deck below, which in rough seas was too heavy to be turned by the whipstaff and required crewmen to pull it over with a block and tackle.
- The shield, bearing the lilies of France, carved on the face of the poop.
- The great double capstan, extending through two decks, was used on the open upper deck to haul sheets and halyards, and on the lower covered 'tween decks to help haul up the anchor lines run aft through the ship from the bow.
- The big wooden bilge pump 'tween decks, spilled its water to run out through scuppers.
- The small swivel guns mounted on the gunwale were *Hermine*'s only armament. These are falconets; loaded with scrap metal they would repel boarders, but were too small to damage enemy ships.
- The long beakhead projecting from the bow under the bowsprit provided a precarious working platform for the men handling the spritsail—the square sail mounted on the yard running athwartship toward the outer end of the bowsprit.
- The cooking arrangements below deck —probably moved topside in good weather—a simple iron shell on which a fire was laid as in a fireplace. The food was cooked in great iron pots.
- The big scuttlebutt was in the forecastle (which at that period had not become the sleeping place of the crew, who slept on the main deck, or topside in warm weather).
- The box-like forecastle itself is a reminder that on medieval ships this really was a "castle," a turret carrying men-at-arms and archers.

Cartier-Brébeuf is a Canadian National Historic Park, which provides an interpretation center on the

Figure 23
Recreation of Jacques Cartier's *Grand Hermine*.

little hill overlooking the ship. Here are models of the *Grande Hermine*, both as completed and partially built to show her framing. Audio-visual shows and other information materials tell the story of Cartier and his ships. There is also a small bookstore and gift/poster shop.

On the grassy bank not far from the ship is a reconstruction of a large Native American longhouse of the type found there by Cartier in the early 16th century. The Indians at Quebec were either Iroquois or Hurons—authorities differ. By the time Champlain returned to the site some 70 years later they had moved away to the west and been replaced by tribesmen of an entirely different culture.

La Grande Hermine, a reconstruction of the type of ship used by French explorer Jacques Cartier in his second and third voyages to New France, is on exhibition at Cartier-Brébeuf Park in Quebec City. Open year round except for Christmas through New Year's and legal holidays. From May 14 to September 1, Tuesday-Sunday, 9:30 a.m. to 5 p.m. September 2 to December 24 and January 2 to May 13,

Monday, 1 to 4 p.m.; Tuesday-Friday, 10 a.m. to 4 p.m. Admission: free. A Canadian National Historic Park. *La Grande Hermine*, 175 de L'Espinay St., C.P. 2474 Postal Terminal, Quebec City, Quebec, Canada G1K 7R3. Telephone (418) 694-4038.

Not far from *La Grande Hermine*, another center of maritime-history interest is the Vieux Port de Quebec, or Old Port Center, on the St. Lawrence wharves, an interpretation center. The center's focus is on both shipbuilding and maritime commerce, particularly lumber exports, in 19th century Quebec. Besides permanent exhibits on four floors, there are talks, a "diaporama," video tape and film presentations on various aspects of the history of the port.

The Port of Quebec in the 19th Century—a part of the National Historic Parks of Canada—is in a large building on the Quebec City riverfront near the Louise Basin. Open December 1 to March 1 by reservation only. From March 1 to mid-June; open Tuesday-Friday, 10 a.m. to noon, 1 to 4 p.m.; Saturday and Sunday, 11 a.m. to 5 p.m. mid-June through Labor Day, Tuesday through Sunday, 11 a.m. to 6 p.m.; Tuesday after Labor Day to November 30; 10 a.m. to noon, 1 p.m. to 4 p.m. Admission: free. The Port of Quebec in the Nineteenth Century, 100 St. Andre Street, P.O. Box 2474. Terminal Post Office, Quebec, Quebec G1K 7R3 Canada. Telephone (418) 648-3300.

Now east some sixty miles down the south shore of the St. Lawrence from Quebec—about an hour's run via the divided lane Trans-Canada Highway—to the handsome little village of Islet-sur-Mer. With its houses—many in the old Quebecois style with high pitched curved roofs—strung out along the river bank, great granite church, and Memorial Cross, Islet is redolent of the spirit of French Canada—appropriately, since French is the language of the town.

Islet-sur-Mer, like a number of little towns along the St. Lawrence, once had a modest ship-building industry. As along the Maine Coast, transportation was far easier afloat than ashore. Timber, pulp wood, and farm products were taken to market in small vessels, predominantly schooners, and these were locally built. From 1860 to 1930, L'Islet yards, manned by carpenters who turned readily back and forth between framing houses and framing ships, launched 25 vessels. Two of them from the yard of Thomas Bernier were quite sizable brigantines—the 98-foot *St. Joseph* of 216 tons (1866) and the 132-foot *St. Michel* of 460 tons (1870).

Islet-sur-Mer also had two other distinctive maritime associations. Many of the men of the town went afloat: it was noted as the home of many seamen and shipmasters. And one of the latter, Captain Joseph-Elzear Bernier, son of shipbuilder Thomas, became a master mariner at an early age and ultimately a distinguished explorer of the Canadian Arctic, making his last voyage in 1925.

At about that time a group of his fellow mariners and townsmen undertook the preservation of the little L'Islet chapel where are inscribed the names of the men of the village who have died at sea. Today the association formed for this purpose also has created and operates a maritime museum in L'Islet dedicated to the memory of Captain Bernier—the Musée Maritime Bernier.

Located in a fine stone building—a former convent—on the river side of the main street, the museum is far more than a personal memorial. Its three floors of exhibits, archives, and library are concerned with preserving the maritime traditions of the St. Lawrence, with special emphasis on the French-Canadian ships and sailors of Quebec. In the river behind the museum is its pride and joy, the large steam ice-breaker *Ernest Lapointe*, completely equipped and beautifully maintained.

The museum is entered on the second floor, where the exhibition galleries contain many interesting shipmodels. Among the vessels represented are:

- the ship *Wasp*, which was wrecked on the Magdalene Islands in the Gulf of St. Lawrence. The only survivor was an Islet man, first mate August La Bourdais, who lost his legs in the disaster. In later years he himself made this authentic model of his old ship—obviously the work of a seaman who knew the ship first hand, rather than a professional model maker;
- a very fine, built-up model of a 19th-century coastal trader, the brigantine *Samuel de Champlain*, typical of the vessels that served the little St. Lawrence river towns;
- another local type in the same service: a schooner or "goélette";
- a huge, nicely finished model of a square-rigged ship—ten feet long, it is big enough to give a clear picture of the complicated rigging and detail of a windjammer; and
- a five-foot model of a 20th-century Canadian supply ship.

There are also a number of builders' half models of schooners built along the St. Lawrence. These include both the keeled type and a distinctive local variation built with no keel and a flat bottom so that the vessel would remain upright when the tide went out and left them high and dry.

Other galleries on this floor are devoted to naval uniforms and weapons. A special exhibit displays photographs and relics of the Canadian Pacific liner *Empress of Ireland*, which sank in the St. Lawrence after a collision.

The third floor of the museum has the library and archives, but the fourth floor has more exhibits, including a gallery—still being installed in 1985—devoted to explorer Bernier. Maps show his voyages to Britain as a very young man in command of timber ships; other graphic displays and pictures portray his family background—the Bernier family arrived in Canada early in the 17th century. A fine larger model portrays his exploration ship, the steam auxiliary *Arctic*, with nice detail.

Other displays deal with his arctic voyages and the Eskimo artifacts he brought back. Also here is a model ship made by a crew member during one of *Arctic*'s voyages to the north.

Of special interest in the fourth floor galleries is a whole squadron of models of Canadian ice-breakers—highly important vessels in the St. Lawrence where ice starts appearing in November and lasts until April. Among these distinctive craft are waterline models of the Canadian Coast Guard vessels

Mikala, early 20th century, and *Lady Grey*, which served from 1906 to 1955. Both have the sharp straight bow designed to break up the ice by brute force when the ship was driven into it head-on. In contrast are later designs, also shown in models, of ice-breakers with bows cut away obliquely at the bottom, so that they slide up on top of the ice and break it by the weight of the ship rather than by ramming.

This distinctive ice-breaker bow can be seen full scale on the Canadian Coast Guard cutter *Ernest Lapointe*, a 1,200-ton steamship docked at the riverbank behind the Museum. About 185 feet long, hull painted the gleaming red of the Canadian flag with white superstructure, the *Lapointe* is a very attractive vessel, made doubly so by the loving care with which she is being maintained from bilges to masthead. She also is striking for the completeness of her equipment, unlike all too many government vessels retired and handed over to private hands for exhibition. Since much of her interior finish went beyond utilitarianism to start with, the result is a very handsome ship.

The *Lapointe* is completely open (in season) to museum visitors. Some things to watch for:

- the big steam engine with eight cylinders that generated 1,000 h.p.: with its huge boilers, six fire boxes (she burned oil), gleaming machinery, it is worth the enthusiast's descent down three levels to the engine-room depths in the stern;
- the enclosed bridge, fully equipped with in-struments, gyro, radio—in top shape so that she looks to be ready to get under way: notice the roomy captain's cabin right behind the bridge;
- the handsome wardroom, mess hall, staterooms—all completely furnished;
- the double steering wheels on deck at the extreme stern—to be used for manual steering in case the steering engines broke down.

Also behind the museum is the DeHaviland experimental hydrofoil, *Bras d'Or*. The museum hopes eventually to add other vessels to its collection. Expected soon is the 80-foot trading schooner—"goélette"—*Jean-Yvan*, the last survivor of the distinctive St. Lawrence type. (There are pictures of her on the fourth floor of the museum.) Called schooners and the descendants of sailing vessels, these craft were really small motor ships with a single mast forward and the pilot house and engine placed in the stern to leave the hold clear. The growth of highway trucking is said to have put these vessels out of business, just as it outmoded the Maine coasters.

Musée Maritime Bernier is in a large granite building on the north side of main street of seafaring village of Islet-sur-Mer, on south bank of the St. Lawrence, about 60 miles from Quebec City. Library/archives. Bookshop. Ship viewable from May 1 to Labor Day. Museum open year round, daily. June, July, and August: 9 a.m. to 8 p.m., balance of year, 9 a.m. to 5 p.m. Sponsored by l'Association des Marins de la Vallee du Saint-Laurent. Musée Maritime Bernier, 55, des Pionniers est, l'Islet-sur-Mer, Quebec, Canada G0R 2B0. Telephone (418) 247-5001.

IV
CANADA'S ATLANTIC PROVINCES

New Brunswick
Prince Edward Island
Acadia/Nova Scotia
Newfoundland

Canada's Atlantic Provinces

The oldest maritime heritage in North America—a heritage that over centuries became ever richer and more varied—is the proud possession of the Atlantic Provinces of Canada.

Here to these wave-girt lands, jutting far eastward from the main body of North America, came 1,000 years ago the first Europeans known to have dared to sail across the Atlantic Ocean.

Here, 500 years ago, began the great Banks fisheries that have continued without interruption to this day.

And here, some 100 years later, a little company of Frenchmen planted a trading post that became the curtain raiser of the European settlement of the Maritimes. At that time, there was not a single European on the North American coast north of Florida.

From these beginnings, geography, history, and economics combined to give the sea and ships a major role in these lands and their peoples. Besides Prince Edward Island, another of the three Maritime Provinces, Nova Scotia, not only includes Cape Breton Island but is in its entirety almost an island, connected to the mainland of North America only by an 11-1/2-mile neck of land. The third province, New Brunswick, has two separate coastlines totaling 550 miles of shore. While Newfoundland, now grouped with the original Maritimes as the fourth Atlantic Province, is a huge island set across the gaping entrance to the Gulf of St. Lawrence.

All these lands are far to the east of both the United States and the rest of Canada. Halifax is some 400 miles east by north from Boston, the most easterly of the great American ports. St. John's, Newfoundland, is almost 900 miles east of Quebec City, the traditional gateway port to mainland Canada. The easternmost point in Newfoundland is less than 1,700 miles from the westernmost point of Ireland. John Cabot, who sailed westward from Bristol, England, to Newfoundland, covered only half the distance that Columbus sailed (although his passage in those stormy seas took just as long).

All four Atlantic Provinces are geographically blessed by being next to, or on, the great Continental Shelf that here extends far eastward out under the ocean. The occasional shallows on the shelf where the waters are only 50 to 400 feet deep are the famous fishing banks—the breeding grounds of plankton and the feeding grounds of enormous schools of fish, particularly of the cod, the fish that led Europeans to frequent the region long before there were any settlements ashore.

The Grand Bank and Georges Bank have long been famous, even among landlubbers, but there are many lesser-known ones. To name only a few, fishermen early found the Green Banquero, Misaines, Sambro, La Have, and Emerald banks. All these and more are out in the Atlantic, while to the northward, in the Gulf of St. Lawrence are many more banks: Pieter, Egmont, Burgeo, Scatarie, des Orphelins, Miscou, Rose Blanche, and Natashquan among them.

All the Atlantic Provinces have coasts fronting the great Gulf of St. Lawrence, through which drains an enormous watershed extending deep into the heart of North America. Newfoundland is set into the seaward end of the Gulf, dividing the outflowing waters into the Straits of Belle Isle to the north and Cabot Strait to the south. New Brunswick and Nova Scotia form the long arc of the western and southern shores of the Gulf. Prince Edward Island is in the southern end of the Gulf, only a relatively few miles offshore.

Both New Brunswick and Nova Scotia also have southern coasts. The two provinces form the two shores of the Bay of Fundy, famous for its enormous tides that flow in and out of the east end of the Gulf of Maine. And finally, Nova Scotia also has a long rocky coast facing southeastward on the open Atlantic, rich in harbors large and small but not much else.

Like much of northern New England, the land is rocky, much of it unsuited even to subsistence farming, but originally covered with fine forests that could be cut for ships' spars and timbers. The forests, together with the long coastlines with their many harbors, and the rich fishing banks offshore, provided a geographical setting where many would find in the sea their major source of income—and sometimes their only hope of survival.

The Norse discovery of Newfoundland had long been forgotten by the time of John Cabot's rediscovery of the island in 1497, only five years after Columbus's crossing. His historic voyage aroused great interest but the ships and seamen that came in his wake were seeking the rich fishing grounds, not places to settle ashore; they sailed over from Europe in the spring and went back with fish-filled holds in the fall.

In the century after Cabot, a number of expeditions—Portuguese, Spanish, French, English—investigated the coast, including ships commanded by such famous explorers as Verrazano, the Corte Reals, and Jacques Cartier. To most of them the land was of secondary interest. They were looking for a passage through North America to the Pacific Ocean and the riches of Asia. They also hoped to come across sources of gold and silver, such as the Spaniards had found in Mexico and Peru. They were disappointed in both hopes, but during their searches they began to chart these complex and often dangerous coasts.

Fishing was the start of European economic activity everywhere in the region, and eventually it was fishing and fur trading that led to settlement. The offshore fishermen who came over from Europe in the spring set up temporary shore stations where they cured their catch in order to preserve it before carrying it back to Europe in the fall. Eventually fur traders followed and established posts. In the first half of the 17th century French farmers were sent out as settlers on the south shore of the Bay of Fundy. The French controlled these early mainland settlements, which they called l'Acadie or Acadia, for most of the century. In the early 18th century Acadia passed to Britain through conquest and became Nova Scotia. Eventually, the French-speaking farmers were expelled from Acadia and English-sponsored settlers—largely New Englanders—took over their lands. The newcomers brought a strong maritime tradition as shipbuilders, seamen, fishermen, and merchant traders. Some of the Acadians managed to stay in the province by hiding in the forest. Later, after the final British conquest, they were allowed to form their own settlements in New Brunswick, together with others who returned from exile.

Maritime activities increased after the American Revolution with a great influx of American Loyalist refugees. Soon more emigrants came from the British Isles; many Scots, as well as Irish and English. By the early 19th century there was a great surge of shipbuilding and shipowning in the Maritimes; Nova Scotia had by now become three provinces, with the separation of Prince Edward Island and New Brunswick. As long as wooden windjammers carried the world's cargoes, the ships, shipmasters, and shipowners of the Maritimes played a significant role.

Meanwhile, fishing had long been flourishing. The little harbors of all the provinces, and especially Nova Scotia, became home ports for fleets of schooners that fished not only on the banks but as far away as Labrador and Greenland.

Fishing was even more important in Newfoundland, in fact for a long time English fishing interests blocked settlement on the island as interference with their summer fish-drying stations ashore.

Eventually, Newfoundland was settled despite the opposition of fishing interests, and the island's own fishermen took over much of the industry. Meanwhile, here as on the mainland, the French and British empires ground against each other, this time competing for the prized shore stations. The outcome was a compromise: The island remained British, but French fishermen retained rights to process fish ashore.

In the 19th century, shipbuilding and shipowning began to flourish in Newfoundland as they were on the mainland. But to this day the great fisheries remain the dominant factor in Newfoundland life, despite hopes that oil beneath the waters off her coasts will provide new sources of income. Newfoundland, incidentally, was not even a part of Canada until after World War II, but a separate British Crown Colony.

Fishing—now from diesel-driven draggers and

trawlers—remains a major activity of all the Atlantic Provinces. Canada is said to be the world's largest exporter of fish products and these provinces play a major role in creating this enormous economic asset, the heritage of five centuries.

No part of North America can boast a longer maritime tradition than the four provinces. And nowhere is that tradition, which has played a major role in the survival of these lands, more highly valued.

While Nova Scotia is the oldest and perhaps most maritime-minded of the mainland provinces, the visitor traveling by auto either from the United States or from other parts of Canada, enters New Brunswick first. Let us therefore begin there, in the only province whose flag and seal portray a ship to remind its people of their seaborne origins.

New Brunswick

Where are the ships I used to know,
That came to port on the Fundy tide
Half a century ago,
In beauty and stagely pride?

In they would come past the beacon light,
With the sun on gleaming sail and spar,
Folding their wings like birds in flight
From countries strange and far.

There all day long you could hear the sound
Of the caulking iron, the ship's bronze bell,
And the clank of the capstan going round
As the great tides rose and fell.

The sailor's songs, the Captain's shout,
The boatswain's whistle piping shrill,
And the roar as the anchor chain runs out,—
I often hear them still.

The fog still hangs on the long tide rips,
The gulls so wavering to and fro,
But where are all the beautiful ships
I knew so long ago?

Bliss Carman, "The Ships of Saint John"

So poet Bliss Carman remembered nostalgically his boyhood in New Brunswick where he was born. The "half a century ago" may have blurred his recollection a little; it seems unlikely that the piping of a Navy bo'sun and a chanteyman's songs were ever heard on the same vessel, but his poem was true in spirit. In 1874, when the poet-to-be was 13 years old, the great New Brunswick port of Saint John was home port for more than 800 blue-water vessels, some 230 of them square-riggers—ships, barks, and barkentines.

Shipbuilding went hand in hand with shipowning not only in Saint John but in all of coastal New Brunswick. The most westerly of the Maritimes, New Brunswick actually has two quite different coastlines. The south shore of the province faces the Bay of Fundy; it is rocky and bold with entering rivers and offshore islands. The other coast, which sweeps in a great arc facing the Gulf of St. Lawrence to the north and east, is gentle and marshy.

Together, these two coasts give the province, which in area is somewhat larger than Scotland but smaller than Maine, a total of about 550 miles of shoreline. Each coast is marked by the mouth of a major river: The Saint John, 450 miles long, flows into the Bay of Fundy, while far to the north the 225-mile Miramichi, seven miles wide at its mouth, drains one-fourth the entire province into the Gulf of St. Lawrence. On these rivers the maritime activities of the province were focused.

Actually, there was little activity in the area—afloat or ashore—until the very end of the 18th century. For almost two hundred years what is now New Brunswick was first part of French Acadia, then, of British Nova Scotia—a vast wilderness of forest between French Canada along the Saint Lawrence, the Acadian settlements on the south shore of the Bay of Fundy, and the New Englanders pushing northward along the coast of southern Maine. Fishermen set up their curing stations on the coast, and inland an occasional trader bartered for furs with the Indians. As the Acadian population expanded, enterprising farmers moved across Fundy, only eventually to lose everything along with their fellow Acadians in the great expulsion. Many Acadians fled into the nearby wilderness, some northward to the Miramichi River and the nearby shores of the Gulf of St. Lawrence, as far away as they could get from the English and Yankees. When the exiled Acadians were allowed to return to the province after the British conquest of Canada, many of them also settled on this northern coast, French-speaking to this day, and became fishermen.

In New Brunswick, as in Nova Scotia proper, local maritime activity really began in the late 18th century with the arrival of settlers from the New England and Middle Atlantic colonies; they had been encouraged by the British authorities to move in to settle the empty farms left by the departed Acadians. Trading merchants from Massachusetts and Rhode Island laid the foundation of commercial activity in the still scanty settlements of the province. The first permanent settlement of Saint John, at the mouth of the Saint John River, was established by a firm of Newburyport merchants with London connections who traded British manufactures for fish, lumber, and produce. The newcomers also brought their Yankee shipbuilding skills; their 10-ton *Betsy*, 1769, which was designed as a cargo carrier between Saint John and Boston and Newburyport, was one of the first vessels built in the area. The *Betsy* was a portent of great days to come.

These were small beginnings: New Brunswick really bloomed when the American Revolution brought a flood of American Loyalists ("Tories" to their late neighbors) to the province. In 1783-84, 12,000 of these refugees settled along the north shore of the Bay of Fundy. That same year New Brunswick was established as a separate province, including all of Nova Scotia west of the narrow isthmus between Fundy and the Gulf of St. Lawrence. On the other side, the western boundary of the new province was in dispute with the United States; some claimed the international line should be as far west as Penobscot Bay. This would have made half of what is now Maine part of New Brunswick, but the border was ultimately set at the Saint Croix River, where it has remained.

Meanwhile, Scottish settlers arrived to add their labor and skills to those of the Loyalists. The great asset of the new province was its magnificent forests, which came down close to navigable waters. New Brunswick replaced New Hampshire as a major source of masts and spars for the King's ships, but that was only the beginning. Not only were boards, great squared timbers, shingles, and barrel staves shipped overseas, but the province built the vessels to carry them. The banks of the Saint John and Petitcodiac rivers in the south, and the Miramichi in the north, resounded with the clamor of new shipyards and the screams of sawmills. At first, the ships were largely for the West Indian trade—lumber and fish for rum and sugar—but later many were sailed directly to England and sold.

Saint John boomed: In the ten years after 1782, the tonnage of vessels entering the port increased 100-fold. The wars between England and France that began in the last decade of the 18th century and lasted until the fall of Napoleon, brought added prosperity to the province; when France cut off Britain's supply of Baltic timber, New Brunswick filled the gap. During the Embargo and Non-Intercourse Acts that closed American ports, in the first decade of the 19th century, New Brunswickers carried on a surreptitious commerce with New England traders. This traffic continued even during the War of 1812, at the very time New Brunswick privateers were harrying American merchant shipping.

The shipbuilding boom started later in New Brunswick than in Nova Scotia, and ended earlier. The major activity was in the 60 years from 1820 to 1880, but the results were impressive. Altogether, New Brunswick yards launched some 2,200,000 tons of wooden ships—almost 6,000 vessels. In the early days, many were cheaply built and rushed overseas for sale; later, much finer vessels were built, many of them owned and registered in the province. At the height of their activities, 1863 to 1871, New Brunswick's shipbuilders launched from 73 to 163 vessels a year; more than 92,000 tons in 1864, the top year.

Among the most famous of the New Brunswick-built ships was the 1625-ton *Marco Polo*, launched in Saint John in 1850. A cargo carrier above the waterline, she was sharper than average below. After she made the round trip from England out to Australia and back in less than six months, her captain claimed *Marco Polo* was the fastest ship in the world. This was an exaggeration (some of the great clippers covered more miles in a 24-hour run) but she was certainly a remarkable vessel. On the outbound leg of her record passage she carried 930 emigrants and a crew of 60.

An outstanding example of a New Brunswick shipping magnate of the province was Jacob Troop. Starting out with a grocery store, he developed a trading business and began to buy shares in small vessels trading to the West Indies. The next step was to order larger ships, either for sale in England or for his own expanding merchant fleet. In its 65-year existence, the Troop firm owned some 90 vessels. The dark side of the great age of sail is reflected in their losses, however: 14 ships, 20 barks, 5 barkentines, 5 schooners (also 2 steamers) lost at sea—almost exactly half the fleet.

The place for an overview of New Brunswick's maritime past is obviously Saint John, the major port of the province. Together with the Saint John River, which is navigable for almost 90 miles from its mouth, and the adjacent Fundy shores the city was a major area of New Brunswick maritime activity. However, Saint John was not by any means the only one. Another centered on the rocky islands just off the coast where Canada and the United States meet at the Saint Croix River and Passamaquoddy Bay.

On the island of Grand Manan, ships have been built and hardy fishermen have wrested a living from the sea ever since their Loyalist ancestors fled over the border from Maine some 200 years ago. Now a little museum is dedicated to preserving records and artifacts that tell about the island and its people.

Leisurely travelers entering New Brunswick from Maine on Route 1 may wish to take a little time en route to visit the Grand Manan Museum, one of the more remote in the province and with a strong salt-water flavor. Grand Manan Island lies close enough to the Maine coast to be visible—and was long claimed by the United States until the Maine-New Brunswick boundary was finally settled. Today it is reached by a ferry from Black's Harbor on the New Brunswick mainland. Sixteen miles long, the island has a 200- to 400-foot cliff on the west shore, but little harbors to the east and south. The Grand Manan Museum, which houses the collection of the Grand Manan Historical Society, is at Grand Harbor in the southeast.

While many of the museum's exhibits cover Grand Manan's birds, rocks, and crafts, the Walter B. McLaughlin Marine Gallery is devoted to the maritime activities that inevitably dominated the island's life. Fishing, shipwrecks and lifesaving, shipbuilding, and navigation are the themes of exhibits that include artifacts, instruments, photographs, and paintings.

The collection was originally gathered, as the name of the gallery implies, by McLaughlin, a man who chronicled the daily life of Grand Manan for half a century, and who for 35 of those years was the keeper of the Gannet Rock Light. Appropriately, the lens and mechanism of the light are major exhibits in the museum.

Grand Manan Museum is at the little fishing port of Grand Harbor on the southeast side of the island. Grand Manan is reached from the mainland by a two-hour ferry ride from Black's Harbor, New Brunswick, which in turn is reached by turning south off Route 1 at Pennfield, about 35 miles west of Saint John. The ferry carries automobiles, but visitors should remember that Grand Manan is only 16 miles long. The Museum is open from mid-June to mid-September; Monday-Saturday, 10:30 a.m. to 4:30 p.m.; Sunday, 1 to 5

Figure 24
The New Brunswick Museum has the largest collection of 19th century ship portraits in Canada. This watercolor of the brigantine *Curlew* was produced by E.J. Russell of Saint John, New Brunswick.
(New Brunswick Museum photo)

p.m. Admission: free. Grand Manan Museum, Grand Harbor, New Brunswick, Canada E0G 1X0. Telephone (506) 662-3524.

Back on the mainland area and continuing eastward to Saint John, New Brunswick's largest city, located on a rocky peninsula where the Saint John River runs into the Bay of Fundy.

Although one of Canada's two major ice-free ports on the Atlantic, Saint John long was handicapped in competing with Halifax because of the New Brunswick city's location on the Bay of Fundy. The tremendous rise and fall of the tides in the bay, among the greatest in the world, the swirling currents that they generate, and the frequent fogs, all made the approaches to Saint John difficult, particularly for sailing ships. This handicap was largely overcome by modern navigational aids. The arrival of the Canadian Pacific Railway helped by tying the port to the population centers of Canada.

Today, Saint John remains a major Canadian port. Her windjammers are long gone, as Bliss Carman noted, but their memory—and indeed that of the province's whole martime heritage—is preserved in the fine collection of the venerable New Brunswick Museum. Founded in the mid-19th century with a collection of natural history specimens and Indian relics, it is the oldest museum in Canada. Today, it is housed in a large handsome stone building with a new wing; its exhibition space has recently been remodeled in order to display exhibits covering every aspect of the life and history of New Brunswick, as well as decorative arts from around the world.

Perhaps the collection can best be described in the words of the maritime specialist on the New Brunswick Museum's curatorial staff: "As a major port during the 19th century, Saint John witnessed the passage of thousands of sailing vessels. The New Brunswick Museum, located in Saint John, holds a large and varied collection of artifacts, which document the Province's marine heritage. The institution has an extensive collection which includes ship portraits, shipbuilding tools, half models, navigational equipment, ship's carvings, scrimshaw, and models. Ethnological material from around the globe, collected by crew members of New Brunswick vessels, shows that ships from the Province ranged far and wide. Archival holdings and a large photographic collection are also important resources at this Museum. Selected artifacts from the New Brunswick Museum's marine collection are on display."

In fact, the maritime collection has grown so large that the museum lacks the space to show it all at the same time. Rather than trying to choose which portions to display and which to relegate to storage,

the museum has decided to abandon permanent exhibits in its maritime gallery and instead rotate the exhibits.

Thus, the portion of the maritime collection on display in the Sea Winds Gallery changes from time to time. Whatever the visitor finds, however, is almost certain to be of unusual interest, since the rotating shows are drawn from one of the finest maritime collections in Canada. The museum's collection of ship portraits alone is considered the nation's largest, for instance.

Saint John can be a difficult city for strangers to find their way around, due in considerable part to the extreme S-curve made by the Saint John River along the city's southern edge, which creates two separate peninsulas. The museum is on the more westerly of these, a long thin neck of land with the river on three sides. Visitors should study the city map in advance and note where to turn off Route 1 to reach the museum's location on Douglas Avenue.

The New Brunswick Museum, 277 Douglas Avenue, Saint John, New Brunswick. Douglas Avenue is on a separate peninsula from the downtown business section. Visitors are advised to study the city map carefully, then watch signs closely. Open all year: May 1 to August 31, daily, 10 a.m. to 5 p.m.; September to April 30, Tuesday-Sunday, 10 a.m. to 5 p.m., closed Mondays. Museum closed major holidays. Archives and library, same hours except closed summer weekends and open 2 to 5 p.m. Saturday afternoons in winter. Admission: $2.00; students, 50 cents; seniors and small children free. Gift shop and bookstore. The New Brunswick Museum, 277 Douglas Avenue, Saint John, New Brunswick, Canada E2K, 1E5. Telephone (506) 693-1196.

From Saint John, the visitor has a choice of going north to the New Brunswick Marine Center on the Gulf of St. Lawrence at Shippagan, where there is a fisheries museum, or east to the little Albert County Museum at Hopewell Cape on the Peticodiac River. We'll go to Shippagan first, driving north via Fredericton.

Fishing has always been an important maritime activity in New Brunswick, although overshadowed in the 19th century by shipbuilding and shipowning. Many of New Brunswick's fishermen, particularly along the shores of the Gulf of St. Lawrence, are directly descended from the original European settlers in the region, the French-speaking Acadians.

In their original Nova Scotia settlements the Acadians had been farmers; but they did not clear the heavily forested inland areas but built dykes along the rich Fundy marshlands so they could farm without tree cutting. Now, in their new home, they turned away from chopping clearings out of the forests for farm fields to farming the sea. There were other reasons also. To crudely translate an Acadian account, written in French: "[They] neglected their land because they served the sea. All the young people had been nurtured by the sea and the sea more than the land had become their home." Acadian fishing villages grew up all along the New Brunswick coast facing the Gulf of St. Lawrence.

Cod and mackerel were abundant, but the Acadians lacked both capital and markets. In the 19th century both came to be supplied by French-speaking merchants from the British island of Jersey in the English Channel. The merchants provided the gear (and sometimes the boats) on credit, then bought the fish, paying with chits on the company store. Acadian writers complain that the fishermen were kept poor and in debt, receiving bottom prices when they sold the merchants their fish and paying top prices when they cashed their chits at the merchants' store.

Eventually, the competition of American buyers pushed up the fish prices while an inability to adapt to new fishing techniques put the Jersey merchants out of business. Today, the Acadians are still fishing out of the little New Brunswick ports along the Gulf of St. Lawrence, but now many sell their fish through a lively cooperative movement.

One of the centers of Acadian fishing activity, the port of Shippagan, has been chosen by the New Brunswick Provincial Department of Fisheries for its Marine Center, which includes a fisheries museum, as well as a fine aquarium and a marine laboratory. Shippagan is at the tip of a cape that extends eastward into the Gulf of St. Lawrence at the northeast corner of the province. Separated from the Gaspe Peninsula on the north by Chaleur Bay, washed on the south by Miramichi Bay, the area is isolated and apparently has few American visitors. Coming up from Fredericton, the traveler drives along next to the Miramichi River through a sparsely settled area devoted to lumbering and sports fishing. Eventually you come out at the sizable towns of Newcastle and Chatham on the lower river. Once shipbuilding and maritime centers, now they are supported by forest products and paper mills.

Suddenly, beyond these towns, out on the peninsula, English disappears and the visitor finds himself in the revived Acadia, where everyone speaks French and only the provincial road signs are bilingual.

Shippagan is one of the largest of the fishing ports that fringe the peninsula. The Marine Center ("Centre Marin" to the Acadians) is in a large modern brick building on the waterfront, north of the local branch of the University of Moncton and close to a great cluster of fishing-boat docks. The upper floors house a marine biological laboratory that focuses on the biol-

ogy and pathology of the economically important fish and shellfish found in the Gulf of St. Lawrence. The fisheries museum and aquarium, both open to the public, are on the ground floor.

The museum portion, although relatively small, is of considerable interest, with models, drawings, photographs, photmurals, and motion pictures. Here are some things to look for:

- The local fishing-boat models portray various types of power trawlers and net fishermen. While well made and detailed, unfortunately they lack captions. Information on how and where each type is used would add greatly to their interest.
- The full size mock-up of the wheelhouse of an ultra-modern fishing vessel. It gives a dramatic picture of the advanced technology used by today's fisherman and is crammed with gleaming instruments of every description. While the visitor can identify some of the more obvious radars, here again explanatory identifications would add a great deal to the interest.
- The inflated rubber raft with canopy, outside the wheelhouse, is laid out and surrounded by its complete outfit of survival gear. The raft is a quiet reminder that despite all the fancy electronics, fishermen and their boats must still cope with disaster.
- A whole bay of photographs clearly explains the building of both wooden and steel fishing vessels.
- Excellent big photos and diagrams show the varous types of fishing gear and how they are used, along with the major varieties of fish.

One museum show not to be missed is a great audiovisual presentation of the historical background of the Gulf of St. Lawrence fisheries and the role of the Acadian fishermen. The aquarium is also first class; note particularly the enormous lobster lurking in the bottom of one of the first tanks you come to.

Marine Center/Centre Marin is located on the waterfront on the north side of Shippagan, New Brunswick. Open May 1 to September 3, Monday-Friday, 10 a.m. to 6 p.m.; balance of the year by appointment. Admission: $3.00; seniors, $2.00; 6-16, $1.50. Gift shop/bookstore. Sponsored by the New Brunswick Provincial Department of Fisheries, Marine Center, C.P. 360, Shippagan, New Brunswick, E0B 2P0, Canada. Telephone (506) 336-4771.

To get a picture of maritime activity in little coastal New Brunswick towns a century ago, take the road southward along the shore of the Gulf of St. Lawrence to the Moncton turn off that will lead you eventually to the Albert County Museum at Hopewell Cape on the Petitcodiac River.

In addition to the Saint John River and the adjacent coasts, a second important area of Fundy shipbuilding in New Brunswick was at the very head of the bay. There, along the more northerly of the two estuaries into which Fundy divides at its head, ships were laid down at every small village with access to timber, particularly along the Petitcodiac River, which connects the sizable city of Moncton with the bay. Records tend to be scanty, but local historians estimate that more than 270 square-rigged vessels—more than 82 thousand tons of ships—were built in the area, plus some 160 schooners.

Some 40 of these vessels, including ships, barks, and brigs, were launched at the little village of Hopewell, now known as Hopewell Cape, on the west shore of the Petitcodiac. There, the great days when the area sent ships across the seven seas are recalled in the Albert County Museum, lodged in a sturdy building that was once the county jail. Like those of most historical society museums, the collection covers a wide range of local memorabilia, from farm tools to a folding bed, but the maritime exhibits are of particular interest: ship models, shipwrights' tools, navigation instruments, ship paintings, and many photographs of local vessels both under construction and in use.

The ship models include a full-rigged ship made by a disabled seaman in hospital around 1876. Of special interest are two small models of the four-masted bark *Andromeda*. When she made a voyage to Japan in 1889-90, four Hopewell Cape men were in the crew; one of them made the models many years later when he was a veteran of 90 recalling his youth at sea.

The museum also has plans and records of ships built in Albert County. The first shipbuilder at Hopewell Cape is said to have been a certain Captain Henry A. Calhoun, about whom little appears to be known but whose name certainly has a fine Cape Cod ring to it. Incidentally, a revealing anecdote makes it clear that shipowning was no royal road to riches. One old-timer gave a succinct account of the "return" on his investment in the large three-master *Gladys McLaughlin*, built locally in 1879. After an initial passage eastward across the Atlantic, the ship returned laden with coal to Barbados and then headed for Jamaica to pick up sugar, but en route she was wrecked on a coral reef and lost. As a shareholder in the ship, the informant was assessed nine dollars to bring home the *McLaughlin*'s crew.

The building that houses the Albert County Museum is of considerable interest in itself. Built in 1845, with 26-inch walls of cut stone, the massive little structure was the county jail for more than a century. The old cell block with steel-barred windows and massive doors remains as it was built in the mid-19th century.

Albert County Museum is in Hopewell Cape, a village on the west bank of the Petitcodiac River. Open June 15 to September 15, Monday-Sunday, 10 a.m. to 6 p.m.; Sunday, noon to 8 p.m. Admission: $1.00; children, 25 cents. Albert County Museum, Albert County Historical Society, Hopewell Cape, New Brunswick, Canada E0A 1Y0. Telephone (506) 734-2003.

From Hopewell Cape, the traveler must return to Moncton, then decide whether to continue north to the Cape Tormentine ferry to Prince Edward Island, or drive eastward to Nova Scotia. We'll vote for the ferry and P.E.I.

Prince Edward Island

One morning as usual we all went out to our trawls. It was thick with fog. All returned but one dory. The men in the lost dory were Eddie Muise 16, Saul Spinny 45. Our Capt was heart broken, a man who loved his crew. We stayed at anchor for two days, while I stayed on the mast head, only coming down for my meals, watching the fishing vessels, if they had a signal of our men. The Capt fired 24 lbs. of powder as a signal for the men, but of no avail . . . . When we came into harbor, Capt went ashore and phoned around with no word of his men . . . . To the surprise of us all, the men turned up . . . . A Norwegian Bark was bound up to some part of New Brunswick, passing along the North Shore of P.E.I., when her Capt had a dream that bothered him. He drempt he seen two men in a dory, such a course and so many miles. He ordered the mate to swing off the ship to the course he drempt. The mate objected, but the course was run. The Capt put over his log and run his miles, hove his ship to, got his spy-glass, and sighted our men. They were out 48 hours, and in bad shape. He took them aboard, gave them a little wine, but no other foods for a few hours, took the men and dory off to Souris, and the dory was left there.

Capt Henry Dicks of Georgetown bought the dory, took her down to the Labrador, and both him and his

son were lost on her. It is a ticklish thing on the banks
or in heavy sea if you do not handle your dory aright.
A safe boat if handled right.

John Hemphill, "Some of My Experiences at Sea,"
in *The Island*, No. 11, 1982.

So, in his old age, a Prince Edward Island
fisherman recalled his first trip in a
banks schooner. As might be expected,
fishing has always been important for
the Island people since the days when it
was Ile St.-Jean and colonized by the
French. Together with the building of
wooden ships, many of them for sale abroad, fishing
has given Prince Edward a lively maritime tradition.

As indeed Prince Edward should have, set as the
island is in the Gulf of St. Lawrence, its jagged crescent
shape matching the great curving bight of the
mainland at the southern end of the gulf. The
Northumberland Strait, 9 to 30 miles wide, separates
the island from Nova Scotia and New Brunswick and
has given Prince Edward, which is only 145 miles long
by 34 miles wide, its status as a separate province. The
island's landmass is further diminished by deep indentations from the sea that divide it into three roughly equal parts, with a total area slightly greater than the
state of Delaware.

During the first century of French settlement the
island saw few Europeans save occasional wandering
fishermen and fur traders. French attempts to get the
Acadians to move there in the early 18th century were
largely unsuccessful, although in 1721 Acadian
craftsmen built the first three vessels launched on the
island: a 25-ton craft for local fishing, a 65-tonner to
carry fish and lumber to the West Indies, and a 100-ton
vessel to trade with Europe.

These three marked the small beginning of what
was to become Prince Edward Island's great 19th-
century industry, the building of wooden ships. Not
until after the British conquest when English, Scottish,
and Irish immigrants began to fill up the empty island
did shipbuilding become a dynamic and successful industry, using the fine forests that were being cleared
away for farmland. In the early years British capital
supplied the financing, and British shipwrights, emi-
grating across the Atlantic, supplied the skills. For
many decades, Britain was also the major market for
the ships; sailed eastward across the Atlantic on their
maiden voyages, they were snapped up as bargains by
British shipowners.

From 1800 to 1810, 35 ships were built on Prince
Edward Island, the largest only 245 tons. By the height
of the building boom in the decades of the 1860s, more
than 900 vessels were turned out by some 60 island
shipyards. From then on, wooden shipbuilding

declined here as everywhere as owners turned first to
iron and then to steel hulls. But in the flourishing years
from 1830 to 1864, Prince Edward Island launched an
average of 70 vessels a year, for a total of 2,363
bottoms, 400,000 tons of ships.

Today, the islanders still build ships—steel fishing
trawlers—but not on the grand scale of their Victorian
predecessors. The fleets of wooden ships turned out
on Prince Edward Island are well remembered,
however. The last of them to survive in Britain, where
so many were bought, was the brigantine *Sela*, built in
1859 and broken up only in 1976. Her ironwork was
saved and sent back across the Atlantic to the fine little
museum that cherishes the relics of Prince Edward
Island shipbuilding: the Green Park Shipbuilding
Museum near the small village of Port Hill.

First, however, a note on how to get to Prince
Edward Island. The most convenient way to reach the
island by auto from any point in New Brunswick is via
the ferry from Cape Tormentine, N.B., to Borden,
P.E.I. This line operates all year, although with a
reduced winter schedule. The trip, in fine large
vessels, takes from 45 minutes to an hour, depending
on the season. Call 1-800-565-9470, toll-free, for
schedules and rates.

From Nova Scotia points, the most convenient
crossing is by auto ferry from Caribou, N.S. (near
Pictou) to Wood Islands, P.E.I. This line also operates
handsome modern vessels, but only from May 1 to
mid-December. Crossing time is about an hour and a
quarter. For information phone (902) 566-3000.

If the visitor takes the east ferry, landing at Wood
Islands, it is suggested that the P.E.I. museums be
visited in reverse sequence from the one in the following section of the guide. Now, back to our report on the
Green Park Museum.

Today, the busy Prince Edward Island yards that
over decades turned out hundreds of wooden ships
have gone with the island forests that supplied their
timbers. Some of the mansions built by the island's
shipbuilding and shipowning magnates remain,
however, and Green Park is one of them. Here, visitors
will find a small museum and a nearby recreation of
portions of the owner's 19th century shipyard, with a
partially constructed schooner on the ways.

Green Park originally belonged to one of Prince
Edward Island's richest and most powerful shipbuilding and shipowning families, the Yeos. The first James
Yeo came over from Devon, England, early in the 19th
century and, according to some accounts, proceeded
to make his fortune in ways that showed that not all
ruthless tycoons lived in Texas. An ex-alcoholic, highly
intelligent, and—according to his critics—none too
scrupulous but a hard worker, Yeo started as an agent
for a British investor. Somehow he acquired a small

lumber business, a store, and a schooner, which he proceeded to parlay into a fortune in land and ships that made him the island's richest man and Sir James.

Yeo and his sons, the oldest of whom managed the English end of the business back in Devon, were responsible for building some 35 ships. The majority were sold in England; the rest were used to carry lumber, fish, and livestock to Britain and bring back both immigrants and manufactured goods to be sold in the Yeo store.

The mansion of Green Park was built by James Yeo, Jr.; several of the Yeo shipyards—there were six altogether—were nearby. Now the estate has become a public park and museum. The house, built in 1865, has been restored and furnished with contemporary Prince Edward Island pieces. While the mansion may not be of direct maritime interest, it gives a fascinating glimpse of the high style of a mid-Victorian shipping magnate.

However, the story of the Yeo's maritime activities and the golden age of Prince Edward Island's shipbuilding is told in the modest museum in the Interpretive Centre on the Green Park grounds. Small but well-arranged, the Centre uses graphic displays, photographs, ship models, and artifacts to illustrate 19th century shipbuilding methods and the life-styles of the shipbuilders, as well as the influence of the industry on Prince Edward Island history.

Among the exhibits are builders' half models used at Prince Edward Island yards, shipwrights' tools, and a photo sequence showing step-by-step the construction of a wooden ship. An unusual display of samples of many different species of Prince Edward Island woods used in shipbuilding is accompanied by clear explanations of what each wood was used for and why.

A map shows the 130 places on Prince Edward Island where there were shipyards. Many of the vessels they turned out can be seen in a fine collection of photographs of Prince Edward Island ships from 1852 to 1920.

The Green Park shipbuilding site by the shore is within easy walking distance of the Interpretive Centre. Here a 75-foot schooner hull is shown in an early stage of construction: keel laid out and the stern and frames set up on it. The hull is based on the half model of a two-masted Prince Edward Island schooner of 150 tons preserved in Britain's National Maritime Museum at Greenwich.

Two small, shingled buildings nearby contain reconstructions of a shipyard's blacksmith and carpenter shops, complete with the special tools of their trades. Here also are the traditional sawpits used for sawing planks and the steam box used to soften them so they could be bent around the frames to sheath the hull.

The original Yeo yard at Green Park launched 24 vessels; it was probably located somewhat further down the open estuary where the water was deeper. The Green Park itself is beautiful, with great sweeps of close-clipped lawns, stands of handsome trees, and views out across the water—an arm of Malpeque Bay, source of the famous Malpeque oysters.

Green Park Shipbuilding Museum is on the one-time estate of wealthy shipbuilder James Yeo, Jr., near the village of Port Hill, facing Malpeque Bay on Prince Edward Island's northwest shore. Open mid-June to Labor Day, daily; 10 a.m. to 6 p.m. Admission: $1.50 (Canadian); children, 50 cents. Part of the decentralized museum system of the Prince Edward Island Museum and Heritage Foundation. The Green Park Shipbuilding Museums and Shipyard, Port Hill, Prince Edward Island, C1A 7I9 Canada. Telephone (902) 831-2206 (winter phone (902) 892-9127).

Visitors who want to see more of Prince Edward Island and get a feel for its maritime past and present may want to visit the "Sea Rescue Park" at Northport, a little fishing village. Northport is located at the far western end of the island where the coastline bends north to terminate at North Cape.

As he approaches Northport village, the visitor suddenly comes upon a heroic statue of a seaman at the helm of his ship beside the quiet country road. A bronze tablet tells the story of the sea rescue that stirred the little village long ago:

On the morning of Nov. 16, 1906, the residents of this community awoke to learn that the A.J. McKean, a vessel of 60 tons, was being shipwrecked on the north bar. Gale force winds and tumultuous waves were fast battering her to pieces. It was apparent to those on shore that if help was to be given, it must be at once. Ten men responded and quickly took their places at the oars of a seine boat. The sight of the men, hanging to the rigging of the doomed vessel, spurred their efforts until finally they arrived within a few yards of the stricken vessel. By signs, because it was impossible to make their voices heard above the gale, they gave the crew orders to fasten a rope to the foremast. Grasping the rope firmly, each man in turn, leaped into the sea. Eager hands reached to pull him to safety. Captain Des Roches was lost however. Valiant efforts were made to save him, but a gigantic wave parted the vessel amidship and he was swept out to sea.

For bravery beyond the call of duty these men were awarded watches and medals by the government of Canada.

The tablet, erected in 1979, goes on to list the two captains and nine men who took part in the rescue.

After this striking introduction, the Sea Rescue Park seemed to one recent visitor something of an anticlimax. The park is a pleasant rough meadow sloping down to the water in the middle of the village. A small neat wooden structure at one end is labeled "Historic Sea Rescue Building." Local informants said it had once stood at the end of a wharf and housed the local lifeboat, but had been moved to the park to preserve it. One section of the building was locked, in the remainder were stored old nets and fishing gear.

A large lifeboat was mounted in the center of the park. According to a tourist brochure, this is the boat that performed the rescue 80 years ago, but to an admittedly inexpert eye it looked much more like a conventional ship's lifeboat of the type carried by passenger liners, with hooks for falls and so forth. A local informant, grandson of a member of the rescue crew, agreed that it was not the original boat but had been placed there relatively recently.

All of which is not to say that Northport is not worth a visit: It is a genuine working fishing village. A boat builder and a fish dealer—the latter with marvelous Malpeque oysters—are next door to the park; fishing boats are hauled out of the water beside stacks of lobster pots; other craft cluster at the wharves. At the Community Center, a block away, there is an ancient photograph of the rescue crew proudly displayed by the grandson, now himself in later middle age. "A good many of their descendents live around here still," he says.

Fishing, of course, had its beginnings far back in Prince Edward Island history. In the later stages of French rule, after Nova Scotia had been surrendered to Britain, Acadians began to move north to the island and some became fishermen along the north coast. Eventually, when the island came under British rule, most of the French-speaking settlers were deported or fled to the mainland. A few hundred Acadian fishermen did remain, though: the ancestors of a substantial portion of the Prince Edward Island population today.

Rich fishing grounds, the many shallow banks in the Gulf of St. Lawrence, lay at the island's door. A British Army doctor who visited Prince Edward in 1801 recorded in his diary: "The Sea surrounding this Island abounds with Fish. Fishing Craft in considerable number come every year from the United States and return with full Cargoes. The principal fish are Cod and Rock Cod, Dog Fish, Herrings, Mackerel, Bass, & Haddock, and in the rivers and bays, Salmon, Sturgen, Perch and Ells. The shellfish are, Lobsters, Oysters, Clams, Rasor Fish & Muscles. Lobsters & Oysters are in such abundance that a middling size Boat may be laden with them in 2 or 3 Hours. They are however inferior in flavour to those of Europe."

But in the early decades under the Union Jack, the new settlers who came out from the British Isles were apparently not attracted to the rugged fishermen's life. Schooners came swarming up from Gloucester and Cape Cod, however, to harvest the fish-rich waters, often in defiance of British laws. According to a local historian, the islanders were criticized because they found it more profitable to service these illegal visitors, who paid cash for bait and gear, "than taking to the sea on their own." And when islanders did go to sea, they found fishing with the Yankees paid better than in local vessels. The extent of this peaceful invasion from south of the border was dramatically illustrated when a great storm hit in October, 1851: 72 American fishing boats were either driven ashore on Prince Edward Island or took refuge in its harbors.

After the ending of a reciprocity treaty with the United States in the mid-1860s, however, island fishing began to boom. From 1870 to 1880, the number of local fishing boats increased about two and a half times, while the number of Prince Edward Island fishermen multiplied four-fold.

For the past century, fishing and lobstering have been an important element in the economy of Prince Edward Island. Both past and present are celebrated at the Basin Head Fisheries Museum near Souris at the far eastern end of the island. Incidentally, the town, an active fishing port on Northumberland Strait, was named for an invasion of mice that ate up the settlers' crops way back when the island was Ile St.-Jean, early in the 18th century.

The little road to the Basin Head Fisheries Museum turns off to the south from the main highway, Route 16, east of Souris. At its end, the visitor finds himself on a high bluff beside a small tidal estuary that cuts through the fine beach at the foot of the bluff and reaches the sea between two breakwaters. Once this was a tiny but active fishing port, but the bar across the channel entrance repeatedly silted up and today there is only one fishing boat left.

The main museum building, the "Interpretive Center," looks out across the water at the seaward end of the bluff, with a marvelous view across Northumberland Strait to where the highlands of Cape Breton Island are dim in the distance. The museum exhibits include many dioramas showing fishing techniques, fishing gear, small craft, ship models, tools, engines, and photographs; the whole covers what would seem to be every aspect of Prince Edward Island fishing from the days of the banks schooners.

The visitor should plan to spend some time exploring for himself, but here are just a sampling of exhibits not to be missed:

• Dioramas illustrate the major commercial fishing techniques. Most of these show a cross section of ocean—a boat or vessel on the surface, controlling nets or lines seeking the fish below. Of special historical interest is the diorama of fishermen sun-drying salt fish on racks set up on the shore, the traditional method that goes back 500 years to the first fishermen who crossed the Atlantic from Europe each summer.

- A collection of stone fishing-spear heads, arrowheads, clam openers found in the area carries the island's fisheries far back into prehistory. Some of these Stone Age tools have been identified as having been made by craftsmen of the Archaic People who lived on Prince Edward island 10,000 years ago.
- A most unusual collection of Bruce Stewart motors will fascinate the engine freak.
- A wall display of half-hull models of skeg and plank boats illustrates the differences between the various types.

For many visitors, the high point will be the museum's collection of regional small craft, ranging up to 34-footers. These include specialized types such as oystermen's boats. They can be viewed, along with fishing gear, in a long line of boat sheds along the west side of the museum grounds. The boat collection continues to grow as more specimens are added.

Another building on the grounds houses the newest addition to the site—a mini-factory for making the little wooden boxes that for generations were the standard packaging for salt fish. A box, roughly eight inches by four with a sliding top, can be bought on the spot. If you don't happen to have any salt cod to keep in it, a box makes a handy holder for pens, pencils, paper clips, and miscellania.

At the foot of the bluff beside the small river is yet another museum facility: an old cannery building where visitors can watch demonstrations of how fish are filleted, salted, and smoked, carried out by a fisherman affiliated with the museum. The building also houses an aquarium where visitors can see living examples of such local fish as cod, hake, sole, and herring, not to mention eels.

On the wharves along the river edge the museum has several sheds for the gear of local fishermen. Visitors arriving early in the morning can go out on a fishing trip from the port, handling lines and nets "with a little jigging on the side." There is no charge for these day trips of hands-on commercial fishing.

Basin Head Fisheries Museum, on the Northumberland Strait shore of Prince Edward Island, between the fishing port of Souris and East Point, the end of the island. Guided tours. Gift shop and bookstore. Open June 20 to September 4, Sunday-Friday, 10 a.m. to 6 p.m.; September 6-22, Sunday-Thursday, 10 a.m. to 6 p.m. Admission: $1.50 (Canadian); children under 15, 50 cents. Museum is part of the decentralized museum system of the Prince Edward Island Museum and Heritage Foundation. Basin Head Fisheries Museum, P.O. Box 248, Souris, Prince Edward Island, C0A 2B0, Canada. Telephone (402) 357-2966.

Travelers with a love for remote, sea-girt fastnesses may want to take advantage of the fact that Souris is the departure point for steamers to the Magdalen Islands. A chain of seven main islands plus islets, connected by storm-washed sandy causeways, the Magdalens are about 50 miles north of Prince Edward Island in the center of rich Gulf of St. Lawrence fishing grounds. (The islands are politically part of the Province of Quebec.)

Jacques Cartier discovered them in 1534, and French and Basque fishermen, whalers, and walrus hunters camped there off and on, but the Magdalens were not permanently occupied until Acadian refugees settled there after their expulsion from Nova Scotia in the mid-18th century. Their French-speaking descendants are still there, some 13,000 of them crammed into 102 square miles, earning their living from the sea: catching cod, and freezing and exporting the fillets.

There have been many wrecks on and around the island over the centuries and these are a major theme of the Musée de la Mer, the maritime museum in Havre-Aubert, on the southernmost island. Devoted to the history of the island people, the museum's exhibits tell about the sailor's world, fish and fishing, and beachcombing. There are reconstructions of such shoreside workshops as a forge and a smokehouse that serviced the fishing fleet and processed the fish.

Musée de la Mer is at Havre-Aubert, on the southernmost of the Magdalen Islands, reached by steamer from Souris, P.E.I.; also from Montreal and Quebec. Open all year. June 15 to August 15, Sunday-Friday, 9 a.m. to 5 p.m.; Saturday, 2 to 5 p.m. Balance of year, Monday-Friday, 9 a.m. to 5 p.m.; Saturday-Sunday, 2 to 4 p.m. Musée de la Mer, Casse Postale 69, Havre-Aubert, Iles-de-la-Madeleine, Quebec G0B 1J0, Canada. Telephone (418) 931-5711.

And now for Nova Scotia and the historic part of Halifax, which has two fine maritime museums. From the eastern end of Prince Edward Island the most convenient route to Nova Scotia is via the Wood Islands Ferry to Caribou, Nova Scotia.

Acadia/Nova Scotia

Si l'homme veut avoir une heureuse fortune
Il lui faut implorer le secours de Neptune
Car celui qui chez soi demeure casanier
Merite seulement le nom de cuisinier!

If man would wish to make his fortune
He must implore the help of Neptune.
A lubber who won't quit his own house
Deserves no better name than louse!

So, with this invocation of the god of the sea, began one of the oldest maritime histories in North America: that of the long rocky peninsula projecting into the Atlantic Ocean, once Acadia, now Nova Scotia. The occasion was a most unlikely performance of amateur theatricals: a masque in verse presented by a little group of Frenchmen at what was at the moment the only European settlement in the entire North American wilderness north of Florida, a tiny fur trading post with a big name—Port Royal. The actors were soldiers, sailors, traders, artisans, gentlemen—adventurers all—dressed up in homemade costumes as Neptune, Tritons, and Indians. The masque, *The Muses of New France*, was written by a lawyer member of the garrison to welcome the return of an exploring party that had sailed down the New England coast. The performance was on November 14, 1606, two years before Jamestown was settled, 14 years before the *Mayflower* arrived at Plymouth Harbor.

The inspired thespians of the 1606 masque could not claim to have founded the first permanent settlement in North America other than the Spanish colonies; politics back in France led to the abandonment of Port Royal the following year. By the time the buildings were reoccupied in 1610, Jamestown had won its place in the history books. In the years that followed, Port Royal was occupied off and on by the French, looted and burned by the English, and even occupied for four years by a party of Scots with a grant from James I. The latter's only permanent contribution was the name Nova Scotia (New Scotland), by which the province is known today. Only after 1632 were there permanent settlements of French-speaking farmers in the Port Royal area; but the farmers eventually prospered and expanded their lands into the legendary L'Acadie, or Acadia. (Whether Acadia referred to the region of ancient Greece admired for its rustic simplicity, or was a corruption of a Micmac Indian word meaning "place" is hotly disputed.)

By now it was clear that Father Neptune was to play a decisive role in the affairs of Nova Scotia/Acadia. The bounty of the sea brought Europeans to these shores in the first place, and the fisheries have been a mainstay of the province ever since. Control of the sea determined which flag would fly over the province. Until very recent times, the sea and its tributary rivers provided the highways for trade and travel; from one town to another, from the province to the rest of the world. And in Nova Scotia's most prosperous days, the commerce of the seas called for ships from Nova Scotia's yards—and tough Nova Scotian mariners to be their masters.

Fisheries, sea power, transportation, shipbuilding and shipowning—these are the four strands of Nova Scotia's maritime history.

Fisheries. Fishermen from overseas had frequented these coasts long before there were settlements ashore. Eventually, New Englanders followed in their little ketches and shallops, and, later, schooners and set up their cod-drying racks in the coves along Nova Scotia's Atlantic coast and in the Gut of Canso, which separates Cape Breton Island from the mainland. During the period of French rule, officials were powerless to stop the Yankees. According to historian W.S. MacNutt, New Englanders felt they had an "inalienable right" to these lands—not for settlement; just the opposite—to keep the region free of settlement for the convenience of their fishery.

The year 1712 saw Acadia surrender to British control and become Nova Scotia, with Annapolis Royal, ex-Port Royal, as its capital. By the middle of the 18th century, Yankees from Cape Cod and Cape Ann were settling along the coast with encouragement from the British government. Farming and fishing went hand in hand. To quote Andrew Hill Clark, a geographer/historian: ". . . that most of Nova Scotia's farmers, for most of its history, remained part-time farmers, with one hand ready to lay on the tiller of a fishing skiff and the other on a woodsman's axe, is to a great degree the result of the fact that farming alone, on the generally indifferent soils and with the limitations imposed by climate, land forms, and drainage, yielded too scanty a living or asked too high a competitive price, in labor and investment."

After the expulsion of the Acadians, who were driven into exile by the British authorities when they refused to swear allegiance to King George, more maritime-minded Yankees moved in and local fishing boomed.

By the 19th century, the fisheries were a major source of income. Farmer/fishermen in small boats worked the inshore fisheries and produced fresh fish for local consumption and bait for the offshore fishermen. The latter went off to the banks—in the Atlantic, the Gulf of Maine, or the Gulf of St. Lawrence—or further, to the shores of Labrador or Newfoundland. Shallops gave way to pinks, pinks to schooners, and schooners ultimately to motor trawlers and draggers. Traditionally, the fish were dried and salted to preserve them for shipment overseas, where the major market was in the West Indies. Today, of course, refrigeration and quick freezing have changed the picture.

Still vitally important to the economy of the province, Nova Scotia fisheries today include lobstering, herring gill netting, and scallop dragging, all inshore fisheries, besides those offshore. Actually, scallops and lobsters bring in more dollars than the traditional cod of the offshore fishermen. With some 3,800 men in the offshore fisheries, 7,500 more fishing inshore, and 4,500 people working in the fish processing plants ashore, the industry is the mainstay of many a tiny coastal town. Canada is the world's largest exporter of fish, and in 1978 more than $185 million worth came from Nova Scotia. A map of fishing ports shows more than 400 along the Nova Scotia coast.

Sea Power. That the New Englanders were able to set up their fishing stations along the coast of Acadia reflected the weakness of French sea power. The only settlements, which consisted of farmers and fur traders, were French, and French rule predominated. But Acadia grew slowly. The main thrust of French settlement was to the northward where the St. Lawrence gave access to the fur-rich interior. English colonies grew in the happier climates and usually better farmland to the southwest in New England and beyond. Nova Scotia/Acadia lay between the two and along the seaward approaches to both of them from Europe. France and Britain each saw a threat if this strategic area were occupied by the other, but for a long time neither was able, or willing, to invest the large sums needed to defend these remote and isolated areas from attacks from hostile fleets.

So the pattern was set for a century and a half of Anglo-French conflict: sudden raids on coastal villages; fishermen seized and their shore stations burned by privateers (pirates, according to their enemies); naval squadrons maneuvering off the coasts. At the climax, the conflict led to wild harbors being turned into great naval bases by one or other of the two powers, and defended by massive citadels.

In general, the British—and New Englanders—were dominant at sea; the French and their Indian allies had the upper hand on land. In a century, Acadia endured some 10 attacks from the sea, some of which devastated Port Royal. Some were British attacks; many were by New Englanders

enraged by French and Indian raids on their frontier villages or by losing ships to French privateers based in the Port Royal Basin. It was a New England amphibious force that eventually attacked and captured Port Royal in 1710 and made it British Annapolis Royal for good and all.

And sea power continued to be a major factor in the maritime activities of the region. Cape Breton Island, at the eastern end of Nova Scotia, had remained French and there the French government tried to make up for the loss of Acadia by building a great fortress to protect the fine harbor at Louisburg. As the Anglo-French wars continued, both England and New England saw Louisburg as a threat. Twice it was captured by amphibious task forces: by New Englanders the first time, then traded back in return for advantages to Britain elsewhere. To counter French Louisburg, Britain now built a great naval and military base on an empty bay on the Atlantic coast of Nova Scotia. Named Halifax, it became the base for the second successful attack on Louisburg when the war with France was renewed. Soon after, Halifax became the staging area for the combined British Army/Navy expedition against Quebec, the final campaign in the destruction of the French empire in North America.

From then on, Halifax was a central element in the Royal Navy's control of the North Atlantic. In the later wars with the rebellious American colonies, with Napoleon, and with the newly-formed United States, Halifax was the base from which Britain controlled the coasts of North America.

Trade and Transportation. From the earliest days, even the farmers and fur traders were basically dependent upon the sea and the rivers. In daily life, rivers and streams were the only practical highways. Visitors commented on how skilled were the Acadians—men, women, and children alike—in handling birch bark canoes; heavy loads were carried in wooden skiffs. And small coastal vessels, hopping from cove to cove along the rugged Atlantic coast, brought supplies and carried away the furs from the trading posts.

Maritime trade was even more important to the Acadians in providing a source of supplies and a market for their crops. New Englanders tended to dominate Acadia's maritime activities in peace as well as in war. Boston, a few days sail away, was far closer than Quebec, which lay beyond hundreds of miles of wild forests, and the Acadians were farmers, not seagoers. Between raids, the little New England vessels brought to Acadia European manufactured goods and West Indian rum and sugar to trade for surplus farm products.

After the British conquest, the sea remained the

common highway for better than 150 years. Not until the coming of automobiles and trucks, and the eventual construction of highways to serve them, did the little coastal schooners lose their essential role as the common freight carriers on the province.

Shipbuilding and Shipowning. While the Acadians built little boats for fishing and travel, it was the influx of Yankees in the mid-18th century that really got shipbuilding started. Many of them had built ships in the small coastal towns of the Massachusetts Bay Colony and in their new homes they found fine ship timbers ready for the cutting in untouched forests. Later, their skills were augmented by those of a new flood of Americans, Loyalist refugees this time, at the end of the American Revolution. At the turn of the century, a great influx of Scots brought yet more skilled shipbuilders.

With skilled craftsmen, forests close at hand to provide ship timbers, and plenty of sites along the shores of protected harbors to set up shipyards, 19th-century Nova Scotia became one of the world's great centers of shipbuilding. All around the province, but particularly along the shores of Northumberland Strait on the north coast, in the little towns along the Minas Basin at the head of the Bay of Fundy, and along the south coast facing the Atlantic, wooden ships slid down the ways. Some were built for local owners, but many were for sale abroad, especially in Britain.

On the Minas Basin alone more than 213 vessels were built between 1843 and 1893. Here, Nova Scotian shipbuilding reached its heroic climax in 1874 when the great ship *W.D. Lawrence*, 2,459 tons, was launched in Maitland. In 1876, Nova Scotians owned 2,867 vessels, totalling 529,252 tons, giving the province a larger per capita tonnage of shipping than any nation in the world. Ships, ship-masters, and seamen from Nova Scotia became known on every trade route.

Ultimately, steel and iron shipbuilding and the triumph of steam propulsion dealt fatal blows to the builders and owners of Nova Scotia's wooden windjammers.

Of the four strands of Nova Scotia's maritime activities—fisheries, sea power, trading and transportation, shipbuilding and shipowning—the fisheries remain the most important in the life of the province. Sea power is still a matter of concern: The NATO navies use Halifax as a base in their defense of the North Atlantic. Trading schooners and coastal steamers were familiar sights until the recent past; now automobiles and trucks have taken over their functions. Ships, particularly large fishing vessels, are still built and owned in the province, but it is no longer a world shipping center.

The memory of all these things is cherished in the province and their relics are carefully preserved. Nova Scotia possesses two maritime museums of the first rank, and a number of smaller collections that are of more than local interest. The maritime-minded traveler will find many places to visit—and in his visits he is likely to gain new perspectives on the role played by the sea in the history of North America.

Two things the visitor to Halifax notices immediately: the magnificent harbor spread out at his feet, and the great granite citadel up the steep hill above him. The two are inextricably linked in history. The harbor is the reason Halifax is on this spot. The citadel was built to guard the harbor.

For Halifax is unique among the great ports of North America. The city did not have its start as a trading post, or as a refuge for religious exiles, or as a commercial center serving inland settlements. From its very beginnings, Halifax was conceived as a great military and naval base, a place where regiments of redcoats and fighting ships of the Royal Navy could be maintained within easy striking distance of the traditional enemy, the French in Canada. And specifically within striking distance of Louisburg, the great French fortress to the northeast, on Cape Breton Island. The "Dunkirk of the West," as it was called, comparing it to the great fortified French naval base on the English Channel.

Halifax came into being overnight in 1749 when a fleet of 16 ships sailed into the broad empty bay of Chebucto on the Atlantic coast side of Nova Scotia. Despite the fine harbor, the shores had remained empty; the early settlers preferred smaller harbors where their trading posts or fishing stations could be more easily defended against pirates that roved the coasts, or, in wartime, against attacks by French privateers.

Now, however, the troops and ships were on hand to defend a base big and strong enough to defy any force that could be brought against it. New Englanders had been particularly eager to have the new base built. An expedition of New England troops had captured Louisburg from the French in 1745, only to see it returned—repaired and rebuilt—to France in the peace treaty of 1748. Britain made the deal in return for advantages elsewhere, but New England was furious: Not only had its young men died in battle—and its treasure been spent—for nothing, but its fishermen and their vessels and stations along the coast were again exposed to French harassment from Louisburg. The only British post of any significance in Nova Scotia was Fort Anne at Annapolis Royal on the Fundy side, and that was useless in protecting the Atlantic coast.

All this began to change as the ships put the troops and laborers ashore in Chebucto, now renamed Halifax to honor the English politician who had pushed the project. On the hill rose the first of a long series of fortresses to be built on the site over many decades, each one embodying the latest in military technology. Along the shore below, a naval dockyard with its workshops, and ultimately a dry dock, came into being to service the King's ships. Between, on the steep hillside, a town was laid out, with barracks for the troops and houses for the settlers.

Halifax had a hard birth. Most of the original 2,800 settlers recruited by the government were poor Londoners, utterly unprepared and unsuited for building a frontier town from scratch on a windswept hillside. The first winter, typhus swept the settlement and 1,000 died—more than one in three. But the British government pushed on. Protestant farmers arrived from France and the Rhineland, Yankees came up from New England, some to fish, some to trade. Frame houses were bought in Boston and Portsmouth, New Hampshire, taken apart, shipped up, and reassembled. Gradually, the town and the docks and the fort to guard them took shape. By 1755, Halifax had become the great advanced base for the final British onslaught on French Canada. Privateers harried French shipping to Louisburg and the St. Lawrence. In 1758, ships and troops moved out of Halifax eastward up the coast to besiege Louisburg. When that great fortress of New France was captured—for the second time—it was demolished and the stonework taken to build the houses of Halifax. And a year later, Halifax was again the base for another great combined-forces expedition, this time against Quebec itself, the final blow that ended French rule in Canada.

So, only ten years after Halifax's foundation, the threat that called the town into being had been blown away. But Halifax survived, and for the greater part of its history the city retained much of its original character: a garrison town and when the King's ships were in, a Navy town. Although the capital of Nova Scotia then as now, in its early days, soldiers and seamen outnumbered civilians five to one and Halifax in the 1760s was reputed to be the most wicked town in North America. When the British fleet that had captured Havana came into Halifax and spent the winter of 1762-63, the men had received the immense sum of £400,000 in prize money. As they spent it carousing in taverns and whorehouses, they made Halifax, in the words of a contemporary observer, "more like a pirate's rendezvous" than a proper naval base.

The French were gone, but Halifax soon proved a most valuable base for dealing with other threats to British hegemony. When the redcoats who had occupied Boston to punish it for rebellious acts were forced to evacuate the city in 1776, the Royal Navy escorted them back to Halifax. With them came the first wave of what was to become a flood of emigrants—Massachusetts Loyalists fleeing the wrath of their neighbors, to whom they were "Tories."

In the war thus begun, the American Revolution, Halifax was the sole base securely in the grasp of the British forces in North America. Transports carrying troops to suppress the rebellion in the colonies to the southward put in at Halifax for orders and supplies. The Naval Dockyard maintained and repaired the warships that controlled the American coast for most of the war. British and Nova Scotian privateers brought their prizes into Halifax—as many as 48 in a single year. American and French prisoners captured in the 13 colonies were brought here.

With the independence of the former British colonies at the end of the American Revolution, Halifax remained the only base for the Royal Navy on the Atlantic coast of North America. During the Napoleonic Wars and the War of 1812, the port was the northern base for the British fleet in the western Atlantic and the place where convoys of merchantmen were made up for the Atlantic crossing. When HMS *Shannon* captured the American frigate *Chesapeake* in 1813, the prize was brought into Halifax. British and Nova Scotian privateers sent in a steady flow of captured American and French merchant ships to be condemned by the Admiralty Court (one Halifax privateer alone took 33 American prizes), and the awards for captured ships and cargoes brought "a golden river" of prize money to the port.

Halifax remained a major base of the Royal Navy for more than a century. Over the years the warships flying the white ensign grew ever larger, sail gave way to steam, wooden ships to steel, bare hulls to armored. On the hilltop, the citadel was repeatedly rebuilt as guns grew bigger and military architecture adapted to them.

Finally, in the first decade of the 20th century, the Royal Navy withdrew to meet more pressing obligations elsewhere, and after a short interim the new Royal Canadian Navy took over.

During World War I, Halifax was the dispatching point for the endless flow of men, munitions, and supplies from Canada to the mother country. Here centered the war against the German U-boats in the western Atlantic, and here convoys formed up—as they had done during the Napoleonic Wars long before—to be shepherded to Britain. And here, on December 6, 1917, an ammunition ship caught fire and blew up in the midst of the crowded harbor; the tremendous blast leveled a large section of the city, killed 2,000 people, and left 6,000 homeless.

World War II saw Halifax again a center of convoy and antisubmarine activity; after Pearl Harbor the

United States Navy shared its facilities. Now Halifax is used by the combined naval forces of the NATO countries.

With its unusually concentrated tradition of naval activity, it is appropriate that Halifax should have a special museum dedicated to the Canadian forces afloat.

For much of the century and a half that Halifax was the Royal Navy's base in the western North Atlantic, the commander in chief of the station had his official residence in Admiralty House. A handsome stone mansion on the hill above the Naval Dockyard, it was built in 1815-18 in the contemporary Georgian style. After the Royal Navy gave up the Halifax station, the building served the Canadian Navy in various less exalted capacities. Now, as the Maritime Command Museum, it has been given duties befitting its venerable age and long association with the forces afloat.

The Maritime Command Museum is charged with collecting, preserving, and displaying artifacts and documents related to the history of the Canadian Maritime Military Forces—the new name given the Royal Canadian navy when the nation's navy, army, and air force were unified into one defense organization. The museum is also concerned with the major role long played by the Royal Navy in the history of Halifax. On display on the two main floors of the building and a good part of a third, are many ship models, dioramas, naval uniforms and insignia, prints, paintings, and photographs, weapons, and equipment, as well as memorabilia of the services.

The ship models are particularly interesting. They include:

- the first ship of the Canadian Navy, RCNS *Niobe*;
- very large—six to eight feet long—waterline models of a minesweeper and the Canadian Corvette *Halifax*;
- many destroyers and destroyer escorts.

Particularly interesting is a diorama giving a bird's-eye view of a great convoy leaving the harbor in World War II; this was a frequent event in Halifax, where convoys were made up for the dangerous crossing of the North Atlantic.

The many naval uniforms displayed include those of World War II WRENS (the Canadian/British equivalent of WAVES), the Volunteer Naval Reserve, and Chaplains. Navy buffs may be particularly interested in the display of today's uniforms, rank and rating insignia, and badges for persons serving with the Maritime Forces—now that there is no longer a Canadian Navy as such.

Other displays include a model gun turret and various light weapons. A whole room is devoted to drawings and paintings of ships and men of the Royal and Canadian Navies. Visitors will find on the landing of the stairs leading to the third floor, one exhibit that definitely sets the Royal Canadian Navy apart from its sister service in the United States—an enormous rum bucket, ready to hold the daily ration of grog.

Maritime Command Museum is on the hillside overlooking the Canadian Forces Base Halifax and the harbor. Admiralty House, containing the museum, is historic stone building in its own grounds on Gottingen Street, between North Street and Russell Street, five blocks north of the Citadel. Parking for visitors available on grounds. Library and archives. Open all year. September to June, weekdays only, 9:30 a.m. to 3:30 p.m.; July and August, Monday-Friday, 9:30 a.m. to 8:30 p.m., Saturday-Sunday, 1 p.m. to 5 p.m. Closed holidays. Admission: free. Maritime Command Museum, Admiralty House, CFB Halifax, Halifax, Nova Scotia B3K 2X0. Telephone (902) 426-5210.

The Naval Dockyard, the fighting ships it supported, and the garrison that guarded it long dominated the life and economy of Halifax, and are still important: in the mid-20th century, defense activities were the city's major source of income. But at the same time other maritime activities were growing over the years: fishing and fish processing, shipbuilding and repair, trade with Europe and the West Indies, transportation of immigrants. With its fine, ice-free harbor opening directly on the North Atlantic, Halifax eventually became Canada's doorway facing Europe.

Halifax's earliest merchants had been shrewd Yankees, up from the Bay Colony to explore the trade opportunities in the new fortress port. In these years before the American Revolution the ties with New England were close; Halifax bought its supplies in Boston rather than London. Many who came to Nova Scotia were already familiar with shipbuilding and with the West Indian trade—fish and lumber to the plantations in return for rum, sugar, and molasses—and used their experience to advantage in their new home.

During and after the Revolution more Americans came to Halifax—a flood of Loyalist refugees. Many drifted away, but some stayed on and built up the mercantile activities of the port. And with the old trade and political ties with the former colonies now broken, Halifax turned to ships, shipping, and overseas trade.

The demand for ships during the early stages of the Napoleonic Wars gave a boost to the infant shipbuilding industry in Halifax, as elsewhere in Nova Scotia, and it has been a major activity ever since. Over the years the industry's prosperity has fluctuated with the world demand for shipping. The California gold rush followed by the Indian Mutiny, for example, led to boom times in the Nova Scotia yards as new ships from the Maritimes replaced vessels pressed into service to carry '49ers or, a few years later, British troops. In the mid-20th century, shipbuilding and repair was second only to defense as an income source.

The famous Cunard Line was born in Halifax, which became its first North American port. Samuel Cunard was a local man who had made a fortune from lumber and sailing ships. In 1838 Cunard bid on and secured a British government contract for a line of steamers to carry the mails between Britain, Halifax, and New York City. In May 1840, the oak-hulled Cunard steamer *Unicorn* steamed into Halifax harbor, 14 days out from Liverpool. Regular Cunard service began in July with the arrival of the SS *Britannia*.

With the arrival of a rail line connecting Halifax with the Great Lakes, the city really came into its own as Canada's major year-round port on the Atlantic, ice free when Montreal and Quebec on the St. Lawrence were frozen in. Passenger and freight lines connected the city to the United States, Europe, and the West Indies. Exports passed through from the mid-Canadian industrial and agricultural centers. Imports—and immigrants—poured in from Europe on their way west.

Today Halifax is not only the business, educational, and cultural center of the Maritime Provinces but continues to be a major Canadian port. The past and present maritime activities of Halifax, and of Nova Scotia as a whole, are the theme of a museum on the Halifax waterfront: It is the largest maritime museum in Canada and one of the finest and most interesting in North America.

The Maritime Museum of the Atlantic is one of a number of museums under the umbrella of the Nova Scotia Museum (itself in Halifax). Housed in a huge old waterfront building that once was a ship chandlery, it has a handsome new exhibition hall attached to provide more space for the rich and growing collection. The museum building backs onto its own wharves; here, its own exhibition ship, the SS *Acadia*, as well as occasional interesting visitors, are berthed.

The Halifax area along and near the waterfront is a maze of one-way streets. Water Street, on which the museum is located, is one-way north, so visitors should be sure to consult a city map and get well south of the museum before entering Water Street.

The museum is extremely well organized, with each of its six galleries focusing on a major topic. In addition, the SS *Acadia*, retired from a long career with the Canadian Hydrographic Survey, offers an opportunity to examine at close range a fine little steamship from the early years of the 20th century.

Here are some things not to be missed:

- The William Robertson & Son Shipchandlery is not a gallery or a reconstruction but the real thing, frozen in time. When the museum bought the building, it also bought the inventory and shop fittings of the retail ship-supply store fronting Water Street. Only minor changes have been made, mostly to restore it to the way it looked around 1910, and the visitor steps through the door into the past, with the counters, shelves, and inventory waiting to serve long-vanished vessels and their captains. Even the indescribable smell seems just right. As the enthusiastic staff member who tends the shop will tell you, old-timers come in and say, "Why, the only thing that's different about the shop is that it's a lot cleaner now." (Get the "shopkeeper" to show you how a boat broom is made from a single birch stick, the end split into wooden curls to do the sweeping.)

- The Navy Gallery is crammed with fine models of 20th-century vessels, but there are also the warships of earlier days. Lovers of sail will be particularly attracted to the handsome little *L'Agneau*, a French cutter captured by the British in 1805.

- The Shipwrecks and Lifesaving Gallery focuses on sinister Sable Island, that strip of fog-bound sand 100 miles off the Nova Scotia coast with perhaps the strongest claim of the several contestants for the title "Graveyard of the Atlantic." The lifeboat, beach gear, wreck photos, nameboards from Sable wrecks, are all of great interest—but don't overlook the public notice that was posted on the island listing the rules governing the behavior of shipwrecked sailors (the Superintendent of the Life-Saving Station was THE BOSS).

- In the Small Craft Gallery Queen Victoria's Royal Barge sits in regal dignity amid humbler craft. Admittedly the barge doesn't have much to do with the maritime heritage of Nova Scotia—after all Her Majesty never came over to be rowed around Halifax harbor—but as an example of beautiful craftsmanship it is a delight. Be sure to climb the open stair beside it for a look down at the magnificent carvings that decorate the interior.

Among the many other interesting exhibits here, small craft enthusiasts are likely to be especially interested in the gundalow. This flat-bottomed, double-ended "hayboat" bears no resemblance to either the gundalow *Edward Adams* in Portsmouth, New Hampshire, or the gondola *Philadelphia* in Washington's Museum of American History—

Figure 25
Ship chandlery in the building on the Halifax, Nova Scotia, waterfront purchased by the Maritime Museum of the Atlantic has been retained with its original fixtures and inventory of everything needed by small vessels in the early 20th century.

evidence of how loosely the name was applied at different times and places. (The name of these craft, originally derived from "gondola," was spelled and pronounced in different ways in different places.)

One other very unusual exhibit looms on the floor there—a windmill pump for shipboard use, displayed with a photograph of one mounted on the *Southern Belle*.

All these galleries are on the ground floor and all but the Chandlery are in the new Exhibition Hall. Now climb the stairs to the second-floor galleries.

- The Age of Steam Gallery is crowded with fine detailed models, most probably made for the owners, of many types of freighters and passenger liners. The most unusual portrays the

Armed Merchant Cruiser *Atlantis*. This German freighter was converted to a commerce raider in World War I and equipped with a variety of disguises that enabled her to sink 22 Allied ships. Accompanying drawings show how her appearance —particularly her silouhette— could be changed quickly from one type of merchant vessel to another, so that she kept one jump ahead of the warnings broadcast about her and could steam to an unsuspecting victim.

Another type rarely seen in models is a cattle ship, the SS *Shenandoah*, built in 1893.

- In The Days of Sail Gallery in the north end of the second floor in the Robertson building there is often an opportunity to see a skilled ship carver working on a figurehead or a fine piece of restoration in a well-equipped demonstration workshop. Here also is a rigger's shop, a very important maritime service in the days of the windjammers. Models portray a variety of ships, barks, and schooners. Notable among them are a fine waterline model of the ship *Tusker*; and a model of the bark *Colburger*, 1890, which in 1917 was the last square-rigged vessel still in service in Canada.

A diorama of a Port Greville shipyard with a vessel on the ways reminds us that shipbuilding is one of the strongest strands in Nova Scotia's maritime heritage. Perhaps most interesting of all is the deck house of the coastal schooner *Royo*, 1919, which has been reassembled on the floor of the gallery. The deckhouse is authentically furnished with marine stove, cabin table, and bunks for four, and the visitor suddenly imagines himself at sea as he hears the slap of waves and sees through the ports the horizon moving slowly up and down—both effects due to audiovisual technology.

The steamship *Acadia*, snug at the dock behind the museum, looks rather like a big handsome yacht, but is a veteran of a rugged 57-year career that included service with the Canadian Navy in both world wars. As a Hydrographic Survey vessel, she charted the coasts of the Atlantic Provinces and up into Hudson Bay. In service, her survey equipment was repeatedly updated with the latest electronics that are preserved just as she was when retired. Her triple-expansion steam engine, coal-fired, is of particular interest.

Maritime Museum of the Atlantic is between Duke and Sackville Streets on Lower Water Street, which runs along the Halifax waterfront one-way north. Public parking lot adjacent. Library. Small bookstore. Museum buildings open all year: May 15 to October 15, Monday, 9:30 a.m. to 5:30 p.m.; Tuesday, 9:30 a.m. to 8:00 p.m.; Wednesday-Saturday; 9:30 a.m. to 5 p.m.; Sunday, 1 to 5 p.m. *Acadia* open May 15 to October 15, closed the balance of the year. Admission: free. The maritime history branch of the Nova Scotia Museum, operated under the Educational Resources Program of the Nova Scotia Department of Education. Maritime Museum of the Atlantic, 1675 Lower Water Street, Halifax, Nova Scotia, Canada 33J 1S3. Telephone (902) 427-7740.

Fishing is the one marine activity not covered in the Maritime Museum of the Atlantic. This is because fishing is so important in Nova Scotia's past and present that an entire separate museum has been dedicated to it: the Fisheries Museum of the Atlantic, down the coast from Halifax in Lunenberg.

Lunenberg is the obvious place for a fine fisheries museum. Like its New England rival, Gloucester, this small coastal town has become a symbol of the white-winged schooners and courageous captains of the historic banks cod fishery. And, also like Gloucester, Lunenberg has successfully made the transition from the age of sail and dory fishing to the age of diesel-powered steel trawlers and draggers. Lunenberg remains in the first rank of the world's great fishing ports.

Incidentally, the visitor soon discovers that Nova Scotians have not forgotten who came out on top when Lunenberg and Gloucester met head-to-head in competition. The schooner *Bluenose*, designed, built, owned, and raced by Lunenburgers, captured the International Fishermen's Trophy by winning a majority of her races against *Gertrude L. Thebaud*, Gloucester's fastest fisherman. *Bluenose* was eventually sold out of the fishing fleet and lost, but *Bluenose II*, an exact replica, has since been built and now cruises along the coasts of the Maritimes (she can sometimes be found berthed at the wharf of the Maritime Museum of the Atlantic in Halifax).

Curiously enough, Lunenburg is one of the few towns along Nova Scotia's Atlantic coast not to owe its origin to a settlement of fishermen. As its name suggests, the town was established by Germans, Protestants who with French coreligionists were settled there by the British government in the mid-18th century. Both groups were farmers and wood cutters from inland Europe, rather than seamen; one reason the Lunenburg area was chosen what that it was one of the few suitable for growing the crops needed to feed Halifax.

However, the village was on a small rocky peninsula next to a fine harbor off fish-filled Mahone Bay, so it was not long before the farmers—or their sons—were building skiffs and reaping a harvest from the waters off their meadows. Alongshore fishing continued to be most important into the early 19th century; after all, as a local man reported, "a man could catch 300 to 400 pounds of codfish a day a mile or two offshore." Before too long the Lunenburgers were catching more fish than they could eat and were drying and salting the surplus and shipping it off to the protein-hungry plantations in the West Indies.

Once they got their feet wet, the Lunenburgers began to push offshore to the so-called Western Banks, the fish-rich shallows on the Continental Shelf off Nova Scotia. This meant building bigger boats—shallops at first and eventually, as longer trips demanded larger vessels, schooners. The larger schooners required more capital, but they could make it to the distant coasts of Labrador where the catches were still better.

Lunenberg, by the mid-19th century, had become not only a fisherman's town but a shipbuilding center and a direct exporter of salt fish to the West Indies. The little port sent out 85 schooners to the banks, the Gulf of St. Lawrence, and Labrador. Fishing with hook and line directly from the schooner deck, the fishermen went after mackerel as well as the traditional cod. Local shipbuilding methods improved and before long Lunenburg-built craft were in demand, known for their high quality. Often a new schooner was sold to fishermen from other ports while on her maiden trip to the Banks. This turnover meant that the Lunenburg fleet was constantly replenished with new vessels.

Bigger schooners meant longer trips, more gear carried, and bigger catches. So did the substitution of fishing with long trawl lines: a mile or more of line with a hook every few feet, tended by two men in a dory launched from the schooner's deck. By the late 19th century, 2,300 men from Lunenburg County were dory fishing on the banks in schooners while 1,100 more were fishing inshore.

And fishing supplied many more jobs than just those handling the lines: The whole economy of the area revolved around the fishing industry and its independent services, making jobs not only for shipwrights, but for sailmakers, coopers, blacksmiths, and even for farmers who supplied provisions for the schooners. The "fish makers," skilled specialists who knew how to salt and dry the catch after it was brought back to Lunenburg so that it would keep for the long voyage to foreign markets, were essential to the system. And local merchants provided the capital, sold the catch, and reaped the profits, while local insurance companies spread the risks of voyages to dangerous waters.

This self-contained economy means that practically all the income from the fishing industry stayed home in Lunenburg. With vessels built, owned, manned, insured, outfitted, and provisioned locally, and their holds filled with locally owned cargoes, all the gross earnings, not just the net, went to the county. As a result, Lunenburg had more maritime income than other Nova Scotian ports that owned several times the ship tonnage in big carriers. These charter freighters, Lunenburgers pointed out, might be far bigger than fishing schooners, but they were manned by foreigners, carried the cargoes of distant owners from one remote port to another, and were serviced far from home: only the net profit came back to the Nova Scotian port where the ship was owned.

The early 1870s were looked back on as the golden age of Lunenburg's traditional fisheries, but at the opening of the 20th century the port's fishing fleet was at its largest with 140 schooners. Then the numbers gradually decreased. Lunenburg was slower than its American rivals to adapt to changing conditions. The port's salt fish had never been of the highest grade, limiting its markets to the poorer countries of the Caribbean; Americans meanwhile shifted to fresh fish, for which there was a demand in the United States, a switch made possible by new cold storage technology.

Despite wars and the depression, however, Lunenburg eventually adapted to change: to diesel power from sail; to steel hulls from wood; to the coming first of cold storage, then of quick-freezing to produce better products for new markets. Now the little town is the base for a modern fleet of trawlers and draggers and claims to be the major fish-landing port on the Atlantic seaboard.

But the past is far from forgotten in Lunenburg. In the Memorial Room at the Community Center are recorded the names of the hundreds of Lunenburg fishermen and dozens of Lunenburg vessels lost at sea over the centuries. Lunenburg yards still build wooden vessels, though not for the banks fishery, to be sure: Among the ships sent down the ways have been the reproductions of HMS *Bounty* for the MGM movie, now in St. Petersburg, Florida, and HMS *Rose*, currently based in Bridgeport, Connecticut. And all its special maritime past is brought into sharp focus at Lunenburg's Fisheries Museum of the Atlantic, which rivals its sister museum in Halifax in the interest of its exhibits.

A final note about the town itself: Lunenburg is very much flavored with the past. Most of its houses have a distinctive form of architecture, perhaps unique to the town, called the "Lunenburg Bump." Popular in the days of the town's greatest prosperity a century ago, the Bump is an overgrown dormer extending out from the roof, typically over the center door. A delightful aberration of Victorian carpenters that give Lunenburg a visual quality all its own.

Now for a tour of the museum.

The Fisheries Museum of the Atlantic is on the Lunenburg waterfront. The on-shore exhibits are housed in a rambling series of large wooden buildings that were formerly part of a fish-processing plant; the museum vessels are tied up along the wharf outside. The exhibits, while all fishery related, cover a wide range: many ship models, dioramas, small craft, full-scale mock-ups, graphic displays explaining past and present fisheries and fishing techniques, and many paintings, drawings, and photographs. In addition, there is a dory shop where summer visitors can watch a skilled boatbuilder at work, a little theater where films about the fisheries are shown, and even an aquarium where the sought-for fish can be seen alive.

For many visitors, the most interesting and informative exhibit will be the "Pictorial History of the Banks Fishery" in the large gallery on the second floor just at the left of the head of the stairs. Here under the solemn gaze of an enormous six-foot carved codfish, a series of graphic displays and beautifully detailed dioramas clearly explain the vessels and fishing techniques used from the 17th century onward.

Visitors with a special interest in small craft will be enthusiastic about the Inshore Boat room on the ground floor. Here, examples of various Nova Scotia types are displayed on the gallery floor while the walls are crowded with pictures of various types of boats as well as huge photomurals of inshore fishing. Boats on the floor include a Bush Island boat, the only type designed for sail (plus engine) that is still actively used.

There are many fishing schooner models on the second floor, with special emphasis, of course, on Lunenburg's own *Bluenose*. Other models portray coasting schooners, which were the transportation link between the little shore villages until fairly recent times, and the large power trawlers that have taken over the offshore fisheries.

Other things to look for:

- a full-scale mock-up of a typical Nova Scotia fish store. Note why they were built with loose floor boards;
- a three-dimensional model (in a corner of the lunchroom) of the bottom contours of the north-west Atlantic, showing locations of the rich fishing banks;
- the dory-building shop (in summer) located on the ground floor at the end of the building farthest from the museum entrance—the shop has its own exterior entrance, facing the wharf;
- displays on rum-running *into* Canada—Many visitors will be surprised to learn that some provinces had their own local prohibition at about the same time that the United States was officially dry;
- films, in third-floor theater, of *Bluenose* and modern fishing methods;
- a dory on the floor with full fishing gear.

Visitors should allow plenty of time to look at the craft berthed at the museum wharf, of course. The museum's prize exhibit, *Theresa E. Connor*, is a historic vessel. With a schooner hull, spoon bow and no bowsprit, lower masts and sails but no topmasts, powered with a huge six-cylinder diesel, *Connor* is typical of the final stages of the banks schooner. Her engines were used for passages to and from the fishing grounds; her cut-down sail rig for moving about on the banks or remaining hove to under riding sail while her dories were out.

The *Connor* was the last of the salt bank schooners and dory fishermen out of Lunenburg. In 1963, already a quarter-century veteran, *Connor* sailed for Newfoundland to pick up a crew to man her dories. No hands could be found, they had all shipped out in the trawlers and longliners, so she returned to Lunenburg and never sailed for the banks fishery again.

Now fully restored, the *Connor* is open to visitors from stem to stern. Take a particular look at her handsome stern cabin where her captain, mates, and senior hands berthed; her big diesel; the galley with menus on the wall; the multi-tiered bunks in the fo'c'sle; the fishery exhibits in the hold; and the dories stacked on deck. When she was on the banks she carried eight dories. Each dory was manned by two men who went out each day to fish with lines, which were anchored and buoyed at each end, as much as a mile and a half long, and carried 2,700 hooks.

The doryman's job was the hardest kind of work: wet, cold, and dangerous. Working along the line, the sternman hauled up the line and removed the fish; the bowman rebaited the hooks and dropped the line back over the side. When the dory was fully loaded with about 1,700 pounds of fish, the dorymen rowed back to the schooner, came alongside, and pitchforked the fish aboard—no easy task if any kind of a sea was running. And always there was the threat of swamping in a sudden squall, or being lost in a fog that would hide them from the mother schooner.

The very different kind of offshore fishing that superseded the dory-fishing schooners is typified by the museum's other major vessel, the 131-foot steel trawler *Cape Sable*, which lies at the dock next to the *Connor*. The *Cape Sable* was built in Holland in 1962, just a year before the *Connor* was retired for lack of dorymen, but trawlers had been fishing out of Nova Scotian ports as early as the 1920s. At first they were bitterly opposed by the dory fishermen, but after World War II they gradually took over the banks fisheries. Instead of catching individual fish on separate hooks, the trawlers trap huge quantities of fish by dragging open-mouthed bags of netting—the "trawl"—through the water. Handling a trawl is hard, often dangerous work, but it is both easier and safer than fishing from dories.

Cape Sable is actually seven feet shorter than the *Connor*, but with far greater fishing and carrying capacity. A relatively new addition to the museum exhibits, she is gradually being overhauled for public viewing. The deck and wheelhouse are the first areas opened; more becomes viewable as the work progresses.

The wheelhouse and captain's cabin of the wooden trawler *Cape North*, recently scrapped by the museum as beyond repair, have been saved and reconstructed on the wharf.

Fisheries Museum of the Atlantic is located on the waterfront of Lunenburg Harbor. Also aquarium, dory-building shop, restaurant, gift shop, bookshop. Open May 15 to October 15, every day, 9:30 a.m. to 5:30 p.m. Admission: $2.00; children, 50 cents. A branch of the Nova Scotia Museum (Halifax). Fisheries Museum of the Atlantic, P.O. Box 1363, Lunenburg, Nova Scotia, Canada B0J 2C0. Telephone (902) 634-4794.

Large, fine museums with their multitudinous exhibits paint the past with broad brush strokes. For the little details that in the aggregate make up the big picture, sometimes the place to look is the small museum. The well-loved if not always topically arranged collection of a local historical society, which is often dependent upon gifts for the collection and volunteers to arrange it, can give unexpected insights into another time and place. The face of a local shipmaster, the portrait of his ship he had painted in some distant port, a ship model carved by an old man remembering his first voyage before the mast, old photographs, pieces of wrecks—all have a story to tell.

Actually, historical society museums come in all shapes and sizes and so do their maritime components. The Yarmouth County Museum, at Yarmouth on the western tip of Nova Scotia, has a large and varied collection dominated by exhibits related to the area's maritime past.

Which is as it should be, since Yarmouth made its living from the sea during most of the 200-odd years since it was founded by Yankee fishermen from Yarmouth on Cape Cod and other New England coastal towns. They came in 1761 after the final conquest of French Canada, to take up British government land grants along the Nova Scotian coast. The settlers had a hard time at first; they farmed but mostly fished from boats and small vessels. They dried and salted their catch ashore, and usually sold it to New Englanders or English traders for export to the West Indies because they lacked the capital to export it themselves.

The coming of the American Revolution put the Yarmouth settlers on the spot. On the one hand, the settlers not only still had close family ties with rebellious Massachusetts but depended on trade with New Englanders for much of their income. On the other hand, they were close to the center of British sea power in Halifax and were already suspected of disloyalty to the King. In a sense, Yarmouth and neighboring towns were as much islands as Nantucket, and, like Nantucket, they tried to remain neutral. Although connected to Halifax by land, a roadless wilderness separated them and the only communication was by sea.

The appeal of Yarmouth's townspeople to be recognized as "divided betwixt natural affection to our nearest relations, and good Faith and Friendship to our King and Country," won them exemption from the Nova Scotia militia but also anger and suspicion from both the British authorities in Halifax and the American patriots in Massachusetts. As it turned out, the trade between Yarmouth and Boston was eventually seen as advantageous to both. Massachusetts told its prize-hungry privateers to go easy on Yarmouth and the other Cape Sable settlements. A contraband trade grew up using British export licenses to British-held ports, and "repatriation" passes from the Massachusetts authorities. Yarmouth and economics proved more powerful than wartime regulations about trading with the enemy.

After the American War of Independence, Yarmouth, like other Nova Scotian towns, received a large influx of American Loyalist refugees. With ample supplies of timber at hand, Yarmouth people turned more and more to building ships. By 1791, 26 ships were owned in the country and the number grew steadily. Eighty years later, 90,000 tons of shipping were Yarmouth-owned. The 19th century saw Yarmouth become one of the great shipowning and shipbuilding centers in Canada; in fact, at one time Yarmouth claimed the largest ship tonnage per capita of any place in the world. From 1800 to 1900, more than 2,000 ships were registered in Yarmouth, totaling nearly half a million tons. The other side of the picture is that up to 1876, 600 of these ships had been lost at sea, some 90 of them with all hands.

With such a heritage, it is not surprising that the Yarmouth County Museum has a major maritime content. Located in a residential section close to downtown Yarmouth, the museum is housed in a one-time church. Cleared of pews, the main floor of the building is now one huge room, crammed with exhibits of every kind—furniture, ship models, china, marine artifacts, carriages, ship prints, costumes, paintings, photographs—check by jowl wherever there is room. In addition, there are more exhibits in the basement below.

This is a museum to prowl in, not to swoop through; you never know what you'll come across next. Keep your eyes peeled for ship models portraying:

- the Cape Islands swordfisherman *Thomas and Burns*;
- the Yarmouth-built bark *James B. Duffus*, 1869, known as the "haunted ship" after the mate was killed on her maiden voyage;
- the steam-auxiliary square-rigger *City of New York*, Admiral Byrd's ship on his first Antarctic expedition;
- the 2,154-ton *County of Yarmouth*, the largest sailing vessel owned in Yarmouth.

There are many other models, including schooners, as well as builders' half models. Also scattered through the exhibits are many paintings of ships. This rather small, general museum is said to have the third largest collection of ship portraits in all Canada. Among the graphics exhibits look for:

- An entire bay is filled with photographic portraits of Yarmouth shipmasters, some 90 of them.
- For many years, starting in 1855, Yarmouth retained its close ties with New England as the Nova Scotia end of the overnight steamer run back and forth to Boston. Paintings of the steamers and photographs of their officers recall those happy days.
- Many will find of special interest an "illuminated address" honoring Captain David Cook of the bark *Sara* for rescuing the crew and passengers of the ship *Caleb Grimshaw*. The scroll, presented by the New York City Common Council in 1850, is fascinatingly decorated with sailors, Indians, and angels, not to mention a vignette of the rescue.

Visitors should be sure to take a look at the wreck relics in the basement; all of them are from vessels lost in the vicinity of Yarmouth. There is something particularly touching about these often commonplace objects, subjected to such wild times before coming to rest in this snug harbor: artifacts from the side-wheeler *City of Monticello*, which sank off Yarmouth in 1900 with the loss of 36 lives; the "saloon table and chairs from the SS *Castilian*, wrecked off Yarmouth 12 March, 1899;" tableware that once graced the dining saloons of vanished vessels.

Yarmouth County Museum is at Yarmouth, historic port on western tip of Nova Scotia, about 180 miles from Halifax via Route 103. Take Yarmouth exit, proceed to Collins Street. Historical research library. Open all year, but hours change with the season. In general, open Monday-Saturday 9 a.m. to 5 p.m. plus Sunday afternoons; Monday-Saturday only, spring and fall; Tuesday-Saturday only, November through April. (Call to confirm hours.) Admission: $1.00; children, 25 cents. Sponsored by Yarmouth County Historical Society. Yarmouth County Museum, 22 Collins Street, Yarmouth, Nova Scotia, Canada B5A 4B1. Telephone (902) 742-5539.

Continuing on around the perimeter of Nova Scotia, the traveler returns to the eastward along the shore of the Bay of Fundy. Half way up the coast is the Annapolis River, site of the first settlements of Nova Scotia/Acadia, much later the bustling little port and shipbuilding town of Annapolis Royal.

Halifax, Lunenburg, and Yarmouth were only three of many Nova Scotian towns where sailing ships were built and owned. Nova Scotia is very nearly surrounded by salt water and little shipyards soon appeared around her coasts and along her rivers, making 19th-century Nova Scotia one of the world's greatest centers, in proportion to population, of shipbuilding and shipowning.

With the passing of the wooden sailing ship, the industry eventually dwindled away. Today, the site of many a bustling shipyard is a quiet village meadow and no one survives who can remember when the last ship went down the ways. In some of these towns people have begun to realize that unless they act now the last relics of their great maritime heritage will be lost forever. The result is the establishment of small

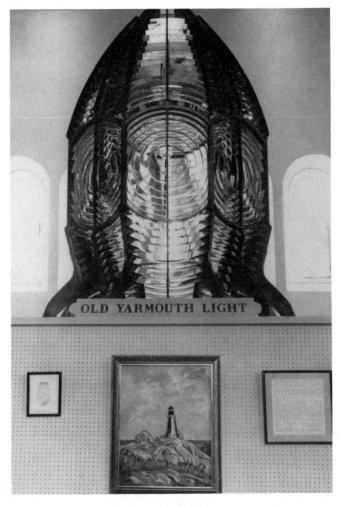

Figure 26
The exhibits in small museums, such as this one in the museum of the Yarmouth County Historical Society in Yarmouth, Nova Scotia, often have a charm and special interest of their own.
(photo courtesy of the Yarmouth County Museum)

museums sponsored by historical societies and preservation groups, where photographs, letters, models, and artifacts are preserved and displayed.

One such is in Annapolis Royal, the little town on the Annapolis River, the most historic town in Nova Scotia. This was the Port Royal of the Acadians, the place where the first settlement in the Maritime Provinces was made. Every visitor to the area will certainly want to visit the magnificent and authentic recreation of the first little French trading post of Port Royal. Now a National Historic Park of Canada, the Port Royal Habitation is built at the site of the 1604 building on the north side of the Annapolis River, a few miles downstream from the present town of Annapolis Royal. Here were the very first beginnings of one of America's oldest maritime traditions north of the Spanish colonies: *La Bonne Renommée* and her sister ships brought the adventurers; here, *Jonas*, their supply ship, was berthed; here, that ship's carpenter and boatbuilder Champdoré built the first vessels launched on these shores, the pinnaces that were used to explore the coast. The visitor will have to use his imagination in reconstructing these maritime beginnings, however. While the Habitation is beautiful, recreated with scholarly care, and tells much about the adventurers' life ashore, there is little information about the maritime aspects of their exploration of this corner of the New World.

The same is true about the other great historic site at Annapolis Royal, Fort Anne. Again, every visitor will want to roam around the maze of bastions, curtain walls, navelins, and glacis—the wonderfully intricate fortifications built by the French and rebuilt by the English to defend the tiny capital of Acadia/Nova Scotia. The fort in its early days protected a base for French privateers, attempted to defend the settlement against repeated sea raiders from old England and New England, and eventually was captured for good by an amphibious force composed primarily of New Englanders. Yet the visitor finds few references to these maritime activities when he visits the nice little museum in the restored officers' quarters of the fort.

Actually, locally based maritime activity did not blossom until the 19th century, long after the original Acadians had been driven out and replaced, first by land-hungry Yankees, then reinforced after the Revolution by American Loyalists.

By the 1830s and 1840s, Annapolis Royal yards were building large square-riggers; and in the second half of the 19th century the town's little riverfront was lined with ships and shipyards. Some of the vessels were pretty large; the *Lawrence Delap*, for example, launched in 1876, was 1,400 tons. The town really boomed with the coming of the railroad in 1869, and continued to be a bustling port until the 1890s, ship-

ping lumber to Europe and the West Indies. Boston, easily reached by ship, was the metropolis where Annapolis people went to shop, to study, or for fun.

The shipyards flourished well into the 20th century, and many of the buildings facing the yards and wharves across lower St. George Street still survive. In one of them, the restored mid-Victorian O'Dell Tavern, a Marine Room has been established as a small maritime museum. The collection consists primarily of prints, documents, photographs, and marine artifacts. Perhaps the most interesting exhibit is a model of the *A.F. Davison*, the only four-masted schooner built at Annapolis Royal; it was wrecked in 1926 after a 17-year career. Photographs show a busy Annapolis waterfront with a schooner on the builder's ways. In the tavern taproom, next to the Marine Room, are two fine primitive shadowboxes, one of a full-rigged ship, the other of the steamer *Jessie Berry*. Both have a notably authentic feeling.

O'Dell Museum is a restored 1850 inn and tavern facing the Annapolis River across Lower St. George Street in Annapolis Royal; easy walking distance from Fort Anne. Open June 1 to September 7, every day, 9:30 a.m. to 5 p.m. Sponsored by Historic Restoration Society. O'Dell Inn and Tavern Museum, Lower St. George Street, Annapolis Royal, Nova Scotia, Canada B0S 1A0. Telephone (902) 532-2041. N.B. Visitors to Annapolis Royal should certainly plan to visit the Port Royal Habitation and Fort Anne, both historic sites of major interest.

Much of the great Nova Scotian shipbuilding/shipowning boom of the 19th century was in the small towns along the Minas Basin, the great tidal estuary that forms the more southerly of the two heads of the Bay of Fundy. In at least 20 towns on both sides of the Minas Basin, spring was marked by the start up of the shipyards, using spruce timber cut in the area during the winter and hauled to the yards on sleds.

Many of the hundreds of ships turned out remained locally owned. In 1881, for example, little Hants County on the south shore of Minas Basin could point to 249 vessels owned or registered locally, totalling 163,000 tons. More than 150 of them were three-masted square-riggers: ships, barks, and barkentines. Fortunes and careers were built on shipbuilding and shipowning. Ezra Churchill started his working life as a wheelwright but after moving to the Hants County town of Hantsport became a shipbuilder; he expanded, grew wealthy (at one time his yard claimed to be the fifth largest in the world), went into politics, and eventually became a senator. His firm, which was carried on by his sons, built almost 90 vessels in some 70 years.

The Cedars, the Victorian mansion in Hantsport built by Ezra Churchill for his son John, has been restored as a community center. Here, appropriately enough, the Marine Memorial Room preserves the memory of Hantsport's shipbuilders, shipowners, and master mariners. This little town was home port for 250 ship captains!

The collection, housed in what was once the Churchill nursery, is a small one but it will appeal to many visitors because it is so intimate, almost like a collection of family heirlooms. Among the exhibits on view are:

- a number of paintings of various ships;
- builders' models from the Hantsport shipyards;
- shipwrights' tools;
- A shadow box model of a bark.
- Photographs of local ships and building yards.
- A list of 215 ships built in Hantsport and vicinity from *Acadia*, 1844, to *William Boothby*, 1918.

Visitors should also be sure to make a little tour of the house itself. Built in 1860, it is amazingly decorated with painted walls and special wallpapers, which have been carefully and lovingly restored. Churchill's wealth enabled him to indulge to an unusual extent in mid-Victorian elegance in decoration.

And there is still another thing to look for: visitors interested in folk art will find a special attraction.

A young Portuguese sailor, named DaSilva, went to sea in Churchill ships and visited many ports. He put down roots in Hantsport and eventually stayed ashore to become a general factotum to the Churchill family. In between his various duties as gardener, carpenter, handyman, and coachman, DaSilva, who had now anglicized his name to Francis Silver, entertained himself by painting murals on the walls of the carriage house and the basement of the mansion. Ships, wrecks, launchings, were among the scenes vividly portrayed, along with such non-maritime subjects as rural landscapes, political cartoons, and scenes from the Bible.

The work of this self-taught artist was little thought of in Hantsport, but today Silver has been "discovered," and his paintings recognized as important and valuable Canadian primitives. Much of his work has been taken on a tour of Canada but will be eventually returned to Hantsport. In the meantime, the remains of some of Silver's murals are still on the walls of the basement at The Cedars. They are worth seeing.

Churchill House—The Cedars is set in the midst of large grounds on the east side of Main Street in Hantsport, Nova Scotia. Hantsport is on the Avon River, which runs into the south side of Minas Basin, about 45 miles northwest of Halifax and 145 miles east of Annapolis Royal, both via Route 101. Take Hantsport exit east to Main Street, turn right; house is on left, back from street in grounds. Open daily, July to September; 10 a.m. to noon, 1 to 5 p.m. Admission: free. Building is now The Hantsport Memorial Community Center. John Churchill House, Main Street, Hantsport, Nova Scotia, Canada B0P 1P0. Telephone (902) 684-3461.

Newfoundland

[Biarni Heriulfsson sailed for Greenland from Iceland in his trading ship. After many days of calms, fogs, north winds, they did not know where they were. Then they saw the sun again . . . hoisted sail, sailed on, and saw land.] Biarni said he did not believe it could be Greenland . . . They . . . soon saw that the land was level, and covered with woods, and that there were small hillocks upon it. [They left this land to larboard and sailed on, finding another flat and wooded land, quite different from the ice mountains of Greenland.] The fair wind failed them then, and the crew took counsel together and concluded that it would be wise to land there, but Biarni would not consent to this. They alleged they were in need of both wood and water. "Ye have no lack of either of these," says Biarni—a course, forsooth, which won him blame among his shipmates. [After a third sighting of land, where Biarni again refused to go ashore, they finally sighted Greenland and completed their voyage.]

[After a trip to Norway, Biarni came again to Greenland.] There was now much talk about voyages of discovery. Leif, the son of Eric the Red, of Brattahlid, visited Biarni Heriulfsson and bought a ship of him, and collected a crew, until they formed altogether a company of thirty-five men . . . . [Lief and his companions] put the ship in order and when they were ready, they sailed out to sea [from Greenland] and found first that land which Biarni and his shipmates found last. They sailed up to the land and cast anchor, and launched a boat and went ashore, and saw no grass there; . . . Then said Leif, "It has not come to pass with us in regard to this land as with Biarni, that we have not gone upon it . . ."

[After sailing on and landing several times] they went aboard their ship again and sailed into a certain sound, which lay between the island and a cape, which jutted out from the land on the north, and they stood in westering past the cape. At ebb-tide there were broad reaches of shallow water there, and they ran their ship aground there, and it was a long distance from the ship to the ocean; yet were they so anxious to go ashore that they could not wait until the tide should rise under their ship, but hastened to the land, where a certain river flows out from a lake. As soon as the tide rose beneath their ship, however, they took their boat and rowed to the ship, which they conveyed up the river, and so into the lake, where they cast anchor and carried their hammocks ashore from the ship, and built themselves booths there. They afterwards determined to establish themselves there for the winter, and they accordingly built a large house. . . .

[Tyrker, the German, went exploring and found vines and grapes.] . . . it is said that their after-boat was filled with grapes. . . . when the spring came, they made their ship ready, and sailed away; and from its products Leif gave the land a name, and called it Wineland. They sailed out to sea and had fair winds until they sighted Greenland . . .

Excerpts from *The Vinland History of the Flat Island Book*,
translated by Arthur Middleton Reeves.

Thus the Icelandic saga described the first European sighting of North America and the first settlement of Europeans on our shores, both around A.D. 1,000. Or at least the first for which there is really conclusive evidence—lacking in earlier legends of seagoing monks and Irish refugees. The settlement was fleeting—the Norsemen were apparently driven out by the Indians—but it was long enough to give Newfoundland a valid claim to the oldest maritime heritage in North America, at least in terms of European discovery.

For after decades of controversy, in which Vinland has been variously located at places along the Atlantic coast from Rhode Island on northward, archaeologists seem agreed that remains of a true Norse settlement have been found at the northern tip of Newfoundland. Here, at a place called L'Anse aux Meadows, the remains of several buildings and a few artifacts have been identified as medieval Norse, while the location largely matches the descriptions in the sagas.

L'Anse aux Meadows has now been made a National Historic Park by the Canadian government. While nothing to be seen there is directly related to the sea, the site marks the tentative beginnings of the most dramatic maritime activity in history—the first of centuries of shiploads of weary emigrants crossing thousands of miles of stormy ocean to seize and settle North America. As such, the National Park may well attract maritime-minded visitors to the most northern of the Atlantic Provinces and to the place where our maritime heritage began.

The island of Newfoundland—set directly across the mouth of the Gulf of St. Lawrence—splits the outpourings of the great St. Lawrence River between the 10-mile wide Strait of Belle Isle to the north (which separates Newfoundland from Labrador), and the 60-mile wide Cabot Straits to the south (which separates Newfoundland from Nova Scotia's Cape Breton Island). Newfoundland's position is sometimes compared to that of the British Isles off Europe. The great island is roughly triangular in shape, almost the same length and breadth, about 316 miles, but so indented by deep fjords and large bays that it has 2,000 miles of shoreline.

From Port aux Basque, where the traveler to L'Anse aux Meadows lands from the Nova Scotia ferry, Route 1 runs northeast to Deer Lake. There the road to L'Anse, Route 430 on the Viking Trail, goes off westward to the coast and follows it all the way up to the tip of the Northern Peninsula, where St. Anthony offers the accommodations nearest the National Park.

For travelers who want to make a flying visit, there is a large commercial airport at Deer Lake, served by Eastern Provincial Airways. From there a feeder airline, Labrador Airways, flies to St. Anthony.

The Norse remains were discovered in 1960 by, appropriately enough, a Norwegian explorer and writer, Helge Ingstad, who had been searching the coast from New England northward. Here, close to the sea, beside a stream running through a peat bog, he found a group of grass-covered mounds that looked man-made. Ingstad and his wife, the archaeologist Anne Stone Ingstad, explored the site and turned up evidence that this was indeed a place where Norse had landed, hauled out their little ships, built houses, and wintered over. The importance of the discovery was emphasized in 1978, when L'Anse aux Meadows became the first historic site to be placed on UNESCO's World Heritage List of cultural and natural sites of outstanding universal value.

The National Historic Park today preserves this remarkable discovery and displays it to visitors; meanwhile, archaeological exploration continues. The mounds discovered by the Ingstads were found to be the foundation of eight 11th-century Norse buildings—three dwellings, four workshops, and a smithy—built of sods laid over wooden frames. Replicas of complete houses have become a major part of the Park exhibits.

Exhibits at the Visitors Reception Center include some of the Norse artifacts that have been found at the site. Various graphic displays and audiovisual shows tell the story of the settlement, and of its discovery and significance.

An expanded Visitors Center is in the works, where it is planned to have a scale model of the kind of full-bodied trading ships that brought the Norse across the Atlantic (the Long Ships of the Vikings were used only for wars or piratical raids).

Incidentally, a replica of one of the medieval Norse merchantmen of this type, called a knarr, has been built in Norway. Based on archaeological discoveries of Norse ships, the reconstructed knarr is a little over 54 feet long and about 16 feet wide with a single sail of almost 1,100 square feet, said to be capable of driving her at 12 knots under favorable conditions. This knarr, the *Saga Siglar*, crossed the Atlantic in the summer of 1984, visited East Coast ports, and went on around the world. Those who missed her brief visit must hope that she will return to the lands found by Biarni Heriulfsson and Leif Ericsson called "The Lucky."

L'Anse aux Meadows, 11th-century Norse settlement site, is in northwestern Newfoundland at tip of Great Northern Peninsula. Short distance by paved road off Highway 430, west-coast road connecting to Port aux Basques ferry. Believed site of community of first Europeans known to have crossed Atlantic to North America. Archaeological digs, artifacts museum, reconstructed Norse sod houses. First historic site on UNESCO World Heritage List. Information: L'Anse aux Meadows National Historic Park, P.O. Box 70, St. Lunaire-Griquet, Newfoundland A0K 2X0, Canada.

Many centuries, half a millenium, passed before Europe again showed an interest in North America or became aware of its existence. But once again Newfoundland was in on the beginnings. When the *Mathew* of Bristol carried John Cabot westward across the North Atlantic in 1497 he ran smack into Newfoundland—figuratively that is; fortunately, his landfall was in daylight on a clear day. Cabot had been commissioned by England's Henry VII to find a passage to the riches of Asia, and conceivably locate Hy-Brasil, the Isle of the Blest, said to be floating around somewhere out there in the mist and possibly a good base for new fishing grounds for Bristol ships.

Cabot found neither a passage to Asia nor the Isle of the Blest, but he hit the jackpot on fishing grounds. The crew of the *Mathew* found that all they had to do was drop a weighted basket overboard on the end of a line and haul it up filled with codfish. (Some historians believe that Basque fishermen may have crossed the Atlantic ahead of him and kept their discovery a trade secret.) Off Newfoundland are some of the richest fishing banks in the world and for most of 500 years fishing has dominated the history of the island. The meeting of the cold Labrador current with the warm Gulf Stream coming up from the south over the shallow places, the famous "banks," in the Continental Shelf, produced a profusion of rich feeding grounds.

These attracted schools of food fish, particularly the codfish, which was much desired because after being salted and dried it would keep almost indefinitely. Thus, codfish caught off Newfoundland in the spring and cured could be kept until the vessel returned to Europe in the fall.

Great fleets of fishermen came across the Atlantic hot on Cabot's heels. French, Spanish, and Portuguese fishermen, all from Roman Catholic countries with many obligatory fast days when fish were in demand, were the most active at first. The English were slower in getting started but eventually became vigorous competitors, particularly after the decline of Spanish and Portuguese sea power—heralded by the defeat of the Spanish Armada—opened up Southern European markets to English ships. Eventually, French and English fishermen came to dominate the North Atlantic fishery, which by the early 18th century had become one of the great industries of Western Europe.

Fishermen of both countries followed the deep-sea fishing technique used universally at the time: the crew took stations along the rail of their little vessel and fished with hand lines over the side.

There were two different methods used to preserve the catch. In the "wet" or "green" fishery, each day's catch was salted and dried on racks on deck, then stored in the hold. The vessel came out across the Atlantic in the spring and might never touch land, staying on the banks until the hold was full, then returning home. There the curing was completed ashore by heavily salting the fish, then sun-drying them for weeks.

This was the method often used by French fishermen, who had plenty of sun and salt at home. In England, both commodities were scarcer, so English fishermen early on began to establish shore bases in Newfoundland, where the fish would be brought and cured ashore; the fish were salted down and sun-dried on racks until they were as hard—and almost as indestructible—as boards.

This fishing technique made the history of Newfoundland different from that of any other North American colony. Settlement on the island was not only not encouraged, it was for a long time actually forbidden. With hundreds of fishing boats swarming to Newfoundland, competition for the best sites to set up fish-drying racks ashore (called stations) was intense. Any settlement was seen as an intrusion, an obstruction to the use of the shoreline by the fishing fleet.

As a result, Newfoundland for centuries had no formal government: no officials, no regular laws, no courts. At the behest of the West-of-England Merchants who owned the fishing vessels, the 1634 Charter of Western Adventurers gave legal force to what had been custom: Each harbor was governed by the captains of the first three fishing vessels to arrive each spring, usually in March. From then until the end of the fishing season in September, the captain of the first vessel in the harbor was admiral of the harbor; the second, the vice-admiral; and the third, rear admiral. All were fully empowered to settle disputes. Colonists were considered transgressors with no right to reside within a quarter mile of the coast.

In 1689, England's Parliament officially confirmed the fisheries claim to exclusive use of the Newfoundland coast. The reasoning behind this remarkable move was the belief that the fishing fleet was a nursery of seamen for the Royal Navy and, as such, was more important to Britain than any colony. This was doubtful; a firmer argument was that the fisheries were a great earner of specie from the sale of salt fish to the Mediterranean countries.

As time went on, the Navy was called upon to take a larger part in keeping order. Despite the prohibition against settlement, fishermen landed to cure the cod, enjoyed their liberty, and managed to avoid returning to England in the fall. Although Newfoundland was described as "a great ship moored for the convenience of the British fishery," settlements did grow supported by farming and inshore fishing, and the residents defied government threats to deport them to Jamaica.

Eventually, chaotic conditions on the island forced the British authorities to assume governmental responsibility; at first through the naval commanders on the station, then, by the end of the 18th century, through a system of courts and colonial officials.

Island residents developed inshore fisheries from small craft and gradually took over a good share of the banks fisheries from the summer fishermen from across the Atlantic. Meanwhile, the French made repeated attempts to seize the island; they failed but preserved fishing rights and the use of the shore along the north and west coasts.

Fishing remains Newfoundland's chief source of income, although steel trawlers and draggers have here as elsewhere long since replaced the wooden schooners. Now the traditional salt fishery accounts for only one-third of the catch; the other two-thirds are fresh frozen. Intense competition for markets, the decline of fishing stocks on the banks, and exchange problems, have all adversely affected the fishing industry.

For most of its history, Newfoundland was a separate colony of Britain. When the mainland provinces united to form Canada, the island remained aloof. Finally, in 1949, it joined the others as Canada's tenth—and poorest—province. Today the island's economic hopes lie in oil, but even here the sea is the major factor in Newfoundland's future. The oil lies many fathoms deep beneath the surface of the North Atlantic, and the drilling platforms are in the path of fierce storms and floating ice. As has been the case for the past 500 years, the men who "go to to sea" on the platforms are at risk; when one platform, reputedly the biggest in the world, collapsed in a gale in February, 1982, all hands were lost with the rig, including a number of Newfoundlanders.

Much of the long maritime history of the island is covered in collections of the Newfoundland Museum in St. John's, the provincial capital. The city is in the diagonally opposite corner of Newfoundland from L'Anse aux Meadows; set on the Avalon Peninsula on the southeast coast and just 1,700 miles west of Ireland, it was the center of the early English fisheries. When European settlements began here is uncertain; fishermen used the fine landlocked harbor as a base from very early times. Here, Sir Humphrey Gilbert landed in 1583 to take formal possession of the island in the name of Queen Elizabeth I. It was a fateful voyage for him; his ship went down with all hands on the homeward passage.

During the prolonged wars between France and Britain in the 17th and 18th centuries St. John's changed hands several times; finally becoming British for good with the collapse of French power in North America in 1762. During both the American Revolution and the War of 1812, the harbor was a base for the Royal Navy and British and local privateers operating against American shipping. In the 19th century, St. John's merchants came to control the fishery and shipbuilding activities of the colony, and by the opening of the 20th century the city was the center of not only the cod fisheries but of the whaling and sealing industries.

Incidentally the St. John's Regatta, held the first Wednesday in August since 1826, is considered the oldest organized sports event in North America.

The Newfoundland Museum in St. John's has devoted the third floor of its branch in the Murray Premises—one-time stone warehouses on the waterfront—to a gallery focused on the maritime and commercial past of the island: "Business in Great Waters: Ships & Shipping in Newfoundland and Labrador, 1500 to the Present."

The gallery traces the maritime history of Newfoundland for 500 years, with of course special emphasis on the cod fisheries, whaling, and sealing. Displays include tools, weapons, instruments, scrimshaw, paintings, and shipbuilder's half models.

- A display is devoted to the Basque seamen who came a'whaling off Newfoundland in the 16th century, and camped on its coasts to try out the blubber and to store the oil in casks. Artifacts found by archaeologists at the site of a Basque shore site are displayed, while an astrolobe found in the remains of a Basque wreck is in the navigational instrument exhibit.

- The navigational instruments display covers the development of the increasingly precise tools of the navigator, from the days when primitive magnetized needles were floated in a bowl of water. The accompanying increase in the accuracy of charts, from the thumbnail sketches of early times to the sophisticated 19th-century surveys, is graphically presented.

The Newfoundland Museum in St. John's includes both the original museum building and an expansion into the Murray Premises on the waterfront, home of the Maritime History Gallery. Open all year. Monday-Friday, 9 a.m. to 5 p.m.; Saturday, Sunday, and holidays 10 a.m. to 6 p.m. Admission: free. Gift shop in main museum building. Museum operated by Historic Resources Division of the Provincial Department of Culture, Recreation & Youth. Newfoundland Museum (Maritime Exhibits), 285 Duckworth Street and the Murray Premises, Beck's Cove, St. John's, Newfoundland, Canada A1C 1G9. Telephone (709) 576-2329.

V

THE MIDDLE ATLANTIC COAST:
RARITARIAN BAY
TO THE NORTH CAROLINA LINE

The Jersey Shore
Delaware Bay I: Philadelphia and Wilmington
Delaware Bay II: The Pennsylvania Canals
Chesapeake Bay I: The Eastern Shore and the Upper Bay
Chesapeake Bay II: The Potomac River and Southern Maryland
Chesapeake Bay III: The Virginia Peninsula and Hampton Roads

The Jersey Shore

Between the great ports of New York, at the mouth of the Hudson River, and Philadelphia, on the Delaware, lies the low sandy coast of New Jersey. The northern edge juts out almost due east from the continent, forming the shore of Raritan Bay. At Sandy Hook, the little peninsula marking the south side of the entrance to New York Bay, the coast turns sharply southward and for 125 or so miles there are almost continuous beaches, the shore turning increasingly toward the southwest until it reaches Cape May at the mouth of the Delaware. The southerly three-fourths of these beaches are on barrier islands, sheltering broad, shallow bays fed by small rivers.

The Jersey shore was a dangerous coast with a well-deserved reputation as yet another of the "graveyards of the Atlantic" along the East Coast of the United States. The inlets between the barrier islands provided the only refuge to a vessel driving onto a lee shore. Most of these inlets were shallow with surf breaking across the mouth; even the few deep enough for light-draft vessels had constantly shifting channels.

A storm might close some entrances entirely while opening up new ones elsewhere.

The *Atlantic Coast Pilot* of 1904 noted without comment that the average distance between lifesaving stations on this shore was less than three miles.

In Colonial times this was a wild coast and a favorite haunt of pirates and smugglers. The pirates lurked in little harbors behind the inlets and preyed on the ships bound for New York and Philadelphia. The few settlers—poor fishermen, traders, farmers—had little enthusiasm for upholding law and order, apparently feeling that these rough fellows at least brought a little money into the neighborhood. In 1699, the Vice-Admiral of Pennsylvania swooped down on pirates operating at Cape May, at the southern end of the Jersey shore, but only managed to capture four of the gang. "I might have with Ease secured all the rest of them and the ship too," he complained, had not local officials, "Entertain'd them with Provisions and Liquors, given them Intelligence and sheltered them from Justice. All the persons that I have employed in searching for apprehending these Pyrates are abused and affronted and called Enemies to the Country for Disturbing and hindering honest men (as they are pleased to call the Pyrates)."

Piracy was perhaps going a bit far, but smuggling seems to have been practically universal along these lonely shores. The British government tried to force the colonies to import their sugar, rum, and molasses only from the British West Indies, although these commodities were far cheaper in the French and Spanish islands. Illegal cargoes would be brought into lonely inlets, landed, and carted off through the Jersey woods to the Delaware River Valley towns to the westward, where customers were glad of a bargain and asked no questions. The Crown Customs officials grew rich on bribes, which the smugglers could well afford to pay: A 10-shilling investment in the trade might bring a return of 50 or 60 shillings.

Not surprisingly, these same little harbors became a great base for privateers during the American Revolution. Again, they found the merchant ships supplying British-held New York a rich source of prizes. Some bold privateersmen from the tiny whaling port of Toms River simply went offshore in whaleboats fitted with a small cannon; they could row faster than a small merchantman could sail. A cutting-out expedition from the Raritan River, two whaleboats and a sailing gunboat under the famous Captain Adam Hyler, captured five vessels at Sandy Hook within a quarter mile of their guard ship, took off cargo, and set four of them afire.

The *Venus*, captured by the American privateers *Chance* and *Sly* in 1778, sold for more than £17,000. Her cargo included fine broadcloths, linens, calicoes, chintzes, silks, satins, stockings, shoes, medicines, books, hardware, beef, pork, butter, cheese, and porter. The following year, 16 American privateers and a frigate were reported at Egg Harbor on the lower Jersey coast; they had captured six ships with cargo worth £80,000 sterling.

But the same characteristics that made the Jersey shore ideal for such irregular maritime pursuits as piracy, smuggling, and hit-and-run privateering, ill-fitted it for peacetime commerce. As merchant vessels grew larger and deeper, few could enter the shallow inlets, and the little harbors were left to fishermen, oyster boats, and coastal small craft. After the Civil War, however, summer visitors discovered the fine bathing beaches, and once-remote villages were transformed into popular seaside resorts; so much so that by the end of the 19th century the *Atlantic Coast Pilot* started its "General Description: Coast from Sandy Hook to Cape May" with the comment: "The characteristic features of this coast are its sandy beaches, numerous summer resorts, and life-saving stations . . ."

In the 1920s, the Jersey shore experienced a brief throwback to the wild times of its Colonial past. Prohibition made liquor smuggling richly profitable and rum runners used the beaches and inlets to land illegal cargoes, much as their predecessors had done two centuries before. Repeal brought a reversion to respectability, however, and the sheltered bays behind the barrier beaches are now the haunt of sport fishermen and are at the same time an important segment of the Inland Waterway along the Atlantic Seaboard.

Several small museums preserve the distinctive maritime traditions of the Jersey shore. Let's start at the north end in an old, old house, haunted with many stories.

From Port Monmouth, a little Jersey village on the shore of Raritan Bay, there is a fine view not only of the protected anchorage in the lee of Sandy Hook but up through the Narrows into upper New York Bay. It is said that during the American Revolution both British and Continental agents used a tavern here as a base to watch shipping all the way from Sandy Hook to the inner harbor.

The building that housed the tavern—really three 17th-century houses that were joined together in the 18th century to form one large house—still stands at Port Monmouth and is now the Shoal Harbor Museum (also called the Spy House Museum Complex).

The curator describes the museum as a learning center where visitors can become aware of the some 300 years of area history. Port Monmouth was a fishing and shipping village, and there are maritime-related artifacts, ship models, gear used in lobstering and eeling, and a model of a fish pond. Children are encouraged to touch the exhibits, many of which are on loan from local residents. "We take the students to the township dock and teach how fish get to their tables," reports the curator.

A copy of a local newspaper feature story sent out by the museum itself in response to a query gives one person's view: "This is not the place to go if you like neatly printed signs and well-lighted displays. This is the place to go if you have a soft spot for a cozy folk museum run in an unsophisticated haphazard manner."

Shoal Harbor Marine Museum is part of the Spy House Museum Complex in a three-centuries-old homestead overlooking Raritan Bay in Port Monmouth, New Jersey, near Red Bank. Open Monday-Friday, 9 a.m. to 3 p.m.; Saturdays, 1 to 3:30 p.m.; Sundays, 2:30 p.m. to 5 p.m.; Donations welcome. Spy House Museum Complex, Wilson Avenue, on the beach off Highway 36, Port Monmouth, New Jersey 07758. Telephone (201) 787-1807 or (201) 291-0559.

Inland, south of Port Monmouth, the land rises approximately 200 feet above the sea. Describing the approaches to New York Bay from seaward, the 1904 edition of the *Atlantic Coast Pilot* noted: "*Prominent objects*—the most prominent landmark southward of the entrance, in approaching from seaward, is the high-wooded ridge forming the Highlands of Navesink, on the side of which, in a cleared space, are two conspicuous lighthouses. The flashing white light shown here is visible 22 miles in clear weather."

This was the Navesink Light, at the eastern end of the Highlands, one of the highest spots on the East Coast. Actually, there were originally twin lights in towers at the two ends of a striking brownstone building erected in 1828, but by the turn of the century the northernly light had been put on standby. Now the tower and the connecting building have become part of a museum complex with special emphasis on lighthouses, lifesaving apparatus, and small craft built and used on the Jersey coast.

The collection also displays the gear used by area fishermen. Maritime artifacts, prints, paintings, and photographs are used to tell the story of the long struggle to increase safety at sea. There is a small auditorium at the south end of the Twin Lights where films and slide shows about the history of the lights are shown.

The Museum at Navesink Lighthouses, Highlands, New Jersey, is part of the Twin Lights Historic Site, a state park. North light tower, 254 feet above sea level, open during museum hours. Gift shop. Open every day, 9:00 a.m. to 5:00 p.m. Admission: free. Operated by New Jersey State Park Service, Twin Lights Historic Site, Highlands, New Jersey 07737. Telephone (201) 872-1814. If no answer, (201) 566-2161.

Sandy Hook is a low peninsula stretching some five and a half miles north from the Jersey coast at the point where it turns sharply from roughly north-south, facing the Atlantic, to roughly east-west, facing Raritan Bay. The Hook forms the southwest side of the entrance to the port of New York and the western entrance channels pass close to it. In sailing ship days vessels found a safe anchorage in its lee, protected from easterly gales.

Many ships were wrecked on and near Sandy Hook and in 1764 the New York Colonial Assembly responded to the pleas of merchants and arranged to have a lighthouse built on the point. Financed by lotteries, the light was only the sixth one built in the American Colonies. Today, Sandy Hook is the oldest operating lighthouse in the United States; the light in its 85-foot tower is visible 19 miles at sea.

Eventually, in 1896-98, Fort Hancock was built on Sandy Hook to house big coast-defense guns to guard the entrance to New York Harbor. Today, military technology has made the fort and its guns obsolete, and it has been turned over to the National Park Service as part of the Gateway National Recreation Area. Within the old fort, the guard house—the post jail—has been made into a museum with some maritime exhibits.

The Sandy Hook Museum in the old guard house of Fort Hancock, on a long spit of sand extending northward from the New Jersey shore. Gift shop. Open daily Memorial Day to Labor Day, 1 to 5 p.m. Balance of the year open Saturday and Sunday, 1 to 5 p.m. Admission: free, but $2.00 parking fee, Memorial Day through Labor Day. Operated by National Park Service, Sandy Hook Museum, Fort Hancock, P.O. Box 437, Gateway National Recreation Center, Highlands, New Jersey 07732. Telephone (201) 872-0115.

Now we'll move down to the other end of the Jersey shore, to the little town of Somers Point, south of Atlantic City on the inland waterway at the mouth of Great Egg Harbor.

The Somers family had roots deep in Jersey's past: Its most famous member was Master-Commandant Richard Somers, U.S.N., a hero of the war with Tripoli. In 1804, as part of the American attack on the port of Tripoli, the ketch *Intrepid* was fitted as a floating mine, filled with 100 barrels of gunpowder plus explosive shells and solid shot. Somers and 13 other officers and men volunteered to take the ketch into the harbor at night and blow her up, if possible in the midst of Tripolitan shipping. They were discovered near the harbor entrance and *Intrepid*'s crew exploded their deadly cargo, destroying an enemy gunboat. Somers and all his crew were lost.

Many Somers memorabilia are preserved in the little museum of the Atlantic County Historical Society

Figure 27
Museum at Navesink Twin Lights; Highlands, New Jersey.

in Somers Point, next door to the Somers family mansion. Beside uniforms and personal weapons of the Naval hero, the museum has half models of local coasting vessels, nine ship models by Ottie, and tools from area shipyards. The society's library has an extensive collection of shipowners' papers and ships' logs.

The Somers mansion next door dates from around 1726. Also opened to visitors by the Historical Society, the house is furnished in the Colonial period.

Atlantic County Historical Society Museum and Library are in Somers Point, a small town on the northern shore of Great Egg Bay, 10 miles south of Atlantic City on the New Jersey coast. Next door, 250-year-old Somers mansion is also open to visitors. Open Wednesday-Saturday, 10 a.m. to noon, 1 p.m. to 4 p.m. Admission: $1.00. Atlantic County Historical Society, 907 Shore Road, P.O. Box 301, Somers Point, New Jersey 08244. Telephone (609) 927-5218.

Now out across the inlet a short distance to the barrier island at the south side of the entrance to Great Egg Harbor.

On the beautiful beaches of the Jersey coast, the era of vacation resorts overlapped the era of wrecks—witness the famous wreck of the *Sindia* at Ocean City. This seaside town was founded in 1879 and eventually acquired such amenities for vacationers as trolley cars and a boardwalk. In December, 1901, the four-masted bark *Sindia* was driven on the beach, just off the boardwalk.

Four months out of Shanghai, bound for New York, *Sindia* was laden with "camphor, silk, matting, camphor oil, and novelties." The crew was taken off by a surfboat of the Life-Saving Service and part of the cargo, badly damaged, was eventually removed on lighters. The expense of removal proved more than the salvage could be sold for, and much cargo remained on the hulk.

Gradually the wreck disappeared, but remains of *Sindia*'s rudder post and tiller are reported to be still sticking out of the sand off the boardwalk at Ocean City's 16th Street. The Ocean City Historical Museum has a special Sindia Room devoted to relics and mementos of the famous wreck. Exhibits include artifacts, photographs, ships' papers, and pieces of the *Sindia*'s cargo that were preserved by local residents. There are also ship models.

Non-maritime exhibits in the museum include costumes, furniture, pictures, household articles, Indian relics, and natural history exhibits.

The Ocean City Historical Museum is at Ocean City, a little resort town on a barrier island on the south side of the entrance to Great Egg Inlet, about 10 miles south of Atlantic City on the New Jersey shore. Open: winter, Tuesday-Saturday, 1 to 4 p.m.; summer, Monday-Saturday, 10 a.m. to 4 p.m. Admission: free. Ocean City Historical Museum, 409 Wesley Avenue, Ocean City, New Jersey 08226. Telephone (609) 399-1801.

Now to Delaware Bay, which separates southern New Jersey from Pennsylvania and Delaware.

Delaware Bay I: Philadelphia and Wilmington

In August 1609, Henry Hudson was poking his way up the Atlantic Coast of North America in the little Dutch "yacht" *Half Moon*. A valiant Englishman in Dutch employ, he was looking for the Northwest Passage, the hoped-for straits that would let European ships pass through the North American barrier and reach the riches of East Asia. He turned hopefully into the wide mouth of a bay fed by a great river. Like all the other estuaries he investigated, however, Delaware Bay proved a disappointment. As his mate recorded in the ship's log: "[In] the Bay we found Shoal; we were forced to stand backe [to sea] again. Steered away to the Eastward on many courses for it is full of shoals. He that would discover the Bay must have sould a small Pinnasse that draw but foure or five foot water to before him."

Hudson went on northward to New York harbor, where he found deep water with few hazards. From the beginning, silted Delaware Bay, with a channel winding among sandbars, has suffered in comparison with New York. Delaware Bay is the drowned valley of the Delaware River; as retreating glaciers melted and the sea level rose, it was filled by the Atlantic Ocean. Originating far to the north, the river cuts through the Appalachians with many shallows and rapids until it reaches Trenton, the head of navigation. From there the Delaware curves like a huge letter C down to Wilmington, then gradually broadens into Delaware Bay, its mouth between Cape May and Cape Henlopen.

Despite its shoals and winding channel, however, Delaware Bay early invited settlement. The Dutch explored bay and river soon after Hudson's visit and built forts, which were largely wiped out by Indian attacks. The Swedes came next (actually, many of their settlers were Dutch), buying a huge tract of land from the Indians and founding Fort Christina where Wilmington is today. After 17 years, aggressive Pieter Stuyvesant seized the Swedish forts for the Netherlands. The Dutch called the Delaware the "South River." Their "North River," which has kept its name until today, is of course the Hudson where it flows past Manhattan Island.

The Dutch early recognized the menace to mariners of the winding channel and the many shoals in the bay and river, and in 1658 they buoyed the most dangerous shoals. They did not have long to enjoy the benefits, however: nine years later the English seized all of New Netherlands. A scattering of Dutch and Swedish settlers stayed on along the Delaware as English immigrants began to move in.

Twenty years later, King Charles II granted an enormous tract of land running westward from the Delaware to William Penn, an English aristocrat and Quaker. Penn's objective was to establish a colony where his fellow Quakers would be free from persecution. In 1682 he founded what was to become one of America's great cities and ports—for many years the greatest port in English-speaking North America—Philadelphia.

The son of a distinguished admiral, Penn was no sailor himself, but he fully recognized the importance of maritime activity to successful colonization. He chose a site on the west bank of the Delaware just upriver from where the Schuykill River runs in from the northwest. He hoped to find a place where the river was deep enough for large vessels to come right alongside the riverbank, rather than having to moor out in the stream to be loaded from lighters. This did not prove possible, but the first settlers of Philadelphia soon built wharves out to deep water.

The chosen site, while probably the best one within Penn's grant, had its drawbacks for a port. Philadelphia was 110 miles from the sea, but the winding channel, which was constantly shifting, made the passage many miles longer—a particularly difficult approach for sailing ships that had to tack between the sandbanks. There is no naturally sheltered harbor on the almost 270 miles of Atlantic coast from Sandy Hook to the entrance to Chesapeake Bay. The mouth of Delaware Bay faces southeast, wide open to the prevailing winds along the coast, and in colonial days there was no shelter anywhere along either the bay or river for any but shallow-draft vessels that could run up the little entering creeks. During the first century and a half of Philadelphia's existence, hundreds of ships were lost in the mouth of the bay and on the adjacent shores. As late as 1820, 55 ships were wrecked within 10 miles of the Delaware Capes. It was

estimated in 1821 that in the preceding 20 years 255 Philadelphia-bound vessels fearful of being blown ashore, were driven out to sea from the open mouth of the Bay. Not until 1828 was a break-water finally built to provide a harbor of refuge at Lewes, on the south side of the bay entrance.

Philadelphia port had another disadvantage, as her merchants soon discovered. Although the city is as far south as Lisbon, Philadelphia turned out to be the most ice-ridden port on the Atlantic Seaboard, surpassed only by Quebec and Montreal on the St. Lawrence. As a result of cold winters and the low salt content of the river at Philadelphia, the harbor froze over regularly and shipping came to a standstill for several months. In the winter of 1809, for example, 17 vessels were lost due to ice. Eventually, so-called ice harbors had to be built along the Delaware. These were piers that broke up floating ice and provided shelter on the downstream side.

The fact that despite these handicaps Philadelphia became a great port is a tribute to the hard work and skills of her people. For Philadelphia has no mean maritime heritage, as Marion Brewington, distinguished scholar of maritime history, has pointed out. Referring to such famous maritime centers as New York, Boston, Baltimore, Nantucket, Salem, and New Bedford, he once wrote:

Ours [Philadelphia's] is equally as interesting, almost as ancient, and in some ways of even greater importance in national history. We can truthfully assure ourselves no port in the United States can produce anything which we cannot duplicate, sometimes as innovators, sometimes as improvers, seldom just as imitators.

The whalemen of New Bedford and Nantucket may well have learned their trade from the men who were working in the Delaware as early as 1633, seven years before the first whalery was organized to the north. The clipper ship designers of Boston and New York certainly owed something to little Philadelphia trading sloops such as the one Jonathan Dickenson had built in 1719, a sloop he described in exactly the same terminology William H. Webb or Donald McKay might have used in 1850, "sharp built." Our ships began the North American trade with our sister continent to the South. Our merchants opened the trade with China and India and at no time from 1784 to 1850 did Philadelphia control less than one third of the investment in East India voyages, but reading the maritime history of Boston and Salem one gathers the idea that they alone navigated the Indian Ocean and the China Seas. Those who think in terms of fighting ships will recall the original Continental fleet sailed from Philadelphia on the first expedition of the War for Independence. They will also remember that the first United States men of war, including the frigate *Constitution*, came from the brain of a Philadelphia

Quaker, Joshua Humphreys. Robert Fulton is popularly credited with the first steamboat; we know better: John Fitch built and operated a steamer on the Delaware almost a quarter of a century before the *North River Steamboat of Clairmont* moved up the Hudson.

Settled by industrious craftsmen and small businessmen, Penn's little city and port flourished almost from the start. Penn made sure that a skilled shipbuilder was among his settlers (he considered shipbuilding so important that he ordered his two sons trained in the craft) and in the first 30 years nearly 300 vessels were launched—mostly little ships and sloops, but supplying the needs of a healthy commerce. Timber, at first from the nearby clearing of farmlands, later rafted down the Delaware, provided ample supplies of oak, both for local shipyards and for export to Europe. The cleared fields supplied the cargo: wheat and flour for shipment to other colonies and to the West Indies. In the islands ships picked up sugar and rum for Europe. If the cargo was sold in an English port, the proceeds were invested in what Pennsylvania needed—such things as iron, textiles, and tea. If the sugar went to Spain and Portugal, there would be a fourth stop; wine for thirsty Britons would be loaded before the voyage home with an English cargo.

With a profit on each transaction, the net returns on a successful voyage were substantial—and kept increasing. In the early days, a merchant could sell the cargo brought home to Philadelphia for some three and a half times his original investment. Seventy years later, in 1768, his return was likely to run eight times the investment.

Assuming, that is, that his ship came in—which was far from assured. Storms took their toll, and during England's frequent wars with other European powers, enemy warships or privateers were happy to snap up a rich Philadelphia cargo. And then there were pirates—at least in the early years—waiting off the entrance to Delaware Bay.

Philadelphia's attitude toward pirates was ambiguous. Piracy was, of course, a hanging offense, and the entrance to many a port was decorated by the body of an executed freebooter swinging on the gallows. But in Pennsylvania, the Quaker authorities were reluctant to undertake the often bloody measures required to wipe out piracy.

And in these early days there was a further piracy problem. Most of the pirates around Philadelphia had committed their major crimes on the other side of the world; based in Madagascar, they looted the rich commerce between Arab ports and India. Many came to Delaware Bay seeking a quiet place to dispose of their booty with no embarrassing questions asked, and there were merchants in Philadelphia quite ready to oblige when the price was right. One pirate even married the daughter of the colony's governor and received the gubernatorial blessing.

That the presence of these freebooters was pretty generally known is evident from reports that appeared in a Philadelphia newspapers of the time. In 1690, for example, readers were told that some 60 pirates had arrived in a ship richly laden with East India goods "besides abundance of money."

Eventually, a combination of circumstances disposed of the pirates. The Penn heirs yielded their proprietary rights to the Crown and the new Royal government had no inhibitions about violence against pirates. The establishment of Admiralty courts in the colonies made it possible to try, convict, and hang pirates and other maritime wrongdoers on the spot.

Meanwhile Philadelphia flourished and became one of the major cities and ports of the American colonies. On a single day in October, 1754, an observer counted 117 large ships in the port. Shipbuilding continued to be an important Philadelphia industry; some family firms started in the 18th century continued to turn out ships for almost a century and a half. Cramp's, a famous Philadelphia yard still going in the 1920s, was the direct successor of a firm founded in 1760. Philadelphia ships were noted for their beauty and fine construction. In 1784 a member told the British House of Commons: "New England has supplied about two fifths of the whole number of American ships employed in Great Britain. But the most beautiful are those built in Philadelphia where this art has attained to the greatest perfection, equal, perhaps superior to any other part of the world."

At the very outbreak of the Revolution, Philadelphia's harbor saw the first American flag raised on a warship by John Paul Jones, First Lieutenant of the Continental warship *Alfred*, as a little Continental naval squadron departed Philadelphia on a cruise that culminated in the capture of the principal town of the Bahamas. Philadelphia yards built a major portion of the Continental Navy, including six frigates and 54 vessels for the Pennsylvania State Navy. Commodore John Barry, often called the Father of the American Navy, was a Philadelphia man who later became Commander-in-Chief of the new United States Navy. Philadelphia privateers raided British shipping, until the Royal Navy slapped a blockade across the entrance to Delaware Bay.

At the outset of the War of Independence, the Port Wardens ordered the removal of all important channel buoys in the Delaware, and forts were subsequently built on islands in the river. Here a small squadron of American gunboats harassed a Royal

Navy task force. The enemy warships came up the Delaware to clear a passage for ships carrying badly needed supplies for the British troops who had already captured Philadelphia. The American gunboats —little 50-foot row galleys—tried to keep the British from removing obstacles that had been sunk to block the channel. The British force, far greater than the defenders, eventually destroyed the forts by gunfire, removed enough obstacles to pass through, and forced the gunboats to retreat up the river. Although British troops evacuated Philadelphia the next spring, Delaware Bay remained closed by the blockade.

During their occupation, the British destroyed all of Philadelphia's seagoing vessels and most of the local river craft, so after the war there was an immediate boom in shipbuilding. Now the yards concentrated on big ships that could be manned by relatively small crews. At the same time, Philadelphia merchants and shipowners began a successful shift from the old West India trade to more distant markets. By the 1790s, Philadelphia ranked first among American ports. The Philadelphia ship *Canton* was a pioneer in the China trade. The ship *United States* of Philadelphia was the first American vessel to enter an Indian port. By 1800, 40 Philadelphia ships were trading with China and about the same number were in the South American trade. In the 65 years after the close of the Revolution, Philadelphia was responsible for one-third of the American China trade. By 1793, Philadelphia's exports were valued at one quarter of the exports from the entire United States.

This period saw other important maritime activities in this bustling port. Inventor John Fitch successfully operated his little steamboat on the Delaware in 1786, but he lacked the financial backing that would have given him Fulton's place in history. When the time came to build a new Navy, Philadelphia naval architect Joshua Humphreys designed the famous first six frigates. Philadelphia established the nation's first school for ship carpenters. Philadelphia ships set a number of speed records to distant ports: Mobile, New Orleans, Rio de Janeiro. The 14-day passage of the Philadelphia-built ship *Rebecca Sims* from the Delaware Capes to Liverpool in 1809 was never equaled by a sailing ship.

In the War of 1812, Philadelphia built and manned small, fast privateers built along the lines of the famous Baltimore clippers, but for most of the war the Royal Navy again blockaded the entrance of Delaware Bay. Philadelphia's chief contribution was in the remarkable career of her captains in the United States Navy: 9 of the 16 gold medals voted by Congress to naval officers went to captains from Philadelphia.

Nevertheless, Philadelphia shipping came to a standstill during the conflict and the port never fully recovered its preeminence afterward. New York, ice-free, close to open ocean, tied to the new Midwest by the Erie Canal, took over Philadelphia's place as the number-one American port. At the same time, Philadelphia capitalists turned their investments away from the sea to the new iron and coal mines opened up in inland Pennsylvania and to the new manufacturing industries that they spawned.

Philadelphia remained, however, in the first rank of American ports. Philadelphia emulated New York by starting a packet line direct to Liverpool, and her ships engaged in a profitable traffic carrying cotton from southern gulf ports to New England and to Europe. Eventually the breakwater at the mouth of Delaware Bay was expanded to provide a harbor of refuge, and a more direct channel was dredged in the shoal-filled Delaware.

Philadelphia's shipyards continued to be an important part of the nation's maritime activities. During the Civil War, Philadelphia turned out monitors and armored ships for the Union Navy. In 1872, a Philadelphia yard launched the first iron ocean liner built in the United States. During World War I, the largest shipyard in the world—housing 50 ways—was set up on Hog Island in the Delaware River. Fed by 300 freight cars a day bringing in steel plates and frames, Hog Island built 1,700 vessels in two years. During World War II, the process was repeated, although new shipbuilding techniques, involving the assemblage of large prefabricated sections, made fewer ways necessary.

Today, Philadelphia, with a new terminal for container ships, ranks fourth among American ports on the Atlantic coast. The active shipping terminals have moved down river to South Philadelphia. The old waterfront has become Penn's Landing, a mooring place for some extremely interesting ships of other days and close to the historic district where many buildings played significant roles in the nation's past.

But although the ships are of great interest in themselves, they don't have a great deal to do with Philadelphia. The place to explore the city's own maritime heritage is the Philadelphia Maritime Museum, so we shall start there.

Located in a fine Victorian building on Chestnut Street, the Maritime Museum is in the heart of Philadelphia's historic district, just a couple of blocks from Independence Hall. The exhibits tell the story of the ships, seamen, and merchants of Philadelphia and the Delaware as well as cover broader aspects of maritime history.

On the first floor of the museum a sampling of ship models, artifacts, pictures, and wall displays gives the visitor an introduction to things maritime. Particularly helpful are two wall-size diagramatic drawings of the famous frigate *Philadelphia*. A bow-to-stern cutaway shows all the decks and spaces, populated by members of the ship's company in typical activities. Next to it, the frigate's masts, spars, rigging, and sails are clearly diagramed. A series of pictorial explanations in the next bay clarifies such often puzzling maritime terms as "displacement" and "propulsion."

Also worth looking for in the first-floor galleries are a colorful set of old prints that satirically describes "sailors ashore." Some remarkably fine ship models include a large and extremely handsome bone model of the three-decker HMS *Caledonia*, 120, one of the largest warships in the world when she was built in 1805.

The first floor also contains The *Titanic* Gallery devoted to the end of that proud liner, which in 1912 sank with great loss of life after colliding with an iceberg on her maiden voyage. Photographs, documents, newspaper reports, mementos, even sheet music, report or comment on the tragedy. Two artifacts vividly bridge the gap of 70 years. One is a battered deck chair that floated away as the ship went down. Across it lies a faded red life jacket. Mrs. John Jacob Astor, whose husband went down with the *Titanic*, was wearing it when rescued. She said a male passenger took it off and gave it to her as they stood on the deck of the sinking liner.

Other special highlights to look for:

- the cocked hat worn by Captain Stephen Decatur, naval hero of the War of 1812;
- the only surviving figurehead, "Peace," known to have been carved by the distinguished Philadelpia sculptor, William Rush. (Rush's figurehead for the ship *Ganges* is said to have been worshiped as a Hindu god when the ship visited India);
- one of the oldest surviving American ship models—an 18th-century schooner—in the fourth floor library of the museum;
- a model of a passenger canal barge, the roof removed to show the interior arrangements;
- a larger-than-life carved figure of a naval officer shooting the sun—originally the shop sign of a marine-instrument maker;
- a nice display of "The Arts of the Sailor"—scrimshaw, string weaving, carving, and so forth.

The second floor of the museum, undergoing renovation, will be used for changing exhibits. On the third floor is a unique section, not to be missed—a "visible storage" gallery where visitors can peer thorugh a glass wall at acquisitions awaiting exhibition.

Like many museums, the Philadelphia Maritime has treasures for which it has not yet display space; unlike most museums, though, the museum has not hidden them away but uses them to give the visitors an idea of how the collection is growing and developing.

Philadelphia Maritime Museum on Chestnut Street in the heart of historic Philadelphia. Open Monday-Saturday, 10 a.m. to 5 p.m.; Sunday, 1 to 5 p.m. Closed Thanksgiving, December 24, 25, and 31, New Year's Day, and Easter. Donations requested. Small gift/book shop. Philadelphia Maritime Museum, 321 Chestnut Street, Philadelphia, Pennsylvania 19106. Telephone (215) 925-5439.

Not all of the Philadelphia Maritime Museum is on Chestnut Street. Just three blocks east of the museum, Chestnut runs into an overpass that takes auto and foot traffic into the parking lot of the new Penn's Landing development. Here, set on a barge in the Delaware river, is the Maritime Museum's "Workshop on the Water," where boat building is demonstrated and periodically taught in classes open to the public. The barge is also used for display of small craft used on the Delaware for work and pleasure.

Actually the Museum Workshop is only a small part of the maritime attractions at Penn's Landing. Here, along an esplanade that rims the riverfront where William Penn and his settlers landed, are berthed a number of historic ships. They vary widely in age and nature, from a 100-year-old barkentine to a World War II submarine, but all are of great interest.

Farthest north, alongside the parking lot, is the huge four-masted bark *Moshulu*, ex-*Dreadnaught*, ex-*Kurt*. The *Moshulu* is an impressive sight. More than 335 feet long, she is one of the few survivors of the remarkable early-20th-century windjammers so efficient as cargo carriers that they could compete with steam tramps. (*Peking* at New York's South Street Seaport is another such survivor.)

What it was like to sail in *Moshulu* around Cape Horn has been preserved in photographs taken by Eric Newby when he took part in the Australian grain race in 1939. In his book, *Windjammer* (*Grain Race* in the English edition), Newby tells how he signed on as a greenhorn apprentice and took photographs while off watch. The photographs are fascinating, the introduction and captions highly informative. Any visitor will get far more out of his *Moshulu* visit if he reads *Windjammer* (now out of print but available in libraries), preferably beforehand, but in any case, afterward.

Stand back and take a good look at her. *Moshulu* is a distinctive type; her size, rig, and design are not the result of whim or chance, but the answers to very practical problems.

Her size: *Moshulu* looks big and for a sailing ship she is; she could carry about 5,000 tons of bulk cargo. Size was an important factor in economical operation. Her crew, including officers, numbered between 28 and 33, an average of about 165 tons of payload per crew member. In contrast, most merchant ships in the 18th century carried fewer than 20 tons of payload per man. It should be added that the small crew was made possible by technology—a donkey engine to hoist the anchors and haul up the heavy yards at the start of a voyage and winches that made it possible for a few men to handle braces and halyards by turning cranks.

Her rig: A four-masted bark, *Moshulu* spread 35 sails, a total of 45,000 square feet of canvas. To carry this huge spread, the three masts of a conventional ship would have had to be so large and heavy that the vessel might be dismasted, so a fourth mast was added, the smaller "jigger" aft, to spread the load. Unlike the other masts, the jigger carries fore-and-aft rig, which makes *Moshulu* a bark instead of a four-masted ship in the strict technical sense. The fore-and-aft jigger made the vessel handier.

Her design: The *Moshulu* is a "three-island" ship with a short head deck in the bow, an amidships bridge deck (sometimes called a "Liverpool House") and a short raised poop at the stern. Beneath the bridge deck were living quarters and galley. *Moshulu* was steered from the bridge deck and much of the sail handling could be done there, above the seas that washed across the main deck in heavy water. Hauling braces in the exposed waist of a conventional windjammer in heavy weather was a dangerous job.

Her lines: From the shore you can get a good look at *Moshulu*'s bow and stern and see her sharp bow and fine run aft. *Mosholu* was known to make 15 knots with her rail underwater. Her best outward-bound passage from Cardiff to Valparaiso was 68 days, made when she was deeply loaded with coal. In 1909, she twice made 300 miles between noon observations.

Now it's time to go aboard. The visitor will quickly notice an anomaly; immediately below her main deck is a row of large plate glass windows that would not have lasted 30 seconds when *Moshulu* was beating around the Horn. The windows reflect *Moshulu*'s double life. Most of the bark has been undergoing a long and careful restoration to her former glory on the day she went down the ways in Port Glasgow, Scotland, in 1904. However, her 'tween decks, immediately under the main deck, has been transformed into an elegant waterfront restaurant.

The effect is incongruous, but under the circumstances it is perhaps the best resolution of a difficult situation. After a long career at sea, *Moshulu* ended up in the 1960s as a mastless hulk used as a float-ing warehouse in Finland. There she was bought by a restaurant company, fitted with new masts and spars in Amsterdam, and towed across the Atlantic. Once in New York, however, she waited at dockside for two years while her owners tried in vain to find some economical way to complete her restoration. Failing this, they had her towed to Philadelphia; one deck was converted to a restaurant, and restoration work continued on the remainder of the ship at their expense. More than two million dollars has been spent on her so far; her use as a restaurant, which does not interfere with the restoration of the upper works, seems a happier fate than ending up a hulk awaiting the scrapyard. Certainly it is easy for the ship-minded visitor to walk through the restaurant, climb to the main deck, and enjoy the spectacle of a massive windjammer being returned to something approaching her original condition.

When you come out on her open deck, take a look aloft at her towering masts and huge spars—her main yards are more than 95 feet long and each weigh more than five tons—and at her marvelously intricate rigging—more than 300 lines come down to be held by belaying pins, cleats, or bits. The mainmast is more than 200 feet high, and in his book, Newby reports that the first day he came aboard as a green apprentice the second mate ordered him to climb to the very top—the last six feet shimmying up a bare pole.

The space below the bridge deck amidships now houses an exhibition area for ship models, prints, and photographs of *Moshulu* during her active career. The restoration work is shown in pictures and explained in a slide show. Besides fine models of two other great barks of similar vintage, *Passat* and *Pamir*, a striking exhibit is the house flag of Siemers, the Hamburg shipping firm for which *Moshulu* was built: a golden star and moon joined on a flaming red field.

The galley and one of the two fo'c'sles housed under the bridge deck—each of which housed ten men—are open for viewing. (Take a sharp look at the calendar in the fo'c'sle—a nice touch.)

The well deck forward of the bridge house has been restored, and photographs of the ship at sea have been mounted on pedestal stands. Particularly amusing is a picture of a couple of the ship's pigs, taken along to provide fresh meat during the passage. One of apprentice Newby's jobs was to take care of the pigs.

The restoration crew is helpful and friendly and, if not too busy, someone is usually happy to take an inquiring visitor down into the hold. Except for a collision bulkhead forward, the entire hold is one open space; practically the entire interior of the steel hull can be seen except for the bilges, which are hidden by sand ballast.

The restoration has already come a long way and *Moshulu* is once again a noble ship, a worthy survivor from the final days of commercial sail.

Bark Moshulu, moored at Penn's Landing at the foot of Chestnut Street, parking adjacent. No admission charge. Open when restaurant is open. Owned by Specialty Restaurants Corp., Chestnut Mall, Penn's Landing, Philadelphia, Pennsylvania 19106. Telephone (215) 925-3237.

Walk southward along the esplanade beside the Delaware and after a quarter of a mile or so you come to a boat basin cut into the riverbank. Here, on a finger pier is berthed the barkentine *Gazela Primeiro*, heritor of one of the most ancient North American maritime traditions.

At first glance *Gazela Primeiro* may seen an exotic stranger in America. More than 100 years old, she spent her working life not in world commerce, but with the Portuguese fishing fleet on the Banks of Newfoundland. Actually, however, *Gazela* is the ultimate survivor of a continuous sailing ship connection between the Old World and the New that is five centuries old. Portuguese fishermen crossed the Atlantic to fish the teeming banks off North America only a few years after Columbus. According to historian Samuel Eliot Morison, by 1506 there were so many Portuguese vessels bringing big catches home from the banks that the King, to protect stay-at-home fishermen, put a duty on fish caught in North American waters. Morison points out that many current place names in Newfoundland and the adjacent mainland are corrupted English or French versions of original Portuguese names given by the first comers.

Gazela was built in 1883 with pine cut from a Portuguese forest preserve planted in 1480 by Prince Henry the Navigator. She is the last of the square-rigged Portuguese fishing vessels that, like the famous Gloucester fishing schooners, served as mother to a fleet of one-man dories, each handling a half-mile trawl line. Crossing the Atlantic to the banks in the spring, she would stay until her hold was full of more than 700,000 pounds of salted cod; sometimes this took six months.

In appearance *Gazela* makes a striking contrast to neighboring *Moshulu*. Some 177 feet long, she has a low freeboard and a beautiful clipper bow. Only 350 tons, she nevertheless carried crews of 30 to 37 men—more than *Moshulu*, which was ten times her size. The men were not needed, of course, to work the ship; their job was to man the dories she carried nested on her decks. The work day was 12 hours or so afloat,

plus more hours cleaning and salting down the catch, day in and day out, until the hold was full.

The fo'c'sle, with its three tiers of bunks where the fishermen lived for long months at sea, is open for viewing. Amidships, the 'tween decks and fish hold have been converted into an exhibit area, with displays of fishing gear, ship's carpenters' tools and similar gear. Visitors can peer down at her four-cylinder diesel engine, which was only installed about 1938 after *Gazela* had served more than a half a century on the banks under sail alone. The addition of an engine was indirectly caused by the migration of cod northward from the banks into Davis Strait. When the fishing fleet followed the cod, several ships without engines were blown ashore in Arctic gales; *Gazela* was given power to enable her to fight her way off from a lee shore.

A steep and winding stair aft, requiring some careful navigation, leads to the officers' little saloon and cabins—carefully labeled in Portuguese "Capitaño" and "Piloto."

Barkentine Gazela Primeiro is tied up on opposite sides of a finger pier in the boat basin at Penn's Landing on the Philadelphia riverfront. Parking lot is reached from the east end of Chestnut Street by an overpass; ships are a short distance south of the lot. When in port the ship is open from noon to 5 p.m. (call to check when the ship is in port). Admission: 50 cents. Sponsored by Penn's Landing, Spruce and Delaware Avenue, Philadelphia, Pennsylvania 19106. Telephone (215) 923-9030.

Move along now to the impressive-looking warship at a nearby berth.

At 5:41 the morning of May 1, 1898, Commodore George Dewey leaned over the rail of the forward bridge of the USS *Olympia* and spoke to her captain, Charles V. Gridley. In a quiet voice, according to a contemporary historian, he said: "When you are ready, you may fire, Gridley." So began the Battle of Manila Bay, which ended later that morning in one of the most one-sided victories in American naval history. Dewey's order caught the public imagination—perhaps because it was so very commonplace compared to the heroics of legendary battle slogans.

The *Olympia*, Dewey's flagship in the battle, has survived to this day, and may be seen at Penn's Landing on the Philadelphia riverfront. She is unique in more ways than one. Besides playing a major role in a historic naval action—a major step in American involvement in East Asia—the *Olympia* is the only surviving United States ship of war to have served in the Spanish-American war. In addition, she is an extremely interesting vessel in herself, representing a transitional period in the evolution of steam warships.

Even in her own time, *Olympia* was a distinctive vessel. Commissioned in 1895, she was, still is, a so-called protected cruiser, a type that has long since vanished form the world's navies. As such, the *Olympia* has no side armor, but a curved protective deck of four-and-a-half-inch steel just above the waterline, covering her vital parts. Like other protected cruisers, she was armed with many small-caliber guns, individually mounted. But she was unique in possessing a main battery of four eight-inchers, the same size as carried by the armored cruisers, the next larger type of almost 50 percent greater tonnage. Her top speed was almost 22 knots, high for her day. A naval historian has called her perhaps one of the best ships in the world of her size and date.

Manila Bay, *Olympia*'s only battle action, came early in her career. In World War I she served with the American expeditionary force sent to Murmansk, Russia, as part of the Allied intervention against the Bolshevik government. In 1921 she had the honor of bringing home for burial the body of America's Unknown Soldier.

Olympia suffered greatly from vandalism and poor maintenance before she was finally turned over to a nonprofit association to be restored and maintained as a naval shrine and museum. But while some sections are still awaiting further work, she is once again a handsome ship and one of the most interesting naval vessels now on display.

The visitor will quickly see that the warship of 100 years ago was very different from today's. Particularly noticeable is the great amount of wood in the interior—paneled walls, bunks, and bureaus in the officers' cabins, and wooden decks. Wood splinters are notorious killers so much of the interior wood partitions are demountable—just as they were back in the days of the *Constitution*—so they could be folded up and stowed out of harm's way before a battle. Some woodwork was even thrown overboard, but it seems that there would have been enough left to set the ship ablaze if she had taken a bad hit.

Olympia's two straight-sided turrets, each containing a pair of 8-inch guns, are visually more reminiscent of the "cheesebox" turret on the Civil War *Monitor* than of the great armored turrets of modern battleships with sloping faceplates. (Actually, the *Olympia*'s turrets are mock-ups; over the years her original turrets and main battery were removed.) The ship's secondary battery, five-inch guns on the upper deck, six-pounders on the deck below, are very much in evidence, as their bays are wide open into the living spaces. Some of the five-inchers are set into the officers' cabins.

Olympia was fitted with twin screws, each with its own triple-expansion steam engine, and visitors should be sure to visit the starboard engine room and stokehold. The fireroom became miserably hot in tropical climates, as a contemporary account noted with considerable understatement: "On Friday [two days before the battle] the weather was very warm and sultry and the work of the coal passers, far down in the bunkers, was extremely debilitating." Incidentally, notice how the coal bunkers were set against the sides of the hull to provide additional protection for the engines and boilers against shellfire.

Outside, the *Olympia*'s most striking features are her flying bridges fore and aft and her tall funnels, typical of the period. The towering masts no longer carry the spars of *Olympia*'s original schooner rig, but they still recall the sailing frigates of an earlier day.

Here are some other things to look out for:

- the simple watertight doors—the beginning of the elaborate compartmentation system used on modern warships to minimize battle damage;
- the huge tank for drinking water—the traditional "scuttlebutt" where crew members exchanged rumors and ship's gossip;
- the ash hoists running up from the stoke hold at the bottom of the ship, which were required to get rid of the endless flow of ashes from her furnaces;
- the sign on the inner side of the hull on the lower deck: "A Spanish shell passed thru the side at this point—damage unimportant." (The entire American squadron came out of the battle practically unscathed; the only casualties were seven men with minor injuries.);
- the exhibits in *Olympia*'s little museum. Among them is a waterline model of the battleship *Maine*, whose loss by explosion in Havana harbor was one of the precipitating causes of the Spanish-American War. American uniforms of the Spanish-American War period are particularly interesting.

Tied up between the *Olympia* and the shore is a warship of quite a different vintage. The submarine *Becuna* was commissioned almost half a century after the historic cruiser, just in time to take part in the final Pacific campaigns of World War II. As shown by the trophy flags painted on her conning tower, she sank 26,000 tons of enemy shipping during her five war patrols. On the surface *Becuna* was almost as fast as *Olympia*, but underwater her speed was reduced to nine knots.

The visitor progresses from the forward torpedo room aft through the central corridor. While there is not a great deal of explanation of how things worked, the diagrams in each space marked "You are here" are very helpful in orienting the visitor. Among the nice personal touches are the uniforms hung up in the cabins. One space has been set aside as a memorial to the American submarines lost in World War II.

Protected Cruiser *Olympia* and Submarine *Becuna* are berthed in the boat basin at Penn's Landing, on the Delaware riverfront of Philadelphia. Open all year except Christmas and New Year's Day. Summers 10 a.m. to 6 p.m. and winters 10 a.m. to 4:30 p.m. (call to confirm hours). Admission: $2.00; children under 12, $2.50. Sponsored by Cruiser Olympia Association, P.O. Box 928, Philadelphia, Pennsylvania 19105. Telephone (215) 922-1898.

Before leaving Philadelphia, some travelers may want to visit the American Philosophical Society. While not specifically maritime in interest, this ancient and distinguished institution possesses some remarkable artifacts from our maritime heritage. The first scientific society in the American colonies, the American Philosophical Society was founded in 1743 with Benjamin Franklin as its moving spirit. Its venerable hall and beautiful library are located on Fifth Street, practically next door to Independence Hall.

Over the years the Society has been presented with a fascinating collection of instruments, models, and artifacts—some of them as supporting evidence for the applications for the Society's gold medal for useful inventions. Among the objects of maritime interest are:

- Inventor John Fitch's model of a paddle system for propelling a vessel. Eight paddles moved by an endless chain are shown mounted on a little boat. Fitch, who eventually built a workable steamboat well before Fulton, made the little paddle boat himself and presented it to the society in 1785.
- A model of a brass log for measuring the speed of a ship, believed to have been made by Commodore David Porter, the 1812 War hero.
- A model of an automatic ship pump, powered by a water wheel hung on the side of a ship, presented by the inventor in 1768.

Particularly interesting are a sailor-made model of the U.S. Sloop of War *Peacock*, and a model of the brigantine *Advance*, which was lost in the ice during the Kane Arctic expedition. A modern *working* model of Fitch's steamboat demonstrates the essential validity of the inventor's pioneering concepts in the development of steam navigation.

The American Philosophical Society has many non-maritime treasures of great interest, of course. Two in particular have an awesome ability to link the viewer with two great Americans. Benjamin Franklin's high-backed leather armchair stands on a platform of honor at one end of the gallery containing the society's wonderful collection of models and instruments. Facing it at the other end of the room is the Windsor armchair of Thomas Jefferson, which he himself specially designed with a broad writing board attached to the right arm.

The American Philosophical Society's hall and library face each other across Fifth Street in the very heart of historic Philadelphia. Visitors interested in seeing the collections should apply at the reception desk in the library. Admission: free. Open all year. Monday to Friday, 9 a.m. to 5 p.m. American Philosophical Society, 105 Fifth Street, Philadelphia, Pennsylvania 19106. Telephone (215) 627-0706.

Not all collections of maritime interest belong to museums or learned societies; some were gathered by private companies whose business was concerned with maritime affairs. Philadelphia is the headquarters of one such concern: the Insurance Company of North America (which merged with another insurance company a few years ago and is now known as CIGNA Corporation).

The insuring of ships and cargo against the perils of the sea, from great storms to mutiny and piracy, is believed to be the oldest of all forms of insurance. Some rudimentary way of spreading the risk seems to have existed in ancient Greece, and marine insurance was established in Europe by the end of the Middle Ages. Not surprisingly, when the Insurance Company of North America was founded in 1792 as the nation's first stock insurance company, marine underwriting was its first business. (Fire insurance was added two years later.)

Over the years, the company—with headquarters in Philadelphia—gathered a remarkable collection of art and artifacts related to the sea and ships. Fine contemporary ship models, seascapes and ships' portraits, books and records, memorabilia, and maps reflect maritime activities of almost two centuries.

Part of this collection, which focuses primarily on American and British activities, has been generously lent to museums and historical societies across the country and some pictures and models have been distributed among the offices of the company. However, many of the company's treasures are on display in a museum at the former INA headquarters building, a block from City Hall in downtown Philadelphia.

A dozen or more fine ship models can be seen in the 16th Street lobby of the building, which is open to the public during normal business hours. Among them are a big bone and ivory model of HMS *Caesar*, 80, made by French prisoners of war in 1805. Unusual is a contemporary model of USS *Jamestown*, an 1845 sloop of war with part of the planking removed to show the framing. Others include an 1880s bark in the American coastal trade, and a Chinese junk.

Arrangements to visit the museum gallery upstairs should preferably be made beforehand by telephone. Prints, paintings, ship portraits, and artifacts make up the maritime portion of the exhibit, with special emphasis on disasters at sea (of painful interest to an insurance company). Among the ship portraits are paintings of the British packet *Owen Potter*, and the *Great Republic*, Donald McKay's largest extreme clipper.

Much of the museum is devoted to pictures and artifacts related to the company's other major activity, fire insurance. Exhibits include fire engines and equipment.

Historical Maritime Collection of Insurance Company of North America is displayed in part at CIGNA Museum. Open Monday-Friday during normal business hours, roughly 8:30 a.m. to 5:30 p.m. Phone ahead for admission to gallery; register on arrival with guard in lobby. Admission: free. CIGNA Museum and Art Collection, 1600 Arch Street, Philadelphia, Pennsylvania 19103. Telephone (215) 241-4894.

One more stop in Philadelphia—this time for a look at the maritime-related exhibits in a venerable institution with a very up-to-date museum.

Philadelphia's Franklin Institute was founded in 1824, named for the city's tutelary genius, and dedicated to "the promotion of the mechanic arts," the first institution of its kind in the country. Today, beside being a national memorial to Franklin with many of his personal effects, the institute possesses a notable library, a planetarium, and a fine Science Museum.

Over the years, the Franklin Institute has also accumulated notable ship models and maritime pictures and artifacts. The Science Museum has used these, together with artifacts from other distinguished museums and private collections, to create a remarkable exhibit: "Shipbuilding on the Delaware." As the museum points out, this is the first time that many of these items have been put on display.

A permanent exhibit occupying 5,000 square feet of display space, "Shipbuilding" covers the rise and decline of the industry on the Delaware River over three centuries. What makes the exhibit particularly fascinating is the imaginative use of a wide range of objects and techniques, from historic artifacts from the distant past to the latest computer-controlled automated devices. Scale miniatures, "hands-on" devices, audiovisual programs, ship models, photographs, builders' plans, text—all are used to tell the story, highlight changes in shipbuilding technology, and show how money, men, and markets all affected the ways ships were built.

Here's a sampling of the many unusual things to look for:

- The 46-foot towing tank ("The only one available for public education in the western hemisphere," according to the institute), which is used to demonstrate how naval architects estimate the resistance of a hull design.
- "Widow Robert's Coffee Shop" where giant puppets of a merchant, shipwright, and sea captain dicker about money and material for a ship.
- Sea Trader: a computer game in which the visitor is challenged to solve problems of maritime trade. The player chooses a ship, a cargo, and a trade route that will make or break his fortune. Actual historical records are programmed into the data base so that the player may experience shipwrecks, mutinies, pirate attacks, typhoons, and so on, just as—and when—they happened.
- Do-it-yourself experiments, in which the visitor learns such things as:

— why sails and hulls are certain shapes;
— why an iron ship floats;
— how a paddlewheel works;
— how to make your own boat plans;
— how a screw propeller operates;
— how to load cargo into a ship's hold, while maintaining stability;
— how to hoist and trim sails;
— how to test ship models.

The Shipbuilding Exhibit was the Franklin Institute's gift to Philadelphia on its 300th birthday. It will fascinate lovers of ships and the sea wherever they may come from.

Franklin Institute Science Museum. Models, towing tank, photographs, ship plans, "hands-on" devices, computers, audiovisual programs portray 300 years of shipbuilding industry, highlighting technological changes. Museum also has planetarium, wide range of scientific, industrial exhibits. Open every day, Monday through Saturday, 10 a.m. to 5 p.m.; Sunday, noon to 5 p.m. Admission: $4.00; children 4 to 12, $3.00. Free weekend parking behind museum, off 21st Street. Taped information about exhibit: (215) 564-3375. Franklin Institute Science Museum and Planetarium, Benjamin Franklin Parkway at 20th Street, Philadelphia, Pennsylvania 19103. Telephone (215) 448-1200.

Now drop down some 30 miles along Delaware Bay to an even more ancient city, Delaware's Wilmington, already a 43-year-old town when Penn's settlers were still living in caves in the riverbank, but it was soon overshadowed by its big neighbor to the north—and has been ever since. Nevertheless, Wilmington has a distinctive maritime heritage of its own, as its people have begun to recognize in recent years.

In 1638 two Swedish ships arrived in Delaware to found a colony. Many of the settlers were Dutch, as was their leader, Pieter Minuit, who chose a hilly site to the west bank of the Delaware a few miles up the Christina River on a little peninsula where Brandywine Creek flowed in from the north. The two streams gave the site five miles of frontage on tidal rivers. Minuit's fort on the riverbank was named, like the river, for the Queen of Sweden, whom many American moviegoers will remember as looking exactly like Greta Garbo.

In the next few years the little settlement changed hands twice, seized first by the Dutch from New Amsterdam, then by the English. Like other Middle Atlantic ports, Wilmington shipped out grain and flour to other colonies and the West Indies. Shipbuilding was important from the very beginning; a ropewalk and a sail loft were among the earliest local enterprises. In the 35 years before the Revolution, most leading citizens of Wilmington had interests in locally built sailing vessels.

After the Revolution, Wilmington's trade with Cuba and the West Indies increased as a new process for kiln-drying corn made possible the delivery to tropical ports of meal free of mould and mustiness. By 1790, half the flour ground in the many mills along the Brandywine was exported. In 1800, Wilmington was described as a port of many brigs, sloops, and schooners in coastwise and West Indian trade.

Local flour milling declined somewhat after the opening of the Erie Canal, but shipbuilding continued to be an important Wilmington industry. In the 1840s, the first iron-ship building yard in the United States was established in Wilmington and four years later the *Bangor* was launched, the first iron propeller steamship built in this country. For a time, the city was the nation's largest producer of iron ships, from ferry boats to passenger liners and America's Cup yachts.

In the 20th century, Wilmington and the Delaware ports around it have become a center for tankers bringing petroleum from overseas. The port of Wilmington itself has shifted, however, to the Delaware riverfront. The Christina Kill is now largely a quiet backwater, where the first steps are being taken to preserve something of the maritime heritage of the nation, and ultimately of the city.

Launched into Wilmington's Christina River in 1934, the Coast Guard Cutter *Mohawk* has now returned to her birthplace like a homing salmon. Here she is being restored and refurbished, largely by volunteers as the first step in developing the banks of the Christina River. In a project sparked by Delaware architect Charles M. Weymouth, the *Mohawk* has become a museum, a memorial to the men who fought in the World War II Battle of the Atlantic against German submarines—a battle in which the cutter served on convoy duty.

Mohawk is also a fully operational cruising vessel, currently limited to inland waters on a "not for hire" basis, although her potential range is 7,000 miles at 14 knots. Today the 167-foot vessel—1,002 gross tons—may well be the only Coast Guard ship on permanent exhibition.

The cutter had a long career with varied duties. *Mohawk*'s regular station as a Coast Guard cutter/icebreaker was off Cape May at the entrance to Delaware Bay. Other peacetime service included a year on the Arctic Weather Patrol, but for the last 30 years of her active career *Mohawk* was stationed at Lewes, Delaware, to put bay and river pilots aboard vessels entering the Delaware.

The *Mohawk*'s story is told in an exhibit room aboard the cutter, which is tied up at a dock in the Christina River, behind the Amtrak railroad station. Her guns have been remounted, the decks show their original teak, and her interior has been completely scraped and painted. The officers' quarters and galley are among the sections already restored. Operated by a volunteer crew, she has already made a number of cruises as a traveling museum and good will ambassador. To help pay for her continuing rehabilitation—and upkeep—she is made available for training or entertaining on a fee basis.

Retired Coast Guard Cutter Mohawk is berthed in the Christina River, behind the Wilmington passenger railroad station, at the southern end of King Street. Open all year; Saturdays, 9 a.m. to 4 p.m.; weekdays by appointment (staff normally aboard). Admission: $1.00. Mohawk Corporation, 901 Washington Street, Wilmington, Delaware 19801. Telephone (302) 656-0400.

Figure 28
Cutter *Mohawk*, based in Christina River at Wilmington, Delaware, is only U.S. Coast Guard vessel on exhibition.

Before we go further down the coast, let's backtrack a little and go a ways up the Delaware well past the head of navigation.

Delaware Bay II: The Pennsylvania Canals

In eastern Pennsylvania, coal and canals went hand in hand. Deposits of anthracite were known in Colonial times, but not until the early 19th century did people learn to burn these hard black rocks properly in their stoves and forges. Then came the problem of how to get the coal from the mines in the Appalachian hills to consumers in Philadelphia and the river towns. To be sure, the Lehigh River ran from the coal country down to the Delaware River, some 80 river miles above Philadelphia, but the Lehigh, full of rocks and shallows, was not navigable.

Less than 400 tons of coal a year were produced until the 1820s, when an imaginative entrepreneur, impressed with coal as a fuel, investigated the possibility of somehow using the Lehigh to carry the coal to market. First, a series of sluices and dams were built on the river to concentrate the water flow so barges could ride down stream. Eventually, a canal was built along the banks of the Lehigh all the way from its headwaters to where it met the Delaware River at Easton. At this point the Delaware itself was not navigable, but within three years another canal was built to continue the waterway southward along the Delaware's bank; now there was an all-water route from the mining country to the coal-shipping port of Bristol on the lower Delaware, just above Philadelphia. In the early and mid-19th century, the canals carried 33 million tons of coal, transforming domestic heating systems and fueling the heartland of America's Industrial Revolution.

In 1855, however, a railroad was built from Easton to Maunch Chunk that eventually took away most of the canal's coal-carrying business. As elsewhere, the years of dwindling traffic saw the canals damaged by floods and lack of maintenance; eventually, in many places, they were filled in and disappeared. At Easton, however, six miles of the canal survive on the south side of the Lehigh River and have become part of a National Register Historic District: Hugh Moore Park. The Park includes three restored locks, a restored locktender's house, and the Canal Museum that is also the home of the Center for Canal History and Technology. Rides on the canal are available in a reproduction of a 19th-century canalboat.

The Canal Museum focuses on such themes as canal technology, the role of canals in economic growth, and what life was like for the canallers—the people who operated the canalboats, lived on them, and made them a distinctive part of American folk culture. Exhibits include a full-scale reproduction of a crew's cabin in a coal-carrying canalboat. The many canal artifacts include cabin furnishings, lanterns, tools, even the harnesses of mules that hauled the boats. Models include canalboats and a canal lock.

A special feature is a map of American canals using fiber optics to highlight the routes. In the museum's small theater, audiovisual shows present the background of the canal era. Photographs from the museum's collection, one of the largest canal picture archives in the country, are used to illustrate the themes.

The *Josiah White*, a reconstructed canalboat drawn by mules, is based about three and a half miles from the museum and offers rides in season Wednesdays through Sundays. About 10 minutes' walk from the canalboat dock is the locktender's house near Guard Lock Number 8 and the Chain Dam in the Lehigh River. The first floor of the house has been restored to show how a locktender and his family lived in the 1890s.

Boats may be rented for individual exploration of the canal and there are picnic areas in the park. The *Josiah White* may be chartered by private groups for special trips.

Canal Museum at Easton, Pennsylvania, is in Hugh Moore Park on the Lehigh Canal and River where they meet the Delaware. Center for Canal History and Technology, archive and research facility, is at museum. Bookstore. Open all year, every day except Thanksgiving, Christmas, New Year's. Monday-Saturday, 10 a.m. to 4 p.m.; Sunday, 1 to 5 p.m. Admission: $1.00; seniors, 80 cents, children, 50 cents. Canal Museum, Hugh Moore Park, 200 South Delaware Drive, P.O. Box 877, Easton, Pennsylvania 18042. Telephone (215) 250-6700.

Canalboat rides are offered in mule-drawn boat *Josiah White*. Trip on restored section of Lehigh Canal takes 45 to 60 minutes. Operates Memorial Day weekend through Labor Day. Wednesday-Saturday, 11 a.m., 1, 2:30 and 4 p.m. Fare: $3.00; ages 5-12, $1.50 (includes Locktender's House, see below). Same address, telephone, as museum.

Locktender's House at guard lock #8, 10-minute walk from canalboat dock. First floor, restored 1890 living quarters and museum. Open Memorial Day weekend through Labor Day, Wednesday-Saturday, plus weekends in September, noon to 4:30 p.m. Admission: 50 cents; ages 5-12, 25 cents; free with canalboat rides. Same address, telephone, as museum.

Below Easton, coal continued on to market on the Delaware Canal, running alongside the river. Started in 1827, the Delaware Canal didn't become fully operational for commercial use between Easton and the downriver terminal at Bristol, Pennsylvania, until 1840. To drop 165 feet, the canal used 25 locks, while nine aqueducts carried it over waterways. In the 1860s, 2,500 to 3,000 boats and barges used the canal, carrying not only coal but limestone and farm produce.

The Delaware Canal has long since ceased to be a bustling commercial waterway. In the little Bucks County town of New Hope, however, visitors can still ride its waters—for a little way. Based on the canal at the south end of the village (long famous as an artists' colony and resort) the New Hope Barge Company operates a small fleet of four canalboats, replicas of 19th-century scows. A stable of nine mules provides the motive power.

The rides along the canal last about an hour and cover about two miles of the canal. Musicians sing folk songs and tell about the history of the canal. The canalboats are available for special charter.

Mule-drawn barge rides on the Delaware Canal are offered at New Hope, in historic Bucks County, Pennsylvania. Trip takes one hour. Operates April 1 to 30, Wednesday, Saturday, Sunday: 1, 2, 3, 4:30 p.m. May 1 to October 15, daily: 11:30 a.m., 1, 2, 3, 4:30, 6 p.m. October 16 to November 15, Wednesday, Saturday, Sunday: 11:30 a.m., 1, 2, 3, 4:40 p.m. Tickets: $4.95; seniors, $4.50; students with ID, $4.25; children under 12, $2.75. New Hope Barge Company, P.O. Box 164, New Hope, Pennsylvania 18938. Telephone (215) 862-2842.

At the height of the canal era, 1,356 miles of waterways were dug in Pennsylvania. Although none survives intact, stretches of canal can still be visited in a number of places in the state in addition to Easton and New Hope. Here is a list compiled by the Pennsylvania Canal Society (which, incidentally, welcomes members: write P.O. Box 877, Easton, Pennsylvania 18042). The sequence is roughly east to west across the state.

Roosevelt State Park. Delaware Division of Pennsylvania Canal, a National Historic Landmark. Towpath trail from Bristol, 59.3 miles to Easton. The canal remains and most of its features are as they were during its commercial operation. Many excellent points at which to view canal along Route 611 from Easton to Kintnersville, then Route 32 to Yardley.

The Locust. P.O. Box 388, Lewiston, Pennsylvania

17044. Telephone (717) 248-3974. Restored section of the Juniata Division of the Pennsylvania Main Line Canal. Located west of Lewiston off Route 22.

Allentown, Bethlehem and Freemansburg. Continuous canal park on Lehigh Canal with six preserved locks. Towpath trail. Original 1828 cut-stone locktender's house at Lock 44 in Freemansburg.

Lehigh Canal. Jim Thorpe to Parryville. Restored Lehigh Canal with 12 well-preserved locks. Towpath trail. Beautiful mountain scenery.

Walnutport. Attractive canal town on the Lehigh Canal. Towpath trail from Lock 22 to Lock 25. Original 1828 stuccoed stone locktender's house at Lock 23.

Delaware and Hudson Canal Aqueduct. Off Route 590 at Lackawaxen. Six-hundred-foot-long suspension bridge built in 1849 by John Roebling.

Tulpehocken Creek Valley Park. Union Canal Lock 47 fully restored with balance-beam gates. Towpath trail. Park follows the Tulpehocken Creek west from Reading. Take Route 422 to Tulpehocken Road and Route 183 to Upper Van Reed Road.

Union Canal Tunnel. Three miles northwest of Lebanon off Route 72. Oldest existing canal tunnel in the United States.

Susquehanna and Tidewater Canal Lock 12. Take Route 372 at the Norman Wood Bridge across the Susquehanna River. Good stone lock in recreation area.

Allegheny Portage Railroad National Historical Site. Take Route 22, two miles east of Cresson. Incline Plane 6, Lemon House, and Skew Arch Bridge. Summit level of the Portage Railroad. First railroad to cross the Allegheny Mountains, it provided a critical link in the Pennsylvania Main Line Canal. Built between 1831 and 1834 it was abandoned by 1857.

Saltsburg. Routes 286 and 981. Attractive canal park on the Western Division of the Pennsylvania Main Line Canal. Town was an important link between the canal and the salt industry of Pennsylvania.

Canal Lock. Route 518 at Sharpsville. Lift lock on the Shenango Division of the Beaver and Erie Canal.

Monongahela Navigation System. Monongahela River south from Pittsburgh to Fairmont, West Virginia. Canalized river had 15 dams and locks. System still in use today by U.S. Army Corps of Engineers.

Chesapeake Bay I: The Eastern Shore and the Upper Bay

The 130-plus miles of Atlantic coast from Delaware Bay to the entrance to the Chesapeake are inhospitable to mariners. There are no real harbors, only shallow, bar-crossed inlets between the barrier islands that rim the shore. From earliest times maritime activity here has been left to oystermen and fishermen. But a few miles to the west, Chesapeake Bay extends 195 miles north and south, from its head, fed by the mighty Susquehanna River, to where its waters meet the Atlantic between Cape Henry and Cape Charles.

Few of America's great waterways are so overflowing with history and maritime traditions as Chesapeake Bay. Here came the three little ships that brought across the Atlantic the men and women who created the first permanent English settlement in North America. At the mouth of the bay was fought the sea battle that effectively secured the independence of the United States. Along the shores of the upper bay, shipwrights created the most famous of distinctively American ship types, the beautiful and wickedly fast Baltimore clipper. In Hampton Roads, off the lower bay, two ironclad warships battled for the first time, and the world's navies would never be the same again. And here is the home of the succulent oysters that led directly to the development of those remarkable bay craft, the bugeye and the skipjack.

Chesapeake Bay was originally a great valley carved out by the Susquehanna. At the end of the Ice Age, melting glaciers raised the ocean level so that the Atlantic moved into the valley. The Susquehanna's tributaries (there are 48 principal ones) now flow into the flanks of the bay and form an important part of the Chesapeake's 4,600 miles of tidal shoreline.

Over the centuries, these rivers have played a major role in maritime activity on the Chesapeake. On the east side of the bay, small tidal streams provided waterways for taking crops to market and harbors for the watermen who harvested the shellfish. On the west side of the Chesapeake, the Patapsco River created the harbor of the great port of Baltimore. Where the Severn flows into the bay is Annapolis, the capital of Maryland and home of the United States Naval Academy. The Patuxent, a few miles further south, was the British highway for the capture of Washington. At the Fall Line of the Potomac, two flourishing ports traded with the West Indies and Europe long before they were overshadowed by neighboring Washington. In Colonial times, the Rappahanock and the York rivers were lined with tobacco plantations, which had their own wharves. At the south end of the Bay, the James joins with the little

Nansemond and Elizabeth to form Hampton Roads, one of the world's great deepwater ports.

Much of the earliest exploration of the Chesapeake was undertaken in the hope of finding a passage through the land to the "East Indies Sea," across which one could sail to the riches of the Orient. This was the goal of Captain John Smith when he and a dozen or so companions set forth from Jamestown in an open boat on two voyages up the bay in the summer of 1608. Coasting along both shores, searching well up the rivers flowing in from the west, Smith eventually reached the head of the Chesapeake. Sixty-odd days of exploration, during which the travelers estimated they covered 3,000 miles, failed to turn up the hoped-for passage, but Smith learned enough about the Chesapeake to enable him to draw a remarkably accurate "mappe of the bay and rivers," which he sent to England for publication.

Finding riches—preferably gold or silver, Oriental or American—was more on the minds of the first settlers than carving farms out of the forest. They had a hard time surviving; not until locally grown tobacco was found to have a ready market in Europe did the colonists prosper. The bay and its rivers turned out to be their road to riches; the first plantation fields were cleared from the forest next to the tidewater and at each plantation a vessel could come in to the wharf to pick up the crop. Meanwhile, another flourishing trade grew up—carrying lumber and provisions to supply the sugar plantations of the British West Indies. By the late 18th century, flour and grain from the inland farms to the north and west, superseded tobacco as the bulk cargoes from the upper bay.

In wartime, Chesapeake Bay saw much naval activity. During the Revolution, bay privateers ravaged British commerce while the Colonies of Virginia and Maryland established tiny state navies to deal with Tories and harass the British squadron that eventually came to occupy the bay. The British ships, in turn, rescued Tories, burned Norfolk, and ravaged the farms and plantations of patriots along the shore. It was the eventual British failure to control the lower bay, following an inconclusive battle with a French fleet off the Virginia Capes, that trapped Cornwallis and forced him to surrender at Yorktown. In the War of 1812, the Chesapeake-based privateers were even more active—and so were the British squadrons that blockaded the bay and then moved up to attack Baltimore and burn Washington.

In the 19th century, local shipping in the bay continued to flourish as small vessels picked up cargoes along the shore to take to the big cities for consumption or export. Sloops and schooners carried the bulk of the trade, until the coming of steam laced the waters of bay and rivers with shallow-draft side-wheelers. At the height of steamboating in the early 20th century, there were 250 steamboat landings along the bay, used for both passengers and freight.

From the early days of settlement there was shipbuilding in the Bay area—much of it small vessels built on plantations for local travel and carrying crops to market. With the increase of both bay and deep-water shipping, shipbuilding grew increasingly important; deep-sea ships and small craft, merchant vessels and frigates, privateers and slavers, windjammers and steamers. But much of the boatbuilding in the little ports was concentrated on small sailing craft; needed for what was becoming the bay's major maritime industry—oystering.

There had always been shell-fishing in the bay and rivers; as far back as 1609, oysters helped some colonists survive the starving time. Oystering was well established in Colonial times, and by the early 19th century the fame of Chesapeake Bay oysters had begun to spread. By mid-century it was a major industry, sending barrels and cans of oysters to distant markets. This maritime industry produced several distinctive types of small sailing craft designed for the special needs of the watermen who dredged and tonged the oysters from the bay beds. These handy little fore-and-afters, which included the famous bugeyes and skipjacks, were built in many of the little towns along the Chesapeake.

The Delmarva peninsula—Delaware, Maryland, Virginia—dangles southward between Chesapeake Bay and the Atlantic Ocean. Long and low, no more than a few feet above sea level at its highest point, the southern two-thirds consists of the famous Eastern Shore, so called by early settlers who moved eastward across the Chesapeake from Virginia and Maryland. The Atlantic coast, rimmed with barrier islands, is lacking in harbors; the inlets between the islands are shallow, with bars across their mouths. In the words of the 1904 *Atlantic Coast Pilot*, the standard government publication on coastal navigation, "These inlets can only be entered by vessels of a limited draft and are not available as harbors of refuge in easterly gales when the bars are covered by breakers."

Elsewhere, the same *Pilot* noted: "Owing to the numerous outlying shoals this coast is a dangerous one for deep draft vessels, and unless sure of the vessel's position by observation, the lead should be used to give warning of too close an approach from seaward."

Not surprisingly, this coast has been largely left to fishing and oystering villages. The west shore facing the Chesapeake, however, is ragged with many little rivers and inlets; this was Colonial tobacco country, dotted with small wharves where planters rolled down their hogsheads to be loaded on shipboard and carried direct to England. Little towns on the rivers became harbors for the small craft of watermen and bay traders.

Until relatively recently, the Eastern Shore has been isolated from the rest of Maryland and Virginia, which could be reached only by a slow ferry-ride across the Chesapeake, or a long trip around the head of the bay. As a result, the Eastern Shore people have traditionally been a breed apart, farmers inland, oystermen and fishermen alongshore.

Now the Bay Bridge at Annapolis has tied the peninsula more closely to the cities on the west shore of the bay, and opened the region to newcomers who love its remoteness and gentle climate. And because the state of Maryland forbids the use of powerboats for oyster dragging, some craft survive the march of progress, becoming the last sailing workboats in America.

In Colonial times and the early years of the republic, the Eastern Shore was cursed by travelers and shipowners as an obstacle to travel to northern cities and ports. With rough roads little better than trails, interrupted by fords and uncertain ferries, travel and the shipment of goods by land was slow and difficult. Coastal schooner or river sloop was far more comfortable for passenger travel, and quicker and cheaper for moving freight. But the length of Chesapeake Bay made water travel to northern colonies from the upper bay slow and difficult. While Baltimore was only 100 miles by land from Philadelphia, a trip by ship between the two ports required a long roundabout sail down the bay and out into the Atlantic, then a passage along the more than 130 miles of harborless coast to Delaware Bay, then finally up the river to Philadelphia—a total of more than 300 miles.

However, the land barrier between the Chesapeake and the Delaware, made even narrower by little rivers on each side, was only 14 miles wide. A combined water/land/water route soon came into use. Passengers were carried by boat to the upper end of Chesapeake Bay, then by stagecoach across the narrow neck to the Delaware. There they either embarked once more on river craft for the voyage upriver to Philadelphia, or, for ports further north or to Europe, took passage on an oceangoing vessel.

As early as the 17th century, farsighted colonists had seen the great advantages of a canal between the two bays that would permit the trip to be made entirely by water. A century after the canal was first proposed, a route across the neck was surveyed, but it took another 70 years before the Chesapeake and Delaware Canal was finally completed in 1829—13 miles long and 10 feet deep, with two locks at each end.

The Chesapeake and Delaware Canal proved so successful that the ditch was repeatedly widened and deepened to permit passage by larger ships, and eventually the locks were removed and the route slightly changed to make possible a sea-level waterway between the bays. One of the original locks of the old canal can still be seen at Delaware City, about two miles north of the eastern end of the present canal.

The old canal had a life of its own. As the Delaware WPA Guide puts it: "Captains of passing barges saluted each other with musical blasts from horns, while their wives hung out the wash on clotheslines rigged abaft and deckhouse. Barge housekeeping included the keeping of chickens and even pigs. Showboats from the Chesapeake circuit tied up here and at other canal towns, and many were the floating emporiums traveling leisurely from place to place with tinware, dress goods, steel-traps, and other things too numerous to mention."

At least twice the Chesapeake and Delaware Canal has proved of great value in time of war. In the first days of the Civil War, Confederate sympathizers blocked the reinforcement of Washington by burning all the railroad bridges north from Baltimore to the Susquehanna River. However, the federal government was able to round up a flotilla of shallow-draft steamers in Delaware Bay and rush them south through the C.&O. Canal to Chesapeake Bay, where they picked up the troops and carried them down to Annapolis, bypassing the blocked railroad.

During World War II, in the first months after Pearl Harbor German submarines inflicted tremendous losses on American shipping off the Atlantic coast. Routing freighters and tankers up Chesapeake Bay, through the canal, and into Delaware Bay, avoided the submarine-infested waters between Cape Charles and Cape Henlopen. Traffic through the canal broke all previous records that year, with 11 million tons.

Today the canal is an integral part of the intercoastal waterway, used annually by more than 22,000 vessels, saving an estimated 40 million gallons or more of fuel oil each year. Travelers can watch the freighters moving through the canal from a vantage point at Chesapeake City, near the Chesapeake Bay end of the canal. At the same time, visitors can learn about the history of the canal, and about some of the specialized vessels that have used and serviced it, at the interesting little museum at Chesapeake City of the Army Corps of Engineers.

Chesapeake City is a tiny village of small 19th-century wooden houses that owes its very existence to the canal: here were originally a lock and steam pump. Today this is the point where all vessels using the canal change pilots: if northbound, from Chesapeake Bay to Delaware Bay pilots; if southbound, the reverse.

The visitor entering Chesapeake City from Route 213 must keep his eye peeled for signs pointing to the Chesapeake and Delaware Canal Museum, which is tucked away on the bank of the Canal beyond a small inlet on the eastern edge of the village. The Chesapeake and Delaware Canal Museum is housed in an ancient stone and brick building, overlooking the canal, that still contains the steam engine and machinery once used to lift water up into the canal lock. The canal has long since been dredged to sea level and the locks removed.

The museum's exhibits are concentrated in the large room that once held the boiler of the pumping engine. The visitor might start by pressing a button that turns on a slide show about the 150-year history of the canal. The neighboring displays fill in the story with models of ships and small craft, dioramas, maps, charts, and artifacts. Of particular interest is a moving model showing how the old locks worked. The various specialized craft that used or serviced the canal—many rarely found elsewhere—are shown in models and photographs. They include:

- a model of a unique type of vessel: a passenger steamboat that was built on exceptionally narrow and shallow lines in order to pass through the canal and locks. The *Lord Baltimore* carried passengers and freight between Philadelphia and Baltimore for almost a century, starting in the mid-1840s;
- a model of a pipeline dredge used in the canal modernization;
- a builder's model of the type of seagoing hopper dredge used to maintain the canal today;
- a diorama of a canal wharf with a showboat alongside. The placard notes that the showboat "brought entertainment to the canal towns and tied up in Chesapeake City";
- a diorama of an old-fashioned covered bridge that for 40 years carried traffic over the canal.

Other displays show models of a wide range of distinctive Chesapeake Bay craft, including a bay pungie (a direct descendant of the famous Baltimore clippers), a "drudger" (used for crabbing), a bateau; a skipjack; a bugeye; and a scow—all small craft rarely found anywhere else in the world.

The visitor should by no means overlook the rooms beyond the museum proper. They contain carefully preserved mid-19th century machinery used to fill the lock with water in order to lift entering vessels to the level of the canal. Most impressive is the enormous wooden water wheel, 38 feet in diameter. Its dozen buckets could lift 1,200,000 gallons of water an hour into the canal. Next door are the steam engines that turned the wheel—magnificent glossy black creations shining with polished brass.

Before leaving, the visitor should cross the small

parking lot to the white frame building that houses the canal's headquarters and traffic control center, operated by the Corps of Engineers. The dispatchers' room is open to visitors by special permission. Seated behind a huge control console, the dispatchers monitor the ships through the various sections of the canal on television screens, and radio them traffic instructions.

Chesapeake and Delaware Canal Museum is at the Army Corps of Engineers Headquarters in Chesapeake City. Open all year. Monday-Saturday; 8 a.m. to 4:15 p.m. and Sundays, May 1 to Thanksgiving, 10 a.m. to 6 p.m. Admission: free. Sponsored by U.S. Army Corps of Engineers, Philadelphia District, Custom House, and Chestnut/Second Streets, Philadelphia, Pennsylvania 19106. Telephone (215) 597-4802. Chesapeake and Delaware Canal Museum, Army Corps Engineer Project, Chesapeake City, Maryland 21915. Telephone (301) 885-5622.

Before heading over to the large and interesting maritime museum at St. Michaels on the eastern shore of Chesapeake Bay, many travelers may wish to detour to the Atlantic coast where there is an interesting little museum at Chincoteague Island, famous for its oysters and its wild ponies. The annual round-up of the ponies bring many visitors every summer; maritime gourmets are likely to be more interested in the salty oysters from the shallow Atlantic tidal waters around Chincoteague, which receive top billing in elegant oyster bars. Appropriately, the docks of the village sprawled along the inshore side of the island are lined with oyster and shrimp boats, the little main street is lined with seafood restaurants, and out on the edge of town the glamorous bivalve is honored with a museum all its own.

The Oyster Museum on Chincoteague Island is in a modest redbrick building on the road east to Assateague, the barrier island facing the Atlantic. Wild ponies sometimes graze quietly on the marsh grass across the way. In the museum yard is a bit of three-dimensional maritime history, the 37-foot oyster boat *R.F.M. Bunting.* Beamy and shallow with a tiny cabin and wheelhouse in the stern, she was built in 1876 and used continuously for a hundred years, being converted from sail to power along the way.

Within, the museum's exhibits cover the oyster from many angles, including its life cycle. An aquarium features local marine specimens including, of course, live oysters. A collection of oyster shells from around the world shows the wide variations in the armor of various species of this important shellfish.

Shellfish farming is explained with a diorama. The lifestyle, and techniques, of the men who harvest the oysters is depicted with photographs of the oyster boats at work and examples of equipment.

The Oyster Museum at Chincoteague Island, Virginia, on the Atlantic Ocean, is at the edge of town on the road east to Assateague. Open Memorial Day weekend through Labor Day; every day, 11 a.m. to 5 p.m. Admission: $1.00; children under 13, 25 cents. Oyster Museum, Maddox Boulevard, or c/o Chamber of Commerce, P.O. Box 258, Chincoteague Island, Virginia 23336. Telephone (804) 336-6117.

Across the Eastern Shore on the Chesapeake Bay side, many inlets and small rivers are dotted with small towns, once active trading ports. Now the chief maritime activity is oyster tonging and crabbing by the Bay watermen. In St. Michaels is the Chesapeake Bay Maritime Museum, dedicated to preserving and recounting the maritime past of the whole Chesapeake Bay area and exhibiting a fine collection of distinctive Bay craft.

St. Michaels is an old, old town. In 1632 it was called Shipping Creek and served as a tobacco port. Some 50 years later, it became St. Michaels and was known as a shipbuilding town. In the early years of the young republic, the USS *Enterprise*, the schooner that was the first of a succession of Navy ships of that name, is said by some historians to have been built at St. Michaels. During the War of 1812, the small port became well-known for building fast little privateers—the famous Baltimore clippers—to harry British commerce, so much so that a Royal Navy squadron tried, unsuccessfully, to burn its half-dozen shipyards.

As shipbuilding dwindled in the late 19th century, St. Michaels became a center for packing oysters in ice for shipment by rail all over the country. Between crabbing and the operation of a dozen schooners to carry produce to Baltimore and bring back coal and fertilizer, the little port was kept busy. Eventually, however, these too faded away. Today, the town, no longer isolated from the Baltimore/Washington metropolitan area since the building of the Bay Bridge, is largely a residential village known for its serenity and beauty.

The Chesapeake Bay Maritime Museum, an offshoot of the Historical Society of Talbot County, is at the western edge of St. Michaels on Navy Point: the land was once the farm of Samuel Hambleton, a veteran of the Battle of Lake Erie and the first purser in the United States Navy. Three ancient houses preserved on their original sites at Navy Point are now the museum's administrative offices.

Alongside the docks at the end of the museum lawn are two historic types of Chesapeake Bay sailing crafts. The *Edna E. Lockwood* is the last log-bottom bugeye still sailing. The ultimate development of the log canoe, the bugeye was built in the post-Civil War period to meet the demand for an inexpensive workboat with enough sail power to haul a dredge over Chesapeake Bay oyster beds. In the words of a pamphlet about the *Lockwood* written by Charles H. Kepner and published by the museum, such a boat "should be decked and fitted for the long runs to market, and it should be shallow draft to get in and out of creeks. It would need to be broad for stability and have low freeboard for easy handling of the dredges. They fitted on extra logs to make the hull wider (than the traditional log canoes), added a little more planking to make it deeper, perhaps put in a few knees to make it stronger, and invented the bugeye." The *Lockwood*, built in 1889, was rebuilt in 1978 with her original lines carefully preserved.

As the cost of building bugeyes increased, oystermen turned to less expensive small craft for oyster dredging and started using the simpler, less costly skipjacks. A traditional Chesapeake skipjack, the *Rosie Parks*, is also at the museum dock. Like all skipjacks, the *Parks* is an overgrown, nearly flatbottomed skiff, decked over with a small cabin, and rigged as a sloop with a massive triangular mainsail and a raked mast.

Both historic Chesapeake Bay small craft are preserved out of the water in the museum's small-craft shed. Among them are five long canoes and the prototypes of two very popular small racing classes: the first Penguin and the first Comet. In the main exhibition building, the Chesapeake Bay gallery, is the v-bottom crabbing skiff *Lark*.

The main exhibition gallery of the museum, the Chesapeake Bay Building, uses models and explanatory displays to make clear the development of Chesapeake small craft, from the "Colonial Bay boat"—a shallop—through the log canoe, the bugeye, v-bottom, and plank-on-frame types. Other handsome models in the gallery include the clipper schooner *Surprise*, the oyster boat *Agnes*, and, from further afield, the 1863 blockade runner *Fergus*. The model of the brig *Peggy Stewart* is of special interest: in the Chesapeake Bay equivalent of the Boston Tea party, "public furor" forced the brig's owner to burn her in retribution for bringing over a cargo of tea. But the most striking display greets the visitor at the entrance to the gallery: here an ingenious combination of huge photomural and a full-scale mock-up of her deck and rail give the illusion of stepping aboard the Baltimore clipper *Lynx*.

Oysters and crabs were far from the only contributions of the Chesapeake to the dining tables of 19th-century America. Then, as now, Chesapeake Bay is a major segment of the great eastern flyway for migrating ducks and geese. In the 19th century many a bay man made his living market hunting these waterfowl, until, that is, the law finally intervened to protect the survivors. How the destruction could be so great as to threaten survival, is made clear in a unique exhibit of boats, decoys, and weapons in the museum's buildings devoted to waterfowl. The boats are small and stealthy, built to slip through the wetlands unperceived. The decoys are beautiful, ranging from crude carvings that only an astigmatic duck would take for a cousin, to true folk art realistically portraying birds feeding, preening, and diving. The weapons are beautiful, too—and deadly: shotguns with extra long barrels for extreme accuracy. Sometimes several of these barrels are mounted on one super-weapon that could bring down half a flock with one blast. Boats, decoys, and guns combined created a hunting system that could knock down hundreds of birds in a day.

On the museum's riverfront is a striking landmark, an entire lighthouse; moved here from Hooper Strait, when replaced by an automated beacon, now open to visitors. One of the last of the screw-pile lights that once dotted the bay, the little tower rises out of the keeper's cottage, built on iron pilings screwed into the mud.

The Chesapeake Bay Maritime Museum offers a unique benefit to the yachtsman: the opportunity to become a "boating member," and thus entitled to dock his boat at the museum wharf and use the showers and restrooms. This ingenious program enriches both the coffers of the museum and the maritime background of the Bay yachtsmen.

Chesapeake Bay Maritime Museum, St. Michaels, is on the shore of the Miles River. Drive through town on Talbot Street—Route 33—and turn right on Mill Street; museum is at end on 16 acres of waterfront. April through December, open daily; January through March, open weekends only. Closed Christmas and New Year's. Summer hours, 10 a.m. to 5 p.m.; winter hours 10 a.m. to 4 p.m. Admission: $4.00; seniors, $2.00; 6 to 12, $1.00. Gift shop. Restaurant nearby. Chesapeake Bay Maritime Museum, P.O. Box 636, St. Michaels, Maryland 21663. Telephone (301) 745-2916.

Now north along the Eastern Shore and across the Chesapeake Bay tollbridge to Annapolis on the west bank.

By Severn shore we learn
Navy's stern call

So have sung generations of midshipmen about their years at the United States Naval Academy, which is set on a point where the Severn River runs into Chesapeake Bay. Annapolis was already almost two centuries old when the Acadamy was established in an old fort, and narrow streets and handsome old houses give the little city a pleasant air of antiquity. The dome of Maryland's modest state house, the oldest in continuous legislative use in America, crowns a gentle hill. To its north, the venerable buildings of two-centuries-old St. John's College are half hidden by noble trees. On the Bay, what is said to be the only 18th-century waterfront in the nation draws visitors by sea and by land to enjoy its lively activities.

Yet with all this, Annapolis remains for most Americans synonymous with the grey granite buildings of the Naval Academy. Since its foundation in 1845, the Naval Academy has educated America's professional naval officers. In so doing it has become the symbol of the naval strand in America's maritime heritage, the traditions and memories of America's fighting ships and seamen from the earliest days of the Republic.

All this is embodied in the Naval Academy Museum, which is housed in Preble Hall, a large, grey brick building just inside the Maryland Avenue gate of the academy grounds and catty-cornered across a green from the chapel. The museum houses artifacts, paintings, ship models, and mementos of naval heroes

Figure 29
The *Rosie Parks*, one of the few survivors of the famous bay skipjacks, is cherished at the Chesapeake Bay Maritime Museum in St. Michaels, Maryland. (The Christmas tree at her mast cap is a traditional holiday decoration.) In the background is the Hooper Strait lighthouse, also a distinctive Bay type, built on piles that screw into the mud. The light was moved to the museum when taken out of service.

from the Revolution onward. The heart of the exhibits is the famous Rogers ship-model collection: more than 100 models of ships and smaller craft, including 17 of the magnificent miniature ships made for the British Admiralty in centuries past. Represented are British warships of all sizes—from fourth- to first-rate—of the 17th and 18th centuries. During most of this time, of course, the Royal Navy was the navy of the American Colonies. Of equal interest is a fine big model of a French 118-gun ship. The model is reputed to represent the *Ville de Paris*, the ship of the line that played a major role in an historic but little-known sea battle of the American Revolution. The finest warship in the world at the time, the *Paris* was the flagship of Admiral de Grasse, commander of the French fleet at the indecisive but strategically important battle with a Royal Navy squadron off the Virginia Capes that was a major factor in the surrender of British General Cornwallis.

Beef-bone ship models, made by prisoners of war from the leftovers of their rations, are of special interest. The bones, a placard explains, were immersed in wet clay to make them more pliable and easier to shape and carve.

Other fine models include one of the British frigate *Shannon*, which defeated the American *Chesapeake* in a famous ship-to-ship duel in the War of 1812, and another of the USS *Lawrence*, Oliver Hazard Perry's flagship at the Battle of Lake Erie. Both the *Merrimack* (CSS *Virginia*) and the *Monitor*, which fought the historic battle in Hampton Roads, are represented by full models; even more interesting is a cutaway model of the *Monitor* showing her gun turret mechanism, engines, and cabins.

But the ship models are only one element of the museum's treasures. Of almost equal interest are:

- The Beverley R. Robinson collection of naval battle prints portraying over a thousand major naval engagements from the 16th century to 1873, most of them contemporary with their subject matter.
- The Malcolm Storer naval medals collection: 1,210 commemorative coin medals from 30 nations, ranging in date from 254 B.C. to 1936.
- The United States Navy trophy flag collection: 600 historic American flags and captured foreign ensigns; including the "Don't Give Up the Ship" flag flown by Oliver Hazard Perry at the Battle of Lake Erie.

The collection of more than 750 oil paintings and sculptures, primarily of naval scenes and portraits, covers two centuries of Navy men and naval activities. Famous sea battles are well represented, but some of the most interesting portray lesser-known activities in the Navy's past. A sampling:

- an enormous, and striking, Harry Reuterdahl oil painting of the Great White Fleet passing through the Straits of Magellan in 1908;
- a painting of the USS *Santiago de Cuba* on blockade duty off the Bahama Islands during the Civil War;
- an on-the-spot sketch of the U.S.N. seaplane NC-4 at Portsmouth, England, after it made the first successful flight across the Atlantic;
- an oil painting of a four-stacker destroyer in a storm, called *Standing By.*

The portraits and photographs of noted naval officers have, of course, a fascination of their own. Two unusual ones are:

- a full-length portrait of Commodore Abraham Whipple, one of the first captains of the Continental Navy;
- another full-length oil of an interesting and sometimes controversial naval officer, Commodore Uriah P. Levy, shown holding a paper inscribed, "Author of the Abolition of Flogging in the United States Navy."

The museum's collection of personal memorabilia often brings us a little closer to some famous, and remote, Americans. Here, for example, is the watch that Captain David Porter U.S.N. gave his stepson, Midshipman David G. Farragut, in 1810 when the nine-year-old boy was just starting a career that was to be climaxed by his becoming the United States Navy's first admiral. (Nearby is a photograph of Admiral Farragut on the quarterdeck after his victory at Mobile Bay.) Here, hung casually on the wall, is a rough plan of a parcel of land drawn by a young Virginia surveyor named George Washington. And displayed nearby is a beautiful quadrant in a remarkable painted case that belonged to none other than John Paul Jones.

Some of the museum's numerous artifacts of two centuries of naval activity are remarkable. Here, for example, is an original broadside, dated April 17, 1776, announcing Commodore Hopkins' successful attack on New Providence in the Bahamas. Against the wall is a rubber raft on which three torpedo-plane crewmen drifted for 34 days after ditching in the Pacific during World War II. Preserved nearby are relics of the battleship *Maine* that blew up in Havana harbor, precipitating the Spanish-American War.

The visitor should not leave the Naval Academy until he has paid a respectful visit to the tomb of John Paul Jones, America's first, and probably most revered, naval hero. Set in the center of a circular crypt under the sanctuary of the huge Academy chapel, the tomb is a magnificent piece of black marble, supported by four bronze dolphins. Contemporary taste may find it somewhat overly ornate but one suspects that Jones, a rather flamboyant man with well-developed—and justified—self-esteem, would have approved. In niches around the wall of the crypt are documents, decorations, pictures, and models relating to Jones's career.

The crypt and tomb date from 1913, more than a century after the captain's death. Jones went to Europe after the American Revolution, served successfully but briefly in the Imperial Russian Navy, and died in obscurity in Paris in 1792. Even his place of burial was forgotten until, in 1905, the then American ambassador to France, Horace B. Porter, made it his personal project to find the grave of this lost American hero. He succeeded, and Jones's body was brought home.

United States Naval Academy Museum, in Preble Hall on the grounds of the academy. Open every day except New Year's, Thanksgiving, and Christmas. Mondays-Saturdays, 9 a.m. to 5 p.m.; Sundays, 11 a.m. to 5 p.m. No admission charge. U.S. Naval Academy Museum, Annapolis, Maryland 21402. Telephone (301) 267-2108 or 267-2109.

Geographically, Annapolis and Baltimore are about 25 miles apart. In other ways, they are half a world apart. Both have a great maritime heritage, but in those few miles the traveler moves from a town looking over its shoulder at the 18th century to a megalopolis banging on the doorway of the 21st; from a tiny waterfront frequented by yachtsmen, oyster draggers, and excursion steamers to one of the world's great ports, fifth largest in the entire country in overall tonnage, its 100 miles of foreshore crammed with shipping from all over the world.

Once, the situation was reversed: Annapolis was the biggest port on Chesapeake Bay when Baltimore was only a tiny cluster of houses around a tobacco wharf. Baltimore didn't exist at all until 80 years after Annapolis was founded. Then a custom house was built on the northwest branch of the Patapsco River for the convenience of tobacco planters nearby, who were supposed to ship only from ports with a resident official to enforce the export tax.

At first the little settlement was slow to grow; a ship that called to pick up tobacco in 1739 found only a single hogshead to add to her cargo. But Baltimore had great assets as a port. For one thing the little village was strategically located where three different economies met. On the tidewater lands to the south, tobacco was the traditional cash crop of colonial Maryland. To the west and north the higher land was fine for growing wheat, and many little tumbling streams powered flour mills. Across the bay on the eastern shore the little river ports became shipbuilding

Figure 30
Magnificent carving graces stern of model French 60-gun ship of the line, late 17th century, in
the U.S. Naval Academy's *Rogers'* collection.

and trading centers, while watermen were already reaping rich harvests of shellfish. And Baltimore's Patapsco River, deeper and broader than most of the little rivers running into the bay, provided a fine harbor and waterfront for loading cargoes for northern ports, the West Indies, and Europe. In the vicinity were local iron ore, plentiful timber, slate, granite, and marble. And the trails leading northeast, north, west, and south encouraged backcountry people to bring their produce to the new little port.

In the days of wooden ships, Baltimore had one other advantage, now long forgotten. A small freshwater creek, navigable for a short distance from its mouth, ran through the town. Fresh water destroys the dreaded teredo worm, swarming in summer in the lower Chesapeake, which attaches itself to wooden bottoms and eats away the hull. To preserve their vessels, skippers would bring them into Baltimore's creek and anchor for a while, until the fresh water killed all the worms.

The true father of Baltimore's maritime prosperity was neither a merchant nor a mariner but an Irish-born physician, Dr. John Stevenson. He knew that flour was in demand in his native land and he arranged for a ship to come to Baltimore to pick up a cargo. The flour sold in Ireland at a good price, the doctor became a prosperous merchant, and Baltimore found the trade that was to make it rich. Exporting grain and flour to Europe and the West Indies, Baltimore by 1776 was overtaking Annapolis as the leading port on the upper Chesapeake. By 1830, the city had grown to be the third largest city in the United States, surpassed only by New York and Boston.

In the meantime, Baltimore ships and Baltimore mariners had taken a very active part in America's two wars with Great Britain. In both, the Royal Navy effectively controlled the Atlantic, and other than the famous ship-to-ship battles, there was little either the Continental Navy or, later, the fledgling United States Navy, could do to challenge it. But with ships and seamen idle in every port, both wars saw great enthusiasm for privateering—nowhere more so than in Baltimore.

A privateer is a privately owned and operated ship of war with an official commission from the government to capture the merchant vessels of an enemy country. American privateers depended on speed; speed both to overtake British merchantmen and to run away from British warships. By the time of the Revolution, Chesapeake Bay was already noted for small, very fast vessels, used as pilot boats, as traders to the West Indies, and, often, by smugglers trying to avoid the British government's restrictions on Colonial trade. Many of these, as well as fishing boats and coasters, obtained privateer commissions. From April 1777, to March 1783, 248 privateers sailed from

Baltimore. They did one million pounds worth of damage to British shipping, leading the British authorities to call Baltimore "a nest of pirates."

Soon the fast Chesapeake Bay schooners developed into the famous Baltimore clippers. Designed with fine lines that sacrificed cargo capacity for speed—sharp bows and high masts sharply raked (that is, leaning aft)—they were fast enough to run down any ship they could capture and to escape bigger ships that could capture them. During the War of 1812, half the privateer commissions and letters of marque (a modified commission issued to armed cargo carriers) went to Baltimore vessels, 126 altogether. Of these, 54 were captured or lost, but among them they took 556 prizes.

The most famous of the Baltimore privateersmen was Captain Thomas Boyle in the *Chasseur*. Cruising off the English coast, in August 1814, Boyle had the audacity to proclaim single-handedly a "strict and rigorous" blockade of the British Isles—an announcement which was posted at Lloyds and sent insurance rates on British merchantmen to record heights. The amphibious attack on Baltimore by a British task force in 1814 was in part designed to wipe out the shipyards that built the privateers and the base that supported them.

After the war, Baltimore faced new problems. The fat profits from privateering vanished overnight. The tobacco trade was in a slump. British laws required that the city's major exports, grain and flour for the British West Indies, be carried in British bottoms. Nevertheless, Baltimore's prosperity eventually returned. European demand for grain and tobacco picked up. In a new and highly profitable trade, Baltimore ships carried grain to Brazil and brought back coffee. Copper and guano were imported from the Pacific coast of South America, and Baltimore became a distribution center for fertilizer for southern farms.

In 1851, the Baltimore and Ohio Railroad, whose eastern terminus was located on the Baltimore docks, reached the Ohio River. With direct rail connections to the Midwest, Baltimore was able to take advantage of its location to attract export shipments. Compared to New York, the city is 140 miles closer to Chicago, 249 miles closer to St. Louis, and 289 miles closer to Cincinnati.

After the Civil War, during which Baltimore built warships for the Union Navy, more and more of the city's foreign trade was carried on foreign bottoms. With the growth of steel mills in the city, however, its shipyards turned to building steel vessels. American-flag shipping continued to decline: At the start of World War I, 12 shipping lines served the port but every one of them flew a foreign flag.

Today, Baltimore remains the Atlantic gateway to

the Middle West. By 1981, 34 million tons of cargo a year passed through the port, with 10 ships arriving or departing each day. The fifth port of the United States in overall tonnage, Baltimore was second only to New York in handling container freight, the wave of the future for ocean shipping.

With such a remarkable maritime past, it is not surprising that Baltimore not only remembers its heritage but cherishes it with both ships and museums. The major centers of maritime interest in Baltimore are the famous USS *Constellation* and other vessels berthed on the original waterfront of the city, which has been recently rebuilt with many tourist attractions; and the Radcliffe Maritime Museum, a few blocks away. In addition, the Baltimore Museum of Technology, on the other side of the Inner Harbor, and the Library of the University of Baltimore are of maritime interest.

A good place to start is the Radcliffe Maritime Museum, which presents a fascinating picture of maritime Baltimore over the centuries.

The Radcliff Maritime Museum is a part of the museum and library of the Maryland Historical Society, which is housed in a handsome building near Baltimore's Washington Monument. Here visual displays, paintings, ship models, dioramas, tools, and artifacts tell about the many facets of Chesapeake Bay and the Port of Baltimore. What makes the museum especially noteworthy is that its collection is not just an assemblage of individual objects: each display is integrated into a carefully organized unit, a little visual essay on some aspect of Baltimore's maritime past. These exhibits are made particularly effective by being related to the social and political background of the period.

Here are the explorers with their maps and reports. Ship models, period documents, and samples of trade goods, tell the story of the little ports along the Chesapeake and the ships that used them. In another section, the life of sailors is portrayed with a mock-up of a 19th-century forecastle. Chesapeake Bay watermen have their own exhibit focusing on the commercial aspects of the distinctive Chesapeake Bay sailing craft, such as the bugeyes and skipjacks.

Steamboating in the bay is reported, not only with ship models and photographs, but with a working model of an 1860s walking-beam engine and a scaled-down recreation of the pilot house of a bay steamboat, housing an audiovisual show of a steamer trip down the bay from Baltimore.

Two segments of exhibits are of special interest. The maritime trades and crafts are displayed with a series of period settings. Shipbuilding, for centuries an important marine industry around Chesapeake Bay, is represented with a reconstructed boat shed, complete with original tools of the trade and a crabbing skiff under construction. Another recreation shows a section of an actual sail loft in the little town of Wenona, Maryland, again equipped with the tools of the trade.

Next to the sailmaker is the shop of another highly skilled maritime tradesman, the maker of such navigational instruments as sextants and quadrants. A ship chandlery is stocked with a sampling of the myriad items required by marine customers.

Appropriately, a special exhibit is devoted to the city's most famous sea child: the Baltimore clipper. Models show the evolution of these famous vessels and their use as pilot boats, West Indian traders, privateers, and—ultimately—slavers and pirate ships. The exhibit makes clear that, as the notable historian of American ship design, Howard Chappelle, has written, "Sired by War, mothered by Privateering and Piracy, and nursed by Cruelty, nevertheless, the Baltimore Clipper will always remain the type representative of the highest development of small sailing craft, as built by American builders."

Maryland Historical Society/Radcliffe Maritime Museum is on West Monument Street, just west of Mount Vernon Place and Baltimore's famous Washington monument. The Museum is in the lower level of No. 201, a large redbrick building on the left housing the Maryland Historical Society. Large gift shop with books, antique reproductions, etc. Open all year. Tuesday-Saturday, 11 a.m. to 4 p.m.; Sunday, 1 to 5 p.m. Closed Mondays and Sundays in the summer. Admission: $2.50; seniors, $1.00; children, 75 cents; families, $4.50. Radcliffe Maritime Museum is part of the museum and library of the Maryland Historical Society, 201 West Monument Street Baltimore, Maryland 21201. Telephone (301) 685-3750.

The Baltimore clipper bore the same relation to contemporary cargo ships that a Grand Prix racing car bears to a delivery truck. The speed of the little schooners was obtained at the expense of cargo capacity and they were built only as long as there were missions where speed was all important—and one by one these disappeared. The type was a favorite with West Indian pirates—until the Royal Navy and the U.S. Navy joined forces in the 1820s and 30s to put an end to piracy. Slavers eagerly bought the clippers—until anti-slavery patrols practically suppressed the trade. The Baltimore clippers gradually disappeared; few were left by the 1860s and none survived to modern times.

Until recently, however, visitors to Baltimore could at least hope to glimpse a Baltimore clipper: if not an original, at least a replica built with the greatest care to reproduce accurately the design, construction, and rig of these famous little vessels. The *Pride of Baltimore* was literally the pride of the port; tragically in the spring of 1986 she was lost with a third of her crew in an Atlantic storm.

Built in 1977 on the shore of Baltimore's inner harbor, the *Pride* was schooner rigged, 90 feet long on deck, with an extreme beam of 23 feet and a draft of only 10 feet. Rather than a reproduction of any particular vessel, she was a fresh design but faithful to all the physical characteristics and style of the original Baltimore clippers.

The *Pride of Baltimore* was based in her native city but cruised extensively as a good-will ambassador, manned by an experienced professional crew. She was returning from one of these cruises, a tour of Europe, when she met her tragic end. According to survivors, the schooner was about 240 miles north of Puerto Rico when she was hit without warning by a so-called white squall. Winds up to 100 m.p.h. knocked her on her beam ends and the crew was thrown into the water. There was a heavy sea running and the *Pride* sank immediately, so quickly that there was no time to radio for help.

The captain and mate dived repeatedly to free a raft from the sinking vessel; they succeeded, eight crew members clambered aboard and survived for four days until picked up by a passing tanker. The captain himself was lost, however, as were three other crew members.

The inner harbor, where *Pride* was formerly berthed, is the oldest part of Baltimore. Here on the shore of the Patapsco River, the tobacco wharf was built close to where a creek ran into the river. In the great era of the bay steamboats, they crammed the little harbor, while large cargo carriers berthed there until new facilities were built further down the river.

Now the area has been rebuilt with a complex of shops and restaurants, an aquarium, a science center with planetarium, several tall commercial buildings; a continuous stream of ethnic festivals is held throughout the summer. More to the point for the maritime-minded visitor, the Inner Harbor contains the berth of the United States Frigate *Constellation*, the first United States Navy ship to put to sea. Here also is the Baltimore Maritime Museum, home of the submarine *Torsk* and the lightship *Chesapeake*. (For information about events, tours, water taxis, etc., at the Inner Harbor, write Baltimore Office of Promotion and Tourism, 34 Market Street, Baltimore, Maryland 21201 or telephone (301) 752-8632. Events Hotline, open 24 hours a day, is (301) 837-4636.)

The Inner Harbor provides graphic evidence of the wonderful variety of sailing vessels. The first American frigates were designed to be big and stable enough to carry a battery of heavy guns and so strongly built that they could go alongside enemy ships and survive an exchange of broadsides, muzzle to muzzle. Yet speed was not forgotten. The *Constellation* proved so fast that she was nicknamed the "Yankee Racehorse."

The *Constellation* is the original 36-gun frigate launched in 1797. No home port could be more appropriate for her than Baltimore, for here she was built to the design of the famous Joshua Hymphreys and launched into the Patapsco in 1797, just a short distance to the east of where she is berthed today. The first ship of the new United States Navy to put to sea, *Constellation* was quick to win fame. Assigned to the Caribbean to protect American merchantmen being harassed by French warships, she engaged and captured the French frigate *L'Insurgente*, becoming the first ship of the United States Navy to fight and win a ship-to-ship combat.

In the years that followed, *Constellation* had a long and distinguished career, including service in the war against the Barbary pirates in 1815. When she was almost 150 years old she served her final active duty assignment as an auxiliary relief flagship of the Atlantic Fleet in World War II.

Now docked in Baltimore's Inner Harbor, *Constellation* is still in the process of being repaired and restored, but almost all the ship is open to visitors. There is a long-standing controversy among expert maritime historians about how much *Constellation* resembles the original frigate. In 1854 she was converted to a 22-gun sloop of war; one deck was removed, 12 feet added to her length, and her original battery replaced with a smaller number of larger guns. Some authorities assert that the rebuilding was a subterfuge to obtain a new vessel at a time when Congress would only appropriate money to repair ships, not to build new ones. Other experts disagree, asserting that she remained the same ship with a new section inserted amidship. According to a staff member of the Constellation Foundation, about 30 percent of the hull is the original construction and the present ship essentially represents the early frigate.

In any case, the current work is aimed at restoring her as she appeared as an 1812 frigate, not as an 1854 sloop of war. And whether she is some 185 years old or a mere 130, the *Constellation* is a most interesting vessel. At the start of his tour the visitor might like to rent a tape player, which presents a recorded commentary on each part of the ship, available at the entrance. Included are general background information and a little on life aboard an early 19th-century frigate; the recorded information is particularly valuable to visitors unfamiliar with the ships and activities of the American Navy in its early years. Also, watch for small copper identifying plates attached to various parts of the ship—sometimes rather hard to see.

The visitor should remember that the restoration has by no means been completed; rough patches are being repaired and missing spars restored as the money is raised to let the work go forward.

For the *Constellation*'s service in World War II with

the Atlantic Fleet a large amount of communications equipment was installed. This required structural alterations that are now complicating her restoration.

Here are things to look for:

• on the spar deck (the open deck): the spritsail spar under the bowsprit. This was used to mount a square sail far forward, primarily to aid maneuverability. First used in the 15th century, the spritsail was disappearing by the early 19th.

• on the gun deck, the first deck below the spar deck:

— the captain's great cabin in the stern. Particularly interesting are the two quarter galleries, the little closets at each of the two after corners of the cabin. One contains the captain's bathtub;

— the ship's pumps, amidships;

— the huge brick ovens in the galley, forward;

— the red paint on the interior sheathing, used for a very practical reason: the paint hid the blood spatters during combat;

— the plaque with the names of all 78 of *Constellation*'s captains;

— the guns, 18-pounders of the period of the War of 1812 (two are originals, the rest are fiberglass replicas).

• on the berth deck, the next deck below the gun deck, the officers' cabins aft. These date from the Civil War period, after the ship had been converted to a sloop of war.

• on the orlop, the lowest deck of all, repairs are going on and it is possible to see a good deal of the ship's structure. Note particularly:

— the ribs and planking;

— the pigs of ballast in the bottom;

— how the foot of the mainmast is set into the keel;

— the many storerooms—locked closets for the various kinds of supplies and gear used to maintain the ship and her crew, including special storerooms for the carpenter and bo'sun, the officers, the sick bay, bread, spirits, and so forth: reminders that the ship was expected to be self-sufficient for months at a time.

From time to time, members of the *Constellation*'s restoration staff, costumed according to the period, relate to visitors such things as what it was like to be a ship's surgeon on antislavery patrol off the African coast, or a member of a gun crew in 1800.

United States Frigate *Constellation*, berthed at Pier One, just off Pratt Street at the Inner Harbor. Open all year, starting at 10 a.m.; closing at 8 p.m. June 15 through Labor day; at 6 p.m. from Labor Day until October 14 and from May 15 to June 14; and at 4 p.m. October 15 through May 14.

Admission: $1.75; senior citizens, $1.00; children 6 to 15, 75 cents. Free to military personnel on active duty. Small gift shop. Sponsored by Star Spangled Banner Flag House Association, maintained and operated by the U.S.S. *Constellation* Foundation, Constellation Dock, Baltimore, Maryland 21202. Telephone (301) 539-1797.

There is a nice model of the *Constellation* on display aboard the frigate and a somewhat larger and finer one in the lobby of the World Trade Center, a short distance to the eastward on the Inner Harbor. Continue a little further east along the waterfront to where the Baltimore Maritime Museum has berthed the submarine *Torsk* at Pier Four, and you'll come to a dramatic demonstration of the contrast between the warships of the original United States Navy and those of the mid-20th century.

The *Torsk*, 311 feet long, is almost twice the length of *Constellation* and her displacement (on the surface) is half again as great. Commissioned in 1944, the *Torsk* made a single war patrol—off the coast of Japan—and had the distinction of firing the last torpedo sinking Japanese combatant ships. In the postwar years *Torsk* served largely as a training submarine; now she is the Maryland Submarine Memorial.

Painted black, with fearsome sharks teeth at her bow, the *Torsk* has a very belligerent appearance, although the namesake fish is similar to the not-very-belligerent cod. Visitors tour the submarine in groups, starting in the after torpedo room and running forward the length of the vessel. More identifying labels would be helpful, but the young guides supply basic information and answer questions. Notable are the paintings and drawings hung in each space, showing crew members at work or leisure in that part of the vessel. Particularly striking is the picture of crew members using the emergency hatch to escape from a flooded compartment. The submarine appears to be well-maintained and to have most of her equipment in place. On the dock beside the *Torsk*, a little house contains a submarine's periscope through which visitors can peer at the harbor.

The Baltimore Maritime Museum has no building. Its headquarters are in the museum's other vessel, the lightship *Chesapeake*, berthed across the wharf from the *Torsk*. *LS 116*, her official designation, was built in 1930 and was stationed for 29 years at the mouth of Chesapeake Bay. The nation's first lightship, incidentally, was also in Chesapeake Bay, and was moored there in 1820.

According to the museum's director, the *LS 116* is kept in active reserve, ready to go on station in an emergency on 24 hours notice. The vessel is certainly well-maintained and fully equipped; the bridge and the adjacent captain's cabin are closed to visitors but can be viewed through windows. Here again more explanatory placards would be helpful.

Baltimore Maritime Museum, consists of the submarine *Torsk* and lightship *Chesapeake*. The vessels are open from May 31 to September 14, 10 a.m. to 5 p.m.; closing half an hour earlier the rest of the year. Admission: $2.50; senior citizens, and children 15 to 18, $2.00; 4 to 14, $1.00. Both vessels available for special tours. Sponsored by the city of Baltimore and operated by Department of Recreation and Parks. Baltimore Maritime Museum, Pier Four, Pratt Street, Baltimore, Maryland 21202. Telephone (301) 396-5528.

A maritime veteran of early 20th-century Baltimore has been preserved at the Baltimore Museum of Industry. The museum itself is in a onetime oyster cannery on the harbor front; behind it, tied up at the dock where oyster boats once dumped their loads, is the steam tug *Baltimore*. Built in 1906, she moved derricks and pile drivers about the harbor, with a sideline of winter ice breaking.

After more than half a century of service, the tug was sold by the city to a private owner. She ended up at the bottom of the Sassafras River, and was donated to the museum. Now, once again afloat, thanks to a contractor friend of the museum, *Baltimore* is gradually being restored to her original condition. Her steam engine is already back in place and is operable, making the tug, according to the museum, the only surviving example of the steam era in the Middle Atlantic states.

Since the work is in progress with the help of devoted volunteers, the condition of the tug at the time of any future visit to the museum is hard to predict. *Baltimore* is already worth a visit, however, and is well on the way to becoming her original handsome self.

The Museum of Technology, although devoted largely to machine tools, printing presses, and other such interesting but non-maritime exhibits, also has a

Figure 31
Glamorous sailing ships and recreations of ancient vessels are not the only vessels exhibited by museums—witness this sturdy steam tug at the Baltimore Museum of Industry. Salvaged from a river bottom, she dates from 1906.

small section concerned with materials-handling in the port. A portion of an old dock, a large industrial scale, and grain handling shovels show how vessels were once laboriously loaded by hand. The visitor can even try hoisting heavy bags of grain with a traditional block and tackle.

Steam Tug *Baltimore*, Baltimore Museum of Industry. Is afloat at a dock on the south side of the old harbor. From the Inner Harbor development area, go west on Lombard Street to Light Street, and turn left. Go south a short distance to where Key Highway enters on the left. The museum is about a mile down Key Highway, on the harbor side of the street. Open all year; Saturday, 10 a.m. to 5 p.m.; Sunday, noon to 5 p.m.; other days by group reservation, 10 a.m. to 5 p.m. Admission: $2.00; student, and seniors, $1.00; children 12 and over, 75 cents. The tug is open by special arrangement. For information contact Mr. Dennis Zimbala at the museum. Baltimore Museum of Industry, 1415 Key Highway, Baltimore, Maryland 21230. Telephone (301)727-4808.

A collection that gives insight into the shoreside activities of the Port of Baltimore is open to the public irregularly at the Brown's Wharf Maritime Museum in the Fells Point section of Baltimore, on the riverfront just east of the Inner Harbor. The wharf was built in 1822 for the coffee trade and long handled general cargo. The museum is sponsored by the industrial company that owns the wharf and is opened on special occasions and by appointment. The exhibits show early cargo handling methods and the life of the waterfront community. Fells Point dates back as the city's traditional sailor's waterfront section to the early years of the port. The "hook" that once formed the tip of the point, now hidden by landfill, is said by some authorities to have supplied the word "hooker" to the English language as a description of the dance hall girls who once hung out there to entertain visiting seamen. (There are, however, other, wholly different explanations.)

Brown's Wharf Maritime Museum is at 1617 Thames Street in the Fells Point waterfront section of Baltimore. From Inner Harbor, drive east short distance on Pratt Street to Eastern Avenue, turn right on Eastern Avenue and continue to Broadway, turn right again to Thames Street, museum focuses on cargo handling and the old waterfront section of the city. Admission: free, but the museum is open only on special occasions and by appontment made with Mr. Bud Nixon, at the sponsor of the museum: Rukert Terminals Corporation, 2021 South Clinton, Baltimore, Maryland 21224. Telephone (301) 276-1013.

For steamboating enthusiasts, Baltimore holds another attraction. Although there are no displays or artifacts, the Steamship Historical Society Collection at the University of Baltimore Library contains more than 4,000 books, as well as periodicals, documents, and 60,000 photographs of American steamships. The collection, invaluable to researchers in the field, is open to the public without charge, but visitors would do well to telephone ahead to make sure that the curator is available at the time of the visit.

Steamboat Historical Society Collection is on the fourth floor of the University of Baltimore Library, on Maryland Avenue. Open Monday-Friday, 8:30 a.m. to 4 p.m. Admission: free. University of Baltimore Library, 1420 Maryland Avenue, Baltimore, Maryland 21201. Telephone (301) 625-3134 or (301) 625-3315, Ext. 3134.

A final note: The visitor who comes to Baltimore by boat is likely to arrive at a buoy unlike any he's ever seen before or ever will again—a nun with a blue cap studded with big white stars and a body painted with red and white vertical stripes. The buoy marks the spot where a little American vessel, the *Minden*, was anchored on the night of Tuesday, August 13, 1814. Nothing special about the *Minden*, just another little Bay craft, except for two things: that particular night, British warships were bombarding Fort McHenry protecting the city, and the *Minden* had aboard a passenger, a lawyer from Frederick, Maryland.

All night long the lawyer—his name was Francis Scott Key—peered up the river to see what was happening to the fort. When dawn came he pulled an old letter out of his pocket and scribbled a few lines about what he saw. His notes have made Baltimore, or at least Fort McHenry, the most sung-about place in the country. You've probably sung about it yourself. One verse goes like this:

> On the shore dimly seen through the mists of the deep,
> Where the foe's haughty host in dread silence reposes,
> What is that which the breeze, o'er the towering steep,
> As it fitfully blows, half conceals, half discloses?

Just in case you haven't guessed the answer—

> Now it catches the gleam of the morning's first beam,
> In full glory reflected, now shines on the stream;
> And the Star-Spangled Banner, in triumph doth wave,
> O'er the land of the free, and the home of the brave!

There's a postscript that tells us something about what kind of a town Baltimore was. On the morning after the nightlong bombardment, with the British fleet barely out of the river, a little note in a local paper announced that the *Chesapeake*, the first and only steamboat in the bay, would take excursionists down the Patapsco, presumably to watch the enemy ships sail away. Dinner, always an important subject to Baltimoreans, was provided on board.

Chesapeake Bay II:
The Potomac River and Southern Maryland

When the steamboats still ran between Baltimore and Washington, the 320-mile trip down the Chesapeake to the mouth of the Potomac and up the river to Washington, with 25 stops, took 37 hours, and was a lot of fun. The last steamer made the run in the summer of 1931; now the visitor must take Amtrak or drive the 40 miles down Interstate 95. In either case, the trip takes about 40 minutes and is a bore. What makes the trip worthwhile, of course, is what you find when you get there: Washington has more interesting things to offer visitors, including travelers on the trail of America's maritime heritage, than almost any city in the United States.

As the nation's capital, Washington has museums that tell the story of the maritime activities of the entire nation. But the city also has a maritime heritage of its own. Washington, 100 miles up a winding river from Chesapeake Bay and 200 miles from the Atlantic Ocean, may see an unlikely place to look for maritime activities, but the Potomac River, draining a 6,000 square mile watershed extending into the Great Valley of Virginia, was once an important waterway in its own right. In early Colonial days the river was lined with small but busy tobacco ports. Well into the late 19th century the Potomac was the home of an important commercial fishery. Most significant of all, the District of Columbia as originally laid out embraced two important blue-water ports on the Potomac, with a third next door.

This was no accident. One of the arguments for choosing the present site for the national capital was that it was on the Fall Line, the head of navigation where the products of inland farms and forests were loaded onto ships for other parts of the country or abroad. Alexandria, across the Potomac from Washington, was founded in 1669. In the mid-18th century the port had become the principal exporter of tobacco and the importer of manufactured goods in the region. By the 1770s, wheat, corn, flour, together surpassed tobacco as an export crop and large oceangoing ships were being built to carry it abroad.

In wartime, the towns and farms along the Potomac soon learned that their great river was as open a highway for enemy warships as it was for peaceful merchantmen. In the Revolution, local patriots formed a "Potomac Flotilla" of 14 small craft—row galleys plus a couple of sloops—to defend the river against raids by the British fleet in lower Chesapeake Bay. During most of the Revolution, however, British landing parties burned homes and mills belonging to supporters of the Continental forces and took off Tory families threatened by their neighbors.

After American independence Alexandria continued to prosper and grow. In the War of 1812, however, Alexandria itself found that access to the sea could be a threat as well as a promise. In 1814, two British frigates and a flotilla of small craft worked their way up the river, sounding the channels all the way, to cooperate with the British Army's overland attack on Washington. Although they easily passed the feeble American riverbank defenses, the 100-mile passage up the channel, winding among sandbars, took 10 days. The frigates arrived to find that the British land forces had already taken Washington, burned the government buildings, and retired to their transports in the Chesapeake. The British ships contented themselves with holding Alexandria for ransom, taking for prizes 21 ships in the harbor, thousands of barrels of flour, and large quantities of tobacco, cotton, and provisions in return for not burning the city. After five days, the squadron retired safely down the Potomac again, having captured or destroyed every boat and larger vessel along the river and burned every shipyard. A remarkable example of the professional skill of the Royal Navy, and of the weakness of American defenses.

When steamboats arrived on the Potomac, progressive Alexandria soon had a steam ferry service to Washington, just up the river. Eventually steamboats linked the port not only to other Potomac River towns but to Norfolk and Baltimore and to Philadelphia and New York. The little city's shipping reached a peak in the 1840s when Alexandria was home port for 39 oceangoing vessels; the largest was 677 tons.

The Civil War and the competition of Baltimore helped to speed the decline of Alexandria port; today, the many merchant ships that once thronged its docks are long gone and the city is in danger of being swallowed up by the Washington megalopolis. However, a fine three-masted schooner now graces its riverfront, thanks to a group of residents concerned with preserving the memory of Alexandria's maritime heritage.

To be sure, the new schooner *Alexandria* is, like the town's original settlers, an immigrant from overseas. She was launched in 1929 as the Swedish cargo carrier *Lindø*. After a busy commercial career, she was wrecked in the Baltic and rebuilt. Eventually, she was brought to this country and operated as a charter boat. In the Bicentennial Tall Ship's race across the Atlantic she came in third.

Today *Alexandria* is the pride of the Alexandria Seaport Foundation, which is dedicated to achieving an ambitious program involving both the restoration and preservation of historic watercraft and providing training in sail handling and boatbuilding. The foundation hopes eventually to establish a maritime museum in Alexandria to house the nautical artifacts that survive from the days when the city was a world port. In the meantime, schooner *Alexandria* is open to the public when she is in port, between cruises in Chesapeake Bay and along the coast.

The schooner is 92 feet long on deck and planked with three-inch oak over eight-inch oak frames. Her interior arrangements include a large main saloon, and five double staterooms.

Schooner *Alexandria* is berthed at Waterfront Park, Alexandria, Virginia. Vessel cruises to East Coast ports, but is open to visitors when in her home port. In commission roughly March 15 through November. Donations accepted. Owned and operated by nonprofit Alexandria Seaport Foundation, P.O. Box 3318/120 North St. Asaph Street, Alexandria, Virginia 22802. Telephone (703) 549-7078.

On the Maryland side of the Potomac at the Fall Line was the port of Georgetown, founded some three-quarters of a century later than its Virginia rival. Georgetown was also a tobacco port until flour, ground in mills up the Rock Creek, took over as the principal export. In the early 19th century, Georgetown benefited by becoming the eastern terminus of the Chesapeake and Ohio Canal, which carried down the coal, stone, and wheat of the upper valley. Soon, however, sediment from upland farms began silting up Georgetown Harbor and big ships were restricted to the deeper channel at Alexandria.

A third port, Bladensburg, grew up at the head of navigation on the Potomac's Eastern Branch, the Anacostia River. In the 18th century, Bladensburg was a bustling harbor, with shipyards, a ropewalk, and fish-salting plants. When Washington sprang up just west of Bladensburg, however, bridges to the new city over the Anacostia hindered shipping. The river eventually silted up and Bladenburg's maritime activities dwindled away. By the 1970s, the shore-to-shore width of the Anacostia River at Bladensburg was only one-fifth its original size.

One reason for the survival of Georgetown and Alexandria as river ports during the 19th century was the construction of the Chesapeake and Ohio Canal. Bypassing the falls and rapids that blocked the Potomac River, the canal linked tidewater to the interior of Virginia and Maryland. Although the canal never actually reached the Ohio—the competing Baltimore and Ohio railroad got there first—the Chesapeake and Ohio waterway was built as far as Cumberland, Maryland, 185 miles from Georgetown. Seventy-four locks lifted, or dropped, canal boats 605 feet. In one place, the canal runs through a 3,100-foot tunnel under a mountain; elsewhere 11 aqueducts carry the waterway over major Potomac tributaries. An impressive feat, considering the canal was largely dug by pick and shovel.

The C & O Canal went out of business as a commercial carrier after a disastrous flood in 1924, but several of the locks have been preserved in a beautiful park at Great Falls, a few miles up the Potomac from Washington. Here, at the Chesapeake and Ohio Canal National Historical Park on the Maryland side of the river, are Locks 17, 18, 19 and 20 and a lockhouse that was also a hotel and tavern. From mid-April to mid-October, 90-minute trips on mule-drawn canal boats are available with constumed guides to describe the canal and its people.

The handsome stone lockhouse, built in 1828, now houses the visitor's center and a small canal museum. The principal exhibit is a large diorama that shows a canal boat being put through the lock. Outside the window, the lock itself, number 20, is just across a small brick terrace. On the other side of the canal, at the foot of a steep bank, the Potomac River rushes furiously by over rocks and ledges—clearly demonstrating why a canal was necessary. An easy stroll along the towpath, overhung by trees, and past a canal boat moored to the bank, brings the visitor to the other three locks in the park.

The canal and house are surrounded by parkland dotted with great trees. Although the Great Falls themselves can be seen only from the Virginia side, the rapids form an impressive backdrop to the park. A very pleasant place—particularly as a respite from tourist-crowded Washington.

C & O Locks and Tavern/Lockhouse are in the C & O Canal National Park in Maryland at the Great Falls of the Potomac, 14 miles west of Washington, D.C. From the west end of Pennsylvania Avenue take its continuation, Route 29. Bear right on MacArthur Boulevard, which leads directly to the park and tavern/lockhouse at Great Falls. Hiking and bicy-cling paths along entire length of the canal. The Tavern is open all year; Wednesday-Sunday, 9 a.m. to 5 p.m. The Park is open all year, daylight to dusk. Admission: free. Great Falls Tavern, C & O National Historical Park, Great Falls, Maryland. Telephone (301) 299-3614. For general park in-formation: Superintendent, C & O Canal National Histori-cal Park, Box 4, Sharpsburg, Maryland 21782. Telephone (301) 739-4200.

Throughout the 19th century and into the 20th, Alexandria and the new city of Washington (which included Georgetown within its borders) continued to comprise a busy port with not only fishermen and river and bay traffic but, in the earlier years, deep-sea ships. The river was thronged with small craft—no fewer than 20 distinctive types, including such esoteric craft as pungy boats, xebecs, and shad galleys. A major problem, despite dredging, was the continuing shoaling of the Potomac with farm run-off from upriver. Nevertheless, 1886 saw almost 2,900 vessels use the harbor, and in 1894 no fewer than 44 steam tugs were still required to move the harbor traffic.

Shipbuilding also flourished. Some authorities claim that in the late 18th century the Potomac River shipyards had more marine artisans than any other river on the East Coast and that this was a factor in selecting the site for the national capital. In the post-Civil War years, the yards largely shifted to building river craft and fishing boats, and enjoyed boom times from 1870 to 1910. As late as World War I, however, 11 oceangoing vessels were built in Alexandria and Washington.

Fishing boomed in the Potomac in the 19th century. In the 1830s there were 450 boats, and 22,500,000 shad were taken in a six-week season. Sturgeon became a big catch after the Civil War, supporting a flourishing business in Potomac caviar; an average of 75,000 pounds of sturgeon was taken from the river.

Today the steamers have faded from the Potomac, the fisheries have been devastated by water pollution, and the river has been largely left to small pleasure craft. There is little in Washington to commemorate the great days of the Potomac, but the maritime traditions of the entire nation, naval and mercantile, are preserved in two of the nation's largest and finest maritime museums.

The Washington Navy Yard, first in the nation, was established on the north bank of the Anacostia River close to where it ran into the Potomac. When the British captured Washington in 1814, the Navy ordered the yard burned to keep its supplies and equipment from falling into enemy hands. Rebuilt after the war, the Yard constructed major ships for the Navy, including the largest wooden vessel ever built in the area, the 3,000-ton steam frigate *Minnesota*. As time went on the Navy Yard concentrated more and more on the development and manufacture of naval guns. Throughout its history the yard has also been concerned with advanced technology: Here were built the nation's first marine railway, the first ship-model basin for testing hull designs in the water, early wind tunnels, and the first successful aircraft catapult for use on shipboard.

Today the Washington Navy Yard is a ceremonial and administrative center, but it is also home of one of the nation's most interesting and least-known maritime collections: the United States Navy Memorial Museum. The exhibits, says the Navy, are "intended to educate, inform, and inspire the public in the traditions, heritage and scientific contributions of the naval service . . ." Housed in a 600-foot building that was once part of the Naval Gun Factory, the museum does all these things, covering American naval activities from the American Revolution through the Space Age.

Without interior supports, and lit by overhead skylights, the uninterrupted open space provides 40,000 square feet of display area for a collection that includes ship models, relics, mementos, tools and equipment, prints and paintings, big guns and personal weapons, space capsules and bottom-exploring submarines, uniforms, and documents.

Facing the visitor as he enters the building is a fighting top of the frigate *Constitution*, erected just the way it once stood aboard Old Ironsides. As John C. Reilly, Jr., describes it in an interesting little booklet called "The Constitution Fighting Top"—well worth owning—the top was brought down from Boston and carefully rigged in the original style. "Every splice and serving was done by hand," Reilly writes, "every ratline was carefully lashed in place in the sailor-fashion of days that are long gone."

The museum's enormous and rich collection—more than 5,000 objects are on display—may seem bewildering at first but it is well organized by topics. Along the sides of the hall, coordinated exhibits are each focused on a conflict or some special event in the U.S. Navy's history: such as Perry's opening of Japan, or the Civil War, for instance. Large individual objects, big guns, contemporary fighting ships, and torpedoes, are displayed down the center of the hall. Still more displays are hung from the ceiling.

Here are some highlights to look for:

- A big model of the *Bon Homme Richard* commanded by John Paul Jones in his victorious battle with HMS *Serapis*.
- The big punch bowl ordered from China by Commodore Truxton, commander of the *Constellation*, with a handsome 44-gun frigate pictured in the bottom.
- 42-pounder cannon from the American privateer *General Armstrong*, which fought an entire British fleet in the closing days of the War of 1812.
- A diorama of Union gunboats firing at Island 10 in a famous Civil War land/sea battle on the Mississippi River.
- A diorama of a steam-frigate gun crew in action in Hampton Roads during the Civil War, with

the *Monitor* and *Merrimack* in the background.

- An unusual collection of models of late-19th- and early-20th-century armored warships. Models of these little-known vessels—part of the modernization of the Navy—are rarely seen. Magnificently detailed, the models were built for the Navy Department at the same time as the vessels themselves. Among them are:
  — the protected cruiser *Baltimore* (1888);
  — the armored cruiser *Brooklyn* (1895);
  — the battleship *Texas*, the Navy's first pre-dreadnaught (1895-1911);
  — the scout cruiser *Salem* (1908), one of the Navy's first turbine-driven warships.
- Many big naval guns, on their original mounts so that children can climb up and work the controls.
- Models of early Navy aircraft and dirigibles.
- A display about the huge mine barrage laid across the North Sea in 1918 to keep German U-boats out of the Atlantic.
- A special submarine room equipped with a working periscope and display models of such early submarines as the *Adder*, a Holland Type VII of 1900, and the S-3, launched in 1918.
- Mounted on stanchions, the original submersible *Trieste*, an underwater exploration vessel, which in 1960 dove 37,000 feet to the deepest place in the ocean. She is the centerpiece of the Undersea Exploration Exhibit.
- The current underwater exploration vehicle *Alvin*, built for deep submergence.
- The big Poseidon nuclear missile, resting on the floor of the museum. While it lacks a label there, descriptive diagrams are in a case nearby.
- An exhibit about the Navy fliers held as prisoners of war in North Vietnam—prison uniforms, a model of the "Hanoi Hilton" prison compound, and mementos;
- A mock-up of the space capsule *United States*, set on the floor, and arranged so that kids can climb into it.

The displays spill out of the building into Willard Park, a two-acre triangular green in front of the museum building. Here there is an assortment of large weapons and pieces of heavy equipment with explanatory labels nearby. Particularly impressive is the huge 16-inch "naval rifle," part of the main battery of the largest battleships, and a whole flock of missiles, airborn and underwater, including an Asroc, Subroc, Talos, and Sea Sparrow. Pieces of 16-inch and 26-inch armor plate—the latter from a Japanese gun turret—are so massive that one wonders how a ship

can carry them. There is even a small vessel: an unmanned platform some 15 feet long and battery operated, called a "Navy oceanographic meteorological automatic device 'Nomad,'" it is a remote sensing device for recording weather data.

The Navy Memorial Museum and its park are not the only things of interest in the Washington Navy Yard. For one, there is the yard itself. The Navy's oldest shore establishment, it occupies land set aside by George Washington for the use of the federal government. Several of the old buildings survived the destruction of the yard in 1814: The "Second Officers Quarters" was built in 1801 but encloses the farmhouse already on the property when the government bought it. The neoclassical Tingey House (1804), is now the official residence of the Chief of Naval Operations. The Latrobe Gate, of which the oldest section also dates from 1804, is the oldest continuously manned Marine sentry post in the nation. A folder is available which maps a walking tour of the yard.

The map also shows the location of two other small museums nearby: the Navy Art Gallery and the Marine Corps Museum. Many artists have had a special interest in naval combat and, in the 50-odd years since the outbreak of World War II, the United States Navy has encouraged this interest—and, at the same time, inspired a striking visual record of its activities. Artists commissioned as naval officers have created a remarkable collection of more than 4,000 paintings and drawings covering not only World War II and the Korean and Vietnam conflicts, but the peacetime activities of the service as well.

The pictures include oils, watercolors, charcoal, and chalk; many can be considered major works of art. In style they vary from near-photographic realism to scenes transformed by the artist's eye almost to the point of abstraction. Some of the pictures show actual battles; more often they report routine but visually striking noncombat operations, such as refueling at sea. Only a few of the pictures can be displayed at the Navy Art Gallery at any one time and the selection is continually changing. Many are highly dramatic, all are of great visual interest.

A personal favorite: the sketch for *PT Boat Gunner* by Mitchell Jamieson.

The United States Marines have, of course, been seagoing soldiers since their inception. Established to keep order aboard warships and to man the fighting tops with sharpshooters, they have since become primarily an amphibious landing force but still an essential part of the Navy, and of our maritime heritage. The Marine Corps Museum, in the first floor of a mid-19th-century brick building, covers all phases of the Corps' activities since its foundation. Uniforms, weapons, memorabilia, and pictures are grouped chronologically. Particularly interesting among the combat dioramas are scenes depicting Marines boarding feluccas in Tripoli harbor during the war with the Barbary pirates; the defense of Bladensburg in the War of 1812; the attack on Mexico City during the Mexican War in 1847; and the deadly battle in Belleau Wood in World War I.

A recent addition to the Washington Navy Yard's exhibits in conjunction with the Navy Memorial Museum is the U.S.S. *Barry*, a destroyer of the Forrest Sherman Class. The 418-foot vessel, which displaces almost 4,000 tons fully loaded, was commissioned in 1956 and saw 26 years of active duty. In Vietnam waters where she won two battle stars, her operations were primarily shore bombardment, firing 2,500 rounds in combat and destroying more than 1,000 enemy structures. Barry's 1967 anti-submarine warfare modernization included installation of ASROL—Anti-Submarine Rocket Launcher—and VDS—Variable Depth Sonar.

Both of these interesting devices remain aboard and can be seen on the carefully organized visitors' tour. With explanations posted at eighteen key points on the ship, the self-guided tour gives the layman a pretty complete picture of how the *Barry* was organized and operated. Of particular interest are the Bridge/Ship-Control Station and the Combat Information Center—respectively, the navigational and combat brains of the ship.

The United States Navy Memorial Museum is in the former Naval Gun Factory at the Washington Navy Yard. The Navy Memorial Museum is open daily from 9 a.m. to 5 p.m. on

Figure 32
Fighting top of frigate *Constitution* dominates entrance to immense, exhibit-crammed hall of U.S. Navy Memorial Museum at the Washington Navy Yard in Washington, D.C.

weekdays; all year, except New Year's Day, Thanksgiving, Christmas Eve, and Christmas Day; 10 a.m. to 5 p.m. on Saturday, Sunday, and holidays. Gift shop. Handicapped facilities available. Admission and parking are free. The Navy Art Gallery is open Monday-Friday, 10 a.m. to 4:30 p.m. Admission free. The Marine Corps Museum is open all year except New Year's and Christmas Day, Monday-Staurday, 10 a.m. to 4 p.m.; Sunday and holidays, noon to 5 p.m.; Friday evenings, 6 p.m. to 8 p.m. Admission free. Gift shop. Handicapped facilities available. Parking is free. U.S.S. *Barry* is open every day of the year from 10 a.m. to 5 p.m. except in bad weather and on Thanksgiving, Christmas Eve, Christmas Day, New Year's. (Also sometimes closed for a few hours for official functions.) United States Navy Memorial Museum, the Naval Historical Center, Washington Navy Yard, 9th and N Streets, South East, Washington, D.C. 20374. Telephone: Navy Yard Information, (202) 433-2878; Marine Corps Museum, (202) 433-3534; Navy Art Gallery, (202) 433-3815.

The development of the United States Navy can be further explored in Washington's other museum with major maritime exhibits, the National Museum of American History, part of the Smithsonian complex on the Mall. Here, among many Navy-related exhibits, is the oldest-surviving American warship. Here, also, are the famous merchant-ship models, along with many historic artifacts in the American Maritime Enterprise collection. And the Smithsonian has still more maritime-related exhibits in the 1876 Centennial Exhibition at the Arts and Industry building. The Smithsonian collections should be a top priority for anyone interested in learning more about the nation's maritime heritage.

At the National Museum of American History, part of the Smithsonian, the hull of the Continental gondola *Philadelphia*, still mounting its original cannon, is berthed in the Armed Forces History section at the east end of the third floor of the History Museum. Gondolas, often called gundalows, were small, shallow vessels sailed with a simple rig or rowed with huge sweeps when the wind failed. They were river or lake craft; the *Philadelphia* served on Lake Champlain and was armed with three guns as part of the tiny flotilla that contested the British invasion from Canada in 1776.

Sitting there on the museum floor, the *Philadelphia* may not seem much to look at; a rather roughly built open boat some 57 feet long, flat-bottomed, drawing only a couple of feet when unloaded, and mounting three corroded cannon. But to those gifted with historical imagination she is more exciting than the most beautiful restoration of a full-rigged ship. Like *Sparrow Hawk* in Plymouth, *Philadelphia* is a direct physical link with America's maritime past. Except for invisible preservative

coatings, this crude little craft is entirely original, looking much as she did when she went down in battle on October 11, 1776. No minor skirmish, either, but a lake battle that may well have changed the course of history.

Afloat, the *Philadelphia* had a short life but a busy one. She was knocked together in a hurry by backwoods carpenters in May 1776, part of the little fleet built to oppose invading British forces moving south from Canada. In October, the *Philadelphia* was lined up with the other American vessels in Valcour Bay in Lake Champlain. All day long they exchanged fire with the superior British squadron. The *Philadelphia* was badly holed and sank that night. The next day the rest of the American squadron was dispersed or destroyed as the ships retreated down the lake.

Tactically, a defeat. But the existence of the American ships delayed the British invasion a month, and, as a result, the British decided to postpone their move south for a year. By 1777 the American defensive forces were strong enough to force the surrender of Burgoyne's invading army. In the words of Admiral Mahan, America's most distinguished analyst of naval warfare: "The little American navy on Champlain was wiped out; but never had any force, big or small, lived to better purpose or died more gloriously, for it saved The Lake for that year."

Alongside the original vessel in the museum is a fine model of the *Philadelphia*, showing her as she originally appeared when fully rigged and armed. Also nearby is a very interesting series of small models showing the evolution of naval cannon from the 15th through the 19th centuries—worth a little study, not only by ship modelers but by anyone interested in understanding battle tactics in the age of sail.

The naval portion of the Armed Forces History section displays a remarkably large and fine selection of models of American naval vessels, from the 14-gun ship *Boston* (1748), to the gigantic World War II battleship *Missouri*. Many are of vessels that are rarely modeled, such as the Revolutionary frigate *Confederacy*; the privateer *Prince of Neufchatel* (1813); Robert Fulton's steam battery (1814); and the 1842 steam frigate *Congress*. The steam frigate *Hartford* is shown fighting it out muzzle to muzzle with the Confederate ram *Tennessee* at the Civil War battle of Mobile Bay. The Civil War era is particularly well-represented, with models of the famous Union gunboats *Benton* and *Carondelet* and an entire flotilla of Confederate ironclads.

The Underwater Exploration section on the same floor of the museum is also of maritime interest. Particularly striking is a life-size diorama of an archaeologist working on the ocean floor, showing how a wreck is marked off with guide lines. A model of the underwater exploration vessel *Trieste* is shown with a full explanation of how it worked and how it was used. (Ideally, the visitor should take a good look at this before going to the Navy Memorial Museum, where he will find the original *Trieste*.)

On the first floor of the National Museum of American History is the famous American Maritime Enterprise section, a wonderful collection of ship models combined with prints and paintings, original artifacts, full-scale mock-ups, documents, and equipment. This permanent exhibition presents, as a Smithsonian brochure puts it, "scenes and episodes from the history of our nation's waterbone commerce." Whole sections are devoted to such topics as the sea commerce of the American colonies; the great age of sail, including whaling; the inland waterways and the coming of steamboats; wrecks and lifesaving services; 20th-century shipping; steamship machinery and equipment; the transatlantic liners; and the seamen that manned American vessels over the centuries.

With a collection of this richness, it is impossible to do more than point out some of the highlights:

- Close to the entrance to the Maritime Section is a very large model of the ship *Brilliant*, a tobacco carrier of 1775, so big that every detail of deck and rigging is easily examined. Next to it is a full-size replica of the base of the *Brilliant*'s foremast, with a section of deck and complete rigging—fife rail, belaying pins, sheets, braces, halyards—just as they are in miniature in the model beside it, making it easy to use the model to visualize the full-sized ship in its entirety.
- The original John Stevens marine steam engine used to power the Stevens steamboat *Little Juliana* in 1804, well before Fulton's *Clermont*, is here. In modern times, this engine, with only a few missing pipes restored, was installed in a replica of the *Juliana* and worked fine. (Models of the Stevens engine, as well as of the John Fitch steamboat engine of 1787, are in the Power Machinery section in the southeast corner of the first floor.)
- Nearby, in an extremely interesting model of an even earlier steamboat, designed by Griffin Greene in 1796. Greene's original plans, shown alongside the model, were used by a Smithsonian expert to build the model and its miniature engine, which have been operated successfully. Also displayed is piece of paper that helps explain why Greene isn't famous as the inventor of the steamboat: a bill for $299.33 for parts. Poor Greene couldn't come up with

the money, so the supplier seized the inventor's engine in lieu of payment, and that was the end of the project.

- The triple-expansion steam engine built in 1920 for the Coast Guard buoy tender *Oak*, provides a dramatic contrast to Steven's primitive engine. In the same display is the *Oak*'s deckhouse with complete gauges, instrument panels, and speaking tubes.

The many, many ship models include the famous National Watercraft collection, inspired, researched, and gathered by the late Howard I. Chappelle, noted historian of American ship design. A sampling shows the range: the schooner *St. Ann* (1730s); the ship *London* (1770); the topsail schooner *Experiment* (early 1800s); the brig *Diligente* (1839); the auxiliary steam packet ship *Massachusetts* (1845); the ship *Tillie E. Starbuck* (1883); and the four-masted barkentine *Kohala* (1901).

The late 19th and 20th centuries are well-represented by models of liners and other steamships. The SS *Philadelphia*, ex-*City of Paris*, built in 1889, is notable for her yacht bow and three masts with fore-and-aft rig. Here, also, are the famous *Leviathan*, ex-*Vaterland*, and the Liberty and Victory ships and tankers of World War II. Of special interest is a model of the *Golden Bear*—a LASH, or Lighter Aboard Ship. A LASH is a special kind of barge that can be hoisted, fully loaded, aboard an oceangoing vessel, carried overseas, and dropped overboard in a port where shallow water prevents a big ship from coming alongside an unloading dock. Memorabilia of the great days of the transatlantic liners include such things as posters, passenger lists, china, menus, souvenir logs, stationery, and oak paneling from the *Leviathan*.

In the Seamen section, the visitor is struck by a life-size recreation of a 1910 tattoo parlor, complete not only with needles, inks, and patterns, but also with a slightly apprehensive looking sailor, already well-decorated, waiting for the tattoo artist to go to work.

In every section, paintings and prints supplement the models and artifacts. Particularly interesting are the graphics in the "For Those in Peril" section dealing with marine disasters and the responsive navigational and lifesaving services. Such lithographs as *The Wreck of the Swallow* (1845), *A Squall off Cape Horn* (mid-19th century), and *They're Saved!* give a vivid report of the perils of 19th-century sea voyages.

The non-maritime portions of the National Museum of American History are also, of course, of great interest, covering everything from railroads to a small house occupied by Mr. and Mrs. Doll and their 10 children.

Figure 33
Huge size, fine detail, and accessibility on gallery floor of model of *Brilliant*, 1775 tobacco
carrier, give visitor wonderful close-up of an 18th century ship at The Smithsonian's National
Museum of American History in Washington, D.C.

The National Museum of American History of the Smithsonian Institution. Open all year, except Christmas Day; 10 a.m. to 5:30 p.m. No admission charge. Gift shop, cafeteria, snack bar, and bookstore. Post office. Demonstrations at various times; special tours by appointment. Part of the Smithsonian Institution. National Museum of American History, Constitution Avenue between 12th and 14th Streets, North West, Washington, D.C. 20560. Telephone (202) 357-2700.

Many aspects of maritime history are to be found in the multi-faceted Smithsonian Institution's "1876: A Centential Exhibition." A mini recreation of the great Centennial Exposition held in Philadelphia in 1876, it includes maritime exhibits originally sponsored by the Navy Department and United States Fisheries Commission. The Centennial exhibit is in the Arts & Industries Building, across the Mall to the southeast of the National Museum of American History.

Here, in the South Hall, is an enormous waterline model of the steam sloop of war *Antietam*, 45 feet long, her masts towering above the visitor. One of the original 1876 Centennial Exposition exhibits, *Antietam* was preserved for a century to teach rigging to Annapolis midshipmen. Alongside is a 10-foot model, dwarfed by its huge neighbor, showing the original *Antietam* on the builder's ways. Nearby are a squadron of models and half models of naval vessels of 1876.

Of special interest to Civil War buffs is the head of a spar torpedo, designed to be filled with explosives and rammed against the side of an enemy vessel to blow it up. Crude though it seems, the spar torpedo was used successfully in the Civil War, notably in the daring Union Navy raid that sank the Confederate ironclad *Albemarle* in the Roanoke River, and in the equally bold Confederate attack that sank the USS *Housatonic* off Charleston.

Close by the *Antietam* are the fisheries and whaling exhibits, which center on a caseful of models of schooners and other fisheries craft. There are no identifying labels, a deliberate omission, since there were few or no labels in the original 1876 exhibits.

1876, a Centennial Exhibition, occupies the Smithsonian's Arts and Science building. Open all year, except Christmas Day. Hours: 10 a.m. to 5:30 p.m. Admission free. Museum shop; Discovery Theater. Arts & Industries Building of the Smithsonian Institution, Jefferson Drive at 9th Street, South West, Washington, D.C. 20560. Telephone (202) 357-1300 or 357-2700.

Now we'll leave the high-pressure atmosphere of the nation's capital and travel only a few miles to a quiet, remote corner where the past is very much present.

Southern Maryland, the wide peninsula between Chesapeake Bay and the Potomac River, was the site of the first European settlement in the colony. That was three and a half centuries ago, and, for most of the intervening time, Southern Maryland has been a sleepy backwater, with little fishing villages and tobacco wharves along its shores and beautiful manor houses decaying amid worked-out tobacco fields. More recently, the explosion of urban Washington into the surrounding areas has turned the northern portion into exurbia. But despite a large Naval air test center at Patuxent and a bridge over the lower Potomac linking the area to Virginia, Southern Maryland remains an out-of-the-way sort of place, far removed from the industrial bustle of Baltimore and the political frenzy of Washington.

Like almost every place along the shores of the great bay, Southern Maryland has an ancient and distinctive maritime heritage. Some 20 different types of small craft have been used at various times along the Potomac. From the very first Maryland settlements, the shallop was the workhorse. When the *Ark* arrived with Lord Calvert's settlers off St. Clement's Island in the lower Potomac after a three month passage, the serving women were sent off in a shallop to wash the party's underwear. Apparently they all leaned over the same side of the shallop and capsized it; most of the first settlers' underwear went to the bottom—a sad loss, since such garments were not part of the wardrobe of the local Indians.

In the early days of the colony, blue-water ships went from one little plantation wharf to the next, loading tobacco for the English market. Most local travel in the bay area was by water in small craft—sloops, shallops, skiffs. When the tobacco fields of the tidewater farms wore out, the people along the shore turned to fishing and oystering. With the coming of the steamboat, each landing on Bay or river became a port of call for passengers and freight. In the Civil War, Union gunboats patrolled the Potomac to cut off supplies smuggled across to the Confederacy from Southern Maryland.

Today the steamboats have gone, the Potomac fisheries have been killed by pollution; shell-fishing and yachting survive to support the watermen. But much of the heritage of the past can be found at the Calvert Marine Museum at Solomons Island, far down on the Chesapeake Bay side of Southern Maryland but within easy driving distance of Washington, Baltimore, and Annapolis.

The little village of Solomons was once a considerable oystering and fishing port with yards that built more bugeyes—the distinctive regional type of oyster boat—than anywhere else on Chesapeake Bay. Now it is a center of recreational boating and yachting. The past is not forgotten, however.

The Calvert Marine Museum is on the side road leading from Route 2 to Solomons village. Housed in a one-time schoolhouse, the museum exhibits ship models, many artifacts, a variety of small craft, and displays related to the paleontology and marine biology of the area.

On the lower level of the museum a ship-model/woodcarving shop offers visitors an opportunity to watch craftsmen at work building miniature replicas of local craft. Nearby is a collection of artifacts recovered from an American gunboat sunk while attempting to block the Royal Navy task force moving up the Patuxent in support of the attack on Washington in 1814.

In the Maritime History Room on the upper level, models, prints, and photographs focus on maritime activities in the Solomons area, including the distinctive Chesapeake Bay watercraft, the old steamboats, and the yachts built in a local shipyard. A reconstruction of a shipbuilder's shack displays the tools of the trade. Of particular interest is a 28-foot Poquoson canoe, a double-ender descended from Indian dugouts; however, its planked sides and clipper bow make it very un-canoelike.

The Watermen's Room on the same floor has exhibits of the various techniques of harvesting fish, oysters, and crabs—the major activities of Chesapeake Bay watermen—alongside a partially reconstructed oyster-shucking shed.

The boat shed behind the museum building displays the *John A. Ryder*, Maryland's first softshell clamming rig, not to mention crabbing skiffs, dory boats, and log canoes. Along the wall is an unusual collection of ancient outboard motors and one-lung inboards.

At the shore on the museum grounds is the old Drum Point Lighthouse. Built in 1883, it is the distinctive Chesapeake Bay screw-pile cottage type with the little light tower rising from the roof of the lightkeeper's cottage, which rests on huge piles that were screwed into the mud of the bay bottom. After marking the entrance to the Patuxent River for 79 years, the lighthouse was decommissioned and eventually moved to the museum grounds. Tied up at the dock next to the lighthouse is the old oyster boat *Wm. B. Tennison*, beautifully maintained and now used to take visitors on cruises along the Patuxent. The *Tennison* is a log-built bugeye but is now operated under power.

Calvert Marine Museum, Solomons, Maryland. From Route 2, turn off about a hundred yards from the east end of the Solomons Bridge. Museum is in a large rectangular building about 500 feet down the road on the left. Exhibits include artifacts, models, small craft, lighthouse. Harbor cruises available May through October in powered log-canoe bugeye. Museum open all year, except New Year's Day, Thanksgiving, and Christmas Day. May through September, open Monday-Saturday, 10 a.m. to 5 p.m.; Sunday, noon to 5 p.m.; October through April, Monday-Friday, 10 a.m. to 4:30 p.m. Saturday-Sunday, noon to 4:30 p.m. Admission: free to museum; small fee for lighthouse and oyster house. Book/gift shop. Dock space available during visit. Sponsored and partially supported by Calvert County, Maryland. Calvert Marine Museum, P.O. Box 97, Solomons, Maryland 20688. Telephone (301) 326-2042.

Even further down into Southern Maryland, the visitor enters one of the oldest areas of English settlement in North America. Here, in 1634, Leonard Calvert, brother of Lord Baltimore, came with two ships, the *Ark* and the *Dove*, carrying gentlemen and workingmen from England (the number ranges from 140 to 320 in different accounts) to found a new colony. Calvert chose a site for his settlement on a high bluff overlooking the St. Mary's River, near where it runs into the broad entrance to the Potomac from Chesapeake Bay. Here he bought an Indian village from its inhabitants and founded St. Mary's City.

The Calverts and many of their settlers were Roman Catholics; their settlement was to provide a refuge for their English coreligionists. St. Mary's became the capital of the new colony, but eventually Protestant jealousy of Catholic influence led to the capital's transfer up the Bay to Annapolis and St. Mary's City dwindled away. Today, a few houses, a small college, and an outdoor history museum with an archaeological dig, a modern recreation of the 17th-century State House, and a Visitors Center are all that mark the site of Maryland's first capital. Nearby are a Natural History Area and a recreated 17th-century plantation.

Plus one other thing of great maritime interest: a fine recreation of a 17th-century vessel.

The recreated vessel is the 50-ton pinnace *Maryland Dove*. The original *Dove* probably carried supplies, while the settlers took passage in the much larger *Ark*. At the very outset of the voyage, when the two ships were delayed in a south coastal English harbor, it was the *Dove* that accidentally got the expedition under way. In the words of Father Andrew White, the Roman Catholic priest who accompanied the settlers: "A strong and favorable wind arose, and a French cutter . . . being forced to set sail, came near running into our pinnance. The latter, therefore, to avoid being run down, having cut away and lost an anchor, set sail without delay; and since it was dangerous to drift about in that place, made haste to get farther out to sea. And so that we might not lose sight of our pinnace, we determined to follow."

During the voyage, the two vessels were separated in a storm. According to White: "The winde grew still lowder and lowder, makeing a boysterous sea, and about midnight we espied our pinnace with her two lights, as she had forewarned us, in the shroodes, from wch time till six weekes, we never see her more, thinke-ing shee had assuredly beene foundred and lost in those huge seas."

But the *Dove* survived, and eventually the two vessels reached the Chesapeake. The *Ark* returned to England; the *Dove*, a chartered vessel, was purchased by the Maryland colony for local use. Unfortunately, after a single trading voyage to Boston, she was sent back across the Atlantic with a cargo of skins and timber and was lost off the coast of England.

The new *Dove* has been built according to plans researched and drawn by the noted historical marine architect, William A. Baker. The term "pinnace" as used in the 17th century was pretty vague, and applied to everything from small, open pulling boats to rela-tively large ship-rigged vessels. In general, it seems to have meant smaller and lighter vessels that could serve as tenders for large ships. No plans for the original *Dove* exist, so Baker designed a small three-masted vessel that might have been sailing in 1633.

The result is the beautiful little vessel that is berthed in the St. Mary's River at the foot of the bluff behind the reconstructed State House near the Governor's Field. Seventy-six feet over all, with a 17-foot beam, she draws only six feet. *Dove* was built by James Richardson at an Eastern Shore shipyard, fami-ly-owned, that has built wooden bay vessels for generations. Her frames are oak and her keel is shaped from a single giant oak log.

The *Dove* is small enough so that her design and rig are easy to take in. Here are some things to look for:

- the great tiller—the *Dove* is too small to need a whipstaff such as Baker installed on *Mayflower II*;
- the "murtherers"—breech-loading culverines mounted on the poop to repel boarders;
- the square spritsail mounted under the bowsprit to help with the steering;
- the strong colors of the decorated trim on her hull—a reminder that in time the original *Dove* was closer to the Middle Ages than to our own era;
- the log pumps and oak windlass;
- the high poop at the stern and the projecting head or beak under the bowsprit, a descendent of the ram used by fighting ships for centuries. Both set the *Dove* apart from the 18th-century vessels with which most of us are more familiar.

Incidentally, St. Mary's is a quiet, out-of-the-way village but there is an ambitious plan to reconstruct more replicas of 17th century buildings.

Figure 34
The *Maryland Dove*, here with a bone in teeth as she enjoys a fine Chesapeake Bay breeze, is an authentic recreation of a 17th century "pinnace." She is based at St. Mary's City where in 1634 the original *Dove* was one of two vessels that landed people and supplies for the first English settlement in Maryland.

Pinnace *Maryland Dove* is docked at the foot of the hill be-hind the reconstructed state house in St. Mary's City; the admission office is in the visitor center about a mile away. Open mid-March through the last weekend in November. Wednesday-Sunday, 10 a.m. to 5 p.m. Admission: $3.00; seniors, $2.00; children 6-12, $1.50. St. Mary's City, P.O. Box 39, St. Mary's City, Maryland 20686. Telephone (301) 682-1634 or 862-1661.

Now south again to the Old Dominion: Virginia, site of the first permanent English settlement in North America, scene of historic naval battles, possessor of a rich maritime heritage that survives today in a commercial port and a naval base, both of major im-portance.

Chesapeake Bay III: The Virginia Peninsula and Hampton Roads

South of the estuary of the Potomac, the west shore of Chesapeake Bay continues to be serrated by rivers—first the Rappahanock, then the York, and finally the James. Like all the Chesapeake's tributaries, these were the Colonial highways—opening the country to settlement, carrying local travelers and freight, providing access for deep-water ships to pick up the golden cargoes of tobacco to be carried across the Atlantic to England. As one early writer put it: ". . .no country is better watered for the convenience of which most Houses are built near some Landing Place; so that any Thing may be delivered to a Gentleman there from London, Bristol . . . with less trouble and Cost, than to one living five miles in the Country in England."

Between the two most southerly of these rivers, the York and the James, is the Virginia Peninsula. Events here marked the beginning of the earliest (continuous) strand in America's maritime heritage—at least of the portion that has come down to us from English-speaking people living in what is now the United States.

In April 1607, with Elizabeth the Virgin Queen just four years dead, three little ships from England sailed between the Virginia Capes into Chesapeake Bay. The *Susan Constant*, *Godspeed*, and *Discovery* were far from the first European vessels to enter the Bay: Dutch, French, Portuguese, Spanish, and earlier English explorers had poked their noses between the capes and gone on. There had even been, briefly, a Spanish mission planted on the Bay, but it had been quickly wiped out by Indians. But these newcomers were neither explorers nor missionaries; they came to settle on the land—at least long enough to make their fortunes.

And fortunes they expected. Had not Michael Drayton, a future poet laureate of England, written:

Britains, you stay too long,
Quickly aboord bestow you,
    And with a merry gale,
    Swell your stretched sayle,
With voys as strong
As the winds that blow you.

And cheerefully at sea,
Successe you still intice,
    To get the pearle and gold,
    And ours to hold,
    VIRGINIA,
Earth's only Paradise;

Where nature hath in store
Fowl, venison, and fish;
    And the fruitfull'st soil
    Without your toil,
Three harvests more,
All greater than you wish.

Those enticing verses had an ironic ring a couple of years later, after the cruel "starving time" had swept away nine settlers out of ten. But on arrival, the crews and passengers must have scrambled ashore, happy to have reached Earth's only paradise after a difficult winter passage of almost five months from London. Captain Christopher Newport, commander of the expedition, had led his little fleet a few miles up the James to a marshy point on the north bank where the water was deep enough for his three small vessels to tie up to the branches of overhanging trees.

Today, the traveler will find *Godspeed*, *Discovery*, and *Susan Constant* berthed in the James River just a few hundred yards from where they arrived more than three and a half centuries ago. Not the originals, to be sure, but vessels carefully designed and built in the old-time manner, based on scholarly research on ships of the period. The ships are there to commemorate a landmark in American history, for the survivors of Jamestown, reinforced by more settlers from England, hung on to establish the first permanent English-speaking settlement in North America. Pearls and gold found they none; fowl, venison, and fish were there aplenty, and eventually rich harvests were to be reaped from virgin fields, but the settlers had to learn through bitter experience that nothing was to be reaped "without your toil."

This first permanent settlement signaled the coming of a dramatic change in the nature of America's maritime heritage. No longer would North American maritime activities consist almost entirely of explorers cautiously coasting along the shore seeking what was beyond the next headland; recording, mapping, reporting back to European sponsors. From Jamestown onward, ships were increasingly concerned with settlement and trade: bringing people and manufactures across the Atlantic from the Old World, taking back the products of the forests, farms, fisheries, of the New. *Discovery*, *Susan Constant*, and *Godspeed* marked the beginning of a new age.

The ships are tied up alongside a pier stretching out into the James River at the Jamestown Festival Park. Established by the state of Virginia to commemorate the first settlement, the park is a short distance from the original site, now largely washed away by riverbank erosion. From the Festival Park exhibition buildings the path to the ships winds through woods, past a recreation of the settlers' fort, to the river bank.

The visitor is likely to be struck right away by how small the Jamestown ships were. They did, after all, carry a whole settlement—105 colonists, plus seamen—three thousand miles across the Atlantic. All three were merchant vessels. The largest, the 76-foot *Susan Constant*, a three-masted ship, was rated at 100 tons, a little more than half the burden of the *Mayflower*. *Constant* probably had a crew of 17 or so, and carried about 55 passengers. She was large enough to be fitted with a whipstaff to assist the steersman in conning the ship.

The other two were less than half *Constant*'s tonnage. The next in size, *Godspeed*, was also three-masted, but only about 40 tons; she is believed to have had a 13-man crew and carried about 39 passengers. The two-masted *Discovery*, the smallest and only half the tonnage of *Godspeed*, carried some 9 crewmen and a dozen passengers.

That the original vessels were well able to cross the Atlantic, despite their small size, was recently demonstrated dramatically. A new *Godspeed* was built at Jamestown, shipped to England on a freighter, dropped into the water, and then repeated her namesake's voyage westward across the Atlantic. She was able to make the entire voyage under her own sail power except for a portion down the English Channel and the final passage around Cape Hatteras and Cape Henry, where she was towed. (Unlike our ancestors, we are unwilling to wait days or weeks for a favorable wind. But then, they had no choice.)

Both the current *Godspeed* and *Discovery* are the second replicas to be built of the original Jamestown ships. Earlier vessels, constructed for the celebration of the 350th anniversary of the settlement in 1957 suffered severe hull damage when the James River silted up and they came to rest on the bottom. The new replicas were recently built by traditional 17th-century methods right on the riverbank nearby, while the largest, the *Constant*, which was also damaged, has had major reconstruction work. The men building the new replicas developed considerable admiration for their 16th-century predecessors. In the words of the master shipwright, Carl Pedersen: "The more you get into these ships, the more respect you have for the men who designed and built them. They have nice lines and sail well."

Now all three ships are again at the exhibition pier. In keeping with 17th-century practice, the hulls of the smaller vessels have been oiled, rather than painted, above the waterline, with the wales (the horizontal strips of planking along the outside of the hull to strengthen it) painted black. The rail caps are picked out in yellows and reds.

The Jamestown ships rank in historic importance with the *Mayflower* and, of course, preceded her by more than a decade. Their replicas, authentic to the types and period of the originals, built with loving craftsmanship, and beautiful in themselves, should be high on the visit list of lovers of America's maritime heritage.

Most travelers will find other exhibits at the Jamestown Festival Park very much worth a look. In the lobby of the entrance building is a special display concerned with the 1985 voyage of the new replica *Godspeed* across the Atlantic. One museum pavilion contains exhibits relating to the Old World background of the Virginia settlement; another presents contributions made to the New World by Virginia-born men and women. At the reconstruction of the palisaded James Fort down on the river bank costumed staff members explain the design of the fort and the primitive buildings of the little village it enclosed.

What remains of the original Jamestown settlement site is now a part of the Colonial National Park, which includes Yorktown of Revolutionary War fame. Close to the Festival Park the National Park Service has reconstructed what has been called "America's first factory," a "glasshouse" where costumed craftsmen demonstrate 17th-century techniques for blowing bottles. The remains of the original glass furnace of 1608 are under a shelter nearby.

Susan Constant, Godspeed, Discovery reconstructions of the Jamestown settlers' ships, are on display at the Jamestown Festival Park, adjacent to the site of the original settlement. The park is open every day of the year, except Christmas and New Year's. September through June, 9 a.m. to 5 p.m.; July and August, later closing hours. Admission: $5; seniors, $4.50; combination tickets with Yorktown Victory Center available. Sponsored by the Commonwealth of Virginia. Jamestown Festival Park. Jamestown-Yorktown Foundation, Drawer JF, Williamsburg, Virginia 23185. Telephone (304) 229-1607.

A few miles to the northeast of Jamestown on the opposite side of the peninsula, is one of those quiet little villages that chance and geography have made historic. Yorktown, on the York River close to where it enters the Chesapeake, was like dozens of other little tobacco ports when General Cornwallis led his British army there in 1781 and dug in to wait for ships bringing him supplies and reinforcements. A French fleet reached the Chesapeake first, however, and when the British fleet finally arrived off the Virginia Capes, it

Figure 35
Susan Constant, *Godspeed*, and *Discovery*, recreations of ships that brought settlers to Virginia in 1607, are moored at Jamestown Festival Park, close to site of first permanent English settlement in America.

only fought an inconclusive battle with the French and sailed away, leaving the French warship in Chesapeake Bay blockading Cornwallis, besieged at Yorktown. The British general was left to his fate—surrender.

Thus, while the battle off the Virginia Capes was inconclusive tactically, it was strategically decisive, and led directly to the achievement of American independence. A statue of Admiral de Grasse, who commanded the French fleet, has been erected on Cape Henry overlooking the waters where the battle took place. In Yorktown, the emphasis has been on the military rather than on the naval aspects of the campaign: the Revolutionary battlefield is preserved as part of the Colonial National Historical Park. In recent years, however, underwater archaeology has begun investigation of the remains of the British ships sunk off the town during the siege.

Dr. James Thacher, a surgeon with the Continental troops at the siege of Yorktown, recorded in his journal of October 1781 the destruction of British ships anchored off the town:

A red-hot shell from the French battery set fire to the *Charon*, a British 44-gun ship, and two or three smaller vessels at anchor in the river, which were consumed in the night. From the bank of the river I had a fine view of this splendid conflagration. The ships were enwrapped in a torrent of fire, which, spreading with vivid brightness among the combustible rigging, and running with amazing rapidity to the tops of the several masts, while all around was thunder and lightning from our numerous cannon and mortars, and in the darkness of night, presented one of the most sublime and magnificent spectacles which can be imagined.

In the course of the siege some 20 other British vessels were sunk, some by the American and French batteries, some by the British themselves to create a barrier in the river against an amphibious landing. Today, the hulks still lie on the river bottom buried in silt, one of the largest known concentrations of wrecked vessels from the American Colonial period.

An archaeological study of these ships is being conducted by the Shipwreck Project of the Virginia division of Historic Landmarks. An unusual opportunity to see marine archaeologists at work is provided by a 500-foot pier built out into the York River to the spot where a hull lies under 20 feet of water. A steel cofferdam has been constructed around the remains; it protects archaeologists who dive down to study the vessel, and permits the river water to be filtered for improved visibility. The pier is located on the riverbank of the York River about a mile from the Yorktown Victory Center, where there is a special exhibit on the Shipwreck Project and the sunken supply ship. Here also is a collection of artifacts salvaged from the vessels, which includes cannon, a ship's bell, glassware and pottery, and personal effects. Of particular interest is a model of HMS *Charon*, whose destruction two centuries ago provided Surgeon Thacher's "most sublime and magnificent spectacle."

Maritime subjects comprise only a portion of the Victory Center's exhibits, which cover the entire American Revolution with multimedia shows, artifact displays, films, and presentations by costumed interpreters.

Yorktown Victory Center of the Jamestown-Yorktown Foundation is on State Route 238, near Colonial Parkway and Route 17. Open daily except Christmas and New Year's, 9 a.m. to 5 p.m.; extended hours in July and August. Admission: $3.50; 6 to 12, $1.75. Combination ticket with Jamestown Festival Park available. Yorktown Victory Center, P.O. Box 1976, Yorktown, Virginia 23690. Telephone (804) 887-1776.

To reach pier that leads to ship excavation, turn right on leaving visitors center and proceed about a mile to pierhead on Water Street. Open Memorial Day weekend through Labor Day, 10 a.m. to 4 p.m. Admission: free, but donation welcomed.

More artifacts from the sunken ships, ranging from cannon to miscellaneous personal items, are on display at the Visitor's Center of the Colonial National Historical park. The major maritime exhibit at the Visitor's Center of the National Park Service is a full-scale conjectural recreation of a portion of the gundeck of HMS *Charon*, the 44-gun frigate sunk by hot shot during the siege of Yorktown. Visitors feel they are actually walking through the ship, and get a first-hand impression of what living conditions were like on an 18th-century warship.

Also of great interest is an electronic orientation map that graphically describes the historic Battle of the Capes, explaining the importance of the outcome in forcing Cornwallis's surrender and, ultimately, in achieving the independence of America.

National Park Service Visitor Center of the Colonial National Historical Park is on Colonial Parkway, Yorktown. Center for battlefield tours. Open mid-June through Labor Day, daily 8:30 a.m. to 6 p.m.; day after Labor Day through October 31, and April 1 through mid-June, 8:30 a.m. to 5:30 p.m.; balance of year, 8:30 a.m. to 5 p.m. Closed Christmas Day. Admission: free. Sponsored by National Park Service. Yorktown Visitor Center, P.O. Box 210, Yorktown, Virginia 23690. Telephone (804) 898-3400.

In the quiet years after the Revolution, Yorktown, like many coastal villages along the Chesapeake Bay, made its living from fishing and oystering. The life of the York River oysterman is recorded at the tiny Watermen's Museum on the bank of the river. Exhibits include pictures of the watermen at work, their gear, and workboat models, including a sailing log canoe, and a menhaden fishing boat of 1910. Displays point up the skills required for crabbing, oystering, clamming, and fishing during the changing seasons. A recent addition is a collection of original tools used in building log canoes. (Incidentally, Chesapeake Bay is said to be the only place in America where the old English term "watermen" is still used, describing the "men and a few women who work on or with the waters of the bay and its tributaries.")

On the museum's grounds are a number of small craft: a 100-year-old renovated log canoe and skiffs and other specialized boats used for crabbing, oyster tonging, and other water trades. An authentic pilot house has been equipped with wheel and compass—a "hands-on" exhibit. Visitors are also encouraged to try their hands at tonging oysters or raising sails, while a simulated tobacco wharf offers a view of the York River.

A Watermen's Heritage Celebration is held in September.

The Watermen's Museum is on Water Street in Yorktown. West of the high bridge that carries Route 17 over the York River. Short distance to the Victory Center on Route 238. Open April through Labor Day (best to check exact opening date). Thursday-Saturday, 10 a.m. to 4 p.m.; Sunday, 1 p.m. to 4 p.m.; closed Monday-Wednesday. Pre-arranged tours may be scheduled any day. Admission: free, but "donations appreciated." Watermen's Museum, P.O. Box 531, Yorktown, Virginia 23690. Telephone (804) 898-3180 or to call the museum directly during the summer, 887-2641.

The lower end of the Virginia Peninsula borders on one of the world's greatest natural harbors, Hampton Roads. Here the James River, flowing in from the west, is joined by the Nansemond and the Elizabeth, smaller rivers from the south, to form a four-mile basin, connected to lower Chesapeake Bay to the eastward by a narrow passage between two points. Around the basin are the port cities of Hampton, Newport News, Portsmouth, and Norfolk; together they form the Port of Hampton Roads, one of the busiest in the nation.

Blue-water ships have frequented Hampton Roads ever since *Susan Constant, Godspeed,* and *Discovery* sailed across it and up the James to found the first permanent settlement. In the Civil War, Hampton Roads won a unique place in naval/maritime history. One March day in 1861 the Confederate ironclad *Virginia* (ex-*Merrimack*) steamed out of the Elizabeth River and wreaked havoc among the wooden Union warships in the Roads, only to be fought to a standstill the next morning by the Union ironclad *Monitor*. When the battle was over, the Federal Navy still controlled Hampton Roads—but all the unarmored warships in the world had been made obsolete in an afternoon.

When the historic *Monitor-Merrimack* sea fight took place, Newport News, now the major port on the north side of Hampton Roads, was open farmland, occupied at that moment by Union troops. Today, Newport News is not only one of the great ports on the Atlantic coast, but a center of maritime interest, particularly noted for a museum that has become one of the nation's most important centers for the preservation of America's maritime heritage.

Few cities have been so intimately involved with a single family as Newport News has been with the Huntingtons. The city owes its very existence to railroad magnate Collis P. Huntington. Dreaming of a rail line that stretched from coast to coast, Huntington extended the Chesapeake and Ohio Railroad from Richmond to a loading pier that he built on the banks of Hampton Roads. His transcontinental railroad never materialized, but his pier, built on a point of land where the James River enters Hampton Roads, became the nucleus of a great rail terminal. With rail lines reaching the Appalachian coalfields and prosperous Midwest farming and manufacturing areas, freight trains could bring cargoes from these areas directly to deep-water ships loading at the pier.

At the same time Huntington bought up all the empty land nearby and sold it to the workmen and tradespeople who came to service the railroad and port, and this became the new little city of Newport News. After a couple of raffish decades in which a local district known as Hell's Half Acre provided saloons and whorehouses for sailors, stevedores, and railroad workers, the town grew into a more staid and solid industrial center.

In the meantime, another Collis Huntington venture was turning Newport News into even more of a maritime city. What is now the Newport News Shipbuilding and Drydock Company was founded in the 1880s to service the ships that came to the Chesapeake and Ohio wharves. The new firm expanded rapidly. When Huntington bid to build ships for the Navy, he declared in an often quoted statement: "We shall build good ships here; at a profit if we can, at a loss if we must, but always good ships."

Today Collis Huntington's Newport News Shipbuilding is one of the largest shipyards in the nation, building both warships and merchant vessels, while in recent years Huntington's loading piers have been crammed at times with colliers loading with coal for energy-hungry Europe.

For the traveler pursuing America's maritime traditions, however, the most interesting Huntington heritage comes from Collis's stepson, Archer Huntington, who in 1930 founded and endowed the famous Mariners' Museum. Set in magnificent parkland on the west side of Newport News, the museum is housed in a large, rather nondescript building, but the moment the visitor walks through the door he knows this is no ordinary collection. On the right-hand wall of the entranceway is an enormous circular woodcarving like a huge spiderweb or the pattern for a giant snowflake. Through the inner doors directly ahead a magnificent golden eagle, its wings 18 feet across, looms over the lobby.

Both pieces are spectacular, both are beautiful, but neither was designed merely as a decorative object for a wall. As with a ship, their beauty is incidental to their function. The carved spider-web was the wheel of a Mississippi steamboat: made so large to give the pilot absolute control as he steered the vessel among the river's shoals and snags. The great 3,200-pound eagle served long years at sea as the figurehead of the steam frigate *Lancaster* of a hundred years ago.

Wheel and eagle raise great expectations; the galleries beyond fulfill them. The Mariners' Museum is today one of the handful of American museums that set the standard by which others are judged. The scope and size of its collections and the high quality of every piece exhibited make this treasure house of American maritime heritage a delight to explore.

There is too much to be seen to recount here; visitors are advised to set aside a day to enjoy the museum's pleasures. Here, however, is a sampling of things not to be missed:

- Start with the Great Hall of Steamships directly behind the eagle. This model collection covers a century and a half of fine vessels—including paddle steamers, Great Lake ore carriers, and transatlantic liners.
- Directly behind the steamship hall is a collection of figureheads and smaller ships' carvings. At times a skilled woodcarver is on hand to demonstrate his art and craft.
- At the left end of the figurehead room is the entrance to two remarkable collections of ship models, both of great interest. One explains the many different reasons why people have built miniature ships over the centuries and the way models differ according to their purpose. Models for training officers are equipped with the complete rigging to be learned, for example. Models made as special gifts may be fantastic vessels of gold or silver. A model created as a thank-offering to a helpful saint for bringing the donor home alive is made with the pious care that reflects the sincerity of gratitude.
- The other model collection is the remarkable Crabtree group, all made by one man to illustrate the development of water-borne vessels from log rafts to full-rigged ships. Take a particularly close look at the magnificently detailed carvings on these tiny craft; everything is exactly to scale. Mirrors in the bottom of the model cases make it easy to view the underside of the hulls.
- The gallery of marine paintings a little further on leaves the visitor with the impression that he has seen at least one example of the work of every fine American and European marine artist from the 16th century to the 20th. Particularly notable for one viewer was the painting of the big fancy Hudson River steamer *Adirondack* of 1895 passing the simple little *Norwich*, built 60 years earlier and believed to have been the oldest steamboat in existence at the time.
- The Civil War coverage is remarkable —particularly the models, paintings, relics, and plans of the famous *Monitor* and *Merrimack* and their battle a few miles away in Hampton Roads. Here also are an actual nine-inch Dahlgren gun, basic cannon of the Union Navy; a detailed model of an 1864 blockade-runner; a model of the ship-based observation balloon and its tender, used by the Union forces in the James River in 1862; and the billethead, cheeks, and

trailboards from the USS *Hartford*, Farragut's flagship at the battles of New Orleans and Mobile Bay.
- Don't overlook the marvelous mini-miniature diorama of a Colonial shipyard. With half-inch figures, and ships and yard in proportion, the scene is presented in great detail, as the blownup photographs on the wall nearby make clear.
- In the Chesapeake Bay gallery a fine 1880 three-log "canoe" is accompanied by a series of photographs illustrating how these unusual Bay craft were built. And even visitors who sneer at stink-pots will have to admit that *Miss Jane*, a 16-foot Dodge runabout built in 1930 of gleaming mahogany, is one of the stars of the museum.

Only a few of the small craft are in the main museum. Most are displayed in a separate building, which is easy to overlook since it requires a detour from the normal traffic flow through the galleries; be sure to check the museum map to find it. Here are such delights as a rare tuck-up catboat from the Delaware River; a Portuguese saveiro, built along centuries-old lines for sardine fishing; and the last whaleboat built by the famous Beetle family of New Bedford.

Figure 36
Enormous gilded eagle, its wings spreading 18 feet, may be largest surviving figurehead in world. Once it graced the bow of U.S. frigate *Lancaster*, it now faces entrance of Mariners' Museum in Newport News, Virginia.

Obviously, this is no museum to be hurried through with one eye on the exhibits and the other on the clock. Such riches—and only a sampling has been mentioned here—require time to savor, digest, and enjoy.

The Mariners' Museum, Newport News, Virginia, is in a large wooded park that extends down to the banks of the James River. Open all year except Christmas Day; Monday-Saturday, 9 a.m. to 5 p.m.; Sunday, noon to 5 p.m. Admission: $3.00; children 6 to 17, $1.50; others, free. Library, giftshop, bookstore. Mariners' Museum, Museum Drive, Newport News, Virginia 23606. Telephone (804) 595-0368.

Newport News is only one, and by far the youngest, of the four cities that comprise the Port of Hampton Roads. Norfolk, on the opposite shore of Hampton Roads, was already two centuries old when Huntington's trains began rattling down to the Chesapeake and Ohio wharves. Unlike the Colonial New England ports that sprang up spontaneously, however, Norfolk was founded in 1680 on empty land by decree of the Virginia legislature as a town where tobacco could be collected, taxed, and loaded for shipment to England. A site a little way up the Elizabeth river was chosen, in part because it was less exposed to such unwelcome visitors as pirates and the privateers and warships of the nations with which England was at war.

This didn't keep Norfolk from being ravaged by the British during the American Revolution. The little village had slowly developed in Colonial times as a port that exported tobacco to Europe, and lumber, naval stores, and provisions to the West Indian plantations. In 1779, British troops landed and burned stores and shipyards; the retreating Americans burned the town.

The coming of steamboats early in the 19th century made Norfolk a port for bay and coastal steamers, but eventually hurt the town as the export point for inland produce: shallow-draft steamers could move quickly up the rivers, while sailing craft, dependent on favorable winds, often took many days. As a result, steamers could pick up export cargoes directly at the Fall line ports and take them to New York for transshipment into deep-water ships for overseas markets.

Meanwhile, rival Baltimore at the other end of the Chesapeake Bay became the deep-water terminal of the Baltimore and Ohio Railroad in 1845. Only after the Civil War, when the Norfolk and Western Railroad connected Norfolk to the West Virginia coalfields, did Norfolk become the great Atlantic port that it remains today.

Norfolk is a big navy town, the headquarters not only of the United States Atlantic Fleet but of SACLANT, the NATO Supreme Allied Command in the Atlantic. This role is reflected in the fine but little-known Hampton Roads Naval Museum at the Norfolk Naval Base. Housed in a two-thirds-sized replica of Philadelphia's Independence Hall, originally built for the Jamestown Exposition in 1907, is a collection of ship models, artifacts, and graphics. The exhibits have a double focus: one on the past, the long history of naval activities in and near lower Chesapeake Bay; and one very much on the present, the current cooperation of the NATO navies.

The latter is emphasized in one of the most interesting exhibits, the models of warships of various Allied navies in the small NATO gallery. Represented are fighting craft from Britain's Royal Navy, the Netherlands Navy, and the fleets of West Germany and Italy. The background of each navy is filled in with a brief written description. The NATO collection is still in the formative stage and additional exhibits are being added.

During World War II, Norfolk was the headquarters for the Battle of the Atlantic. An audio-video show explains the significance of the war against German submarines attempting to block the flow of American troops and supplies to Europe.

Exhibits concerned with earlier eras of naval history include:

- A handsome model of the 104-gun *Ville de Paris*, the flagship of the French fleet at the historic battle between French and British fleets off the entrance to Chesapeake Bay, which led directly to Cornwallis's surrender in 1781.
- A fine Civil War exhibit including models of the *Monitor* and the *Merrimack* (CSS *Virginia*), which fought their historic battle practically in sight of the museum's windows. Relics of the USS *Cumberland*, sunk by the *Virginia*, are also on display.
- Interesting American naval models from the latter half of the 19th century, when armored steam vessels were superseding wooden sailing ships. Not often seen are such vessels as the protected cruiser *Chicago*, 1881, and the heavy cruiser *Brooklyn*, a veteran of the Battle of Santiago in the Spanish-American War. Here also are models and pictures of the Great White Fleet that went around the world in 1906.

The Hampton Roads Naval Museum is relatively new and the collection and displays are still being expanded. Ship model enthusiasts will find more to look at when they pick up the required entrance pass at the Tour and Information Building on Hampton Boulevard, a short distance outside the principal entrance to the naval base. Here at the Information Building are naval prints, photographs, and maps as well as several very large models of such modern naval vessels as the USS *Fargo*, USS *Thomaston*, and a variety of landing craft.

Both municipal and Navy buses depart from the Information Building on tours around the base with Navy guides, for which tickets must be purchased. Stops are made at the museum.

Hampton Roads Naval Museum is in Pennsylvania House on Admiral's Row in the Norfolk Naval Base. On Route 64, main north-south interstate through Norfolk, watch for naval base exit signs a short distance south of the tunnel under Hampton Roads. Admiral Taussig Boulevard leads to Gate Two of Base. Get museum pass at Tour and Information Building just outside gate on Hampton Boulevard; exact directions to museum are on back of pass. Open all year; every day, 10 a.m. to 4 p.m. Closed New Year's Day, Easter, Thanksgiving, Christmas. Admission: free. Hampton Roads Naval Museum, Pennsylvania Building, Commander Naval Base, Norfolk, Virginia 23511-6002. Telephone (804) 444-3827.

Early in the 18th century Norfolk spilled across the Elizabeth River, where the establishment of shipyards resulted in another little town, Portsmouth, in 1750.

Portsmouth has been a shipbuilding town from its earliest days and in Colonial times the Royal Navy used it as a ship repair station. During the Revolution, a private shipyard there was taken over and used by the new state of Virginia and was later burned by the British. When the U.S. navy was established in 1798, the yard became the Gosport Navy Yard, one of the first of the new Navy's six Navy yards.

Here was installed one of the first stone dry docks in the nation. When the CSS *Virginia* came steaming out of the Elizabeth River to attack the Union warships in Hampton Roads, she came straight from this great stone dry dock at the Gosport Navy Yard in Portsmouth, where she had been rebuilt from the lower hull and machinery of the burned United States frigate *Merrimack*.

The Union forces retook Portsmouth a couple of months after the Monitor-Merrimack battle and for the rest of the Civil War the Gosport yard was a major base for Union warships. Since then, the Yard, usually referred to as the Norfolk Navy Yard and more recently as the Norfolk Naval Shipyard, has been a major building and repair facility of the United States Navy.

Norfolk Naval Shipyard, Portsmouth, Virginia. Open by advance arrangement with the public relations officer. No regular hours. Admission: free. Norfolk Naval Shipyard, Portsmouth, Virginia 23709. Telephone (804) 396-3000.

The history of the Norfolk Naval Shipyard and naval activities in the Portsmouth area is the theme of an attractive little museum on the bank of the South Branch of the Elizabeth River in Portsmouth. The lawn in front of the two-story brick building of the Naval Shipyard Museum is lined with many varieties of ship-borne weapons, from 12-pounders of the Revolutionary period to Polaris missiles. Within, the varied collection, which is exhibited in one large room, is particularly notable for models, guns, and pictures related to the rebirth of the U.S. Navy in the late 19th century.

Two models of special interest from this era are the 4,500 ton protected cruiser *Chicago* (1889), still with partial sail rig, and the somewhat smaller protected cruiser *Raleigh*, which was part of Commodore Dewey's command at the battle of Manila Bay.

The ordnance exhibits include an 1880 Gatling gun and a five-barrelled Naval Hotchkiss gun of 1889. Two striking models are those of the 78,000-ton attack carrier *Forrestal*, and the nuclear submarine *Nautilus*, the pioneer atomic type. A diorama of the town of Portsmouth in 1776 shows the shipyards and the ships in the harbor; another, the Norfolk Naval Shipyard in 1945 at the height of its World War II activity.

Of special interest are a variety of uniforms, dress swords, and other naval memorabilia. Documents tell the story of the surrender of the Navy Yard to Confederate troops at the outbreak of the Civil War. Of particular local interest is a fine model of the USS *Delaware*, the first ship of the line of the U.S. Navy, built here in the yard in 1820.

Next door to the Naval Shipyard Museum, Lightship WAL 524 is on display. A 101-foot vessel painted lightship red, she now carries "Portsmouth" in huge white letters along her sides, in token of her last berth on a green lawn on the Portsmouth riverfront. In almost half a century of active duty she served at five different posts along the Atlantic coast.

Visitors will be particularly interested in the huge anchors in her bow and the big openings just below the waterline for her anchor cables—the essential gear for keeping her exactly on station despite gales and hurricanes. The ship may be boarded for a close look at her deck gear and interior. Artifacts displayed include uniforms, Coast Guard equipment, photographs, and models of other lightships.

The Portsmouth Naval Shipyard Museum and **The Portsmouth Lightship Museum**, both part of the Portsmouth Museum System, are side by side on the banks of the south branch of the Elizabeth River. Both museums are free, and open Tuesday-Saturday, 10 a.m. to 5 p.m.; Sunday, 1 p.m. to 5 p.m. Both museums are closed

Mondays. Portsmouth Naval Shipyard and Lighthouse Museum, on the Elizabeth River waterfront at the foot of High Street, Portsmouth, Virginia 23709. Telephone (804) 393-8591.

Now a few miles eastward, out to the storm-battered Atlantic coast just south of Cape Henry.

In late March 1891, a 60-knot northeast gale swept the Atlantic off Cape Henry at the mouth of Chesapeake Bay. Off the cape the Norwegian bark *Diktator*, bound for Europe with a load of Florida pine, was hard hit. At the time she was already leaking badly and heading for shelter in the Chesapeake, the crew exhausted from endless pumping. Now the fresh gale opened the seams wider and Captain J.M. Jorgensen saw nothing for it but to run for shore in hopes of beaching *Diktator* before she went to the bottom.

Diktator made it and ran ashore on Virginia Beach, the ocean face of Cape Henry. She had been sighted by the nearby Seatrack Life-Saving Station and the surfmen were able to rescue 10 of the 17 persons aboard. Captain Jorgensen attempted to tie his wife to a spar but she was washed away. The Captain tied himself to his four-year-old son and tried to float ashore on a ladder, but the child drifted away from him. Mother and child were lost.

The figurehead of the lost *Diktator*, a woman, was salvaged and set up on the shore; people came to call it the *Norwegian Lady*, remembering Mrs. Jorgensen. For the Seatrack Station life-saving crew the wreck and the rescue were all in a day's work. The Virginia Beach station was kept busy year in and year out: In 1894, for example, there were two dozen sea rescues as 13 vessels went ashore, but no lives were lost. There have been 185 wrecks on Virginia Beach since records were first kept in 1875.

Today, the transformation of the remote village of Virginia Beach into a bustling seashore resort has lined the once lonely beach with multistory hotels and condominiums behind 30 blocks of boardwalk. But the *Norwegian Lady* still overlooks the beach, gazing out to sea; not the original figurehead to be sure, she was badly damaged in a later storm and replaced by a bronze replica. This second statue was a gift of the people of the Norwegian town of Moss, the *Diktator*'s home port, who also set up a twin replica on their own waterfront, gazing westward.

The Seatrack Life-Saving Station is also still on the beach; a larger building that replaced the original one in 1903. Although no longer housing a crew of surfmen, the station is still very much concerned with the angry Atlantic and the wrecks it drives ashore. The Seatrack Life-Saving Station is now the home of the Virginia Beach Maritime Historical Museum, and

among the major exhibits are relics salvaged from the *Diktator* and other vessels that hit the beach. But wrecks are only one of the museum's interests concerning the 350 years of maritime activity at the Virginia Capes.

The first floor of the old station is now devoted primarily to the history and activities of the surfmen who once were based there. Exhibits tell the story of the Life-Saving Service—which eventually became part of the Coast Guard—particularly in relation to Virginia Beach, where from 1878 to 1969 there were four stations on the shore. Lifesaving gear on display includes a Lyle gun for hurling a lifeline to wrecked ships, and the "faking box" in which the line is stowed in an elaborate pattern so that it runs freely without tangles. The museum has two 16-foot surf boats—about two-thirds the size of the originals but built on identical lines—which are used in lifesaving demonstrations. There are many wreck relics, and more continue to appear on the beach.

The second-floor gallery displays nautical instruments, scrimshaw, and maritime artifacts. Of particular interest is a valentine elaborately carved of wood by some lovelorn sailor on a long passage in the 1890s. The collection of ship-models centers on the pilotboats in which the Virginia pilots waited offshore for incoming vessels, but includes many other types: tugboats, a shrimper, schooners, and Coast Guard vessels.

A special exhibit tells about the Battle of the Capes, the action between the British and French fleets at sea off Cape Henry in 1783 that led directly to the surrender of Cornwallis and the achievement of American independence.

The museum's research program concentrates on the Life-Saving Service and the surfmen who manned the lifeboats. The photographic collection has many pictures of Virginia Beach activities. The Seatrack Station that houses the museum has been placed on the National Register of Historical Places.

The Virginia Beach Maritime Historical Museum is located on the beach facing open Atlantic where 24th Street ends at Atlantic Avenue. From Route 64, exit eastward on Route 44, Virginia Beach Norfolk Expressway, which becomes 21st Street. Continue to Atlantic Avenue, turn left three blocks. Museum is housed in 1903 Life-Saving Station. Open Memorial Day to September 30, Monday-Saturday, 10 a.m. to 9 p.m.; Sunday, noon to 5 p.m. Balance of the year, Tuesday-Saturday, 10 a.m. to 5 p.m.; Sunday, noon to 5 p.m. Admission: $1.50; seniors and service personnel, $1.00; ages 6 to 18, 50 cents. Building on National Register of Historic Places. Operated by private, nonprofit membership group. Virginia Beach Maritime Historical Museum, P.O. Box 24, Virginia Beach, Virginia 23458. Telephone (804) 422-1587.

VI
THE SOUTH FACING THE ATLANTIC

South of Cape Henry to Cape Fear: The North Carolina Coast
Cape Fear to the St. Mary's: South Carolina and Georgia

South of the Virginia Capes the Atlantic coast pretty much follows the pattern that started at Sandy Hook: low marshy shores, fringed with strips of sand that have been piled up by ocean currents into barrier islands. But there are two major differences and both hamper maritime activity. Missing are the drowned valleys of great rivers, such as Chesapeake Bay and Delaware Bay, that make possible such port cities as Philadelphia and Baltimore more than a hundred miles from open ocean, their feet in tidewater and their arms reaching out to grasp great markets far inland.

The other difference is that a ways south of Cape Henry the barrier islands cease to hug the mainland and instead curve seaward to form Cape Hatteras. To make matters worse, treacherous shoals stretch even further into the Atlantic out of sight of land. In season, fierce storms ride up the coast from the Caribbean to take toll of ships at sea and structures ashore.

South of the Cape Fear River, there is a brief stretch of open coast, then the pattern of barrier islands separated from the mainland by narrow shallow waterways resumes. Where these are barrier islands, the inlets between them are shallow with constantly shifting bars. There is only one fine natural harbor, Charleston, on the whole coast. Other ports, such as North Carolina's Wilmington, and Savannah in Georgia, are found some distance up rivers. They were originally established inland in hopes of making them less vulnerable to attack by enemy warships or piratical marauders.

For this section of coast has had more than its share of conflict—conflict between Spaniards and Frenchmen who planted lonely colonies that were bloodily removed by their enemies; conflict between Europeans and coastal Indians who soon learned to distrust these strange invaders; conflict between Spain pushing up from its outposts in Florida, and England pushing south from Virginia and the Carolinas; and conflict between King's ships and the pirates who preyed on the ships of every nation.

The French gave up early in the game. The Spanish were primarily interested in keeping control of the Florida Strait between the mainland and the Bahama Islands, through which their treasure fleet from Mexico had to pass each year on the way to Spain. After several unsuccessful attempts to drive the English from South Carolina and Georgia, marked by bloody sea battles in the sounds, they grudgingly accepted the St. Mary's River as the limit to their domain. The English, first interested in the Indian trade, then in settlement, consolidated their hold on the Carolinas and Georgia, the southernmost of their American colonies.

Which didn't end the conflicts. England was repeatedly at war with other European powers, whose ships of war and privateersmen raided the little English settlements along the coast. Pirates found these frontier regions safe bases—for a while—and levied tribute from ships and settlers. And, of course, in three wars these coasts were attacked by hostile fleets. In the American Revolution, the British twice attacked Charleston, capturing it the second time from the land side. In the War of 1812, the Southern ports were closely blockaded, but managed to maintain a lively coastal traffic behind the barrier islands, interrupted by Royal Naval cutting-out parties rowing in through the inlets. And in the Civil War, not only was the coast closely blockaded by the United States Navy, with major sea-land combat at the mouth of Charleston harbor, but the Union forces landed and occupied one Southern port after another.

Meanwhile, tidewater plantations and Southern forests produced cargoes that brought many ships to the region's ports—in Colonial times, rice and indigo; later, naval stores and cotton. Before the War of 1812, one-third of the exports of the United States were from Southern ports. Most of the ships that carried these exports, however, were built and owned elsewhere, in the North or in Europe. Here in the South, fortunes were to be made ashore, not on the high seas. With rich virgin lands and few ports, rather than New England's rocky fields fringed by a string of little harbors, the South regions bred relatively few hardy mariners forced to earn their living by carrying other people's cargoes across the world.

Today, of course, dredging and jetties keep deepwater channels open and create new ports in shallow bays. The Intra-Coastal Waterway makes use of the barrier islands to provide a sheltered route for small craft. The islands themselves sprout condominiums along the shores. But still the sands shift, still tropical storms beat against the coast, still Hatteras takes its toll.

South of Cape Henry to Cape Fear: The North Carolina Coast

Unlike the colonies on either side and despite its 320 miles of oceanfront, North Carolina was not first settled from the sea. In the 16th century, attempts to establish an English settlement on Roanoke Island in Pamlico Sound failed twice: The first colonists gave up and thumbed a ride home after a year; the second group, the famous "Lost Colony," simply disappeared. When a permanent English settlement was finally established, it was in Chesapeake Bay to the north. When the Carolinas were granted to royal favorites late in the 17th century, the ships carrying the first settlers headed for the fine harbor of Charleston to the south. North Carolina was largely left for settlement by people pushing overland from the two sides, seeking fur trade with the Indians and new fertile lands for the golden crop, tobacco. In time they found that their best-selling exports were provisions and naval stores—tar and turpentine from the pine forests.

Maps of North Carolina are likely to be misleading. If small-scale, they tend to fill in the two vast watery sounds behind Cape Hatteras—Albemarle to the north, Pamlico to the south—and make the cape look like a bold promontory instead of what it actually is: a fragile line of sandy islands, scarcely more than overgrown sandbars. If large-scale, a map shows these sounds as huge lakes, and the viewer wonders why these broad waters, protected from the Atlantic, did not become the scene of thriving maritime activities as did Delaware Bay and Chesapeake Bay. The maps do not reveal that these sounds are full of shoals and bars and are whipped by winds that produce a short brutal chop as they pass over long reaches of shallow water. The few openings, or inlets, between the barrier islands into these waters are partially blocked by constantly shifting sandbars: The ships that carried Raleigh's first settlers to Roanoke Island all ran aground when entering Pamlico Sound through Whalebone Inlet.

Invisible on ordinary maps is Cape Hatteras's greatest hazard. The same ocean currents that created the barrier islands have piled up more sand in dangerous shoals far out to sea. Diamond Shoals, off the tip of Cape Hatteras, and Frying Pan Shoals, off Cape Fear, extend many miles offshore so that hapless captains run aground out of sight of land. Since the days when the first Europeans came to North America, thousands of ships have been lost on Cape Hatteras, Cape Lookout, and Cape Fear, and their attendant shoals. They continue to be a major source of danger to vessels approaching the United States from the south and east.

Scientists are unsure what caused this sandy projection into open ocean. One theory that seems to have considerable support, however, attributes capes and offshore shoals to a combination of factors. Deposits of sand, it is believed, gradually washed down from the Carolina uplands to the west. Along the coast, the Gulf Stream moving northward ran into other currents moving south—the remnant of the Labrador Current plus outpouring from Chesapeake Bay. The meeting of these two currents piled up the sand in barrier beaches and shoals along the coast.

Simultaneously, a rise in the sea level, which resulted from melting glaciers, flooded the lowlands behind the coastal dunes, forming the shallow sounds behind barrier islands.

Most U.S. Colonial shipping in the sounds was local traffic—canoes, flatboats, sailing scows—based in little ports that grew up where rivers entered. At the point where the Chowan River reaches the Albemarle Sound, for example, the small town of Edenton had shipyards, and local merchants exported naval stores and provisions. Small vessels continued to use the port for half a century after the Revolution.

These little ports had many handicaps, however. To reach the ocean, vessels had to travel considerable distances across the shallow sound waters and then thread through the dangerous inlets to open ocean. As an alternative, cargoes could be taken to the small town of Portsmouth, where the sounds opened on the ocean at Ocracoke Inlet, and there transferred to deep-draft, oceangoing vessels for export. Alternatively, they could be taken to the deep-water ports in Chesapeake Bay—at first in little coasters that went out through the inlets and north in a rough ocean passage around Cape Henry; later, through a canal built through the Great Dismal Swamp in order to connect Albemarle Sound with the Chesapeake.

An additional hazard was pirates. Although they used the inlets as places where they could retire between cruises to overhaul their ships and enjoy their loot, they were not above plundering any coastal shipping that came their way. In one three-year period, 1715 to 1718, Stede Bonnet and Blackbeard (Edward Teach) were both active in the area.

In addition to Portsmouth, Colonial North Carolina had two other ports with direct access to the Atlantic, both in the southeast corner of the state. Beaufort, just down the coast from Cape Lookout, boasted a good harbor between barrier islands and the mainland, but suffered from having only a roundabout water connection to the hinterland that produced the export cargoes. Today, its place as an active port has been taken by neighboring Morehead City. Further south and west, settlements on the Cape Fear River became deep-water ports in the 18th century. The little village of Brunswick, a short distance upriver from the entrance, was the first port. After it was looted by Spanish privateers in the mid-18th century, however, the residents moved for safety further upriver to Wilmington, which became and remains today the principal port of North Carolina.

To reach Beaufort or Wilmington from the north, the traveler must detour around Albemarle and Pamlico Sounds. The main route runs westward around the inland edge of the Sounds. The longer but more interesting route is to the eastward along the thin strips of barrier islands that separate the sounds from the sea. Most maritime-minded travelers are likely to prefer the latter approach, which also has the advantage of facilitating a visit to historic Roanoke Island by making a small side trip.

The barrier islands are the outer banks that form Cape Hatteras, one of the most remote, interesting, and—for ships—dangerous sections of the Atlantic coast. The sea permeates and dominates the lives of the people who for generations have lived in the tiny villages among the sand dunes.

From Norfolk, the traveler turns south from Interstate 64 on Route 17, which goes along the canal through the remains of the Great Dismal Swamp to Elizabeth City, North Carolina. This is a venerable town; it was a shipbuilding center as early as the 17th century; and a considerable port in the early 1800s.

At Elizabeth City, the route to Cape Hatteras and Roanoke Island turns east and south on Route 158. The highway runs along the narrow barrier islands, which in this northernmost section of Cape Hatteras have been heavily developed. About eight miles south of Nag's Head, Route 64 turns off to the right, crossing a series of causeways and bridges to Roanoke Island. The island was the focal point of the earliest intensive English maritime activity in what is now the United States, and today is the home port of a beautiful reconstruction of an Elizabethan merchant ship.

This small island, set in the narrow waterway that connects Albemarle and Pamlico Sounds, almost outranks Jamestown and Plymouth in significance as the earliest site of English settlement in North America. Almost but not quite, for although the two Roanoke Island settlements came years earlier than either of the others, they did not survive to become permanent colonies. The story of these failures has long fascinated Americans, however, and they are worth a little detour four centuries back into history.

Brilliant, handsome Sir Walter Raleigh sent out both groups of settlers. A great favorite of Queen Elizabeth, he had obtained from the Queen an enormous grant of land in North America—not quite as generous as it sounds, though, since it was more of a hunting license than a title deed. In the words of Raleigh's letters-patent from the Queen, he had her permission "to discover search fynde out and viewe such remote heathen and barbarous landes Countries and territories not actually possessed by an Christian Prynce." These he could colonize and govern according to the laws of England—at his own expense.

A two-ship scouting expedition sent out by Raleigh in 1584 returned with a glowing account of the advantages of a settlement somewhere in the sheltered sounds behind the Cape Hatteras barrier islands. Here were reported fertile soil, forests teeming with game, and friendly Indians. (Also the sounds could provide a strategic base from which English privateers could attack the Spanish treasure fleets on their way from Mexico to Spain.)

Raleigh named his prospective colony Virginia in honor of the Virgin Queen and sent out a colonizing expedition the following year, 1585. The Queen lent the largest vessel, the *Tyger*, of a little squadron that included Raleigh's own ship, the *Roebuck*; the bark *Red Lion*, of Chichester; a smaller bark, the *Elizabeth*; and several small pinnaces. Queen Elizabeth would not allow Raleigh to leave her court, so he appointed his kinsman, the veteran and valiant soldier Sir Richard Grenville, to command. The 100 or so colonists, all men, included an artist, a scientist, and a mining expert (so they'd recognize any signs of gold or silver they came across).

The voyage out was by way of the West Indies, where Grenville took several Spanish ships as prizes. Arrived at Cape Hatteras, *Tyger* grounded trying to enter Pamlico Sound through an inlet and many essential supplies were lost. Nevertheless, the sounds were explored in small craft and Roanoke Island was chosen as the colony site.

During the mild Carolina winter, the colonists further explored the sounds in their pinnaces and even pushed north around Cape Henry into Chesapeake Bay, which they found far better suited for settlement than the shallow Carolina sounds. Come spring, however, they ran out of supplies—and what was worse, quarreled with the local Indians who had been selling them food. Open hostilities broke out. The colonists were fearfully waiting for the Indians to attack in overwhelming force when Francis Drake appeared with a large fleet, on his way back to England after a profitable raid on the Spanish West Indies. The colonists saw escape at hand. They persuaded Drake to carry them all back to England, and abandoned the settlement.

Not easily discouraged, Raleigh promptly sent out another expedition in 1587, this time including whole families with wives and children. The new landing site was supposed to be in Chesapeake Bay, but the ships carrying the expedition called at Roanoke Island on the way and through mischance, misjudgment, or bad faith the colonists were dumped there.

Here, later that summer, the famous Virginia Dare, granddaughter of the governor, became the first English child born in North America. Soon afterward, her grandfather returned to England in the only ship that had been left with the colonists, planning to arrange support for the little colony. His report is the last word we have about the fate of the settlement. Raleigh did not forget his colonists, but the following year, 1588, the Spanish Armada came up the

English Channel and England needed every available ship to fight off the threatened invasion; none could be spared for a Virginia voyage. Three years passed before Raleigh could send ships. The relief squadron wasted time privateering along the way, and when the ships finally reached Roanoke—after a five-month passage from England—the settlers were gone and the fort and houses were vine-covered ruins. Before a search of the area could be made, a threatening storm forced the relief ships to leave this dangerous coast and they never returned.

Despite many theories, the mystery of the colonists' disappearance has never been conclusively solved. Seventeen years passed before the first permanent English settlement in North America was established in the Chesapeake Bay area, where Raleigh had intended to plant his second settlement. Roanoke and Virginia Dare have passed into history as the Lost Colony, wrapped in romantic legend.

To commemorate the 400th anniversary of the Lost Colony, one of the vessels in the first colonizing flotilla has been reconstructed and placed on display at the town of Manteo on Roanoke Island. (Manteo is named for an Indian boy who visited England and returned with the settlers, eventually becoming a tribal chief.) The vessel chosen to be reproduced was the 50-ton *Elizabeth*, a bark probably owned by her captain, young Thomas Cavendish, High Marshall of the 1585 expedition and later famous for making a privateering voyage that became the third known circumnavigation of the globe.

Elizabeth was the smallest of the three larger ships in the squadron. As in the case of all the early vessels that have been "reconstructed" in recent years, no plans for the original *Elizabeth* survive if indeed they ever existed. *Elizabeth II* represents a typical late 16th-century merchant ship of the size and rig of her namesake: 69 feet long with an eight-foot draft; three-masted with the mizzen—aftermost—mast lateen rigged. Preliminary plans were researched and prepared by William Avery Baker, the architect of *Mayflower II* and other reproductions, and completed by Stanley Potter, naval architect of Beaufort, North Carolina.

The visitor will find *Elizabeth II* moored in a creek opening into Shallowbag Bay off the Manteo waterfront. Visitors reach her by driving over a little bridge from the town to Ice House Island where the Visitors Center is.

To modern eyes, *Elizabeth II* seems an exotic craft, brightly decorated in reds, blues, and yellows, with a diamond pattern along her poop and vertical stripes on her beakhead. The narrow poop raised above her main deck, the boxlike fo'c'sle (literally a "fore-castle"), and her beakhead projecting from the bow are distinctive features that remind us that this is a ship design four centuries old. Aboard the bark, the visitor finds more such reminders, so that he feels he has stepped into the past. Among other things, watch for:

- The whipstaff, the huge spar that is fastened vertically to the tiller so that the helmsman gains enough leverage to steer the ship. This was a great improvement over previous methods that required several men with a block and tackle to control the ponderous tiller of a sizable vessel in any kind of a sea. (The whipstaff was, of course, eventually superseded by the even more efficient steering wheel.)
- The "great cabin" in the poop with its single berth for the captain—in a vessel of this size, quite small and cramped.
- The galley, simply a brick hearth built on the deck in the fo'c'sle.

Incidentally, in the reconstruction the height of the ceiling between decks has been raised a foot over the 16th-century standard in order to minimize bumped heads among visitors. (The lower deck is the original height.) The *Elizabeth* probably carried 50 or 60 people across the Atlantic, as well as supplies for the new colony.

Elizabeth II was built and launched right on the Manteo waterfront. In order to increase strength and minimize maintenance problems, some concessions have been made to modern materials and technology. The fastenings are of steel and galvanized iron, rather than the traditional wooden pegs. The rigging is Dacron, stained to look like natural fiber. The original *Elizabeth* was almost certainly built of English oak, but her namesake has been constructed with a pressure-treated yellow pine frame and juniper planking—more resistant to rot in the Carolina climate. Modern tools were used in her construction, but pieces have been finished with adze and ax so that they show the distinctive marks of hand tools that would have appeared on the original.

The original *Elizabeth* actually never made it in through the barrier islands to the settlement site: she drew too much water and had to remain at anchor outside in the ocean while her passengers and cargo were taken through the inlets to Roanoke Island in small craft. Shallow water is still a problem. The channel up to Manteo from the inlets had silted up and had to be redredged by Army engineers before *Elizabeth II* could leave her harbor. Now, however, cruises are planned to other North Carolina ports in the the spring of 1987, so anyone planning a visit at this time should check ahead as to her whereabouts.

In the Visitors Center are a series of wall graphics,

Figure 37
At Manteo, North Carolina, seaman in 17th century costume climbs rigging of *Elizabeth II*, sailing recreation of ship that brought settlers to Lost Colony on Roanoke Island in 1586.

and various audiovisual programs can be viewed. In the summer, living history interpretations are presented aboard the ship.

Most travelers will not want to leave this historic ground without visiting what is believed to be the site of the Lost Colony, about three miles north of Manteo. Here Fort Raleigh has been excavated and restored. Not far away is the Waterside Theater where a symphonic drama, "The Lost Colony," is presented outdoors from mid-June through late August.

Elizabeth II is on display at Manteo, North Carolina, on the north-east shore of Roanoke Island, in the passage connecting Pamlico and Albemarle sounds. Book/gift shop in visitors center. Open November through March 31, Tuesday-Sunday, 10 a.m. to 4 p.m. April 1 to October 31, every day, 10 a.m. to 6 p.m. Admission: $3.00; seniors, $2.00; students and children 6 to 12, $2.00. Admissions include audiovisual programs at center. *Elizabeth II*, P.O. Box 155, Manteo, North Carolina 27954. Telephone (919) 473-1144.

To continue along the outer banks to Cape Hatteras, the visitor goes back to where he turned off the barrier island road. At this point, Route 158 becomes Route 12 as it enters the Cape Hatteras National Seashore. Cape Hatteras, which technically is made up of only the tip of Hatteras Island, the easternmost point of the outer banks, is 45 miles south of Route 12.

Here is the Cape Hatteras Island Visitor Center which is concerned with the history of the area and the development of lighthouses. Next door is the 196-foot high Cape Hatteras Lighthouse, the tallest brick lighthouse in America.

The first Hatteras lighthouse went into service in 1797. The cape and its shoals had already earned a grim reputation as the "Graveyard of the Atlantic." The light warned mariners to stand off, but gales and currents continued to drive ships onto the shoals or through them onto the beach. As totaled in 1968 by Ben Dixon MacNeill, a long-time Hatteras resident, in his book *The Hatterasman*, 2,268 ships had been lost in the previous 400 years; since then more ships have undoubtedly been added to the somber list.

Cape Hatteras Island Visitor Center. Open all year, 9 a.m. to 5 p.m. Admission: free. Operated by the National Park Service, Cape Hatteras Island Visitor Center, Cape Hatteras Seashore Park, Buxton, North Carolina 27920. Telephone (919) 995-4474.

Every wreck is a tragic drama, but three stand out as being particularly memorable. One is legendary: In 1737 the *Prince of India* is said to have broken up on Ocracoke Island while carrying a cargo of Arabian—or at least Middle Eastern—horses. Some of the horses and their Arabian attendants made it to shore and the descendants of both are still on the island.

The *Mary Varney* is also remembered for her cargo. When she drove on the shoals in 1857, she was carrying gold bars from San Francisco to New York. Her hull was still in one piece when, gold and all, she was swallowed up by the sand.

The third disaster led directly to reforms that established an effective national lifesaving service. The USS *Huron*, a new gunboat, went ashore on the northern side of Cape Hatteras and, despite the best efforts of semi-volunteer lifesaving crews, 103 lives were lost. National outrage, spurred by cartoons by the famous Thomas Nast, led Congress to establish the United States Life-Saving Service as an independent, full-time organization with stations all along the coast.

From earliest times, wrecks helped the islanders to supplement their meager living from fishing. Many a house in the little villages is said to be built of lumber that floated ashore from a schooner on the shoals. In fact, the island families themselves appear to have arrived on Hatteras by way of the beach. According to Ben Dixon MacNeill, the progenitors of most of the families whose origins he traced were originally castaways.

Service on lifesaving crews has been an islander's job since the middle of the 19th century, when Congress subsidized local self-organized crews for the hurricane season. In some families several generations have been surfmen, and the need for every man to pull his weight in the boat has become part of the local ethic. Ben Dixon MacNeill gives a revealing glimpse of this. After describing how the bankers made lifetime careers out of manning the surfboats, MacNeill continues: "And the worst judgment that can be put into words about any man is simple, 'I'd not like to have him in a boat with me.' "

MacNeill also quotes an aesthetic judgment made by a 90-year-old islander: " 'I've seen a lot of pretty things in my life and I've had me three wives and all of 'em I took because they were good to look at, but all of 'em put together, all the women I've ever seen in my life, were not as pretty as a clean barkentine with all sails set in a fair wind.' "

From Cape Hatteras Light, Route 12 continues southwestward until, after 10 miles, it comes to Hatteras Inlet, the outlet from Pamlico Sound to the sea between Hatteras and Ocracoke islands. Before 1847 the inlet was too shallow to be navigated, but that year a September storm scoured out a channel. For a while thereafter the little village on the inlet became a port of entry where cargoes were transshipped from shallow-draft sound vessels to oceangoing ships. During the Civil War the Union Navy captured the Confederate forts here and established a base that for a brief period was called the capital of North Carolina.

The traveler crosses Hatteras Inlet on a free ferry and continues 16 miles along Ocracoke Island to Ocracoke village and inlet. Here Blackbeard made his base until 1718, when he was surprised one November morning by a task force of shallow-draft sloops, armed and manned by the Royal Navy and sent down from Virginia. The pirates resisted desperately aboard their ship the *Revenge*, but Blackbeard was cut down in hand-to-hand combat: His severed head went off nailed to the bowsprit of a Virginia sloop. Blackbeard's headless ghost is said to frequent the vicinity still.

Across Ocracoke Inlet the next barrier island, Portsmouth, has largely washed away, and the site of once-flourishing Portsmouth town has disappeared. Long ago, beginning in the late 17th century, Portsmouth was the most active port between Norfolk and Charleston. Enterprising mainland traders built log warehouses where small craft brought tobacco, timber, provisions, and turpentine across the Sounds to be stored until picked up by oceangoing ships for export overseas. Despite its exposed position, Portsmouth survived until after the Revolution. Eventually, however, as the trees were cut down and cattle ate the grass, the town was wasted away by wind and water, and sand shoaled the little harbor. Today its site can be reached only after a long wade through tidal shallows.

At Ocracoke, the southbound traveler must take another ferry. Bypassing the remains of Portsmouth Island, the ferry crosses Core Sound to Cedar Island, where Route 12 continues across a bridge to the mainland. There the highway eventually becomes Route 70 and runs along the shore to Beaufort, an ancient port and home of the North Carolina Maritime Museum. (N.B. The Hatteras ferry is free; the Ocracoke-Cedar Island ferry charges a toll. They fill up quickly at some seasons and travelers are advised to phone ahead to ensure a place. Reservations may be made at Ocracoke by telephoning (919) 928-3841, and at Cedar Island by telephoning (919) 225-3551.)

Beaufort, on Old Topsail Inlet—now called Beaufort Inlet—is behind Cape Lookout at the southern end of the outer banks. The third-oldest town in North Carolina, Beaufort (pronounced "Bo-fort") was founded in 1713 to take advantage of one of the few deep-water harbors along the coast. The port soon became a busy place, bustling with merchants, shipyards, fishermen, and whalers who hunted on the Outer Banks. The harbor also attracted pirates; Blackbeard is said to have careened his ships there. Later pirates were less welcome; the town is said to have been twice pillaged in the summer of 1747. When American privateers used the harbor during the Revolution, British troops landed and occupied the town for a couple of weeks.

Privateers were again active out of Beaufort in the War of 1812. In the early days of the Civil War, Beaufort was a base for Confederate blockade-runners until the town and nearby Fort Macon were captured by Federal troops in 1862. For the rest of the war it was a Union base and an R & R town for sailors from the Union blockading fleet. Beaufort was not highly esteemed as a liberty port: One young bluejacket described Beaufort as "a string of houses, a number of churches, and a lot of sand." Another, as "a sleepy Rip-Van-Winkle, dead-alive, gone to seed, fishing-smack town." Recreation centers, he reported, consisted of a bowling alley, "where poor beer was sold," and a billiard saloon.

By this time the main port activity had been transferred to a new town just to the westward, Morehead City, which was connected by rail to inland North Carolina. After the war, Beaufort remained an isolated little town, used by fishermen and coastal ship-

ping. With only one road leading into it, most travel was by water; Beaufort was said to have more direct communication with New York and Philadelphia than with the inland cities of its own state.

There are more roads leading into Beaufort today, but it still has the feeling of a quiet, out-of-the-way place—qualities more highly valued by current visitors and winter residents who come to enjoy its fine climate and snug harbor for yachts. Among maritime-related attractions from the past is the Hammock House on Hammock Lane off Fulford Street, said to have been built by Blackbeard, using timber and ballast from captured ships. His third wife is reputed to have been murdered there and to be buried nearby. The oldest house in Beaufort, it is still a private residence and not open to visitors, but imaginative travelers may view the exterior and picture that fierce, bearded face peering from a window.

In the Old Burying Ground on Ann Street, between the Methodist and Baptist churches, is the tomb of Captain Otway Burns, surmounted by the barrel of a cannon taken from his privateer, the *Snapdragon*. In the spring of 1814, Burns and *Snapdragon* are said to have captured two British barks, five brigantines, and three schooners, with a total value of one and a quarter million dollars. Later, Burns built the steamboat *Prometheus* and took her in through Frying Pan Shoals to become the first steam vessel on the Cape Fear River.

At the east end of the cemetery is a marker for the sailors who froze to death when the *Crissie Wright* was wrecked on the Shackleford Banks in January, 1886. "Cold as the night the *Crissie Wright* went ashore" is said to be a local expression still.

A model of *Snapdragon* is on display at Beaufort's center of maritime interest, the North Carolina Maritime Museum (until 1984 the Hampton Mariners Museum). With a new name better reflecting its role as the state's only maritime museum, it has acquired a new home with more than four times the space of its predecessor. A handsome two-story building facing Beaufort harbor, its design recalls the early lifesaving stations along the North Carolina coast. When the visitor enters he feels that he is in the hold of a large wooden ship.

The North Carolina Maritime Museum's ship models, artifacts, and photographs are focused on the history of North Carolina's maritime activities and man's relationship with the sea. Particularly interesting are models of a Beaufort shrimp trawler, a Carolina sharpie, and an oyster schooner. An appealing scene caught by some long-ago photographer is "A Family Outing in the Sharpie *Julia Bell*." *Julia* was a craft of modest size, but for that outing she carried eleven grown ups and two kids.

A special display of photographs and artifacts portrays the men and boats of the lifesaving crews once stationed along that dangerous coast.

Across Water Street from the main building, regional small craft are on display at the museum's watercraft center. The collection includes both original boats and modern replicas of such craft as a spritsail skiff and sharpies. There is also a boatbuilding shop; a boatbuilder periodically demonstrates his art for visitors. (The museum shop built the replica of a 16th-century ship's boat that now attends the *Elizabeth II* at Manteo, North Carolina.)

Each year the museum sponsors a traditional wooden boat show with a regatta and rowing and sailing races. The museum also conducts a variety of field trips, including visits to the little boatbuilding yards "down east"—which in Beaufort means Carteret County along the coast to the eastward. Other trips explore various aspects of the natural history of the North Carolina coast, another concern of the museum.

The North Carolina Maritime Museum (formerly the Hampton Mariners Museum) is on the harborfront in Beaufort, North Carolina. Open year around, Monday-Friday, 9 a.m. to 5 p.m.; Saturday, 10 a.m. to 5 p.m.; Sunday, 2 to 5 p.m. Admission: free. Watercraft center across street displays regional small craft; boatbuilding shop. Open all year, Monday-Friday only; 9 a.m. to 1 p.m. and 2 p.m. to 5 p.m. Admission: free. North Carolina Maritime Museum, 315 Front Street, Beaufort, North Carolina 28516. Telephone (919) 728-7317.

Figure 38
Maritime artifacts and pictures line the flag-draped main exhibition gallery of the North Carolina Maritime Museum in Beaufort, North Carolina.

Now we'll keep going south along the Carolina coast.

The biggest port in North Carolina and one of the largest on the southern Atlantic Coast is Wilmington, about 100 miles down the coast from Beaufort. Founded in the mid-18th century, the city is at the upper end of the 30-mile tidal estuary of the Cape Fear River. The river's mouth is sheltered by one of the characteristic barrier islands, which extends out into the Atlantic to form Cape Fear, southernmost cape of the Hatteras complex.

Why "Cape Fear"? In 1879, a former attorney general of the Confederacy suggested an answer:

Looking then to the Cape for the idea and reason of its name, we find that it is the southernmost point of Smith's Island, a naked bleak elbow of sand jutting far out into the ocean. Immediately in its front are Frying Pan Shoals pushing out still farther 20 miles to sea. Together they stand for warning and woe; and together they catch the long majestic roll of the Atlantic as it sweeps through a thousand miles of grandeur and power from the Arctic to the Gulf. . . . Its whole aspect is suggestive, not of repose and beauty,

but of desolation and terror. . . . There it stands today, bleak and threatening and pitiless, as it stood three hundred years ago when Grenville and White came near unto death upon its sands. And there it will stand bleak and threatening and pitiless until the earth and sea give up their dead. And as its nature, so its name, is now, always has been, and always will be the Cape of Fear.

Cape Fear and its river played major roles in the most exciting period of Wilmington's maritime history: the Civil War. The Confederacy, with little industry of its own, depended heavily on Europe for arms and supplies of every kind. It could only pay for them by exporting cotton, its major cash crop. To cut off this commerce, the Union Navy blockaded the more than 3,000 miles of hostile coastline. One by one, the entrances to the few deep-water ports along the South Atlantic and Gulf coasts were either captured or tightly patrolled until Wilmington was almost the only port where blockade-running was still possible on a regular basis.

Two things enabled the blockade-runners—fast, shallow-draft steamers—to continue to slip in and out of Wilmington's Cape Fear River. One was the difficult approach: The dangerous Frying Pan Shoals stretched out to sea from Cape Fear, and the narrow entrance, already cluttered with sandbars, was further blocked by Confederate underwater obstructions. Even more important was Confederate Fort Fisher at the river's mouth, whose heavy guns, nestled among sand dunes, outranged those of the blockading ships and kept them at a respectful distance.

After the close of the Civil War, the master of a successful blockade runner using the pseudonym of Captain Roberts wrote a little book, *Never Caught, The Story of a Blockade Runner*, telling what it was like:

> The inshore squadron off Wilmington consisted of about 30 vessels, and lay in the form of a crescent, facing the entrance to Cape Clear [Cape Fear] river, the centre being just out of range of the heavy guns mounted on Fort Fisher; the horns, as it were, gradually approaching the shore on each side. The whole line or curve covered about 10 miles.
>
> The blockade-runners had been in the habit of trying to get between the vessel at either extremity; and the coast being quite flat and very dangerous, without any landmark, excepting here and there a tree somewhat taller than others, the cruisers generally kept at a sufficient distance to allow of this being done. The runner would then crawl close along the shore, and when as near as could be judged opposite the entrance of the river, would show a light on the vessel's inshore side, which was answered by a very indistinct light being shown on the beach, close to the water's edge, and another at the background. These two lights being got into a line, was a proof that the opening was arrived at; the vessels then steered straight in, and anchored under the Confederate batteries at Fort Fisher. More vessels were lost crawling along this dangerous beach than were taken by the cruisers. I have seen three burning at one time; for the moment a vessel struck, she was set fire to, to prevent the blockaders getting her off when daylight came.

Not until a Union amphibious operation captured Fort Fisher in the final months of the war was Wilmington closed to blockade-runners. By then these vessels, almost all British owned, had made well over 400 successful runs through the blockade, bringing in more than $65 million worth of supplies desperately needed by the Confederacy and carrying back bales of cotton for Lancashire textile mills.

Today, wind, rain, and the sea have eaten away at Fort Fisher until only the remains of the landward face survive and it takes imagination to see these as more than a row of sand hills. North Carolina administers Fort Fisher as an historic site with a small but interesting museum, which focuses largely on the fort itself,

with many artifacts and relics dug up on the spot. Artifacts from sunken or beached blockade-runners, a Confederate mine that washed ashore a century after it was laid, and pictures of blockade-runners are the principal exhibits concerned with activities afloat.

Nevertheless, the displays, together with charts and an audiovisual show, give a good idea of the importance of the Cape Fear River to blockade-runners—and the problems it presented to the Union Navy. The fort and the park surrounding it, which extends from the Atlantic on one side to the Cape Fear River on the other are an attractive spot for a casual visit. Certainly the fort is of interest to anyone concerned with amphibious warfare.

Fort Fisher, or the remains of it, is located on a sandy spit of land at the east side of the mouth of the Cape Fear River. The museum is in the visitors' center at the entrance. Open all year round: Monday-Saturday, 9 a.m. to 5 p.m.; Sunday, 1 p.m. to 5 p.m.; closed Mondays. No admission charge. Small gift shop. Fort Fisher Historic Site, P.O. Box 68, Kure Beach, North Carolina 28449. Telephone (919) 458-5538.

Now to the blockade-runners' goal: Wilmington, where they sold their European cargoes and loaded with cotton for the run back. The city is still North Carolina's major deep-water port with a dredged channel down the Cape Fear River to the sea. The past is not forgotten, however, behind a restored waterfront.

The Blockade Runner Museum, (formerly near Fort Fisher, North Carolina) has gone out of existence but its outstanding collection, which focuses on the ships and men who ran the Union blockade of the

Figure 39
Blockade runners tied up along the Wilmington riverfront during the Civil War are faithfully reproduced to scale in this huge model at the New Hanover County Museum in Wilmington, North Carolina.

Cape Fear River during the Civil War, is now at the New Hanover County Museum in Wilmington. This large and notable collection includes big dioramas and more than 600 artifacts, comprising ship models, small arms, paintings, ship guns, and relics salvaged from sunken vessels. A considerable portion of the collection, as much as there is space for, is on display in two museum galleries. Included is a huge diorama of the Wilmington riverfront in 1863, showing the blockade runners, the shipyards, forges, and sail lofts that serviced them, and the warehouses that held the cotton they carried on the return run out through the blockading Union squadron.

Other exhibits to look for include:

- A smaller diorama of a blockade runner being boarded at sea by a Union warship;
- A third diorama of an auction in Wilmington, during the Civil War, of the cargo a runner had brought in through the Union blockade;
- Surviving examples of goods the blockade runners brought from Europe, including medical kits, clothing, and Confederate uniforms.

New Hanover County Museum. Small bookstore. Open all year: Tuesday-Saturday, 9 a.m. to 5 p.m.; Sunday 2 p.m. to 5 p.m.; closed Mondays. Admission: free. New Hanover County Museum, 814 Market Street, Wilmington, North Carolina 28401. Telephone (919) 763-0852.

Across the Cape Fear River from Wilmington looms the city's pride: the beautiful World War II battleship *North Carolina*, berthed in a narrow slip cut into the river bank. More than 700 feet long, displacing nearly 45,000 tons fully loaded, armed with nine 16-inch guns, able to steam at 28 knots, the *North Carolina* was the only battleship to fight in all 12 Pacific battle actions. Now she is a memorial to the nearly 10,000 North Carolinians who lost their lives in World War II.

When the *North Carolina* was laid down in the fall of 1937, she was the first new American battleship built in 16 years. Finishing her took three and a half years; she was still undergoing shakedowns when Pearl Harbor came. *North Carolina* reached the Pacific in the spring of 1942 and served 40 months in combat zones during the balance of World War II. In September 1942, she took a Japanese torpedo but was repaired in two months and returned to action.

The *North Carolina* is exceptionally well-maintained and appears to have practically all of her gear and equipment in place. To tell the visitor what he is looking at, an excellent tape-recorded description of each point of interest is available at the press of a button.

A big battleship is an immensely complex weapons system, and the visitor will do well to buy the illustrated brochure, available at the gift shop alongside, entitled "Ships Data 1 USS North Carolina (BB55)." Here are some suggestions for things worth special notice as you tour the ship:

- The main battery gun turrets are open for inspection, each with three huge naval rifles capable of hurling a projectile over 23 miles. The voice explanation of how the shells, weighing more than a ton apiece, were hoisted up from the magazine below and loaded into the guns is fascinating.
- Watertight compartment doors are frequent throughout the ship, ready to be dogged shut to compartmentalize the vessel when she went into action.
- The crew's living quarters are scattered all through the ship so that men bunked near their work stations.
- The galley saw eight-million meals prepared and served.
- The engine room with its enormous propeller shafts is striking.
- The bosun's gear laid out in a case can be identified by the check-off list alongside.
- The combat information center, the brains of the ship, is preserved with all the plotting boards and other gear in place.
- Museums with photos of the ship's history, the crew's personal photos and mementos, and the Memorial Hall with an honor roll of 10,000 names are at various points in the ship.

The seaplane mounted on the stern, a Vought Kingfisher of the type used by the battleship for spotting long-range gunfire, has an interesting history. The *North Carolina* originally carried three of these float planes, which were launched by catapult. Upon return to the ship, the aircraft would land on the sea in the battleship's wake and be hoisted aboard by a crane mounted in the stern. (Sketches mounted near the plane show the retrieval process.) When the *North Carolina* was being prepared for exhibition, no surviving Kingfisher could be found. Eventually the wreck of one was located on an island off British Columbia, where it had crashed a quarter of a century earlier. The pieces were carefully picked up, flown to the manufacturer's plant, and there painstakingly put together to form the restored aircraft now on display. (Radar eventually took over the spotting job, making the planes obsolete.)

Figure 40
The USS *North Carolina*, The "Show Boat" battleship of World War II, is now retired to a berth in the Cape Fear River opposite Wilmington, North Carolina.

When the *North Carolina* was undergoing her trials off New York City she became a familiar sight and was nicknamed "Show Boat"—and it stuck. Today, she is literally a showboat. Nightly at 9 p.m. during the summer months the battleship is the centerpiece of a sound-and-light show in which the spoken word, stirring music, lighting, and such sound effects as gunfire and explosions are woven into a 70-minute history of the ship.

One final note. As a visitor starts to climb the gangplank, he is greeted by a modest sign:

Visitors: Please do not catnap us. We cats are working members of the crew—the memorial's anti-mouse squad.
Thank you. Cleo III, Chief Cat

USS North Carolina Battleship Memorial, in the Cape Fear River at Wilmington. Open every day all year. Hours: September to June, 8 a.m. to sunset; June through Labor Day, 8 a.m. to 8 p.m. Admission: $3.00; children 6 to 11 $1.50. Owned and sponsored by North Carolina Battleship Commission, USS North Carolina Battleship Memorial, P.O. Box 417, Wilmington, North Carolina 28402. Telephone (919) 762-1829.

Cape Fear to the St. Mary's:
South Carolina and Georgia

Except for a comparatively short stretch immediately west of the Cape Fear River, the Atlantic coast continues to be fringed by barrier islands all the way to the Florida line. Unlike the Outer Banks of Hatteras, these islands hug the coast; the sounds behind them are long narrow waterways. Nor are there shoals along this coast to match the terrible Diamond and Frying Pan that reach far out to sea from the North Carolina shore to trap the unwary mariner.

In much of the Colonial period, what is now South Carolina and Georgia was disputed ground, where the Spanish and British empires ground against each other. Little fleets moved up and down the coast and through the sounds. Island forts were boldly attacked and hotly defended. The English held fast and the St. Mary's River eventually became the northern boundary of Spanish Florida.

As settlements grew, the area soon became plantation country, with the Sea Islands and tidewater mainland producing rich crops, first of indigo and rice, then of more and more cotton. The crops were loaded on flatboats or other small craft and poled or sailed to a deep-water port—Charleston or Savannah—where they could be loaded on oceangoing ships for transport to Europe or the north.

The maritime traditions of these ports were primarily concerned with the booming export trade. Before the American Revolution more than 400 ships were employed trading to England, Europe, and the West Indies. Some vessels were locally built, owned, and manned; more came from Northern colonies or Europe, Southern ports provided supportive services—the maritime trades needed for maintenance and repair of sailing ships.

Charleston, on a point between the Ashley and Cooper rivers in South Carolina, early became the most important Southern port, the only one to rank with Boston, New York, Newport, and Philadelphia, the leading cities of the Colonies. With nine miles of waterfront and a deep harbor extending seven miles in from the ocean, Charleston had only one major problem: a bar across the harbor mouth that required deep-draft ships to wait for high tide before crossing.

In Colonial times, Southern exports to England—mostly tar, marine stores, rice, and indigo—were of greater value than the exports of New England, New York, and Pennsylvania put together.

In the 19th century, cotton took over as the main export and on the eve of the Civil War, Charleston ranked third as a cotton port, being surpassed only by New Orleans and Mobile. The port of Charleston declined in the late 19th century but revived after World War II; by 1960 Charleston was ranked 15th among all American ports.

The first permanent English settlers to arrive at Charleston were sent out in 1670 by the Lords Proprietor, prominent noblemen to whom Charles II had granted the Carolinas to form a new colony. When their three ships arrived in Charleston harbor, however, the leaders did not choose the site of the present city between the Ashley and the Cooper rivers. Instead they staked out a settlement and built a fort a little way up the Kiawah River, as the Ashley was then called, on a high point of land, easily defended behind marshes and a creek. Ten years later the town was moved to the present location between the rivers for easier access to the ocean.

The site of the original Charleston fort and village is now part of a state nature preserve and historic park called Charles Towne Landing. For travelers concerned with maritime history, the prize exhibit is the ketch *Adventure*, a modern reconstruction of a small 17th-century vessel such as colonists used not only for coastal trading but for voyages to the West Indies or Newfoundland. Designed by the noted historical marine architect William A. Baker, *Adventure* is not a reproduction of any known ship, but is based on shipbuilding contracts and other records.

Adventure, which is open to visitors, is about 53 feet long over all, and has a cargo hold slightly more than seven feet deep. In the 17th century she would have been rated at 43 tons. She is double-ended, a feature of colonial-built ketches, according to Baker. A typically 17th-century detail is the hanging knees secured to the sides of the beams. The rig and spars are based on contemporary descriptions and pictures of ships of the period. The ketch is fitted with a simple forecastle, with a brick hearth for cooking, and a cabin aft. The *Adventure* goes on periodic cruises and has proved a handy vessel.

There is another vessel designed by Baker at Charles Towne Landing. A fine model of the *Carolina*, one of the ships that brought the first settlers, is on display in one of the galleries of the park's unique underground museum. Once again, no plans of the original vessel exist so the miniature *Carolina* is based on a similar merchant ship launched on the Thames in 1676. The model is built to an unusually large scale (half an inch to the foot) and the hull above the water-line is planked as in the original ship. The large size permits the use of scale rigging throughout; "a close examination will show splices in all the proper locations," Baker has written. The museum, called the "Interpretive Center," is largely devoted to artifacts of Colonial South Carolina.

Also of maritime interest at the Landing are dugout canoes—the small watercraft originally used by the Indians and adopted by the settlers. The canoes on display are each hollowed out from a single huge cypress log. According to experts, this shows that they were not Indian-built; the Indians, lacking iron tools, hollowed out their dugouts by controlled burning and experiments have demonstrated that cypress logs can't be charred out in this manner. The dugouts at the Landing include a standard "model T" type, a very wide and long cargo-carrying dugout, and a particularly beautiful carved canoe. One has a hinged plate set into the stern so that an outboard motor can be attached—evidence that dugouts have been in use in recent times.

Other interesting attractions at Charles Towne Landing include not only archaeological digs at the site of the original fort, but replicas of Colonial buildings, a 1670 crop garden, and an "Animal Forest"—all set in more than 600 acres of beautiful wooded parkland.

Ketch *Adventure*, reconstruction of a typical 17th-century vessel, is in the water at Charles Towne Landing at the site of the original settlement at Charleston, South Carolina. Take Route 17 bridge over the Ashley River, south from Charleston, turning right almost immediately onto Routes 61 and 171. Where the two routes divide, keep right on 171. Gift shop and restaurant. Open daily, 9 a.m. to 5 p.m. in winter; to 6 p.m. in summer. Admission: $3.00; senior citizens, $1.50; children, 6 to 14, $1.00. Sponsored by the South Carolina Division of State Parks. Charles Towne Landing, 1500 Old Town Road, Charleston, South Carolina 29407-6099. Telephone (803) 556-4450.

When war came to the south Atlantic coast, Charleston, with the finest harbor for hundreds of miles, was a prize to be fought for. In the Revolution, the British attacked twice: The first time, the harbor forts fought off a Royal Navy squadron; the second time, British troops were put ashore and captured the city from the land side. In the Civil War, attempts by the Union Navy to capture Charleston by battering down the harbor forts did not succeed; the Confederate Army only abandoned the city a few weeks before Appomattox. Early in the war, however, the Union blockade closed in tight: Scores of U.S. Navy ships, including converted merchantmen, whaleships,

Figure 41

Ketch *Adventure* is an authentic reproduction of a 17th century type used by the first Carolina settlers. She is berthed at Charles Towne Landing, historic site where the original Charleston settlement was made.

even ferry boats, ringed the harbor entrance just out of range of the forts. Traffic in and out of the port was cut to a trickle; only the wiliest, and luckiest, blockade-runner could slip through the iron cordon.

The Confederates retaliated by harassing the blockade ships as best they could with their limited resources. Two armored rams successfully attacked the Union ships and briefly broke the blockade, but it quickly snapped shut again, reinforced with Union ironclads. In another attempt, the Confederates built small semi-submersible torpedo boats, called "Davids": One successfully rammed dynamite into the hull of a Union ironclad. The most imaginative of the Confederate anti-blockade craft was a true submarine, named the *H.L. Hunley* for its inventor/designer. The *Hunley* was also the most deadly of the Confederate craft—particularly for the brave volunteers who manned it.

A replica of the *Hunley* is on display on the terrace of the Charleston Museum at 360 Meeting Street. Not an impressive craft to look at, it resembles a big iron tank, 30 or 40 feet long and some five feet in diameter. But the *Hunley* was a memorable vessel: a milestone in the history of submarining. And its brief history was marked by repeated displays of a raw courage that went far beyond the courage of the battlefield.

The *Hunley* was submerged by opening a valve that admitted water to the ballast tank; in theory she was surfaced by handpumping the water out of the tank. Once submerged, the only light in the interior was from candles that increased the rapid consumption of the limited oxygen supply. Under these conditions, her crew had to perform the hard physical labor of turning cranks that spun the propeller shaft, and thus pushed her through the water. Simultaneously her officers had to aim the vessel in order to ram a spar torpedo into a target ship and then after the attack—in theory—carefully adjust the valves to pump the submarine to the surface again.

Only *Hunley* never reached the final resurfacing stage. During trials in Mobile, where she was built, the *Hunley* had killed one crew by failing to surface. In Charleston, where she had been sent by rail, *Hunley* dived twice and, again, each time failed to surface, killing two more crews. After that, Confederate General Beauregard forbade her operation completely submerged, even though there was no lack of volunteers to take her down. For her final and most successful operation, therefore, she was used as a semi-submersible with her bulbous hatches a few inches above the water.

Her target was the USS *Housatonic*, a sloop of war in the Union blockade squadron. Approaching on a moonlight night, the *Hunley* got within a few yards before she was detected. Too late: The tiny craft rammed in, her torpedo, explosives on the end of a spar like a bowsprit, struck the Union ship on the quarter and blew a big hole in her bottom. The *Housatonic* went down at once in shallow water, her masts and spars filled with men, remaining above the surface.

And the *Hunley*? No one knows. Presumably she was caught in the explosion and went down too, but divers who examined the wreck could find no trace of her. The *Hunley*'s last crew disappeared with their ship. In her earlier dives she had killed 25 men including her designer/builder.

Replica of the Confederate submarine *Hunley*, is on the terrace of the Charleston Museum. There is no explanatory information; interested visitors should see *The Civil War at Charleston* by A. M. Wilcox and W. Ripley, available at the museum bookshop. This inexpensive paperback gives a full account of the *Hunely* and the "Davids" (as well as many other aspects of the sea/land battles at Charleston). Open daily 9 a.m. to 5 p.m. Admission: $2.00; children 3 to 18, $1.00. The Charleston Museum, 360 Meeting Street, Charleston, South Carolina 29403. Telephone (803) 722-2996.

Not all the maritime interest of Charleston is centered on ships and events centuries past. At Patriot's Point, on the north side of Charleston harbor, are almost 70,000 tons of mid-20th-century vessels: three warships and a most unusual merchant vessel. The aircraft carrier *Yorktown*, the destroyer *Laffey*, the submarine *Clamagore*, and the *Savannah*, the world's first nuclear-powered merchant ship, are all tied alongside an L-shaped pier angled out into the harbor. As you approach down the long walkway, you are con-

fronted by the 900-foot *Yorktown* across your bow, looming larger and larger as you move closer until the eye can no longer take her all in. The coast here is low and flat, and with her many decks topped by her skyscraping "island," the carrier looms up like a Park Avenue apartment house in an Iowa cornfield.

Let's start, however, with the *Savannah*, berthed across the east end of the pier.

Savannah is a unique ship with a unique career. Named for the pioneering *Savannah*, the first ship to cross the Atlantic partially under steam, this *Savannah* is herself a pioneer. Not only the world's first nuclear-powered merchant ship, she is also the only one ever built in the United States. Technologically successful, she was an economic failure. As an experimental ship she was not expected to earn the high cost of her nuclear propulsion system, but a combination of labor problems and changes in cargo handling methods made her unprofitable even with a subsidy.

Savannah is a beautiful ship as she sits there gleaming white at the end of the pier. The only clue to her distinctive propulsion system is the lack of any funnel, even the measly exhaust stack of some diesels. The upper decks—she was designed as a combination passenger liner and cargo carrier—and engine room are open to visitors. The most interesting aspect of the ship is, of course, her nuclear propulsion system.

For the technically minded, *Savannah* was powered by a pressurized-water atomic reactor with 32 fuel elements. The engines can be viewed from observation platforms, where the visitor should take a good look at the schematic diagram mounted on the wall at a turn in the passage. This show how the heat from the nuclear reactor is used to make steam to operate three turbines: one for high power ahead, one for low power ahead, one for power astern.

The nuclear reactor itself, which takes the place of the firebox and boilers of a conventional steam engine, is out of sight beneath the passageway. What is both visible and significant is the enormous control board from which the reactor is operated. Dotted with a multitude of red and green lights, the board is all lit up like a Christmas tree—striking evidence of the complexity of a nuclear system.

Back along the pier, the submarine *Clamagore*, commissioned too late to see action in World War II, offers a good opportunity to see the interior of a standard submersible. She has been well cared for. Little touches help the visitor to visualize her 80-man crew crammed into her tiny living spaces: the picture of a little girl in the ship's office; the lived-in look of the officers' cabins; the sign on a bulkhead, "There are two kinds of ships—submarines and targets."

One visitor followed a group in which a ten-year-old boy assumed the function of guide, explaining each area's purpose and operation as he came to it—pretty accurately, too. Asked how he knew so much, he replied matter-of-factly, "Dad's a submariner."

The destroyer *Laffey*, tied up alongside *Clamagore*, is a proud veteran of battle and a wartime comrade of *Yorktown*. While escorting the carrier off Okinawa in April 1945, she was massively attacked by 22 Japanese bombers and kamikazes. She shot down 11 of them, but in turn was hit by five kamikazes and three bombs, and had two near-misses. Almost one-third of her crew was killed or wounded. That she survived to serve on active duty for 30 more years is a tribute both to the heroic damage-control operations of her crew and to the basic strength of her design and construction.

The preparation of the *Laffey* for public viewing is an ongoing operation. The bridge, one of the most interesting parts of the ship, is open and visitors will be particularly interested in the maneuvering board, used to help maintain the destroyer in her proper position in a carrier task force formation. A five-inch gun turret also can be visited. A Memorial Room dedicated to the two Laffeys, this vessel and her predecessor of the same name, has been established in the wardroom. (The earlier *Laffey*, DD 459, was sunk off Guadalcanal in 1942.) Here are on display the Presidential Unit Citations that each ship received, casualty lists, and paintings of both the destroyers in action.

More recently a Laffey Museum has been installed in the crew's mess, where a variety of memorabilia of the ship and her crew are on display.

Interesting though these ships are, they are overshadowed by the *Yorktown*, the famous "Fighting Lady" of World War II. As the spearhead of the famous Fast Carrier Task Force, she was the heroine of the film *Fighting Lady*, which won an Academy Award in 1944.

Most visitors will get more out of their tour of the ship if they buy a copy of *Aircraft Carrier*, on sale in the gift shop. The little paperback is, in effect, the journal of Lieutenant Commander J. Bryan's four months on the *Yorktown* in 1945. Too long to read through on the spot, it will add a lot to your later appreciation of what you've seen. Bryan, a professional writer, gives the reader an intimate picture of what it was like aboard a carrier in combat. One part that is particularly significant and short enough to be read before starting the tour is the description (pp. 70-76) of the Sunday afternoon in March, 1945, when *Yorktown* took a bomb that exploded at the level of the hangar deck on the starboard side of the ship. The account does not make pleasant reading, but helps to destroy the illusion—inevitable after trudging through her myriad spaces—that the ship was too big, too strong, too technologically advanced to be damaged in battle.

And trudge you will. A visit to the four ships is fascinating but it is for the brave of heart and strong of wind and limb. Seeing the first three ships takes somewhere between an hour and a half and two hours; the arrow-guided tour through the *Yorktown*, at least as much or more. The tour is thorough, and covers portions of every deck down to the engine room. One corridor tends to look pretty much like another, so the visitor does well to stick to the arrows and not try short cuts.

Some idea of the size and complexity of the ship can be gleaned from Bryan's description of what it meant to get from his cabin to his battle station on the flag bridge when general quarters sounds. (Everyone had to move fast before the watertight doors were closed.)

"Here's the course, beginning at my room on the second deck:

"Run forward about seventy-five feet and up two ladders to the gallery deck; run forward twenty feet, up a ladder to the flight deck, up another to the first superstructure deck and up another to the flag bridge—six (puff) steep (wheeze) ladders (cough!)."

The hangar deck is used as an exhibition gallery. At the forward end is the "Arlington of Naval Aviation"—a plaque for each carrier with the names of her lost fliers. Aft is an exhibit on Doolittle's bombing flight over Tokyo, while nearby on the deck is a B-24 bomber of the type used in the carrier-launched raid. Elsewhere on the hangar deck are an F-6F Hellcat, an F4U Corsair, and a torpedo bomber. A plaque tells the torpedo bomber's story: "This TBF Avenger torpedo bomber is gratefully donated by the surviving members of Torpedo Squadron Five and One in loving memory of their heroic squadron mates who gave their lives while operating from the USS *Yorktown* CV-10 during World War II."

Some other things to watch for below decks:

- The engine room, three decks down, is impressive with its huge boilers and big brass control wheels. The posted explanations here are particularly helpful.
- The "Tailhook Award" (displayed on hangar deck) lists pilots making 1,000 or more "arrested" landings on the carrier; 16 names are recorded from 1962 to 1976.
- The wonderful collection of "Dilbert" cartoons has its own little gallery. Dilbert was the mythical naval aviator who made all conceivable stupid mistakes and was used to teach others to avoid them. Beautifully drawn, they make their point incisively.
- The ready-rooms where aviators on watch waited to be called to their planes is a poignant

reminder that at a moment's notice they could be hurled into the sky to face deadly enemies.
• The big model of the Japanese super-battleship *Yamato*.

Visitors should be sure to visit the open flight deck above the hangar deck and from there climb up to the bridge. You get not only an overview of the whole vast vessel but a look at the carrier's brains—the combat intelligence center, flag plot, pilot house, and flag bridge. A passage from Bryan helps you to understand what you see:

Flag bridge hangs on the forward end of the island, 315 feet from the bow, 545 feet from the stern, and 80 feet above the waterline. It is a narrow, horseshoe-shaped balcony about five feet wide at the toe, tapering three feet along the shanks . . . . Flag plot, which flag bridge encloses on three sides, is the Admiral's battle headquarters. Just as Captain Comb's battle headquarters—the pilothouse, on the next level above—is the nerve center of the ship, flag plot is the nerve center of the task group. All battle information funnels through this cramped room. Radiomen rush in with sheaves of fresh dispatches. Coded messages to and from the other commands rasp over TB CQ. A red light flashes on the squawk-box, and air plot makes its report. Returned pilots stumble up from their planes, sweating under their heavy flight gear, and tell the Admiral what they have seen and done. Signalmen bring in the messages they have just taken down from blinker or semaphore. Through the speaking tubes come the ghostly voices of the observers outside on flag bridge. A desk phone, or a Marine orderly, or an Intelligence officer brings more news. Still more comes from needles, dials, pin-point lights: the compass; the speed log; the anemometer, reporting the velocity and relative direction of the wind; the DRT—Dead Reckoning Tracer, also known as 'the bug'—automatically plotting the ship's course; the PPI scope—Plane Position Indicator—reflecting the positions of the ships around us.

Bryan quotes a new verse to the hymn "Eternal Father Strong to Save" that he heard sung aboard the *Yorktown*. It seems the proper note on which to end the visit:

When storms are nigh and clouds are dark,
Guide Thou the hand that steers their bark,
Far above the land and sea
By day and night their Pilot be.
Hear, oh, hear our earnest prayer.
For all who travel through the air.

Amen.

Patriots Point, berthing site of carrier *Yorktown*, submarine *Clamagore*, destroyer *Laffey*, nuclear ship *Savannah*. From

Charleston, take Route 17 northward over the Cooper River bridge; at end, bear right on Coleman Boulevard, avoiding the Route 17 bypass. All ships open to visitors daily; April 1 through September 30, 9 a.m. to 6 p.m.; October 1 through March 31, 9 a.m. to 5 p.m. One admission covers all ships: $6.50; seniors and uniformed military, $5.50; ages 6 to 11, $4.00. Patriots Point, P.O. Box 986, Mount Pleasant, South Carolina 29464. Telephone (803) 884-2727.

South from Charleston the coast remains much the same, edged with an endless fringe of low-lying marshy islands, separated from the mainland and each other by a labyrinth of winding tidal channels. After a hundred miles, however, the pattern is interrupted by the mouth of the greatest river below the Chesapeake: the Savannah.

Draining more than 10,000 square miles, the Savannah River provided the water road that opened the back country of Georgia and South Carolina—the river is the boundary between them—to exploration and settlement. Even before Georgia was established as a colony, flatboats were floating great bundles of deerskins down the river. At the mouth, the boatmen turned up the coast and poled their way through the inshore channels to Charleston, where their cargoes were loaded on ships for England. The trip took four or five days; the trip back, laboriously poling empty boats upstream, took 20 days. Fifty thousand skins a year were sent out of the wilderness in this way—until there were few upland deer left.

Meanwhile the Colony of Georgia had come into being, led and fostered by the remarkable James Oglethorpe, a unique combination of successful general and thoughtful social reformer. Oglethorpe obtained a royal grant for a proposed settlement in America where he proposed to give wretched outcasts of London a fresh start. In 1733, he arrived at the mouth of the Savannah River in the ship *Ann* with his first settlers. About 18 miles up the river he came to the first high land, a 40-foot bluff on the south bank. Here, Oglethorpe wrote home: "Ships that draw twelve foot of water can ride within ten yards of the bank . . . . The river is pretty wide, the water fresh, and from the key of the town you can see its whole course to the sea, with the island Tybee, which forms the mouth of the river . . . "

Oglethorpe's settlement, Savannah town, became the port where cargoes were brought in small craft to be loaded on blue-water ships for export to Europe or the West Indies. Indigo and rice from the Sea Island or tidewater plantations were rowed or sailed through the narrow channels between the barrier islands and the mainland. Cargoes of fur and hides, beef, corn, wheat, and tobacco came down the Savannah River from inland Georgia and South Carolina. In either case, finished goods and supplies from England were taken back to isolated plantations or lonely inland farms and settlements.

Historians say that one reason Georgia was far less angry about the 18th-century British Navigation Acts than the Colonies in the north was that few of the ships that loaded at Savannah for overseas were Georgia-built or owned. Then, and later, the city's exports were largely carried by ships from other Colonies, other regions, other nations.

In the post-Revolution era, Eli Whitney's gin made cotton an immensely profitable crop and it became Savannah's major export. In 1805, one-fourth of all the American cotton destined for Liverpool was shipped from Savannah. For some 20 years after the War of 1812, cotton moved Savannah to first place among Southern ports. By 1826, cotton shipments had increased seven-fold over the 1805 figure.

Steam came early to the Savannah River; some local authorities even claim that only the Hudson saw steamships earlier. At any rate, between 1820 and 1865, 70 different steamboats at one time or another ran between Savannah and Augusta, the town at the head of river navigation. No fewer than 30 of these came to a sad end: 6 blew up, 11 sank, and 13 burned.

Savannah today remains an important deep-water port, but its local maritime traditions tend to concern local river and coastal small craft. Nevertheless, the city has a considerable maritime museum on its riverbank, close to where Oglethorpe came ashore to found his city.

The high bluff that led Oglethorpe to choose the site for his city is still the dominant feature of Savannah's beautiful old waterfront. Along the top of the bluff runs Bay Street, the traditional street of the merchants and shipping agents. Their offices were, some still are, in multi-storied buildings built on the low riverbank at the foot of the bluff, entered from Bay Street at the third-story level over little bridges. The narrow lane between the buildings and the river is paved with cobblestones that were originally brought across the Atlantic as ship ballast. Today large ocean freighters pass a few yards from the river bank on their way to and from the industrial waterfront area upriver: Savannah is both an active port and a center of the pulp and paper industry.

In one of these venerable buildings is a handsome maritime museum, Ships of the Sea, with a third-floor Bay Street bridge entrance on the south side, and a ground floor entrance from River Street on the north. The museum covers an unusually wide time range, from the Phoenicians to the nuclear age.

Ship models form the core of the Ships of the Sea collection. Included, appropriately, are models of Oglethorpe's *Ann* and both the *Savannahs*, the original transatlantic paddle wheeler of 1819, and the big nuclear-powered merchant ship now at Charleston. Of special interest are almost 60 tiny ship models built in bottles. Built by Peter Barlow, a British naval officer, writer, photographer, and obviously fine craftsman, the collection provides a mini-history of the sailing ship.

The ship-model collection is a fine one, including such unusual vessels as HMS *Cressy*, a turn of the century armored cruiser. The model of CSS *Atlanta* portrays an ironclad that was converted from a blockade runner right here in Savannah.

Other exhibits include a weapons collection, a ship carpenter's shop, a chandlery, and a special display on the cotton export trade, which at one time made Savannah one of the busiest ports on the eastern seaboard. The British and American marine paintings on display include a number of works by Leslie Wilcox. Nautical instruments, marine artifacts, fine furniture, and lusterware make up the balance of the collection.

Incidentally, don't overlook the utterly ridiculous figureheads interspersed— without comment —among genuine ones. Also take a look at the small carved wooden figures caricaturing maritime types; some bear a remarkable facial resemblance to well-known personages of today. This is a museum with a sense of humor.

Ships of the Sea is a maritime museum on the old Savannah riverfront. Open all year except New Year's Day, Thanksgiving and Christmas Day. Hours: 10 a.m. to 5 p.m. Suggested donations: $2.00; children 7 to 12, 75 cents. Gift shop. Ships of the Sea, 503 East River Street and 504 East Bay Street, Savannah, Georgia 31401. Telephone (912) 232-1511.

On the river bank a few yards from the museum is a larger-than-life statue of unusual maritime interest. It portrays Florence Martus, the sister of the keeper of the Tybee Light at the entrance to the Savannah River, who became a familiar figure to ships entering or leaving port. Florence waved at every passing ship, and was always answered with a whistle blast.

The Savannah riverfront, with its many shops, is itself of considerable interest. Here, visitors will find restaurants, basket shops, gem stores, craft shops, clothing stores, leather shops, and so forth. Tours of Savannah Harbor aboard small river boats are available year-round.

Now a trip all the way across Georgia to the Alabama line and the Confederate Naval Museum at Columbus with its unique exhibits: the only surviving remains of the Confederate Navy's river gunboats on display.

That the Confederate Naval Museum is more than 150 miles from salt water up the Chattahoochee River is a tribute to the aggressive activities of the

Union Navy. The recapture of the Navy yards and commercial shipyards at Norfolk, Pensacola, and New Orleans early in the Civil War deprived the Confederacy of most of its coastal shipbuilding and repair facilities. At the same time, the penetration of Southern coastal rivers and sounds by Union gunboats and raiding parties showed that facilities near the coast were very much exposed to attack. As a result, the Confederate Navy Department established a building yard at Columbus, Georgia, on the Chattahoochee River well away from both the exposed Atlantic and Gulf coast.

Here Confederate Naval engineers and shipbuilders struggled for years to build river gunboats, despite an almost complete lack of the guns and armor plate needed to equip them. In 1861, the ram *Muscogee* (officially the CSS *Jackson*) was laid down. Some 250 feet long, she was planned on the general lines of the *Virginia*, ex-*Merrimack*, a steam-powered ram, heavily armored and carrying six guns. The Confederate Navy Department hoped she would not only be able to defend the Georgia rivers but would also break the Union blockade of east Gulf ports.

Engines, armor, and guns had to be built from scratch; her construction dragged on for years. When Union cavalry raided Columbus nearly a week after Appomattox, delivery of armor and guns was still two weeks away. The Union troopers set the *Muscogee* afire; her cables burned away, and she drifted off in flames to sink 25 miles downriver.

Meanwhile, the Confederate Navy had ordered a gunboat built by a private shipyard in the area. A shallow-draft steamer, 130-foot *Chattahoochee* was equipped with sails but her rig is unclear: one source describes her as a "square-rigged schooner," a contradiction of terms. She was undergoing major repairs in Columbus in April 1865 when the Confederates themselves set her afire to prevent her capture.

The remains of these little warships have now been located, raised from the river, and established in a small museum of their own in Columbus. While they never saw combat, they are of real historic interest as rare evidence of the desperate Confederate attempts to build a navy.

The *Muscogee/Jackson* and many artifacts were raised from the bottom of the Chattahoochee River just before a dam backed up another 40 feet of water over the site. Buoyed by flotation tanks, the remains were towed upstream to Columbus. Largely as a result of the public interest in the *Muscogee*, a 30-foot section of the gunboat *Chattahoochee* was later also raised from the river. Her engine, recovered at this time, is said to be the only Confederate-built steam engine to survive.

The two ships—or what's left of them—together with the salvaged artifacts, form the core of the Confederate Naval Museum exhibits. The remains, preserved under an open-sided pavilion, are pretty impressive, but visitors will do well to pause first for at least a quick look at the little museum gallery alongside. Here models of the *Chattahoochee* and *Muskogee* show how they looked before they were sunk; from them the viewer can better understand the battered relics.

Raised platforms next to the pavilion permit overviews of the ships. The visitor is likely to be struck by the size of the *Muskogee*, (as the Confederate ram *Jackson* is usually called) spread out on the ground. She burned to the waterline when she was scuttled, but her bottom, lower sides, bow, and stern survived as a unit and give a good idea of her general shape. Her distinctive flat bottom makes it clear that despite her size she was intended for use only on inland waters.

Walking around the ships, the visitor will find many interesting artifacts, including naval cannon, displayed beside them. These include four Confederate Brooke guns and an 11-inch smoothbore said to be the only one of its type still in existence. Here also are sections of 2-inch armor plate and the *Chattahoochee*'s drive shafts. Also notice particularly the *Muskogee*'s armored fantail with plating to protect her propellers.

In the gallery the museum displays scale models of a number of other Confederate ironclads, part of a growing collection. The museum, according to the curator, attempts "to touch on all major aspects of Confederate naval operations, i.e., blockade running, submarine and torpedo warfare, commerce raiders, development of the ironclad, etc." The collection includes paintings, photographs, and memorabilia.

Confederate Naval Museum is on Second Avenue in downtown Columbus, just south of Victory Drive, which carries Route 80/280 to the bridge over the Chattahoochee River. Open year round six days a week except Thanksgiving and Christmas. Tuesday-Saturday, 10 a.m. to 5 p.m.; Sunday, 2 p.m. to 5 p.m.; closed Mondays. James W. Woodruff, Jr., Confederate Naval Museum, P.O. Box 1022, Columbus, Georgia 31902. Telephone (404) 327-9798.

VII
THE GULF COAST

Tampa Bay to the Mississippi
The Mississippi to the Rio Grande

The Gulf of Mexico coast of the United states from Key West, Fla., to the Rio Grande," says the United States Coast Pilot, "is low and mostly sandy, presenting no marked natural features to the mariner approaching from seaward; shoal water extends well offshore."

Key West is, of course, on a key at the extreme southern end of the Florida peninsula; from here the Gulf coast runs north and south, all of it low, some of it behind barrier islands, much of it marshy. The only important natural harbor is Tampa Bay, about 20 miles long and six to seven miles wide, separating the principal deep-water ports of St. Petersburg and Tampa.

At the end of the peninsula the coast makes a sharp bend to the west. Behind this section of coast a rolling plain extends northward for hundreds of miles. At the bend the Apalachicola River drains an extensive hinterland, but the little port at its mouth is primarily used by fishermen and oyster dredgers. The major port of this section is Mobile to the west where an interlaced river system empties into the head of Mobile Bay.

The dominant feature of the Gulf Coast, of course, is the mouth of the Mississippi, draining with its tributaries a million and a quarter square miles of Middle America. Here are the greatest ports of the region, historic New Orleans and its upstart rival, Baton Rouge.

To the west of the Mississippi, 250 miles of swampy lowlands—the Louisiana bayou country—fringe the coast, protected by barrier islands. Beyond the Sabine River, the Texas boundary, there is a rare stretch of 50 miles where the mainland confronts the open gulf. Then the barrier islands begin again, providing Galveston with its fine bay/harbor. The island fringe continues all the way to the Rio Grande, marking the border between Texas and Mexico.

Map 1
Florida Coast

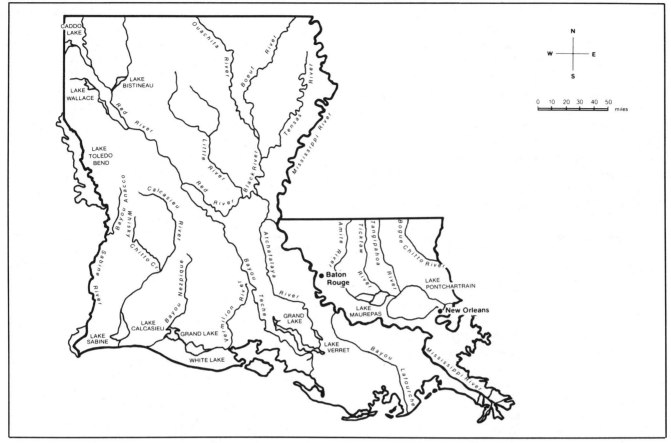

Map 2
Louisiana and Mississippi Delta

Tampa Bay to the Mississippi

When the traveler reaches the shores of the Gulf of Mexico, he leaves behind the maritime traditions of Colonial America. While the English settlements were planted and sprouting along the Atlantic Coast, the Gulf Coast was claimed and controlled by France and Spain. None of the original thirteen colonies touched the Gulf: not until the Louisiana Purchase did the United States obtain access to its waters, and then only for a few hundred miles of coast on either side of the mouth of the Mississippi.

The first European voyage along these shores was tragic and fascinating. In 1582, Pànfilo de Narvàez, a Spanish soldier who was exploring inland Florida, missed connections with his ships; he, his men, and their horses found themselves stranded at the head of Apalachee Bay, where Florida turns sharply to the westward. Narvàez's men built five open boats, the first European-type vessels built on these coasts, forging tools from spurs and stirrups, making lines from

pine fiber and horsehair, sewing shirts together for sails. In these rough craft, each about 33 feet long, 245 men started out for Mexico, which they knew only was somewhere to the west.

It was a torturous— and ultimately tragic —voyage. Sailing along the coast, they landed at Pensacola Bay, went on to cross the mouth of Mobile Bay, and finally reached the Mississippi in about five weeks. On they struggled, losing their boats one after another—wrecked, capsized, drifted off—and many lives. Some 80 survivors wintered on the coast of Texas, perhaps somewhere near Galveston Bay. In the spring, 15 were still alive. Soon there were only four, and they lived as guests/slaves of local Indians. Eventually, however, these four made it on foot to Mexico. They arrived almost eight years after they had lost their boats.

Pensacola Bay is the best harbor on the eastern gulf. A Spanish attempt to plant a colony there in the 16th century failed and more than a century passed before Spanish settlement took root there. Soon afterward, the French settled at Mobile Bay, Biloxi, and—eventually—New Orleans. Before the ultimate annexation to the United States, some areas of the Gulf Coast changed hands among France, Spain, and Britain no fewer than 12 times.

Although the eastern Gulf has such fine harbors as Pensacola and Mobile bays, only New Orleans showed much sign of becoming a great port before the 19th century. The reasons are clear: No matter how good a harbor, ships have little use for it unless there are cargoes to be loaded or unloaded. New Orleans, strategically located upriver from the mouth of the Mississippi, received export crops from the French settlements upriver and along the coast. Mobile and Pensacola became bases for great French and Spanish networks of Indian traders, who received furs and deerskins from hunting grounds far inland, but these bases remained little more than villages around a fort.

Not until American settlers crossed the Alleghenies after the Revolution and began flatboating their farm and forest products down the Mississippi did New Orleans fully come into its own. And not until American settlers from the east and north pushed the Indian tribes out of western Georgia and Alabama in the early 19th century did Mobile flourish as the port where the vast cotton crops from new plantations were loaded for export. Pensacola lagged still longer, until there was demand for the timber in its hinterland.

Later, both Pensacola and Mobile went through periods of decline but today both are once again bustling ports. Smaller cities along the coast, such as Port Saint Joe, Biloxi, and Pascagoula, are active with paper and chemicals, fishing, and shipbuilding. And, of course, New Orleans, located strategically almost at the mouth of the premier river in North America, is the mightiest of them all.

Most of the historic ships and museums of maritime interest are west of Apolachee Bay, but before investigating them, let's drop southward down the Florida coast for a brief look at the *Bounty* on Tampa Bay.

Tampa Bay, incidentally, was visited by both de Narváez and de Soto in the early 16th century, but Europeans and colonists alike long shunned the region because of the fierce hostility of the Indians of the area: three centuries passed before there was permanent settlement on the bay.

Few tales of the sea have so caught and held the public imagination as the mutiny that disastrously ended the South Seas voyage of HMS *Bounty*. The true story of overbearing Captain Bligh and the desperate mutineers who set him adrift while they took his ship to Tahiti has been told and re-told many times, includ-

ing the wonderful recreation in the Nordoff and Hall trilogy of novels.

The mutiny has also been the subject of several motion pictures with such distinguished actors as Charles Laughton, Clark Gable, and Marlon Brando in the leading roles. These necessarily required the recreation of the leading non-human actor in the drama, the *Bounty* herself. The vessel used in the 1930s film is reported to have ended up as part of a breakwater. The *Bounty* sailed by Marlon Brando in the 1960 MGM version, however, has been preserved and is on exhibition at St. Petersburg on Florida'a Gulf Coast.

The design of this *Bounty* was based on contemporary records of the original ship and built in Nova Scotia; for the filming she is said to have made a remarkable 33-day passage to Tahiti. Now *Bounty* is moored in the Vinoy Basin next to St. Petersburg's municipal pier on Tampa Bay. There she is on exhibition, fitted with contemporary furnishings and gear. Mannequins represent participants in the historic mutiny.

The adjacent dock has been given a "Tahitian setting" reminiscent of the islands where the mutineers took refuge. There also is a replica of an 18th-century long boat similar to the one in which Captain Bligh and loyal crew members rowed and sailed almost 4,000 miles across the Pacific to Timor in the East Indies.

Present plans call for the ship to be moved to Miami in the relatively near future.

MGM's Reconstruction of HMS *Bounty* has been preserved and is on exhibition at the Tampa Bay waterfront of downtown St. Petersburg, Florida, pending move to Miami. Open all year, daily, when not on tour. Check schedule, hours, admission fees. Bounty Exhibit, 345 Second Avenue, N.E., St. Petersburg, Florida. Telephone (813) 896-3117.

In 1825 when the United States was seeking the best location for a naval base on the Gulf of Mexico, a Navy board wrote to President John Quincy Adams:

> The Bay of Pensacola is extensive and capacious, easy of access from sea and affording secured anchorage for any number of vessels of the largest class.

These advantages had been recognized long before. The bay, formed by the estuaries of two rivers and sheltered behind Santa Rosa Island, was chosen by the Spanish as the site of a settlement in the mid-16th century. Their aim in planting an outpost so far east of their empire in Mexico was to get ahead of the French, who were reported to have plans to move into the area. After two years, however, the colony had not prospered and was abandoned in 1561, leaving to St. Augustine, founded four years later, the undisputed claim of being the oldest city in what is now the United States.

When the Spanish tried again at Pensacola in 1673, it was only to head off the French once more. In the decades that followed, the little settlement changed hands between France and Spain repeatedly (four times between 1719 and 1723 alone) since it was not feasible to support a shore garrison in the Pensacola fort large enough to resist the hostile fleets that came sailing into the bay. Much later, in 1763, Britain received Florida as the spoils of war. The colony grew rapidly as English settlement was encouraged, but in 1781, Spain, then allied with the American colonies, retook the little city with overwhelming force. In the years that followed, Pensacola was variously occupied by British, Spanish, and American troops until finally, in 1821, Spain ceded all of Florida to the United States. In 1826, work was started at Pensacola on an American Navy yard and protective forts. The Navy has been there ever since, except for a brief interval of Confederate occupation in the first months of the Civil War.

In 1914, the rapid growth of the Navy's interest in aviation led to the conversion of the old Navy Yard, then inactive, to Naval Air Station Pensacola. Since then, Pensacola has been the Navy's center for the development of aircraft and the training of Naval aviators.

As for non-Navy Pensacola, it remained a modest port until after the Civil War. Starting around 1870, however, Northern forests began to give out and lumber from the rich stands of yellow pine along the Gulf came to be in demand. For half a century, Pensacola prospered by shipping timber. Then the Southern forests in turn were cut over—and Pensacola went into a slump.

Since World War II, however, new industries, including chemicals and wood products are once again providing cargoes in and out of Pensacola and taking full advantage of its greatest asset: the finest natural harbor on the Gulf of Mexico.

Pensacola's Seville Square Historical District is reached from Interstate 10 by turning off on Route 1-110 south to exit 1-A. Proceed to first light and turn left on Alcaniz Street. In a few blocks you'll arrive at the north side of Seville Square. A good place to start is the West Florida Museum of History, a block west of the square. Devoted to the early history of Pensacola, including some of its maritime aspects, the West Florida Museum of History is lodged in a 100-year-old warehouse converted to exhibition space.

The museum displays include a variety of dioramas, artifacts, photographs, paintings, and ship models. Of particular maritime interest is a section relating to the building of wooden ships. Besides displays of tools and other artifacts, the shipwright's craft is explained with drawings and photographs. The entry of the Spanish fleet into Pensacola Bay in 1781, when the town and fort were captured from the British, is portrayed in an interesting diorama.

Travelers with children will probably find them clamoring to visit the Transportation Building across the street, where exhibits include wagons, carriages, and automobiles, not to mention a railroad station.

West Florida Museum of History is in Pensacola's Seville Square Historical District, just a block west of the square itself. Open all year, except Thanksgiving, Christmas, and New Year's. Monday-Friday, 9 a.m. to 5 p.m.; Saturday, 10 a.m. to 5 p.m. Admission: free. Operated by State of Florida, West Florida Museum of History, Zaragoza and Tarragona Streets, Pensacola, Florida 32501. Telephone (904) 432-6717.

Pensacola became a major port after the Civil War when its harbor was filled with ships loading lumber for the north and Europe. This maritime aspect of the city's history is covered in the Pensacola Historical Museum, which is lodged in a one-time church on Seville Square itself. Photographs, models, artifacts, and maps are on display in this small but attractive building.

Of particular interest is a special exhibit about Stephen R. Mallory, a Pensacola native who became the Confederate Secretary of the Navy. A nice, rough waterline model, carved by a sailor, represents the four-masted bark *Angelina*, while photographs give a vivid picture of the 19th-century port in full swing, with sailing ships loading at the docks. The museum's collection of documents includes the 1781 log of the ship *Meteor*.

The museum building itself is of considerable interest. Brick, with a handsome square tower, it was built in 1832 as an Episcopal church; during the Civil War it was used at various times as a hospital and a prison. Non-maritime exhibits include costumes, Victorian silver, Indian pottery, and household items.

Pensacola Historical Museum is in the one-time Christ Church building facing Seville Square. Open Monday-Saturday, 9 a.m. to 4:30 p.m.; closed Sundays and holidays. Admission: free. Operated by Pensacola Historical Society. Pensacola Historical Museum, 405 South Adams Street, Pensacola, Florida 32501. Telephone (904) 433-1559.

For thousands of Americans, Pensacola means one special thing: naval aviation. Since 1914, when pioneer seaplane pilots established the Naval Air Station there, the city has been the Navy's center for the training of Navy pilots and development of the technology of flying aircraft off aircraft carriers. This 70-year history is told at the Naval Aviation Museum on the Air Station.

The Naval Air Station is easily reached by auto from the Historic District, but visitors should try to avoid the mid-to-late-afternoon hours, when approaches to the station are jammed with traffic. All visitors are required to stop at the station entrance and go to the office on the right-hand side to fill out a brief form and receive a pass. Be sure to pick up a little map showing how to find the museum on the station grounds.

Naval aviation calls upon both aeronautical and maritime skills. From the very beginning in 1910, when a plane was flown off an improvised platform on a cruiser, the two have been intermingled, as is made clear at the Naval Aviation Museum. The museum in its current phase—it is still growing—concentrates its aircraft displays in an enormous open room as big as an indoor arena; it is crowded with aircraft of all shapes and sizes grouped chronologically from the earliest pioneers to post-World War II models. Balcony galleries display photographs, huge ship models, and special exhibits—all related to aircraft carriers.

The alpha and omega of the aircraft in the museum are the Navy's very first airplane, a reproduction of the Curtiss A-1 Triad of 1911, and the Skylab command module of 1973. For many visitors, the most impressive exhibit will be the first airplane to fly the Atlantic—the original Navy flying boat NC-4. This wooden Curtiss biplane—wingspread 126 feet, almost as much as a Boeing 707—carried a crew of six in a 45-foot wooden hull. The flight from Newfoundland to Lisbon in 1919, including a refueling stop in the Azores, took 11 days.

Altogether there are some 80 air- and space-craft rotated on display. Exhibits to be watched for:

- a fine model of a balloon boat used by the Union forces in 1861;
- a Ford Tri-Motor aircraft;
- a Curtis N-9;
- a 1914 Jenny trainer, built of fabric, wood, and wire;
- a display on the mezzanine balcony depicting the evolution of aircraft carriers from the USS *Langley*, the original carrier converted from a collier, to the gigantic nuclear-powered super-carriers of the present day.
- the big model of USS *Ranger*, 1934, the first designed from the outset as an aircraft carrier.

Before leaving the Naval Air Station, many visitors will want to check whether the USS *Lexington* is in port. Now based in Pensacola and used for training naval aviators, the aircraft carrier is open to visitors between cruises.

Naval Aviation Museum is located at the Naval Air Station in Pensacola. Open every day except Thanksgiving, Christmas, New Year's: 9 a.m. to 5 p.m. Admission: free. Small book/gift shop. Naval Aviation Museum, Naval Air Station, Pensacola, Florida 32508. Telephone (904) 452-3604.

Now, west along the Gulf coast again.

Over the years the Navy has been the source of not a few striking phrases that have caught the public ear and entered the language, from "We have just begun to fight" to "You many fire when ready, Gridley." Perhaps most widely quoted of all is that epitome of daring resolution, Farragut's "Damn the torpedoes! Full steam ahead!"

Admiral Farragut was not, of course, engaged in phrasemaking, but shouting an angry order at a desperate moment in the Battle of Mobile Bay. Today the scene of battle—the east side of the entrance to the bay, about 40 miles west of Pensacola along the Gulf coast—is surprisingly little changed. The principal Confederate defense, Fort Morgan, still stands on its point overlooking the entrance channel, and nearby a small museum tells the story of fort and battle.

Mobile Bay is a great estuary, extending 30 miles inland from the Gulf Coast and fed by two interconnected rivers, the mouths of the Alabama/Tombigbee River system. They are the outflows of a vast network of waterways, extending hundreds of miles through inland Alabama, that once brought to Mobile the huge cotton crops that made the port one of the busiest in the gulf.

To cut off these profitable Southern exports during the Civil War, Union ships blockaded the entrance to Mobile Bay. In order to prevent the Federal squadron from entering the bay and attacking the city, the Confederates closed the entrance with sunken piles and a field of moored mines, then called "torpedoes." A single narrow channel, only 100-yards wide and right under the heavy guns of Fort Morgan was left open so that blockade runners could slip in and out. And by 1864 the Confederate Navy had managed to build, upriver from Mobile, a heavily armored ram, the *Tennessee*, designed to sortie out of Mobile Bay to sink or drive away the Union blockaders. She was one of the most formidable vessels in contemporary navies.

Faced with this threat, Admiral Farragut, the Union commander, was determined to fight his way past Fort Morgan, sink the *Tennessee*, and close Mobile Bay completely to the Confederate commerce raiders and blockade-runners that were still able occasionally to evade the blockade.

This plan meant taking his ships in through that 100-yard channel between the minefield and the fort. The four armored monitors of the Union fleet led the column. The cannonade from the shore batteries, in the words of an eyewitness, seemed to envelope the whole fort in flames, tearing into the Union ships at almost point-blank range. The lead monitor, the USS *Tecumseh*, impatiently tried to take a shortcut through a mined area. The next moment, according to a witness, "the *Tecumseh* reeled a little to starboard, her bows settled beneath the surface, and while we looked, her stern lifted high in the air with the propeller still revolving and the ship pitched out of sight. . . . "

This disaster threw the Union column into confusion. The other monitors slowed, and the USS *Brooklyn*, next in line, mistook a row of floating ammunition boxes for mines, stopped, and drifted across the channel. The fort's fire redoubled, smashing the halted ships. Farragut, lashed high in the rigging of his flagship *Hartford*, next in the column, saw that he must risk the minefield to cut out around the ships halted ahead of him. "Damn the torpedoes! Full steam ahead!" he ordered. The *Hartford* passed safely through the minefield and, followed by the rest of the fleet, steamed past the fort into the bay. Later that morning, the *Tennessee* was captured when she attacked the Union ships single-handed. Fort Morgan eventually surrendered to a land attack by Union troops. Mobile Bay was occupied and shut tight to Confederate ships.

Fort Morgan is still there, an elaborate brick and stone structure on the European model. Having been used as a military post into the 20th century, the fort is well-preserved; despite the removal of its guns and a few modernizations, it is very easy to visualize the Fort as it was 120 years ago. Mobile Bay is still under its gun ports and little imagination is required to see the Union ships passing close under the casemates. The fine little museum at the entrance to the fort makes it still easier, displaying drawings, photographs, models, and artifacts that tell the history of the fort and the story of the battle.

A buoy to the north of the point is a grim reminder of the battle. The *Atlantic Coast Pilot* notes under "Dangers": "The wreck of the Civil War vessel *Tecumseh* is N of Mobile Point Light . . . marked by a buoy with orange and white bands. The vessel is reported to be in an unstable condition, and ammunition and powder aboard the wreck could be detonated if the vessel shifts."

Fort Morgan State Historic Park, on Mobile Point at the east side of the entrance to Mobile Bay. Open all year except Thanksgiving, Christmas, and New Year's: 8 a.m. to 5 p.m. Admission: Adults, $2.00; children 6 to 18, $1.00. Fort Morgan State Historic Park, Mobile Point, County Route 180, Alabama 36542. Telephone (205) 540-7125.

In its almost three centuries of history, Mobile at the head of its bay has at various times flown the French, Spanish, and English flags, and been an Indian trading post, a colonial capital, and a great cotton port. Today, Mobile is one of the major Gulf of Mexico ports and its bustling docks serve a wide region.

The French were there first. In 1702 they planted a settlement at Mobile, a Louisiana outpost against the Spanish and English to the eastward. Briefly it was Louisiana's capital until New Orleans was founded on the Mississippi and became the chief town of the colony. Mobile has played second fiddle ever since.

From the beginning, Mobile's great asset has been its location at the point where the outlet of the great Alabama/Tombigbee river system meets Mobile Bay with direct access to the Gulf of Mexico. In Colonial times this made the village the base for a vast network of French fur trappers and Indian traders competing with the Spanish and English as far inland as the Southern Appalachians.

Mobile remained a frontier trading village, however, until the early decades of the 19th century. Then, within the space of a few years, three things happened to turn it into a busy port. In 1813, Mobile and its bay were annexed by the United States, a move that united it politically and economically with inland Alabama. Simultaneously, American settlers moved into the interior, driving out the Indians and establishing flourishing cotton plantations. And in 1818-20 the newly invented steamboat came to Alabama and multiplied the usefulness of the river system by making two-way traffic possible. River steamers cut the three-month trip upriver from Mobile to Montgomery to somewhere between five days and two weeks. Now, vessels that carried cotton down to Mobile for export could carry back upriver the supplies needed by plantations. Mobile became one of the world's greatest cotton export ports, only surpassed by New Orleans. It was the only town of any size in the whole of Alabama.

After the Civil War, however, Mobile slumped as new railways tied inland Alabama directly to northern markets. The cotton trade, although still important, declined. Eventually, however, the cutting of Northern forests led to a demand for Southern timber, and Mobile became an important lumber-shipping port.

Today, Mobile's own industries provide much business for the port. Petroleum, chemicals, bananas, bauxite, paper, and iron and steel products from upriver Birmingham are among the cargoes that keep the docks filled with ships. Since World War I, the city has also been a major shipbuilding and ship-repair center.

Despite Mobile's long maritime tradition, however, the visitor will find little evidence of it except the miles of busy docks. Nevertheless, the area has a special attraction for travelers interested in America's Navy during World War II; the retired battleship *Alabama* awaits visitors at a mooring east of the city.

The World War II battleship *Alabama*, together with the retired submarine *Drum*, is berthed where the Tensaw River enters the head of Mobile Bay. The battleship, which earned nine battle stars in the later stages of World War II in the Pacific, is extremely well preserved and maintained. To enable visitors to adjust their inspection to their available time, interest, and leg power, arrows of various colors identify tours of the forward and after sections of the interior while a third tour covers the upper decks. A battleship is an enormous vessel—the *Alabama* is 680 feet long with many decks—and not every visitor will want to take all three tours. Incidentally, tall visitors will appreciate the fenders buffering the tops of the low door openings in the bulkheads.

Some things of particular interest to watch for:

- a big diorama of the Fast Carrier Attack group in formation; *Alabama* was the flagship of the group;
- the three 16-inch gun turrets—all open to inspection but unhappily without any explanation of the complex loading and firing mechanism;
- the *Alabama*'s enormous battle ensign;
- the combat information center—the brains of the ship in action—with the instruments all lit up as if in use;
- the Main and Secondary Battery Plotting Room, where information from radar and range finders was used to aim both the main battery of 16-inch guns and the secondary 5-inch battery;
- the engine room—particularly the huge reduction gears used to transform engine speed to desired propeller speed.

Visitors who want to limit themselves to only one tour will probably find the "yellow arrow" tour of the upper decks the most interesting. Climbing upward, the visitor comes to a series of facilities from which the ship and its guns were controlled. From the open deck up three ladders to the Flag Bridge; up another flight to the navigating bridge, conning tower and captain's sea cabin; up a flight to the fire control tower—this level provides a sweeping view of the after portion of the ship. And finally, for the super-energetic, three more ladders take you to the secondary conning station.

The submarine *Drum*, SS228, is tied up next to the *Alabama*. She is also exceptionally well maintained, with an apparently full complement of guns and deck gear—not always the case with submarines retired for exhibition. Also unusual is the fact that her conning tower, with its impressive array of instruments, is open to inspection. Besides her operating gear, the *Drum* is displayed with such housekeeping equipment as table silver and dishes, giving her a very much lived-in look. Unhappily, there is a minimum of explanatory material.

In the *Drum*'s after crew compartment there is a memorial to the submarines and submariners lost in World War II. Of the 264 underwater craft, which made a total of 1,682 war patrols, 52 were lost—almost one out of five.

A number of aircraft are on display on the riverbank next to the ship.

The Battleship *Alabama* and Submarine *Drum* are on display in a memorial park on Route 90 at the head of Mobile Bay two and a half miles east of the city of Mobile. Ships are open every day except Christmas; 8 a.m. to sunset. Parking, $1.00. Admission to the two ships: $4.00; children 6 to 11, $2.00. Gift shop. USS Alabama Battleship Commission, P.O. Box 65, Mobile, Alabama 36601. Telephone (205) 433-2703.

For some 70 miles along the coast west of the entrance to Mobile Bay, a string of low, narrow offshore islands separates Mississippi Sound from the open gulf. Along this sheltered waterway were the first French settlements and, for some 20-odd years, the capital of Louisiana on Biloxi Bay. As French settlements moved up the lower Mississippi valley, however, the governor shifted the seat of government to a more central location on a great oxbow bend in the Mississippi, 110 miles upriver from the sea. Here in 1718 the little settlement of Nouvelle Orleans was laid out on the east bank at the point where the Indians had a portage between the Mississippi and Lake Ponchartrain. The site was swampy, and difficult for sailing vessels to reach up the river (a Spanish squadron took three weeks) but it had the advantage of being midway between the French settlements upriver and on the coast.

And of course New Orleans had the immense advantage of being located on one of the world's greatest rivers, draining half a continent. From the Appalachians to the Rockies, a network of tributary and navigable rivers funnels down to New Orleans some 40 percent of all the water flowing into the rivers of what is now the United States. In 15 years the river brings down a cubic mile of solid materials; over the centuries, the river silt filled in the whole lower Mississippi Valley.

From the outset, this vast inland empire fed the port of New Orleans. The French network of woods runners and trappers in the Ohio Valley and along the lower Mississippi brought their furs downriver to New Orleans—by the mid-18th century £80,000 worth of furs a year from the advanced post of St. Louis. Eventually the fur exports were overshadowed by rice, indigo, tobacco, and lumber—largely exported to the French West Indies—and by cotton exported to Europe. New Orleans merchants and brokers grew rich on wharfage, brokerage, and forwarding fees.

From the beginning, New Orleans' maritime activities reflected the fact that it was both a river town and a deep-sea port. As American settlements crossed the mountains into the Mississippi Valley, the easiest way to get their crops to market was to send them down the river on rafts and flatboats to New Orleans. After the United States purchased Louisiana from France this traffic doubled and tripled. Thousands of crude river craft brought lumber, grain, and provisions down the Mississippi each year.

In 1816, the first steamboat arrived after a river trip of many months from Pittsburgh where it had been built. For the rest of the century the steamboats ruled the rivers, feeding New Orleans the cargoes that multiplied the prosperity of the city.

The 1840s and 1850s were boom years for the river packets. Running upstream to St. Louis, they averaged 14 miles an hour from point to point against the current for more than 1,200 miles. In 1860, more than 3,500 steamboats arrived at New Orleans, where they were tied up two deep along the levee; New Orleans exported two million bales of cotton a year.

The coming of steam also made a big difference on the stretch of river between New Orleans and the Gulf: Steam tugs towed up the cotton packets so that they no longer had to tack up 110 miles of narrow channels. Tugs were also needed to haul ships over the bars building up at the passes (entrances) to the Mississippi. By the 1830s, the newest and largest ships were nevertheless having great difficulty reaching the city, sometimes lying grounded on the bars for weeks. One result was that the cotton carriers, owned in New York and New England, were designed to be shallower than the usual merchant ship; some mariners argued that this increased their speed and applied it to the design of clipper ships.

In 1821, New Orleans exports totalled $16 million; by 1848, they were $77 million. Imports arrived from Europe, Cuba, the West Indies, South America, Mexico, to be transshipped to river steamboats and carried up the river. By the 1840s, New Orleans claimed to be not only the second largest port in the United States but also the fourth largest in the entire world. But significantly, seven-eighths of the shipping firms were connected to the great houses of the Atlantic seaboard.

Early in the Civil War, Farragut's squadron successfully ran past the forts on the Mississippi below New Orleans, brushed aside a handful of Confederate gunboats, and received the surrender of the city. For the rest of the war New Orleans was in Union hands. Cotton brought through the lines and exported to Europe and the North made big profits for speculators; the Mississippi River steamboats were replaced by gunboats, and the flow of midwestern cargoes simply ceased.

After the war, New Orleans never recovered its dominant place in the commerce of the Mississippi Valley. During the conflict, the upper Midwest had shipped its crops eastward by rail or water to Atlantic ports, and much of this east-west traffic continued in the postwar years. Many of the river packets that had been destroyed during the war were never replaced.

In 1879, the problem of the silted entrances to the Mississippi was tackled when the federal government paid for a jetty system at the South Pass entrance to the river. This concentrated the current to scour out the channel rather than dumping more silt. But although a 30-foot channel was dredged up to the city, the tonnage moving through New Orleans didn't reach the pre-Civil War level for almost 25 years after the war. Not until 1912 did the port traffic of New Orleans and Baton Rouge combined surpass in value the prewar figure for New Orleans alone.

Today, however, New Orleans is not merely the largest port on the bustling Gulf Coast, it is again one of the largest and most active in the nation. Its docks stretch for 30 miles along both sides of the Mississippi, with 50 miles of frontage for deep-water vessels on the riverbanks and private wharves. New Orleans is also the heart of some of the busiest grain export areas in the world; its public docks can handle 85 ships at a time, and major air and rail routes tie the city to all parts of the United States. The river flowing endlessly past its levees is the lower end of navigable waterways to Minneapolis, 1,600 miles to the north and Pittsburgh, 1,700 miles to the northeast.

Meanwhile, the little settlements along the Mississippi Sound where French Louisiana was born, have grown into busy ports in their own right. Pascagoula, where the Pascagoula River enters the sound, is a major shipbuilding and repair center. Biloxi, on a peninsula 40 miles further west, is a center for commercial seafood. Gulfport, next door, is a major fishing port and a manufacturing city. But all are overshadowed by the Crescent City, the hub of the gulf, strategically sited on the mightiest river in North America.

The varied maritime heritage of New Orleans—and Louisiana—is the theme of the Louisiana Maritime Museum. Two floors are devoted to pictures, artifacts, and—in particular—ship models. The storied steamboats of the Mississippi River, the freighters that visit a great port, the special craft used in the offshore oil industry in the Gulf of Mexico, all receive special attention.

Here are some exhibits to watch for:

- Mississippi river craft, including the famous steamboat *Robert E. Lee*, and a big model of the steamer *St. Paul*, which was built in 1883 originally as a passenger/freight carrier on the upper river but shown as converted to the excursion trade with an enormous dance floor. Here also are models of the stern-wheelers *Sewanee* and *Queen City*. Lovers of primitive Americana will be fascinated by a model of the side-wheeler *Rambler*; simple to the point of crudity, but obviously made by someone familiar with her general appearance. A more recent type of riverboat is represented by a river towboat, which actually pushes, rather than tows, barges.
- Oceangoing freighter models include the British *Crafter*, built in South Shields in 1951, and the German-built, Norwegian owned M.S. *Nopal Progress*.
- The special craft devised for the offshore oil industry, now active off Louisiana's coasts, are represented by a fine big testing model of a Shell Oil Company barge used to build a rig capable of drilling in deep water. The accompanying explanation shows how the barge drops the feet of the drilling tower onto the ocean bottom.
- Other special craft, also rarely seen in models, include a couple of experimental surface-effect vessels. Of particular interest is a model of a LASH-type vessel, the *Delta Mar*. (LASH stands for "Lighter Aboard Ship.") As shown on the model, specially designed barges that can be loaded in shallow inland rivers and towed down to a deep-water port are picked out of the water, stowed on the deck of the LASH ship, and carried across open ocean. At the terminal port the process is reversed: the loaded barges are dropped overside to be towed to the unloading dock. The LASH system is particularly designed for Third World ports where there are no docks for freighters to come alongside for direct shore-ship loading and unloading.
- Naval vessels are naturally represented by a fine 10-foot model of the cruiser *New Orleans*. There are also models of earlier naval vessels, including the auxiliary steam frigate *Mohican* of the Civil War period.

The Louisiana Maritime Museum is just one block west of Canal Street on Carondelet Street, the continuation of the French Quarter's Bourbon Street. Open all year, Monday-Saturday, 10 a.m. to 4 p.m. Admission: $1.00; children, 50 cents. Louisiana Maritime Museum, 130 Carondelet Street, New Orleans, Louisiana 70130. Telephone (504) 581-1874.

A historic vessel, the Confederate submarine *Pioneer*, is displayed on Jackson Square, right in front of the historic Presbytere, just east of the Cathedral, which is now occupied by the Louisiana State Museum. The *Pioneer* was designed and built in New Orleans in 1861; although she never saw combat, she is said to have been the first successful Confederate submarine torpedo boat. When Commodore Farragut's squadron was about to capture New Orleans in 1862, the little craft was scuttled in nearby Lake Pontchartrain to avoid seizure by the Union Navy. She was raised from the lake bottom in 1878 and placed on exhibition. Cigar-shaped, some 20 feet long, the *Pioneer* was powered by a hand-cranked propeller. The riveted iron hull is badly eroded in spots, but still gives a clear picture of the appearance of these primitive submarines.

The Louisiana State Museum formerly had a notable maritime/riverine collection on display in its Mississippi River gallery in the Cabildo on Jackson Square. Besides many fine paintings of the river and its packet boats, blue-water sailing ships, and early ocean steamships, the gallery had a number of interesting ship models and artifacts. A reorganization of the museum's collection for the Louisiana World Exposition has led to much of the maritime/riverine collection being placed in storage, but a number of the paintings are on exhibition in the Louisiana State Museum's new display space in the former United States Mint Building on Esplanade Avenue at the down-river end of the French Quarter. These include such interesting subjects as ocean liners of the 1880s—when steamships still carried auxiliary sails—shown with a variety of rigs. Several of the paintings are by the well-known marine artist Edward Arnold. The museum hopes to gradually expand the maritime collection in the Old Mint building as funds become available. The Old Mint, incidentally, also houses the Jazz and Carnival Museums.

The Louisiana State Museum currently displays a portion of its maritime/riverine collection in the one-time U.S. Mint Building on the Esplanade, the north-east boundary of the French Quarter. Exhibits consist primarily of 19th-century paintings. Open all year, Tuesday-Sunday, 10 a.m. to 6 p.m. Admission: $2.00; children under 12, $1.00. Louisiana State

Museum at the U.S. Mint Building, 400 Esplanade Avenue, New Orleans, Louisiana 70176. Telephone (504) 568-6968.

Now a few miles up the Mississippi to another world port, which has come to rival New Orleans itself—Baton Rouge.

Isaac Campbell Kidd, Rear Admiral, U.S.N., was the first flag officer of the United States Navy to be killed in action—on the bridge of his flagship, the battleship *Arizona*, as he directed air defense at Pearl Harbor on December 7th, 1941. The Admiral was posthumously awarded the Medal of Honor for conspicuous gallantry and, following Navy custom, a ship was named for him—the 2,050 Fletcher-class destroyer *Kidd*, commissioned at the Brooklyn Navy Yard in 1943.

Today, as the *Kidd* rests in honored retirement as a naval museum at Baton Rouge, Louisiana, eight battle stars show she lived up to the fighting name she bore. Wasting no time in getting into the thick of the Pacific War, she escorted the task force at the Bougainville landings in October, 1943, fighting off Japanese air attacks while rescuing downed American airmen. Screening carriers off Tarawa, *Kidd* downed two enemy bombers. During the Marshall Islands invasion the destroyer moved in to shell Japanese shore installations. At the Battle of the Philippine Sea, *Kidd* was again part of the carrier screen and fought off air attacks, serving the same function at Guam as well as providing fire support for the landing. Again, these were her duties at the invasion of the Philippines, and in February, 1945, she supported raids on the Japanese islands.

Kidd's World War II service was climaxed by heavy combat off the Okinawa beachhead. While screening battleships against kamikazes, she provided early warning of air attacks, rescued downed pilots, and sank floating mines with gunfire. And there on April 11th, 1945, she was hit by a kamikaze coming in low over the water. The suicide plane carried a 500-lb. bomb that blew up the destroyer's forward fire room, killing 38 and wounding 55 of her crew.

Kidd managed to stay afloat, moving under half power while damage-control parties rushed emergency repairs—all the time under intensive air attack. Eventually the destroyer made it back to California, where she was under repair when Japan surrendered. This did not end *Kidd*'s combat service, however. During the Korean War she was active in bombardment of enemy shore positions and patrolling hostile coasts.

Moth-balled in 1964, destined ultimately for a last voyage to the scrapyard, the historic *Kidd* was saved by being chosen as a memorial to Louisiana war veterans. Since 1982 she has been on public exhibition on the

bank of the Mississippi River, just north of the Interstate-10 bridge at Baton Rouge.

The *Kidd* rests on concrete cradles at the foot of a high levee and from a distance looks at first glance like a gigantic mantelpiece shipmodel. That is, if you arrive in the summer or fall when the river is low. The Mississippi at this point rises and falls over a span of 40 feet; when the river is high, usually from early spring to mid-June, the destroyer floats off its base and is once more water-borne, held in place by an ingenious system of loose steel collars that ride up and down tail pilings as the water level changes.

Afloat or ashore, the *Kidd* is very much worth a visit. Not only does the *Kidd*'s exceptional combat record make her a historic vessel, but the high level of her repair and maintenance, the careful attention to accurate detail with which she is being restored to her World War II condition, and the imaginative touches that give the feeling of a living, working ship all combine to make her a stand-out among the retired warships that have been placed on exhibition.

This happy situation did not come about by chance. One reason that the *Kidd* was chosen as a memorial ship was that she had not been cannibalized when retired, unlike many sister vessels that were stripped of everything usable when moth-balled. Not only did the destroyer have much of her original electronic equipment but she was close to her World War II configuration, retaining her five 5-inch guns and her pole mast. Where changes had been made in the post-war years, gifts of armament and equipment from many sources, including the United States and foreign navies, made restoration possible.

Even so, restoration has been no easy job. Staff and enthusiastic volunteers put in long hours removing the moth-balling guck and making the many repairs and replacements the *Kidd* needed after 18 years in the reserve fleet. Both the interior and exterior had to be repainted; the latter returned to the blue-gray tones of measure-22 camouflage she wore in wartime.

The restoration is still going on, as missing pieces of WW-II equipment, now hard to find, are tracked down. To show visitors how much had to be done just in simple clean-up, one small compartment has been left as it was when the destroyer arrived at Baton Rouge.

What many visitors will most appreciate are the hundreds of little touches throughout the *Kidd* that give the feeling that time has rolled back forty years and the World War II crew may return at any moment. Many "personal artifacts," from ship's clocks to Jane Russell pin-ups, were contributed after a public appeal. Flak jackets hang by every bunk, helmets are at the ready, family photos are on the bureaus, 1944

Figure 42
U.S. Destroyer *Kidd*, moored at the levee in Baton Rouge, Louisiana, rests entirely on the bottom when the Mississippi River is low. As the water level changes she slides down or up along the pilings at left, which keep her on an even keel.

magazines lie around, the wardroom mess is set for a meal. The Torpedo and Ordnance Workshop is strewn with tools apparently in use; typewriters in the ship's office are merely pausing in the flow of Navy paperwork.

The *Kidd*'s location is a striking one. Baton Rouge, besides being Louisiana's capital, is the nation's fifth largest port and ships and barges move busily past on the Mississippi. Ashore, behind the levee, the building of the U.S.S. Kidd Interpretive Center has been erected and is scheduled for opening in the spring of 1986. The center will be a museum that will not only tell more about the *Kidd* but will exhibit historic naval artifacts.

Also behind the levee by the destroyer is "Catfish Town," a riverfront section of old warehouses con-

verted to specialty shops and restaurants. Just upriver is the Baton Rouge Centroplex, a complex of government buildings and the Louisiana Arts and Science Center.

USS *Kidd* is mounted on supports on the bank of the Mississippi River at Government and Front Streets, Baton Rouge, Louisiana. Small book/gift shop. Open all year, daily except Christmas, 9 a.m. to sunset, but schedule subject to revision, so advance telephone check suggested. Admission: $3.00; seniors, children 6 to 12, $2.00. Louisiana State War Memorial Commission, USS *Kidd*, P.O. Box 44242, Baton Rouge, Louisiana 70804. Telephone (504) 383-9096.

Now west again along the coast of the Gulf of Mexico to the mouth of the Rio Grande.

The Mississippi to the Rio Grande

From the Mississippi entrances 250 miles west to Sabine Pass, the Gulf Coast is faced by low sandy beaches backed by miles of empty marsh. Offshore, shoals extend out of sight of land. Behind the marshes, swamps stretch 75 miles inland, crisscrossed by canals and bayous. This is Cajun country, sparsely settled by fishermen and muskrat hunters except where little ports service the modern offshore oil rigs. Lake Charles, the city on the lake of the same name, 32 miles in from the Gulf, is the only major port in western Louisiana and a center of petroleum processing.

Scattered along the coast are several shallow bays separated from the Gulf by long, narrow islands. In the early 19th century, Barataria Bay, connected to the Mississippi River by a maze of inland waterways, was the base for Jean Lafitte's activities as a smuggler and privateer attacking Spanish shipping. The notorious privateersman—pirate to some—had a shop in New Orleans where he sold his loot. Eventually he and his men were pardoned for fighting bravely on the American side in the defense of New Orleans against British attack in the War of 1812. After the war, Lafitte moved west to Texas where he established a new base on Galveston Island.

The boundary between Louisiana and Texas is at Sabine Pass, which connects the Gulf of Mexico to the Neches and Sabine rivers and to the ports and industrial cities of Beaumont, Port Arthur, and Orange. The 50 miles of coast westward from there to Galveston Inlet is bare beach, ending in a long point, parallel to the shore, that stretches westward and protects East Bay, the eastern end of Galveston Bay.

When Lafitte and his men shifted their base to Galveston Island after the War of 1812, Texas was a part of Mexico and the only settlement on the island was a little village. Lafitte took it over and gathered 1,000 men ostensibly as privateers authorized by rebellious South American colonies to capture Spanish ships, but in fact for his attacks on shipping in the Gulf. The town became a city of freebooters, supplying their needs and pleasures. In 1820, however, some of Lafitte's followers so far forgot themselves as to attack American ships. Soon a U.S. Navy task force arrived at Galveston and ordered him out—and Lafitte and his men disappeared from history.

But the little settlement remained—and so, of course, did Galveston Bay, which competes with Pensacola for the title of finest natural harbor on the Gulf of Mexico. Thirty miles long and 15 miles wide, the bay is protected from the Gulf by long, low

Galveston Island. Galveston—village, town, city—grew up on the landward side of the island. The Trinity and San Jacinto Rivers run into the bay and provide the best navigable water routes into inland Texas. The currents swirling through the bay entrance are said to be so strong that they keep sandbars from forming across the mouth—the curse of harbors from Newburyport to New Orleans.

As American settlers moved westward into Mexican Texas in the early years of the 19th century, Galveston became their principal port. During the War of Texas Independence, Texas had a tiny navy of its own—two of them in fact. The first, organized in 1835, policed the Gulf shipping lanes between Galveston and New Orleans and cut off the flow of shipborne supplies to Santa Ana's army. Eventually, however, its four small vessels were captured or wrecked. In 1839 and 1840 a second Texas navy of six ships was commissioned. This one devoted most of its time to helping Yucatan in its attempt to separate from Mexico. The surviving four ships eventually became part of the United States Navy when Texas joined the Union. Paintings of the activities of the two Texas navies by Robert Moak can be seen at the Lykes Maritime Gallery of the Rosenberg Library in Galveston at 2310 Sealy Avenue; open 9 a.m. to 5 p.m.; closed Sundays and holidays. Telephone: (713) 763-8853. There is no admission charge. The Lykes Gallery also displays a permanent collection of ship models, marine paintings, and artifacts.

The Texas settlers rapidly turned the virgin land of Texas into prosperous cotton plantations. The bales came down the rivers to Galveston, at first on timber rafts but by the 1850s carried by shallow-draft steamboats. On the eve of the Civil War, two-thirds of the cotton grown in the whole of Texas was shipped out through Galveston. The port's merchants owned and operated both sailing vessels and steamers; 65 vessels traded regularly between Galveston and Europe, almost 500 more were in the coastal trade. To service these ships, sail-makers, engine shops, and ship-repair yards sprang up along the waterfront. In the first six months of 1860, Galveston's exports were worth $11 million; imports in this period averaged about half as much.

With eleven foreign consuls, Galveston, in the decade before the Civil War, was described as a small, handsome, and cosmopolitan city of six or seven thousand people. The city's prosperity had a grim side, however. The high profits of the cotton plantations depended on an ample supply of black slaves, both to replace those worked out and to supply new work gangs to farm the new cotton plantations that were starting up as the cotton economy spread across eastern Texas. Demand sent the price of slaves soaring. Importing slaves from Africa had long been illegal and United States Naval vessels cruised off the African coast to catch slave ships, but the tremendous profits lured many into the trade. Ships were pretty openly fitted out in Galveston to buy slaves in Africa and bring them back to be landed on deserted inlets along the Texas coast and smuggled inland. Many of the slave ships, however, were built, owned, and manned in Northern ports—Boston, New York, even Portland, Maine, for example. Almost all of the 50-odd captured slavers brought into New York in the 1840s were Northern owned.

So great was the demand for slaves in Texas, and so unscrupulous were the slave traders and the local authorities, that Galveston became a highly dangerous port for free black sailors, even those of foreign citizenship. Shipowners recruited crews of free blacks in Northern ports, and sent the ships to Galveston, where the freemen were arrested as vagrants and sold into slavery despite their protests. Free Negroes coming into port in British-flag ships from the West Indies would mysteriously disappear, reputedly kidnapped and sold to become field hands on inland plantations.

Filibustering, another illegal maritime activity centered in Galveston and New Orleans, also resulted from the high profits to be made in cotton culture using slave labor. With further expansion of cotton westward blocked by the dry plains, Southerners eyed the little countries of Central America, newly independent of Spain, as possible areas where cotton plantations—and slavery—could expand. Several armed expeditions set out from Galveston and New Orleans during the 1850s and for a brief period American filibusters actually controlled parts of Nicaragua.

During the Civil War, Galveston remained in Confederate hands and in the final months the port was almost the last source of cotton for blockade-runners. After the war, the port boomed again for a while but the new city of Houston, an upstart rival 50 miles inland on Buffalo Bayou, took an increasingly larger share of the lucrative cotton trade. Even before the war Houston had managed to bring in the railroads that were opening up the interior. Now some major merchants began to move their warehouses to Houston to take advantage of the rail connections, sending cotton and timber down to Galveston for export by sea.

One of Houston's advantages was that it was less exposed to coastal storms. Most of Galveston Island is less than five feet above high water, and although the city and its wharves were built on the bay side, in the 19th century, they were little protected. In 1900, a hurricane sent a great wave smashing across the island, which drowned some 6,000 people and did immense damage. Since then a sea wall has been wrapped around the Gulf side of the city, and subsequent storms, including one in 1983, flooded parts of the city but caused little loss of life and did relatively little damage.

The 1900 catastrophe set back the economic progress of the city for years. Fifteen years later it suffered an even greater competitive blow when Buffalo Bayou was dredged and straightened into the Houston Ship Canal, giving large oceangoing vessels direct access to the inland city. Since then, Houston has ballooned into a megalopolis but Galveston has nevertheless survived as a thriving international port—and a city with an increasing interest in its heritage from the past. Not only have historic districts been established but Galveston has become the home port for a beautifully restored square-rigger, built more than a century ago.

In 1883 the British bark *Elissa* sailed into Galveston Harbor with a cargo of bananas. She was a handsome vessel, only six years from her builder's yard in Aberdeen. Built of iron, she was typical of hundreds of such ships that carried the world's cargoes in the last decades of the age of sail. She came again to Galveston three years later and then no more for almost a century as the search for cargoes in the face of increasing competition from tramp steamers took her all over the world.

Now, the *Elissa*, more handsome than ever, is once again in Galveston, berthed at Pier 2 on the waterfront. The story of the *Elissa* between her last two visits encapsulates the decline and fall of the square-rigger. On a happier note, her rebirth in Galveston since her return in 1979 is heartening evidence of America's growing recognition of the significance and importance of the nation's, and the world's, maritime heritage.

As she grew older and dingier and less profitable to her owners, *Elissa* repeatedly changed names and flags. In 1898 she was sold to Norwegian owners and became the *Fjeld*. Thirteen years later she was sold again and became the Swedish *Gustaf*. During World War I she was re-rigged as an auxiliary schooner and flew the Finnish flag. From then on it was all downhill as she passed from owner to owner and flag to flag, eventually ending up in the mid-1960s as the *Christophoros* in the hands of Greek smugglers. She suffered a final indignity when her beautiful clipper bow was removed as the result of a collision—which incidentally made her less recognizable as she slunk along illegal coasts. Finally she was abandoned off the wreckers' beach near the port of Athens.

No one would guess this tattered history seeing *Elissa* today. From the figurehead on her restored Aberdeen bow to her classic stern, from royal mast to keel, she has been rebuilt, re-rigged, and refinished, and work continues on the final touches. Many persons have shared in *Elissa*'s rebirth: distinguished maritime historians who recognized one of the few surviving square-rigger hulls beneath the grubby motor cargo carrier; the historical foundation that bought her in Greece; the volunteers who went there to arrange repairs to enable her to be towed across the Atlantic; the many foundations, government agencies, and private contributors who provided the millions of dollars needed for her restoration; the professional craftsmen and enthusiastic volunteers who teamed up to do the work.

Here are some of the things to notice aboard the *Elissa*:

- The little signs posted about the decks with sketches and diagrams are extremely helpful in showing the function of each part of the vessel. The placard at the pumps, for example, not only explains their use but also points out that *Elissa*'s iron hull meant that she leaked a lot less than earlier wooden vessels.
- In the hold, which is open for inspection, you can see the barrels of ballast stacked in the bilges.
- Between decks, before-and-after photographs show not only *Elissa*'s dramatic transformation from ancient hag to vibrant beauty, but also several earlier stages in her career, such as when she was a World War I barkentine and when she flew the Finnish flag as a three-masted schooner.
- The beautiful new figurehead was especially carved for *Elissa*'s restored bow.
- On the dock alongside *Elissa* is another vessel—designed to delight small-fry too young to appreciate *Elissa* herself. The *Sea-Child* is a pretend ship that children can climb aboard; here, they can turn the steering wheel, peer into the hold, and sail away to distant islands on the seas of imagination.
- A film about *Elissa* is shown aboard the vessel and also at the Strand Visitors Center, about a block from the ship.

The *Elissa* is berthed in the heart of Galveston's bustling waterfront. The Dock Line Railroad shuttles cargo back and forth across the wharf entrance. At the big dock next door, the visitor is quite likely to find a Russian freighter loading cotton. At the head of Elissa's dock is a rough-hewn seafood restaurant where visitors can buy shrimps, then eat them outside on a little deck overlooking the ships and the harbor.

Bark *Elissa*, built in 1877 and now restored to her original condition, is berthed at Pier 1 on the Galveston waterfront. Open all year, daily from 9:30 a.m. to 6 p.m. Route 45, from Houston becomes Broadway after entering Galveston and runs along parallel to the waterfront. Turn left on Kempner Street (22nd Street), which leads to Pier 2, three blocks away. Open all year; daily, from 9:30 a.m. to 6 p.m. Admission: $3.50; seniors and teenagers, $3.00; children over 6, $2.50. Gift shop. *Elissa*, Galveston Historical Foundation, P.O. Drawer 539, Galveston, Texas 77553. Telephone (713) 765-7834.

Two other vessels on display in Galveston tell of a very different time and kind of maritime activity. The submarine *Cavalla* and destroyer escort *Stewart* are tied up alongshore at Seawolf Park, on the eastern tip of Pelican Island, a peninsula sticking out into Galveston harbor.

Figure 43
The bark *Elissa*, beautifully and expensively restored, is shown under full sail off her home port, Galveston, Texas. She was built of iron in Scotland more than a century ago.

The *Cavalla* is described as "the luckiest submarine in the fleet," having made—and survived—six combat patrols during World War II in which she sank a Japanese aircraft carrier, a destroyer, and two cargo vessels. In retirement, her deck has been covered with a concrete walkway and her deck gear removed. The interior is open to inspection but the lack of identifying information about many of the spaces and equipment leaves much for the visitor to figure out for himself.

The *Stewart*, at the next berth, is a veteran of North Atlantic convoy duty in World War II. When visited, she was closed below the main deck and no information was provided about the spaces in the bridge island that are on view. The visitor can climb a ladder to the passage behind the bridge and peer through the door at the wheel, engine room, telegraph, and so forth. Restoration work, preparing the ship for public viewing, is said to be continuing.

Destroyer Escort *Stewart* and Submarine *Cavalla* are berthed at Seawolf Park on Pelican Island; from I-45 (Broadway) turn off on Seawolf Parkway (51st Street). Open all year, daily from dawn to dusk. Admission: $2.50; children, $1.00. Parking, $1.00 Gift shop. Sponsored by U.S. Submarine Veterans World War II, Texas, Inc. Operated by the Park Board of Trustees of the City of Galveston. Information: Seawolf Park, Pelican Island, Galveston, Texas 77550. Telephone (409) 744-5738.

Some 40 miles north of Galveston is its great rival, Houston, which since the Ship Canal was built providing deep-water access to the gulf, has far outstripped the coastal city both as a port and as a metropolis. For the visitor looking for our maritime heritage, however, the major interest is not in Houston itself but in the USS *Texas*, the oldest surviving American battleship, now moored in a lagoon off the San Jacinto River Houston Ship Canal.

I had just gone up the ladder to the Admiral's bridge when the shell struck. It hit just under the captain's bridge. I ran down the 12 feet into thin smoke and stillness. The wheel stood unmanned. The helmsman and the other seamen I had left just a minute earlier lay unconscious on the curved deck plates; a lone telephone lay beside a jagged hole. It had happened so fast that I could not take it in. To stop a rising sense of hysteria I began snapping pictures.

Thus Time-Life correspondent Wilmot Ragsdale remembers the moment when the USS *Texas* suffered a direct hit by an 11-inch shell. Although the blast reported by Ragsdale killed the helmsman of the *Texas* and wounded 13 others on the bridge, the veteran battleship, fighting her second war, went on shelling the German-held forts around Cherbourg on the tip of the Normandy peninsula. The time was June, 1944, the Allies had landed in Normandy, and American forces were attacking Cherbourg from the land side. The *Texas*, with her mighty battery of 10 14-inch guns, was continuing her support of the invasion by shore bombardment: she fired almost 900 rounds, starting on D-Day with an artillery engagement with the strong German defenses at Omaha Beach where American forces went ashore.

The hit off Cherbourg, and a later shell that penetrated her bow but failed to explode, did not keep *Texas* from doing her job well. As the U.S. Army's Major General Collins wrote later: "I witnessed your naval bombardment on the coastal batteries and the enemy strong points around Cherbourg which were engaged by your guns on 25 June. The results were excellent and did much to engage the enemy's fire while our troops stormed into Cherbourg from the rear."

Texas had already been active in World War II. First she did convoy duty in the North Atlantic. Then at the first of the successive American landings, in North Africa in November 1942, the battleship's long-range guns laid down a barrage that turned back Vichy French reinforcements rushing to resist the American troop landings at Port Lyautey.

And Cherbourg did not end her service. Later that year, in 1944, the *Texas*'s 14-inch batteries provided fire support for the Allied landings in southern France. The following year, after being refitted, *Texas* moved to the Pacific where she earned the last two of her five battle stars at Iwo Jima and Okinawa.

A fine record—five battle stars and four medals—but not unique among the American battlewagons. But it is a good deal more than her World War II combat activities that today makes the *Texas* perhaps the most interesting of the four American battleships now retired and on exhibition. The visitor to the USS *Texas*—in Texas, outside of Houston, where else?—will find a unique vessel, a survivor of a historic development in the history of fighting ships and naval warfare. Commissioned in 1914, *Texas* is the only existing ship of the United States Navy to have fought in both World Wars. Even more striking, she is the only survivor of the dreadnaught era—a "super dreadnaught," actually—the huge, heavily armored all-big-gun ships, that all the naval powers raced to build in the decade before World War I. For a few months the 27,000-ton *Texas*, with five heavily armored turrets each containing twin 14-inch guns, threw the heaviest broadside in the world—14,000 pounds of high explosives. (In 1915, Britain, by then at war with Germany, commissioned the even more powerful *Queen Elizabeth*.)

After America entered World War I, *Texas* served with the British Grand Fleet in the North Sea, but her only action was to elude a U-boat torpedo and counterattack the submarine. In the mid-1920s, when the Naval Arms Limitations Treaties forbade the construction of new battleships, the *Texas* was extensively rebuilt and modernized in the light of British battle experience in the recent war. Her basket masts were replaced by the tripod type, great "blisters" were added along her waterline to detonate torpedoes before they could reach her hull, and her engines were converted from burning coal to oil. By the late 1920s, when she became flagship of the commander-in-chief of the United States Fleet, *Texas* looked much as she does now.

Today the visitor will find her in a lagoon off the Houston Ship Canal at the San Jacinto Battlefield and Monument, the historical park on the site of the decisive battle of the Texas War of Independence. Modernized though she was in the 1920s, and later modified again during World War II, the *Texas* still shows her dreadnaught origin. Even before going aboard, the visitor will note:

- Her bulbous "nose" projecting forward from the bow at the waterline. Not really a ram, this distinctive bow nevertheless is a design survival of the period in the 19th century when battleships were expected to fight by crashing into each other at full speed.
- The casemates that scallop her sides amidships, set into the hull just below the open main deck. Empty now, these armored compartments originally held her secondary battery of five-inch guns, designed to knock out high-speed torpedo boats or destroyers moving to launch torpedoes. By the 1920s modernization of the *Texas*, however, such attacks were no longer considered to be serious threats, and since the casemates were flooded by heavy seas in bad weather, they were closed off. All the five-inch guns were removed except for six that were relocated on the main deck, where they can be seen near the base of the main (forward) tripod mast.

Once aboard, the visitor will find an extremely interesting vessel. Basically her interior layout remains the same as it was 70 years ago; although the modernizations thickened her deck armor to increase resistance to plunging fire, this change cannot be seen. The ship seems more open, with fewer watertight compartments, for example, than the World War II battleships on display.

Curiously, the ship's two enormous triple-expansion steam engines were already obsolescent when installed. By 1914, the latest dreadnaughts were powered by steam turbines and the *Texas* was designed for them. American manufacturers were apparently unable to provide turbines of this size, however, and the Navy had to go back to the already old-fashioned triple-expansion engines. The engines of the *Texas* are now a National Engineering Landmark; one is open to view, and worth a climb down into the bowels of the ship for the engineering minded.

The layout of the *Texas* can be bewildering; the tour path mapped in the little information folder handed out at the ticket office is a great help. The open areas of the ship currently include most of two decks; a portion of a third; an engine room; the superstructure and bridge; and the interior of her massive number three turret, with its pair of 14-inch rifles and the accompanying complex gear for hoisting and loading ammunition.

In addition to the ship herself, here are some other things to look for on a tour of the *Texas*:

- Two magnificent silver table services displayed, one that belonged to this battleship *Texas*, the other the service of the pre-dreadnaught *Texas* (1895), which includes a tray with a beautiful engraving of the ship. (The earlier *Texas* ended her career as the *San Marcos* and was sunk as a target for naval gunners.) Here also is a wonderful silver model of a galleon presented to the *Texas* by the Netherlands in gratitude for rescuing the crew of a Dutch freighter sinking after a collision at sea in 1915.
- The *Houston* Memorial Room, with a fine big model of the cruiser *Houston*, sunk in the Battle of Sunda Straits in the early months of World War II. Here also are big blown-up photographs of a second *Houston* taking a hit from a torpedo later in the war (she survived).
- The Texas Navy Room with handsome models of the various small fighting ships that comprised the seagoing forces of the rebellious Texans during their War of Independence.

Not all of the *Texas* interior has been restored from the dilapidation of retirement; more spaces will be opened as they are brought back to their original condition. Actually, the restoration and preservation of the *Texas* is a never-ending process. Located close to an oil-refining and chemical-processing center, the old battleship is in a damaging environment. For three months in the fall of 1986, the *Texas* will be taken away to be drydocked for a major overhaul and further restoration, including replacement of a concrete slab main deck with wood, the original covering.

At this time the *Texas* will be repainted in the battle colors she wore at the time of Normandy in 1944: dark gray on the lower portions, light gray above. The goal of the restoration program is the ship's complete restoration to the way she looked in June, 1944. (While some Navy history buffs might dream of returning *Texas* to her 1914 configuration as a dreadnaught, financial considerations, and probably technological ones as well, make a 70-year rollback out of the question.)

USS *Texas*, BB 35, commissioned 1914, is now retired and on display at San Jacinto Battlefield and Monument, historic park about 25 miles east of Houston, Texas. From I-10, main east-west highway, take San Jacinto Memorial Park exit, proceed southeast on Lynchberg Road. (Includes brief ferry ride over arm of San Jacinto River; free, but may require wait at rush hours.) Can also be reached from Houston by driving east on SR 225; exit on SR 134, drive three miles north. The 570-foot San Jacinto monument, near ship, can be seen from afar. Almost all of ship is open to visitors; follow tour route in folder. Open every day year round, September through May, 10 a.m. to 5 p.m.; June through August, 10 a.m. to 5:30 p.m. Admission: $2; children 6 to 12, $1.00. Owned by State of Texas; administered by Texas Parks and Wildlife Department. Battleship Texas, 3527 Battleground Road, La Porte, Texas 77571. Telephone (713) 479-2411.

Ashore near the *Texas* is the Seawolf Memorial. Dedicated to a submarine lost on patrol with all hands, it also commemorates all 52 American submarines lost in World War II. "Still on Patrol" is the legend.

The *Texas* is moored in a park marking the battlefield of San Jacinto, the decisive Texan victory that gained Texas independence from Mexico in 1836. Close by is the San Jacinto Memorial Tower and Museum of History, which commemorates the struggle for Texan independence and tells the history of the region from Indian times to the Civil War.

Before proceeding further along the Texas coast, some Navy buffs will want to make a visit inland.

A unique naval vessel, apparently the only one of its kind on exhibition, can be seen at the Pate Museum of Transportation, a few miles outside of Fort Worth, Texas. There displayed is the MSB-5, the first of a class of 54 small minesweeping boats that the U.S. Navy put in commission between 1952 and 1956. (MSBs 1 through 4 were older craft taken over from the Army.) Powered by a pair of diesels that gave them 12 knots, these little sweepers were built of wood and equipped with nonmagnetic machinery so that they wouldn't trigger magnetically-activated mines. According to *Jane's Fighting Ships*, vessels of this class were designed to be carried aboard a large assault ship to an operational area and there dropped overside. However, the

sweepers—drawing only four feet but 57 feet long and weighing 39 tons fully loaded—are said to have proved too big to be easily handled by shipboard cranes and were therefore reassigned to harbor-clearing duties.

Jane's listed the MSBs under "Combatant craft," and in South Vietnam from 1966 to 1972 they grimly earned the title. With a beefed-up armament of machine guns and fitted with removable fiberglass armor, the little sweepers went to work keeping rivers free of Viet Cong mines. For the six-man crews it was very much a combat assignment; around each river bend an enemy ambush might lurk in the jungle. That at least one of these craft has been preserved should remind us of the many that fought in this dangerous, dirty, unglamorous, little-recognized sector of an unpopular war.

MSB-5 is exhibited on a platform on the grounds of the Pate Museum of Transportation, located on Highway 377 South, about 14 miles southwest of Fort Worth, and three miles from Cresson, Texas. (Museum also exhibits models of modern freighters, automobiles, aircraft, railway cars.) Open all year, Tuesday-Sunday, 9 a.m. to 5 p.m. Closed Mondays and some holidays; check. Admission: free. Supported by Pate Foundation. Pate Museum of Transportation, P.O. Box 711, Fort Worth, Texas 76101. Telephone (817) 332-1161.

Now southwestward, back to the Texas coast at Corpus Christi.

Sometime in the year 1554, the galleon *San Esteban* and at least two other merchant vessels set sail for Spain from the Mexican port of Vera Cruz. A long, dangerous voyage through the Gulf of Mexico into and across the Atlantic lay ahead, but the *San Esteban* and her two companions had barely started when they were driven ashore on Padre Island, near the present Texas port of Corpus Christi. All three vessels were wrecked. The survivors struggled ashore only to be confronted by hostile Indians. In the end, 300 Spaniards lost their lives.

Now marine archaeologists have located the wreck of the *San Esteban* and recovered relics that are displayed at the Corpus Christi Museum. Here in the north wing are portions of the keel of the galleon and a variety of gear and artifacts, including her anchor, a cannon, a section of rail, and a crossbow.

Nearby in the museum is another maritime-related exhibit, one that illustrates the history of naval aviation at Corpus Christi. The port has long been an important center for the training of U.S. Navy pilots; during World War II it was the largest such center in the world.

Exhibits in the south wing of the museum include a collection of ships' carpenter's tools, a number of marine artifacts, and models of such windjammers as *Star of India* and the clipper *Red Jacket*. Also, says the curator, "a few pirate artifacts."

The Corpus Christi Museum, in Corpus Christi, Texas, on the Gulf of Mexico. Open all year, Tuesday-Saturday, 10 a.m. to 5 p.m.; Sunday 2 to 5 p.m. Admission: free. A department of the city of Corpus Christi. Corpus Christi Museum, 1900 North Chaparrel, Corpus Christi, Texas 78401. Telephone (512) 883-2862.

Inland again now for a final Texas visit.

A little town deep in the heart of Texas hill country, 165 miles from the nearest salt water, may seem an unlikely place for a maritime museum. Fredericksburg, Texas, however, has personal ties to the far-away Pacific: Fleet Admiral Chester W. Nimitz, Commander-in-Chief of the U.S. Naval Forces in the Pacific in World War II, was born and raised here, a descendant of the German immigrants who founded Fredericksburg.

When Fredericksburg was a Texas frontier settlement, the Steamboat Hotel on Fredericksburg's Main Street was owned by Admiral Nimitz's grandfather, a one-time shipmaster in the German merchant marine. Now the old hotel, restored to its appearance in 1891, houses the Museum of the Pacific War, the principal building of the Admiral Nimitz State Historical Park, named for the little town's most famous native son and the last of America's five-star admirals.

Much of the museum is devoted to Nimitz memorabilia, including uniforms, decorations, portraits, photographs, and various personal items. Of particular interest, and with somewhat ironic overtones, are photographs of Nimitz as a young American naval officer visiting Admiral Togo, the father of the Imperial Japanese Navy, long before World War II.

There are a number of fine ship models, most of them either related to Admiral Nimitz's career or to the war in the Pacific. Among them is the USS *Decatur*, the four-stacker destroyer that was Nimitz's first command. An interesting model of PC590, a World War II antisubmarine patrol boat, was made by a former member of the crew. The bulk of the collection is made up of many weapons, documents, photographs, and artifacts of various kinds related to the war in the Pacific. A reminder of an earlier period of American naval activity around Japan is a model of the USS *Susquehanna*, the steam frigate that was Commodore Perry's flagship when he made his historic visit to Japan in the 1850s.

Behind the Pacific War Museum is the beautiful Garden of Peace, a gift from the people in Japan. Within it is a replica of Admiral Togo's study, brought from Japan and assembled on the site. The gift was in response to Admiral Nimitz's kindly gestures toward Japan in the years after World War II, particularly in starting a fund to restore Admiral Togo's flagship, the *Mikasa*.

The "Pacific War History Walk" leads through adjacent side streets. Along the way are displayed airplanes, including a Kawanishi NIKI fighter seaplane, cannon, small naval craft, and other relics of the war in the Pacific such as the conning tower of the U.S.S. *Pintado*, the submarine that sank Japan's largest merchant ship.

Admiral Nimitz agreed to the request that the museum be named for him, but asked that it be dedicated to the two million men and women who served with him in the Pacific War.

Admiral Nimitz State Historical Park centers in the old Steamboat Hotel on Route 290 in Fredericksburg, Texas. It includes the Museum of the Pacific War, the Garden of Peace, and the Pacific History Walk. Open daily all year: 8 a.m. to 5 p.m. Admission $2.00; ages 6 to 12, $1.00. Gift shop. Admiral Nimitz State Historical Park, 340 Main Street, Fredericksburg, Texas 78624. Telephone (512) 997-4379 or 997-7269.

PART TWO

MIDDLE AMERICA'S RIVERS AND LAKES

VIII
THE OHIO COUNTRY

"The Beautiful River"
From Lake to River: The Canals of Ohio and Indiana

"The Beautiful River"

The French who found the Ohio River
named it
La Belle Riviere, meaning a woman easy
to look at.

Carl Sandburg, *Whiffs of the*
Ohio River at Cincinnati

The gentlemen explorers and wild *coureurs de bois*—fur traders and trappers—of New France and their opposite numbers in the English colonies were probably well matched in courage and hardihood—but the Frenchmen and Canadians had the edge in language. When they found beauty in the wilderness, they gave it a beautiful name. The Anglo-Americans might have been equally impressed but when it came to names they too often came up with something like "The Big Stinky."

Running through the heart of the smokestack America, the Ohio may not be quite as belle as it was 300 years ago, but it remains a mighty and impressive river. The Ohio has always been overshadowed by its giant neighbor, the Mississippi, into which its waters flow; otherwise its 981-mile length would have long ago won recognition as one of the world's great rivers. Draining more than 200,000 square miles, the Ohio delivers more water to the Mississippi than the Missouri, two and a half times as long.

The untiring and intrepid Sieur de la Salle is thought to have been the first European to have penetrated to the Ohio River. The record is not wholly clear, but in 1669 he apparently canoed up a river running north into Lake Erie, at the head portaged across the watershed to a river running south, and canoed on down into the Ohio.

All through the Colonial period the Ohio Valley remained Indian country. The French Canadians from the north and the Anglo-Americans from the east each sought to dominate the fur trade and on occasion fought battles in the wilderness. Fort Duquesne, at the Forks of the Ohio, where the Monongahela and Allegheny join to form the larger river, was a key post in the French attempt to form a great inland empire from New Orleans to Quebec.

During the British conquest of French Canada, however, Fort Duquesne became Fort Pitt. Anglo-American traders used the river as a highway for their boats laden with furs or trade goods. Soon land speculators back in the coastal Colonies, particularly in Virginia, became interested in the possibility of acquiring large blocks of land along the river for future resale to settlers. Among them was a Virginia plantation owner who had served with Colonial troops in western Pennsylvania during the French and Indian War: in 1770, George Washington traveled by boat down the Ohio from Pittsburgh (formerly Fort Pitt) to the mouth of the Great Kanawha River looking for likely tracts to buy up, thus making the Ohio the only western river visited by the Father of His Country.

During the Revolution, the Ohio was a back door to the Colonies in revolt; an American agent succeeded in buying 98 barrels of gunpowder in New

Orleans and bringing it all the way up the Mississippi and Ohio rivers to supply the Continental troops. Even while the Revolution was still going on, squatters moved into Indian lands along the river. While these illegal settlers were later removed by American troops, eventually and inevitably the Indians were driven out and a stream of emigrants took to the Ohio on rafts and crude flatboats to float downriver to take up land in the newly opened territories. Until the opening of the Erie Canal, the Ohio River was the preferred water route to the West.

The most significant event in the Ohio's maritime history came more than a decade before that, however. In 1809, Nicholas Roosevelt, an associate of Robert Fulton, arrived with his bride at Pittsburgh, at the Forks of the Ohio. He had a flatboat built and set out down the Ohio to see whether the Western rivers were suitable for Fulton's new-fangled steamboat. After traveling down the Ohio and Mississippi all the way to New Orleans he made a favorable report. The following year he was back in Pittsburgh with Fulton's plans, a crew of New York workmen, and a substantial amount of money or credit. Putting them all together, Roosevelt spent almost $40,000 building the *New Orleans*, a 116-foot steamboat based on Fulton's design.

In October 1811, *New Orleans* started down the Ohio on a historic voyage, the first steamboat passage on a Western river. Roosevelt and his wife were the only passengers; nobody else dared venture on such a vessel. It was a slow trip. Each day the *New Orleans* had to tie up to the riverbank while the crew went ashore and cut enough wood to fuel the steam engine for that day's run. At that time of year, the Ohio River was low and the *New Orleans* was delayed by lack of water to float her over the rapids at Louisville. (While they were waiting, Mrs. Roosevelt gave birth to a baby!) Finally the river rose just enough to allow *New Orleans* to run the rapids. Immediately afterwards the whole region was shaken by a tremendous earthquake, with great shocks continuing for several days. When they reached the Mississippi, the steamboaters found the face of the country altered and the channel still shifting as the shocks continued. Nevertheless, the *New Orleans* reached Natchez safely, picked up a load of cotton, and carried it downriver to New Orleans—the first steamboat freight on the Mississippi.

The *New Orleans* never saw the Ohio River again, her steam engine was too weak to drive her upstream against the strong current. The *Enterprise* was the first steamboat to make it back up to Louisville, completing the 1,500-mile trip in 25 days in 1814.

From then on, steamboats flourished on the Ohio as on the Mississippi. In the 20th century, traditional steamboating has faded away but the Ohio remains an important waterway. With locks around the Louisville rapids and a nine-foot channel maintained for its entire length, the river carries great clusters of big barges loaded with bulk cargoes and pushed by powerful diesel "tugs." There is even hope that the river, long heavily polluted with industrial waste, coal-mine drainage, and city sewage, may once again become La Belle Riviere as states and the Federal government unite to clean it up.

Before visiting the museums on the Ohio, let's take a look at the distinctive craft that developed on the Western rivers.

All the great rivers of Middle America have been highways since long before the coming of Europeans. Native Americans ran them in canoes—birch bark in the north, dugouts further south—on trading expeditions or war parties. The white settlers, however, wanted to use the rivers to transport heavy loads; the household goods and supplies of settlers moving west, and, soon, farm crops and lumber to be carried to market. Rafts and flatboats were the earliest craft. Flatboats were crude barges 20 to 60 feet long, drawing only a couple of feet fully loaded so they could pass over the innumerable shallows that clogged the creeks and rivers. They were rowed with a single huge sweep on each side, but could make headway only downstream; once they reached their destination the flatboats were broken up and sold as lumber.

The keelboat came next; the keel improved steering and the pointed bow and stern made for easier handling. They could be rowed or sailed, or poled in shallow waters. Upriver passage was possible but tediously slow and laborious as the crew poled against the current, or towed the boat along the riverbank at the end of a long hawser.

Nowhere were the new steamboats more useful than on these Western rivers that long provided the only highways through the wilderness. Flatboats and keelboats continued to be used for downriver trips, but the steamboat became the backbone of the transportation systems of the new Western states and territories.

Although descended directly from Fulton's pioneer steamboats, the vessels on the Western rivers were different from their deep-water cousins; developed into a very distinctive type in response to the different conditions found in the Mississippi Valley. The Western rivers were full of shallows and sandbars with constantly shifting channels and extremes of high and low water. The current was often swift. Passengers and freight had to be delivered and picked up (along with wood to feed the boilers) at places that were often little more than clearings on the riverbank, without a dock.

The evolution was gradual, but some characteristics eventually became universal.

Hulls were very light draft, flatbottomed, with

engines and boilers mounted on the main deck rather than in the shallow hold. Stems were raked so that the main decks overhung the bows, permitting a vessel to nose up to the river bank without damage where there was no wharf. Decks were built out from the hull along the sides. Called the "guards," these overhangs provided as much as 75 percent extra area on the main deck for cargo, protected the protruding housings for side paddle wheels, and were used as passageways fore and aft along the deck.

Engines in the Western river steamers were horizontal, using steam under high pressure—as much as 100 psi—exhausted into the air. (In contrast to Fulton's vertical engine, which condensed the steam with a jet of cold water.) The horizontal engines gave a long slow stroke, suitable to turning the big paddle wheels. They had great reserves of power, really only limited by the strength of their parts, particularly when the safety valve was tied down in a race. In the early days boiler explosions were not uncommon. The high-pressure engines were noisy, but they were cheap to buy and to repair, lighter, and more compact.

The power of later steamboats was increased by installing two engines, each with its own boiler, at the sides of the main deck. Each engine drove one paddle wheel, making it possible to turn a vessel sharply by running one wheel forward and one in reverse. The arrangement also left more center space for cargo.

Propulsion: The queens of the river fleets were side-wheelers. The huge paddles on each flank provided speed and easy handling, and their position amidships added stability and reduced vibration.

Stern-wheels had the advantage of being protected against damage if the boat hit a snag or banged against a dock. Their use enabled the hull to be wider and to draw less water, particularly useful on shallow tributaries as well as during periods of low water on the big rivers. Stern-wheelers were also superior for pushing heavy loads, and when the steamers eventually became barge pushers instead of cargo carriers the big stern-wheelers were almost universally adopted.

Today, of course, the river towboats (barge pushers) have diesel engines that drive propellers.

Fuel: The first steamboats, and those that followed for decades afterward, were wood burners. Their fuel consumption was tremendous; not only did the stacked firewood take up a lot of valuable cargo space but it was used up so quickly that the steamer had to keep stopping at wood yards along the river to refuel. Starting in the 1840s, as the hitherto seemingly endless forests began to be cut away, the steamboats became coal burners. Forty years later coal was used everywhere except on remote rivers, such as the upper Missouri. In the 20th century, the last surviving steamboats were converted to oil.

Today's diesel towboats, of course, burn their own special fuel.

Superstructure: Over the decades the steamboats kept adding decks, until the floating palaces of the mid-19th century towered over the river. In general, however, there were three principal decks, with distinctive names. Lowest was the main deck, which carried the engines and boilers as well as heavy cargo. Next above came the boiler deck, so called despite the fact that it was over the boilers. On this deck was the main cabin, used as a lounge and dining room, and the staterooms. Above this was the hurricane deck which was usually open except for a deckhouse called the Texas, which held the crew's quarters. Finally, at the top came the pilothouse, the highest point on the vessel, giving the pilot full visibility in all directions.

Now back to the rivers.

The first settlement on the Ohio River, other than illegal squatters, was built at the point where the Ohio was joined by the Muskingum River. There, in 1788, an advance party of New Englanders went to take up land that had been purchased from the federal government by the Ohio Company. The settlers, who included Harvard and Yale graduates, had strong New England ties and included many former officers in the Continental Army. They named their town Marietta in honor of Queen Marie Antoinette of France as an expression of gratitude for French aid to the Colonies during the American Revolution. In the course of time Marietta became a prosperous Ohio River town with a considerable shipbuilding industry.

As Ohio's first settlement, Marietta is naturally very conscious of its historic past. Of special interest to the maritime enthusiast is the Ohio River Museum. Housed in three buildings raised on stilts and connected by covered walkways, the museum has a fine model collection, riverboat artifacts, and the oldest surviving steamer pilothouse. Tied up to the bank of the Muskingum River next to the museum buildings is a stern-wheel steam towboat, veteran of 35 active years on the Ohio River and its tributaries. The *W.P. Snyder, Jr.* (ex *A-1*, ex *J.L. Perry*, ex *W.H. Clingerman*) was built in 1918; today, the steel-hulled, 175-foot vessel is one of the last of her breed, replaced by diesel-powered vessel.

Steamboat specialists will take note of *Snyder*'s low pilothouse, designed to permit her to pass under low bridges on the Monongahela River, where she pushed coal barges. Also of particular interest is her "hogchain" cable support system that keeps her from buckling in the center. Stateroom and cabin construction, engine-room telegraph, and pilot wheel follow traditional riverboat design.

One building of the museum focuses on the discovery and exploration of Ohio's many rivers. The displays include a diorama of a river habitat of 200 years ago. Exhibits in a second museum building concentrate on the development of river steamboats. Here there are many models of historic vessels of the past, including not only the famous *Robert E. Lee*, and Roosevelt's *New Orleans* that inaugurated steamboating on the western rivers, but less widely known steamboats such as the *Sunshine, Homer Smith* and *Betsy Ann*. Artifacts from river steamers and graphics tie the exhibits together.

A third building is concerned with more recent river activities. Here, the models and artifacts are of modern diesel towboats.

Beside the *Snyder*, the Ohio River Museum has several other river craft on display. Among them is the

dugout canoe that was the original ferry between frontier Marietta and Fort Harmon across the Muskingum. Other craft include a full-scale reproduction of a flatboat similar to those that brought the earliest settlers floating down the Ohio, and a 19th-century river skiff.

Other exhibits include the pilothouse from the steamer *Tell City*, the oldest known to survive, and engines from the ferry *Oweva*.

The museum was initiated by the Sons and Daughters of Pioneer Rivermen, which lent many of the exhibits. It is a facility of the Ohio Historical Society, which has its headquarters in Marietta as well, a general historical museum a block away on the same grounds as the River Museum. There, at the Campus

Figure 44
S.S. *W.P. Snyder, Jr.*, veteran sternwheel steam tugboat, shown here on the river at Pittsburgh, Pennsylvania, is now on display at the Ohio River Museum in Marietta, Ohio.

Martius State Memorial Museum, is preserved one of the original fortified houses built by the first settlers as a refuge against Indian attacks.

Also nearby, at Washington and Front Street, is the wharf of the *Valley Gem*, a modern replica sternwheeler that cruises along the Muskingum and Ohio rivers on weekends and holiday afternoons in spring and fall, and every afternoon but Monday during June, July, and August.

The Ohio River Museum is at Washington and Front Streets on the Muskingum River at the foot of St. Clair Street, in Marietta, Ohio. Open March through November. Hours: March, April, October, November, Wednesday-Saturday, 9:30 a.m. to 5 p.m.; Sunday, noon to 5 p.m. May through September, Monday-Saturday, 9:30 a.m. to 5 p.m.; Sunday, noon to 5 p.m. Admission: $2.00; youths, $1.00; children, free. A facility of Ohio Historical Society. Ohio River Museum, c/o Campus Martius Museum, 601 Second Street, Marietta, Ohio 45750. Telephone (614) 373-3750.

Steamboats were built in many places along the Western rivers, but a major source were the towns along the Ohio. Between 1820 and 1880, the Ohio River shipyards turned out some 6,000 vessels: Pittsburgh, Wheeling, Marietta, Cincinnati, and the Indiana towns of Madison and New Albany all launched famous steamboats. One of the largest and most successful yards was the Howard Shipyard and Dock Company at Jeffersonville, Indiana. Here were built the Anchor Line packets and such well-known steamboats as *John W. Cannon*, *Natchez*, *Belle of the Bends*, *Spread Eagle IV*, and *J.M. White III*, 1878; the latter has been described as "probably the finest and fastest boat in the Western river service."

Jeffersonville is a river town on the Ohio opposite Louisville. The Howard yard operated from 1834 to 1941 and its memory is kept fresh by a unique museum, located in the Howard family mansion across the road from the riverbank site of the yard itself.

Figure 45
Sternwheeler *Belle of Louisville* is one of last surviving passenger riverboats. Based in the Ohio River at Louisville, Kentucky, she takes visitors on short cruises, and races each year against her rival steamboat, *Delta Queen* of Cincinnati.

The Howard Steamboat Museum naturally focuses primarily on the Howard family, and many of the exhibits are artifacts from the yard. The first floor of the big 22-room house, built in 1890, is devoted to the Howards and their way of life. The two upper floors tell the story of the shipyard and the steamboats on the river. A fine model collection includes the *Natchez*, *Sprague*, *Tell City*, and *Cape Girardeau*. Here, also, are the builder's half-hulls from the shipyard.

A number of steamboat engines are also on display. Of special interest is the huge pilot wheel of the steamboat *Northern*. The earliest river activities are represented by a collection of miniature Indian canoes. The graphics display—paintings, prints, and photographs of riverboat activity—is highlighted by such treasures as a painting of the SS *J.M. White*, the floating palace of 1878.

Howard Steamboat Museum is in Jeffersonville, Indiana, across the Ohio River from Louisville; turn off east from I-65. Open all year, every day except holidays (Christmas, New Year's, Easter, Memorial Day, Labor Day). Hours: Monday-Saturday, 10 a.m. to 3 p.m.; Sunday, 1 to 3 p.m. Admission: $1.50; students and seniors, 75 cents; children, 50 cents. Sponsored by Clark County Historical Society. Howard Steamboat Museum, 1100 Market Street, Jeffersonville, Indiana 47130. Telephone (812) 283-3728.

Visitors who want a taste of steamboating on the Ohio can embark on a river ride on the *Belle of Louisville*. This 1914 stern-wheeler has been restored as a day cruiser and is based on the Louisville river front. Now 170 feet long, more than 12 feet more than her original length, she draws only four to five feet. Originally coal-fired, her boilers are now oil-fired, and her hull has now been divided into 35 watertight compartments.

In her long career, the *Belle* started out as a Memphis-based day packet but later became an excursion boat. In World War II she was put to work towing barges. Over the years, she has steamed all over the Western rivers, from Omaha on the Missouri to Pittsburgh at the head of the Ohio, from New Orleans to Stillwater, Minnesota, many hundreds of miles up Old Man River to the north. Now the *Belle* cruises every afternoon from Memorial Day to Labor Day, with twilight and evening cruises once a week.

Belle of Louisville is berthed in the Ohio River at Louisville, Kentucky. Annual spring steamboat race with SS *Delta Queen* at Kentucky Derby time. Operates Memorial Day through Labor Day. Monday-Saturday, call ahead for hours. Open balance of the year for private cruises. Fare: $5; seniors, $4.50; children, $2.50. Belle of Louisville, Fourth Street and River Road, Louisville, Kentucky 40202. Telephone (502) 582-2547. (Winter address: 27th Street and Portland Canal, Louisville, Kentucky 40212. Telephone (502) 778-6651.)

Before going on to the Mississippi, we'll take a look at the canals that once linked the Ohio River to the Great Lakes.

From Lake to River: The Canals of Ohio and Indiana

There's a little silver ribbon runs across the Buckeye State,
'Tis the dearest place of all the earth to me,
For upon its placid surface I was born some years ago
And its beauty, grandeur, always do I see.
Cleveland is the northern end and Portsmouth is the south,
While its side cuts they are many, many, Pal
And where e'er we went we took along our
Home, Sweet Home, you know,
In those balmy days upon the old canal.

So, according to the Ohio Historical Society, the canalboat people sang about their life on the Ohio & Erie Canal, built in the early 19th century to connect Lake Erie, at Cleveland, with the Ohio River, at Portsmouth.

John Quincy Adams, former president of the United States, had less happy memories of a ride he took on the canal in the 1840s.

. . . [we] took passage on the canal boat Rob Roy. This boat is 83 feet long, fifteen feet wide and had about 20 other passengers. It is divided into six compartments, the first in the bow, with two settee beds, for the ladies, separated by a curtain from a parlor bed-chamber, with an iron stove in the center, and side settees on one of which four of us slept, feet to feet; then a bulging stable for four horses, two by two by turns, and a narrow passage, with a side settee for one passenger to sleep on, leading to the third compartment; a dining hall and dormitory for thirty persons and lastly, a kitchen and cooking apparatus with sleeping room for cook, steward and crew and necessary conveniences.

So much humanity crowded into such a compass was a trial such as I had never before experienced . . . and I reflected that I am to pass three nights and four days in it . . .

The most uncomfortable part of our navigation is caused by the careless and unskilled steering of the boat in and through the locks, which seem to be numberless . . . The boat scarcely escapes a heavy thump on entering every one of them. She strikes and grazes against their sides, and staggers along like a stumbling nag . . .

Despite ex-President Adam's grumbling, travel on the Ohio & Erie was probably a good deal more comfortable than riding a stagecoach on country roads. Certainly it was cheap: The full 80-hour trip from Cleveland to Portsmouth cost $1.70. In any case, the primary function of the canal was to carry freight, not passengers. In this the Ohio & Erie was a great success; for a quarter of a century, the 308-mile ditch bisecting the state north and south was of the greatest economic importance to Ohio.

The O & E was started hard on the heels of the Erie Canal and finished seven years later, in 1832. While the Ohio & Erie never achieved the legendary fame of Clinton's Ditch, mainly because it was never part of the great emigrant route to Western lands, the canal was a major factor in opening up the farmlands of central Ohio. Wheat sales at Cleveland jumped from 1,000 to 250,000 bushels a year. The cost of manufactures from the East dropped with the drop in transportation costs. Little towns sprang up along the canal route, particularly at the locks—there were 44 of them—where passengers and crews ate and drank away the time while waiting for their boat to be locked through. Coal and iron deposits were developed now that there was a way to carry away the product, while water flow from the spillways drove grist mills, saw mills, and woolen mills.

And the work of building the canal brought a much needed cash flow to the frontier barter economy. The canal was dug largely with pick and shovel; the laborers, mostly local settlers and immigrant Germans and Irish, earned 30 cents a day. As the route skirted mosquito-haunted swamps, they died by the hundreds from malaria and other epidemics.

The Ohio & Erie cost four and a quarter million dollars, but it more than paid off the cost in tolls. Traffic reached its peak in 1852; after that, the newly arrived railroads increasingly took away its customers. The canal survived, however, until 1913, when devastating floods washed it out and practically destroyed it. Today, most of the canal has been filled in; in several places highways run along the old bed. Only a branch called the Muskingum Improvement, extending 91 miles from the Ohio River at Marietta north to Dresden, remains in use, now greatly deepened and enlarged for barges and their towboats.

However, visitors can still get a taste of what it was like to travel on the Ohio & Erie 150 years ago. At two places along the route where the canal survives, replicas of the original canalboats, drawn by horses or mules, offer short rides through the countryside.

As its name makes clear, the village of Canal Fulton was born when the Ohio & Erie built lock 4 there, 35 miles south of Akron and 56 miles from the northern end of the canal at Cleveland. Today, some 90 buildings survive from the great canal era, when the town was not only a station but originated cargoes of wheat and coal.

An energetic group of volunteers, organized as the Canal Fulton Heritage Society, have built the *St. Helena II*, which they call the first authentically built canalboat in the country. Sixty feet on the keel, the *St. Helena* weighs 22 tons empty and draws a foot and a half of water. Volunteers worked 15,000 hours (in addition to 1,000 man-hours paid labor) on her construction; she is built of one-and-a-half-inch oak planks. Designed to represent a typical canal freight boat, she now takes visitors on a trip along a surviving stretch of the Ohio & Erie, drawn by two sturdy mules.

The regular trip lasts a little less than an hour. Lock 4 has now been restored, however, and passengers on the final trips Saturdays and Sundays are taken down through the lock and back up again for the return trip. The lock gates are opened and closed by hand just as in the old days.

The Canal Fulton Heritage Society also sponsors two museums in the village and one of them, the Canal Days Museum in the Heritage House, a one-time saloon, displays a collection of canal photographs and memorabilia, maps, and tools used by canal workmen. There are also guided walking tours.

St. Helena II, reproduction canalboat, operates on surviving portion of Ohio and Erie Canal at village of Canal Fulton, Ohio. Walking tours. Special events. Restaurants. Rides: June, July, August, Tuesday-Saturday, 1:30, 2:30, 3:30 p.m.; Sunday, same, plus 4:30 p.m. May and September 1 to October 15, rides Saturday and Sunday only, same times. (Mules rest Mondays.) Tickets: $3.00; seniors, $2.50; children 2-12, $1.50. Operated by Canal Fulton Heritage Society, P.O. Box 584, Canal Fulton, Ohio 44614. Telephone (216) 854-3808.

Canal rides are also to be had at Roscoe Village, some 75 miles further south on the Ohio & Erie, across the Muskingum River from Coshocton.

There was a frontier settlement at Roscoe Village, where the Walhonding and Tuscanawas rivers join to form the Muskingum, but it was the coming of the Canal, with triple locks nearby, that turned it into a prosperous town. Beside becoming a substantial wheat and wool shipping canal port, Roscoe developed many retail businesses and services, as well as small industries such as cooperages, brickyards, foundries, and potteries.

But like most towns that lived by the canal, Roscoe almost died by it. As the canal traffic disappeared, so did Roscoe's prosperity. Finally in the 1960s, a restora-

Figure 46
Mules provide the motive power for today's recreated canalboats as they did for the original craft 150 years ago. Here a team hauls the *St. Helena II* along the Ohio and Erie Canal at Canal Fulton, Ohio.

tion project started by a Coshocton businessman led to the formation of a nonprofit foundation dedicated to preserving the old village.

In the old canal Toll House, one of the buildings now restored and on display with costumed staff, there are canal-era artifacts, model canalboats, and a working model demonstrating the operation of double locks.

A reconstructed canalboat, the *Monticello II*, offers rides on the surviving portion of the Ohio & Erie Canal. The trips take about 45 minutes and leave from the end of the Towpath Trail, about a mile north of the village.

Reconstructed Canalboat *Monticello II*, on Ohio and Erie Canal near Coshocton, Ohio, about 100 miles south of Cleveland. Offers rides on canal weekends, mid-May to June 1 and after Labor Day to mid-October; daily, June 1 through Labor Day. Hours 1 to 5 p.m. Ride lasts 45 minutes; departures hourly. Tickets: $2.50; seniors, $2.25; 8-18, $1.25. Owned and operated by City of Coshocton. Monticello II, P.O. Box 644, Coshocton, Ohio 43812. Telephone (614) 622-3415. Canal toll house in nearby Roscoe Village. Historical museum nearby; both open year round, except Thanksgiving, Christmas, New Year's. April through December, 11 a.m. to 5 p.m.; January through March, limited schedule. Ticket for self-guided tour of exhibit buildings, including toll house: $4.00; 8-18, $2.00; children, free. Operated by private nonprofit foundation. Roscoe Village Foundation, 381 Hill Street, Coshocton, Ohio 43812. Telephone (614) 622-9310.

Eventually, a second canal, the Miami & Erie, was built all the way across the state of Ohio, north and south between Lake Erie and the Ohio River. This second waterway, some historians say, was born of the need to win the support of the southwestern Ohio counties for spending state money to build the Ohio & Erie; voters in the southwest of the state were promised a canal of their own, to run from Cincinnati to Dayton with a future extension all the way north to Toledo. The Miami & Erie Canal was started the same year as the Ohio & Erie, 1825 and reached Dayton four years later, in 1829. Progress on the northern extension was delayed by lack of funds and political disputes, however, and the *Banner*, the first boat through the entire length, didn't make the passage from Cincinnati to Toledo until 1845.

The Miami & Erie played an important role in the development of Dayton as a flourishing manufacturing town, but the through route was completed too late to be profitable. The railroads were already pushing westward and after the mid-1850s the canal systems did not pay off.

Today, a few stretches of the Miami & Erie survive. On one of them, near Piqua, Ohio, visitors can go for a ride on the replica 1840s passenger/cargo canalboat *General Harrison*.

An Indian village near Piqua was a major fur-trading post in the 18th century and eventually Fort Piqua was built there on the frontier. The house and farm of the Indian agent who lived there in the early 19th century have been restored and are now part of the Piqua Historical Area. Not far from the house is the landing on the Miami and Erie Canal where visitors embark on the *General Harrison*. The trip, in which the canalboat is drawn by mules, covers about a mile of the restored canal.

The Historical Area, a facility of the Ohio Historical Society, also includes a museum of artifacts, a prehistoric earthwork, and various farm buildings.

***General Harrison*,** replica of 19th century canalboat, offers rides on surviving portion of Miami and Erie Canal at Piqua Historical Area on Route 66, 3 1/2 miles north of Piqua, Ohio. Open Memorial Day through Labor Day, Wednesday-Saturday, 9:30 a.m. to 5 p.m., Sunday, noon to 5 p.m. September through October, Saturday, 9:30 a.m. to 5 p.m., Sunday, noon to 5 p.m. Rides leave 12:30, 1, 2, 3, 4 p.m., weather permitting. Ticket included in admission to Piqua Historical Area: $3.00; under 12, free. Piqua Historical Area, 9845 North Harding Road, Piqua, Ohio 45356. Telephone (513) 773-2522.

Like Ohio, Indiana saw in canals the answer to one of its big problems—getting the crops of its frontier farmers to market. A canal from the St. Joseph River in northeast Indiana to the Wabash River in the west provided a water route across the state from Lake Erie to the Ohio River in 1835, but was eventually abandoned. Soon afterward an elaborate state plan for a network of canals and railroads was financed by $10 million in state bonds, but speculation, financial panics, depression—and the inevitable triumph of rails over ditches—ruined the project and it collapsed before many years.

Among the projected canals was the Whitewater, planned to run from Indianapolis to Cincinnati on the Ohio River. A portion was built, but the full route was never finished. Today, however, a 14-mile stretch survives in southeastern Indiana and has been made part of the Whitewater Canal State Memorial, a park near the restored canal village of Metamora.

A canalboat has been built according to the plans of the 19th century originals, and visitors can ride it along a two-mile stretch of canal. The section includes an operating lock. Metamora Village has old houses of the canal era, craft shops, a restored grist mill, and restaurants.

Whitewater Canal State Memorial, just south of Metamora, Indiana, on Route 52, southeast of Indianapolis. Small museum. Bookstore. Canalboat rides operate from mid-April to October 31, Wednesday-Saturday, 9 a.m. to 5 p.m. Sunday and Tuesday, noon to 5 p.m. Closed Mondays, and all holidays except Memorial Day, July 4, Labor Day. Fare: 75 cents; under 12, free. Information: Whitewater State Memorial, c/o Indiana State Museum and Memorial, 202 North Alabama Street, Indianapolis, Indiana 46204. Telephone (317) 232-1634, or, at Memorial (317) 647-6512.

Now back to the rivers—and the mightiest of all.

IX
THE MISSISSIPPI

Old Man River I:
The Lower Mississippi and the Arkansas River
Old Man River II: The Upper Mississippi
Big Muddy: The Missouri

Old Man River I: The Lower Mississippi and the Arkansas River

No river in America has so gripped and held the imagination of the American people as the mighty Mississippi. The river's immense size, draining the whole heart of the North American continent; catastrophic floods, when the Mississippi overflows and challenges human ingenuity to contain its terrible forces; the colorful people who have lived along it ashore and afloat; the great steamboats that once raced hundreds of miles between its ports; the Civil War battles that raged on its waters and its banks—all these have given the Mississippi a unique place in the consciousness of Americans. At the same time, the maritime, or riverine, contributions of the Mississippi have been of the greatest economic importance, providing the highways for pioneer farmers to send their crops to market and still carrying much of the grain and soybeans of the upper Midwest down to the Gulf of Mexico. And to top it all, one of the greatest of American writers was born on its banks, worked on its waters, and made the river the setting for his works.

From its very beginning, no city has been more closely associated with commerce on the Mississippi than Memphis, the river town par excellence. Chickasaw Bluff, on which the little frontier village of Memphis sprang up around 1820, had attracted human activity long before. The Mississippi River at its foot habitually overran its banks and flooded the

countryside; the Bluff rose 40 feet above high water and provided a dry camp ground for the Chickasaws, a safe stopping place for travelers up and down the river, and a logical site for French and Spanish colonial governors to plant forts. On its bluff, Memphis continued to grow as the bottomlands around it became rich cotton plantations, until eventually it became the great steamboat port of the middle Mississippi.

Fought over in the Civil War, Memphis survived to grow and flourish as a commercial center, despite devastating epidemics in the late 19th century. Today, the river city is the metropolis of a great region, a financial and commercial center—and still a river town that cherishes the heritage of its long and close association with the Mississippi.

In *Life on the Mississippi*, Mark Twain explained why the big river steamers, which disappointed Charles Dickens, seemed like "floating palaces" to people who lived along the Mississippi:

When he [a passenger from a Mississippi River town] stepped aboard a fine steamboat, he entered a new and marvelous world: chimney-tops cut to counterfeit a spraying crown of plumes—and maybe painted red; pilot-house, hurricane deck, boiler-deckguards, all garnished with white wooden filagree work of fanciful patterns; gilt acorns topping the derricks; gilt deer-horns over the big bell; gaudy symbolical pictures on the paddle box, possibly; big room boiler-deck, painted blue, and furnished with

Windsor arm-chairs; inside, a far receding snow-white "cabin"; porcelain knob and oil-picture on every stateroom door; curving patterns of filagree-work touched up with gilding, stretching overhead all down the converging vista; big chandeliers every little way, each an April shower of glittering glass-drops; lovely rainbow-light falling everywhere from the colored glazing of the skylights; the whole long-drawn resplendent tunnel, a bewildering and soul-satisfying spectacle! in the ladies cabin a pink and white Wilton carpet, soft as mush, and glorified with a ravishing pattern of gigantic flowers . . . . Every state-room had its couple of cozy clean bunks, and perhaps a looking-glass and a snug closet; and sometimes there was even a washbowl and pitcher, and part of a towel which could be told from mosquito netting by an expert—though generally these things were absent, and the shirt-sleeved passengers cleansed themselves at a long row of stationary bowls in the barber shop, where there were also public towels, public combs, and public soap.

Take the steamboat that I have just described, and you have her in her highest and finest, and most pleasing, and most comfortable, and satisfactory estate. . .

Mark Twain, *Life on the Mississippi*, Chapter 38

The last of the great Mississippi River steamers of the Mark Twain era vanished long ago. However, the traveler can have at least the illusion of stepping aboard one in a fine museum dedicated to the river in Memphis, Tennessee. On the upper level of the Mississippi River Museum is a full-scale reproduction of the forward third of an 1870s steamboat, the *Belle of the Bluffs*. Here you can wander through the pilothouse and the ladies cabins, see the grand lounge, and listen—thanks to the wonders of modern technology—to throbbing engines, lapping waters, and the conversations of passengers and crew.

The simulated Belle is only one of the extremely interesting exhibits at the Mississippi River Museum on Mud Island, a short distance out in the river off downtown Memphis. In another gallery, the visitor is startled to find Mark Twain himself telling about his life on the Mississippi. Of course, it is an animated figure but it looks so realistic in the darkened gallery that for at least a moment you are convinced that you are listening to Sam Clemens reminiscing.

Maritime activities on the Mississippi began well before steamboats arrived; in the museum a particularly fine display of scale models shows the evolution of Mississippi River transportation from the very beginning. Starting with the log rafts of 1700, the sequence includes the flatboats of the early 1800s, the keelboats of a few years later, and finally such side-wheel packet steamers as the *George Washington* of 1825. Many other models show the immense variety of Mississippi River craft: showboats, ferries, dredges,

snagboats. A 15-foot model portrays the diesel towboats and barges of today. All are carefully explained with good captions and illustrative pictures.

In another gallery are the silver pitcher and cups given to a Mississippi River steamboat captain for saving lives from a burning steamer in 1855. The "Theater of River Disasters" tells of bad times on the Mississippi: steamer blowups, collisions, ice jams, earthquakes. One gallery is devoted to the engineering of the river: levees, dikes, bridges, spillways, and channels.

And, of course, no Mississippi River museum would be complete without the music which burst forth along its banks—ragtime, blues, jazz—and spread across the nation. There are exhibits of musical scores and instruments and the music itself is played for the visitor.

Many of the river actions of the Civil War were fought not too far from Memphis itself. A full-size mock-up of a portion of the gun-deck of a Union gunboat surrounds the visitor with the sounds of a battle against a Confederate shore battery. In the adjacent Civil War gallery are models of the Union and Confederate gunboats and rams that fought it out on the river; artifacts from the ships themselves; and a special display of Civil War medical equipment, particularly relevant to Memphis, which was a Union hospital depot during much of the Civil War.

This is a fine museum and one which anybody visiting the Central Mississippi Valley should see to get a clearer idea of the past and the historical significance of this great river. The Mississippi River Museum was built by the city of Memphis and can be reached from the city's riverfront either dramatically, by an aerial monorail; or prosaically, by a walkway over a pedestrian bridge. Two floors of the five-story River Center on Mud Island, which is also the terminal building for the monorail, are given over to museum exhibits; others are devoted to craft shops and restaurants. Surrounding the center is a 50-acre park in the midst of which is a magnificent 2,000-foot-long reproduction to scale of the entire Mississippi River system with all its tributaries. Water flows through the mini rivers from the uppermost reaches near the Canadian border to where they all join together in Old Man River and just keep rollin' along until at last they reach the gulf of Mexico.

The Mississippi River Museum is on Mud Island, opposite Adams Street and Riverside Drive, Memphis, Tennessee. Riverside Drive is the northern continuation of Route 55 segment of circular expressway; parking at mainland terminal of bridge and memorial. Paddlewheel excursion boats dock at island. Shops. Picnic ground. Open all year. Daily, April through October, 10 a.m. to 10 p.m.; November through March, 10 a.m. to 3:30 p.m. Admission: $4.00; children, $2.50. Supported by city of Memphis. Mississippi River Museum, Mud Island, 125 N. Main Street, Memphis, Tennessee 38103. Telephone (901) 576-7241.

Now we'll head downriver to a museum which focuses on the days when the river was a battlefield and the riverboats were fighting ships.

On the Yazoo River, the morning of December 12, 1862, dawned cool and cloudy. The Yazoo is a tributary of the Mississippi, entering just above Vicksburg, and a little Union Navy flotilla was steaming upstream to reconnoiter Confederate activities. Second in line was the heavy gunboat *Cairo*, a 175-foot Eads double-ender, flatbottomed for work in shallow waters. Armored with two-and-a-half-inch iron plates, she carried a 13-gun battery; altogether a formidable veteran of combat on the Mississippi.

As the *Cairo* proceeded up the river, the light gunboat ahead of her, the *Marmora*, was destroying floats to which the Confederates had attached mines. These mines (then called "submarine torpedoes") were made by filling five-gallon glass whiskey demijohns with black gunpowder, putting a primer in the neck, then wiring it to an electric battery ashore. When the circuit to the battery was closed, the current set off the primer and exploded the mine. Very primitive but potentially deadly.

The captain of the *Cairo* grew impatient of clearing the mines, particularly when distant Confederate shore batteries opened fire, and ordered his powerful vessel to push ahead up the channel. At this point, 11:55 a.m., there were two explosions, one under the port quarter, the other under the starboard bow. The *Cairo* began to fill rapidly and the captain headed for the riverbank. As she ran ashore, the crew escaped onto the land or into boats, but the vessel slid off the bank and settled into the water. A total loss, she went to the river bottom in just 12 minutes.

In the chronicles of the Civil War, this was a minor incident; but in the history of naval warfare, it was a historic moment. For the first time, a warship had been sunk by a submarine mine fired by electricity. For the crew and officers of the *Cairo* it was devastating; they had lost their ship and, incidentally, all their personal possessions. One more Union vessel gone to the bottom, victim of the desperate ingenuity of the Confederate engineers. No more *Cairo*.

Only, by a freak of history, this turned out not to be true. Today, the sunken *Cairo*, lifted from the river bottom and brought ashore, is the only survivor of the scores of Union gunboats that fought and won a desperately important campaign of the Civil War on the Mississippi and its tributary rivers. The gunboat's

remains can be visited at Vicksburg, only a few miles from where she was sunk, where she acts as a reminder of the importance of naval warfare on inland waters in the Civil War.

Visitors will find *Cairo* at the extreme northwestern end of the semi-circular battlefield park that preserves the entrenchments of the siege of Vicksburg. The *Cairo*—or what's left of her—rests in an open shed, protected by a roof from erosion by sun and rain. The pieces that survive include portions of her armor, planking, and beams, her guns, and the great propulsion wheel in the stern. These have been mounted on a wooden framework that fixes them in the same relative positions that they had originally.

To get a really good idea of what the *Cairo* was originally like, however, the visitor should be sure to take a look at the small museum of the National Park Service on the hillside next to the gunboat. Here, a scale model of the remains on their supporting structure is displayed next to a model of the *Cairo* as she originally appeared, built according to her plans, which have survived. By comparing the two it is easy to visualize how the original vessel looked and the role of each of the parts that have been salvaged.

Because the *Cairo* sank so quickly, the crew had no time to save either the ship's gear or their personal possessions. Much of these were found still in place aboard the gunboat when she was raised, remarkably well-preserved by the Yazoo mud, which had formed an airtight seal. The considerable supply of live ammunition was gingerly taken ashore and exploded by a U.S. Navy demolition team. Thousands of artifacts were removed, cleaned, and identified: the mess gear of officers and crew, the galley equipment, wine, whiskey, soft drinks, boots, medicines, combs, toothbrushes, pens and pencils, neckerchiefs and ribbons (silk; wool and cotton disintegrated), personal jewelry, leisure-time carvings, pipes (both kinds), fifes, dominoes, muskets, revolvers, and so on and so on.

All of these treasures have added greatly to the interest and importance of the salvage of the *Cairo*. The weapons and gear tell the naval historian a good deal not previously known about the equipment of the river gunboats. At the same time, the personal items give even the most casual viewer some sense of personal contact with these young men of long ago. Over 1,200 artifacts are on display in the museum.

The preservation of the *Cairo* did not come easily. The position of the sunken gunboat on the bottom of the Yazoo was known roughly, and in 1956 she was located more precisely magnetically and by probing the mud. Eventually, in the 1960s, the remains of the gunboat were lifted from the bottom. Unhappily, at that point the funds ran out and for many years the poor old *Cairo*, having lost her protective coating of mud, deteriorated in the hot sun and searing breezes of the Gulf Coast where she had been deposited in a shipyard. Finally, historically-minded congressmen voted Federal funds that enabled the remains to be taken back up the Mississippi and installed at the Vicksburg Battlefield Parks, a unique exhibit.

USS Cairo Museum is on a hillside overlooking the Yazoo Canal (formerly Mississippi River) at the extreme northeastern end of Military Park Tour Road, next to National Cemetery. Open every day, 8 a.m. to 5 p.m. Admission: free. Operated by National Park Service, U.S.S. Cairo Museum, Union and Connecting Avenues, Vicksburg National Military Park, 3201 Clay Street, Vicksburg, Mississippi 39180. Telephone (601) 636-2199.

Before leaving the lower Mississippi, some visitors may want to take a side trip up the Arkansas, which enters the Mississippi from the west between Memphis and Vicksburg. Close to the head of navigation, at Muskogee, Oklahoma, is a notable fighting ship of World War II.

Muskogee is in the heart of what was until fairly recently Indian Territory and it seems natural to find there the Five Civilized Tribes Museum. Most visitors are likely to be pretty surprised, however, to find that another major museum in this small city, many hundreds of miles as the crow flies from the nearest salt water, is a blue-water ship—and no ordinary one at that but one of the fightingest ships in the U.S. Navy of World War II.

There she sits, the submarine *Batfish*, all 312 feet of her, drydocked at the edge of the Arkansas River. A museum and war memorial, the *Batfish* in her retirement is bringing the United States Navy to the attention of a region more likely to be concerned with cattle ranches and oil wells than naval warfare.

Not but what Muskogee has actually been a port ever since 1971, thanks to an elaborate chain of dams and locks on the Arkansas River. These have opened navigation to substantial vessels all the way up to Tulsa. Thus it was possible to bring the 1,465-ton *Batfish* up some 800 miles of inland rivers from the Gulf of Mexico to her new home.

The submarine brought with her a most impressive combat record. Commissioned in 1943, in seven combat patrols in the Western Pacific *Batfish* sank some 37,000 tons of enemy shipping. In a little more than a year and a half she sank 14 Japanese ships and damaged three others. Other activities included picking up downed American fliers. The high point of her career was her sixth patrol in February, 1945, which drew an unusual comment from the Commander, Submarine Force Pacific:

> This illustrious patrol was outstanding in every sense of the word. The splendid planning, judgment and daring displayed in the attacks is best described in the fact that three enemy submarines were destroyed in a period of four days.

For these activities, members of *Batfish*'s crew were awarded ten bronze stars, four silver stars, and a Navy cross, in addition to a Presidential Unit Citation.

All of this historic vessel is now open to visitors except the conning tower.

USS Batfish, World War II submarine, is drydocked at edge of Arkansas River in Muskogee, Oklahoma, in Port of Muskogee, off Muskogee Turnpike. Watch for highway signs. Open daily March 15 to October 15. Monday-Saturday, 9 a.m. to 5 p.m.; Sunday, noon to 5 p.m. Admission: $1.50; children 6 to 16, 75 cents. Oklahoma Maritime Advisory Board, P.O. Box 253, Muskogee, Oklahoma 74401. Telephone (918) 682-6294.

Old Man River II: The Upper Mississippi

Steamboats came later to the Upper Mississippi, north of where the Ohio flows in at Cairo, Illinois—or at least to that portion above the mouth of the Missouri, just above St. Louis—than to the lower river. Not until 1823 did the little steamboat *Virginia* work its way almost 700 miles up the Mississippi to where the Falls of St. Anthony closed all further navigation at what was to become St. Paul, Minnesota. For a decade afterward the region remained Indian country; most of the few steamboats on the upper river were troop carriers, moving soldiers to frontier posts. Only after the Sacs and Foxes lost their last battle for their homeland in the Black Hawk War did white settlers start pouring in.

The steamboats did not find the Upper Mississippi an easy waterway into the northland. For one thing, the river froze over for four months or so in the winter; an average of 143 days at St. Paul, while even at St. Louis there was more than a month of ice. In the spring, melting snow and ice sent great freshets sweeping downriver making navigation dangerous. At other times, the water level dropped so low that there was not enough water over the shallows and rapids to float a steamboat.

Two such hazards on the upper river were made even worse by low water. North of where the Des Moines River enters at Keokuk were the dangerous Des Moines rapids, created by a limestone ledge running across the Mississippi River bed; the rapids closed the river at this point to all but the smallest vessels even at normal water levels. As far back as the 1830s, Lieutenant Robert E. Lee of the Army Engineers had urged that a canal with locks be built to carry vessels past these rapids, but it was almost half a century before it was done. The second hazard was north of Rock Island, near Davenport, Iowa, where there was another set of dangerous rapids.

Until the rapids were tamed by locks and canals, the steamboats that served the Upper Mississippi river towns struggled as best they could with ice, freshets, low water, and rapids. Inevitably there were delays, and sometimes wrecks. All this made it difficult for the riverboats to compete when the new railroads reached the river in the 1850s. The Civil War slowed change, but in the postwar decades the railroads, which were faster than steamboats, able to go anywhere, and kept fairly regular schedules the year round, took over passenger traffic and general freight in the upper river region.

For a while, the construction of locks and canals, as well as dams and sluices to keep the river channel scoured free of shallows and sandbars, enabled barges to take over as freight carriers; they were powered by stern-wheel steamers—"towboats," even though they pushed instead of towed. By the turn of the century, however, even the bulk cargoes were being carried by rail.

What brought freight traffic back to the river was World War I. The railroads couldn't handle the enormous increase in shipments and in 1918 the Federal government started a barge line to carry the overload. River operations proved so successful that after the war Congress financed a river improvement campaign. First the Ohio River and then the Upper Mississippi, were completely "canalized" with dams and locks, thus ensuring a constant water level in the channel all the way to the head of navigation. When, in 1939, the last stretch of Old Man River was locked-in, there were 26 locks and dams between St. Louis and St. Paul.

Meanwhile, towboat efficiency was increased by replacing the stern-wheel steamers with vessels powered by diesel engines driving propellers. Today steamboats survive mostly as museums, but barge traffic on the Mississippi and its tributaries remains an important part of the nation's transportation system.

Before we start looking at the Upper Mississippi steamboats and museums, we'll pause for a brief visit to a blue water naval vessel that has found a retirement home at St. Louis.

Mines started sinking fighting ships at least as long ago as the Civil War (when they were called "torpedoes") and continue to be an important naval weapon to this day. As recently as the Korean War, the U.S. Marine landing at Wonson was held up for 15 days by the need to sweep approach paths through the mines that blocked the harbor. Minesweepers, vessels that clear away enemy mine fields, have become a valued element in our naval forces.

Navy buffs will have a hard time, however, locating vessels or museum artifacts related to this important but little publicized service: There are only three minesweepers among some 60-odd vessels in the U.S. Navy's list of historic naval ships preserved in the United States. One is the MSB-Minesweeping Boat, built in the fifties, now at a museum near Fort Worth, Texas. The other two are veterans of the 185-foot "Admirable" class, 795-ton vessels built in 1944.

One of the Admirables is the USS *Inaugural*, moored to the Mississippi River bank at St. Louis, just below the famous Gateway Arch. The *Inaugural* won two battle stars in the last months of the War in the Pacific where she patrolled off the beachhead at the Okinawa landing, fighting off both enemy submarines and kamikazes. After the Japanese surrender, the sweeper returned to her regular duties; she was credited with clearing 84 mines from the harbors of Japan, Korea, and Saipan.

Inaugural was decommissioned in 1946 and spent many years in the mothballed reserve fleet before being restored and placed on exhibition. She is said to retain most of her wartime mine detection and sweeping gear. Work is continuing to completely return her to her original appearance, but most of the vessel is already open to visitors.

The nearby Museum of Western Expansion, underground under the Gateway Arch, has little of maritime or riverine interest other than a wall of fine photo murals of Mississippi river steamboats. However, one exhibit displays, without identification, what appears to be one of the famous "Buffalo boats" used by Indians on the Upper Mississippi and Missouri rivers. Much like an Irish coracle in appearance, the saucer-shaped craft consists of a buffalo skin stretched, fur outward, over a roughly circular wooden framework about five feet in diameter and a couple of feet deep.

USS *Inaugural*, World War II minesweeper, is berthed in the Mississippi River at St. Louis, close to the Gateway Arch at the Jefferson National Expansion Memorial. Open May 1 to October 1, every day, also weekends in October when weather favorable. 10 a.m. to dusk; Admission: $1.75; children 6 to 12, $1.25. Owned and exhibited by St. Louis Concessions, 400 Mansion House Center, Suite 2510, St. Louis, Missouri 63102. Ship address: USS *Inaugural*, 300 N. Wharf Street, St. Louis, Missouri 63102. Telephone (314) 421-1511.

A sister ship to the *Inaugural*, the USS *Hazard* (AM240) is on display in the Missouri River at Omaha, Nebraska.

USS *Hazard*, retired 1944 minesweeper, along with T1-class submarine *Marlin*, is moored in the Missouri River at Omaha, Nebraska. Ships are at Freedom Park. Open 1 to 5 p.m. Greater Omaha Military Historical Society, Box 9056, Station C, Omaha, Nebraska 68110. Telephone (402) 733-4654.

Now, back to the Mississippi and the historic craft that made the great river synonymous with steamboating. Just let your imagination take you back 60 years to when cargo carriers on the upper river staged a comeback. Two loud blasts on the steam whistle, please.

A few minutes after 10 o'clock in the morning of August 15, 1927, the huge paddle wheel at the stern of the steam towboat SS *Thorpe* began to turn and she pushed her three barges out into the channel of the Mississippi River at St. Louis. Fresh from the Dubuque builder's yard, she was off on her maiden voyage, 668 miles upriver to Minneapolis, delivering 900 tons of New Orleans sugar and 700 tons of St. Louis freight.

As the *Thorpe*'s St. Lawrence-type whistle marked her departure, it also marked a historic moment in river history: the inauguration of modern barge traffic on the Upper Mississippi. Under the impact of railroad competition, the steamboats that once crowded Old Man River had gradually dwindled away. Where once there had been thousands, by 1918 there were only 300 left and many of the surviving floating palaces had been stripped down to become excursion boats or mobile dance halls in the river towns.

Now the Mississippi was staging a comeback as a key transportation route for bulk cargoes. When the *Thorpe* reached Minneapolis after a 10-day passage, her arrival was celebrated as "Minneapolis to the Gulf Day."

The first of the *Thorpe*'s 10 ports of call on her maiden voyage was Keokuk, Iowa, a little more than 170 river miles up the Mississippi from St. Louis, where her arrival was seen as a harbinger of better days to come. The *Gate City*, Keokuk's newspaper, commented that the *Thorpe*'s barges brought "a small consignment of freight for Keokuk, the first time anything has been brought here by river for many a year. The *Thorpe* is the first steamboat to make a

through trip from St. Louis to Minneapolis in twelve years. And it is said to be the first of a fleet of boats and barges which will be placed in service."

The *Thorpe* was indeed the harbinger of a small fleet of stern-wheel towboats operated by the Inland Waterways Corporation, successor to the Federal Barge Lines, which established regular freight service on the Upper Mississippi. She served for 13 years on the Mississippi and then was sold, partly as a result of the competition of new towboats in which diesel engines drove propellers, not paddle wheels. New owners renamed her the *George M. Verity*, and for the next twenty years she was active on the Ohio River, where, it is estimated, she pushed barges delivering more than 10 million tons of coal.

Now, as the *Verity*, she is back in Keokuk. Ashore in a dry berth on the riverbank, she houses the Keokuk River Museum, which is dedicated to preserving the memory of Upper Mississippi River history, and is herself its principal exhibit.

Keokuk's ties to the river have been close since its foundation near the point where the Des Moines River enters the Mississippi. The original village was at the foot of the rapids in the Mississippi that for many years required all steamboat cargo to be unloaded from river steamers and either lightered through the rapids or hauled around past them on land. In 1873, a seven-mile canal was built with three small locks to carry river traffic around the rapids. Forty years later, a hydroelectric dam backed up a 40-mile lake over the rapids. Now one of the largest locks on the Mississippi (1,200 feet long) enables barges to handle the 38-foot difference between the level of the lake and the river below the dam.

Close to the downstream entrance to the lock sits the 578-ton *Verity* in a Keokuk river-front park. All 162 feet of her is open to visitors, including her engine room its tandem-compound steam engine with its high and low pressure cylinders, which generated 1,000 hp at full stroke. Particularly interesting:

- her pilothouse, which was raised a full deck higher early in her career as the number of barges in a tow increased;
- the cabins; more were added for traveling steel company officials when *Thorpe* moved to the Ohio and became *Verity*;
- the crew's quarters; when the steamer went into service she was amply manned by a crew of 28, including two waitresses, a laundress, and a cabin boy. She also carried a "watchman," which is river lingo for a second mate. Later, on the Ohio, her complement was reduced to 17, including three women cooks.

• the huge paddle wheel abaft the stern—the stern-wheel, 19 by 22 feet. This normally made 19 revolutions a minute when *Verity* was under way. The stern-wheel is of an unusual shallow-V design, intended to avoid the hull-shaking vibrations set up by the conventional wheel as each paddle hit the water.

Exhibits in the *Verity* include photographs of river steamers and river activities as well as artifacts from long-gone vessels: whistles, wheels, bell pulls, and so forth.

The Keokuk River Museum is housed in the stern-wheel steamer *George M. Verity*, in Victory Park on Mississippi river front of Keokuk, Iowa, about 150 miles north of St. Louis. Open April 1 to October 31, daily, 9 a.m. to 5 p.m. Admission: $1.00; children 6 to 19, 50 cents. Keokuk River Museum, P.O. Box 268, Keokuk, Iowa 52632. Telephone (319) 524-4765.

Some 100 miles further up the river at Davenport, Iowa, one of the Quad Cities at a great east-west bend in the Mississippi, the River Boat Room in the Putnam Museum preserves relics of the riverine past. Exhibits include steamboat models and artifacts. Notable are the huge pilot wheels used to guide steamers through the intricate river channels. There are also paintings, and an extensive collection of steamboat photographs.

The Putnam Museum's principal exhibits cover a wide range, from the Far East to Middle America.

The Putnam Museum with Mississippi River collection in River Boat Room is on West 12th Street in Davenport, Iowa. Open all year, except major holidays. Closed Mondays. Open Tuesday-Saturday, 9 a.m. to 5 p.m.; Sunday, 1 to 5 p.m. Admission to museum: $2.00; seniors, $1.50; children 7 to 18, $1.00; free to all, Saturday, 9 a.m. to noon. Putnam Museum, 1717 W. 12th Street, Davenport, Iowa 52804. Telephone (319) 324-1933.

Now a 15-minute run east (parallel to the Mississippi at this point) to the little town of Le Claire.

Don't let the name Buffalo Bill Museum mislead you. Le Claire, Iowa, indeed dedicated its museum to native son William Cody but the town is very conscious of its close ties to the mighty river flowing past its door. Not only does the Buffalo Bill Museum collection cover the river, but its major exhibit is a steamboat, the *Lone Star*, said to be one of the oldest to survive and one of the few remaining wooden-hulled river vessels.

Built in 1890, the *Lone Star* was originally a wood-burning side-wheeler; later she was converted to a stern-wheeler, burning coal. When she retired in 1968, she was the last stern-wheel towboat to operate on the Upper Mississippi.

The Buffalo Bill Museum exhibits include a number of steamboat models, photographs, and record books, as well as records and memorabilia of river captains. The collection also focuses on James B. Eads, who was not a steamboat master or pilot, but nevertheless a most significant figure in Mississippi River history. An engineer, he invented a diving bell used in the salvage of vessels sunk in the river; designed and built a fleet of Union gunboats that did much to win control of the Mississippi during the Civil War; and designed the great bridge across the river at St. Louis. His greatest achievement was the design and construction of the jetties at the mouth of the Mississippi that created self-scouring channels that did not silt up, enabling New Orleans to remain an ocean port.

SS *Lone Star*, ancient stern-wheeler, together with riverine collection, are at the Buffalo Bill Museum at 206 N. River Street, Le Claire, about 15 minutes east of Davenport, Iowa. From I-80, major east-west route, take exit closest to west end of Mississippi River bridge, look for museum directional signs in small town. Open every day, May 1 to October 31; 9 a.m. to 5 p.m. Rest of year: Saturday and Sunday only; 9 a.m. to 5 p.m. Admission: $1.00; teens, 50 cents. Buffalo Bill Museum, Box 284, Le Claire, Iowa 52753. Telephone (319) 289-5580 or 289-4330.

Upriver again, this time to a showboat that is also a river museum.

Showboats arrived on the western rivers almost at the same time as the first settlers and their river craft. As early as 1817, a little company of professional actors bought a keelboat in Nashville and headed down the Mississippi to New Orleans, fighting off river pirates on the way. According to Norbury Wayman's *Life on the River*, an English Shakespearean company built a theater on a barge in 1831 and went on tour. They started in Pittsburgh and were then pushed by a steamboat from town to town. Apparently they did well, for five years later they bought a steamboat and their theater became self-propelled.

Showboats multiplied; one at least is said to have been big enough to hold a whole circus performing before 3,400 people. In the latter 19th century, theater families had their own showboats, where they performed not only vaudeville acts, but thundering melodramas. The boats got bigger and fancier, but on the river, as elsewhere, the coming of motion pictures eventually killed the stock companies. By the time Edna Ferber wrote *Show Boat*, which, with Jerome Kern, she turned into a classic operetta in the mid-1920s, the originals were disappearing from the rivers.

The visitor will find a recreation of one of these riverine theaters on the Mississippi river front at Clinton, Iowa. The showboat, which also houses a small river museum, began her career afloat as the two-deck stern-wheel tug *The Omar* on the Ohio River in 1935. After a quarter century pushing barges—she was powered by two Marietta compound steam engines developing 1,000 hp—*The Omar* was presented to the state of West Virginia. With her gallery area and crew's quarters converted to a 225-seat theater, and a third deck added to provide for a balcony and exhibition space, she became the showboat *Rhododendron*. Now, shifted from the Ohio to the Upper Mississippi, she is the *City of Clinton*. After being moored in the river for several years, the showboat was eventually moved ashore. She now lives atop a levee where she is protected from the winter river.

The main deck, lounge, and second deck captain's quarters have been preserved and are open to visitors. In the exhibition gallery at the forward end of her third deck, there is a display of steamboat artifacts and photographs.

During the summer months the resident theater company presents old-time melodramas, comedies, musicals, and children's plays.

City of Clinton **Showboat**, on the river at Clinton, Iowa, about 30 miles north of Davenport, 50 miles south of Dubuque. From I-80, main east-west route, take Route 67. Exit north to Clinton, where it runs into Second Street. Turn right on Sixth Avenue North, proceed to Riverview Drive where showboat will be visible at river. Boat is open June 1 through August 31, 1 to 6 p.m. Admission to exhibits: 50 cents; under 12, free. Operated by Clinton Parks and Recreation Department. City of Clinton Showboat, 1401 11th Avenue North, Clinton, Iowa 52732. Telephone (319) 243-1260 weekdays; (319) 242-6760 summer afternoons only.

Now to one of the great historic river ports of the upper Mississippi, where both a steamboat and a museum await the visitor.

The major river museum on the upper Mississippi is at the old Iowa river town of Dubuque. From its beginnings in the 1830s, Dubuque has been a first-ranking river port. (Many years before that, when Iowa was still Indian country in 1788, Julian Dubuque built his cabin on the bluff and started mining lead.) Dubuque has also long been a major shipbuilding center where many of the Upper Mississippi's steamboats, towboats, and barges were constructed. And until the forests of Wisconsin and Minnesota gave out, Dubuque was filled with lumber mills. The logs were floated downriver in enormous rafts.

Dubuque is also the native place of Richard Bissell, who wrote a novel about the Upper Mississippi and its people, *A Stretch on the River*. A great success, the book led to Bissell's being hailed as the modern Mark Twain—apparently somewhat to his discomfort, since he later wrote another book wryly titled *My Life on the Mississippi or Why I Am Not Mark Twain*.

Dubuque has preserved the traditions of the Upper Mississippi in a river steamboat and a museum. The veteran steam dredge *William M. Black* and the Fred W. Woodward Riverboat Museum, both sponsored by the Dubuque County Historical Society, are side by side in the Port of Dubuque on the Mississippi river front. They are dedicated to telling the story of the Mississippi over the three centuries since the first Europeans canoed down the Illinois and out into the mightiest river of them all.

The *Black* is a 277-foot "dust-pan" dredge, used by the Army Corps of Engineers for nearly 40 years to keep the channels of inland waterways from silting up. Ultimately she was replaced by more efficient craft—keeping steam up in her boilers used 7,000 gallons of fuel a day. Three decks—main, boiler, and hurricane—are open to visitors, as is her pilothouse. The housing that once covered one of her side paddles has been turned into a little theater where river films are shown.

Next to the side-wheeler is the Riverboat Museum. Full-sized dioramas with lifelike costumed figures depicting historic scenes such as Joliet and Marquette on the Mississippi. Among the museum's steamboat artifact collection is a rare copper eagle that once graced the top of an 1890s steamboat.

Of particular interest is a huge 30-foot model of the steamboat *Dubuque*, 1867, built to an exact one-eighth scale. One side of the hull and superstructure have been removed so visitors see a cross-section of the vessel; small carved figures represent passengers and crew. Another unusual exhibit is a 12-foot log raft (mirrors give an illusion of greater size) that apparently floats, so that when the visitor steps aboard the raft bounces beneath his weight (actually, the raft "floats" on springs, not water).

Dubuque's past is recalled with a lumber boat included in the museum's small craft collection. Other craft on view include a clamming boat with gear (Mississippi clams are raked up to make pearl buttons, not chowder), a 1950s fishing boat, several historic canoe types, and the 43-foot diesel towboat *Tavern*. Queen of the fleet is the 1905 pleasure launch *Rosalie*, powered by a two-cylinder gasoline engine. The museum also exhibits a collection of outboard motors dating back to 1915.

SS *William M. Black*/Woodward Riverboat Museum/Port of Dubuque are on Dubuque's river front north of the Julian Dubuque Bridge. River rides available nearby, on *Spirit of Dubuque*. SS *Black* and Woodward Riverboat Museum open daily May 1 to October 31, 10 a.m. to 6:30 p.m. Admission:

$3.00; juniors, $1.00. Sponsored by Dubuque County Historical Society. Port of Dubuque, P.O. Box 305, Dubuque, Iowa 52001. Telephone (319) 557-9545.

Winona in southeastern Minnesota, some 120 miles up the Mississippi from Dubuque, was once the proud possessor of the retired river steamboat *Julius C. Wilkie* (ex-*James P. Person*) which served as a museum in a riverside park. Unhappily, in 1981 the steamboat, like many of her sisters in days gone by, was lost by fire. Winona still possesses a Wilkie Steamboat Center, however. The name now graces a steamboat-shaped building housing a new museum dedicated to steamboating and the Mississippi River.

The Center is so designed that half of the first floor, the lower deck, serves as the museum; the upper deck is a steamboat saloon. The exhibits include steamboat models, tools, and many prints and photographs.

Also on display is an extensive collection of artifacts, including a big paddle wheel from a stern-wheeler. Other artifacts include engines, a capstan, pumps, anchors, and even a bow and a smokestack from old-time river boats.

The Julius C. Wilkie Steamboat Museum is housed in a building that looks like a steamboat in Winona, Minnesota, a little over 100 miles southeast down the Mississippi River from Minneapolis/St. Paul. From I-90, transcontinental interstate, exit north at Wilson or Dakota (longer, but runs along river). Museum is in Levee Park at Mississippi River (north) end of Main Street. Open May 1 to Memorial Day weekend, Sunday-Friday, 10 a.m. to 5 p.m.; Saturday, 10 a.m. to 7 p.m. Memorial Day weekend through Labor Day, Sunday-Thursday, 9 a.m. to 5 p.m.; Friday-Saturday, 9 a.m. to 7 p.m. After Labor Day through October 20, Sunday-Friday, 10 a.m. to 5 p.m.; Saturday, 10 a.m. to 7 p.m. January 1 to April 30, Thursday-Saturday, noon to 5 p.m. Admission for guided tours Memorial Day through Labor Day, $1.50; children 5 to 11, $1.00; balance of the year, 75 cents; children 5 to 11 cents. Julius C. Wilkie Steamboat Museum, P.O. Box 1157, Winona, Minnesota 55987. Telephone (507) 454-5315.

Now for a very quick look at the Mississippi's mightiest tributary, the Missouri, itself one of the world's great rivers.

Big Muddy: The Missouri

What is the longest river in North America? The Mississippi, you say? Not so. Old Man River may be the greatest, the most glamorous, the most written and sung about, but he can't match the length of his mightiest tributary: the Missouri. From its sources high in the Rocky Mountains to where it flows into the Mississippi just above St. Louis, the Missouri measures 2,600 miles head to tail. With its many tributaries, some themselves great rivers, the Missouri drains more than half a million square miles. At the mouth, it is 3,000 feet across and pours an average of 120,000 cubic feet of water into the Mississippi every second.

All the recognition this giant among rivers has received for its gargantuan dimensions, however, is to be known as "the Big Muddy," both as a nickname and literally: *Missui* means "big," *Souri* means "muddy," in Algonquin Indian. But there's some justification for the name. For most of its length the river runs through easily eroded grasslands, picking up millions of tons of silt and sand along the way.

Early travelers, largely French-Canadian fur traders, voyaged by canoe and mackinaw boats drawing only a few inches so that they could be easily shoved

off any sand bars they couldn't ride over. When the steamboats came, however, it was a different story. The first steamer was the *Independence* in 1819, closely followed the same year by the *Western Engineer*, which went all the way up to the future site of Omaha. *Western Engineer* was no ordinary looking steamboat: A sable serpent's head projected from her bow, spewing smoke and steam through its open mouth and frightening the Indians along the river banks—perhaps its purpose.

The pioneer steamboats and the others that soon followed, quickly discovered that the Big Muddy was no easy river for steam navigation. Not only was the channel clogged with sandbars but they were constantly shifting; this meant a pilot couldn't depend on the knowledge of the river he had gained on previous trips, which slowed travel considerably. What was worse, the silt suspended in the river water used to feed the boilers clogged the valves and pipes. Still another hazard was the hostility of the Plains Indians, who had an unpleasant habit of ambushing steamboats when they pulled into the riverbank to load wood.

There were even whirlpools on the Big Muddy large enough to sink steamboats, as happened to the *Bishop* in 1867.

The early steamboats on the Missouri were deep-draft side-wheelers but they proved ill-suited to the shallow and dangerous river. Gradually, a distinctive Missouri River type developed: extra shallow and very light, broad of beam, and driven by a big paddle wheel at the stern instead of side paddles, so increasing maneuverability in shallow water.

In the beginning, the Missouri steamboats were primarily used in the fur trade, taking supplies upriver. At first, the fur traders met the steamers part way, bringing their fur and, later, buffalo hides down from the upper Missouri in bateaux and mackinaw boats. Eventually, the steamboats pushed farther and farther up the river, however, carrying not only supplies but Indian agents, troops, and, later on, gold

miners. In 1860, the SS *Chippewa* reached Fort Benton in western Montana. Five years later, the *Tom Stevens* steamed to the head of navigation 35 miles beyond, where the Great Falls of the Missouri blocked further progress.

As the settlers moved into the plains country, they were carried by steamboats, but in due time the coming of the railroads took away the passenger business and the Missouri River packets disappeared. Freight continued to move on the river, however, as it does to this day on barges. The Missouri still remains part of the great inland waterway system of the Mississippi Valley.

As far back as 1838, Congress started appropriating funds to improve the Missouri River by removing

Figure 47
Collection of the Museum of Missouri River History is housed in the veteran river dredge *Captain Meriwether Lewis,* now mounted in the bank of the Missouri River in the small river town of Brownville, Nebraska.

snags, dead trees or branches, that could rip out the bottom of a steamboat. The river has demanded attention ever since. It is most appropriate, therefore, that the Museum of Missouri River History is housed in a retired river dredge. Operated by the Army Corps of Engineers, the *Captain Meriwether Lewis* roamed the Missouri for almost 40 years, sucking up the endless silt deposits that constantly threatened to block the channel. Now she sits in a dry berth on the bank of the Missouri at Brownville, Nebraska. *Lewis* herself is the chief exhibit of the museum, but she also displays an interesting collection of riverine models, artifacts, and photographs gathered by the Nebraska State Historical Society.

The vessel is named, of course, for Meriwether Lewis, the pioneer who in 1804-5 joined with William Clark to become the first Euro-Americans to explore the Missouri from its mouth to its headwaters. The steamboat's main deck, which contains the engine room, boiler room, and shop, has been restored to the way it was when she was working on the river. The crew's quarters on the boiler deck above, have been modified to display the museum exhibits, which include models of typical craft used in early traffic on the Missouri. Among those portrayed are a keelboat, and the lesser-known bull boat, which is constructed of buffalo-bull hides stretched over a framework (an Indian version of the Irish coracle?) Exhibits in the former officers' staterooms focus on the influence of the Missouri River on Nebraska history.

Among the ship models are portrayals of the 1931 stern-wheel steam towboat *John James*; the *Western Engineer*, the first steamboat to reach Nebraska waters, in 1819; and a modern towboat. The museum also has many photographs of both old and contemporary Missouri River vessels, although the Nebraska State Historical Society's main collection is in its headquarters in Lincoln.

Brownville is an old river town, founded in 1854, and very conscious of its history. There are 19th-century restored houses, museums, and galleries. Excursion boat cruises on the Missouri are available in July and August.

The Museum of Missouri River History is lodged aboard the side-wheeler dredge *Captain Meriwether Lewis*, drydocked beside the Missouri River in the little southeast Nebraska town of Brownville. From Interstate 29, the principal north-south route along the Missouri side of the river, exit west across the river on the Route 136 bridge; turn off on Main Street Brownville. *Lewis* is on the river front south of the bridge; ask local directions. Open April through October, Monday-Saturday, 8 a.m. to 5 p.m.; Sunday, 1:30 to 5:00 p.m. Museum of Missouri River History, P.O. Box 124, Brownville, Nebraska 68321. Telephone (402) 825-3341 ("let it ring").

X
"THOSE GRAND
FRESH-WATER SEAS OF OURS"

Lake Ontario
Lake Erie (and Lake Chautauqua)
Lake Huron and Georgian Bay
Lake Michigan
Lake Superior

Now gentlemen, in square-sail brigs and three-masted ships, well nigh as large and stout as any that ever sailed out of your old Callao to far Marrilla; this Lakeman, in the land-locked heart of our America, had yet been nurtured by all those agrarian freebooting impressions popularly connected with the open ocean. For in their interflowing aggregate, those grand fresh-water seas of ours,—Erie, and Ontario, and Huron, and Superior, and Michigan,—possess an ocean-like expansiveness, with many of the ocean's noblest traits; with many of its rimmed varieties of races and of climes. They contain round archipelagoes of romantic isles, even as the Polynesian waters do; in large part, are shored by two great contrasting nations, as the Atlantic is; they furnish long maritime approaches to our numerous territorial colonies from the East, dotted all round their banks; here and there are frowned upon by batteries, and by the goat-like craggy guns of lofty Mackinaw; they have heard the fleet thunderings of naval victories; at intervals, they yield their beaches to wild barbarians, whose red-painted faces flash from out their petty wigwams; for leagues and leagues are flanked by ancient and unentered forests, where the gaunt pines stand like serried lines of kings in Gothic geneologies; those same woods harboring wild Afric beasts of prey, and silken creatures whose exported furs give robes to Tartar Emperors; they mirror the paved capitals of Buffalo and Cleveland, as well as Winnebago villages; they float alike the full-rigged merchant ship, the armed cruiser of the State, the steamer, and the beech

canoe; they are swept by Borean and dismasting blasts as direful as any that lash the salted wave; they know what shipwrecks are, for out of sight of land, however inland, they have drowned full many a midnight ship with all its shrieking crew.

Herman Melville, *Moby Dick*, Chapter 54

Almost a century and a half have passed since Melville's invocation of those grand fresh-water seas of ours. A few batteries still frown here and there, but for the edification of tourists rather than to guard a sullen frontier. The ancient and unentered forests are long gone, cut away to build the cities of Middle America. Many of the wild Afric beasts of prey are on the endangered species list. The full-rigged merchant ships have followed the beech canoe into the mists of the past.

But the inland seas remain—and so do their ships. For actually, when Melville wrote, the Great Lakes were only on the eve of a tremendous expansion of maritime activities. New and even mightier ships have repeatedly taken over the lakes, until today they float huge 1,000-foot vessels built especially for their waters. Sharing the ship lanes are blue-water ships flying flags from distant corners of the world.

And the direful Borean blasts still sweep these inland seas, and still sometimes drown a midnight ship and crew.

247

As a result, here in mid-America is a maritime tradition as rich and dramatic as any on the coasts, and as separate and distinct.

Remarkable bodies of water, these inland seas, deserving of their own maritime traditions. Familiar with them on every map of the United States and Canada, we tend to forget just how remarkable they are. Among them, the five lakes contain one-half the fresh water in the entire world. They drain an area larger than Britain, and their combined shorelines total 8,000 miles.

Gouged out by glaciers during the Ice Age, the bottoms of all the lakes except Erie are below sea level. The terminal moraine formed by the earth and rocks the glaciers pushed ahead of them blocked drainage to the south, and as the warming land melted the ice the run-off found an outlet to the eastward.

The result was a continuous water route between the Atlantic Ocean at the mouth of the St. Lawrence and the western end of Lake Superior, 2,300 miles deep into North America, 1,200 of them on the lakes. At the same time, short portages (canoe carries) across the watersheds at the heads of various rivers flowing into the lakes provided access to the Ohio and Mississippi valleys leading south to the Gulf of Mexico, and to Lake Winnipeg and the rivers running north into Hudson Bay.

The surface of Lake Superior averages more than 600 feet above sea level; by the time the joined waters of all five lakes reach the St. Lawrence the level has dropped more than 350 feet. There are, however, three interruptions in the flow of the Great Lakes waters eastward to the sea. At the head of the St. Mary's River, which connects Lakes Superior and Huron, there is a fall of about 20 feet in about a mile, resulting in tumbling rock-filled rapids. Even more of an obstacle is the Niagara River which carries Lake Erie's waters into Lake Ontario; it drops 314 feet in 34 miles, including of course the 167-foot plunge at Niagara Falls. And finally, there are rapids in the St. Lawrence River above Montreal. The falls blocked all passage: The rapids required canoes and small craft bound upstream, to be dragged along the shore or taken out and portaged. Larger vessels were completely blocked: their cargoes had to be unloaded, carried around, and loaded on other craft on the other side. Not until these three obstacles were by-passed by lock canals in the 19th century could the Great Lakes approach their maritime potential as a system of water highways to the heart of the continent.

Long before the canals were built, however, the inland seas were a dominant factor in the political and economic history of the upper midwest. The European exploration, conquest, settlement, and economic exploitation of the region have each in turn depended in large part on maritime activity on these magnificent natural highways.

For 150 years, the lakes were the great road to the West for French explorers, missionaries, fur traders, and soldiers based on the settlements of New France along the St. Lawrence. Samuel Champlain himself traveled to Lake Huron's Georgian Bay, and went on to cross Lake Ontario as early as 1615. Sometime in the next 10 years, one of the explorers Champlain sent out to the westward probably saw Lake Superior. Another, Jean Nicolet, penetrated into Lake Michigan by 1634. Because of the hostility of the Five Nations of the Iroquois, Lake Erie was the last to be explored. Only after the Iroquois had been temporarily subdued by a French punitive expedition did the first French explorers canoe along Lake Erie in 1669.

The earliest explorations of the lakes were in search of the Pacific Ocean and the coast of China. As the hoped-for China Seas, the lakes proved a disappointment—they did not even provide a water route through North America to the Pacific. But if the French were frustrated in their hopes of reaching China via the Great Lakes, they early found there were rich profits to be made in the fur trade. At first, the tribes nearest the European settlements served as middlemen. Soon, however, French Canadian woods runners were pushing along the lakes and inland up the tributaries to trade with tribes deep in the surrounding forests. Often these early explorers and traders were accompanied by French missionaries seeking to convert the tribesmen to Christianity.

For a century and a half, the canoes and open boats of these early travelers were almost the only European maritime activity on the lakes. The birch bark canoe, light enough to be easily repaired with materials at hand in the wilderness, was borrowed from the Indians. Their canoes seem to have been small, carrying two or three people. The fur traders needed to carry heavy loads, however, and their canoes grew steadily larger over the years until the *canot du maitre*, or Montreal canoe, designed specifically for use on the big lakes, was 35 feet or more in length. These could carry four-ton loads, which could mean eight or nine men plus gear, supplies, and trade goods or furs, yet when unloaded were light enough to be carried by four men over a portage. The cargo was stowed in 90-pound packs, carried over the portages two at a time.

The voyageurs also traveled in wooden boats, which were rowed or paddled. Sturdier than canoes, they were less easily damaged and could carry heavier loads, but they were so heavy that they had to be painfully dragged rather than carried along the portages. There were several types. One of the commonest was the bateau, a clinker built double-ended boat, flatbottomed, that the French brought with them from Europe; experts say it was descended from a common medieval type. It is variously described; some say it averaged 25 feet long, others that it ranged up to 50 feet or more. Another type, the Mackinaw boat, is described by one expert as being built of bark over a double-ended frame, much like an extra large canoe. Another, however, calls it a planked boat, similar to a bateau.

Flotillas of these craft were used to take traders on long voyages out through the lakes; they averaged about 35 miles a day. If there were favorable winds, square sails were hoisted and the boats covered greater distances; otherwise, they were paddled or rowed. The voyageurs stayed close to the shore of the lakes so they could pull in to take shelter if a storm came up, and so they could camp each night. Sometimes, however, they had to cut across open water to save time—a risky course because of sudden lake squalls.

For a century and a half after their settlement in Canada, the French dominated the Great Lakes. The inland seas were central to their immensely profitable fur trade in the upper Midwest. And in time the lakes came to be seen as a vital connecting link between French Canada and French Louisiana, one that could create a vast inland empire, encircling the English Colonies and pin them to the Atlantic Seaboard.

During all this time there were no true sailing vessels on the four western lakes, with one exception: The ill-fated *Griffin* (or *Griffon*, as often spelled), was built by the Sieur de La Salle, greatest of the French explorers of the West. In 1679, he managed to convey ship's gear and shipwrights to the shores of the Niagara River above the Falls; here, they built the *Griffin*. One of America's truly historic ships, she carried on her bow a carved griffin—half eagle, half lion—the mythical beast emblazoned on the arms of Count Frontenac, the Governor of New France. *Griffin* was a square-rigged two-master, 45 tons burden, said to be armed with five small cannon.

Under La Salle's command, *Griffin* reached the east end of Lake Erie in three days. Then north through Detroit River, across Lake St. Clair and into the St. Clair River, where part of her crew had to go ashore with a hawser and tow her through against the current. Eventually, *Griffin* sailed around what is now Michigan and down Lake Michigan to an island off the Wisconsin shore, the passage from Niagara taking a total of 44 days. La Salle sent her back east with a load of furs which had been collected by an advance party. That was the last of *Griffin*; an autumn storm swept the lake soon after she sailed and she was never seen again. (Ship timbers and a keel that may be the remains of *Griffin* have been found buried in an island beach in northern Lake Huron.)

This was also the end of sailing vessels on the western lakes for some 100 years, at least as far as the records go. (The discovery of ship remains with 17th-century coins has raised questions.) There was more sailing ship activity on the easternmost lake, Ontario. Soon after the French had built Fort Frontenac at the eastern end of Lake Ontario, on the site of Kingston, Ontario, they had constructed several small sailing vessels; described as two-masters, and variously called barks or luggers, they were around 50 feet long. Some of these vessels were employed by La Salle to carry the supplies and gear for *Griffin* across Lake Ontario.

With their little fleet based on Fort Frontenac, the French held undisputed control of Lake Ontario until the final stages of the war with Britain. After her conquest of New France, Britain took control of all the lakes. Ever ship-minded, the British saw the advantages of using sailing vessels to control the western lakes, and to maintain communications between the military and trading posts they had taken over. Shipyards in the Niagara River and Detroit turned out small naval vessels and schooners, which were used to carry supplies and furs. During the American Revolution, and for many years afterward, British naval power dominated on the lakes. Eventually, during the War of 1812, the United States rushed to build squadrons on both Lake Ontario and Lake Erie, and whole fleets of British and American warships, including full-rigged vessels, maneuvered and fought on the two eastern lakes. The naval battles on Lake Ontario were a draw, but on Lake Erie, Perry's victory meant that the international boundary remained where it had been set at the end of the Revolution; that is, running along the center of Ontario, Erie, Huron, and Superior.

After the war, steamboats arrived on the lakes; the first sailed on Lake Ontario only a decade after Fulton's *Clermont*, quickly followed on Lake Erie by the famous *Walk-in-the-Water*. The early steamboats could not compete with sail as ordinary cargo carriers. Their primitive engines, weak though they were, took up a large amount of valuable cargo space. Worse, they burned enormous quantities of wood. Even after decades of improving engine efficiency, the average side-wheel lake steamer of the 1840s burned two cords of wood an hour. Since a cord occupies 128 cubic feet, this meant the wood for a single day's run displaced more than 6,000 cubic feet of cargo. Combined with the added expense of engines and paddle wheels, this pushed steamboat freight rates much higher than those of sailing vessels.

The big advantages of the steamboats, of course, were speed and liberation from dependence on favorable winds. While travel or shipment by a sailing vessel was cheaper, it was also slower—much slower if the vessel had to wait for a change of wind. For passengers and "package freight" (boxes and barrels rather than such bulk cargoes as grain or lumber), the saving in time made up for the extra cost and the steamers took over this business from sailing ships between the main lake ports.

Meanwhile, schooners were proving the most useful type of vessel for the lakes, as on the coast. Their shallow draft enabled them to enter the little lake ports, which were often merely shallow river mouths. Handy and maneuverable—important qualities in the close quarters often found on the lakes—they were also fast and could sail far closer to a wind than square-riggers. Cheap to build, they were also cheap to operate, needing only a small crew. Soon schooners became the standard Great Lakes vessel of the 19th century.

By the 1820s, both sailing vessels and steamers were kept busy carrying westward the settlers seeking to homestead the cheap, rich lands opening up around the lakes. They came first from New England and the seaboard states, then from Europe; families and whole groups of families seeking a new start.

Two historic events multiplied the flow of incomers in the 1830s. In 1825 the Erie Canal was opened, bypassing Niagara Falls to provide a direct water route between Lake Erie and the Hudson River, New York City, and the Atlantic Ocean. Now immigrants crossed New York state in canal packets, transshipping to lake vessels at Buffalo. At about the same time, Canada built the Welland Canal to lift vessels from Lake Ontario to Lake Erie. Together with a canal built around the rapids on the St. Lawrence River, the Welland locks permitted small oceangoing vessels to enter the Great Lakes for the first time.

The other key event was the Black Hawk War, fought in 1832 between United States troops, regulars and militia, and the Indians of Wisconsin and northern Illinois, who were making one last despairing stand to block white settlement in their hunting grounds. The first steamboat to reach the head of Lake Michigan at Chicago carried troops. When, inevitably, the Indians were defeated, the tide of immigration moved westward to the Lake Michigan shores of Wisconsin and Illinois.

Passenger steamers, improved in efficiency and built in many little ports along the lakes, multiplied and generally prospered until the coming of the railroads just before the Civil War took away much of the business. Freight traffic on the lakes continued to boom, however; in 1860, there were 1,122 sailing vessels and 335 steamers.

Another whole chapter in Great Lake maritime activity opened with the discovery of iron ore on the shores of Lake Superior. The third great era of maritime traffic on the lakes thus launched continues to this day. To smelt the ore and produce iron and steel required huge quantities of coal. The industry soon found that the most economical place to bring the ore and the coal together was on the southern shore of Lake Erie. There was a major problem, however: The St. Mary's River rapids, which blocked the outlet of Lake Superior into Lake Huron, made it necessary to unload all cargoes, carry them around the rapids in carts, and reload them onto different vessels.

Again, a massive feat of engineering solved the problem. A canal with locks to carry ships around the rapids was opened at Sault Ste. Marie in 1855. Since then, the locks have been repeatedly enlarged as the ore ships have grown bigger and bigger. Today, 1,000-foot vessels, equipped with their own machinery for loading and unloading so that they can dock almost anywhere, bring iron pellets from the west end of Lake Superior to the Lake Erie steel ports.

For a time in the 19th century, lumber schooners crowded the lakes as the virgin forests of Michigan and Wisconsin were leveled and carried down the lakes to build new cities. More enduring were the grain shipments that started flowing east over the lakes, starting with the first settlements in northern Ohio. As settlements moved westward, the grain cargoes came back east from more distant lake ports, often on sailing ships and steamers that had carried immigrants on the outward passage. Buffalo became for many years one of the world's great grain receiving ports, crowded with storage elevators.

Sailing ships survived on the lakes into the early decades of the 20th century, but dwindled away as the survivors were scrapped or demasted and converted into barges. By 1941, there were only a dozen sail left—six schooners and six schooner barges. The big lakes passenger liners lasted longer, but now they too have disappeared. Today, the huge bulk carriers rule the lakes.

The major event in the 20th century history of the Great Lakes has been the building of the St. Lawrence Seaway. A joint Canadian-American project, the Seaway includes locks and a deep waterway in the St. Lawrence River and an enlarged Welland Canal between Lake Ontario and Lake Erie that provides passage for oceangoing vessels up to 730 feet long and 28,000 tons cargo capacity. Opened in 1959, it enables the manufactures and bulk cargoes of central North America—iron ore, wheat, coal—to be carried to the lower St. Lawrence River and on out into the Atlantic to foreign ports.

The usefulness of the Seaway is diminished by a factor that has been a continuing problem ever since maritime activity began on the lakes: ice. From December to April most of the lakes freeze hard, and even where they don't, such as in the south end of Lake Michigan, pack ice blown in around the shores is a hazard to navigation. Many of the ship losses over the years have come at the end of the season, during November and December, when shipowners try to make one last voyage before laying up their expensive vessels for the winter.

Over the years, the use of icebreakers to keep open channels through the ice and compressed-air bubblers to prevent ice formation in the locks has made it possible to stretch out the season more and more. Whether anti-ice technology will ever enable ships to keep moving through the Seaway, the locks, and the lakes, the year round, no one knows, but such an achievement would enhance the value of the Great Lakes port facilities and the vessels that use them.

Meanwhile, the maritime traditions of the Great Lakes are being preserved with an increasing number of restored ships, as well as maritime museums, and maritime galleries in museums of general interest. The tradition they cherish is a distinctive one: the sailors of the lakes have always been a breed apart with

their own lore of ships and men. One Great Lakes story tells of the prayer with which a shipmaster started every meal until after hearing it three times a day for voyage after voyage his officers knew it by heart. In part, it went:

> . . . Let the hand of prudence guide our helm, the winds of love fill our sails, and the Good Book be our compass. And Almighty God, whose patience with humanity is everlasting, keep all hidden rocks of adversity off our course; let our bow cut clean the fresh waters of righteousness; steer us clear of Satan's derelicts; and may the bright rays of hope never die out of the lighthouses along the shore that we may make the run of life without disaster . . . . Let not our eyes be darkened by fogs of evil; keep ringing loud for our guidance the bell-buoys of faith. And when at last we have sailed into and anchored in the very port of death, may the good skipper of the universe say: Well done, thou good and faithful mariner, come and sign the log and receive eternal happiness as your salvage reward.
>
> Amen.

Lake Ontario

Stretching only 200 miles in its longest dimension, roughly southwest to northeast, Lake Ontario, the easternmost of the Great Lakes, is also the smallest. Ontario has seen more human conflict, however, than the other four put together. For two centuries after the first Europeans reached its shores and for an unknown time before that Lake Ontario was a combat zone. Flotillas of canoes carried Indian war parties across the lake to ravage enemy villages on the other side. By the early 19th century, whole fleets of square-riggers, armed with the latest in naval artillery, were maneuvering in battle from one end of Lake Ontario to the other. In between, the lake was the highway for troops attacking enemy forts and bases.

For Lake Ontario was on a political fault line where rival nations ground against each other. Even before the Europeans arrived, the lake separated most of the warlike Iroquois from their bitter enemies (and cousins), the equally warlike Hurons. As the lake closest to European settlements, Ontario came to lie between the frontiers of the rival colonial empires of France and Britain. During the American Revolution, the lake was again roughly the dividing line between the British and Tory forces based in Canada and the Americans on the New York frontier. And finally in

the War of 1812, Britain and the United States faced each other across the lake and each built fleets to drive the other's ships from its waters.

But Lake Ontario was worth fighting over not merely because it was a no-man's water between enemies, but because it was also the great highway to the west over which passed explorers, missionaries, fur traders, and government agents, on their way to the lower lakes and the Ohio and Mississippi valleys.

Etienne Brulé, a young Frenchman sent by Champlain into the wilderness to enlist Indian support, was the first European to see Lake Ontario. Later that same year, 1615, Samuel Champlain himself crossed it, accompanying his Indian allies on a raid against Iroquois villages south of the lake. The Iroquois were the enemies of New France from then on, and for some decades French traders bypassed both the upper St. Lawrence and the lake for fear of Iroquois attacks, using instead northern routes via the Ottawa and French rivers leading to Georgian Bay and Lake Huron. The Iroquois repeatedly raided north across Lake Ontario, and ultimately wiped out the Huron villages and the missions that had been established among them by French priests.

Eventually, in 1666, the French government sent a regiment of regular troops to Canada, and a punitive expedition burned the Mohawk and Oneida villages in the Mohawk valley. During the two decades of uneasy peace that followed, Governor Frontenac built a fort, which was named for him, at the mouth of a little river on the north shore of Lake Ontario, close to where its waters flow into the St. Lawrence. Here, now the site of the city of Kingston, European maritime activity began, not only the first on Lake Ontario but the first on any of the Great lakes. With great difficulty, Frontenac's men dragged two flat boats up along the shore of the St. Lawrence past the rapids. These craft were fitted with sails, mounted with cannon, and painted with "strange devices" in red and blue. At the fort building site, where the Iroquois had gathered, Frontenac pointed to the gunboats to back up his warnings to the Iroquois to keep the peace: Sea power had arrived at inland America.

Other maritime firsts soon followed. The French at the fort built the first true sailing vessels on the lakes. Small versions of ocean craft, they were square-rigged, around 50 feet long, and variously described as barks or luggers. The French used them to carry men and supplies on the lake, to overawe hostile Indians, and to cut off fur trade with the English to the southward. Soon one of this little squadron, the 40-ton *Frontenac*, became another first on the maritime records of the lakes when she was wrecked in a gale on Christmas day, 1678. She was the first of many thousands of sailing vessels and steamers lost over the centuries in the terrible storms that swept the inland seas.

France dominated Lake Ontario during most of the late 17th and early 18th centuries, sending raiding parties across or around the lake to ravage the English settlements now spreading westward in New York's Mohawk River valley. Only at the very end of the long struggle between the two great European powers did the British build ships where the Oswego River ran into Lake Ontario on the south shore. The remains of one of these vessels, the snow *Halifax*, have been found. (A snow was a two-master very similar to a brig.) Built in 1756, the *Halifax* was about 75 feet long on the keel; the interior was laid out much as in an oceangoing vessel of the period. Whaleboats and bateaux were still often used on the lake, however, and indeed the task force of Colonial troops that finally captured Fort Frontenac was carried across the lake in such small craft. One result of this British/Colonial victory was destruction of the entire French Navy on the lake—nine vessels, carrying eight to eighteen guns.

The American Revolution saw a replay of the attacks from Canada southward across Lake Ontario, only now the invaders were British troops and their Tory allies attacking the American settlements. Control of the lake remained firmly in British hands, with Kingston, formerly Fort Frontenac, holding the eastern end of the lake, and British Fort Niagara hold-ing the entrance from the west at the Niagara River. The British advance base on the south shore of the lake was the fort at the mouth of the Oswego River. The Oswego was an important invasion route southward into New York and the fort had been a key point during the French and Indian War.

After the Revolution, many American Loyalists, particularly those from New York State, settled on the Canadian north shore of Lake Ontario. Little townships sprang up where once there had been Huron villages. In 1793, the British government decided to make a separate province out of Upper Canada, the new English-speaking settlements as distinct from French-speaking Lower Canada down the St. Lawrence. A site on Toronto Bay, on the north shore toward the western end of the lake, was chosen for the capital of the new province. At the other, eastern end of the bay, a small naval base was built at Kingston.

During the War of 1812, Kingston became the center of British naval activity on Lake Ontario. Control of the lake was hotly contested. The Americans on the south and east sides of the lake, engaged in a naval building race with the British on the north side, each hoping to gain complete control of its waters. The British naval squadron based in Kingston was commanded by Sir James Yeo, an intelligent and energetic officer of the Royal Navy. The American commander, based on Sackets Harbor, a few miles south of the entrance to the St. Lawrence on the east side of Lake Ontario, was Commodore Isaac Chauncy, equally distinguished. Able organizers, each was determined not to risk a decisive battle for control of the lake until he was sure that he had a preponderance of ships. Both had shipbuilding facilities at hand, which were turning out naval vessels throughout the war; neither outbuilt the other, however, and the Lake Ontario naval campaigns on the lake were inconclusive. The two squadrons sailed back and forth, whichever feeling the stronger chasing the other, but never really coming to grips. When peace came, the line between Canada and the United States remained where it was before the war—roughly down the center of Lake Ontario to the Niagara River and up the middle of the river to Lake Erie.

After the War of 1812, treaties with the Iroquois opened previously closed areas of the south shore of Lake Ontario to settlement. However, the building of the Erie Canal, 1817-25, which went directly from the Hudson River to Lake Erie, bypassed Lake Ontario entirely, diverting the flow of American traffic away from the lake. This was a legacy of the recent war. Routing the canal to Lake Ontario and then building another canal on the American side past Niagara Falls to Lake Erie, would have required less construction.

However, this would have placed a large portion of the route in international waters on Lake Ontario. With the naval combat on the lake during the recent war fresh in everybody's mind, the American planners preferred to keep the canal entirely within New York State.

As a result, the great flow of westward trade and settlement followed the Erie Canal 12 to 25 miles south of Lake Ontario. The southern shores of Lake Ontario remained relatively sparsely settled except for Oswego, connected by branch canal to the Erie Canal, and Rochester on the Genesee River.

On the Canadian side of the lake, things were very different. With the government actively encouraging settlement, a dozen busy little ports in addition to Kingston sprang up along the north shore. York, later Toronto, pulled ahead to become a major city.

Today, the major commercial activity, along with small cities and the great metropolis, are on the northern, Canadian side of the lake.

Steamboats came to Lake Ontario very soon after Fulton's *Clermont* made its historic voyage up the Hudson. The SS *Frontenac*, built in 1817 on the Canadian side of Lake Ontario, was the first steamer on the Great Lakes and was quickly followed by the American SS *Ontario*. Soon Lake Ontario became laced with local steamer traffic. Oswego was the chief American shipbuilding center on the lake and here in 1838 was launched the *Vandalia*, the first steamer of what became the typical Great Lake design, with engine installed far aft, leaving the entire hull available for cargo as it is in today's enormous lake ore carriers.

The 1850s saw the height of passenger steamer traffic on Lake Ontario. Soon steamers began to lose business to the railroads that had crept out from the east around the lakes.

The growth of commerce on the Canadian side was increased by two canals. One was built around the St. Lawrence rapids, which had always made it difficult for even canoes and bateaux to push their way up the river from Montreal. The other, on the Canadian side of the Niagara River, was the Welland Canal, whose locks made it possible for ships to detour Niagara Falls and pass from Lake Ontario to Lake Erie. With these two canals, four of the Great Lakes became accessible to shipping from the St. Lawrence. In 1855, a full-rigged ship, the *City of Toronto*, was built on Lake Ontario and sailed down the St. Lawrence, out into the ocean, and across the Atlantic to Liverpool and back.

In spite of the growth of steam, the second half of the 19th century saw many topsail schooners still on the lake. Fishing vessels were dependent on sail well into the turn of the century.

Since 1959, a joint Canadian-American project costing billions of dollars, the St. Lawrence Seaway, has considerably increased ship activity on Lake Ontario, although much of the traffic continues to be between Canadian ports on Lake Ontario and those on the upper lakes.

In the last decades of the 19th century and the early 20th century, recreational yachting and boating appeared on the lake, particularly around a magnificent island area at the eastern end of Lake Ontario. Here, the Thousand Islands, in the entrance to the St. Lawrence, became a summer playground. Many wealthy Americans and Canadians built houses on the islands and enjoyed sailing and, increasingly as time went on, motorboating among the islands.

All of these strands of Lake Ontario's maritime past have been collected in museums on Lake Ontario, most of them on the Canadian north shore. We'll start, however, with a look at two places on the American lake shore, then cross the St. Lawrence to Canada's Ontario Province.

To drive along the drowsy streets of Sackets Harbor, a little village on the east side shore of Lake Ontario, on a spring evening before the summer people come is to feel that you have stepped back in time. Surely this is how houses and harbor, serenely quiet in the twilight, must have looked 100 years ago.

But if our time machine, or imagination, could carry us back further, to the early 19th century, we'd find a very different scene. In 1812, this tiny frontier village on Lake Ontario was suddenly transformed into the United States Navy's major base on the lake, the harbor filled with warships fitting out, more warships on the ways, the streets crammed with Navy ratings, United States Marines, shipwrights, militiamen, U.S. Army regulars.

Britain, with whom the United States was at war, had had warships on Lake Ontario for many years, and was building more. Even before hostilities began, relations between the two nations grew tense and the Navy saw the need for a base on Lake Ontario to challenge British control of the lake should war come. Sackets Harbor, which had been settled only 10 years before, was chosen for its fine little harbor on Black River Bay, the only good harbor on the American side of the lake.

During the war, Sackets was protected by a small fort manned by New York militia and U.S. Army regulars. British forces based on Kingston on the Canadian side of the lake made several naval attacks on the harbor—once landing troops—but were fought off and this battlefield is now a New York State Park.

Meanwhile, the British navy was also feverishly expanding its squadron on the lake and there was a naval building race as each side sought to achieve sufficient superiority in ships and guns to win an overwhelming victory. Neither succeeded; control of the lake remained in dispute until the end of the war. The real hero of the Lake Ontario naval operation on the American side, was a civilian, Henry Eckford, a successful New York shipbuilder and ship designer. Eckford came out to Sackets Harbor with a party of workmen, and set up a shipyard in the wilderness. He proceeded to turn out warships for the United States Navy in an average time of forty days apiece, starting with living trees in the surrounding wilderness and ending with finished vessels. This was a remarkable feat in any case, but made doubly so by the location. All armaments, munitions, supplies, and ships' gear had to be brought overland, most of it hundreds of miles from New York City. The roads were so bad that when possible shipments were sent down the Oswego River to its mouth, then barged 40 miles along the shore of Lake Ontario, despite the exposure to British attack. Eckford both built vessels of war from scratch and converted commercial schooners to fighting ships, creating the Navy's Lake Ontario fleet in minimal time from minimal resources.

Incidentally, after the war, Eckford eventually went to Turkey and built big three-decker ships of the line for the Sultan.

Sackets not only continued to be an American naval and military base for decades after the War of 1812, but became for a while a busy commercial port and shipbuilding center. Here, in 1817, *Ontario*, the first American steamship launched on the Great Lakes, was built for service between Sackets and Niagara at the other end of Lake Ontario. By 1819, 100 ships a season were calling there. During tensions between the United States and Britain in the 1830s and 1840s, the naval base—which had been allowed to run down—was rehabilitated with new buildings.

A couple of these later buildings are now all that survive of the Navy's facilities. The houses of the commander and second-in-command of the naval shipyard, which were built in the 1830s and 1840s, have been restored with appropriate period furnishings and are open to visitors. While none of the original 1812 period buildings remain, the nearby Visitors Center, in an historic stone hotel built shortly after 1812, has interpretive exhibits and a slide program that tells about the wartime activities at Sackets.

Admittedly, not much that is obviously maritime-related is left at the little village today other than the harbor itself, now home port for recreational craft. (Marine archaeologists complain that New York State allowed the sunken remains of an 1812 ship on the bottom to be covered by concrete for a marina.) However, the battlefield, scene of the repulsed British landing, is interesting. Every year, military buffs from

Canada come over to meet other enthusiasts from New York State to once again reenact the Battle of Sackets Harbor in a bloodless get-together. Nearby, is a historic military post, Madison Barracks, of which the oldest part—a beautiful stone barracks—is now falling into ruins.

Sackets is really a place for visitors with a sense of history and some creative imagination. For them the little village will once again be the naval counterweight to Kingston across the lake 170 years ago, bustling with American warships—building and fitting out, some moored in the harbor, some starting out on cruises, some fighting off enemy attacks.

Sackets Harbor, once the principal U.S. naval base on Lake Ontario, on east shore about 40 miles southwest of outflow into St. Lawrence River. From Interstate 81, main north-south route, take exit 45 (Watertown) and proceed west eight miles on Route 3, turn off one mile. Buildings open Memorial Day weekend through Labor Day, Wednesday-Saturday, 10 a.m. to 5 p.m.; Sunday, 1 to 5 p.m. Admission: free. Part of New York State's Thousand Island State Park. Sackets Harbor Battlefield State Historic Site, Sackets Harbor, New York 13685. Telephone (315) 646-3634.

Now let's look at a very different recollection of Lake Ontario's maritime past.

The Adirondack Mountains, which form the northernmost part of New York State, continue north across the eastern end of Lake Ontario—but here they are underwater, their tops forming a myriad of islands where the Lake Ontario waters flow eastward into the St. Lawrence. Although they are called the Thousand Islands, there are probably more than 1,500 of them. In this beautiful part of the world (the Iroquois called it *Manitonna*, which means "the garden of the Great Spirit"), there grew up in the last decade of the 19th century a resort area where wealthy Americans and Canadians came to sail, fish, and socialize among the islands. Here, also, fishermen and guides developed such distinctive types of boats as the St. Lawrence skiff: a 22-foot clinker-built double-ender, the only known type of small craft that could be sailed without a rudder or a guiding oar.

Today, the millionaire resorts are gone, but the memories of the rich watercraft inheritance of the area are preserved in a fine museum at Clayton, a little village on the south shore where the St. Lawrence skiff probably originated in the late 1860s. Called the Thousand Islands Shipyard Museum, it is located on the village waterfront, facing the ship channel of the St. Lawrence Seaway, in buildings formerly part of the last shipyard to survive in the area. The museum is dedicated "to the preservation of fresh water nautical history along the beautiful St. Lawrence River"; it has as its particular specialty not only the St. Lawrence skiff and similar regional craft, but classic powerboats. Its collection of such powered small craft is probably the finest anywhere in America.

A remarkable number of boats of many different kinds are on display—in the museum, on covered outdoor racks, and in the water—ranging from birch bark canoes to fishing boats and luxury runabouts.

Among the particularly notable craft to be seen are:

- The launch *Ariel*, built in 1880 and originally owned by President Garfield.
- The Gold Cup racers, *Moike*, a 36-footer built in 1904; and *Dixie II*, which not only won the Harmsworth Trophy three years in a row but held the power boat speed record in 1910 at 45 miles an hour; the last displacement boat to be the record holder before the planing hulls took over.
- The 42-foot *Mohegan*, an open power boat that carried the mail among the islands.
- The 25-foot naphtha-powered launch *Anita* of 1902.

One of the museum's newest exhibits shows the evolution of the St. Lawrence skiff from a small rowing boat to a large fish and guide vessel, 20 to 25 feet long. Here, also, are special types of regional small craft, not only Native American canoes, but Rushton wooden canoes, and the ice boats inspired by the frigid winters of the area. The 50-foot sightseeing boat *Narrah Mattah*, built in 1902, is the largest of the museum's fleet of waterborne classics.

The museum also displays what is said to be the oldest outboard motor in America; part of a large collection of boat engines.

Other exhibits at the museum include models, paintings, and photographs of small craft. The emphasis, however, is very much on the boats themselves, particularly those from the late 19th century and the early years of the 20th. These were the years when the small powered boat was just coming into its own with the introduction of the internal-combustion engine, and when rivercraft were receiving respectful attention from millionaire Americans. The highpoint of the museum year is the Antique Boat Show, usually held in early August, to which owners bring hundreds of classic boats for a series of competitions, displays, and festivities.

Thousand Islands Shipyard Museum, said to be world's largest motorboat museum, is in Clayton, New York. From I-81, connecting Syracuse and Thousand Islands International Bridge, take exit 50S to Route 12, then west five miles to Clayton; there right on Theresa Street. Museum, at end of Mary Street, is in several buildings of former shipyard.

Book/gift shop. Library. Open mid-May to June, Thursday-Monday, 10 a.m. to 4 p.m.; mid-June to Labor Day, daily 10 a.m. to 5 p.m.; day after Labor Day to mid-October, Thursday-Monday 10 a.m. to 5 p.m. Admission: $4.00; seniors and students, $3.00. Includes boat ride in the summer. Thousand Islands Shipyard Museum, 750 Mary Street, Clayton, New York 13624. Telephone (315) 686-4104.

From Clayton, it's an easy drive to where I-81 crosses the St. Lawrence to the Canadian side and then west to Kingston, the historic little city on the north shore of Lake Ontario.

Kingston stands on historic ground, close to where Lake Ontario's waters enter the St. Lawrence. Perhaps no other place has been so deeply involved in major events in the early maritime history of the Great Lakes. For it was here, at the mouth of the Cataragui River, that Governor Frontenac of New France chose in 1673 to build his fort to dominate Lake Ontario, the Indians, and the fur trade. Among other things, this led to:

- The first application of the European concept of mobile sea power on the Great Lakes, when Frontenac brought to the site of the fort two sailing flatboats, each mounting a row of cannon, and used them to overawe the Iroquois who met him there.
- The first use of European marine technology on the lakes, when La Salle built four sailing vessels at the fort: two-masted "barks," said to resemble luggers. (But Francis Parkman, the great historian of New France, says canoes continued to be used ordinarily.)
- Establishment of a fortified port (first French, then British) at which were built and based the little warships that dominated Lake Ontario—and hence the water route to the west—well into the 19th century.
- Construction of the SS *Frontenac*, the first steamship on any of the Great Lakes, built in the Kingston area in 1818.

Today, Kingston is a pleasant university town where maritime traditions are preserved in a museum on the harborfront. The Marine Museum of the Great Lakes, which is housed in one-time shipyard buildings next to an ancient stone dry dock, bears an inscription at the entrance that reads: "Kingston—where sail and steam began on the Great Lakes." The museum focuses primarily on Lake Ontario and, naturally, on the activities at Kingston as its oldest and most historic port.

Photographs, artifacts, prints, paintings, ship models, and slide films all tell the story. One unusual and very impressive exhibit is a shipbuilding gallery in which a long sequence of very large photographs with accompanying text shows in detail, almost day by day, how a steel freighter was built in 1922.

A highlight of the ship model collection is a typical Canadian corvette of World War II, similar to those built in Kingston. Other models include lake ore carriers, Canadian Coast Guard cutters and patrol boats, and a ship shown towing a huge timber raft.

One unique exhibit is an "iceboat"; it was adapted for coping with the special conditions a boat faced in coming ashore from a lake island in winter, when the passage meant crossing patches of both solid ice and open water. Essentially a punt on runners, it was pushed along by the crew who jumped aboard as they felt the ice give way beneath them.

One wall of the museum is covered with striking builders' half models, dating from 1883 to the 1920s, taken from Kingston shipyards; equally impressive is a nearby wall of photographs of lake steamers. The gallery of underwater archaeology shows artifacts brought up from wrecks at the bottom of Lake Ontario, including relics of the steamship *Comet*, which sank after a collision in the lake.

The steam engines and pumps used to pump out the stepped-stone dry dock adjacent to the museum building are still in place. The museum hopes eventually to restore them to their original condition.

The Marine Museum of the Great Lakes is on the Lake Ontario shore at Kingston, Ontario. Parking. Blacksmith shop. Educational program. Library. Gift shop/bookstore. Open mid-April to October 31, every day, 10 a.m. to 5 p.m. November 1 to mid-December, Tuesday-Sunday, 10 a.m. to 5 p.m. Admission: $2.50; seniors and students, $1.50; families, $3.50. Marine Museum of the Great Lakes at Kingston, 55 Ontario Street, Kingston, Ontario K7L 2Y2, Canada. Telephone (613) 542-2261.

Many visitors to Kingston will want to see Old Fort Henry, built during the War of 1812 to protect the naval base from American attacks. Here the "Fort Henry Guard," dressed in historic British uniforms, demonstrate the infantry drills and artillery salutes of other days. There are 15 museums, galleries, and historic sites in the Kingston area.

From Kingston, Route 401 runs up along the north shore of Lake Ontario directly to Toronto.

There are curious parallels between the histories of Toronto and Washington, D.C. Both were founded by conscious government decision, rather than the choice of settlers, and both were planned as capital cities; in Toronto's case, capital of the new province of Upper Canada (now Ontario). Both were captured by enemy troops during the War of 1812, and both were burned, although under quite different circumstances.

Unlike Washington, however, Toronto went on to become Canada's major industrial, commercial, and financial center, as well as the greatest of its lake ports. Sited on a large, shallow bay where the river Don enters Lake Ontario, Toronto grew steadily as a port; at first, a lumber port, until the nearby forests were cut away. As its shipping expanded, the city deepened and improved and eventually outgrew its harbor, spreading its port facilities out along the lake for many miles. As the province filled with people, Toronto became the distribution point for a large part of Canada's population. Today, of course, it is not only Canada's largest English-speaking city and the center of a huge metropolitan area, but also a world port, thanks to the St. Lawrence Seaway, which opened the Great Lakes to large oceangoing vessels.

Toronto's maritime heritage is recognized and cherished in the Marine Museum of Upper Canada, located right on the Toronto lakefront. The museum is housed in the former officers' quarters of British troops who were stationed in Toronto. In its own words, the museum tells "of our marine heritage on the waterways of Central Canada and development of commerce on the Great Lakes."

The museum is carefully organized by topic with galleries devoted to such subjects as warships, underwater activities, commercial vessels, canoes and kayaks, the fur trade (largely waterborne by canoe), and the activities of tugs, freighters, and passenger ships in Toronto's harbor. Of particular interest:

- The mock-up of a 1928 wireless room. Notice that the operator still used the Morse code key at that time rather than voice signal.
- Another mock-up showing part of a sailing warship's bulwark with cannon in place, presumably a vessel of the period of the War of 1812.
- A third reconstruction presents a fur trader's shop, with furs and a counter where the Indians swapped their winter's trapping for trade goods. Furs and trade goods were the cargoes of the earliest, canoe-borne commerce of the lakes.
- The many delightful ship models: freighters, tankers, tugs, lake sailing craft, schooners and fishermen, side-wheeler steamers, ore carriers, great ocean liners, and such historic vessels as La Salle's ship *Griffin*.
- A remarkable collection of ships' steam whistles, which are periodically sounded off for the benefit of audio-minded visitors.
- A full-sized birch bark canoe, as well as many models showing the variation in canoe design

from region to region and from one Indian tribe to another.

There are also, of course, many artifacts, such as navigational instruments, sailmakers' and shipwrights' tools, and charts. On the walls are paintings, prints, and photographs of Toronto and Lake Ontario in various stages of maritime development.

Outside, on the lawn next to the museum, is a veteran Toronto tug, the *Ned Hanlan*, named for a famous Toronto oarsman who won many medals around the turn of the century. The tug is open to visitors, who will get a good idea of how such a craft is organized: engine room, wheelhouse, and so on. (Inside the museum, a whole room is devoted to Hanlan the oarsman and his outstanding athletic career.) In front of the museum, in a glass case, is a triple-expansion steam engine that is motor-driven to demonstrate how the different parts work in relation to each other.

There is a good restaurant on the lowest floor of the museum; recommended.

Marine Museum of Upper Canada is in the grounds of Toronto's Exhibition Place, beside Lake Ontario. Ship Inn Restaurant. Bookshop. Open daily, all year. Monday-Saturday, 9:30 a.m. to 5:00 p.m. Sundays and holidays, noon to 5 p.m. Admission: $1.50, seniors and children, $1. Owned by City of Toronto, operated by Toronto Historical Board. Marine Museum of Upper Canada, Stanley Barracks, Exhibition Place, Toronto, Ontario M6K 3C3. Telephone (416) 392-6827.

Look toward the lakefront, a little to the westward of the Museum, and there she lies quietly at her retirement berth: HMCS *Haida*, long, lean, grey. Her paint as spic and span as the day she left the builder's yard, *Haida* does not look like a grizzled combat veteran of two wars. But if ships could dream, *Haida* would have plenty to dream about. Certainly, none of the almost 250 men who were in her ever forgot that night in April 1944, when *Haida* went on combat patrol off the coast of France with her sister Tribal Class destroyer, HMCS *Athabaskan*. (The Tribal Class ships were named for Indian tribes: The Haida, pronounced "Hy-da," live on Canada's Pacific coast.)

Here, somewhat compressed, is how William Sclater tells of the climactic events of that night in *Haida*, his lively history of the ship. (Which is worth owning; it can be purchased at the ship.) The time was past three a.m. off the Ile de Blas; moon had set; two German destroyers were on the radar screen in toward the French coast: Now, Sclater:

Information coming from the Plot gave the range of the enemy ships as 7,000 yards now.

"Ignite," said the Captain.

"Three stars, spreading left, fire!" ordered the Illumination Control Officer through his telephone, and the guns at X mounting fired with a crack like a whip as the ship sped onwards.

"There they are . . . two of them."

"Red five o, two enemy destroyers," called an observer.

"Open fire," said the Captain.

Haida's for'd gun mountings came into action then and the ship rolled with the recoil. *Athabaskan* was firing too, with starshell and main armament.

"Enemy making smoke and turning to Eastward," came a report.

The Captain studied the situation briefly. It was a critical moment. If he turned too soon the enemy might still get past to the Westward. Deciding to take a chance on that he gave the order.

"Port 20, executive to *Athabaskan*." The two Tribals heeled over as they started to come around, maintaining their fire at the same time . . . . Enemy starshell was bursting over and between them and the whistle of other shells passing overhead could be heard as he brought his main armament into action.

Just then came a cry, "*Athabaskan*'s been hit," which made every head on *Haida*'s bridge turn around.

They could see her plainly. She was right on station, close astern, and had not yet lost her way. From somewhere aft of the bridge, a great column of flame was shooting up, outlining her foresection in bold relief. Even as they looked her B gun fired.

From the enemy ships there came a frenzied burst of gunfire as they sighted the burning destroyer and turned all their guns on her in an endeavour to give her a knockout blow.

His face grim, the Captain of *Haida* spoke briefly. "Make smoke," he ordered; "we'll put a screen across to protect *Athabaskan*. Tell them what we're doing," he added . . . *Haida*, alone, and with the fire of both German destroyers converging on her, was carrying the fight to the enemy. If her gunners had been fast before, they fought desperately now . . . .

"A hit." The tell-tale glow of fire broke out amidships on the first German destroyer and smouldered through the smoke. Something was happening over there. The second enemy ship appeared to be slowing and was falling behind the first. Studying the situation, the Captain decided to change targets and *Haida*'s guns swung on the second enemy ship.

One salvo punched out at her; another and another, as the guns were ranged and directed, and then came a hit. High amidships flames mounted on the German's superstructure.

"It's a hit," came the relieved shout. Another salvo shuddered into her and the flames spread. Then suddenly the burning enemy destroyer gave out with a vicious burst of close-range fire directed towards her fleeting consort.

It was answered by a return burst from the other ship. In the confusion they seemed unable to tell friend from foe.

A deep rumble and the noise of a tremendous explosion from somewhere astern caused *Haida*'s bridge crew to look back again. They saw an awesome sight. Hundreds of feet above the black pall of the smokescreen and lighting it from above, a great column of flames and debris was shooting up into the air above where their sister ship had been.

"There goes the *Athabaskan*," said an officer sadly . . .

But here, close at hand was the burning enemy ship. She was badly hit and *Haida*, with a double motive now, surged forward for the kill.

"Reefs ahead," sang out the Officer of the Watch.

"Port 20," said the Captain, and *Haida* heeled over and swung away from the shore. The enemy destroyer, burning furiously, had driven up on the beach out of control. Swinging round, *Haida* let her have it, again and again, to finish her off. She was well afire and intermittent explosions were bursting through the smoke and flames when they finished . . .

. . . *Haida* turned back toward where the *Athabaskan* had been.

Only two nights before this action, *Haida* had played a major part in sinking one German destroyer and putting two or three others to flight. In one three-month period in the spring and summer of 1944, *Haida* was in on the sinking of 14 enemy ships, including four destroyers and a submarine. Later, she served two tours of combat duty in the Korean War. No wonder Canadians call *Haida* the fightingest, and best-loved, ship in the Royal Canadian Navy. Now she is a memorial to the men and women of the sea service, on display in Ontario Place on the lake next to Exhibition Place.

Haida was built on Britain's Tyne in 1941-43; a 3,000-ton vessel, 370 feet long. Manned by 248 officers and ratings, she carried a main battery of four-inch guns plus antiaircraft and smaller weapons. At her stern, she carried so-called squid bombs, an advanced type of depth charge.

The *Haida* has been beautifully maintained and, where necessary, restored. With almost all parts of the vessel open to visitors, you should be warned that the complete tour involves a strenuous trip up and down real ladders, not just steep stairs, and is not for those who are easily tired. The engine room is of particular interest, even though you have to climb way down into the bowels of the ship to see it. The *Haida* is propelled by two steam turbines, which drove her at 36 1/2 knots.

Navy buffs will be interested in comparing *Haida* with the various retired American destroyers of roughly the same vintage, several of which have been placed on exhibition in various parts of the United States. In the *Haida* fo'c'sle, notice the bars on which hammocks were slung. Hammocks disappeared from the American Navy many decades ago, but they remained in the British and Canadian Navies until fairly recently, survivors from the fighting ships of the days of Nelson's HMS *Victory*, and the USS *Constitution*.

HMCS *Haida*, moored on Toronto waterfront at Ontario Place, adjacent to Exhibition Place, on Lakeshore Boulevard West and Strachan Drive. Open daily mid-May to the weekend after Labor Day, 10 a.m. to 7 p.m. General admission to Ontario Place (includes various shows, concerts, etc.): $4.25; $2.50, youth; $1.00, children. Senior citizens, free. Admission to *Haida*: 75 cents; children, 50 cents. HMCS *Haida*, Ontario Place, Exhibition Place, 955 Lakeshore Boulevard West, Toronto, Ontario M6K 3B9, Canada. Telephone (416) 965-7711.

Toronto's maritime exhibits are not limited to the Marine Museum of Upper Canada and the *Haida*. The Ontario Science Centre, a wonderful, sprawling institution covering a wide range of human activities, has fine maritime displays in its Transportation Division and Canadian Resources Section.

The transportation division displays a number of unusually fine ship models, including a 1650 Dutch cargo ship, *Houtpoort*; a very handsome five-foot planked model of the famous clipper *Sovereign of the Seas*; and a small, nice model of the Prince Edward Island brigantine *Raven* of 1875. There is also an extremely interesting diorama of a shipyard in St. John, New Brunswick, in 1851, showing the famous *Marco Polo* nearing completion on the ways.

Most of these models, and the diorama, are the works of a remarkable craftsman-in-residence, model maker Ben Verburgh. For the past 20 years, he has been building beautiful models for the museum in a little glass-walled shop set up in the gallery so that museum visitors can watch him at work. A friendly and approachable man, Verburgh is happy to talk about what he is doing and about the ships that he builds with infinite care and craftsmanship. On display during a typical visit, for example, was a Grand Banks schooner cut-away, showing the fish hold and a number of dories stacked on deck. Equally interesting was the steamship *Royal William* of Quebec on which Verburgh was working at the time. (The model has since been put on display in the adjacent Hall of Technology.) The original *Royal William*, a 175-foot side-wheeler built in Quebec, was of historic importance not only in Canadian but in world maritime history: In 1833, she crossed the Atlantic from Canada to England entirely under steam power alone—the first all-steam ocean crossing ever.

In the Canadian Resources Section, in the mezzanine of the same building as the transportation division, is a model of Roald Amundsen's little vessel *Gjoa*, in which the explorer became the first person to sail through the long-sought Northwest Passage from the Atlantic to the Pacific, through the Arctic ice around the north of Canada. Here, also, is a beautiful diorama of a Norse shipyard as it would have looked 1,000 years ago: Its caption explains that in such a yard were built the vessels that brought the Norsemen westward to become the first Europeans known to have landed on North America.

An animated model demonstrates the operation of St. Lambert's Lock in the St. Lawrence Seaway. When a visitor presses a button, a freighter enters, goes into the lock, rises as the water—theoretically—lifts it, then steams out the other end.

Ontario Science Centre is at the southwest corner of Eglinton Avenue East and Don Mills Road (connecting to Don Valley Parkway North) on a hilltop overlooking Toronto. Fine large hands-on general science/industry museum. Maritime exhibits mostly in Transportation Division, in lower level building at far rear, reached via elevators/escalators. Get museum map; watch for signs. Bookstore. Gift shop. Cafeteria. Open all year, daily except Christmas; 10 a.m. to 6 p.m. (may be open longer hours in the summer). Admission: $3.00; youth, $2.00; children, $1.00; seniors, free. Parking, $1.00. An Agency of Ontario Ministry of Citizenship and Culture. Ontario Science Centre, 770 Don Mills Road, Don Mills, Ontario, M3C 1T3. Telephone (416) 429-4423 or 429-4100.

Now we'll proceed westward for one last visit on the shores of Lake Ontario. At Hamilton, a flourishing city and lake port, is a fascinating report on a remarkable archaeological discovery on the bottom of the lake.

August 7, 1813

> . . . night shut in with the two opponents sailing in parallel lines, heading north, with the wind at west; the Americans to leeward and in rear of the British. At two in the morning, in a heavy squall, two schooners upset, with the loss of all on board save sixteen souls. Chauncey reckoned these to be among his best, and, as they together mounted nineteen guns, he considered that 'this accident gave the enemy decidedly the superiority' . . .

> Alfred Mahan,
> *Sea Power in its Relations to the War of 1812*

Thus, briefly, naval historian Alfred Mahan referred to the loss of the American schooners *Hamilton* and *Scourge* in a Lake Ontario squall. And thus their loss might have gone down in history (with a correction: 19 were saved) as little more than a footnote, except . . .

Except for two things. The first is that one of the survivors of the *Scourge* had been a shipmate of James Fenimore Cooper and years later gave the author a vivid first-person account of the catastrophe, which Cooper used as the basis for his book *Ned Myers; or a Life Before the Mast*. The second is that Canadian historians and marine archaeologists became interested in finding where the schooners went down. In 1973, they located two sonar targets in the general area 300 feet underwater and two years later, using an experimental diving device carrying a television camera, were able to see and photograph one of them. They identified it as one of the lost vessels, still in a remarkable state of preservation. (The other "target" was later also tracked down and found to be the other schooner.)

Just what was found is shown in detail in beautiful pictures accompanying a full take-out in the March, 1983, issue of *National Geographic*, which also includes excerpts from Cooper's version of his friend's narrative of the sinkings. The icy waters in the depths of Lake Ontario have kept the hull, fittings, guns, and even the bones of trapped sailors where they were when the schooners sank almost 175 years ago. While the rigging has gone and the spars have fallen on the decks, three of four masts still stand. The hulls appear undamaged.

Whether the two ships will ever be brought to the surface is uncertain. Preservation of such finds presents problems. For instance, it is uncertain what would happened to wood that has been well-preserved in dark, cold, fresh water if it's dried out and exposed to light, warmth, and air. While preservation techniques have been developed using absorption of a waxlike substance, they are difficult, and costly, and the results are far from certain. For the time being, the vessels are being left on the lake bottom while marine archaeologists devise new techniques for precisely mapping and recording the nature, position, and condition of every part of the ships and their contents.

Which does not mean that the public will have no view of this wonderful find. At an interpretive center in the City of Hamilton's Confederation Park, the marine archaeological project is explained by an audiovisual program and graphic displays. The ships are shown in a Jacques Cousteau film and video tapes, and literature is available describing the vessels, their background, and their discovery.

A memorial garden with the names of the American sailors lost with the schooners has been dedicated at the site, and marked by a replica of *Scourge*'s 65-foot foremast. Incidentally, a complete account of the Hamilton-Scourge Project will be found in *Ghost Ships-Hamilton and Scourge*, by Emily Cain.

Hamilton-Scourge Interpretive Center is in Confederation Park on Lake Ontario at Hamilton, Ontario. Park is at the north end of Highway 20 just off Queen Elizabeth Highway, at the south end of the Skyway Bridge. Open July to Labor Day, every day, 10 a.m. to 6 p.m. Bookstore. Admission to center free, but required parking costs approximate $2.50. Hamilton-Scourge Project Headquarters, Hamilton City Hall, 71 Main Street West, Hamilton, Ontario L8N 3T4. Telephone (416) 526-4601.

One final note before leaving Hamilton. The Hamilton Military Museum includes the Royal Canadian Navy in its coverage, and from time to time

has special exhibits on various aspects of the sea service. The museum is housed in historic Battery Lodge in Dundern Park and is open every day except Christmas and New Year's. Summer hours, mid-June to Labor Day, are noon to 5 p.m.; for the rest of the year, 2 to 5 p.m. The park is on York Boulevard at Dundern, and the telephone is (416) 523-5681.

Now back to the United States at Buffalo on Lake Erie, the southernmost of the Great Lakes.

Lake Erie (and Lake Chautauqua)

The wind came on to blow a gale . . . It rained incessantly, the night was very dark, and to add [to] the danger of the situation, the boat began to leak badly. About 8 o'clock, the Captain, finding it impossible to proceed further, put about and started back to Buffalo.

The sailing master proposed running the boat into the Niagara River and anchoring, but the Captain said it was so dark that she might strike the pier in the attempt, and in such a case, no human power could save a soul on board. The boat was run to within a few miles of the pier, as the Captain supposed . . . Three anchors were dropped, one with a chain and two with hempen cables. The boat plunged heavily at her anchorage . . . the leak continued to increase. The whole power of the engine was applied to the pumps. The boat dragged her anchors . . . It was the impression of the great number on board that we should never see the morning.

The water gained gradually in spite of every exertion, and it was evident, as the night wore on, that the bark must founder or be run ashore . . .

About half-past four in the morning the Captain sent down for all the passengers to come on deck. He had decided . . . to permit the boat to go ashore. The chain cable was slipped and the two hempen ones cut. Drifting before the gale, the Walk-in-the-Water, in about half an hour, grazed the beach. The next swell let her down with a crash of crockery and glass, the third left her further up the shore, fixed immovably in the sand, the swells made a clear breach over her. Some of the ladies were in their night clothes and all were repeatedly drenched.

When daylight came, a sailor succeeded in getting ashore in a small boat, with one end of a hawser, which he tied to a tree, the other end being tied on board. By the aid of the hawser, all the passengers were taken ashore in a small boat.

Personal narrative from the
Buffalo and Erie County Historical Society Archives

Thus, Mrs. Mary A. Witherell Palmer recalled the sad end of *Walk-in-the-Water*, the first steamboat on Lake Erie, on the last day of October 1821. Mrs. Palmer had boarded the side-wheeler at Buffalo at 4 o'clock that afternoon, homeward bound for Detroit after a visit to New York. The three-year-old *Walk-in-the-Water*, rigged as a handsome topsail schooner with a carved Oliver Hazard Perry on her bow, was a total loss but her engines were salvaged and installed in another steamboat.

The only unusual aspect of the wreck of Lake Erie's first steamship was that no lives were lost. The lake was already a notorious ship-killer. Next to smallest of the Great Lakes, it is by far the shallowest, a bowl averaging only 90 feet in depth. At the same time, it is located at the meeting place of competing weather systems. Harlan Hatcher, in *Lake Erie*, a notable book devoted to the lake, vividly describes what happens:

The shallow basin and the position of Lake Erie also make it the most tempestuous and choppy of the Great Lakes. The wide frontal storms roaring down over Lake Huron from Upper Canada and Hudson Bay strike Lake Erie with great force. The subtropical highs press in from the south. They engage in conflict over and around Lake Erie, and its shallow waters plunge and toss furiously. The winds can whip up tremendous seas on the surface almost without warning. The navigation charts are figured on low-water datum of 570.5 feet above sea level. The actual level fluctuates widely from half a foot below this datum in winter to four feet above it in certain summers. And the wind alone, sweeping up from southwest to northeast along the axis of the lake, may lower the level at Toledo by eight or more feet; while the depth of the harbors at the east end may rise by several feet.

Likewise a strong east wind lowers the water at Buffalo and has, at times, actually laid bare the rock bottom of the lake near Fort Erie.

All through its maritime history Lake Erie has been unpredictable. Uncounted numbers of disasters, tragedies and shipwrecks have overtaken the men who have sailed over her blue surface.

Although the east end of Lake Erie, where its waters flow out through the Niagara River into Lake Ontario, is only a little more than 200 miles from the head of the St. Lawrence, Erie was the last of the Great Lakes to be visited and explored by Europeans. The long delay—more than half a century after Champlain reached Lakes Huron and Ontario on either side—was due to the hostility of the Iroquois who long controlled the approaches to the lake from the eastward. As a result, French explorers and fur traders took a northerly route to the west via the Ottawa River from Montreal to Lake Huron, bypassing both Lake Erie and Lake Ontario. Only after a French military expedition into the eastern Iroquois country forced a temporary peace were the lower lakes safe for travelers.

Thus, it was only in 1669 that Louis Jolliet, returning from a prospecting trip to Lake Superior, came back down Lake Huron, entered Lake Erie and canoed along the northern shore. Jolliet was the first European visitor by only a few days, however, for crossing to Lake Ontario he met the famous Sieur de La Salle headed westward on his first exploration trip.

Ten years later, La Salle established a base on the Niagara River above the falls and there had built the *Griffin* (or *Griffon*), the first ship on Lake Erie. Returning with a cargo of furs from Lake Michigan, on her maiden voyage, the *Griffin* was lost with all hands; and there were no more ships on Lake Erie for almost 100 years. Small craft were often on its waters, however, as the lake became an important link in the water route that tied together the French network of forts and fur trading posts that spread around the Great Lakes and across the upper Ohio and Mississippi valleys. Canoes, bateaux, and whaleboats (so-called) carried fur traders, missionaries, and soldiers not only back and forth the length of the lake, but also up the little rivers that run into Lake Erie from the south. A short paddle reached the low watershed; here, an easy portage took travelers to rivers running south into the Ohio, providing a water route to the Mississippi and down that river to Louisiana.

To control entry to this key section of the French wilderness empire, forts were built at the two ends of Lake Erie—Detroit in the west, and Niagara in the east—early in the 18th century. The final British conquest of New France, however, swallowed up the

French posts throughout the Great Lakes region and the upper Mississippi Valley.

When Major Robert Rogers and his Rangers traveled westward along the lakes to receive the surrender of the French garrison at Detroit in 1760, they paddled and sailed in a column of 15 whaleboats, camping ashore each night; the trip from Montreal took 76 days. However, the British set to work at once to build schooners, and established a shipyard on the Niagara River. The *Huron* and *Michigan*, two 60-foot vessels armed with three cannon each, were launched in 1763; they proved invaluable in keeping a flow of supplies moving across Lake Erie to Detroit during Pontiac's War, which broke out almost at once. Ten years later a second British naval shipyard was established in Detroit. The two yards turned out a little fleet of armed schooners and commercial vessels to supply the British garrisons and trading posts. British sea power—lake power—kept Lake Ontario as well as the other Great Lakes firmly under British control long after the American Revolution ended. When the British belatedly turned over the fort at Detroit in 1796, the American troops who received it had to hire two ships to take them up Lake Erie and the Detroit River.

The flow of American settlers westward after the Revolution brought no immediate increase of shipping on lonely Lake Erie. A waterway to the West it might be, but Lake Erie already had a bad reputation for furious and unpredictable storms, and even in good weather the current—and frequently the wind—was from west to east, which meant arduous rowing in open boats. Not surprisingly, emigrants preferred the Ohio River; with no storms or high waves, and a current flowing south and west, it was an easier route, along which they could float on flatboats or even rafts. When settlers did come to take up lands along the southern shore of Lake Erie, they frequently preferred to drive their wagons and cattle along the beaches that rimmed the lake rather than risk them afloat.

Thus, when the War of 1812 came, much of the Ohio lakeshore was still wilderness. The British naval squadron on the lake, based on the Canadian side of the Detroit River, was tiny—just three small vessels, the largest 17 guns, plus armed trading schooners—but it dominated the lake. The American naval forces were almost nonexistent: a transport schooner and a brig undergoing repairs; both were quickly captured. The lack of naval power to protect the flow of supplies from the East was one factor in the quick surrender of Detroit by American forces in the early months of the war.

In 1813, the United States Navy established two shipyards, first at Black Rock on the Niagara River and then on Lake Erie itself at Presque Isle (Erie, Pennsylvania), and set about building ships to challenge British control.

The major American ships, two brigs and three schooners, were built at Erie in record time, despite the fact that the shipwrights and supplies had to make a five-week journey through the wilderness from the Atlantic coast. The timber was cut in April; the ships were afloat and ready for battle in August. Meanwhile, thanks to a fortuitous fog, the smaller vessels from the Niagara River evaded British attempts to intercept them and joined those at Erie. In September, Oliver Hazard Perry, who had superintended the whole operation, led his little fleet into battle against the British squadron off Put-in-Bay at the west end of Lake Erie. The resulting defeat and capture of the British ships insured that when peace returned the lakes would remain the boundary between the two nations. In 1817, Britain and the United States agreed that neither would keep more than one lightly-armed warship on the Great Lakes. Despite minor violations, the agreement has essentially remained in effect to this day.

After the war, sails began to appear on the hitherto lonely lake. The revived fur trade required shipping supplies to the western lakes and bringing back cargoes of pelts. Settlers began to travel Lake Erie out to the growing town around the fort at Detroit. Buffalo had only a shallow harbor but the village was nevertheless the obvious terminal port at the east end of the lake. Little villages sprang up at the mouths of the small rivers that ran into the lake from the south; soon they began to build their own schooners to carry passengers and local produce along the lakeshore and to Buffalo for market.

Despite *Walk-in-the-Water*'s dire fate, the advantages of steamboats on Lake Erie, with its strong currents and head winds, were obvious and the engine of the wrecked vessel was quickly salvaged and used in a new steamer. But what really made Lake Erie shipping boom was the opening of the Erie Canal in 1825. Connecting Lake Erie directly to the Hudson River, the canal created an all-water route for passengers and cargo all the way from New York City to Illinois and Wisconsin.

The Erie Canal was quickly followed by another from Lake Erie to the Ohio River, via the Cuyahoga and Muskingum rivers. Even before this canal was finished, the cargoes brought down from inland Ohio farms made the little village of Cleveland at the mouth of the Cuyahoga a bustling port, giving it a vital head start toward becoming the major port on the south shore of the lake.

At almost the same time, a third key waterway was built in Canada: the Welland Canal provided a route around Niagara Falls, so that lake vessels could travel directly between Lake Erie and Lake Ontario. The canal fever was catching; before the builders were done, three more were tied into Lake Erie, making it the center of a network of waterways. These later canals suffered heavily from the competition of the new railroad lines being constructed, however, and none was as successful as the Erie.

Soon steamboats were being built in many towns along the lake. Many were lost in storms, explosions, collisions, or else were capsized; but better ones were built, with more efficient engines, and as the western lands were settled there were cargoes, notably grain, to carry back east to Buffalo. Eventually, Buffalo became a major grain port, its harbor lined with storage elevators.

By 1833, 11 steamers were carrying 50,000 immigrants a season from Buffalo to ports on the western lakes. And the wood-burners not only multipled in number but in size and efficiency. In 1838, the *Great Western*, which was built especially to carry settlers, became the first steamer with cabins above her main deck, a feature that greatly increased her human payload. Three years later, the lake steamer *Vandalia* became the first commercial steamer in the world to use John Ericsson's ship propeller instead of paddle wheels, permitting more compact engines that consumed far less fuel. Eventually, however, more efficient side-wheel steamers were designed; in shallow waters they were better balanced and faster than their propeller rivals. One of the most famous passenger liners on Lake Erie, the 500-foot *Seeandbee*, was a side-wheeler: Built in 1912-13, she was one of the last of the Great Lakes passenger carriers.

Meanwhile, sailing vessels—primarily schooners—continued to be the workhorses of the lake. The shallow waters of most of the Lake Erie ports dominated ship design, requiring light-draft vessels. Around 1825, a distinctive lake-schooner type developed, said to have been pioneered at yards in Lorain and Huron. Drawing less than five feet, these vessels had a broader than average beam in relation to their length. To increase stability and sailing qualities, experiments were made with leeboards but the fierce lake storms tore them off; finally centerboards and dagger boards solved the problem. At the same time, the conventional two-masted schooner rig is said to have been modified by increasing the space between the masts, permitting a larger foresail.

Meanwhile, the discovery in the mid-19th century of immense deposits of iron ore near Lake Superior brought an endless flow of ships all the way down through Lake Huron to the Lake Erie ports. The coal needed to smelt the ore lay to the south of Erie. Since at the outset it took about four tons of coal to make a ton of iron or steel, it was obviously more economical to bring the ore to the vicinity of the coal than the other way around. Railroads brought the coal up from western Pennsylvania and southern Ohio to the lake ports; bulk carriers, which grew even larger over the years, brought the ore down through the lakes to Cleveland, Toledo, Erie, Buffalo, Detroit, and other smaller ports where the steel mills boomed.

The lack of such a wedding of ore and coal was one reason why the Canadian, northern, shore of Lake Erie never developed ports to match those on the south. In sharp contrast to Lake Ontario, the maritime action on Lake Erie has all been on the American shore; the little Canadian ports on the lake lacked the cargoes, in or out, to make worthwhile the dredging and breakwaters needed to turn shallow river mouths into fine harbors. Actually, none of the ports that serve the Canadian region north of the lake is on Lake Erie; Windsor, on the Detroit River, and Sarnia, on the St. Clair River, are the maritime outlets to the west while Hamilton and Toronto on Lake Ontario provide shipping points to the east.

In the late 19th and early 20th centuries, Lake Erie still swarmed with shipping, carrying primarily freight but still many passengers. As everywhere, first the railroads, then highways and automobiles enticed away both cargoes and passengers. But the great bulk carriers still survive, bigger than ever. And the traditions of an earlier maritime Lake Erie, from canoes to supercarriers, are preserved in a number of maritime museums along the Erie shore.

Let's start with Buffalo, at the east end of the lake, then follow around the south shore.

Drive down to Buffalo's waterfront and right away it's clear what once made the city one of America's great inland ports: Huge grain elevators still loom over the harbor like the massive towers of medieval fortresses. Here, at the eastern end of Lake Erie, where the lake waters flow out to Lake Ontario, Buffalo long received a golden flow of grain from the west, some to be processed, some to be sent on by barge or rail still further east. In the 1930s, one-fifth of all the grain grown in the United States passed through Buffalo's 40 grain elevators. Added to other bulk cargoes such as iron ore and limestone, these shipments made Buffalo at that time the first port on the Great Lakes with respect to the value of gross tonnage.

What gave Buffalo its real start as a port was its selection as the western terminus of the Erie Canal. Even though it was the home port for the short-lived *Walk-in-the-Water*, first steamboat on Lake Erie, Buffalo was little more than an overgrown village before the canal arrived. The entrance to the basin at the mouth of Buffalo Creek, which formed the harbor, was shallow and dangerous. Black Rock, almost three miles down the nearby Niagara River, had a better harbor, but as the river rushed to plunge over Niagara Falls, the current was so strong that ships often had to be towed out to the lake by oxen. Lake Erie already had a bad reputation for rough weather and head winds and most west-bound immigrants in the early 19th century preferred a more southerly route via the Ohio River.

But the Erie Canal changed all this: To become the terminus for the canal, Buffalo dredged its harbor entrance and became a viable port. When the canal was completed in 1825, travelers and freight could be carried all the way from New York City to Buffalo by water, and there transferred to a lake vessel. Some went on by sailing ship, which was cheaper but much slower than the new steamboats. Just eight years after the canal opened, however, 11 steamers out of Buffalo carried 50,000 passengers a year to Great Lakes ports further west. Each year bigger, faster steamships were built. And soon, as the newcomers cleared and planted the rich farmlands of the upper Middle West, the immigrant ships were coming back to Buffalo with cargoes of grain.

The first result was a tremendous back-up of grain ships in the harbor. Each barrel or bag of grain had to be hoisted out of a vessel's hold, weighed, and laboriously carried by hand to a warehouse. In the 1840s, a Buffalo man, Joseph Dart, found the answer: an endless belt of buckets, driven by a steam engine, that scooped up the grain from a vessel's hold and carried it up into a storage elevator. In the decades that followed, Buffalo's harbor became ringed by enormous grain elevators.

Soon after the turn of the century, Buffalo also became a steel center, taking advantage of regional coal mines that had long provided cargoes for the grain carriers returning to western lake ports. The steel mills brought the great ore carriers to Buffalo. In the 1940s, the city boasted the third largest steel works in the country.

By the mid-1980s, however, the picture had changed. The steel industry, contracting in the face of declining sales, had left the city. The grain trade had sadly shrunk; some of the great elevators had been razed, many of the survivors had been closed down. Nevertheless, Buffalo remains a huge sprawling city, a metropolis of more than a million and a quarter people that long ago swallowed up rival Black Rock. The New York State Barge Canal replaced the Erie many years ago, but still provides the city an all-water route to the Hudson River and the Atlantic. Thanks to the St. Lawrence Seaway, blue-water freighters can now share the harbor. The port dozes, waiting for better times.

The maritime traditions of Buffalo and its environs go back to the earliest European explorers. Nearby, on the Niagara River, La Salle built the *Griffin*, the first sailing ship on Lake Erie. Here, also, the British built many of the armed schooners with which they dominated the western lakes for half a century after the fall of New France. At Black Rock, on the river, now swallowed up by Buffalo, was built half the little fleet with which Perry won the Battle of Lake Erie in the War of 1812. And, of course, the famous *Walk-in-the-Water*, Lake Erie's first steamboat, had Buffalo for a home port.

The visitor will find models and pictures of many of these historic vessels in various Lake Erie museums. The two vessels on display at the Buffalo waterfront, however, belong to a very different and much more recent era of maritime history. *The Sullivans*, a destroyer, is a veteran of some of the fiercest battles of the Pacific in World War II. Her berthmate at Naval and Servicemen's Park, the guided missile cruiser *Little Rock*, is of great interest as an example of the U.S. Navy's transition from the age of guns to the new era of self-propelled missiles.

The Sullivans owes her unusual name to a World War II naval disaster when the cruiser *Juneau* was sunk off Guadalcanal with heavy loss of life. Among the casualties were five Sullivan brothers who served together on the same ship. The 2,000-ton destroyer named for them was commissioned in 1943 and served in the Marshalls, Carolines, Mariannas, and Philippines. Later, she again was active in the Korean War and the Cuban Blockade.

Figure 48
USS *Little Rock*, only missile cruiser on display in U.S., towers over Buffalo, New York waterfront. Astern is USS *The Sullivans*, a destroyer.

Long and lean—her 376-foot length is almost ten times her beam—*The Sullivans* is a fine example of World War II destroyers. Among the many areas on display, those likely to be of special interest include the bridge, combat information center, the wardroom with its memorial to the Sullivan brothers, and the captain's two cabins—one for use at sea, one for use in port.

The *Little Rock*, six times the tonnage of the destroyer, was commissioned in mid-1945, too late to see action in World War II. Originally a light cruiser, she was converted in 1960 to carry Talos guided missiles, then the latest technological advance in naval armaments. The 30-foot Talos, driven by a 40,000-hp ramjet engine, is guided by radar against either aircraft or surface vessels as far as 70 miles distant. The missile magazine and handling room are among the 21 areas aboard the *Little Rock* that are on the visitors' tour.

The *Little Rock* was the flagship of the U.S. Navy's Sixth Fleet in the Mediterranean in the late 1960s. Honorably retired in 1976, she came to Buffalo two years later.

Crew quarters, mess decks, galleys, gunmounts (she retained some cannon), the wardroom, and flag bridge are among the high spots of the tour. Navy buffs will be particularly interested in the *Little Rock*, not only for her armament but because she is the only 20th century cruiser of the U.S. Navy now on exhibition.

The USS *Little Rock*, a retired guided-missile cruiser, and the USS *The Sullivans*, a destroyer, are berthed on Buffalo's Lake Erie waterfront at Naval and Servicemen's Park, located at the south end of Main Street, close to Routes 190 and 5. Open every day, April through October, 10 a.m. to dusk; November, Saturday and Sunday only 10 a.m. to dusk. Admission: $3.50; seniors and children 6 to 16, $2.50; children under 5 free. Naval and Servicemen's Park, 1 Naval Park Cove, Buffalo, New York 14202. Telephone (716) 847-1773.

Let's make a short detour to a much smaller body of water, Lake Chautauqua, with two reconstructed vessels of the past, very different in every way except their great interest for the visitor.

Chautauqua in southwestern New York state has a firm niche in American social history as the home of the famous Assemblies, a landmark in adult education. The maritime history of its 18-mile lake, however, has been largely limited to being part of an early canoe route from Lake Erie to the headwaters of the Allegheny River, plus little lake steamers in the 19th and early 20th centuries.

That is, until very recently. Today, however, this mini-mini sea with no navigable outlet to a larger body of water boasts two very substantial recreations of historic vessels of the past that would be the pride of a major port. *Sea Lion* is a careful, scholarly reconstruction of a 16th-century three-masted merchant ship. *Chautauqua Belle* is an authentic reproduction of a small Mississippi River steamer of the 1890s. Both have their origins in the devoted efforts of individuals fascinated by the great ships of the past.

Chautauqua Belle arrived on the lake first, in 1976, the realization of a dream of an area industrial executive. James Webster remembered his own youthful pleasure in riding lake steamers and wanted others to enjoy the experience. The *Belle*, a 98-foot stern-wheel steamer weighing 65 tons, was built on the shore of Lake Chautauqua and upon launching became the first steamer on the lake in 20 years. She has a crew of four and can carry as many as 110 people on summer mini-cruises up and down the lake.

Chautauqua Belle has become so popular that reservations should be made ahead, according to the Sea Lion Project, which has leased *Belle* from Mr. Webster. Lake Chautauqua's other recreation of a vessel of the past, *Sea Lion*, is also the result of one man's dream. Ernie Cowan, an artist and carpenter, enlisted two close friends—who were augmented by many volunteers as the project progressed—to research and build a vessel of 400 years ago, using only the tools and methods of the shipwrights of that time. Three and a half years were spent in research. The hull was designed according to the method described in a 1586 shipbuilding treatise, using only a compass and straight-edge. The white oak of her hull came from 400-year-old trees growing near the lake. The tools were those of the traditional wooden shipwrights; some were contributed or borrowed, some that could not be found were made from scratch. Her keel was laid in 1977. Since then most of the work has been done at the same lakeside yard where the *Chautauqua Belle* was built.

More than 30,000 volunteer hours went into building *Sea Lion*, and the completed vessel is estimated to represent one million dollars in labor and materials. The Sea Lion Project, Inc., a nonprofit corporation, was formed to sponsor and obtain financial support for the ambitious and very costly operation.

Today, *Sea Lion* floats in triumph, in summer months, on Lake Chautauqua, ready with a trained crew—trained aboard her, that is; there were few experienced 16th-century seamen available in upstate New York. Visitors will find a remarkable and fascinating vessel. *Sea Lion* carries three masts, square-rigged on fore and mainmast, lateen on the mizzen. She weighs 90 tons; with ballast she displaces 155 tons and draws six or seven feet: She is the largest sailing vessel ever on Lake Chautauqua. Her armament is six brass cannon.

Sea Lion is a striking vessel, strange to our eyes but an example of naval architecture of the days when English fighting ships out-sailed their enemies in the Spanish Armada. The long beakhead under the bowsprit is a survival of the medieval ram and helped keep the box-like forecastle as dry as possible in a heavy sea. Her high, narrow stern is the high "after castle" that served as command post and provided shelter for the captain and important passengers.

Sea Lion Project has still a third vessel on the lake: a ferry that is operated by cables on a 180-year-old route across the narrow waist of the lake between Bemis Point and Stow. A bridge now carries the road traffic so the ferry is retired, but volunteers operate it for the benefit of the nostalgic.

SS *Chautauqua Belle* and Replica 16th-Century Ship *Sea Lion* are both berthed in season at Mayville on Lake Chautauqua in southwestern New York State. Open June 1 to September 30. Rides: June and September, Sundays only; July and August, every day. Hours: 1, 2:30, 4 p.m. Tickets: $5.50; ages 6-16, $2.75. *Sea Lion*, same dock, same season; times and prices to be announced, check in advance with sponsors. Rides also available on Bemis Point/Stow cable ferry at historic lake crossing. Operating Friday-Sunday, Memorial Day and Labor Day weekends; Saturday-Sunday, in July; every day July and August. Hours: noon to 10 p.m. (extended hours on weekends). Sea Lion Project, Ltd., R.D. One, Sea Lion Drive, Mayville, New York 14757. Telephone (716) 753-2403.

Now, back to the shore of Lake Erie and the port of Erie, Pennsylvania.

Other than the fact that it is Pennsylvania's only outlet on Lake Erie, the modest city of Erie, population 125,000, may seem to the casual observer little different from the other smaller ports along the lakeshore. Actually, however, Erie belongs among the handful of places where maritime activities changed the course of history. The visitor soon discovers that Erie proudly remembers, and has enshrined, its unique maritime tradition in a restoration of the historic ship that played a central role, the USS *Niagara*.

The United States and Britain were at war. The time was the spring of 1813 and the Royal Navy had the only fighting ships on Lake Erie and completely controlled its waters. Partly as a result, British forces had captured Detroit and the American troops there, and had defeated an American invasion of Canada. If they continued to hold the area when the end of the war came, the upper Midwest might easily become British territory.

Both Britain and the United States had warships on Lake Ontario to the eastward, both were building more, each hoping to crush the other, but the result was a standoff. The U.S. Navy was also building ships at Black Rock on the Niagara River, just off Lake Erie, in order to challenge British control of the lake. British forces were just across the river, however; the shipyard was exposed to enemy fire and vulnerable to raids. Commodore Isaac Chauncey, the U.S. Navy commander on the lakes, ordered the shipbuilding shifted to a safer spot.

The base he chose was the tiny village of Erie, about 100 miles southwestward along the Lake Erie shore, away from the Niagara River and the enemy. Erie had a protected harbor behind Presque Isle, a big sandspit that paralleled the shore for several miles. A good road led 15 miles to the headwaters of the French River, which ran into the Allegheny, providing a direct barge route from Pittsburgh.

During the winter and early spring of 1813, a 200-man work force was assembled at Erie, the last contingent arriving after a five-week journey through the snowy wilderness from the East Coast. Most of the supplies, ships' gear, and fittings had to be brought 400 miles, some from the Philadelphia Navy Yard, some, like the ships' guns, from Washington. The timbers—black oak, and white pine—were cut in the nearby forest in April.

Two brigs, the *Niagara* and the *Lawrence*, as well as three schooners were built at Erie. Working at red-hot speed, the shipwrights had the brigs launched before the end of May. The entire squadron was afloat, rigged, and armed by July 23. Included were the five little vessels from Black Rock, which had slipped out of the Niagara River and down the lake to Erie in a fog, eluding British ships that tried to cut them off.

The little fleet was delayed, however, by a shortage of seamen. Finally Oliver Hazard Perry, who was in command, would wait no longer and determined to go out with his vessels manned by little more than half their normal crews.

But now came the critical point that gives Erie—Presque Isle—its special place in maritime history. Over the bar at the mouth of the harbor was only four or five feet of water; Perry's brigs could pass over it out into the lake only if they were lightened. To do this they had to be stripped of everything movable, including their guns, and lifted by pontoons to reduce their draft. At this point, of course, they would be completely defenseless. The British ships had been cruising off Erie; if they arrived and attacked at that moment, the American fleet, the control of the lake, quite possibly possession of the Northwest Territory, might be lost.

The first week in August Perry made the attempt. Fortune was with him. The British ships left their position off Erie on July 30; on August 4 they returned to find that the brig *Lawrence* had been floated across the bar of the harbor and that the schooners, which drew less water, were also past the bar. While the other brig, the *Niagara*, was still being floated out on pontoons, the American vessels already in the lake appeared too strong to be attacked and the *Niagara* was successfully taken over the bar without being molested.

Perry took his ships westward to Put-In-Bay, whence he sailed on September 10 to win the Battle of Lake Erie.

The *Niagara* was a 500-ton brig carrying 18 32-pounder carronades and two long 12-pounders, giving her roughly the fighting power of the famous sloops of war *Wasp* and *Hornet*. During the early stages of the Battle of Lake Erie, she lagged and so escaped major damage from enemy fire, so Perry transferred his flag to her when his own vessel, the *Lawrence*, was knocked out.

Figure 49
At Erie, Pennsylvania, a gun crew in action on the deck of the rebuilt U.S. Navy brig *Niagara* demonstrates what naval warfare was like when Commodore O.H. Perry won his victory on Lake Erie in 1813.

After the war, *Niagara* remained on Lake Erie, but was eventually allowed to sink into Misery Bay, near the port of Erie, which over the years, became a busy harbor, receiving ore, wood pulp, and grain, and shipping out coal. When the time came to celebrate the centennial of the Battle of Lake Erie in 1913, the remains of the *Niagara* were lifted from the bottom. Her keel was still sound and was built into a restored *Niagara*. No plans of the original vessel survived, so the new *Niagara* had to be based on the general concept provided by contemporary accounts. After being sailed around the lake as part of the celebration, she was returned to Erie as her permanent home port.

Today, the *Niagara*, which was for many years preserved ashore in a park on the Erie lakefront, certainly gives a clear picture of the general size and armament of the original brigs. However, like all wooden vessels kept out of the water in the open, the *Niagara*'s structure has suffered. Happily, the state of Pennsylvania has budgeted one million dollars for her repair and restoration to a seaworthy condition where she can be put back in the water and eventually sail the Great Lakes. During the restoration, more of the original *Niagara*'s timbers will be incorporated in the brig; such a step is made possible by advanced wood-preservation techniques. Plans call for the entire restoration process to be open to view, but visitors may want to check ahead to see what stage has been reached before planning a special visit.

A waterfront complex has been proposed for the Erie shorefront at the east end of Presque Isle Bay. This would include a huge shipyard building converted into a museum; the *Niagara* would be moored alongside in the summer, and brought into a sheltered graving dock in the winter.

USS *Niagara*, incorporating parts of the original 1813 brig, is on exhibition out of the water in a park near the lakefront in Erie, Pennsylvania. Open all year, Tuesday-Saturday 9 a.m. to 5 p.m.; Sunday noon to 5 p.m. (Open some holidays.) Admission: $2.00; seniors, $1.50; children 6 to 17, $1.00. Administered by Pennsylvania Historical and Museum Commission. Sponsored by the Commonwealth of Pennsylvania. Flagship Niagara, 80 State Street, Erie, Pennsylvania 16507. Telephone (814) 871-4596.

Our next stop is a small town along the lakeshore to the westward.

Much of the maritime tradition of Lake Erie originated in the smaller ports along the south shore. The river mouths provided harbors of a sort—at the outset usually shallow and poorly protected from onshore gales on Lake Erie, but the best there were. As New Englanders came out to Ohio after the American Revolution, they settled villages at the mouths, and gradually improved the harbors by dredging channels and building breakwaters. The little rivers themselves—little because the final terminal moraine of the retreating glacier, the watershed between the lake and the Ohio Valley, is only a few miles south of the lake—provided access to the interior.

These small Lake Erie ports—such as Huron, Vermilion, Lorain, Conneaut, Erie, Dunkirk, Silver Creek, Ashtabula, Cattaraugus, Cleveland, Painesville/Fairport—became increasingly prosperous after the War of 1812. Outlets for the crops of farms up inland, many lake villages built their own schooners to carry cargo and passengers along the lake to Buffalo or Detroit: *Fire Fly*, *Zephyr*, *Ranger*—wonderfully imaginative names from frontier villages.

Painesville's port, Fairport Harbor, three miles down the Grand River at its mouth, was home port for the schooner *Widow's Son* (the name perhaps a reference to her owner). Fairport was a favorite landing place for Yankee settlers, and the improvement of its harbor was one of the first public undertakings in the area. During the War of 1812 boats were built at Painesville to carry American troops for the invasion of Canada.

Fairport Harbor is east of Cleveland, roughly half way to Ashtabula on the Lake Erie shore. Fairport Harbor like many of the little lake ports, was eventually overshadowed by its larger neighbors, particularly, of course, Cleveland. But also like its fellows, Fairport Harbor itself became a receiving port for iron ore from the Lake Superior mines, and a shipping point for coal brought by rail from mines to the southward.

Today, Fairport Harbor has kept in touch with its maritime past with an interesting small museum on the Grand River. The Fairport Marine Museum is lodged in the Fairport Harbor Light, a 60-foot stone tower built in 1871, and the lightkeeper's house next door. (The lighthouse has now been retired, supplanted by a combination light and foghorn out on the west breakwater.)

Exhibits in the small museum, which is sponsored by the Fairport Historical Society, include full ship models as well as the half-hull models used as a guide by shipbuilders. Navigation instruments and ships' carpenter's tools are also on display. Lifesaving gear includes two of the Lyle guns that hurled lifelines to wrecked ships, and a covered lifecar, used to carry shipwrecked crewmen from wreck to shore. The lens of the original Fairport light is on display and, of course, there are photographs and paintings of ships.

Attached to the museum building is the pilothouse of the Great Lakes ore carrier *Frontenac*. Fully equipped with ship's wheel, binnacle, and instruments, it offers landlubbers of all ages a chance to steer a hypothetical ship through imaginary seas. The museum flagpole, incidentally, is the mast of the USS

Wolverine, an iron naval vessel whose bow has been preserved at Erie.

Fairport Marine Museum is lodged in a former lighthouse and the adjacent keeper's cottage at the northwest corner of Second and High Streets on the east side of the Grand River, at the north end of the business district of the village of Fairport Harbor. Open from Saturday before Memorial Day through Labor Day on Saturdays, Sundays, and legal holidays, and group tours April through October, Monday-Friday by appointment. Hours: 1 to 6 p.m. Admission: 50 cents. Sponsored by Fairport Harbor Historical Society. Fairport Marine Museum, 129 Second Street, Fairport Harbor, Ohio 44077. Telephone (216) 354-4825.

From a small lake town, we move to one of the major ports of the Great Lakes and to the maritime gallery of a major museum.

The maritime activities of the village of Cleaveland, 200 miles west of Buffalo along the south shore of Lake Erie, were slow in getting under way. To be sure, Moses Cleveland laid out his town on the flood plain at the mouth of the Cuyahoga River. But the Connecticut general didn't even arrive there by boat; he walked down the Lake Erie shore, leading his fellow Yankees to the promised land in Ohio's Western Reserve (reserved by the state of Connecticut when it gave up its claim to western lands).

That was in 1796. In 1808, Cleveland launched its first schooner, the *Zephyr*. Schooners were the links connecting the Erie shore villages with each other and with Buffalo and Detroit, carrying passengers and cargo where there were few roads. Then years later Cleveland had a small fleet: *Neptune*, *American Eagle*, *Fairplay*, *Aurora*. But there was little indication that Cleveland would ever outstrip the rival ports on the lake. Lorain, then known as Black River, had a much better natural harbor, deep enough to take the biggest vessels of the time. Vermilion's shallower harbor was easily dredged and the town soon became a shipbuilding center. In contrast, the mouth of the Cuyahoga at Cleveland was choked by a sandbar that at low water turned the lower end of the river into a stagnant pool, which not only smelled bad but was blamed by the residents for their recurring attacks of fever and ague.

But Cleveland had a couple of less visible assets. One was the fact that the Cuyahoga River was the northern end of an Indian canoe route south to the Ohio River that required only a short portage at Akron to the head of the south-flowing Muskingum River. Cleveland's other asset was a young lawyer named Alfred Kelley. He convinced first the Ohio legislature and then the Federal government, that a north-south canal from Lake Erie to the Ohio River would do just as great things for Ohio as the Erie Canal was projected to do for New York State, and that the

Cuyahoga-Muskingum route was the way to go, making Cleveland the northern terminus.

The first spadeful of the Ohio-Erie Canal was dug in 1825. A federal appropriation helped clear a channel through the sandbar at the mouth of the Cuyahoga. Two years later the first section, as far south as Akron, was rushed to completion; by 1833 the entire 307-mile route was open. The effect on Cleveland was dramatic; from a village of 500 people in 1825, it grew to 6,000 in a decade. The canal brought down the crops of the rich interior, and took back supplies and manufactures: By the mid-1830s, almost 2,000 lake vessels a year were calling at the port.

Although canals were later built to other lake ports, Cleveland had gotten the jump on its rivals and was never bested. In 1844, a Cleveland yard launched the largest ship yet built on the lake, the 260-foot steamer *Empire*. By the 1850s, there was overnight steamer service to Buffalo and Detroit. Shipbuilders and shipowners moved to Cleveland from other lake ports. Manufacturing boomed. Soon railroads linked the city to the coal fields and furnaces to the south.

As a result, Cleveland was in a key position when it became evident that the most economical way to process the great iron deposits around Lake Superior was to carry them by ship down the lakes to the Erie ports. Many Ohio harbors received the ore ships but Cleveland was the leader. In the words of one historian, Cleveland was "the controlling brain center of both the ore fields and the shipping companies." The bulk ore carriers have been the major element in Lake Erie shipping for more than a century. The heart of this unique maritime tradition is in the port at the mouth of the Cuyahoga, long the largest Ohio port on the Lake.

The History Museum of the Western Reserve Historical Society, in the University Circle section east of downtown Cleveland, includes the maritime past of the city and of the Great Lakes in its gallery devoted to transportation. A highlight is an extensive collection of models of vessels used on the lake and the canals of the region.

Particularly notable are a builder's model of the 1896 ore boat *Frank Roosevelt*, and a very large model of the side-wheel passenger liner *Seeandbee*. Unusual is a sailing model of an international class racing yacht.

Very pertinent to the rise of Cleveland from a small village to a major port, is a diorama that shows a canalboat going through a lock on the Ohio and Erie Canal. It was this canal that brought the cargoes to Cleveland from inland Ohio, which first made it an important port of call for Lake Erie shipping. A painting of special interest shows the steam brig *Superior*, 1824, the vessel that received the engine from the wrecked *Walk-in-the-Water*.

The History Museum of Western Reserve Historical Society is in the heart of the University Circle, Cleveland, on East Boulevard east of its circle junction with Liberty Boulevard. Library. Open all year, Tuesday-Friday, 10 a.m. to 3 p.m., Saturday and Sunday noon to 5 p.m. Admission: $2.50; seniors and students, $1.50; free Tuesdays noon to 3 p.m. Other museum exhibits include furniture, decorative arts of region; auto/aviation museum adjacent. History Museum of the Western Reserve Historical Society, 10825 East Boulevard, Cleveland, Ohio 44106. Telephone (216) 721-5722.

Also on exhibit in Cleveland is the submarine *Cod*, between East Ninth Street and Burke Airport. The *Cod*, a *Gato* class submarine built in 1943, is open to visitors from Memorial Day to Labor Day. For information telephone (216) 566-8770. Her address is 1069 East Ninth Street, Cleveland, Ohio 44114.

The next stop is in a little town that once dreamt of surpassing Cleveland. That dream has vanished, but the town, Vermilion, Ohio, is the home of one of the leading maritime museums on the Great Lakes.

Vermilion, at the mouth of the Vermilion River between Loraine and Sandusky, is today a quiet little resort and fishing town. In the early 19th century, however, it was a vigorous competitor in the struggle to become the top port on the south shore of Lake Erie. Vermilion's prospects certainly looked better than those of rival Cleveland on its smelly, stagnant river, for while the Vermilion River mouth was shallow, it was easy to dredge. Founded in 1808, the village had built its own schooner, the *Ranger*, before a dozen years were out. Captain Alva Bradley, who became one of Ohio's great shipping magnates, chose Vermilion in preference to other Lake Erie ports when he began his career as both a builder and captain of lake schooners.

What ended Vermilion's hopes, and those of many of the Lake Erie ports, was the edge given Cleveland by its transportation links to the south—first the Erie-Ohio Canal, and then the rail lines. Captain Bradley moved his headquarters from Vermilion to Cleveland just before the Civil War, and his shipyards followed him in 1868. Vermilion was left to become a satellite of the metropolis to the eastward that it had once hoped to leave behind.

Today, Vermilion is very conscious of its maritime heritage. Two annual events, a Fishing Festival in June and a Boat Regatta in August, celebrate its relations with Lake Erie. What visitors will particularly appreciate is that Vermilion is the home of the finest maritime museum on Lake Erie, home indeed of one of the top-ranking collections concerned with Great Lakes ships and shipping in the entire region. The collection has been gathered by the Great Lakes Historical Society and housed in a one-time mansion, now much expanded, overlooking Lake Erie and

Vermilion harbor. Convenient to the Ohio Turnpike, the museum is a must stop for the maritime-minded traveler crossing northern Ohio.

A fine model of Perry's famous brig *Niagara* is one of the stars of the model collection, and timbers from the original *Niagara* herself are also on display. An entire exhibit is devoted to the Battle of Lake Erie. The model collection also includes examples of most of the many types of vessels that have sailed or steamed on the Great Lakes. A huge model represents the ill-fated ore carrier *Edmund Fitzgerald*, which sank with all hands during a November gale on Lake Superior in 1975.

Besides commercial vessels and warships, the model collection includes a number of examples of sail and power yachts. These are part of an exhibit chronicling the history of the Inter-Lake Yachting Association, which serves the Great Lakes. The exhibit also displays trophies, pictures, and memorabilia of the Association.

A striking exhibit is the 500-hp steam engine from the harbor tug *Roger*, 1913. The monster is part of what the museum believes to be "one of the largest collections of marine engines in North America." An assortment of the gauges with which the engineers of several well-known lake steamers received instructions and controlled their charges, is displayed on a special panel.

Other exhibits to watch for:

- a ship's cabin, removed from a 1913 lakes tanker;
- the Fresnel lens from the Spectacle Reef Lighthouse;
- shipwright's tools;
- navigational instruments;
- lifesaving gear;
- wreck relics.

A simulated ship's bridge or pilothouse is attached to a wing of the museum overlooking the lake. The bridge is completely equipped with binnacle, gyrocompass, radar, pelorus, and even a whistle pull so that the visitor gripping the wheel and peering ahead over the lake can dream for a moment that he is guiding a 1,000-foot ore carrier along the inland seas.

Beside a well-known collection of paintings and prints of Great Lakes maritime subjects, many contemporary with their 19th-century subject matter, the museum displays a huge mural depicting many of the fascinating vessels, sail and steam, that navigated the Great Lakes in the century between 1869 and 1969.

The Museum of the Great Lakes Historical Society is housed in a mansion overlooking the harbor of Vermilion, Ohio. Library. Bookshop. Gift shop. Open all year. April through December, every day. January through March,

Saturday and Sunday only. Hours: 10 a.m. to 5 p.m. Admission: $2.00; seniors, $1.50; children, 75 cents. Great Lakes Historical Society Museum, 480 Main Street, Vermilion, Ohio 44089-1099. Telephone (216) 967-3467.

We've seen Perry's ship and a lot of exhibits about his victory. Now let's look at where the Battle of Lake Erie was fought.

After successfully floating his new ships out into the lake at Erie, Oliver Hazard Perry took them westward up the lake and established his base at Put-in-Bay on South Bass Island. This was 30 miles southeast of Malden where the British squadron was based on the Canadian side of the lake. From Put-in-Bay, Perry successfully cut off the flow of supplies along the lake to the British forces and the many thousands of their Indian allies who had gathered nearby. This was a major factor in forcing the British ships, which were short both of men and provisions, to come out and fight at a disadvantage.

After the battle, the survivors of the two fleets, victors and vanquished, returned to Put-in-Bay. There, both the American and British officers killed in the battle were buried ashore with full military honors.

Today, their resting place on South Bass Island is marked by the 352-foot granite shaft of the Perry Memorial, which was dedicated on the centennial of the battle. An elevator is available to take visitors to the top of the tower; Middle Sister Island, near where the battle was fought, can be seen in the distance. The monument is now known as Perry's Victory and International Peace Memorial and is a facility of the National Park Service. The Visitors' Center at the Memorial displays graphics about the battle and occasional exhibits of related artifacts.

Perry's Victory and International Peace Memorial is on South Bass Island off southwest shore of Lake Erie. Reached April through November by auto ferry from Catawba or Port Clinton; also air service. Open daily: late April to mid-June, 10 a.m. to 5 p.m.; mid-June to Labor Day, 9 a.m. to 6 p.m.; post Labor Day to mid-October, 10 a.m. to 5 p.m. Admission: free; elevator, 50 cents. Operated by National Park Service. Perry's Victory and International Peace Memorial, P.O. Box 549, Put-in-Bay, Ohio 43456. Telephone (419) 285-2184.

Our next stop is a fine big maritime museum on an island right in the middle of the Detroit River. So back to the mainland, and head around the west end of Lake Erie.

The maritime, or riverine if you prefer, element in Detroit's origins is embedded in its name: "*d'etroit*," meaning "of the narrows" or straits. Cadillac built the fort that became Detroit at the narrowest part of the river that carries the waters of the upper Great Lakes down into Lake Erie. Built on a high bluff in 1701, his fort commanded the water highway and was intended to block English penetration of the Great Lakes fur trade from the south. The French held the fort until the final British conquest of Canada, when Major Robert Rogers, the famous Ranger, led a whaleboat expedition the length of Lake Erie to receive Detroit's surrender in 1760.

Three years later, Detroit came under Indian attack and siege during Pontiac's War and was held only because the Navy-minded British had built two armed schooners on Lake Erie. The *Huron* and *Michigan* were able to fight off Indian attacks as they brought supplies the length of the lake from Niagara to Detroit. (At the same time, British whaleboat expeditions up the lake were either wrecked or ambushed on the shore.) Subsequently, the British started a shipyard at Detroit and turned out about a dozen small warships plus trading schooners; these vessels dominated the lakes, supplied far-flung trading posts, and brought out rich cargoes of furs.

Detroit nominally became American at the end of the Revolution, but the British garrison did not leave until 1796. Even after that, however, Britain's little fleet retained control of the lakes, and was a factor in the American surrender of Detroit to British forces early in the War of 1812. Perry's victory on Lake Erie put control of the lake in American hands and once again Detroit changed hands.

Despite its strategic location, for some years Detroit was slow to grow after the war; immigrants to the frontier lands preferred the easier route to the West down the Ohio River. *Walk-in-the-Water* began steamboat service to Detroit during her short career, but here as elsewhere on the lake it was the opening of the Erie Canal that brought boom times. With an all-water route direct from the Atlantic Coast, immigrants poured into Buffalo, transferring to sailing packets and steamers to take them on west across Lake Erie and through the Detroit River to the further Great Lakes. Detroit became an important port, not only fueling, supplying, and servicing the carriers, but building them as well. From 1832 to 1854, 16 steamers were constructed there.

Detroit developed as a manufacturing town gradually during the second half of the 19th century, then with explosive speed as it became the center of automobile manufacturing. The city remained an active port, however, and at the height of the great steamboating era on the Great Lakes had regular steamer services to Buffalo, Cleveland, and Chicago. As late as 1913, the great sidewheel steamer *Seeandbee* was built in Detroit with 12,000 hp engines, 33-foot paddle wheels, a capacity of 6,000 passengers plus freight, and a top speed of 22 mph. (She ended up during World War II being converted into an aircraft carrier which was used to train naval aviators on the Great Lakes.)

As befits a major port, Detroit has a major maritime museum. Sponsored and supported by the city itself with the participation and cooperation of such organizations as the Great Lakes Maritime Institute, the Detroit Historical Society, and the Mariner's Church of Detroit, the Dossin Great Lakes Museum is "involved with displays, events, and activities which highlight the history of the Great Lakes." The museum is located on Belle Isle in the middle of the Detroit River, just a little way upstream from the bluff where Cadillac built his fort.

The museum has a number of striking exhibits, one of which greets the visitor as soon as he steps in the door. When the luxury passenger liner *City of Detroit III* was scrapped, the elaborate carved paneling in her smoking room, the "Gothic Room," was preserved and much of it has been installed at the entrance to the museum's main exhibition hall. She was the largest side-wheeler in the world when launched in 1912, and the room not only represented the culmination of steamboat magnificence but was remarkably handsome in itself.

Another high point of the museum collection is the 40-foot unlimited, multiple-step hydroplane *Miss Pepsi*. Raced from 1949 to 1954, she was the first to qualify at more than 100 mph. There is also a series of exhibits on powerboat racing in the Detroit River.

The Dossin Great Lakes Museum has a fine ship model collection, of course, covering the development of Great Lakes vessels from La Salle's *Griffin* of 1679, the first sailing ship on the four western lakes, to that same *City of Detroit III*. What makes the collection of particular interest is that all the models are built to exactly the same scale, making it possible to compare their relative dimensions. Among the more unusual vessels portrayed are the *Onoko*, 1855, the first steel ore carrier on the lakes; the *Alpena*, 1909, the first self-unloader; and the *South America*, 1914, one of the last overnight passenger liners on the Great Lakes.

Here are other interesting exhibits to watch for:

- a topographical model of the entire Great Lakes system;
- an early ship-to-shore wireless station;
- antique navigation instruments;
- a replica of a Great Lakes steamer's bridge at the turn of the century;
- builders' half models;
- an operating marine radio, tuned to pick up the conversation of today's passing steamers.

The Dossin Great Lakes Museum is on the south side of Belle Isle in the Detroit River. Open all year; Wednesday-Sunday. Closed Mondays, Tuesdays, and all legal holidays. Hours: 10 a.m. to 5:30 p.m. Admission: donation requested. Museum is part of Detroit Historical Museum of the City of Detroit. Dossin Great Lakes Museum, Belle Isle, Detroit, Michigan 48207. Telephone (313) 267-6440.

Lake Huron and Georgian Bay

The maritime traditions of Lake Huron, west and north of the lower lakes, don't include such fleet battles as marked the War of 1812 on Lakes Erie and Ontario. Near Mackinac Island, however, there was a remarkable cutting-out action worth preserving in the naval annals of the lakes. Most Americans are probably unfamiliar with it, perhaps because the U.S. Navy came out the loser.

After Perry's victory at the Battle of Lake Erie, two U.S. Navy schooners, *Scorpion* and *Tigress*, had been assigned to prevent supplies reaching the fort on Mackinac Island, which the British had captured at the beginning of the war. By then the last British naval vessel on Lake Huron, the supply schooner *Nancy*, had been tracked down and sunk. Her crew had escaped ashore unharmed, however. Their commander, a valiant and energetic young officer, Lieutenant Miller Worsley, R.N., determined to break the American blockade, which threatened to starve the fort into surrender. Reinforcing his 18 navy ratings with 70 soldiers borrowed from the British garrison at Mackinac, Worsley set out in open pulling boats to attack the American ships. The little task force found the *Tigress* at anchor, came quietly alongside one dark night, boarded, and captured her in a surprise attack. Worsley kept the American flag flying on his prize and a few days later took *Tigress* alongside the unsuspecting *Scorpion*, and captured her too. As a result of these daring actions the British were able to supply and hold Fort Mackinac until the end of the war.

The fort was in the Straits of Mackinac, originally Michilimackinac, which connects Lake Huron to Lake Michigan and had been a key point on the lakes from the earliest European exploration. Jean Nicolet canoed through the straits in 1634 looking for the Pacific Ocean—he found Lake Michigan instead. Soon there were a French mission, trading post, and fort on the north shore of the straits. The mission was later abandoned and over the years the post and fort were shifted to other locations on the straits, but Mackinac remained a major center of the fur trade and a strategically important military post for control of the upper lakes.

Most travelers from French Canada to Mackinac and beyond saw little of Lake Huron, however. To avoid hostile Iroquois along the lower lakes, the canoe route from Montreal was via the Ottawa and French rivers, only reaching Lake Huron at its northern end close to the straits. And while Huron was the first of the Great Lakes to be seen by Europeans (Champlain's

advance scout and the explorer himself both reached it in 1615), they traveled this northern river route and then canoed south down Georgian Bay, which is so separated from the rest of Lake Huron by a peninsula and islands as to be almost a sixth Great Lake. Half a century elapsed before a European first traveled the 250-mile length of the main lake; then Louis Jolliet, returning from a prospecting trip to the west, was taken down the full length of Lake Huron and into Lake Erie by his Indian guide.

Although at Mackinac Straits the upper end of Lake Huron turns toward the west, for the greater part of its 247-mile length Huron runs roughly north and south. Its width averages about 100 miles and the maximum depth reaches 750 feet. Lake Huron receives not only the waters of Lake Michigan through the straits but also the outflow of Lake Superior, which comes rushing down the St. Mary's River to enter the lake about 60 miles east of the straits. Thus, the shipping lanes of Lake Michigan and Lake Superior come together on Lake Huron.

At its south end, Lake Huron empties into the St. Clair River, which eventually becomes the Detroit River, flowing on into Lake Erie. The St. Clair was long an obstacle to ships headed north both because of shallows across the entrance from the lake and a strong head current. When the first European ship on Lake Erie, La Salle's *Griffin*, tried to sail up the St. Clair, her crew had to take a hawser ashore and haul her through by main strength.

Although Lake Huron long remained under French control, with a fort at Detroit blocking access from the south, La Salle's ill-fated *Griffin* has long been thought to have been the only sailing ship on the lake until after the British conquest of New France in the mid-18th century, but recent wreck discoveries have raised questions. In any case, the new British masters of the lake built a whole fleet of small sailing craft—sloops, schooners, brigs, and snows, both warships and trading vessels—to control the lakes and supply Mackinac and the other fur trading ports scattered around the lakes. Although the west shore of Lake Huron became part of the United States after the American Revolution, British armed vessels dominated the lake until Perry's victory in 1813.

Lake Huron was a major segment of the 19th-century water highway to the West. But few of the steamboats and sailing packets that picked up immigrants at Buffalo and carried them through the lakes to Chicago or Milwaukee stopped along the west shores of Lake Huron itself: Michigan, heavily forested, was left to the fur trappers who discouraged settlement by spreading stories that the land was poor. Depletion of the fur-bearing animals practically ended the Michigan fur trade in the mid-1830s, but 10 years later there were still only a few cabins on the western Lake Huron shore north of Port Huron, at the southern tip of the lake. The lake steamers kept right on going past.

Eventually, however, well into the 19th century, lumber schooners appeared on Lake Huron. Spurred by the tremendous demand for lumber to house the rapidly growing nation, the lumberjacks moved up the Michigan peninsula, cutting the state's wonderful forests. In each valley of the little rivers running down into Lake Huron the logs were floated downstream; as soon as the ice was melted in the spring, a fleet of schooners arrived at the river mouth and loaded up. As each valley was stripped, the logging crews moved on north to the next one, the schooners following. Sometimes logs were formed into huge rafts, as much as 1,000 feet long, and towed down lake by tugs. The forest produced maritime perils as well as cargoes, however. Enormous fires swept through the Michigan woodlands and huge clouds of thick black smoke, blown out over the lake by the prevailing wind, produced impenetrable "black fog."

By the 1860s, the schooners were carrying away the white pine of northern Michigan. A quarter century later the best wood was disappearing and so was the Huron lumber fleet.

Meanwhile, Lake Huron remained an essential link in the water highway. Down it steamed the ore carriers on their way from Lake Superior to the Lake Erie iron and steel ports. Down it also came the grain ships; some headed for Buffalo, some for the Canadian grain ports on Georgian Bay and at Goderich, on the east shore of Lake Huron itself. The only bulk cargo originating on Lake Huron was limestone, which began to be shipped out early in the 20th century.

Like all the Great Lakes, Lake Huron has been notorious for fierce storms. Even in this chronicle of disaster the great 1913 gale stands out grimly: For 16 hours the wind averaged 65 mph, blowing continuously but with rapid changes in direction, churning the lake surface into 35-foot waves. Eight ships sank on Huron (plus two on Lake Superior). There were no survivors.

A happier note: A chronicler of Lake Huron has recorded how steamboat language permeated everyday talk in the little ports along the lake. "Will you take in wood?" was an invitation to have some refreshments. (The early wood-burning marine steam engines consumed enormous amounts of fuel, requiring frequent stops to reload.) "Is your steam up?" meant "Are you ready to go?"

So—steam's up, ring "slow ahead" as we pull out from the dock, then "ahead full" and we're off to Port Huron, Michigan, at the southern end of the lake.

Port Huron, Michigan, is at the strategic point where the waters of Lake Huron pour into the St. Clair River in the first stage of their journey down to Lake Erie. The little city has had a close association with the lake for most of the almost 200 years since the first settlement. In the decade after the American Revolution, French-speaking lake fishermen, together with trappers gathering beaver pelts, were the first to build their cabins there. In the final stages of the War of 1812 the American forces built Fort Gratiot at this point, to dominate the narrows where the lake waters tumbled out into the river.

Lumbering brought people to the area: By the 1840s, there were 40 sawmills in the country and lumber schooners frequented the little port at the mouth of the Black River. Lumbering reached its peak in the 1870s; after that, the industry—and the schooners—dwindled. By then, however, a flourishing shipbuilding business had been built up in the town: From 1838 to 1908, 180 vessels were built at Port Huron, more than half sail. After 1890, only steamships were turned out.

Eventually, Port Huron became a predominately manufacturing city, but it retained one close tie to the lake at its doorstep: The Port Huron mail boat carried a mail bag out to the big freighters coming down the lake, who picked it up without stopping.

The Museum of Arts and History in Port Huron is very conscious of the community's maritime heritage. In addition to marine artifacts from the age of sail to the big lake steamships, the museum's exhibits include a turn of the century pilothouse, handsomely paneled and equipped with a wheel and instruments from scrapped ships.

The archives of the museum are housed in a reconstructed ship's cabin. They include the shipping records of the Huron Customs District, and a century of local marine news. The museum also has hundreds of pictures of Great Lakes sailing vessels from the Capt. H.C. Inches Memorial Collection.

The museum is closely associated with the Lake Huron Lore Marine Society, which declares that "if you like living along the Blue Water, you will like us!" A more unusual group also has its headquarters there: "The Great Lakes Society for the Preservation of Side Ship Launching." This august body gathers every ten months or so to watch the side-launching of a vessel across the lake at Collingswood, Ontario. (The shipyard there is said to be not only the only Great Lakes yard launching ships sideways, but the only yard on the lakes still building merchant vessels.)

A final note. The museum has a fine steamship whistle collection which it plans to link up to live steam at a local utility power house—and have a blast.

Museum of Arts and History is in Port Huron, on the west shore of Lake Huron at the point where it meets the St. Clair River. Open all year, Wednesday-Sunday, 1 to 4:30 p.m., closed major holidays. Admission by donation. The Museum is affiliated with the Lake Huron Lore Marine Society. Museum of Arts and History, 1115 Sixth Street, Port Huron, Michigan 48060. Telephone (313) 982-0891.

Now, we'll drive up along the Michigan shore of Lake Huron to one of the most historic spots on the Great Lakes: Fort Michilimackinac.

The Straits of Mackinac, the narrow passage through which the waters of Lake Michigan run into Lake Huron, was a strategic center—military, political, commercial—from the 17th century onward. Throughout the colonial Period and into the 19th century, it was the meeting place between Indians bringing furs from the wilderness and the traders—French, British, eventually American—who paid for pelts with guns, whiskey, cloth, traps, and tools. Here also was the central distributing point for the smaller trading posts around the lakes and the traders who penetrated the wilderness beyond.

The first French fort and mission were at St. Ignace on the north side of the straits. Cadillac moved the garrison down to Detroit when he built a fort there; but the fort, Michilimackinac, was reestablished a few years later on the south side of the straits.

After the fall of New France, Fort Michilimackinac, commonly shortened to Fort Mackinac, was taken over by a British garrison like all French posts. Shortly afterward, Chippewa tribesmen captured the fort by strategem. Playing lacrosse against visiting Sauks, the Chippewas knocked the ball through the open gate of the fort and raced in after it. Once inside, the warriors seized guns that squaws had brought in under their blankets and proceeded to massacre the British garrison almost to a man.

Until now the maritime activities in and around Mackinac had been confined to the canoes, bark boats, and bateaux of the Indians, woods runners, and fur traders, craft that had to hug the shore when braving the dangerous open waters of the lakes. The British, however, built a little navy of sloops and schooners on the lakes and reoccupied Fort Mackinac in 1764. From then on, the fort was supplied by sailing craft and Mackinac became a base for commercial sloops and schooners that served the outlying fur trading posts around the lakes. The Royal Navy controlled the lakes until the final defeat of the British squadron at the Battle of Lake Erie in 1813.

At one point during the American Revolution, there were rumors of a combined American-Spanish invasion of the region from the south. Alarmed, and fearful that Fort Mackinac on the south shore was vulnerable to a surprise attack, the commandant decided to move it bodily out to Mackinac Island in the middle of the straits. In 1780, he employed the little sloop *Welcome* and another small vessel, the *Angelica*, to move the men, guns, and stores of the fort—lock, stock, and barrel—out to the island.

Welcome had been built as a private trading vessel at Mackinac in 1775 by John Askin. Askin had come to America as a soldier in a Highland regiment and remained to become a fur trader. He married a woman of the Ottawa tribe and became a leading merchant with far-flung fur trading activities around the lakes. He was also the first shipping magnate of the upper Great Lakes, owning several small sloops and schooners (one of them was the first vessel to be taken up through the St. Mary's River into Lake Superior). Askin had sold *Welcome* to the British Army for £900 in 1779. The sloop spent the winter of 1780-81 at Mackinac, but later that year was lost in the lakes with all her stores.

Today, the *Welcome* is back in Mackinac Straits—not the original vessel, to be sure, but a careful reconstruction. She is a 55-foot sloop, drawing seven feet, and rated at 45 gross tons. To visitors accustomed to 20th-century sloops, her rig will appear strange. In the colonial manner, her single mast not only carries the usual fore-and-aft mainsail and jib, but also two cross yards on which she carries a square topsail and course, enabling her to take full advantage of a favorable breeze.

Built to help us remember the exciting times around the straits, and to "recapture Michigan's rich maritime tradition," the sloop is on display at Mackinaw City on the south side of the straits. Here, the fort of 1715-1780 has been reconstructed on the original foundations. Called Fort Michilimackinac, the original long name, to distinguish it from Fort Mackinac, which still survives out on Mackinac Island, the restored fort is set in a 27-acre maritime park at the southern end of the Mackinac Bridge across the straits.

The new *Welcome* was built near the shipyard site where the original sloop was constructed more than 200 years ago and is berthed at the Mackinaw City Marina. Decked over, with cargo hold and crew's quarters below, she is a compact and sturdy vessel, and typical of the first small sailing craft that appeared on the lakes during the period of British control.

Mackinaw City is the mainland terminal of the ferry to Mackinac Island. The fort built on the island with the help of the original *Welcome* still survives. Control of the fort was transferred to the United States some years after the American Revolution, but the

Figure 50
Sloop *Welcome*, recreation of a Great Lakes trading sloop taken over by the British Army during the American Revolution, heels in a fresh breeze in the Straits of Mackinac. She is based at the same place as the original vessel, a fort on the shore of Lake Huron in what is now Mackinaw City, Michigan.

British took the fort by surprise at the beginning of the War of 1812. The British garrison beat off an American attack and held the fort until it was returned to American control by the treaty that ended the war. The fort survived all this without damage and remained a U.S. Army post until 1894.

Welcome, recreation of 18th-century Great Lakes trading sloop, is docked at Marina on Main Street in Mackinaw City, Michigan, on straits between Lakes Huron and Michigan. At nearby Mackinac Maritime Park, former lighthouse has become small maritime museum; also 18th-century Fort Michilimackinac has been reproduced on site of original structure. *Welcome* is open June 15 through Labor Day, every day, 11 a.m. to 7 p.m. Admission: $1.00; children, free. Admission included in Fort Michilimackinac ticket. Sloop *Welcome*, Mackinac Island State Park Commission, Fort Michilimackinac, Mackinaw City, Michigan 49701. Telephone (616) 436-5563.

Now, a look at the east side of Lake Huron, which is dominated by Georgian Bay, almost big enough to be a great lake in its own right.

Georgian Bay is a bulge—100 miles long and 50 miles wide—on the east side of Lake Huron. It is almost a separate lake, cut off from the main part of Huron by a long peninsula to the south and islands off the northern shore.

More than 400 miles due west of the tiny French settlement at Quebec City, the first French foothold on Canada, Georgian Bay was even further away by the devious canoe route up rivers and across lakes used by the early explorers. Nevertheless, the bay was the first part of the Great Lakes seen by a European; probably Etienne Brulé, a young Frenchman whom Champlain had sent into the wilderness to live with the Indians and learn their language.

Samuel de Champlain himself visited Georgian Bay the same year, 1615. To avoid hostile Indians on the direct route up the St. Lawrence, he had canoed up the Ottawa River, across Lake Nipissing at the head, and down the French River into the northern end of Georgian Bay. Because of the lake's great size, he wrote, "I named it the fresh water sea." On his way to fulfill a promise to accompany his Huron Indian allies on an invasion of the country south of Lake Ontario, Champlain continued by canoe down the east shore of Georgian Bay and landed at one of the little harbors across the southern edge.

The Hurons lived in fortified villages in the area between Georgian Bay and Lake Ontario, and there they were visited soon after Champlain's expedition by French missionaries. In the middle of the 17th century, however, Iroquois war parties crossed Lake Ontario and spread destruction throughout the area; the missions were wiped out, along with the Huron villages and the Huron nation itself.

In the years that followed, the fur-trade canoe routes to the west crossed the upper end of Georgian Bay and Lake Huron, but the shores and islands of Georgian Bay itself were left largely to trappers and fishermen for a century and a half. However, when the British lost control of Lake Erie and the Detroit River after Perry's victory in the War of 1812, which cut off communications to the upper lakes, they found a substitute route making use of rivers and lakes to carry supplies across the peninsula between Lake Ontario and Georgian Bay. From there, cargoes were carried by boats to the major fort the British had captured at Mackinac Island.

In the years after the 1812 War, tensions continued along the Canadian-American border and a British naval and military base was built on a protected harbor at the south end of Georgian Bay. Meanwhile, lumbermen attacked the forests of the region, and settlers from Europe and eastern Canada gradually moved into the area between the bay and Lake Erie, and along the shores of Lake Huron and the bay itself.

In the late 1840s, shipyards in the little harbor towns along the south shore of Georgian Bay began to launch trading schooners. They coasted along the lakeshores, exchanging manufactured goods for farm crops. During the next decade, railroads reached the bay, providing direct connections all the way east to New England. Steamboat lines began regular service from these Canadian ports to Chicago, and through the new Sault Ste. Marie Canal all the way to Lake Superior, carrying immigrants from Europe on their way to the western lands. Soon grain was coming back east to Georgian Bay harbors where cargoes of wheat were transferred from lake carriers to rail cars. Shipbuilding flourished (steel steamships eventually) to supply vessels for these trades.

All this busy shipping faced serious hazards—partly from notorious lake storms, partly from the tricky channels and the many reefs along the shore. Georgian Bay has swallowed many vessels and broken hundreds more upon its shores. The tales of lost ships are many: Poignant to this day is the story of how the little wooden steamer *Asia*, overloaded with passengers and freight, sailed from the Georgian Bay port of Owen Sound one September day in 1882 and was never seen again. Eventually, the only two survivors were picked up in a lifeboat.

In the latter part of the 19th century, the Georgian Bay region was discovered by summer visitors, particularly by Americans who came north to escape the heat. Here, small steamers prospered as they provided the main means of communication for the small towns on the bay and along the inland lakes.

All these varied activities have given the Georgian Bay area a very distinctive maritime heritage of its own, something that has been recognized and preserved at a number of little ports along the bay's southern shore.

We'll start at Collingwood, westernmost of the Georgian Bay museum towns.

In the early decades of the 19th century, the lands between Georgian Bay and Lake Erie, empty since the destruction of the Huron villages, slowly began to fill up with settlers as would-be farmers moved in, some from England and Scotland, some from the French settlements in Quebec. Along the shores, little villages sprang up and became fishing and trading ports.

In 1855, one of these small villages, Collingwood, became the terminus of a railway from the east. At once ships started bringing grain from Chicago and the western lakes to be shipped on by rail to Atlantic ports for export to Europe.

Before the American Civil War, Collingwood was for a while also a terminus of a different kind of railroad. Slaves who had escaped in Southern states and made their way as far north as Chicago on the Underground Railroad were smuggled aboard grain schooners and brought over to Canada where they were safe from being sent back South under the Fugutive Slave Act.

Collingwood eventually became an embarkation point for European immigrants, particularly from Scandinavia. Bound for Wisconsin and Minnesota, they were carried around the lakes on side-wheel steamers. As late as 1900, Collingwood was the center of a whole network of steamer services to ports as far away as Thunder Bay on distant Lake Superior.

Collingwood was always a sailor's town and so considers itself today. Local men served on ships all through the lakes. When a great storm swept Lake Huron in 1913, 26 Collingwood men were lost, probably more than from any other port.

The town's big celebration came each year at the end of the shipping season when the ice was about to close in and everything became somnolent until the following spring. Each shipping line held a big wind-up supper upon its flagship, inviting all the shipping bigwigs, the ships' officers, city officials, and railroad men to a feast prepared by the ships' cooks.

Along with shipping went shipbuilding. First came the wooden ships, some square-riggers, but more particularly schooners and brigs. Later, of course, steel vessels were built. As recently as World War II, Collingwood was the center for the construction of corvettes for the Royal Canadian Navy.

Shipbuilding is among the local maritime activities displayed and explained in the interesting little Collingwood Museum. Here is a fine collection of shipbuilding documents, ledgers, and letter books, as well as the tools of the shipbuilders and more than

2,000 photographs of lake boats from early schooners to the present, many of which were built in the little port. In addition, there is a very considerable collection of ship models, including the side-wheelers *Gore* and *Decora*; the lake steamer *Majestic*, which was built in Collingwood; the *Edmondton*; and a more recent Collingwood steamer, the motor vessel *Yankcanuck*, 1963.

There are also two reconstructed wheel houses. One is from the *John Ericsson*, one of McDougall's whalebacks, the distinctive ore carrier designed with a rounded deck like the back of a whale. *Ericsson* was built in 1892 and served until 1965. The other was salvaged from the *Gray Beaver*, built in 1927. Small craft enthusiasts will be particularly interested in the models and photographs of a distinctive local type, the Collingwood skiff, a two-masted double-ender developed on Georgian Bay in the mid-19th century. The personal, human side of the maritime history of the port is recorded in the library of oral histories.

Collingwood Museum is housed in a former railroad station in Memorial Park, Collingwood, Ontario, Georgian Bay port. Open Victoria Day (May 24 or closest preceding Monday) to Canadian Thanksgiving (second Monday in October), Monday-Saturday, 10 a.m. to 5 p.m.; Sunday, 12 noon to 4 p.m. Open balance of year, Wednesday-Saturday, 12 noon to 5 p.m.; Sunday, noon to 4 p.m. Closed Easter and Christmas. Admission: 50 cents; children, 25 cents. Collingwood Museum, Memorial Park, St. Paul Street, Box 556, Collingwood, Ontario L9Y 4B2, Canada. Telephone (705) 445-4811.

Now to a battle site—and the remains of a ship destroyed in the War of 1812.

"The schooner will be a perfect masterpiece of workmanship and beauty. The expense to us will be great, but there will be the satisfaction of her being strong and very durable. Her floor timbers, keel, keelson, stem and lower fettock are oak. The transom, stern post, upper fettocks, top-timbers, beams and knees are all red cedar. She will carry 350 barrels." So wrote a Montreal fur merchant, John Richardson, one of the owners of the schooner *Nancy*, when she was launched in 1789.

Almost 200 years later, we can see that his praise was justified: Today, the remains of the schooner *Nancy* can be viewed in a museum; her bottom timbers are still strong and her fine workmanship is evident. And this despite the fact that she was sunk by cannon fire and left at the bottom of a river for over 100 years.

How the *Nancy* got from Montreal in 1789 to a museum on the south shores of Georgian Bay in the 1980s, takes a little telling. The schooner was built for the fur trade on the Great Lakes. When the War of 1812 broke out, the *Nancy* was taken over by the Royal

Figure 51
Sidelaunching, a traditional technique in the Georgian Bay shipbuilding town of Collingwood, Ontario, is recorded in a photograph from the archives of the Collingwood Museum. This launching, of the *Sir Wilfred Lawrier*, a Canadian Coast Guard icebreaker, occurred in 1985, but the method goes back to early days.

Navy and used as a supply ship. The defeat of the British squadron on Lake Erie by Oliver Hazard Perry in 1813 left the *Nancy* the only British vessel on the upper Great Lakes. The loss of Lake Erie cut the supply route to the British posts on the upper Great Lakes, particularly Fort Mackinac, where Lake Huron and Lake Michigan come together. The British authorities set up a new overland route from York, now Toronto, on Lake Ontario to rivers running into Georgian Bay, where the supplies were loaded on the *Nancy* and carried up Lake Huron to the northern post.

In 1814, three U.S. naval vessels assigned to cut off the new supply route searched for the *Nancy*. Aware of the search, the British hid the ship in the

Nottawasaga River where it runs parallel to the bay, separated from it by a low, narrow point. There the American ships discovered the *Nancy*, bombarded her, and set her on fire. She sank where she lay and over the years her hulk formed a sandbar in the river that eventually grew into an island. This island is now the Nancy Island Historic Site and the ship herself has been dug out and put on exhibition in the Nancy Island Museum.

Here on her own island the *Nancy*'s remains rest in honored dignity, her bottom timbers and keel sheltered in a handsome glass building, humidity and temperature carefully controlled for maximum preservation. The timbers are pretty impressive in themselves, and next to them is a fine big model of the *Nancy* as she looked in her prime in the early 19th century.

There is more to this nice little museum than the *Nancy* and her story, though. The War of 1812 as it was fought on the western lakes is fully described with graphic displays on the causes, the battles, and the outcome. The supply route across the rough wilderness from Lake Erie to Georgian Bay is shown, and the costumes of the voyageurs, British naval officers, and the Ojibway Indians are recreated and displayed. Wall graphics illustrate the fur trade routes, and show how water travel was conducted in the early 1800s. A diorama portrays Schoonertown, a little settlement two miles up the river where a British base was established for a few years at the end of the War of 1812.

The museum also recounts an incident of the war that will be of particular interest to visitors from below the border, to whom it is little known: the story of how the naval crew of the sunken *Nancy*, now operating in small boats and reinforced by British soldiers from Fort Mackinac, eventually succeeded in surprising and capturing two American naval schooners at the upper end of Lake Huron.

Nancy Island Museum is at Wasaga Beach, on the Nottawasaga River almost at the point where it flows into an arm of Georgian Bay. Open daily Victoria Day weekend (May 24 or closest preceding Monday) through Labor Day weekend, 10 a.m. to 6 p.m. Admission: $2.50 per vehicle, walk in free. Nancy Island Historic Site, Wasaga Beach Provincial Park, Box 183, Wasaga Beach, Ontario L0L 2P0, Canada. Telephone (705) 429-2516.

Next stop also has a naval background, and a long name.

The peace treaty that ended the War of 1812 did not end tensions between Britain and the United States on the western frontier. With the Detroit River between Lakes Erie and Huron under the guns of an American fort, the British government developed a less exposed route to its posts on the upper Great Lakes, sending supplies and men across the peninsula between Lake Ontario and Georgian Bay via rivers and Lake Simcoe. At Georgian Bay they were transferred to schooners at Penetanguishene and sent on up the lakes.

The deep, protected harbor at Penetanguishene (the jaw-breaking Huron word means "the place of the rolling wind sands") was a key link in the route and for almost 40 years the combined naval and army base there was the center of British military activity in the eastern Great Lakes. In 1817, a naval dockyard was built there, followed over the years by storehouses, quarters for soldiers and sailors, and administrative

offices, all of which were spread along the hillside above the harbor. But then, in the 1850s, British military responsibilities in faraway parts of the world—the Crimea, India—led to closure of the base. Over the years the buildings gradually fell into ruins. Now the old base is being restored as a historic site by the Province of Ontario and there is already a great deal for the visitor to see.

Naturally, the place to start is the Visitors' Center. There, models of various ships of the area are on display, and a slide film tells the history of the base. Water rushing alongside the simulated deck of a schooner gives the illusion that the whole deck and its imaginary vessel are moving through the bay.

There are guided tours of the base every half hour, but visitors are welcome to ramble at their own speed along the shores of the harbor. Buildings of the original base have been recreated on the hillside above the harbor. Here have been reproduced the homes of staff officers, the school, the quarters for seamen and troops, the dockyard area, and the workshops, manned by costumed staff who explain their functions. The Senior Officers' Quarters, which has survived because it was built of stone, remains as the only original building on the base.

Maritime-minded visitors are likely to be particularly interested in the large naval storehouse, and the recreation of HMS *Bee*, one of the British naval vessels on the lower Great Lakes. The storehouse is stocked with all the varied gear needed to maintain the schooners based at the harbor. The *Bee*, just under 50 feet in length with a five-foot draft, represents one of the transport vessels that operated here from 1817 to 1831. Although the *Bee* has such modern equipment as a diesel engine and safety gear, permitting her to carry passengers on the lake, these have been carefully concealed so that to the visitor she appears much as such a vessel must have looked 150 years ago.

Incidentally, the Establishment is only a few miles from another restored historic site. The reconstruction of Sainte Marie among the Hurons, 17th-century French mission to the Indians, is just east of Midland, the next town to Penetanguishene.

Historic Naval and Military Establishments are at Penetanguishene on a protected harbor off Georgian Bay. In Penetanguishene, follow directional markers—white cannon on red field—to end of Church Street, proceed on through grounds of mental health center. Free parking, boat docking. Open every day, Victoria Day weekend (May 24 or nearest preceding Monday) to Labor Day, 10 a.m. to 6 p.m.; last admission, 4:30 p.m. Admission: $1.25; students, 75 cents; family rate, $3.00. A part of Ministry of Tourism and Information of Ontario Province's Huronia Historic Parks, Historic Naval and Military Establishments, P.O. Box 1800, Penetanguishene, Ontario L0K 1P0. Telephone (705) 549-8064 or 526-7838.

Now a trip to a small but interesting museum at Midland, Ontario.

When, in 1872, the railroad came to the little village of Mundy's Bay on the shore of Georgian Bay, the town was transformed. Under the new name of Midland it became a very considerable grain and shipbuilding port. Here, grain ships from the upper lakes discharged cargoes to be carried by rail to Montreal for export to Europe. Midland also became the home port for several shipping companies that survived into the 1920s, as well as a substantial shipbuilding center. Built in 1926, the *LeMoyne*, at 633 feet the longest bulk freighter built on the lakes up to that time, went on to break a wide variety of records for carrying huge cargoes. During World War II, Midland yards built corvettes, minesweepers, and other small naval vessels.

Today, the recollection of these shipping and shipbuilding activities is preserved in the little Huronia Museum. As a general historical museum, the Huronia is concerned with all the different activities of the region back to Indian times, but the maritime section is of special interest since, according to the curator, it comprises one of Canada's best collections of photographs of Great Lakes shipping outside of Ottawa. Here, also, is a half model of the Midland-built grain carrier *Midland Queen* and ship models that include the schooner *Deloma Rose*. A double ship's wheel from the lake passenger steamer *Midland City* is the center of a display of artifacts and mementos from the shipping lines that used the port. A small collection but an interesting one.

Incidentally, only a short distance away in the same park is a replica of a Huron Indian village, commemorating the Indians whom Champlain found here when he visited the area early in the 17th century.

Huronia Museum is in Lake Park on west side of King Street. Open daily, Victoria Day (May 24 or nearest preceding Monday) to Canadian Thanksgiving (second Monday in October); Monday-Saturday, 9:30 a.m. to 5:30 p.m.; Sunday, 11 a.m. to 5:30 p.m. Admission: $1.50; students, 75 cents. Huronia Museum, Ltd., P.O. Box 638, Midland, Ontario L4R 4P4. Telephone (705) 526-2844.

Now we'll jump from the past to the present to a ship that's survived alive and returned to active service.

Inland from the southeast corner of Georgian Bay, a chain of three beautiful little lakes—Muskoka, Rosseau, and Joseph—became a popular resort area in the latter part of the 19th century. Millionaires built their estates along the shores, and great resort hotels in the comfortable tradition of the times drew visitors from all over Canada and the United States. Until good roads and automobiles eventually put them out of business, little lake steamers tied together the small resort towns scattered here and there. Today, one of these steamers, the *Segwun*, has been revived to give the visitor a pleasant picture of what it was like in the heyday of 19th-century steamboating.

The *Segwun* is a 128-footer, about 270 tons, an iron-hulled steamer built in Scotland in the late 1880s. Originally a side-wheeler, and now a propeller ship, she was long on the lakes as the *Nipissing II* and then was retired after an accident in 1957. Eventually, she was relaunched and now she is back in operation as a passenger vessel, with Gravenhurst on Lake Muskoka at the south end of her run as her home port.

Segwun is an attractive vessel. While there is no regular program for showing the ship to visitors, travelers in the vicinity should inquire if she is in port between cruises and whether she can be seen. If so, take a took at her original steam engine and boilers, coal-fired by stokers shoveling it in by hand. With her lounges and dining room she is obviously a comfortable little ship and inviting for a cruise on the lakes, and cruises are available during the summer months for periods varying from two hours to two days. While *Segwun* no longer has cabin accommodations (passengers on overnight cruises stay ashore in the grand old hotels that still survive along the lakes), meals are served aboard in the Royal-Muskoka dining saloon in the stern.

Segwun's operators frankly avow that their big selling point is nostalgia; if you would enjoy a brief voyage into the past, this small handsome steamer seems a remarkably pleasant vessel in which to make it.

RMS *Segwun*, restored lake steamer, is based just east of Route 169 at Gravenhurst, extreme south end of Lake Muskoka. Daily cruises June to Canadian Thanksgiving (2nd Monday in October). Inquire for type of cruises, they change from day to day. Season-long cruise schedule available on request. Muskoka Lakes Navigation & Hotel Co., Ltd., Box 68, Gravenhurst, Ontario P0C 1G0. Telephone (705) 687-6667.

Lake Michigan

They [a delegation of Wisconsin Indians] meet him, they escort him, and carry all his baggage. He [Jean Nicolet] wore a grand robe of China damask, all strewn with wild flowers and buds of many colors. No sooner did they perceive him than the women and children fled, at the sight of a man who carried thunder in both hands, for thus they called the two pistols that he held.

Thus, Father Vimont described the landing of the great explorer Jean Nicolet, his close friend, on the shores of Lake Michigan in 1634. Nicolet had carried his grand robe packed away in his canoe all the way from Quebec, in order to be prepared for what he hoped to find. Rumors had reached Quebec, the tiny heart of New France, that far to the west, farther than any European had yet explored, lived the "People of the Sea." These people, according to the Hurons, lived beside the "Stinking Water." The French, still hopeful that America was but a narrow land barrier blocking the way to the riches of Asia, decided that the "Stinking Water" must mean salt water and the "People of the Sea" must be Chinese or other Orientals living on the shores of the Pacific. For Nicolet to meet the Emperor of China or the Khan of Tartary dressed in his rough woodsman's canoe costume would never do, so Nicolet took along the damask robe in order to make a proper impression.

Alas, instead of the Pacific Ocean, Nicolet discovered Lake Michigan; the "People of the Sea" he found there were Indians with no more connection with India or anywhere else in Asia than the other natives of North America. Just the same, the French long called Green Bay, where Nicolet landed, the "Bay of Puants," or "Stinkers."

Actually, Lake Michigan was no mean inland sea, even if not the Pacific Ocean. Roughly 300 miles long north and south, and up to 120 miles wide, it covers 22,000 square miles. As the French soon discovered, it was of considerable strategic value. In 1673, two other great French explorers, Louis Jolliet and the missionary priest, Jacques Marquette, canoed into Lake Michigan; they then paddled and portaged across Wisconsin to the Mississippi River, returning by another canoe route—the Des Plaines and Chicago rivers—to the lake.

Soon afterward, Lake Michigan saw its first sailing ship: to be the only one for almost a century. She was La Salle's *Griffin*, a two-master on which he sailed all the way from the east end of Lake Erie to Green Bay on the west shore of Lake Michigan. Here, an advance party had accumulated furs by trading with the Indians. La Salle loaded the *Griffin* with furs and sent her back with instructions to return with supplies while he went on down along the lakeshore by canoe. The *Griffin* with her crew disappeared forever. According to one Indian account, her pilot refused to believe their warnings of bad weather and left a protected anchorage only to be hit and sunk by a terrific gale—the first of many ship losses on the Great Lakes, losses which have continued into the 20th century.

La Salle made a second trip to Lake Michigan a few years later, in 1682. This time he followed a third portage route all the way to the Mississippi River and canoed down it to the Gulf of Mexico, claiming the Mississippi Valley for the King of France. Lake Michigan became a key link in the chain of lakes and rivers connecting Canada to Louisiana in what the French hoped would be a great empire in the heart of North America.

In this empire of remote posts peopled by Indians, fur traders, and missionaries, Lake Michigan's maritime activities long consisted of flotillas of canoes, Mackinac boats, and bateaux passing up and down the lakes. Coming from the east in the fall, loaded with supplies and trade goods, these fur brigades wintered in the wilderness collecting pelts and returned eastward across the lakes in the spring.

The situation remained much the same when the Lake Michigan posts were turned over to the victorious British after the conquest of French Canada. The British built small sloops and schooners on the lakes, but remote Michigan saw only an occasional government vessel or trader's craft. The shift to American sovereignty belatedly brought the Stars and Stripes to Lake Michigan waters in 1803 when the American sloop *Tracy* carried supplies for the establishment of Fort Dearborn on the Chicago River. Long after that, however, a single yearly voyage by a U.S. government supply ship was the principal shipping event on the lake.

After the War of 1812, in which Britain held control of the western lakes, American vessels returned to Lake Michigan carrying troops to establish American military posts. This was the task of the famous *Walk-in-the-Water*, which became the first steamship to enter Lake Michigan when it brought 200 soldiers around from Detroit to Green Bay in 13 days.

But it was not until after the defeat of Chief Black Hawk in 1832, that ships appeared on Lake Michigan in any numbers. With the end of Indian opposition to settlement there was a rush of immigrants to take up land in northern Illinois and Wisconsin. A steady stream of steamers and sailing packets brought out settlers, but shipping was hampered by the lack of good natural harbors on the lake south of Green Bay. The little river mouths were shallow and often closed by bars: Ships had to anchor offshore in open water and send freight and passengers in by small boats. In a region notorious for sudden storms, this was a chancy mode of operation. Only gradually were the rivers dredged and breakwaters built to provide shelter for docks.

By 1833, the 156-foot *Michigan*, the leviathan of the lakes, was making a couple of special trips a year into Lake Michigan; the first steamer on the lake other than those carrying government supplies. Four years later, there was regular steamboat service from Buffalo the lengths of Lakes Erie, Huron, and Michigan to Chicago. Although it was estimated that a steamer burned 600 cords of wood on this run—which meant the cutting of a 10-acre woodlot—travel was cheap: A passenger could cover the 1,054 lake miles from Buffalo to Chicago for just two dollars a day, five meals a day included.

As steamboating boomed, so did the Lake Michigan ports, particularly Chicago and Milwaukee. They became the principal arrival points for the flood of immigrants, many of whom were completing four or five thousand mile journeys from Germany or Scandinavia. The earnings of Lake Michigan steamships ballooned from $4,355 in 1833, to $226,352 just eight years later. The number of steamers on the upper lakes rose from 48 in 1841 to 60 in 1845.

The bottom dropped out of the steamboat passenger business in the 1850s when the railroads reached Chicago, eventually providing a through line all the way from New York City. Freight traffic held up for the steamboats, however, and by now the new settlers were producing enough crops to have a surplus to send to market back East. As early as 1839, immigrant ships that had formerly had to ballast with sand for the return passage east found that they could now load with grain for Buffalo.

Most of the earlier development was on the Wisconsin, western, side of Lake Michigan. Here, the little ports between Green Bay and Milwaukee provided access to some of the richest farmland in the West. The Michigan, eastern, shore, which was heavily forested, attracted far fewer settlers and in any case was more easily reached overland from Detroit. Lumbering, however, eventually brought schooners to newly settled Michigan shore towns, which later turned from sawmills to manufacturing, but which still depended on little lake steamers for passenger and package freight service.

As the upper Middle West developed, first into the nation's major farming area, then into an important industrial region as well, Lake Michigan's big ports of Chicago and Milwaukee became two of the most important shipping centers on the Great Lakes. Chicago, in particular, has made Lake Michigan part of the great ocean highways of the world, linked by the St. Lawrence Seaway to the Atlantic.

A final, less happy note. Like all the Great Lakes, Michigan has a long and dismal record of storms taking tremendous tolls of ships and lives. Nor were these confined to the frail sailing ships and side-wheelers of the 19th century. A storm in November 1913 destroyed a dozen vessels and took more than 200 lives. As recently as 1940, several large freighters were driven onto the Lake Michigan shore with a loss of more than 60 persons.

We'll start our tour of Lake Michigan ships and museums on the eastern shore and proceed clockwise around the southern end of the lake and up the western side.

The harbor of the small port of Ludington, Michigan, on the eastern shore of Lake Michigan is formed by the river and lake named for Pere Marquette. In 1675, Father Jacques Marquette, who with Louis Jolliet had first crossed from Lake Michigan to the Mississippi River, fell ill. His companions decided to carry him back up the lake by canoe to Mackinac, but on the journey his illness grew worse and he was taken ashore at the mouth of a little river, where he died and was buried.

For almost 200 years, the harbor at the mouth of the river, now named for the famous explorer-missionary who had died nearby, was left to wandering trappers and fishermen. In the mid-19th century, however, James Ludington came across Lake Michigan from Milwaukee, bought a small sawmill and a tract of pine forest, and started lumbering. As elsewhere along the Michigan lakeshores, the first real shipping activity involved the lumber schooners that carried off the forests as they were cut away. When the forests disappeared, so did the schooners.

In the 20th century, however, Ludington's harbor gained special importance as the eastern terminal for rail ferries across Lake Michigan. The first such ferry had begun operation in the 1890s, with wooden vessels carrying trains across the lake between Frankfort, Michigan, and Wisconsin ports. The service saved hundreds of rail miles around the southern end of Lake Michigan, and other railroads started their own ferries, including lines between Ludington and the west shore ports of Manitowoc and Milwaukee.

Freight cars were rolled onto parallel tracks laid lengthwise in the interior of the ferry. Before the loading techniques were perfected, it is said, several cars rolled off the stern of one such ferry in a storm. Certainly the ferries met plenty of bad weather. They were the only lake vessels built to run all winter, defying the ice packed by storms along the edges of the lake. In 1910, the car ferry *Pere Marquette 18* of Ludington was lost in the lake.

Ludington's maritime past is remembered and its relics preserved in the collection of the Rose Hawley Museum of the Mason County Historical Society. Among the maritime exhibits are models of train ferries and lumber schooners as well as other types of sailing vessels and steamships. Special displays focus on local lighthouses. Coast Guard equipment, artifacts, paintings, and photographs are included in the museum. The Mason County Historical Society, incidentally, also sponsors nearby White Pine Village, a collection of historic buildings.

Rose Hawley Museum downtown in Ludington, Michigan, on West Loomis Street, just a block south of Ludington Avenue, the town's principal street. Open all year, Monday-Friday, 9:30 a.m. to 4:30 p.m. From Memorial Day weekend through Labor Day weekend, also open Saturdays, 9:30 a.m. to 5:30 p.m. Admission: free. Small gift shop. Open all year, Monday-Friday, 9:30 a.m. to 4:30 p.m.; June through August open Saturday. Mrs. Molly Perry, Mason County Historical Society, 115 West Loomis, Ludington, Michigan 49431. Telephone (616) 843-2001.

South along the eastern shore again, now, to visit a handsome lakes liner.

Although the great boom in steamers carrying immigrants to the west was ended by the coming of the railroads in the 1850s, passenger liners continued to cruise the lakes for more than a century. Some competed with the sleeping cars in providing comfortable overnight travel between big cities. Some serviced small lakeside towns by carrying passengers along with mail and package freight. Some made runs through several lakes for passengers who valued comfort and convenience—and the beauty of the lakes—more than a fast trip.

One of the most enduring of these services was operated by the Canadian Pacific Railway (CPR). Despite its name, the CPR was a great shipping company early on, operating the famous Empress liners across both the Atlantic and Pacific oceans. The Great Lakes service came about because the difficult terrain between Toronto and Fort William on Lake Superior delayed completion of this section of the CPR's trans-Canada rail line. With the rail line completed the rest of the way to the Pacific, the railway provided through service by establishing a steamship line between the Georgian Bay port of Owen Sound, connected to Toronto by rail, and Fort William. Started in 1884, the service ran three times a week: three hours by rail from Toronto to the CPR dock at Owen Sound, two and a half days by lake steamer to Fort William, then back on the train for the rest of the trip.

The service proved so popular that the Canadian Pacific Railway continued it even after the final rail link in the transcontinental line had been completed. In 80 years of service on the tempest-wracked lakes, notorious for ship disasters, there was only one fatal accident on the run. In 1885, the *Algoma*, carrying sail before a heavy wind while heading west through a snowstorm at night, overran her reckoning and struck a rock near Isle Royale. Forty-five lives were lost. (The ship's engines and boilers were salvaged and used in her replacement, SS *Manitoba*.) Otherwise, the line had a remarkable safety record and the original steamers were replaced by new, larger liners, also built in Scotland, in 1907. But what the lake gales could not achieve, time, economics, and increasingly strict construction standards accomplished. Canadian Pacific Railway ended steamer passenger service in 1965 and sold off the coal-burning SS *Keewatin*, one of the last two ships on the run, to a scrap dealer.

Today, however, the *Keewatin* has not only been rescued but is on display in the little harbor of the twin Michigan towns of Saugatuck and Douglas, on the east shore of Lake Michigan. Not merely rescued, but saved with all her gear and equipment right down to the table silver before a hand could be laid on her, thanks to the fact that she was frozen into her dock so there was a delay in hauling her off to the scrapyard. *Keewatin* was saved by a happy accident: Three people interested in Great Lakes ships, and able to do something about preserving them, happened to learn of *Keewatin*'s fate and were able to buy her from the scrap company. Now Roland E. Peterson and Roland J. Peterson, father and son, and the younger Peterson's wife, Diane, own and cherish the steamer in her new home in the Kalamazoo River, where she is docked at a pier close to the Blue Star highway.

Like her predecessors on the run, *Keewatin* was built on the Clyde and crossed the Atlantic under her own power in 1907. Her 350-foot length wouldn't fit through the locks in the St. Lawrence and Welland canals, so she was cut in half in Montreal, towed up in two sections, and then riveted together again in Buffalo. Rated at 3,856 tons gross, she has quadruple expansion engines, and burned coal under her four Scotch boilers. Visitors accustomed to coastal steamers will find her appearance unusual. Like the Great Lakes freighters, *Keewatin* has her bridge and island way forward in the very bow of the ship, while her funnel ("smokestack" on the lakes) is in the after third, above her engines.

The ship has been handsomely and lovingly maintained and the visitor will find it easy to imagine that *Keewatin* is about to pull out from the dock with a whistle blast and set out across the lakes. Actually, you'll almost certainly see more of the ship than the average passenger ever did, for the guided tour covers five decks, from cargo hold to the pilothouse.

Here are some suggestions of things to watch for:

- the captain's cabin, with the shoes of her last commander by his bunk where he left them;
- the observation lounge in the stern, with carvings of various peoples of the British Commonwealth;
- the dining room with the original silver, china, and table linen, not to mention the dinner menu;
- the grand stairway and Flower Well lounge with hand-painted clerestory windows;
- the galley with its 14-foot coal-burning stove;
- the crew's quarters in the bow;
- the wheelhouse with the navigation and control devices; *Keewatin* is said to have been the first ship on the Great Lakes to be equipped with radar;
- the cabins, made up ready for the passengers to move in.

The three Petersons own two other interesting vessels, the tug *Reiss*, said to be the last steam-powered tug on the lakes, and the *Helen McLeod*, last of the Lake Erie fishing sailboats. These will eventually also be on exhibition.

SS *Keewatin* is moored on the Kalamazoo River where it runs into Lake Michigan between the little Michigan towns of Douglas and Saugatuck. Take exit 44 or 36 off I-196, which runs along this section of the east shore of Lake Michigan. Gift shop. Open Memorial Day through Labor Day, daily, 10 a.m. to 4:30 p.m. Admission: $2.50; children $1.00. Owned by Peterson Steamship Company, SS *Keewatin*, Box 511, Douglas, Michigan 49406. Telephone (616) 857-2151, ext. 26.

Now south again, this time to South Haven, Michigan.

Like all the Great Lakes, Lake Michigan has taken a fearful toll of ships and people over the years. For example, the schooner *City of Green Bay* was wrecked off the port of South Haven, about 18 miles down the coast from Douglas, and in January 1895 the steamship *Chicora* went down in the same area with a loss of 26 lives. Which makes it particularly appropriate that among the various small craft preserved and displayed at the Lake Michigan Maritime Museum in South Haven are a 26-foot surf boat and a 36-foot motor lifeboat, both retired from the Coast Guard.

South Haven, Michigan, has a good harbor and was long an important regional port. For a time, until the forests were cut away, schooners flocked here to pick up lumber. When freight and passengers traveled by steamer from town to town along the shore and across the lake to Chicago, South Haven was not only the distribution point for the many resort villages of the area but a port of entry for foreign vessels. There was also considerable shipbuilding, mostly of schooners and small lake steamers.

These varied maritime activities make a rich background for the exhibits at the Lake Michigan Maritime Museum. Five galleries are concerned with the evolution of Great Lakes vessels over three centuries, while two others show how the lakes were mapped and portray 19th century shipbuilding. The museum's ship model collection has examples not only of the sailing vessels and steamships of later years, but also of the canoes, bateaux, and Mackinac boats that were used by the earliest Europeans on the lakes.

Not that the age of steam is overlooked. Among the models are such propeller steamers as the *H.W. Williams*, built right in South Haven in 1888, and later and larger vessels such as the *City of South Haven* and *City of Kalamazoo*.

Other models include working schooners and yachts, steam tugs, and ore carriers. The museum also has a considerable collection of artifacts, as well as many photographs, paintings, and prints of lake shipping.

Besides the Coast Guard boats, the small craft collection includes birch-bark and dugout canoes and the 60-foot fishing tug *Evelyn S.*

The Lake Michigan Maritime Museum is carrying out research on a sunken vessel discovered on the lake bottom off South Haven. The wreck has been tentatively identified as *Rockaway*, a 106-foot scow schooner lost in 1891.

The Lake Michigan Maritime Museum is in South Haven, Michigan. Open all year. May through October, Tuesday-Sunday, 10 a.m. to 5 p.m. November through April, Tuesday-Saturday 10 a.m. to 4 p.m. Closed Thanksgiving, Christmas, New Year's Day. Admission: $1.00; seniors, students, 50 cents. Lake Michigan Maritime Museum, P.O. Box 534, Dyckman Avenue at the Bridge, South Haven, Michigan 49090. Telephone (616) 637-8078.

On around the head of Lake Michigan to its southwest shore brings us to Chicago.

Conceivably, the great inland port of Chicago owes its existence to a long since forgotten swamp known locally as Mud Lake. In mid-summer, the "lake" usually dried up. Filled by heavy rains or melting snow, it overflowed in two directions. Eastward the water ran into the South Branch of the Chicagou River and eventually into Lake Michigan. Mud Lake also overflowed to the westward, and this water ran into the Des Plaines River, which runs into the Illinois, which runs into the Mississippi. For Mud Lake, set in a patch of nearly level prairie, was right on the watershed between the Atlantic Ocean and the Gulf of Mexico.

As such, it was a major portage point between Lake Michigan and the Mississippi River. In a wet season, travelers might canoe right across the watershed; after a dry spell they might have to drag their canoe, loaded with trade goods, for as much as 100 miles over dried-up swamp and river bottoms. But either way, the little Chicagou River, whose name was soon shortened to Chicago, marked the northern and eastern end of a major North American trade route used by Indians, trappers, soldiers, and missionaries traveling between the Mississippi Valley and the Great Lakes.

Louis Jolliet and Father Jacques Marquette, returning from their historic exploration of the Mississippi, were the first Europeans known to have used the Chicago portage. La Salle and his men went the same way in the winter of 1681-82, hauling their canoes on sleds over the frozen river and portage on the start of their famous voyage down the Mississippi to the Gulf of Mexico.

Indians and fur traders gathered at the portage. By 1698, it was estimated that three or four thousand lived in two villages. The French briefly established a fort and mission at this important passage between French Canada and French Louisiana, but intertribal wars led to their abandonment after a few years. During the 18th century, Chicago was left to the Indians and fur traders.

Finally, in 1803, came more activity: The U.S. Army built Fort Dearborn there. The Americans found the Chicago River so low that the troops walked across the bar at the mouth without getting their feet wet, and the penned-up water was so stagnant that it was unusable. The government sloop *Tracy*, which brought the supplies for the troops, had to lie out in the lake and send its cargo ashore in boats, and this was the custom of the Army's supply ships for many years.

For the maritime activities of fur traders and Indians, no harbor was needed. A report of the Illinois Fur Brigade of the American Fur Company, which traveled from Mackinac to the Illinois River via the Chicago portage in 1818, gives a picture of the times. About 100 men traveled down Lake Michigan in a dozen open boats, rowing and hoisting square sails when the wind was favorable. In a good day, they made about 70 miles; when the wind was against them or the weather was bad, they took refuge in the mouths of little creeks. Traveling along the east shore of Lake Michigan and around the south end of the lake, they

reached the Chicago River in 20 days. Poling and dragging through the mud, the voyageurs took three days to cross the divide to the Des Plaines River.

Hostile Indians wiped out Fort Dearborn during the War of 1812, and although the post was reestablished later, it was not until the Black Hawk War ended the threat of Indian attack that Chicago really became firmly established. The *Sheldon Thompson*, which brought out troops in 1832, was the first steamship to reach Chicago and she still had to anchor out in the open lake. The rush of settlers to the rich farmlands of northern Illinois led the village to take the first steps toward making a harbor in the river mouth, cutting a channel through the bar in 1833. Soon breakwaters were built, creating an artificial harbor.

As steamboats and sailing ships brought a stream of immigrants to the new port of Chicago, they began for the first time to find return cargoes to supplement the rapidly dwindling supply of furs. The 100-ton schooner *Napoleon* is said to have been the first to return with the new kind of cargo; she loaded up with beef, tallow, and hides in 1833. Six years later, the *Oceola* loaded the first considerable cargo of grain—3,678 bushels of wheat bound for Buffalo. Grain elevators, crude at first, were built to hold the golden harvest waiting for shipment, and Chicago was soon launched on its role as the gateway port to the incredibly fertile farmland of the upper Midwest.

Chicago's harbor was repeatedly improved to meet the exploding demand for shipping. In 1848, the old portage route was replaced by the Illinois and Michigan Canal, providing a direct barge way between Lake Michigan and the Mississippi River. By 1846, 1,400 vessels sailed from Chicago. By 1882, there were 26,000 arrivals or departures of vessels a year, and Chicagoans could proudly boast that this figure exceeded the combined totals for the ports of New York, New Orleans, and San Francisco.

In the early decades of the 20th century, auxiliary harbors at the head of the lake, just south of Chicago itself, were built to receive Lake Superior iron ore for the steel mills of South Chicago, Hammond, and Gary. The canal to the Mississippi was broadened and deepened over the years, and during World War II naval frigates built on the lakes were floated through it on pontoons to be taken downriver to the Gulf of Mexico.

Today, of course, Chicago is a world port, thanks to the St. Lawrence Seaway. We'll start our visit with a look at a historical fighting ship from the other side of the Atlantic.

In June, 1944, a U.S. Navy task force—a small carrier with destroyers—tracked down a German submarine 150 miles off French west Africa and heavily depth-bombed it, forcing the U-boat to the surface where the crew fled overboard under fire. A boarding party from one of the American destroyers managed to land on the U-boat as it ran in circles uncontrolled. The task force commander, Rear Admiral Daniel V. Gallery, U.S.N., tells what happened next.

No one in that boarding party had ever set foot on a submarine of any kind before—to say nothing of a runaway German sub. Anyone who ventured down that conning tower hatch might be greeted by a blast of gunfire from below! Even if abandoned, the ship might blow up or sink at any moment. That sewerlike opening in the bridge leading down under the seas looked like a one way street to Davy Jones's locker for everyone in the boarding party.

They hit the floor plates at the bottom of the ladder ready to fight it out with anyone left aboard. But the enemy had fled for their lives and were now all in the water watching the death struggle of their stricken boat. My boys were all alone on board a runaway enemy ship with machinery humming all around them, surrounded by a bewildering array of pipes, valves, levers, and instruments with German labels on them. They felt the throbbing of the screws still driving the ship ahead and heard an ominous gurgle of water coming in somewhere nearby.

But the submarine was all theirs. All theirs, that is, if they didn't touch the wrong valve or lever in the semi-darkness of the emergency lights and blow up or sink the boat. [Lieutenant Albert] David yelled up to the boys on deck to tumble down and lend a hand while he, Knispel and Wdowiak ran forward for the radio room to get the code books. They smashed open a couple of lockers, found the books and immediately passed them up on deck, so we would have something to show for our efforts in case we still lost the boat.

The sub was now in practically neutral buoyancy, was riding about ten degrees down by the stern and was settling deeper all the time.

One of the first to plunge down the hatch in response to David's call from below was Zenon B. Lukosius. As soon as Luke hit the floor plates he heard running water. Heading for the sound he ducked around behind the main periscope well and found a stream of water six inches in diameter gushing into the bilges from an open sea chest. By the grace of God the cover for this chest had not fallen down into the bilges where we wouldn't have been able to find it, but was lying on the floor plates. Luke grabbed it, slapped it back in place, set up on the butterfly nuts and checked the inrush of water. By this time the boat was threatening to up-end like the U-515 any minute. If she had, she would have taken the whole boarding party with her. Luke got his little chore done just in the nick of time. Another minute might have been too late.

Meantime, I had reversed course, got back to the scene of action and sent over a whale boat with

Commander Earl Trosino and a group of our "experts" in it.

I cannot speak too highly of the job that Trosino did in keeping that sub afloat. He too had never been aboard a submarine before. But he had spent most of his life at sea as a chief engineer in Sun Oil tankers. He is the kind of an engineer who can walk into any marine plant, whether it is installed in the "Queen Mary" or a German U-boat, take a quick look around the engine room and be ready to put the blast on any dumb cluck who touches the wrong valve at the wrong time.

He spent the next couple of hours fighting to keep the sub's head above water. It was touch and go whether he would succeed or not and they had to keep that conning tower hatch closed. A lot of the time Trosino was down in the bilges under the floor plates tracing out pipelines. Had the sub taken a sudden lurch and up-ended herself, as it was quite probable she would—Earl wouldn't have had any chance whatever to get out.

Trosino got the right valves closed and didn't open any of the hundreds of wrong ones. While he was doing this, Gunner Burr went through the boat looking for demolition charges. Our intelligence reports told us we would find fourteen five-pound TNT charges placed against the hull, several in each compartment. We had no information on their exact location or how the firing mechanism worked. Gunner Burr found and disarmed thirteen while Trosino was bilge diving. They found the fourteenth in Bermuda three weeks later! The Germans had been so sure when they abandoned ship that this sub was on the way to the bottom within minutes, that they hadn't set the firing devices!

Trosino reported that as long as the sub had headway, she rode about ten degrees down by the stern. But when he slowed her down, she lost the lift of her stern diving planes, settled to a steeper angle and submerged the conning tower hatch. The "Pillsbury" reported a DE couldn't do the towing job, so I headed over to take her in tow myself. As we drew near, Trosino pulled the switches and stopped the sub . . . . I cracked off an urgent top secret dispatch to CinCLant and Cominch, "Request immediate assistance to tow captured submarine U-505." That dispatch really shook the staff duty officers back home. At first they didn't believe it and demanded a recheck on the decoding—but lost no time getting necessary action underway in the improbable event that it was true.

Rear-Admiral Daniel V. Gallery, U.S.N.
Condensed from *20,000 Tons Under the Sea*

And that is why the U-505 today sits on the lawn behind the Museum of Science and Industry in Chicago instead of on the bottom of the Atlantic Ocean. Rear-Admiral Gallery, an ebullient and imaginative naval officer, had conceived the possibility of capturing an enemy submarine with the hunter-killer task force (a jeep carrier with destroyer escorts) he commanded. The account is a sharply condensed excerpt from Admiral Gallery's book *20,000 Tons Under the Sea*, which is highly recommended as not only an exciting but a thoughtful and insightful account of antisubmarine warfare in the Atlantic during the later stages of World War II.

The U-505 is probably the only survivor of Hitler's submarine fleet: By agreement among the Allied powers, all the U-boats that surrendered at the end of the war were either scrapped or taken out to sea and scuttled. And as Gallery notes, to capture an enemy vessel by boarding is a unique achievement in modern naval warfare. The capture succeeded only because Gallery had thoroughly prepared his boarding parties to race aboard a surfaced sub, close the seacocks, and remove the demolition charges.

The captured U-505, a long-range fleet submarine of the 1X9C class, may be unique but after World War II her future was uncertain. For years after the war she rusted away at a dock at the Portsmouth, New Hampshire Navy Yard. Fortunately, Chicagoans who realized that the submarine was an irreplaceable historical artifact were able to find a home for her and to persuade the Navy to release her for public exhibition. Towed through the St. Lawrence into the Great Lakes, U-505 arrived at Chicago in 1954. There, she was lifted out of the water in a floating dry dock, mounted on a steel cradle, floated in through a specially dredged channel to the museum's Lake Michigan front, and rolled ashore on rails over a pier. Fifteen thousand people watched as the submarine was hauled slowly across the Outer Drive where a sign warned motorists: "Drive Carefully—Submarine Crossing." She was dedicated as a memorial to the 55,000 Americans lost at sea in World War II.

Today, U-505 is the centerpiece of the Sea Power Exhibit of the Museum of Science and Industry. She is reached through a covered ramp from the museum building. Heated and lighted, the 258-foot vessel is displayed as she was captured, with her original equipment in working order. Navy buffs will be particularly interested in comparing the German boat with American submarines of the same period that are on exhibition in many parts of the country (including one, the USS *Silversides*, a few miles away at Chicago's Navy Pier).

As might be expected in a museum notable both for the breadth and the detail of its collections, U-505 is only one element in the Museum of Science and Industry's maritime exhibits. The balance of the Sea Power Gallery is on the ground floor of the museum adjacent to the submarine, where there is a full-size replica of a portion of the gun deck of one of the United States Navy's original frigates of 1797. Many of the exhibits are presented by the U.S. Navy, including a simulated Fleet Ballistic Missile System that the visitor can operate himself, firing at the lighted outline of a submarine. Ship models include two extremely large representations of fighting craft: an inch-to-the-foot cutaway of a World War II fleet destroyer, and a 20-foot model of the aircraft carrier *Coral Sea*. A special section recounts the history of naval aviation with aircraft models and action video tapes. There are also sections on oceanography and weather studies.

The Navy plans to replace many of these exhibits in the next few years with new displays embodying the latest naval technology.

The other major maritime exhibits are also on the ground floor of the museum, in the central section of the building. Here in the Ships Through the Ages Gallery is a parade of 50 to 60 miniature vessels, from the river craft of the ancient Egyptians to the roaring steamships of the 19th century. The collection of models, many made for the museum, covers an unusually wide range. Included are such out-of-the-ordinary models as representations of Phoenician and Roman ships, Viking long ships, Chinese junks, Venetian galleys.

The mock-up of the quarterdeck of a 19th-century sailing ship in the gallery includes such details as the pinrail and spankerboom. A model of the Newport News Shipbuilding Company's Graving Dock 2 shows the liner *City of New York* in the basin. Figureheads, scrimshaw, and marine artifacts of various kinds complete the collection.

Before we leave the Museum of Science and Industry, let's give the last word to Dan Gallery, the only naval commander to capture a submarine at sea—and thus provide the museum with its prize maritime exhibit.

"The U-505 will be alongside the Museum for many years to come, perhaps over a hundred if it isn't blasted to atoms by a hydrogen bomb in the meantime," Gallery wrote in his book. "It should serve as a constant reminder to us that seventy per cent of the earth's surface is salt water, and that the United States owes a great deal to the sea which carried our ancestors to freedom and a new way of life on a virgin continent, was the bulwark that protected us when the country was young and weak, and gave us access to the markets and resources of the world to make our industry thrive and grow."

The Museum of Science and Industry, on the lakefront of Chicago's Jackson Park. Open all year, Monday-Friday 9:30 a.m. to 4 p.m. Saturday and Sunday 9:30 a.m. to 5:30 p.m. Admission: free. Museum of Science and Industry, Jackson Park at 57th and S. Lake Shore Drive, Chicago, Illinois 60637. Telephone (312) 684-1414.

Figure 52
U-505, only modern vessel captured by boarding and only surviving German World War II submarine, nestles cozily against steps of Chicago's Museum of Science and Industry, where entire vessel can be visited.

The U-505 is not the only submarine to find a retirement home in Chicago. At the Turning Basin, further north on the Lake Michigan waterfront, the Great Lakes Naval and Maritime Museum has on exhibition the USS *Silversides*, a veteran of 14 combat patrols in the Pacific during World War II. A member of the 312-foot Drum class, *Silversides* served throughout practically the entire war and is credited with sinking 23 enemy ships totaling 90,000 tons. Her kill record—third highest in number of ships and fifth highest in tonnage of the entire U.S. submarine fleet—earned *Silversides* a Presidential Unit Citation.

The *Silversides* was also the scene of a famous incident in which a Navy medic performed an emergency appendectomy on a crew member, an incident later dramatized in the movie *Destination Tokyo* with Cary Grant. Although she served as a training

vessel after the war, *Silversides* has been restored and is being preserved as she appeared in 1945 at the end of her combat tours. The vessel is fully open to inspection and makes an interesting contrast with the U-505 at the Museum of Science & Technology.

The submarine is only one of several vessels at the Great Lakes Naval and Maritime Museum. The SS *Rachel Carson*, still in commission, has also had an active and varied career. Originally she was the USS *Crockett*, P.G. 88, a 115-foot gunboat of the Asheville class built in 1967 for use in Vietnamese waters. Retired 10 years later, she was renamed for the noted marine biologist and conservationist and converted to serve as a Great Lakes research vessel for the Environmental Protection Agency. Now the *Carson* belongs to the museum, but she is still used on occasion for research on the lakes.

Beside being an interesting vessel in herself, with laboratories, classrooms, and gear for underwater research, the *Carson* also serves as a museum. Here, on display, are pictures and artifacts of U.S. Navy training ships on the Great Lakes; notably the aircraft carriers *Wolverine* and *Sable*, converted from side-wheel passenger liners, and the training gunboat *Willamette*, once the notorious lakes steamer *Eastland*, which in 1915 capsized at her dock drowning hundreds of passengers.

A third vessel on display at the Navy Pier is the *Marquette*, a 102-foot tug retired from service with the U.S. Army Corps of Engineers. Built in New Orleans in 1941, she served during World War II as the *Col. John Adams*. Then, in 1948, she became the tender of the enormous steam dipper dredge *Gaylord*, not only working all over the Great Lakes but helping to dig the St. Lawrence Seaway.

Great Lakes Naval and Maritime Museum is at the Turning Basin on Chicago's Lake Michigan waterfront. From Lake Shore Drive northbound, take Randolph exit ramp which leads directly to Basin. Open January and February weekends, weather permitting; March 1 to May 1, all weekends; May 1 to October 1, every day; October 1 to December 1, weekends. Hours: noon to 6 p.m. Closed December. Admission: $2.00, seniors and children, $1. Special overnight stays on *Silversides* or *Carson* available to youth groups; make reservations well ahead. *Carson* may be chartered for research. Great Lakes Naval and Maritime Museum, P.O. Box A 3785, Chicago, Illinois 60690. Telephone (312) 819-0055.

From Chicago, we'll head up the west shore of Lake Michigan to Manitowoc, Wisconsin, which started building ships when it was still a frontier village.

To a casual observer, Manitowoc, Wisconsin, 1,000 miles from salt water, must have seemed peacefully remote from the fierce naval combat of World War II. Actually, however, the little city on the western shore of Lake Michigan was playing an important role in the Navy's war: From the shipways along the Manitowoc River came no less than 28 submarines for the nation's underwater fleet.

Shipbuilding achievements were nothing new for Manitowoc. Just before the war, the city's yards had launched the huge passenger/auto ferry *City of Midland*, then described as the "Queen of the Lakes," for the service across Lake Michigan. In fact, Manitowoc's shipbuilding tradition began long before, almost with the first settlement: In little more than a decade after the first settlers arrived in 1836 they started building vessels. With forests at hand to provide the raw materials and a strong demand for bottoms to carry the settlers westward through the lake to take up newly opened lands, it was a boom time for shipbuilders. What with cargoes of grain becoming available for the voyage east, it was not unusual for a vessel to pay for herself in her first season of operation.

The city's shipbuilding, from early sailing packets to recent fighting ships, is a major theme of the notable Manitowoc Maritime Museum, located on the bank of the little river that forms the harbor. The USS *Cobia*, a submarine just like those built at Manitowoc, is berthed alongside a bulkhead by the museum building on the river front. The *Cobia* is open to visitors from stem to stern, including her bridge and conning tower, which are not always viewable in submarines on exhibition. Recorded sounds of a crash dive and combat action add a very realistic note to a tour of the boat.

The museum has long been outgrowing its quarters, and in the fall of 1986 it moved into a new and larger home just across the river. The additional space provides room for expanded exhibits on steel shipbuilding and the activities of Manitowoc shipyards during the two World Wars. Marine engine development, an important aspect of maritime activity covered in few other places, gains an exhibit of its own. A full-scale reconstruction of a cross-section of the fast lumber schooner *Clipper City*, built in Manitowoc in 1854, demonstrates the wooden shipbuilding techniques of the period. ("Clipper City" was the nickname of Manitowoc.) Shipwrights' tools and artifacts fill in the picture.

In the main hall of the museum a striking reconstruction of the buildings on the waterfront of old Manitowoc emphasizes the maritime trades, such as ship chandlery. The Maritime Arts and Crafts Gallery displays a fine fleet of miniature vessels, including both scale and folk models as well as the half models used by shipbuilders. Represented are not only sailing ships but the lake steamers, from the famous sidewheeler *Michigan* to the elegant propeller liners of a later era.

Special exhibits, which are changed periodically, are devoted to such subjects as the lake fisheries, lifesaving, and the various types of small craft.

Manitowoc Marine Museum is downtown on the river in Manitowoc, Wisconsin, on the west shore of Lake Michigan. Adjacent in Manitowoc River is USS *Cobia*, retired submarine. Book and gift shop. Open all year, every day except holidays. Museum hours: April through October, daily 9 a.m. to 5 p.m.; November through March, Monday-Friday, 9 a.m. to 5 p.m., Saturday and Sunday 10 a.m. to 4 p.m. Admission to submarine and museum: $4.00; children, $2.00. USS *Cobia* is open daily May 1 to October 31; 9 a.m. to 5 p.m. Admission to museum and submarine: $4.00; children, $2.00. Manitowoc Maritime Museum, 809 South Eighth Street, Manitowoc, Wisconsin 54220, until autumn 1986. After that, 75 Maritime Drive. Telephone (414) 684-0218.

Still further north along Lake Michigan we'll come to Sturgeon Bay, another noted shipbuilding center.

Some people say that the Door Peninsula, which separates Wisconsin's Green Bay from Lake Michigan, is the nearest Midwestern equivalent to New England's famed Cape Cod. Not only does it have water on three sides but, also like Cape Cod, the narrow neck that ties it to the mainland has been cut by a canal, making it really an island. Little fishing villages nestle along the shore. The visitor feels he is entering a separate world, as distinct from "America's Dairyland" as Cape Cod is from the milltowns (or the High Tech) of the Bay State.

Figure 53
The Manitowoc Maritime Museum's submarine *Cobia*, at her berth in Manitowoc River, reminds us that the Lake Michigan port was a major submarine building center during World War II.

And, curiously, Door County (common usage for the peninsula) saw a sailing ship in the 17th century, not too long after the first European settlement on Cape Cod. The great French explorer La Salle arrived at an island off the tip of the peninsula in his little 45-ton, two-masted *Griffin* in 1679. Here, he loaded her with furs to be carried back through the lakes to Niagara; the ill-fated voyage in which she disappeared with all hands.

The odd name of the peninsula, which sounds as if it were named by a house carpenter, has as direct a maritime origin as Cape Cod—but more doomful. Between the tip of the peninsula and Washington Island is a narrow channel, used by vessels making a passage between the Lake Michigan ports to the south, such as Chicago and Milwaukee, and the port of Green Bay at the head of the bay. Not only was this a dangerous route in itself, but it was bedeviled by what one expert describes as "brief furious thunder squalls that ripped with unexpected suddenness through the passage at the headlands of the Door Peninsula." These sudden storms were the doom of many a vessel, and the passage became known as "Death's Door," giving part of its name to the adjacent land.

Door County is rimmed with rock rather than sand; its soil is good enough for cherry orchards rather than the cranberries and beachplums of the Cape, but while it never developed the major maritime traditions of New England, the peninsula did become the home of fishermen and shipbuilders—the latter particularly at Sturgeon Bay, at the base of the peninsula. Thanks to the St. Lawrence Seaway, ships can be built there now for service in remote parts of the world. Sturgeon Bay is also a center of yacht building. The canal through the peninsula here provides a short cut between Lake Michigan and Green Bay, making unnecessary the long voyage around the tip through Death's Door.

Appropriately, Door County is preserving its maritime heritage in a museum, or rather two museums under the same sponsorship but at opposite ends of the peninsula: Sturgeon Bay at the base and Gills Rock at the tip.

The Sturgeon Bay Marine Museum is appropriately lodged in a building that was once the headquarters of a steamship company; one of the exhibits is the owner's private office, which is kept just as he used it for many years. The museum also has the refurbished pilothouse of a lake steamer.

The major exhibits of the museum, however, are small craft. Besides turn-of-the-century pulling and sailing boats, they include the launch *Wanda* and a Chris-Craft "speed boat." Another important element is a collection of marine engines, ranging from antique outboards to the one-lungers that were once used to drive every type of small craft. Among them is a ponderous Kollenburg that looks big and heavy enough to drive anything.

At the outer end of the peninsula, the Gills Rock Marine Museum emphasizes the commercial fisheries that have been an important regional activity since early times. A centerpiece is a full-size fish tug, once employed as a gill-netter. Fishing gear and artifacts include a number of marine engines used in the lake fishing fleet. And, appropriately for a museum that's at the threshold of Death's Door, there is a wide-ranging collection of objects recovered by scuba divers from the multitude of wrecks at the bottom of Green Bay and nearby Lake Michigan.

Both museums have large collections of maritime pictures and photographs.

The Door County Maritime Museums are at opposite ends of the Door Peninsula, reached by Route 57 from Green Bay; from Milwaukee, I-43 north to Manitowoc, then Route 42 to Sturgeon Bay. *Sturgeon Bay Marine Museum* is off Third Avenue, close to the corner of Georgia Street in Sturgeon Bay at entrance to peninsula. Book store. Open May 28 through September 5, daily, 10 a.m. to noon, and 1:30 to 4 p.m. Admission: donation encouraged. Sturgeon Bay Marine Museum, Sunset Park, Bay Ship and Third Avenue, Sturgeon Bay, Wisconsin 54235. Telephone (414) 743-8139. *Gills Rock Marine Museum* is at tip of Door Peninsula. Just before Gills Rock ferry landing, turn right on road to North Port, then left on Wisconsin Bay Road, museum is on right. Book store. Open May 28 through September 5, daily, 10 a.m. to 4 p.m. Admission: donation encouraged. Gills Rock Marine Museum, Gills Rock Memorial Park, Gills Rock, Wisconsin 54235. Headquarters, Door County Maritime Museums, 6427 Green Bay Road, Sturgeon Bay, Wisconsin 54235. Telephone (414) 743-5809.

For a look at a victim of Death's Door, we'll drive back down the peninsula, around the head of Green Bay, and up the west shore.

On June 29, 1884, the brigantine *Alvin Clark*, in ballast and with her hatch covers off to air the hold, was bound for the little lumber port of Oconto, Wisconsin, near the head of Green Bay. She was under full sail, close-hauled, beating against a moderate breeze rising out of the south-southeast, but now beginning to back. Astern, a rain shower coming across the water obscured visibility.

When the first raindrops reached the *Clark*, her crew would have felt the wind drop abruptly. Then, within a minute, they were struck by a powerful gust from the northeast. [The Captain], again at the helm, had seen it coming and quickly put the helm down to avoid a jibe. The *Clark*, having little way on, responded slowly at first but then, with gathering momentum, rounded up while nearly rolling her starboard rail under. With the gust came a tremendous clap of thunder, finally warning Durnin that this would be no light shower.

Now aware of the danger, Durnin shouted his orders to loose the 'course tacks and haul the buntlines. Cray, meanwhile, fetched an axe. The deck was now inclined steeply under the press of another gust and, with the last of his footing, Cray reached the forward shrouds. The gust passed and the *Clark* struggled upright. Working with one hand, Cray cut the backstays. Then, sensing another gust, Cray let fly at the topgallant shroud lanyards and then parted the topmast shrouds. By this time, the *Clark* was fully broadside to the wind with her sails still trimmed for sailing close-hauled. Dunn had tried to let go the foresheet, but found it had become jammed. The next gust struck furiously. The topgallant mast snapped above the doubling and settled alongside the lee rail. The topmast soon followed, creating an appalling mass of wreckage. Still the squall grew stronger. Cray had abandoned the axe and now grasped the windward rigging with both hands. His legs went from beneath him, and he knew that the *Clark* was going over and that without hatch covers in place would fill quickly. It was too late to save her. Swinging his legs up and over the rail, Cray found himself lying on the bulwarks across the port chainplates. Now pelted by driving hail, he could hear nothing but the gale.

Then, almost as abruptly as it had set upon them, the storm passed off to the southwest. Only Cray and one other seaman remained aboard, clinging to the mainmast shrouds. Francis Higgie, aboard the *Dewitt*, had seen the *Clark* capsize and soon brought his ship close in, lowered the yawlboat, and picked up the two men. The others had drowned.

Thus, C.T. McCutcheon, Jr. imaginatively recreated for the readers of the magazine *Wooden Boat* the afternoon long ago when the *Alvin Clark*, an 18-year-old lake carrier, suddenly went to the bottom of Green Bay, carrying her captain, mate, and a seaman with her. She lay there for 103 years, sitting upright on the bottom in 110 feet of water. Then scuba diver Frank Hoffmann found her. In the late fall of 1967, he was called on to dive in Green Bay in order to release a commercial fisherman's net that had been snagged underwater. Hoffmann found it caught in the rigging of a two-masted vessel, later identified as the *Alvin Clark*.

The *Clark* sits today in a little dry dock next to the Menominee River, in Menominee, Michigan, which is on the west shore of Green Bay. How Hoffmann raised her from the bottom with the help of scuba-diving friends, sought—so far apparently in vain—for help in preserving her, and installed her in what he calls the Mystery Ship Seaport in Menominee is a long and complicated story, filled with practically every human emotion but dominated by determination and frustration. The story is told and discussed in detail from three different viewpoints in the May/June 1983 issue of *Wooden Boat*, which should be read by everyone interested in the preservation of old ships, whether or not they ever expect to get to Menominee to see the *Clark*. (It should be noted that Hoffmann himself naturally has a fourth viewpoint.)

The future of the *Clark*, believed to be the only original Great Lakes sailing vessel on display, has been uncertain from the beginning, and according to Hoffmann, there is a good possibility that she will be moved to another site. The vessel is reported to have deteriorated badly from exposure to the sun and air after being removed from the water, and Hoffmann has long sought support for her restoration and preservation.

When on display, the *Clark* is open below decks. Because of the speed of her final catastrophe, the vessel was found completely equipped with crew clothing, dishes, lamps, tools, compass, octant, and so forth, and these objects are in the museum. The seaport also has a 28-minute film showing the process of raising her from the bottom, which visiting groups can arrange to have shown.

Also on display are a fine 27-inch model of the *Alvin Clark* as she looked in her prime and portions of another vessel, the 79-foot steamer *Erie L. Hackley*. Top-heavy, the *Hackley* capsized and sank in Green Bay in 1903. Artifacts from the vessel include compass and bell, as well as stores and tools, not to mention some plows that were presumably cargo.

Mystery Ship Seaport is at Menominee, in the far southwest corner of Michigan's Upper Peninsula, just across the Menominee River from Marinette, Wisconsin; 60 miles from Green Bay, via Route 41. Seaport is three blocks east of Interstate Bridge on 13th Street, in River Park. "Mystery Ship" is topsail schooner *Alvin Clark*, built 1846, sunk 1864; raised, 1967. Vessel in pumped out drydock. Open June 14 to September 14, every day, 9 a.m. to 6 p.m. Admission: $3.50; 7 to 14, $1.50; younger children free. Owned by nonprofit Mystery Ship Preservation Society. Mystery Ship Seaport, P.O. Box 235, Menominee, Michigan 49858. Telephone (906) 863-8721.

Lake Superior

In the early evening of November 10, 1975, the 729-foot steamer *Edmund Fitzgerald* was headed eastward on Lake Superior, bound for Detroit from Superior, Wisconsin, with a cargo of 26,116 long tons of taconite pellets (concentrated iron ore). An autumn storm had produced northwest winds as high as 58 knots, and some seas of as much as 25 feet. At 7:10, a vessel following behind conversed by radio with the *Fitzgerald* and saw her on the radar screen, nine miles ahead. Shortly after that she vanished—from the screen and from the lake.

The *Fitzgerald*, a relatively new ship, and her crew of 29 were never seen again.

An underwater survey the following spring found her hull, broken into two sections, on the lake bottom under 530 feet of water. Lake Superior had claimed another victim.

Largest of the Great Lakes, 350 miles long and 160 miles across at its widest point, Lake Superior has taken its toll since ships first appeared on its water. In this century, to give just two examples, a November storm in 1913 sank a dozen ships, drove 16 aground, and took the lives of more than 250 seamen. Another storm in November, 1940, sank five ships and left 67 dead. In the 19th century, when ships were smaller and navigation aids fewer, the losses were proportionately greater. Superior's storms, which arise very quickly, have been dreaded for centuries. In many places, dangerous reefs lurk below the surface; everywhere, the water is killing cold.

The lake, whose surface is 600 feet above sea level, is almost 1,300 feet deep in spots. Some 32,000 square miles in area, Superior is a drowned river valley, widened and deepened by glacial action. As the continental ice sheet retreated, the melt, trapped between terminal moraines and the glacier front, formed a lake and the overflow ran out to the southeastward through the rapids-filled St. Mary's River into Lake Huron where the level is 28 to 42 feet lower.

Superior is shaped roughly like a strung bow, with a long curved coast on the north and a much straighter shore on the south. No great rivers enter: Terminal morains to the south and rocky ledges cut off the drainage. Yet the headwaters of the little rivers running into the north shore are close to the heads of rivers running north through the wilderness to Hudson Bay, providing—with portages—a canoe route for fur traders far into upper North America.

Curiously, this remote lake, the furthest west and the furthest north of the five great inland seas, was discovered by Europeans at about the time when the Pilgrim fathers were still barely hanging on by their fingertips at the very edge of the continent. Like much of the early exploration of North America, the discovery of Lake Superior probably resulted from attempts to find what didn't exist: the fabled Northeast Passage through North America to the riches of Asia. To look for it, Samuel de Champlain, father of New France, sent men far to the west; in 1623 two of them crossed the north end of Lake Huron and are believed to have gone up the St. Mary's River and had a first glimpse of Lake Superior. Within a few years the lake appeared on French maps.

Thus, Lake Superior was actually explored before lower lakes much closer to French Canada. To avoid hostile Iroquois along the lower lakes, French explorers and fur traders canoed northwest on the Ottawa River, portaged across headwaters, and went down the French River into upper Lake Huron. Traveling westward they came to the mouth of St. Mary's River, which took them, after a short portage past rapids at its head, to the east end of Lake Superior. This long route was used by Indians bringing furs from the west, until posts were established to trade with them along the lakes.

From the beginning, the newcomers found Lake Superior and its shores difficult places to survive in.

A Jesuit missionary reported in 1668 what it was like to fish in the lake: "It was a sight to arouse pity to see poor Frenchmen in a Canoe, amid rain and snow, borne hither and thither by whirlwinds in these great Lakes, which often show waves as high as those of the Sea. The men frequently found their hands and feet frozen upon their return, while occasionally they were overtaken by so thick a fall of powdery snow, driven against them by a violent wind, that the one steering the Canoe could not see his companion in the bow. How then gain the port? Verily, as often as they reached the land, their doing so seemed a little miracle."

The highly profitable fur trade was taken over by the English when they captured French Canada at the end of the Seven Years War. While the Hudson's Bay Company continued to have a monopoly of the trade in the huge region drained by rivers flowing north into the Bay, the wilderness to the south was open and dominated by merchants based in Montreal. Lake Superior was a key to access to the region, and in the 20 years after the conquest the fur trade around the lake reached its peak.

Travel on Lake Superior was carried out in great canoes, as much as 30 or 35 feet long; they were so large that they were sometimes rowed, the oars held in loops of rawhide, rather than paddled the hundreds of miles along the lake. By the 18th century, canoes were often superseded by rough wooden Mackinac boats and bateaux, simple flatbottom craft used on the rivers of New France. As early as 1735, however, sailing vessels began to appear upon Lake Superior. In that year, a decked vessel was built on the lake to carry supplies to an abortive mining venture. Forty years later, British sloops as large as 40 tons, with four guns, were being constructed on the lake.

In the early 19th century, attempts were made to run sailing vessels built on the lake down through the rapids on the St. Mary's River, but several small schooners and sloops were wrecked in the attempt.

Sailing craft, mostly schooners, multiplied on Superior in the first half of the 19th century. By 1846, 10 schooners were carrying supplies, missionaries, would-be miners, and soldiers. The late 1860s were the Golden Age of schooners.

Mining is what brought great fleets of ships to the lake. The Indians of the area had always known that there was copper there; but modern copper mining did not begin until 1844. From then until 1925, half of the world's copper came from the United States and for the first forty years of this period the greater part of this copper came from the upper peninsula of Michigan—and was carried away over the waters of Lake Superior.

Almost simultaneously in 1844, a great iron ore range was discovered on the south shore of Lake Superior and, soon afterward, the town and port of Marquette came into being to ship the ore. As more discoveries were made along the south shore, more little ore ports, such as Ashland, sprang up. Starting in 1892, Minnesota's Great Mesabi Range, inland from the west end of Lake Superior, produced tremendous amounts of iron ore and today is still a source of shipments of low-grade taconite. Here, as in the case of copper, cheap transportation provided by Lake Superior bulk carriers made possible the utilization of iron ores from what was then a very remote part of the United States.

To process the ore required an ample supply of low-cost fuel, and there was plenty in the coal mines of Pennsylvania, Ohio, Kentucky, and West Virginia, south of the lower lakes. Thanks to the four-to-one coal-iron ratio, and the nearness of the lower lakes to markets for steel, producers found it most economical to carry the iron ore down to the vicinity of the coal, shipping it from Lake Superior through the St. Mary's River to Lake Huron and down the lakes to such Lake Erie ports as Cleveland and Erie. The St. Mary's rapids were a major obstacle, however; cargoes had to be unloaded, and reloaded on different vessels for the remainder of the trip. With ore shipments booming, the problem was solved by the construction in 1855 of the first of a series of lock canals at Sault Ste. Marie, carrying ships around the rapids. A portent of things to come, the steamer *Illinois* was the first ship through the new canal. Eventually, side-wheelers took over ore carrying, increasing their cargo capacity by lashing sailing ships loaded with ore on both sides and taking them down through the lakes. In the 1860s and 70s much of the ore traffic came to be handled by steam tugs: a tug like the *Champion* could tow seven or eight sailing vessels loaded with ore.

A steamship was designed especially for ore carrying for the first time in 1869 when the *R.J. Hackett* was built with her engines way aft in the stern, leaving the main body of the hull entirely open for loading bulk ore through hatches. This has been the pattern that the ore carriers have faithfully followed ever since, although they grow steadily in size to take advantage of large locks at the Sault Ste. Marie Canal. In 1900, four 500-foot steamers were ordered. The largest of today's vessels are over 1,000 feet long and carry nearly 70,000 tons of ore; the newest ones have their own equipment for loading and unloading so that they can dock anywhere.

While iron ore has been the major Lake Superior cargo it has been far from the only one. Starting in the 1880s, the forest around the lake produced a steady flow of lumber for almost half a century. The first sizable craft built on Lake Superior were lumber barges, some self-propelled and each able to carry one million board feet of lumber. Wisconsin lumber from the south shore of the lake could be shipped to Chicago by lake vessel from the Ashland/Bayfield area at half the rail rate. By 1925, however, the great native forests had been cut down and the lumber trade dwindled, although some lumber and pulpwood are still carried on the lakes today.

Meanwhile, the movement of settlers westward into the prairie lands of Minnesota, the Dakotas, and Manitoba brought another rich flow of cargoes to Lake Superior: wheat. As the great grain elevators in Superior/Duluth at the west end of the lake and of Fort William and Port Arthur on the Canadian north shore attest, grain to this day provides major cargoes. Some, loaded on salt-water ships, are carried through the St. Lawrence Seaway directly to overseas markets.

At one time fishing was a major activity on Lake Superior. Early, European explorers commented on the good catches found in the lake, and fish were an indispensable part of the diet of the Indians and fur traders who lived along its shores. In the 1830s, the American Fur Company (the American rival to the Hudson's Bay Company) established lake fisheries to provide a commodity to sell in the settlements that would pay for provisions. The company established fishing stations along the north shore of the lake and particularly at Isle Royale; the schooner *John Jacob Astor*, launched in 1835, was designed to carry both furs and fish. Whitefish was the most esteemed; authors of contemporary accounts said they had never tasted a fish to equal it.

With ups and downs, fishing by "steam tugs" lasted well into the 20th century. By the 1880s, however, the fishing grounds were already becoming depleted, and by 1920 the whitefish and sturgeon were virtually extinct along most of the American shore of the lake. In fact, practically all of the other fish had declined, except herring and trout.

One final note: Lake Superior is one of the few places, perhaps the only place, in North America where there has been a sworn sighting of a Merman. On November 13, 1812, a man appeared before the Court of King's Bench in Montreal and swore that:

> On May 3, 1782, traveling by canoe from Grand Portage to Mackinac, [he had] camped for the night at the south end of Pie Island.
>
> He went out and set his nets, and came back ashore. As did so, saw not very far away a man-shaped creature, the size of a 7-8 yr old child, half out of water, looking at him and companions with curiosity but uneasiness.
>
> [He] tried to shoot [the creature] but was stopped by an old Indian woman in party who warned him that this was the God of the Waters and Lakes and that all who saw him must die. Man disappeared in water. Indian woman climbed up steep bank to avoid storm she predicted. At 10 p.m., intense storm; lasted three days.
>
> [The witness] told the court that Indians and others had frequently seen this strange creature in this area and that God of the Waters lived there.

We'll start our trip around Lake Superior at the east end where the Soo Canal locks 1,000-foot ships in and out of the lake.

The key to Lake Superior is the St. Mary's River, Superior's outlet to the other four Great Lakes and eventually to the sea. Sixty-three miles long, the St. Mary's is a small river as North American rivers go, yet measured by the flow of water through it, or the flow of ships over it, the river is one of the world's great waterways. As the only outlet from Lake Superior, the St. Mary's receives an average of 71,700 cubic feet of water every second. Over its surface flows all of the water traffic between Superior and the rest of America and the world: ore ships and grain ships in particular, and in past days the lumber schooners and fishing vessels of the lakes.

But the St. Mary's was not naturally a shipway at all. As it leaves Lake Superior, the river drops 20 feet in something over a mile of tumbling waters. Nothing larger than a canoe could shoot down the rock-filled rapids; passage upstream was completely blocked. Indians and after them the fur traders and explorers made a portage here, lifting their canoes out of the river, carrying them for a mile along the riverbank, and launching them again at the other end of the rapids. Later, very substantial vessels were portaged: sailing ships, even one of the first steamers on Lake Superior was dragged over the portage route. (It took seven weeks, in the winter of 1846, to haul the steamer *Julia Palmer* that one mile around the rapids up to Lake Superior.)

Portaging could be endured until deposits of copper and iron ore were discovered close to the south shore of Lake Superior. The first lake ore had to be carried to Sault Ste. Marie in a schooner, unloaded, and the ore trundled in carts around the rapids, then reloaded on other vessels on the river below. There was great demand for locks to carry ships around the rapids, and in 1855 a canal was built. The first locks were 350 feet long, which set an automatic limit to the size of the ore ships. As the mines continued to pour out their bulky cargoes, however, new locks were repeatedly built to take bigger ships. In 1881, the new lock was 515 feet long; in 1896, 800 feet; in 1914, 1,300 feet. Today, the canal takes huge 1,000-foot ore carriers, lifting or dropping them the 20 feet necessary to get around the rapids.

The river is the international boundary, separating twin cities: Sault Ste. Marie, Michigan, U.S.A., and Sault Ste. Marie, Ontario, Canada. Ancient towns, they were originally centers of the fur trade. The maritime-minded visitor should be sure to watch today's vessels going through the locks of the great canal. The U.S. Army Engineers have built observation stands beside the locks on the American side, and from this vantage point a visitor can watch a procession of ships, big and small, rising or falling. A park walkway right along the edge of the canal leads to a "tower of history" that gives the visitor a fine overall view of the river, canal, and locks.

For most visitors, however, the most interesting things to see will be two Great Lakes steamships, one berthed at each of the two Sault Ste. Maries.

Let's look first at the SS *Valley Camp*, on the American shore of the river.

Not far from the locks visitors have an opportunity not only to look at ore carriers but to explore one to their heart's content. The SS *Valley Camp* is a veteran of the lakes; she passed through the canal many times carrying ore through Lake Superior down to the steel works on Lake Erie and Lake Michigan. Built in 1917, she logged more than three million miles in nearly 50 years of operations. Now she is a museum, tied up alongside the shore and open to visitors.

Five hundred and fifty feet long, displacing almost 12,000 tons, the *Valley Camp* was a big ship for her day, although overshadowed now by the monsters that cruise the lakes. Here are some of the things you should look for:

- From the deck house, look along the open cargo deck and note the multiplicity of hatches. Many hatches make for quick loading of bulk cargoes, and quick turnarounds cut operating costs.
- Climb down to the engine room in the stern of the ship; her triple-expansion steam engine is open for viewing from a catwalk. This workhorse is becoming rarer and rarer as steam has been superseded by diesel power for marine propulsion.
- In the two deck houses, bow and stern, you can get an idea of how crew and officers lived during their voyages up and down the lakes. The black gang, the engine room crew, and the engineers lived in the after deckhouse above their engine. The deck gang and the deck officers lived in the forward deckhouse. Just below the navigating bridge are the captain's quarters with his office, bedroom, and head, and the guest cabin for visitors.
- The wheelhouse is open; here are the instruments for navigating the lakes, which can be just as tricky as the open ocean. In fact, considering the restricted navigational area, the number of rocks and shoals, and the sudden, vicious storms, the lakes are in some ways more dangerous and more demanding for navigators.

In the cavernous open holds where the ore was carried are a number of exhibits. The most interesting are a number of fine models of ore carriers, including the 1,000-foot motorship *James R. Baker*, a self-unloader that was the biggest vessel on the lakes in 1976. An enormous model, 30 feet long, portrays the bulk carrier *Belle River*, another 1,000-footer built in the same year. Another fine model shows the whaleback *John Ericsson*, a distinctive type superseded by later and larger designs in the early decades of the 20th century.

In the gallery around the outer edge of the hold, is an aquarium holding specimens of the aquatic life of the lakes. In the forward hold, the memorial to the steamship *Edmund Fitzgerald* and her crew will be of particular interest to ship-minded visitors. The *Fitzgerald* was the 700-foot ore carrier, less than 20 years old, that disappeared with all hands in a Lake Superior storm in 1975. Her two battered lifeboats, found adrift after the storm, are on exhibition in Valley Camp's museum, together with the roster of the lost crew, a model of the *Fitzgerald*, and a number of articles and news stories which are worth looking at for the various reasons the writers suggest for the vessel's tragic loss.

In the small information center on the dock next to the ship there are more exhibits, including a number of models of steamers and fishing boats. Of particular interest is a model of the SS *Atlantic*, an 1870 passenger steamer, carved from wood by her captain during the long winter layup when the lakes froze. Here, also, is a fine wooden eagle salvaged from the steamship *Vienna* after she was sunk in a collision in 1892.

Maps, artifacts, and photographs of ice-bound ships in the lakes are also displayed in the center. On the wall, a series of diagramatic pictures portrays the silhouettes of ore vessels from the earliest types to the latest, all drawn to scale to point up the enormous increase in their size over the 130 years since ore-carrying began on Lake Superior.

SS *Valley Camp*, retired Great Lakes ore carrier, is tied up at the old Union Carbide dock on the south side of the St. Mary's River, a short distance east of the locks in Sault Ste. Marie, Michigan. Parking. Book/gift shop. Open May 15 to June 30, and September 1 to October 15, daily, 10 a.m. to 6 p.m. July 1 to August 31, open daily, 9 a.m. to 8 p.m. Admission: $3.00; children, $1.50. SS *Valley Camp*, Le Sault de Sainte Marie Historical Sites, Inc., P.O. Box 1668, Sault Ste. Marie, Michigan 49783. Telephone (906) 632-3658.

Now, across the bridge to Sault Ste. Marie, Ontario, and another interesting but very different lake steamer.

The SS *Norgoma* spent the greater part of her active career as a passenger liner on Lake Huron and Georgian Bay. A striking contrast to the *Valley Camp*, she gives an idea of the wide variety of vessels that cruised the lakes during the heyday of water transportation. One of the last overnight passenger carriers active on the lakes, *Norgoma* is in retirement today, one of the few survivors of that once-great fleet.

The black-hulled vessel with two white passengers decks is only half the length of *Valley Camp*, but she slept 100 passengers, in addition to carrying a load of freight, and cruised three or four knots faster than the ore carrier. As an Owen Sound Line steamer, *Norgoma* ran back and forth between the port of Owen Sound, at the south end of Georgian Bay, and Sault Ste. Marie, calling at lake ports in between. The round trip took five days. Later, she was an auto ferry between Manitoulin Island and the mainland.

Retired in 1974, *Norgoma* had deteriorated badly by the time she started a new career as an exhibition ship six years later. She is still being restored under the sharp eye of a blue-water master mariner from the Maritime Provinces, but much of the ship is already open to visitors.

A number of cabins can be viewed, and they give the feel of travel on the lakes. On the deck below are the lounges where the passengers took their ease. Here is a little museum with ship models and artifacts. Also open is the wheelhouse with its navigation instruments.

SS _Norgoma_, a retired Lake Huron passenger/freight steamer, is tied up to a dock in St. Mary's River east of the locks in Sault Ste. Marie, Ontario. Open daily June 1 to June 30 and Labor Day to October 10, 10 a.m. to 6 p.m., July 1 to Labor Day, 9 a.m. to 9 p.m. Closed October 11 through May 31. Admission: $2.50; seniors and youth, $2.00. Vessel is owned by City of Sault Ste. Marie, Ontario. SS _Norgoma_ Museum Ship, Norgoma Marine Park Dock, Foster Drive, Sault Ste. Marie, Ontario, Canada PGA 5X6. Telephone (705) 942-6984.

Now, back to the American side. We'll head westward along the south shore of Lake Superior.

In 1844, the first large bodies of iron ore discovered in the North American continent were found close to the south shores of Lake Superior. They were soon exploited and a forge built at the mouth of the nearby Carp River. The little town that grew up around it was named for Father Jacques Marquette, the French missionary who in the 17th century traveled over much of this area preaching Christianity to the Indians. Here, in 1856, an ore dock was built and Marquette became the first ore-shipping port on Lake Superior. The first steamer designed specifically as an ore carrier, the 211-foot _R.J. Hackett_, was built to run to Marquette to carry away the output of the Jackson mine nearby.

In the latter half of the 19th century, Marquette was also a major lumbering and fishing port, but eventually the forests of the Upper Michigan peninsula were cut over and the fish supply depleted. A lifesaving station that was established here was kept busy, succoring the vessels in distress in the storms that swept Lake Superior.

Although the original rich ores are no longer pouring out of the mines near Marquette, the port still ships low-grade ores that have been pelletized. And, today, a brand new maritime museum is dedicated to preserving the traditions of 130 years of major involvement with Lake Superior shipping.

The museum was opened by a group of enthusiastic volunteers in the spring of 1984, in an old city waterworks building on the lakefront next to the Coast Guard station. The building was in terrible condition, and much of their first efforts went to making it sound and tight. The core of the exhibits come from the personal collections of the founders, which have been steadily augmented by gifts from others.

In one of the most interesting displays, an early Marquette dock is reproduced in replica. A walk-through fish shack is hung with lines and nets, a coffee pot on the stove, a lantern at the side of the tin plate on the weathered table, as if the occupant had just stepped outside to check the weather.

Inevitably on the shores of Lake Superior, wreck artifacts make up a considerable part of the collection. There is a special display on the ill-fated _Edmund Fitzgerald_, the huge ore carrier that went down in a November storm in the 1970s, carrying all hands with it. A display of small engines reminds the visitor that the first outboard engines are said to have been manufactured in Marquette. Charts, navigation aids, and photographic displays showing the development of Great Lakes ships from the early sailing vessels to the great modern freighters, are also in the collection.

The museum is still in its formative years and undoubtedly will acquire new exhibits as it becomes established.

Marquette Maritime Museum is at 501 East Archer Street on the corner of Lake Shore Boulevard, at the west end of the harborfront. Open May 1 through September 30, Tuesday-Sunday, 1 p.m. to 5 p.m. Admission: $1.50. Marquette Maritime Museum, P.O. Box 1096, Marquette, Michigan 49855. Telephone (906) 494-2669.

Up the hill in the city, the Marquette Historical Society has a maritime gallery displaying artifacts and photographs concerning the history of the port and the lake.

Now continue westward, passing from Michigan's Upper Peninsula to Wisconsin—really one region geographically, but politically divided by historical accident.

The little village of Bayfield in Wisconsin, on the south shore of Lake Superior, has many summer visitors today as the departure point for the boats to the Apostle and Madeline Islands. Once, however, it was best known as a major fishing and lumber port. Together with the neighboring ore-shipping port of Ashland, it kept Chequeamegon Bay filled with busy maritime traffic.

Bayfield, named for a Royal Navy officer who conducted a magnificent survey of Lake Superior in the early 19th century, was founded by people who hoped that it would become terminus of a railroad to connect the Mississippi River with Lake Superior. The railroad never materialized but gill-netters and lumber schooners took over the harbor. Today, the lumber schooners are long gone and while there is still some commercial fishing, the village is more concerned with sports fishermen and yachts that tie up at the marina near the waterfront piers.

Some of the artifacts from the maritime past of the little town are on display at the museum of the Bayfield Heritage Association, housed on the lower floor of the old courthouse building on North Washington Street (which also serves as the area headquarters of the National Park Rangers). For some time, local enthusiasts have proposed founding a maritime museum based in a one-time shipyard where there were still small craft surviving from an earlier period. Visitors who pass this way (Route 2 runs along the lake, turn north at Ashland) might do well to visit the Historical Society Museum and to inquire how the plans for a maritime museum have progressed.

Our next destination is Superior at the western end of Lake Superior, one of the lake's major ports.

Superior, Wisconsin, faces its twin city, Duluth, Minnesota, across St. Louis Bay, the estuary at the mouth of the St. Louis River, where a fur-trading post was the original settlement. Duluth was named for the Sieur du Lhut, a French explorer who came here in 1679 to hold a great council with the Chippewa. Until the middle of the 19th century, the lands around this end of the lake were Indian territory and no settlement was allowed. However, a treaty with the Indians in 1842 permitted settlement on the level Wisconsin side of the St. Louis River, and another treaty, 12 years later, opened up what became Duluth on the hilly Minnesota side of the river.

The twin cities early grew and prospered, thanks to railroads that connected them with the rich wheat lands that were being opened up in Minnesota and the Dakotas to the west. The grain brought by rail was loaded on ships at Duluth/Superior and carried to terminals at Buffalo or other ports on the lower lakes. In 1887, the Mesabi range, a fantastically rich body of iron ore, was discovered inland north of the ports; a railroad from the Mesabi to Duluth provided cargoes for the ore carriers that now joined the grain ships in the harbor.

The Duluth/Superior harbor itself is an unusual one. A natural sandspit, six and a half miles long, across the end of Lake Superior provided protection from storms. The harbor is entered by an artificial passage called the Ship Canal, which was cut through this spit in 1871 and kept from filling in by breakwaters on either side. Duluth/Superior claim to be the furthest inland of any of the world's seaports. On their 17 miles of waterfront, 1,200 to 1,500 vessels a year call for the taconite that has replaced the rich Mesabi ore, the coal from new western open-pit mines, and the grain from the prairies. The opening of the St.

Lawrence Seaway has provided the ports with a direct connection to the high seas and more than 200 million bushels of grain a year leave via Lake Superior and the seaway for distant markets.

Tied up alongside an open meadow at the Superior end of the twin ports harbor, is a unique vessel: The SS *Meteor* is the only surviving whaleback. The name refers to the appearance of these vessels: their topsides curved inward toward the center of the ship, so their rounded decks resembled the backs of whales.

Founded only on the Great Lakes, the whalebacks were designed to carry grain and ore in bulk. The theory of the extreme tumblehome was that this would allow rough seas to wash harmlessly over a vessel's decks without impeding her progress.

The whaleback type was originally invented by a Scottish-born sea captain, Captain Alexander McDougall, who was trying to find ways to make bulk carrying on the lakes more efficient. McDougall left a record of how he arrived at the first whaleback: "While captain of the Hiawatha . . . I thought out a plan to build an iron boat cheaper than wooden vessels. I first made plans and models of a boat with a flat bottom designed to carry the greatest cargo on the least water, with rounded top so that water could not stay on board; with a spoon-shaped bow to best follow the line of strain with the least use of the rudder and the turrets on deck for passage into the interior of the hull."

McDougall was unable to interest lake shipbuilders in his design and finally, in 1887, he went into the shipbuilding business himself in West Superior. Ultimately, more than 40 whalebacks were built, many of them in Captain McDougall's yard, and they continued in use on the lakes well into the 20th century.

Eventually, however, the design proved uneconomical in competition with the newer and larger bulk carriers that were being turned out on conventional designs, and there was some talk that they were unstable when running empty. Also, the tumblehome lost cargo space compared to a conventional ship of the same size. The whalebacks had about one-third the capacity of the present bulk carriers on the lake. However, this is not so much a matter of design as the fact that today's bulk carriers are far larger than those at the turn of the century.

The whaleback at Superior was launched as the *Frank Roosevelt* in 1896, and for 30 years she was an ore carrier. Subsequently she carried a variety of cargoes, including grain, sand, coal, and even automobiles. Eventually, in 1943, she was converted into an oil carrier and renamed *Meteor*. Unhappily for the historically minded, at that time the characteristic whaleback shape was largely hidden under a flat deck so that it no longer shows, but underneath the superficial deck she is still a whaleback just the same.

In touring the *Meteor*, particularly notice the gyrocompass in the pilothouse. A special problem in the iron ore carriers is the fact that their cargo throws off magnetic compasses; the gyro is essentially for navigation. In the chart room, notice the original logs.

Within the entrance to the midships is a museum with many half models of vessels, navigational instruments, and photographs of ore carriers, particularly the whalebacks. Especially interesting are detailed photos of *Christopher Columbus*, the only passenger whaleback ever built. *Columbus* was constructed by Captain McDougall to carry passengers to the Chicago World's Fair in 1892, and proved a great success. Among the other models in this little collection are fine ones of the whalebacks SS *Pillsbury*, *John Ericsson*, and *Alexander Halley*.

On the shore next to the ship are a couple of rather battered small craft: the pilot boat *Milwaukee* and a coast Guard motor lifeboat. More striking is a heroic statue of a seaman, almost twice life-size, cast of solid brass. Dedicated to the memory of the seamen of the Great Lakes, particularly those lost in the great storms that sweep the lakes, the huge figure will not soon be forgotten.

SS *Meteor*, last surviving whaleback ore carrier, is tied up on Barker's Island on Superior Bay. From I-35, the main Duluth-St. Paul highway, turn south on Route 535 over Blatnik bridge across St. Louis Bay. At the south end of bridge, keep left on Route 53; watch for *Meteor* sign on left. Gift shop. Open Memorial Day to Labor Day, daily 10 a.m. to 5 p.m.; day after Labor Day through October, Saturday and Sunday, 10 a.m. to 5 p.m. Admission: $2.25; seniors and children, $1.75. SS *Meteor*, Box 775, Superior, Wisconsin 54880-0775. Telephone (715) 392-5742.

Many of the diverse types of lake vessels developed over the decades have now disappeared. No longer are there the swift package freighters that carried the boxes and barrels of mixed freight, nor the cruise ships that brought summer tourists by the hundreds up from the lower lakes for a tour of the cool Superior waters. The whalebacks, the pig boats, are gone except for the *Meteor* at the other end of the bay. For that matter, so are the steam tugs that once hauled barges up and down the lakes.

That is to say, all these vessels are gone from the lake waters; actually, however, all of them can be seen in miniature in the fine museum right next to the distinctive Ship Canal in Duluth, Minnesota, at the north end of the Superior/Duluth harbor. The Canal Park Marine Museum was founded and built in 1973 by the U.S. Army Corps of Engineers, which is responsible for harbor maintenance. Later enlarged, today's very

substantial building houses a fine collection. The museum is so close to the harbor entrance that visitors can look out the window and watch the big lake freighters—and sometimes oceangoing steamers—passing in and out just a few feet away.

Besides no fewer than 60 models of lake ships, all built to the same scale, the museum has a fascinating collection of artifacts, and all kinds of special displays and background information about Great Lakes shipping. Among the exhibits:

- Ship models of vessels of the fur and lumber trades start with La Salle's *Griffin* of 1679. Here, for example, are the merchant sloop *Welcome* of 1775, the trader *Algonquin* of 1839, and the steam barge *Rhoda Emily* of 1884.
- Models of lake passenger steamers and the package freighters range from the 1833 sidewheeler *Michigan* to the ocean freighter *Gadsden* built at Duluth in 1944.
- The evolution of the bulk carriers, backbone of the lake-borne water traffic, is shown from the five-masted barkentine of 1881 to the 1974 self-unloader *Wolverine*. These are particularly beautiful models and, as in the case of all the models in the museum, their interest to the visitor is enhanced by the full descriptions in the accompanying captions.

Models are by no means the only attractive exhibits in this large and varied museum. A reconstructed pilothouse of a lake steamer is equipped with charts and instruments salvaged from lake ships as they are scrapped. Three cabin mockups, one from a two-man berth of a 1870 schooner recovered from a wreck, another from a two-man crew cabin from a 1910 freighter, and a third from a second-class cabin from a 1905 passenger liner, show how light, space, and ventilation improved over time.

In the stairwell between the first and second floors is an enormous steam engine, a compound high/low pressure marine type taken from the 1908 tugboat *Essayons*, an immensely impressive piece of machinery.

A special wreck exhibit, inevitable on wreck-strewn Lake Superior, includes artifacts from lost ships, statistical analysis of the causes, and models demonstrating the underwater position of the broken hull of the *Edmund Fitzgerald* at the bottom of Lake Superior where it was eventually found by divers after its mysterious disappearance in a November storm. A wall map shows the location of the hundreds of other wrecks that have occurred on the lake over the years.

Beside the exhibits, the museum's library collection includes 35,000 vessel photographs and dozens of ships' logs.

Figure 54
One of the last of its type, the huge 15-ton "fore and aft compound" steam engine from the 1908
tug *Essayons* fills a stairwell at the Canal Park Marine Museum in Duluth, Minnesota.

Canal Park Museum is right alongside the Duluth Ship Canal, entrance to Duluth/Superior harbor. From Superior Street (here Route 61) running along Duluth lakefront, turn south on Lake Avenue. Free parking. Open all year. Summer, every day, 10 a.m. to 9 p.m. Spring and fall, every day, 10 a.m. to 6 p.m. Winter, Friday-Sunday, 10 a.m. to 4:30 p.m. Admission: free. Restaurants nearby. Sponsored by Detroit District, U.S. Army Corps of Engineers. Canal Park Marine Museum, Duluth, Minnesota 55802. Telephone (218) 727-2497.

Much of the north side of Lake Superior is part of Canada's province of Ontario. Here, where once fur traders gathered to make the long canoe trip north into the wilderness, one of the earliest sailing vessels on the lake has been brought to life again in a handsome reconstruction.

After the conquest of New France, Britain opened the Montreal-based fur trade, previously a semi-monopoly, to licensed traders. A period of savage competition followed, until finally fur merchants and traders got together and formed the North West Company. With headquarters in Montreal, the North West Company centered its activities in the same region as its French predecessors: around the upper Great Lakes, particularly Lake Superior, south of the monopoly granted to the Hudson's Bay Company. To cover this enormous region, the company employed more than a thousand traders and voyageurs in addi-

Figure 55
At Old Fort William on Lake Superior, a big 36 foot Montreal-type bark canoe passes the schooner *Perseverence*, a recreation of the craft that replaced the big canoes as carriers of heavy cargoes across the lake for the fur traders.

tion to many guides, interpreters, and clerks. North West's chief post on the upper lakes was at Fort William, where the Kaministkwia River runs into Lake Superior at Thunder Bay, the starting point of a canoe route into the northern wilderness.

At Fort William, trade goods were distributed and pelts collected. To supply the post, the company built a number of small sailing vessels, which picked up provisions and trade goods at Sault Ste. Marie and carried them across Lake Superior to the fort, taking back furs on the return run.

Now one of these little vessels, the sloop *Perseverence*, has been reconstructed and is on view to visitors at Fort William Historic Park, on the river a few miles from the site of the original trading post.

No plans exist for the original *Perseverence*, built in the early 19th century at Pointe aux Pins on the St. Mary's River, so the reconstruction follows the general design of a lake schooner of that size and period: approximately 83 feet overall, including an extremely long bowsprit. *Perseverence* has been loaded with trade goods such as the original would have carried, giving visitors an idea of how these little vessels were used.

While the new schooner has been fitted with an engine and modern safety gear, so that she may carry passengers on the lake, these have been carefully concealed. The schooner was built right at Fort William Historic Park, as one of many park projects portraying activities of the past. The fort has been reconstructed according to surviving records of the original post.

Perseverence, reconstruction of an early 19th-century schooner of the North West Company, is displayed at Thunder Bay on the north shore of Lake Superior on Route 17. Plans to make occasional cruises afloat. Hours and admission are those of the fort, a historical park of the Ontario Ministry of Tourism and Information. Open mid-May to last week in September, every day. Hours: until Labor Day, 10 a.m. to 6 p.m.; after Labor Day, 10 a.m. to 4 p.m. Admission: $3.00; students, $1.50. Fort William Historical Park, Broadway Avenue, Thunder Bay, Ontario P0T 2Z0. Telephone (807) 577-8461.

For our final visits in the heartland of North America, we'll head north along the route of the fur traders to the Red River.

XI
TO THE NORTH: MANITOBA

Winnipeg and the Red River

Winnipeg and the Red River

Canada's great central province of Manitoba and its metropolitan center of Winnipeg—which lie almost exactly half way between the Atlantic and Pacific Oceans—may seem an unlikely place to look for maritime traditions or a maritime museum. Here as in much of inland North America, however, streams, rivers, and lakes were for centuries vital highways; first for Indians, European explorers and traders, and the beginning of settlement; later as the communication links between new towns and with the outer world, by canoe, river boat, and—ultimately—by steamer.

Manitoba possesses one very large lake, Lake Winnipeg, several middle-sized ones, and is laced with many, many smaller lakes. Lake Winnipeg, a major travel route as far back as the 17th century, is 280 miles long north and south and covers 9,100 square miles. Into the southern end of the lake flows the Red River of the north, which is 310 miles long, and runs north across the border from North Dakota and Minnesota. Out of Lake Winnipeg to the north, the Nelson River flows up into Hudson Bay. In fact, Manitoba has a number of great rivers, including the Saskatchewan, the Churchill, the Winnipeg, the Red, and the Assiniboine, all of them utilized by the first Europeans that came into the country.

Manitoba even has a saltwater coastline on Hudson Bay, with a modern grain port at Churchill where the great wheat crops of the Canadian prairies are fed into oceangoing vessels to be taken to Europe.

Churchill is not too far along the coast from York Factory, the very first English settlement in Manitoba. The Factory, a fort, trading post, and headquarters, was built at the mouth of the Nelson River in the 17th century by the Hudson's Bay Company, the fantastic combination of private enterprise and semi-government that dominated the whole Canadian West for 200 years.

Winnipeg, a great city and capital of Manitoba, is the center of efforts to preserve the maritime heritage of middle Canada. Here or nearby are a museum gallery enclosing a magnificent reconstructed vessel, lake steamships retired ashore, a rare example of a truly historic boat, and a collection of ship models. All are worth a visit.

Let's start with a look at the Museum of Man and Nature in downtown Winnipeg. Thread your way through a maze of galleries, interesting exhibits unrelated to the sea or maritime affairs, what you might expect in the midst of prairies equally far from the Atlantic and Pacific. Turn a corner into yet another gallery . . . and suddenly three centuries and thousands of miles fade away. You are standing on a dock in 17th-century London. Alongside is a beautiful ship, her masts towering far above you. The falling tide has left her sitting on the bottom of the little pool and her tender stranded at the landing opposite. A row of waterfront buildings—a tavern, a sailmaker, sailors' lodging house—line the wharf facing the ship.

She is *Nonsuch*, a square-rigged ketch, mainmast amidships, smaller mast stepped aft on the poop. The wonderful carving everywhere—bow, sides, stern—shows that she was designed in an age when a ship was as much a work of art as a transport machine. She is berthed in her permanent home, a recreation of the Deptford docks where her original probably berthed a little over three centuries ago.

What's going on here? Has this magnificent vessel anything to do with a 20th-century city in the middle of the Canadian prairie? Or is this some antiquarian irrelevancy to make the tourists gape?

Far from it. *Nonsuch*—the 17th-century original, of course—is for Manitoba the ship that started it all, in quite a different way from how *Carolina* launched the Charleston settlements in almost the same year but of equal significance in the history of a proud people. To find out the role that *Nonsuch* played and why she is remembered and revered, look back briefly to what was going on 300 years ago.

In the 17th century the merchants of Montreal grew rich shipping Canadian furs to France. The trappers were Indians who traded pelts for European products such as metal tools and utensils and woolen cloth. A major source of the finest furs were the tribes to the west of the French settlements who arrived in great canoe flotillas for annual trading sessions.

These Indians were not themselves the fur trappers, however, but middlemen who obtained their furs by trading with other, more remote tribes far in the interior of North America. The furs were brought to Montreal from the far-away west and north through a long series of lakes and rivers and ultimately down the Ottawa River to the St. Lawrence and Montreal. From there the pelts were picked up by ships at Quebec and carried to France.

By controlling the St. Lawrence outlet to the sea, the Montreal merchants and colonial officials effectively controlled this valuable fur trade as a monopoly. In 1659-60, two enterprising and aggressive French traders, the Sieur des Groseilliers (Medard Chouart), and Pierre Esprit Radisson, explored far westward both to trade and to find out more about where the furs came from. They learned that the major source of the best furs was the country of the Cree Indians in the wilderness that stretched away north of Lake Superior toward Hudson Bay. When they returned to Montreal they suggested that the Cree might be reached directly, by going by sea around Labrador to the coast of Hudson Bay. This would cut out the middlemen, the tribes between the Cree and Montreal, and thereby provide a much more reliable supply—and, not so incidentally, cut out the middlemen's profits.

In Montreal neither the fur merchants nor the government officials of New France were interested in this proposal. Both were satisfied with the existing system, which worked fairly well from their point of view and which insured that all the furs passed through Montreal and Quebec. If they allowed an alternative route to be set up, it would be much more difficult to control who got the profits and whether those persons paid their taxes to the French government.

So the Hudson Bay route was turned down, first in Montreal and later in France. The innovative pair took their proposal elsewhere. Eventually, they went to London where they explained their plan to a group of bigwigs: noblemen, rich merchants, courtiers, financiers, even some scientists. The English were interested; here was a plan that provided a way for an end run to the rich fur country now blocked off by French control of the St. Lawrence outlet. But, first, the Londoners wanted to see whether a northern route was practical, so in 1668 a group of interested backers sent out the ketch *Nonsuch* on an experimental trading voyage to Hudson Bay.

The *Nonsuch* made a successful passage and arrived in James Bay, a large teardrop off the bottom of Hudson Bay. She spent the winter there, and began trading in the spring with the Cree, who brought furs from the interior. The ship returned to England that summer with a cargo of beaver pelts, then tremendously in demand for the making of fashionable beaver hats. On the basis of this successful demonstration that direct trade was possible via the Hudson Bay route, Charles II granted a charter to "the Governor and Company of Adventurers of England Trading into Hudson Bay," usually known thereafter as the Hudson's Bay Company.

The company was given enormous powers. It had not only a complete monopoly of the fur trade in what amounted to the entire area drained by the rivers running into Hudson Bay, but also governmental powers, with the right to hold courts and judge cases according to the laws of England. For almost 200 years, the Hudson's Bay Company *was* the government of western Canada, eventually expanding across the Rocky Mountains to the shores of the Pacific Ocean.

By the latter half of the 19th century, however, a private government had become an anachronism and the Hudson's Bay Company sold out to the Canadian government. Today, the Company operates trading posts but is best known for its chain of retail stores.

Obviously, *Nonsuch*, the ship that started it all, is remembered in central Canada in something of the same way that the *Mayflower* is remembered in New England. But how did the new *Nonsuch* get to Winnipeg?

To celebrate the Centennial of Canadian Confederation in 1967 and its own Tercentenary three years later, the Hudson's Bay Company agreed to have a replica of *Nonsuch* built; eventually, the replica was to become part of a new Winnipeg museum complex.

The first problem was to design the ship. Scholarly research found mention of a Royal Navy vessel of 1650 believed to be the original *Nonsuch*, but only the length of keel and cargo capacity were given. Plans were drawn up, however, based on research into mid-17th century vessels of a similar size, and the ship was built in North Devon out of stout English oak. Engines and electricity were added for safety's sake, and to enable the vessel to travel around to be shown in various Canadian ports on the two oceans and the Great Lakes.

After sea trials in the English Channel, *Nonsuch* was carried across the Atlantic on a freighter. For two years she cruised the Maritimes, the St. Lawrence, and the Great Lakes, then she was carried by land across to the Pacific Coast where she cruised some more to Canadian and American ports of the Pacific Northwest. Finally, after she had been viewed by many thousands of people, *Nonsuch* was dismantled and carried to Winnipeg by truck. There, she was mounted in a special dry dock that had been built next to the new museum, and a building was erected around her and roofed over. Once under cover, *Nonsuch* had her mast and rigging restored and a replica of a 300-year-old English waterfront scene was constructed alongside.

At the museum, there are several guided tours a day of the *Nonsuch*; she is shown from stem to stern. Here are some of the things to look for as you go over the ship:

- The marvelous carvings that decorate the vessel, completely authentic to the time and place of the original. For example, the wreaths around the gunports, the life-size crouching dogs at the break of the rail between the waist and the poop, the female figures across the stern under the cabin windows, and the mermaids supporting the catheads. Viewers will be reminded of the beautiful yachts of Charles II and James II.
- The paneled cabin in the stern. Remember this is a small vessel and the so-called great cabin is very cramped but nevertheless handsomely finished.
- The 17th-century navigation tools: the hourglass that was turned periodically, the cross staff used to find the ship's position by the stars, and the traverse board used to keep track of the various courses that the ship took as she tacked back and forth across the Atlantic.
- The great tiller in the stern: it took a lot of strength, a couple of men at least, perhaps even more, to handle it in a storm.
- The eight two-pounder cannon.
- The beautifully made shallop, the small boat tied up at the landing across the pool. Walk around for a look.

Notice also the great care that is being taken to preserve all this wonderful woodwork, with humidity checks all through the vessel.

Before leaving, most visitors will want to poke around in the buildings across the dock from the ship. The tavern, lodging house, sailmaker's loft, have been reconstructed as they would have appeared in *Nonsuch*'s day. Give your imagination full play: A trip back three centuries is worth making—we don't get such an opportunity very often.

Manitoba Museum of Man and Nature, on the eastern edge of downtown Winnipeg. Home of sailing reconstruction of 16th-century ketch *Nonsuch* now drydocked in gallery. Book/gift shop. Open all year. May 15 to September 15, Monday-Saturday and holidays, 10 a.m. to 9 p.m.; Sunday, 12 noon to 9 p.m. September 16 to May 14, Monday-Saturday, 10 a.m. to 5 p.m.; Sundays and holidays, 12 noon to 6 p.m. Also open 10 a.m. to 9 p.m. the first Monday in every month. Admission: $2.50; students, $1.25; seniors and children, $1.00. Manitoba Museum of Man and Nature, 170 Rupert Avenue, Winnipeg, Manitoba, Canada R3B 0N2. Telephone (204) 956-2830.

Winnipeg was the original site of the important Hudson's Bay Company post of Fort Garry, but this was later moved to higher ground a few miles down the Red River. There, at Lower Fort Garry, we'll find a little-known craft that had a major part in the fur trade of central Canada.

Historic vessels vary widely not only in every physical characteristic but in public recognition. Tell the average North American that the last original York boat survives near Winnipeg, and the odds are that you'll get a blank stare—even from maritime buffs. Yet over thousands of square miles of the continent, the York boat was as historically important as the whaleboat or the Gloucester dory in other parts of the world.

For these roughly built planked boats were the humble workhorses that enabled the Hudson's Bay Company to move heavy cargoes through trackless wilderness, from the icy bay south almost to the Great Lakes; from Labrador westward to where rivers faded to rivulets in the Rockies.

Originally, these cargoes—trade goods going in, furs coming out—were transported in great canoes: 36 feet long, and able to carry up to four tons, including eight or nine men with their provisions and gear. These birch-bark canoes were light enough, about 600 pounds, to be portaged from one stream to the next or around rapids on the shoulders of four men. They were fragile but easily repaired; birch bark patches were sewn with spruce roots, and caulked with spruce pitch.

However, the key entry point for the Hudson's Bay Company was York Factory, far to the north on the

Figure 56
Nonsuch, full-sized sailing recreation of 17th century ship that played a major role in
the foundation of the Hudson's Bay Company, lies at simulated London dock in the
Manitoba Museum of Man and Nature in Winnipeg.

shore of Hudson Bay near the Hayes River. Here, the ships came from England, bringing out trade goods and carrying back the furs for which they were exchanged.

This system required a round trip of some 700 miles between Lower Fort Garry, near Lake Winnipeg, and York Factory and return. This arduous journey took many weeks each way; the southern portion on the broad waters of Lake Winnipeg, further north on north-running rivers through treeless tundra. Without birch or spruce on the spot, repair materials had to be carried along. A good deal of time was lost in repairing canoes. In addition, the canoes did not sail well on the lakes. And as trade increased, there was demand for more carrying capacity.

Eventually, sometime in the late 18th or early 19th

century (authorities differ), the fragile canoes began to be replaced by wooden boats built of planks. Used primarily on trips between York Factory and inland posts, they became known as York boats. In design, they seem similar to Orkney fishing boats, which was not surprising since many Hudson's Bay men had been recruited in the Orkney Islands off Scotland. Double-ended, flatbottomed, with long sharp overhanging bow and stern, they averaged around 35 or 40 feet in length. Too heavy to paddle, they could be either rowed or sailed, or sometimes towed against the current by men along the river bank hauling a line from the boat.

The York boats were far less easily damaged by rocks than the big canoes, and carried bigger loads in proportion to crew. On the lakes, they were not only safer and better sailors, but they could venture out in the kind of stormy weather that kept canoes on the beach. When, at the beginning and the end of each season, the voyageurs had to navigate through the floating ice, the heavy wooden boat was far less likely to be cut than the fragile birch-bark canoe.

These advantages were paid for when you came to a portage. The York boat was far too heavy to be lifted and carried; the crew had to literally drag the boat on its bottom over the rough stony trails between one stream and the next. The weary voyageurs called the York boat a man-killer and swore that they dragged it more miles than they rowed or sailed, but the York boat nevertheless became the backbone of the Hudson Bay transportation system.

The York boats largely disappeared with the enormous fur-trading empire they once served. What is said to be the only original York boat left is at Lower Fort Garry, located just a few miles northeast of Winnipeg on the bank of the Red River.

Built some 150 years ago as a major center for Hudson's Bay Company activities, Lower Fort Garry is today a National Historic Park of Canada. The original York boat is preserved under a shelter against the outer wall of the Fort, on the south side, near the Furloft building. This boat was brought down from Norway House, the Company's post at the northern end of Lake Winnipeg.

There are several other York boats at the Fort but these were all built in the last few years as part of the Historic Park's recreation of life on the Canadian frontier a century and a half ago. Visitors should not leave without touring the Fort, which is fascinating if not maritime related. The handsome stone buildings within the fortified wall include the mansion of the governor, the trading house, dormitories for the river men, barracks for troops, and workshops. All are furnished and equipped according to the period and staffed by costumed experts who play the roles of the Hudson's Bay Company's servants—as all employees were called—in the early days of the Fort.

Lower Fort Garry, on the banks of the Red River. Book/gift shop. Restaurant. Open mid-May through to Canadian Labor Day and the following three weekends; 9:30 a.m. to 6 p.m. Admission: $2.50; Children, $1.00. Lower Fort Garry National Historic Park, Box 37, Grp 343, RR 3, Selkirk, Manitoba R1A 2A8, Canada. Telephone (204) 482-6843.

Now for a look at a later phase of Lake Winnipeg's maritime activities, after steamboats took over. A short drive downriver to Selkirk brings us to two veterans of an almost vanished era.

As the fur traders gradually dwindled away and trappers, fur traders, and Indians were pushed aside by settlers, farmers, and townspeople, canoes and York boats were also superseded and lake and river steamers took over. In time, here as elsewhere in North America, railroads, improved highways and the automobile cut deeply into steamer traffic. One by one, the side-wheelers and propellers were converted into excursion boats, or laid up for good at some out-of-the-way dock.

Three of Lake Winnipeg's steamers survive in honorable retirement at the Maritime Museum of Manitoba at Selkirk. This little town is a half hour run northeast of Winnipeg, on the Red River close to where it enters Lake Winnipeg. The visitor will find the vessels at their mooring, high and dry in a meadow at the entrance to Selkirk Park, surrounded by a number of smaller craft. The largest steamship is the SS *Keenora*, long active on the lake. Another is a former government ship-of-all-work, the SS *Bradbury*. Both are interesting and well worth a look. Very recently added, and undergoing restoration, is the *Chickama II*, a smaller companion ship to *Keenora*, once owned by the same line.

Keenora, built in 1897, originally served a gold mining area on the Rainy River, then briefly was a dance-hall ship. Eventually, she came into her own on Lake Winnipeg, carrying passengers and freight from Selkirk most of the way up to Norway House at the far northern end, where once the fur brigades of the Hudson's Bay Company set out on the last leg of their long journey to York Factory. *Keenora* was too large for the final leg and turned her passenger and crew over to *Chickama II* to take them through the water-way between Warrens Landing and Norway House.

Keenora made the round trip in a week, stopping at all the little settlements along the shores, their only link to the rest of the world. Lake Winnipeg had not been charted since 1906 and the channel was shallow and tricky; *Keenora*'s principal navigation aid was the memory of her officers.

Here are some things to look for as you go over the *Keenora*:

- A large photographic exhibition amidships on the main deck.
- The staterooms, on the next deck above; some of them are already restored and others are being restored. Some are used as special little photo galleries for such subjects as trading posts, small craft of the area, fishing gear, and so forth.
- On the top deck, notice the Red River-Lake Winnipeg Chart in the wheelhouse.

Another vessel at the museum is the steamer *Bradbury*, which is reached via a gangway from the main deck of the *Keenora*. Built in 1915, *Bradbury* was at various times a fishery patrol vessel, an icebreaker, and a tug. One hundred and sixty-one feet long and built especially for the government, she was considered a particularly luxurious work vessel. Notice the fancy paneling, which was covered over when she went to grubby work as a tug, but is now restored. The captain's cabin below the wheelhouse is particularly handsome. The 10-cylinder diesel engine, below in the engine room, is worth peering down at.

The *Chickama II*, also on the grounds, will eventually be opened to visitors. So will a fourth vessel, the fish packer *Lady Canadian II*, brought to the museum for restoration in 1986.

Also on the grounds of the museum are a huge steam engine, the stack of a tug, and a number of small craft. These include the tug *Peguis II*, modern replicas of York boats, and several fishing vessels. The museum is a young one, and the restoration work is on-going.

Marine Museum of Manitoba is at the entrance to Selkirk Park, on the Red River, in Selkirk. Open every day, third weekend in May through August; 10 a.m. to 7 p.m. September, Sundays only, 11 a.m. to 6 p.m. Closed balance of year. Admission: $2.00; seniors, students, $1.00; children, 50 cents. Marine Museum of Manitoba, P.O. Box 7, Selkirk, Manitoba R1A 2B1. Telephone (204) 482-7761 or (204) 482-4321.

For maritime-minded travelers with a little time, there are a couple more places in Winnipeg to take a look at.

In Winnipeg, the building housing the enormous Olympic swimming pool in the southwestern section of the city also contains a collection of ship models and nautical memorabilia. While not easily examined—many of the models are on shelves above the visitor's head—the collection nevertheless contains some interesting vessels.

Included are a sailor's model of the clipper *Fiery Cross*, a big model with a sense of authenticity, and a somewhat rough model of the square-rigger *Joseph Conrad* (the original ship is now at the Mystic Seaport). There is also a good small model of the *Archibald Russell*, 1905, the last square-rigger built on the Clyde.

Beside several 16th, 17th and 18th century ships, the model collection includes a number of distinctive Oriental types, junks and proas, as well as a Thames barge. The famous Lunenberg fishing schooner *Bluenose*, winner of the International Fisherman's Trophy, is also represented.

The models, which belong to Winnipeg's Cutty Sark Club, are in the second floor lobby. On the stairs are ship prints and 18th century recruiting posters for the Royal Navy.

Cutty Sark Club ship model collection is in the Aquatic Hall of Fame and Museum of Canada. Open all year, daily 9 a.m. to 10 p.m. No admission charge. Pan American Pool Building, 25 Poseidon Drive, Winnipeg, Manitoba. Telephone (204) 284-4030 or 284-4031.

Finally, there's one other maritime collection that Navy buffs may want to visit before leaving Winnipeg: the Naval Museum HMCS Chippewa. Located at 51 Smith Street, Winnipeg, the museum's collection includes British and Canadian naval artifacts, from World War I to the present. The museum is ordinarily open only by appointment; arrangements for a visit can be made by letter or by telephoning (204) 943-7027. There is no admission charge.

PART THREE

THE PACIFIC COAST AND HAWAII

The Pacific Coast

When the American colonies were ruled by Britain, all trade with lands rimming the Pacific Ocean was a monopoly of the East India Company. Scarcely was the ink dry on the treaty ending the American Revolution, however, when adventurous captains were carrying the Stars and Stripes around Cape Horn to investigate the opportunities for trade in the Pacific. They quickly found that the beautiful pelts of the sea otter, which was hunted along the North American coast, brought fabulous prices when sold across the Pacific in China. Before long, American ships were trading for furs from the Indian villages that dotted the sounds and inlets of the far Northwest to the tiny Spanish mission settlements of Alta California.

These enterprising captains found a coast far different from the Atlantic shores they had left 15,000 ocean miles behind them. Not here the dozens of little harbors of the fretsaw coast of New England; no great wide-mouthed, open estuaries like those that enabled deep-water ships to sail deep into the Middle Atlantic states; not even the little protected waterways between barrier islands and flat sandy shores found along the Atlantic coast of the South. These Pacific coasts were beautiful, empty—and hostile to ships and sailors. For hundred of miles there were few natural harbors. In most places, hills (often real mountains) came right down to the sea to end in a wall of cliffs. Huge standing rocks and hidden shoals stretched out to sea to catch the unwary mariner who stood inshore for a closer look.

The narrow entrance to San Francisco Bay was often fogbound and guarded by off-shore reefs to catch the unwary. Even the wide-mouthed Columbia in the north offered no easy refuge; much of the time seas breaking on the entrance bar made it extremely dangerous to enter. Only at the Strait of Juan de Fuca, almost 200 miles further north, was there easy access to sheltered waters—Puget Sound and the strait between Vancouver Island and the mainland.

Ashore, the Pacific coast was also very different from the Atlantic shores of the United States. Although the first Spanish explorers had sailed northward along the coast from Mexican ports early in the 16th century, they were primarily looking for a water passage eastward through North America and they found little to interest them, particularly no short cut to the Atlantic. The coast remained unsettled by Europeans until the second half of the 18th century, well after the Atlantic coast was populated by millions and had half a dozen thriving ports. And when it finally came, settlement was no spontaneous push into the wilderness but the planting of tiny mission villages up the southern California coast by the Spanish authorities in Mexico who were worried that Russian and British fur traders, coming by ship from Alaska or Europe, would challenge Spain's claim to the land on the basis of coastal exploration that had taken place centuries earlier.

The chain of missions went no further north than San Francisco Bay. From there northward was only wilderness—empty, mountainous, and almost without harbors. The Columbia River was only discovered in 1791, as were the Strait of Juan de Fuca and the sheltered waters of Puget Sound and Georgia Strait to which it led.

Actually, there is some evidence that blue-water sailors had arrived on these coasts a thousand years or more before the Spaniards. Chinese archives record that in the fifth century an explorer named Hwui Shan reached North America; he established settlements in Mexico, and 40 years later sailed back across the Pacific to China. Some 25 disabled Japanese junks are known to have been carried eastward on the Japan Current and wrecked on the American coast. But these vague contacts with Asia had no permanent impact, and in the closing years of the 18th century outside of the Spanish mission villages these shores were left to the Native Americans: wandering hunters and food gatherers in the south; skilled boatbuilders and fishermen in the north.

Even where there were settlements in the south there was no local shipping; trade with the tiny California mission villages was legally forbidden even to Spanish vessels except for the few official ships sent up from Mexico by the colonial government.

That two centuries later these inhospitable shores boast some of the great ports of the world is to no small degree due to the enterprise of the mariners who came to the coast, some to trade, some to settle. In the process, some became rich, some died paupers, but all added to the maritime heritage of the region. Today in the great ports of this long, historic coast, this heritage is being preserved in fine museums ashore and tall ships afloat.

XII
CALIFORNIA

The San Diego River to Monterey Bay
The Golden Gate to Oregon

This wind (the south-easter) is the bane of the coast of California. Between the months of November and April (including a part of each,) which is the rainy season in this latitude, you are never safe from it, and accordingly, in the ports which are open to it, vessels are obliged, during these months, to lie at anchor at a distance of three miles from the shore, with slip-ropes on their cables, ready to slip and go to sea at a moment's warning. The only ports which are safe from this wind are San Francisco and Monterey in the north, and San Diego in the south.

[How to land at the other, open, harbors.]

[At Santa Barbara] We pulled strongly in, and as soon as we felt that the sea had got hold of us and was carrying us in with the speed of a race-horse, we threw the oars as far from the boat as we could, and took hold of the gunwale, ready to spring out and seize her when she struck, the officer using his utmost strength to keep her stern on. We were shot up upon the beach like an arrow from a bow, and seizing the boat, ran her up high and dry, and soon picked up our oars, and stood by her.

Richard Henry Dana
Two Years Before the Mast, Chapter 9.

The coast of California stretches almost 800 miles along the Pacific from the Mexican border to where it abuts the state of Oregon, a line set by treaty with Great Britain long ago. There are only three states on the entire Pacific coast and the California coast is almost twice as long as the other two put together. The northern half of California lies pretty much north and south; the southern half bends off in a southeasterly direction.

Two mountain ranges, one along the coast, one far inland, run the length of the state, enclosing between them a great central valley whose rivers unite and turn eastward to reach the ocean through a single outlet: San Francisco Bay and its Golden Gate. Since the mountains elsewhere are close to the coast, the other rivers reaching the sea are relatively small and their entrances offer few safe havens to the mariner. San Francisco has the only fine natural harbor in the state, although other harbors have been improved and artificial harbors built where needed.

At the far south, the San Diego River was scarcely more than a sandy creek and dry part of the year; although its mouth formed a protected harbor, it was shallow and full of sandbars. Now the harbor has been vastly improved by dredging and has become a great naval base.

At the opposite, northern end of California, Humboldt Bay provides a small harbor for the once busy lumber port of Eureka. Between San Diego and San Francisco, the entirely man-made harbors of San Pedro and Long Beach service the busiest port on the entire California coast.

"California," the earliest Spaniards called this coast, apparently taking the name from a popular romance of the period. Soon after the conquest of Mexico, Cortez sent expeditions northward up the Pacific coast. In 1542, two ships commanded by Juan Rodriguez Cabrillo reached somewhere around what is now the northern edge of California. Thirty-five years later Francis Drake arrived on the coast after a buccaneering expedition, ravaging ships and settlements along the Pacific shores of Spanish America. He careened his ship in a little harbor just

Map 3
California Coast

California, the peninsula that extends southward along the Mexican coast, was a barren place (and is only sparsely settled to this day); and Alta California, to the northward, could only be reached by an arduous voyage, frequently against headwinds and adverse currents, or by an equally arduous land journey from the northernmost Mexican settlements across deserts and mountains.

Not until other European empires began to show an interest in the Pacific coast did the Spanish government decide to occupy Alta California in order to back up its claims, which were based on Cabrillo's voyage and another by Sebastian Vizcaíno 60 years later. Russians seeking furs had moved across the Bering Sea to the Aleutian Islands, where they had established trading posts. Britain, having taken Canada from France, had become interested in the Pacific; naval expeditions were exploring the South Seas, while fur traders were pushing westward across northern North America. To the Spanish government, both nations looked ready to gobble up any land left unoccupied, regardless of Spain's prior claims.

This activity led Jose de Galvez, the Spanish Viceroy in Mexico, to send land and sea expeditions in 1769 to explore and plant settlements in Alta California. Soldiers and a few settlers accompanied Franciscan priests who founded a chain of missions along the coast from San Diego to San Francisco Bay. These mission villages were tiny, usually made up of cattle ranchers attracted from Mexico by the offer of free land, the mission fathers who quickly gathered Indian converts, and sometimes a handful of soldiers. Maritime activities were minimal. The only trade permitted the Californians by the Spanish government was with one or two government ships that came each year to bring supplies and to take away the hides and provisions produced by the settlements.

At least this was the theory. After the value of sea otter pelts became known in the last years of the 18th century, foreign ships would slip in to California harbors and trade for furs, often under the pretext of seeking shelter.

In the early 1820s, Mexico achieved independence from Spain. Although the new government allowed foreign ships to trade on the California coast, it imposed high duties on imported goods, so illicit trade continued. By now overkill had almost wiped out the otters, but Californians found they had a new export: cattle hides. Early in the 19th century, some shrewd Yankee traders observed that when cattle were slaughtered for meat on the California ranches the hides were left to rot for lack of a market. Soon a vigorous trade sprang up as New England ships came around Cape Horn loaded with the provisions and manufactures that the Californians wanted and went

north of San Francisco Bay, and then sailed on to complete his voyage around the world on the *Golden Hind*. Curiously enough, neither Cabrillo nor Drake discovered the entrance to San Francisco Bay; it remained unknown for another two centuries.

Throughout the Spanish colonial era, the galleons bringing luxury goods from the Philippines across the Pacific to Mexico took advantage of favoring winds by heading for California and then coasting southward to their home ports. They did not land along the way, however. For almost 200 years there was little further exploration of the coast north of Mexico. Today, it seems strange that the Spaniards, who had explored and settled not only Mexico and Central America but most of both coasts of South America, ignored the Pacific Coast lands to the north of Mexico. But the Spanish explorers were primarily interested in finding precious metals and there was no indication that in California there was the gold and silver that had enriched the conquistadors in Mexico and Peru. Baja back with hides to be sold at a fat profit to the shoe factories of Massachusetts. This trade produced one of the great sea narratives of American literature: Richard Henry Dana's *Two Years Before the Mast*, which gives a vivid picture of the trade, of the Yankee hide ships and their crews, and of the sleepy California ports in the 1830s.

The Mexican War, which made California part of the United States, and the discovery of gold that quickly followed changed everything. The Gold Rush brought thousands of Americans from the East Coast to the new territory, some by ships around Cape Horn, many more by steamers via the Isthmus of Panama. A few became rich; many stayed as settlers, California farmers, and lumbermen. The '49ers turned the tiny settlement of Yerba Buena in San Francisco Bay into California's first great seaport: San Francisco. In the years that followed, wheat from California farms and lumber from the state's forests provided cargoes for the ships that crowded the bay.

In the last decades of the 19th century, San Francisco inherited from New Bedford the dying whaling industry: Her fleet of steam auxiliary whaleships hunted dangerously far up into the edge of the Arctic. For many decades schooners brought lumber down the coast from the Northwest and northern California. And around the turn of the century, the Alaskan salmon fishery was served by ships—usually veteran windjammers come down in the world—that carried fishermen and cannery workers up to Alaska each spring, then brought them back in the fall along with a hold filled with tons of canned salmon.

Today, California is not only immensely wealthy and the largest state in terms of population, but it possesses two of the nation's most active ports and carries on an extensive trade across the Pacific to the Antipodes and Asia. And in California, as in other ports of the country, Americans are at last remembering and starting to preserve the maritime heritage that has been all too rapidly disappearing from the scene.

San Diego to Monterey Bay

. . . hauling our wind, brought the little harbor, which is rather the outlet of a small river, right before us . . . . A chain of high hills, beginning at the point, (which was on our larboard hand, coming in,) protected the harbor on the north and west, and ran off into the interior as far as the eye could reach. On the other sides, the land was low, and green, but without trees. The entrance is so narrow as to admit but one vessel at a time, the current swift, and the channel runs so near to a low stony point that the ship's sides appeared almost to touch it. There was no town in sight, but on the smooth sand beach, abreast, and within a cable's length of which three vessels lay moored, were four large houses, built of rough boards, and looking like the great barns in which ice is stored on the borders of the large ponds near Boston; with piles of hides standing round them, and men in red shirts and large straw hats, walking in and out of the doors. These were the hide houses.

Richard Henry Dana
Two Years Before the Mast, Chapter 15.

s Dana noted, San Diego's little harbor was enclosed by a sand spit that gave it perfect protection from the Pacific. In the 16th century, the earliest Spanish explorers—having missed the Golden Gate—admired San Diego as the only protected harbor on the coast.

Nevertheless, the harbor remained deserted for more than two centuries after its discovery. Even when a Franciscan mission was established there in 1769, the tiny settlement became a village of priests, Indians, soldiers, and cattle ranchers, not fishermen or seamen. Here, as elsewhere in California, the Spanish colonial authorities strictly forbade trading with any vessel except the ships they sent up from Mexico.

The harbor did not remain entirely empty, however. Foreign ships would arrive in San Diego under various pretexts; the ruses were happily accepted by the San Diegans, including the mission fathers, eager as they were for broader opportunities to trade. One early Yankee came into port under the plea that his crew needed treatment for scurvy, then proceeded to secretly buy $20,000 worth of sea otter pelts. Others quietly anchored in offshore islands while the settlers sent out small boats loaded with the precious pelts.

After Mexican independence, the Spanish ban on foreign trading ships was replaced in 1822 by a system of high custom duties, which were frequently evaded. Yankee ships came out around the Horn with cargoes of trade goods: tea, coffee, spices, hats, shoes, calicoes, silks, staple groceries, rum. San Diego was the first port of call and it was said that the ladies of the little village were never more than a year behind the latest East Coast fashions.

Thanks to its protected harbor, San Diego became the depot for the hide trade; ships would make several cruises up the coast as far as there were settlements, selling their "Yankee notions" and picking up hides at each little village. The hides were then brought back to San Diego, and taken ashore to one of the crude "hide houses" on the beach, where they were pickled, scraped and dried so they wouldn't rot, and stored away. When enough hides had accumulated to fill the ship's hold—perhaps 50,000 of them compressed into tight bundles—they were loaded aboard ship for the voyage home. San Diego's protected harbor was absolutely essential to the trade. Once treated, a hide had to be kept completely dry or it would be ruined; San Diego was almost the only place where dry loading was possible. At such open roadsteads as San Pedro, Santa Barbara, and Monterey, the hides had to be carried out through the surf on the heads of sailors and arrived aboard ship soaking wet.

Like all California ports, San Diego became American territory during the Mexican War: A landing party from the U.S. *Cyane* raised the American flag there in July 1846. For some time, however, the little harbor remained a sleepy, out-of-the-way place, too shallow for many blue-water ships. The hide trade gradually died away and the rough hills behind the little town did not produce any substitute cargoes. The California Gold Rush was hundreds of miles away. Not until San Diego's happy climate was discovered by visitors after the Civil War did the town begin to grow slowly, and the port to be used for coastal passenger/freight steamers to Los Angeles and San Francisco. Successive real estate booms spread the town around the shores of the bay.

Eventually, the tuna fishermen found San Diego a fine base from which to exploit the rich fishing grounds to the southward, off the Mexican coast. San Diego became an important port, however, only after it aroused the increasing interest of the United States Navy. In 1900, the battleship *Iowa* had to anchor outside the harbor because there wasn't enough water over the bar. The harbor was gradually improved and by 1917 the port had become the principal operating base of the Pacific Fleet, although during World War I, naval action was focused on the Atlantic and San Diego saw little activity. In contrast, during World War II San Diego was the scene of furious activity as a mainland supply and service base for Pacific operations.

Today, San Diego remains basically a Navy town; it not only has a large naval base in its harbor, it is also the home of many Navy veterans who have retired there after leaving the service. Meanwhile, tourism, business, and industry have combined to expand the city to the second largest in California; as a commercial port, however, San Diego remains overshadowed by its rivals up the coast. The city is home port for a fleet of large, technologically advanced tuna-fishing vessels, although in the mid 80s the industry has faced hard times. San Diego's center of interest for us, however, is a very different kind of vessel: a beautifully restored square-rigger berthed on the waterfront.

On November 26, 1865, the future—if any—of the ship *Euterpe* seemed very doubtful. Only two years from the builder's ways, the iron ship had already had more than her share of bad luck: on her maiden voyage she had been rammed by a brig off the English coast and a semi-mutinous crew forced her return to port for repair. Now she was in the Bay of Bengal where for three days she had been battered by a cyclone. As the captain's notes recorded:

Nov. 23, 1865, Madras—This day we slipped from Madras to avoid an approaching Cyclone which unfortunately overtook us on the 26th & to save the Ship from foundering we were obliged to cut away the Masts, after which the sea broke over the ship in terrible fury, Severely injuring a great portion of the Crew . . .

Euterpe did survive, thanks to desperate efforts of her officers and crew—"With the remainder of the Crew we erected Jury masts & made the best of our way towards the land . . . Dec. 4, 1865—This day we arrived in . . . Trincomalie." In the years that followed she continued to survive: innumerable gales, more collisions, Arctic ice, groundings, over a total of 60 years at sea. And then during 30 years of retirement she survived the often more deadly threat of neglect and decay.

Today, *Euterpe* has survived to become the oldest merchant ship afloat. Far more than survive, actually. Painstakingly restored to the beauty of her youth, her masts towering over the waterfront, *Euterpe* is the pride and joy of the San Diego Maritime Museum, where she is known by the name of her later years, *Star of India*.

Star of India owes her long life to two things. The first is her sturdy iron hull, built on the Isle of Man. The second was the resolve of a handful of San Diegans 60 years ago to find and preserve a square-rigged ship as a maritime museum. This was in 1925, long before the present surge of interest in ships of the past. At that time there were still a number of windjammers left on the West Coast but they were rapidly disappearing as they were sold to the scrapyards or abandoned on the mudflats. The San

Diego group raised enough money to buy the *Star of India* (she cost only $9,000) and brought her to San Diego in 1927. And then the whole project went hard aground, and remained stuck hard and fast for 30 years.

Maintaining, never mind restoring, a large sailing vessel is tremendously expensive. What with the Great Depression, soon followed by World War II, the *Star of India*'s supporters were not able to do much more than keep her afloat and she rusted away alongside her dock for three decades. Finally, inspired by Alan Villiers and the example of the restoration of *Balclutha* in San Francisco, sponsors found new funds and in the late fifties restoration began. By her 100th birthday, in 1963, *Star* was a respectable ship again, although there was still much work to be done. Since then she has several times spread her wings and made sail off San Diego Bay. Today, the fine details of restoration are still being carried out—can such a task ever be really finished?—but *Star* has long been the beautiful queen of the San Diego waterfront and, of course, the Maritime Museum.

Before going aboard, stop for a moment on the dock. There is much to admire:

- *Star*'s beautiful lines are a visual delight. Not that she was a clipper in any sense, but a hardworking ship of all trades—in fact, a rather slow sailor on long passages.

- The towering masts surrounded by an intricate maze of rigging, each line with a very precise function. As often as we marvel at the rigging of a model, it takes the real thing, full-scale, to bring home its tremendous and highly ordered complexity.

- The beautiful carved figurehead of the goddess Euterpe, which survived all the ship's vicissitudes, albeit somewhat battered. *Euterpe*, the muse of music and lyric poetry, was carved by a Glasgow sculptor.

The *Star* served in several different trades during her long life at sea. The result is changes that the visitor can pick out as he goes over the ship, although the museum plans to restore her to her original condition as a general cargo and passenger carrier. Her figurehead, the picture of Euterpe herself painted on the glass at the after end of the cabin skylight, and the beautifully paneled main cabin all reflect the initial period of her career.

After a few years as a cargo carrier, *Euterpe* (not yet renamed the *Star of India*) became an emigrant ship, making 22 round-the-world voyages to New Zealand carrying Britons to seek their fortunes halfway around the world. When you visit her 'tween-decks, where most of the emigrants who couldn't afford separate cabins were berthed, try to imagine what it was like to spend four months at sea there. To help your imagination, here are the recollections of a woman who made the passage on *Euterpe* as a child with her parents in the mid-1870s:

> I have heard parents say how closely they were crowded, the married people and small children all in together and the only privacy being a small curtain in front of their bunks. The single girls were in a part of the vessel called the poop [actually the after 'tween decks] and they were all gathered together after the evening meal and were not allowed on deck again until the next morning. The food at times was very bad and once when a complaint was made regarding the soup, an investigation revealed a man's sock in the stock pot.

Look for the huge map at the forward end of the 'tween-decks space that shows the track of *Euterpe*'s passages as an emigrant ship—out to New Zealand around the Cape of Good Hope, home to Britain around Cape Horn—so that each was an eastward voyage around the world. And look for the excerpts from the ship's log mounted beside the map, with its succinct account of the fate of young John Campbell, who in March, 1885, stowed away in *Euterpe*'s coalhole.

For a brief period at the end of the 19th century, *Euterpe* was in the timber trade, carrying lumber from the Pacific Northwest to Australia. Relics of this phase are the two large square ports cut into her stern, so that long timbers could be slid aboard end first. After that, *Euterpe* was purchased by the Alaska Packers Association in 1901 and five years later was renamed *Star of India*. Every spring she took fishermen, cannery workers, and supplies to Alaska, spent the summer at anchor at a mother ship for dory fishermen, and returned in the fall loaded down with canned salmon and the fishing and cannery crews. It was at this time that she was altered from a ship to a bark, her square-rigged mizzen mast replaced by a new one with a fore-and-aft rig. This change, which made her easier to handle by a small crew, has been retained in her restoration.

The *Star* is only one of three interesting vessels owned and exhibited by the San Diego Maritime Museum. The museum has no base ashore and its offices and library are in the one-time San Francisco ferry *Berkeley*, tied up next to the *Star*. To an older generation, the big auto ferries such as once crisscrossed San Francisco Bay were such a familiar sight that it may seem odd to see one preserved in a

Figure 57
The bark *Star of India*, built in 1863, at sea following her restoration—with loving care, years of hard work, and great expense—at the San Diego Maritime Museum.

museum. Today, however, all but a few ferries have been replaced by bridges or tunnels. Each year a few more of the survivors disappear until before long they will be as hard to find as the long-vanished windjammers. So take a good look at *Berkeley*, a handsome example of her type, embodying a good deal of maritime history. Built in 1898, she was the first successful propeller ferry on the Pacific Coast and served on various runs in the bay for 60 years. Her big moment began on April 18, 1906, when she ran for 24 hours a day evacuating refugees from the San Francisco earthquake and fire.

A large and fine collection of ship models has been installed on the *Berkeley*'s main deck. Included are some vessels that are rarely seen:

- the ill-fated cruiser *San Diego*, the only American naval vessel lost to enemy action in the First World War;
- several of San Diego's own harbor ferryboats;
- various types of tuna-fishing boats, showing their evolution from simple small craft to the big, technologically advanced tuna clippers.

Be sure to take a look at *Berkeley*'s original triple-expansion steam engine, still in place and in operating condition. Her boiler room and fuel bunkers have also been restored.

The museum's third vessel is the beautiful steam yacht *Medea*. The epitome of luxury in a gilded age, 140 feet overall, she is a marvel of varnished teak and oak. Built in Scotland in 1904, she cruised in European waters from the Mediterranean to the Baltic until 1969. When you peer in at her carpeted cabins, however, don't forget that this rich man's darling is a veteran of two wars. At various times she has flown the flags of the British, French, and Norwegian navies. Today, she is a vigorous octogenarian, able to cruise the bay at 10 1/2 knots, as she periodically demonstrates in local waters.

The Maritime Museum of San Diego is housed in three vessels moored on the city's Embarcadero, close to where Ash Street enters Harbor Drive. Gift and book shop. Open every day of the year, 9 a.m. to 8 p.m. Admission: $4.00; seniors and students 13 to 17, $3.00; children 6 to 12, $1.00. Motels and restaurants within easy walking distance. Maritime Museum Association of San Diego, 1306 N Harbor Drive, San Diego, California 92101. Telephone (619) 234-9153.

Now let's drive north along the rugged California coast and look for other museums that tell of the maritime past. They are worth finding.

On the bluffs at Dana Point between San Diego and Laguna Beach is the Nautical Heritage Museum. Exhibits include paintings and lithographs of ships and marine scenes; a carving of Lord Nelson made from wood taken from HMS *Victory*, Nelson's flagship; a notable collection of antique firearms; an antique figurehead of Commodore Perry; and a wide variety of ship models.

The pride of the museum, however, is the two-masted schooner *Californian*, a reconstruction of a 19th-century vessel designed along the lines of the Coast Guard cutters active along the California coast in the late 1840s. The *Californian* is based upon plans used by the Treasury Department in that period for a class of seven new revenue cutters, as described by H.I. Chappelle, the noted researcher and historian of the development of marine architecture. She was built from scratch by traditional methods. Designated the official tall ship of California, *Californian* has an extensive cruising program up and down the Pacific Coast with 13 ports of call.

The museum also has its own little flotilla of small craft, kept in the water and in use. Among them are the Swedish-built diesel launch *Skol* and a number of small sloops, including the 35-foot racing sloop *Aurora* and the cruising sloop *Shanmor*.

The Nautical Heritage Museum overlooks the Pacific Ocean at Dana Point, just off the Pacific Coast Highway between San Clemente and Laguna Beach. Museum open Tuesday-Saturday, 10 a.m. to 5 p.m. No admission charge. Schooner schedule varies; check in advance. Nautical Heritage Museum at Dana Point, 24532 Del Prado, Dana Point, California 92629. Telephone (714) 661-1001.

North again, this time to San Pedro, the port of Los Angeles.

This, they told me, was a worse harbor than Santa Barbara, for south-easters; the bearing of the headland being a point and a half more to windward, and it being so shallow that the sea broke often as far out as we lay at anchor. The gale from which we slipped at Santa Barbara, had been so bad a one here, that the whole bay, for a league out, was filled with the foam of the breakers, and the seas actually broke over the Dead Man's Island.

Richard Henry Dana
Two Years Before the Mast, Chapter 15

As Dana accurately reported, in the 1830s the so-called harbor at San Pedro was an open windswept bay, the very opposite of the snug little port at San Diego down the coast. Yet, Dana discovered, this was a very important calling point for the hide ships.

I also learned, to my surprise, that the desolate-looking place we were in was the best place on the whole coast for hides. It was the only port for a distance of eighty miles, and about thirty miles in the interior was a fine plane country, filled with herds of cattle, in the centre of which was the Pueblo de les Angelos [sic]—the largest town in California—and several of the wealthiest missions; to all of which San Pedro was the sea-port.

Dana's comments summed up the history of the port of San Pedro: Its minimal natural advantages as a harbor were outweighed by the fact that there were cargoes to be landed and cargoes to be loaded. For the port had an invisible asset that became of tremendous value over the years. It served a hinterland that was to become both productive and a rich market.

As the cargoes appeared, the open roadstead was gradually transformed into what an expert has described as the most convenient and efficient harbor on the Pacific Coast.

The cargoes, of course, resulted from the change of the sleepy little village of Los Angeles and the sparsely populated cattle ranges around it into a prosperous city in the midst of a rich agricultural region. At first, however, cargoes other than manufactured goods traded for hides and tallow were slow to come. Annexation by the United States brought no great changes to this part of California; the main impact of the '49 Gold Rush was to provide a market for cattle driven northward overland. However, a little dock was built, and lighterage started to take passengers and freight out to ships anchored in the roadstead. But when Richard Henry Dana, who was by now a distinguished Boston lawyer, revisited San Pedro a quarter century after he came there as a foremast hand, there were still only two houses by the shore, although the small new settlement of New San Pedro had appeared up a little creek by the new wharf—New San Pedro, which later became the town of Wilmington.

The Civil War brought Fort Drum to Wilmington, businesses to serve it, and cargoes of lumber and supplies. At this stage the little town up the creek was more important than San Pedro itself, thanks to rail connections to Los Angeles opened in 1869. Eventually, San Pedro was also linked by rail to Los Angeles, which had already been connected to a transcontinental line in the mid-1870s. The population of the whole region grew dramatically—and so did the cargoes and the port to handle them. As Los Angeles started on the road to becoming an immense metropolis there was steady demand for seaborne lumber and supplies; and as ranches were replaced by irrigated farms and orchards, there were agricultural crops to ship out by sea.

San Pedro's harbor was steadily improved to meet the demand for a better port. A breakwater was built in the 1870s to form an inner harbor, followed by a channel dredged through the sandbar that had forced all but small craft to anchor offshore. At the end of the 19th century, other nearby coastal towns sought to replace San Pedro as the port of Los Angeles, but after a good deal of political maneuvering San Pedro won out over these rivals. Officially chosen as the city's deep-water port, San Pedro now received a massive (for the time) federal appropriation for a man-made harbor. For 11 years, freight trains and barges brought an endless flow of huge granite blocks to the harbor, where they were dumped to form a breakwater nearly two miles long. The towns of San Pedro and its neighbor Wilmington officially became part of Los Angeles in 1909 when the city annexed a strip 16 miles long and a mile wide, connecting it to the harbor. Together the two towns comprise the port of Los Angeles.

As Los Angeles burgeoned into a megalopolis in the 20th century, the port grew with it. The discovery and exploitation of oil in the region added fleets of tankers to the harbor traffic. By 1925, lumber imports and oil exports made San Pedro the busiest harbor on the West Coast, and the next year the port was second only to New York in total tonnage among all American ports.

Since then, Los Angeles has continued to improve its harbor, which it shares with the independent port of Long Beach next door. The one-time open roadstead facing barren hills is now one of the world's busiest harbors and the gateway to the sea of southern California, one of the richest, most productive, and fastest-growing regions of the country.

A series of huge photographs telling the story of the growth of San Pedro harbor—construction of the enormous breakwater, modernization of docks, dredging of the channel—is one of the interesting exhibits in the relatively new Los Angeles Maritime Museum. The museum has been established in a one-time ferry terminal on the San Pedro waterfront, actually part of Los Angeles although a long way from Los Angeles' downtown. When the building opened in 1980, the museum's staff wondered how they would ever fill the cavernous spaces: Today, the galleries are so crammed with interesting displays that the staff wonders how to find room for all the exhibits they have received.

Focused on the maritime activities of California, San Pedro in particular, the museum's exhibits include artifacts from the harbor, a large number of prints and photographs, and many fine ship models covering four centuries of maritime history. Models of Liberty ships remind us that hundreds of these workhorses were built at San Pedro and Long Beach during World War II. A model of the battleship *Maine* portrays the vessel that exploded in Havana Harbor and helped bring on the Spanish-American War. In the model room to the left of the entrance are vessels rarely portrayed by model makers: the U.S. Navy's Great White Fleet that President Theodore Roosevelt sent around the world in 1908. These ships represented the entry of the United States onto the world scene as a major naval power.

In the great hall to the right of the entrance is an enormous model of the *Titanic*, 18 feet long, cut away down the middle lengthwise from the bilges to the top of the boat deck. All of the compartments and cabins of the ship are shown with small figures, representing crewmen or passengers, to make clear the scale. A taped account of what happened when the *Titanic* collided with the fatal iceberg lends the model special interest: explaining why the huge liner's much-touted watertight bulkheads were unable to prevent it from going to the bottom with the loss of 1,800 lives.

Another exhibit of more than usual interest is a one-eighth-scale replica of a South Sea trading brig. The original, *Warragul*, which traded out of Melbourne, Australia, was 100 feet long, so the replica measures 12 feet, big enough so that all of the details of gear and rigging can be easily examined and their functions understood. According to the museum's experts it fairly represents the brig *Pilgrim*, in which Dana made his famous voyage to the California coast.

A very different period of maritime history is reported in a mock-up of the bridge of the World War II heavy cruiser *Los Angeles*. Here, the visitor may view the equipment used in the original vessel.

There are many fine sailing-ship models on the upper deck, reached by the old passenger ferry ramp. A number of famous windjammers are portrayed; especially interesting are the West Coast lumber schooners, with their distinctive regional peculiarities.

The museum is particularly proud of its collection of maritime watercolors by Navy artist Arthur Beaumont. All of its exhibits are of interest, however, for in a remarkably short time the museum has managed to gather an outstanding collection. Southern California has a distinctive image in the minds of most Americans. Now thanks to the Los Angeles Maritime Museum we are made aware of a very different facet of its past: a 150-year-old maritime tradition.

Los Angeles Maritime Museum is in the former Municipal Ferry Building at Berth 84 in the Port of Los Angeles, near the corner of Harbor Boulevard, and Sixth Street in San Pedro. Open May through September, Monday-Friday, 9 a.m. to 5:30 p.m.; Saturday and Sunday 10 a.m. to 6 p.m.; October through April, Monday-Friday, 9:30 a.m. to 4:30 p.m.; Saturday and Sunday, 10 a.m. to 5 p.m. Closed Christmas and New Year's Day. Admission and parking free. Sponsored by City of Los Angeles Harbor and Recreation/Parks Departments. Los Angeles Maritime Museum, Berth 84, Foot of Sixth Street, San Pedro, California 90731. Telephone (213) 548-7618.

Moored alongside a dock in San Pedro's sister port of Long Beach is one of the great ships of the 20th century, the *Queen Mary*, largest and fastest passenger liner of her time. The one-time queen of the North Atlantic has now been converted into a luxury hotel, but visitors can tour the mammoth ship from the shaft alley far below the waterline to the bridge and wheelhouse far above.

The *Queen Mary* was the pride of the Cunard Line when she was launched on the banks of the Clyde in 1934: more than 81,000 gross tons, 1,020 feet long, with 12 decks, and capable of carrying more than 1,900 passengers at a cruising speed of 28.5 knots. She retired to California—where else?—after more than 30 years of service, including dodging submarines as a troop transport from 1940 to the end of World War II.

Here are some highlights to watch for on the Queen Mary shipwalk route:

- the engine room where massive steam turbines turned out 40,000 hp;
- the enormous propeller shafts;
- the restored First Class facilities in various parts of the ship, including the boarding lobby, drawing room, playroom, gymnasium, and staterooms;
- the wheelhouse and bridge;
- wireless and radio room with equipment used by the *Queen Mary* at different periods;
- officers' quarters, including captain's suite;
- various films and audiovisual shows, including such subjects as the construction and launching of the *Queen*, engine room activity, and how a near collision emergency would be handled in the wheelhouse.
- Hall of Maritime Heritage, which exhibits marine paintings and models of *Queen Mary* and the famous *Mauritania*, as well as other ships of the past;
- World War II exhibit, showing how the luxury liner was transformed into a troop carrier;
- Model Builder's Workshop, which features a resident ship model builder and his current projects;
- nautical demonstrations, given at scheduled intervals, including knots and splices, navigation, semaphore, and lifeboat drill.

There are a number of restaurants of various types and sizes on the ship, as well as many shops.

Nearby is the *Spruce Goose*, the largest aircraft ever built. A wooden seaplane constructed by Howard Hughes as a troop carrier, the aircraft has a 320-foot wingspan. It is preserved under an aluminum dome alongside the *Queen Mary*.

Queen Mary, 81,000-ton North Atlantic passenger liner, moored at Long Beach; luxury hotel but open to visitors as a historic ship. Located at southernmost point of Long Beach Freeway. Restaurants, shops. Open all year, Monday-Friday, 10 a.m. to 4 p.m.; Saturday and Sunday, 9:30 to 4:30 p.m. Admission: $10.95; children, 5 to 11, $6.95. Combination ticket with *Spruce Goose* available. Senior citizens discount. Owned by Wrather Port Properties, Ltd., *Queen Mary*, Pier J, P.O. Box 8, Long Beach, California 90801. Telephone (213) 435-4747.

Now—again north along the coast.

On a stretch of coastal plain between Los Angeles and Santa Barbara is an interesting small museum devoted to the achievements of one of the newer and less publicized branches of the Navy, the Construction Battalions, commonly known as Seabees. The Seabee Museum is at the Naval Construction Battalion Center, the hub of Seabee activities on the Pacific Coast, near the little town of Port Hueneme. Appropriately enough, the core of the museum is formed by two huge Quonset huts, the quickly erected, corrugated-metal buildings that the Seabees have built all over the world.

The Seabees were formed in 1942, during World War II, when the U.S. Navy found that the Pacific theater presented a new problem. Island-hopping, one amphibious landing after another, required the repeated construction of forward shore bases and port facilities. These had to be built fast, far from the sources of supply, sometimes under enemy fire, often with little equipment.

The Navy had had a Civil Engineer Corps since 1867, but these engineering specialists built permanent shore stations in the United States under peacetime conditions. Now the Navy needed a great many skilled construction workers who could do a lot with a little in a hurry—and, if necessary, fight their way in to do the job. The answer was the U.S. Navy Construction Battalions, men recruited from the building trades and trained for amphibious landings on the remote beaches and islands of the Pacific.

Difficult, dangerous, the Seabees' operations were often overlooked as news stories focused on dramatic combat, but the battalions were an essential element in the Pacific victory. In the European theater they built roads for the advance of the Allied forces across Europe. Later they were playing their essential and little-publicized role in Korea and Vietnam. Now Seabees have their own museum to preserve, and tell about, their history and achievements all over the world.

The visitor can't miss the huge three-dimensional bee, the Seabees' symbol, lodged atop a pole outside the museum. Each leg of this enormous many-legged insect holds an object related to the Seabees' many construction skills: a wrench, a hammer, a carpenter's square, a telephone pole, even a flash of lightning to indicate its electrical skills. One leg carries a machine gun, a reminder of the fact that the Seabees fight as well as build. Also marking the museum entrance is an enormous totem pole, carved by a Seabee unit based in remote Kodiak, Alaska, in the 1950s.

The exhibits inside the museum reflect the Seabees' far-flung activities over more than four decades, from the remote Pacific bases of World War II to more recent activities of base-building in Alaska and Asia. A number of dioramas portray large Seabees construction projects. One of the most interesting shows a typical amphibious landing and the establishment of a beachhead camp during the Pacific War.

The Uniform and Arms gallery exhibits a wide range of uniforms and weapons, not only of the Seabees, but of other branches of the U.S. Navy as well as the armed forces of other countries, including one-time enemies. Other galleries recall the 120-year history of the Civil Engineer Corps and some of its most distinguished officers: for example, Rear Admiral Robert E. Peary, U.S.N., a civil engineer who discovered the North Pole in 1909.

Very different but equally interesting is a mock-up of the control panel of a nuclear power plant that the Seabees built in the Antarctic to provide electricity thousands of miles from any other source.

Working on major construction projects, Seabees tend to stay longer in one place than most military units and thus to develop closer ties with local peoples. As a result, the battalions have received every kind of gift from local friends all over the world. Many, reflecting faraway cultures, are on display at the museum. Exhibits range from paintings and musical instruments to farm implements, exotic articles of clothing, and primitive tools and weapons.

The Civil Engineer Corps/Seabee Museum is in Naval Construction Battalion Center, Port Hueneme, California. From Interstate 101, the Los Angeles-Santa Barbara Freeway, take the Vinyard Avenue exit and proceed south to Gonzalez Road. Turn right and continue to Ventura Road. Turn left; the entrance to the center is at the right on Ventura Road just past Channel Islands Boulevard. Closed holidays. Open weekdays, 8 a.m. to 4:30 p.m.; Saturday, 9 a.m. to 4:30 p.m.; Sunday, 12:30 p.m. to 4:30 p.m. Admission and parking free. CEC/Seabee Museum, Building 99, Naval Construction Battalion Center, Port Hueneme, California 93043. Telephone (805) 982-5163.

Figure 58
Huge three-dimensional emblem of U.S. Navy's Construction Battalions (Seabees) at entrance to Seabee Museum, Port Hueneme, California carries symbols of equal readiness to build or battle.

Now, this time quite a long move northward to one of the most historic ports on the Pacific coast, a former capital of California.

As to what this harbor of Monterey is, in addition to being so well suited in point of latitude for that which His Majesty intends to do for the protection and security of ships coming from the Philippines: in it may be repaired the damages which they may have sustained, for there is a great extent of pine forest from which to obtain mast and yards, even though the vessel be of a thousand tons burden, very large live oaks and white oaks for shipbuilding, and this close to the seaside in great numbers. There is fresh water in great quantity and the harbor is very secure against all winds.

So Sebastiano Vizcaíno wrote the Spanish Council of the Indies following his exploration of the California coast in 1603. Vizcaíno was searching for a protected harbor where the Philippine galleons that every year came eastward across the Pacific with precious goods from Asia could repair storm damage before proceeding on southward down the California coast to Mexico. However, his encomium on the Monterey harbor was only half true. Monterey Bay is indeed protected from the prevailing southeasterly gales which harass the coast in the winter, and also partially sheltered on the west by Point Pinos. Essentially, however, Monterey Bay was, and is, an open roadstead, completely exposed to winds from the northwest and the north.

As it turned out, the Spanish authorities decided to seek a harbor of refuge for the galleons on the Asiatic side of the Pacific where they were more likely to suffer storm damage. So Monterey, like the rest of the California coast, long remained empty of European settlement. Eventually, one of the chain of Franciscan missions sponsored by the Spanish colonial government in 1769 was established there. Monterey also received a presidio, or garrison, and this tiny settlement became the capital of Alta California.

Sixty-odd years later Richard Henry Dana visited Monterey as a foremast hand in the brig *Pilgrim*. In his classic work, *Two Years Before the Mast*, he described the bay far more accurately than had Vizcaíno. Much of Dana's description holds true today:

The bay of Monterey is very wide at the entrance, being about twenty-four miles between the two points, Año Nuevo at the north, and Pinos at the south, but narrows gradually as you approach the town, which is situated in a bend, or large cove, at the south-eastern extremity, and about eighteen miles from the points, which makes the whole depth of the bay. The shores are extremely well wooded (the pine abounding upon them,) and as it was now the rainy season, everything was as green as nature could make it—the grass, the leaves, and all; the birds were singing in the woods, and great numbers of wildfowl were flying over our heads. Here we could lie safe from the south-easters. We came to anchor within two cable lengths of the shore, and the town lay directly before us, making a very pretty appearance; its houses being plastered, which gives a much better effect than those of Santa Barbara, which are of a mud color. . . .

When Dana was on the California coast in 1835, the harbors of both Monterey and San Pedro were open roadsteads. Monterey, having the advantage of providing a lee against the prevailing gales, was an established town, while San Pedro had but one house on its bare hill. Today, San Pedro is one of the largest and most active ports in the world, while Monterey is still a quiet little coastal town. Cargoes build ports; the dynamic hinterland behind San Pedro—Los Angeles and the region around it—eventually could provide the cargoes that create a great port. The countryside inland from Monterey could not.

As long as California was part of Mexico, Monterey was the only official port of entry; all trading ships had to go there and pay customs duties on their cargoes. The rates were very high, at least in theory, but so were the trading profits. In 1842, a rumor of war between Mexico and the United States led the U.S. Navy commander on the station to seize the little town, which made no resistance. A few days later he discovered his mistake and withdrew with an apology. When war between the two countries did come four years later, the capture was repeated. After the peace treaty was signed, legally transferring California to the United States, American settlers voted to move the state capital from Monterey to Sacramento as a more central location.

Since then, Monterey has been largely a quiet fishing town. For a while during the 1860s and 70s, whaling was a local activity; not the kind of whaling in which ships make long voyages to distant waters, but the original type carried on in small boats launched from shore. When lookouts posted on the hills behind Monterey sighted whales migrating along the coast, they signaled the whalemen to row out to the attack. Harpooned whales were towed back to shore, cut up and the oil boiled out of the blubber right on the beach. Monterey whaling reached its height in 1861, but by the end of the 1870s overfishing had cut the supply of whales and the industry faded away.

In the early 20th century, sardine fishing was tried experimentally, using Italian techniques, and by 1913 there were four sardine canneries in the little town. After World War I, Monterey was for a time the third largest fishing port in the entire world in terms of size of catch. Again overfishing slowed, then killed the industry: The sardines gave out, the canneries closed, and while there is a "Cannery Row" left in Monterey, today it is largely a tourist attraction.

Monterey well remembers its past, not only in its many well preserved and restored old houses but in the small but choice Allen Knight Maritime Museum, which concentrates on its maritime aspects. The museum's collections, originally gathered by a banker as a hobby but since greatly added to, comprises artifacts, paintings, prints, and above all, ship models. Most interesting are the models of vessels that played a part in the maritime history of California; especially, of course, of Monterey itself. Here is the *San Diego*, flagship of Sebastian Vizcaíno, the first European to enter Monterey Bay. Another fine model is that of the United States frigate *Savannah*, flagship of the American Pacific squadron when Monterey was seized at the outbreak of the Mexican-American War.

Also of special California interest is the model of the ship *Isaac James*, built in 1854, which made the Philadelphia to San Francisco passage in 108 days; 22 years later the ship was lost south of San Francisco. Two models portray distinctive regional types: The scow schooner *Regina S.*, 1885, used in the protected waters of San Francisco Bay to carry farm produce to the city, and a purse seiner, probably built by a fisherman who knew such a vessel.

In one model case, New Englanders will find an old friend, the whaleship *Charles W. Morgan* of New Bedford, not inappropriately since most her whale hunting was in Pacific waters. There are many *Morgan* models, of course, but the one here is of particular interest, not merely for its fine workmanship but because in the case with it are models of a number of whales carved to exactly the same scale, making clear the relative size of the ship and its prey.

A captain's cabin from a sailing ship, paneled and with furniture from several historic vessels, is another notable exhibit. The museum's collection also includes a number of fine models of Chinese junks, with the various types and uses well labeled. Long before Europeans arrived, this coast had seen Asiatic junks—swept across the North Pacific by the Japan Current and wrecked on the shores of North America, so this exhibit has more regional pertinence than may be immediately apparent.

The Knight Museum is in a historic section of Monterey, in the same block as the house built in 1835 by the American hide trader, Thomas O. Larkin, who later became the first and only American consul to Monterey. Only one floor is available to the museum, however, and the collection has outgrown the space. One proposal would move the museum to a larger building at Custom House Plaza so visitors should make sure of the current address.

Incidentally, immediately behind the present museum building is Colton Hall, where the California Constitutional Convention was held in the fall of 1849. This attractive mid-19th-century building is of historical importance and well worth a visit.

Allen Knight Maritime Museum is located in a historic section of Monterey, California (plans are afoot to move the museum to a larger home on Custom House Plaza). Research library. Open every day except Monday. Weekday hours: June 15 to September 15, 10 a.m. to 4 p.m.; September 15 to June 15, 1 p.m. to 4 p.m. Saturday-Sunday hours: year round, 2 p.m. to 4 p.m. Admission free. Sponsored by Monterey History and Art Assn. Allen Knight Memorial Museum, 550 Calle Principal, P.O. Box 805, Monterey, California 93942. Telephone (408) 375-2553.

The Golden Gate to Oregon

San Francisco is at once one of America's favorite cities and one of the world's great ports, and both its glamour and its economic importance owe much to the magnificent bay at the city's doorstep. San Francisco began as a village on the south side of the passage which connects the bay with the Pacific through the famous Golden Gate. At right angles to the entrance passage, the bay, 450 square miles at low tide with a 100-mile shore line, extends almost 40 miles to the southeast and 10 miles to the northeast, where it connects with San Pablo Bay.

This smaller northeasterly arm of the bay is the one that feeds its waters: Down through San Pablo Bay come the united outpourings of the Sacramento River, which flows from the north 382 miles through California's Central Valley, and the 350-mile-long San Joaquin River, which drains the southern half of the Central Valley. All the surface water from more than 700 miles of valley, trapped between two mountain ranges, runs into San Francisco Bay and then out into open ocean through the Gate, an opening less than a mile wide between the hills of the Coast Ranges.

Curiously, San Francisco Bay, the only fine natural harbor on the entire coast of California and the best on the Pacific Coast of the United States, went undiscovered for centuries after the first exploration of this coast. The Spanish expeditions from Mexico sailed right past the Golden Gate without noticing it. Sir Francis Drake not only passed the entrance, but on his return down the coast landed in a bay sheltered by Point Keyes—only 35 miles north of the entrance of San Francisco Bay—and spent five weeks there careening the *Golden Hind* to repair a leak. Before sailing off westward across the Pacific to complete his famous voyage around the world, Drake nailed to a post an engraved metal plate claiming the land for Queen Elizabeth. Such a plate has been found on the shore of San Francisco Bay, but, according to maritime historian Samuel Eliot Morison, the scholarly consensus is that the find is a fake and that the great English navigator never saw the great bay.

Neither did the few other Europeans who sailed along the coast during the next 200 years. There was a good reason. Seen from seaward, the narrow opening of the Golden Gate is usually visually filled by bay islands and distant hills; no entrance appears. In addition, the early explorers had learned to fear currents and reefs along the California coast and were leery of standing in too close to shore without a good reason.

When San Francisco Bay finally was discovered by Europeans it was by land not by sea; a hunting party from the 1769 expedition establishing missions stumbled on the huge estuary quite by accident. But discovery brought little settlement. Except for the two inland missions of San Francisco and Santa Clara, the bay area was left largely uninhabited for years. Not until 1775 did the first ship come through the Golden Gate: the Spanish *San Carlos*, whose pilot spent 40 days charting the bay. For decades the only other ships were occasional traders who came to buy the hides sent down the rivers in small boats from the missions. The situation was just beginning to change when Richard Henry Dana came here in 1836. He described it as, "A magnificent bay, containing several good harbors, great depth of water, and surrounded by a fertile and finely wooded country . . ." Later he continued:

We sailed down this magnificent bay with a light wind, the tide, which was running out, carrying us at the rate of four or five knots. It was a fine day; the first of entire sunshine we had had for more than a month. We passed directly under the high cliff on which the presidio is built, and stood into the middle of the bay, from whence we could see small bays, making up into the interior, on every side; large and beautifully-wooded islands; and the mouths of several small rivers. If California ever becomes a prosperous country, this bay will be the centre of its prosperity. The abundance of wood and water, the extreme fertility of its shores, the excellence of its climate, which is as near to being perfect as any in the world, and its facilities for navigation, affording the best anchoring-grounds in the whole western coast of America, all fit for a place of great importance; and, indeed, it has attracted much attention, for the settlement of "Yerba Buena," where we lay at anchor, made chiefly by Americans and English, and which bids fair to become the most important trading place on the coast, at this time began to supply traders, Russian ships, and whalers, with their stores of wheat and frijoles.

In 1847, the traders who built the first scattered houses at Yerba Buena on the south shore of the bay decided to rename their tiny settlement San Francisco after the bay and this bit of public relations may have played a part in making the tiny village the leading settlement in the area. Certainly Yerba Buena—San Francisco—itself had some drawbacks as the site of a major port town. The hills of the coastal range came down steeply to the water, making it difficult to unload cargoes. The cove around which Yerba Buena straggled was filled with mud flats so that no ship could come in close to the shore; all cargoes had to be first unloaded into small boats.

When the United States annexed California in 1848, the village, population 1,800, was seized without resistance by a landing party from the American sloop of war *Portsmouth*. But then the port and the whole region was transformed: In 1849, gold was discovered on the Sacramento River. Overnight California, or at least the region inland from San Francisco, became the target of adventurers from the United States, Europe, the Antipodes. The easy water route from the coast to the gold fields was through San Pablo Bay and on up the Sacramento River. In a few months San Francisco's population grew to 20,000, and the hitherto empty harbor was crammed with ships, many of them deserted by their crews who had set out to make their way inland to the gold fields. By 1851, the lonely village had exploded to a city of 80,000 people.

And because of the Gold Rush, ships were bringing San Francisco not only eager '49ers but cargoes of every kind, particularly lumber and provisions from the great forests of the Puget Sound and the fertile new farms of Oregon's Willamette Valley. Manufactures came around Cape Horn from the cities of the East. In order to bring out both men and supplies to the area as fast as possible, clipper ships were diverted from the China tea trade, while new clippers were hastily built to meet the demand for ultra-fast passages to El Dorado. Sometimes the trip around Cape Horn, from the East Coast to the Golden Gate, took as little as 110 days—occasionally even less.

As San Francisco was transformed from a tiny trading village to a world port, the mud flats were first covered by finger piers stretching out into the deep water. Then the space between the piers was filled in, partly by scraping the tops off the surrounding hills, partly by dumping trash. Some of the fill was made up of the hulls of ships abandoned in the harbor.

Few made fortunes in the gold fields but many disappointed miners stayed on, attracted by the rich farmland of the central valley and the wonderful climate. Other immigrants came across the continent in covered wagons, and before the decade of the fifties was out California was producing wheat for export to other parts of the world. For the rest of the century, San Francisco's Embarcadero was crowded with tall ships. In addition to being the hub of the Pacific Coast from the Mexican border to the Arctic Circle, San Francisco was also a center of overseas trade: with Europe, with the East Coast of the United States, and with Australia and China across the Pacific. The ships that came and went around Cape Horn were largely built and owned either by Easterners or by Europeans; the latter from the British Isles particularly. San Francisco's own shipping magnates invested their capital in commerce with Australia and the South Sea Islands. A flourishing trade sprang up with the Kingdom of Hawaii where sugar provided desirable return cargoes.

All port cities tend to be tough; San Francisco was exceptionally lawless, starting with the flood of reckless, gold-hungry '49ers, but remaining so for decades afterward. Along the waterfront, sailors drank and whored away in a few days the money hard-earned from months-long voyages around Cape Horn. The Barbary Coast of San Francisco, with its red light districts and endless saloons, became notorious for violence. At the same time, few seamen called San Francisco their home port: native San Franciscans could make a better living ashore than by the hard life before the mast. When ships sailed from San Francisco they filled their fo'c'sles with men from incoming ships who had been paid off and spent all their money on the Barbary Coast. Broke again, they were supported on credit by boardinghouse masters who took their advance pay to settle their debts when a crew was called for. Not all went to sea voluntarily; many a man was knocked on the head or drugged, then woke up to find himself outside the Golden Gate in the fo'c'sle of a ship headed for Australia or around the Horn.

Blue-water ships and hard-case crews were not unique to San Francisco: It was the many other maritime activities in the bay that made her distinctive among American ports. Where else in North America, indeed in the world, could a visitor look out across the harbor and see such an exotic range of vessels, large and small, as thronged San Francisco Bay at the turn of the century? Off the waterfront, a New Bedford whaler—only now her home port is San Francisco and a smokestack has sprouted among her masts—is getting up steam to head for a summer's whaling on the edge of the Arctic. A flotilla of feluccas are hoisting their traditional lateen sails to head out from Fisherman's Wharf for the offshore fishing grounds. A Chinese junk, a fresh breeze filling her venetian-blind sails, bowls past looking as though she's come straight from Hong Kong.

Over there, a big side-wheeler heads up the bay, bound for some inland river port: Sacramento, Stockton, or perhaps little Petaluma. Gliding majestically past her is a big liner chartered to the Occidental and Oriental Steamship Company, outward bound for Yokahama—a big screw steamer but with four masts, two square-rigged, two fore and aft, ready just in case. Coming in through the Golden Gate is a smaller liner, the night boat from Los Angeles, while behind her comes a lumber schooner down to her marks with a heavy load of redwood from some little dog-hole port (really an open cove) far up the California coast. She's passing another schooner outward bound, her deck stacked with yellow dories, headed for the cod banks off Alaska. Still another schooner—a little scow—is coming in from the country down bay: At first glance she looks more like a haystack than a vessel; her deck load is six bales high, fodder for San Francisco's horses. And in every direction are ferries, big and small, bustling self-importantly as if conscious that they tie the whole bay area together.

All these, of course, were in addition to the deep-water sail—the grain carriers and tramping windjammers who crowded the harbor. While most of the big square riggers were foreign built and owned, many of the diverse coasting, harbor, and fishing craft—even the Mediterranean feluccas and Oriental junks—were built in local yards. San Francisco Bay shipbuilding really got going when the Gold Rush created a hot market for river and coastal vessels. Wooden ships continued to be built until after World War I, but steel shipbuilding began back in the 1880s when the Union Iron Works, originally a builder of mining equipment for '49ers, launched the 800-ton collier *Arago*, the first steel steamer built on the Pacific Coast. Over the years, the Union Iron Works and other bay yards turned out everything from scows and barges to the latest type of battleships, cruisers, submarines. At the same time, the shore line sprouted repair yards, graving docks, marine railways—all the ship-servicing facilities of a great port.

As elsewhere, the great boom in shipbuilding came during the two World Wars when bay area yards turned out freighters—Liberty and Victory ships and tankers in World War II—by the dozens. In World War II, of course, San Francisco was a major supply base for our forces in the Pacific.

Not only the square riggers but much of the other shipping in San Francisco Bay has faded away over the years. The railroads that reached San Francisco Bay in 1869 gradually took away from the river and coastal steamers the express passenger and freight trade between major cities. Decades later, the growing network of roads made truck delivery easy and knocked out most of the remaining Bay freight carriers. The beautiful feluccas gave way to engine-driven steel trawlers and draggers. Women threw away their corsets, the price of whalebone collapsed, and the whaleships disappeared. Even the great fleet of ferries dwindled away as bridges and tunnels took their place.

As for the deep-sea shipping, San Francisco's neighboring rivals in the bay took much of this business away from the city in the years after World War II. Sacramento and Stockton, up the rivers but with deep-water channels to the ocean, became major exporters of the lumber and farm products of inland California. Redwood City became a center of bulk salt exports. Petroleum shipments centered on San Pablo Bay. Oakland became a great container port. For a while, San Francisco wharves grew emptier and emptier and

much of the old waterfront became a recreational area. In recent years, however, the development of new cargo handling facilities further south, with emphasis upon container shipments, has started to bring ships back to the city.

And meanwhile many San Franciscans have come to know and value the heritage of a great port. With fascinating exhibits ashore and great ships afloat, one of the nation's outstanding maritime museums has made that heritage available to everyone.

To a remarkable extent, the rich variety of San Francisco's maritime past is reflected in the vessels and exhibits of the city's great National Maritime Museum. Like the Mystic Seaport in Connecticut and South Street Seaport in New York, the National Maritime Museum combines a museum ashore with historic vessels afloat. The museum's flotilla includes a great steel square-rigger, a big three-masted schooner, and a survivor of the ferries that once thronged the bay. Ashore, the museum has on exhibition an unusually large and fine collection of ship models, artifacts, prints, paintings, and other memorabilia of our maritime traditions.

Remarkable institutions are often the reflection of remarkable men: The National Maritime Museum is the reflection of Karl Kortum, who had the insight to see that the relics of San Francisco's rich maritime heritage were fast disappearing, had the imagination to dream of a museum to preserve them, and, finally, had the persuasive enthusiasm and endless energy to turn his dream into reality. In 1951, thanks to Kortum's mustering of community and press support, San Francisco established a maritime museum on the Embarcadero. The famous Clark/Spreckels collection of ship models formed the core of the museum; its founder, Kortum, was its first director. Originally a city museum, the National Maritime Museum is now part of the Golden Gate National Recreation Area and is administered by the National Park Service, but Karl Kortum is still its Chief Curator and guiding spirit.

The museum collection is primarily focused on Pacific Coast maritime activities in general and San Francisco Bay in particular. Over the years it has grown immensely. In 1955, Kortum spearheaded efforts that led to the purchase of the windjammer *Pacific Queen* and her restoration under her original name, *Balclutha*. She and other vessels since acquired by the museum are now on display at docks within easy walking distance of the museum building.

Let's first take a look at the museum itself, which is housed in a handsome white building at the foot of Polk Street, facing the basin of the Aquatic Park. From the beginning, Kortum followed the example of the famous National Maritime Museum in Stockholm, preserving large segments of scrapped vessels for display. On the main floor, interspersed among the models, pictures, photographs, prints, and other exhibits, the visitor will come upon such unique relics as a section of a sailing-ship mast with cross trees or the beakhead and bow decoration of the four-masted schooner *Commerce*, built in Alameda. Here, also, are the stern of a scow schooner from the San Joaquin delta, an anchor from the *Independence*, and a complete ship's steering mechanism. A number of very fine figureheads portray such personages as David Crockett, Mary Queen of Scots, and Lord Clive; all saved from wooden sailing ships when they went to the scrapyard.

The models in this gallery are primarily sailing ships; of particular local interest is the model of the USS *Portsmouth*, the 20-gun sloop of war that sent a detachment of sailors ashore to raise the American flag over San Francisco at the outbreak of the Mexican War. Nearby is an impressive eight-foot representation of the enormous bark *Preussen*, accompanied by a good description; according to Alan Villers, *Preussen* was the ultimate development of the sailing ship. A cutaway model of *Zenobia*, showing its construction in detail, is a marvel of beautiful workmanship.

On the terrace at the rear of the entrance floor is the 19-foot sloop *Mermaid*, in which a 23-year-old Japanese sailed solo from Osaka to San Francisco in 1962. His 5,000-mile voyage in this handsome little vessel took three months.

In the Steamship Room, reached via the rear terrace, are many fine models not only of modern vessels but of historic steamships of the past, many of which are rarely seen in museum collections. Here, for example, the visitor will find an unusually fine model of the famous *Great Western*, whose transatlantic crossing in 1838 marked the development of marine steam engines to the point where they could be used efficiently on the high seas. Nearby is an even bigger model of the unsuccessful *Great Eastern*. (The lack of scales on the model labels makes it difficult to compare the size of the originals.)

Other interesting ships modeled in this gallery include the battleship *Oregon*, which steamed eastward around Cape Horn from the Pacific Coast to join the Atlantic fleet at the outbreak of the Spanish-American War. A steam-schooner model portrays a type unique to the Pacific Coast, based in San Francisco. A collection of unusual late-19th-century and early-20th-century models of passenger liners is particularly rich in vessels active in the Pacific.

On the second floor of the museum are still more ship models, including river craft. Of particular interest is a big model of the *Fort Sutter*, a Sacramento River steamboat built in 1912, a stern-wheeler that made overnight runs from San Francisco up the bays and river to the state capital. Look also for the half models on the east wall showing how the lines of the clipper ship differed from those of ordinary cargo carriers, and the way the clipper sacrificed carrying capacity and ease of handling for speed. Here also is a fine collection of photographs, prints, and artifacts, as well as unusual graphic wall displays on various aspects of life at sea. Be sure to look for the one on Bucko Mates.

A nice model of the hide-trading brig *Pilgrim* recalls Harvard-dropout Richard Henry Dana who sailed in her to the California coast, and wrote a maritime classic about his two years before the mast. A sailor's half model of a down easter called "Scudding Under Reduced Canvas" has a delightfully authentic feeling.

A large diorama of the Mare Island Naval Shipyard in 1870, showing a frigate under construction, reminds us that San Francisco has been an important naval base practically from the moment the Bay became part of the United States.

Many photographs are displayed on this floor, including shots of the San Francisco Bay ferries, and river steamers, and the famous steam schooners that carried lumber up and down the coast. Here are famous photographs showing San Francisco harbor during the Gold Rush, jam-packed with windjammers, many of them abandoned by their crews, run away to the gold fields.

In addition to an extensive library, the museum boasts a remarkable archive of 160,000 photographs, including many of vessels closely related to San Francisco and San Francisco Bay. Most unusual is the museum's collection of tapes; they record the recollections of seafarers whose memories, thus preserved, will long outlive them.

National Maritime Museum is on San Francisco's bay front in a large white building on Beach Street, at the foot of Polk, backing up on the lagoon of the Aquatic Park. Book/gift shop. A facility of the National Park Service but with major local input. Open daily, 10 a.m. to 5 p.m. Admission free. Museum's several ships in the water are at different locations but in easy walking distance; see below. National Maritime Museum, Beach Street at the foot of Polk, San Francisco, California 94109. Telephone (415) 556-8177.

After a good look at the National Maritime Museum's marvelous models, pictures, and artifacts, stroll eastward a short distance along the Embarcadero to the Hyde Street Pier. Here are berthed three of the museum's historic vessels: the lumber schooner *C.A. Thayer*, the bay ferry *Eureka*, and the tug *Hercules*. Other small vessels belonging to the museum, not yet ready for visitors, are moored off the pier.

On the pier itself are a number of major artifacts, as well as small craft that should not be overlooked as you head for the ships at the outer end. Here are some things to watch for:

- The hugh stern wheel used to propel the river steamer *Petaluma* from 1913 to 1950. When the *Petaluma* retired, 103 years of stern-wheel steamer activity on San Francisco Bay and its tributaries came to an end.
- A little further along you will find the *Matilda D.*, a modern replica of a classic San Francisco felucca. Found nowhere else in America, the feluccas were built in bay yards for Italian immigrant fishermen who wanted the same kind of small boat they had used in the old country. Almost entirely decked over except for tiny cockpits for the helmsmen and crew, and with a lateen sail instead of a conventional fore-and-aft rig, this direct transplant from the Mediterranean is uniquely San Franciscan.
- Just beyond the felucca is another exotic craft with roots deep in San Francisco's past. As she sits on the pier, the *Lewis Ark* looks more like a cottage than a boat; actually the *Ark* is both: a houseboat of a type used by wealthy San Francisco families to summer in quiet northern backwaters of the bay. She is frequently not open to visitors but you can peek in through the windows—and be a little envious of those really relaxed summers 80 years ago.

But the really exciting exhibits, of course, are the two fine vessels berthed at the end of the pier. The 156-foot, three-masted schooner *C.A. Thayer*, built for the lumber trade, later a dory fisherman in Alaskan waters, looms on the left. Beautifully maintained, she represents a segment of the American maritime tradition that has almost been forgotten. *Thayer* originally loaded lumber in Grey's Harbor, up on the Washington Coast, for San Francisco or perhaps for San Diego or even the South Seas. For a while, she carried salted salmon from Alaska to San Francisco. Finally, she was converted to carrying fishermen and their dories north to fish for cod in the Bering Sea. In 1950, the last year that she was in this trade, the *Thayer* was the only sailing vessel still in active commercial use on the entire Pacific Coast.

As a lumber schooner, *Thayer* carried only a four-man crew, who were housed in a deck house on the main deck. As a fisherman, however, she carried 28 men who went out each day in dories to hand-line for cod off the Alaskan coast. In her hold, open to visitors, is a typical dory; basically the same as those used on the cod banks off New England, it is a so-called improved type fitted with a canvas shield forward. The shields made the dories less likely to ship water in rough

Alaskan seas but impossible to stack the way they were on the decks of Gloucester fishermen.

Sidelight: If you are lucky, you may board the schooner on one of the mornings when a young National Parks Ranger becomes the inspired chantey man who leads the schoolchildren who swarm aboard the *Thayer*. Organizing them into watches, each assigned to haul on a halliard, he soon has them pulling together and piping the chorus he lines out.

Across the pier from the *Thayer* is the side-wheel ferry *Eureka*, built in 1890; now retired after a long, successful career carrying passengers and freight across San Francisco Bay. At one time *Eureka* was not only the world's largest passenger ferry but also claimed to be the world's fastest double-ended passenger ferry, able to make 18 knots across the bay. *Eureka* ended her active days carrying passengers and railroad freight and made her final run in 1957. Now she is gradually being restored to her handsome youth as a super-fast passenger/vehicle carrier.

In her prime, the *Eureka* could carry 2,300 passengers and 120 automobiles. The massive walking-beam steam engine which drove her 27-foot paddle wheels can be visited only with a guided tour, but it can be viewed from above through windows opening onto the passenger deck.

The sign on the little newsstand on the ferry's upper deck, reads "Will return at 11:50." What year is not stated, but on the counter are 1935 newspapers and the *Literary Digest*, *Delineator*, and *Blue Book*, all magazines long departed from the scene.

Many visitors will be fascinated by the automobiles and trucks waiting patiently on the vehicle deck for *Eureka* to dock so that they can go ashore. Dating back to the early decades of this century, they are in beautiful condition—a wonderful collection to match the ferry itself.

Further out at the very tip of the pier, but closed to visitors, is the large oceangoing steam tug *Hercules*, a magnificently powered vessel, still undergoing restoration. She had an active career on the West Coast from 1907 to 1962 and her triple-expansion steam engine could handle the largest vessels of the day. (Today, such tugs are diesel powered.) The *Hercules* is being returned to her original condition. When the work is completed, visitors will be able to examine one of the finest American steam tugs, an essential part of the maritime tradition of a busy port.

Moored off the end of the pier are two other Maritime Museum vessels. The *Alma*, built in 1891, is a San Francisco Bay scow schooner, a distinctive, square-ended workhorse. This 59-footer carried hay, coal, sand, lumber—all kinds of heavy loads—across the bays and up the shallow-entering creeks, her flat bottom enabling her to nose in where other types of cargo carriers would run aground. In her later years, *Alma* was an oyster dredge; now she makes demonstration cruises, manned by museum staff, in summer months.

Also moored off the pier is the side-wheel paddle tug *Eppleton Hall*, built in 1904. An English tug, rescued from a scrap yard by an enthusiast and restored in England, *Eppleton* steamed under her own power across the Atlantic and through the Panama Canal to a new home in San Francisco Bay.

Schooner *C.A. Thayer* and San Francisco Bay ferry *Eureka*, two of the National Maritime Museum's restored vessels, are berthed at the outer end of the Hyde Street Pier, which forms the east side of the Aquatic Park lagoon. Moored off the pier are scow schooner *Alma* and side-wheeler tug *Eppleton Hall.* Open daily. October through April, 10 a.m. to 5 p.m.; May through September, 10 a.m. to 6 p.m. Admission free. Hyde Street Pier, 2905 Hyde Street, San Francisco, California 94109. Telephone (415) 556-6435.

In 1886, Scottish-built *Balclutha* made her maiden voyage around Cape Horn to San Francisco to load grain. A century later she is back in the bay, not to pick up cargo but permanently, in honorable retirement as the queen of the National Maritime Museum flotilla. She is a ship to be proud of, as visitors can see for themselves by walking a little way eastward to where *Balclutha*'s tall masts tower over the Embarcadero.

Steel-hulled, 301 feet overall, 1,689 gross tons, *Balclutha* has been beautifully restored to her condition as a general cargo carrier. She made four more voyages to San Francisco in the 1880s and 1890s, bringing out from Europe such varied cargoes as wine and spirits from London, hardware from Antwerp, coal from Wales; on each trip she carried back California grain. In between, she went all over the world; around Cape Horn 17 times, loading rice in Rangoon, nitrates in Iquique, guano in Callao, wool in New Zealand.

Eventually, after a brief stint as a lumber carrier to Australia, under Hawaiian registry, she was bought into the Alaskan salmon trade and came under American registry with San Francisco as her home port. Every spring for 28 years she carried as many as 300 fishermen and cannery workers to Alaska, returning in the fall loaded with canned salmon. In 1906, she went aground on an Alaskan reef and was sold for salvage where she lay for $500.

Balclutha was a sturdy ship, however. Her new owner hauled her off, patched her up, and gave her a new name—*Star of Alaska.* She continued in the salmon trade for a quarter century more, eventually retiring in 1930, the last sailing ship in the trade.

For more than 20 years the veteran was used as an exhibition ship and in occasional movies, only to be finally left to rot away on a San Francisco mud flat. Her rescue by the museum was followed by a year-long restoration by volunteers, including members of 18 bay area labor unions, with supplies and services contributed by more than 90 business firms.

Today the *Balclutha*'s gear, paint, and brightwork are kept in beautiful condition all over the ship. Visitors will find particularly helpful the excellent notes posted in various parts of the ship to explain the purpose of equipment or methods of construction.

Here are some things to notice as you go around the ship:

- sea chests in the fo'c'sle with wonderfully painted inner lids;
- the pig pen just forward of the deckhouse at midships with an enormous wooden pig in it—a symbolic representation of the live porkers that were carried to provide fresh meat on long voyages;
- the paneled captain's cabin aft, more accurately his suite of cabins—sitting room, berth cabin, and bathroom complete with a zinc tub—luxuries not always found ashore, never mind a ship at sea in the 1890s;
- the open 'tween decks displays of photos and drawings of a series of maritime-related topics including such things as hellships, the Cape Horn trade, the lumber trade, and shipbuilding: also the fine figureheads on display here;
- the ballast at the bottom of the open hold, contained in tubs so it could be shifted easily for repairs and so forth;
- also in the hold, a big diorama of a typical salmon cannery with a square-rigger alongside the dock.

Balclutha, the National Maritime Museum's full-rigged steel ship of 1886, is moored at Pier 43, on Embarcadero at the foot of Powell Street. Short walk from museum building and Hyde Street Pier. Open daily, 9 a.m. to 10 p.m. Admission: $2.00; children, $1.00. Ship *Balclutha*, Pier 43, Embarcadero, San Francisco, California 94109. Telephone (415) 982-1886.

The other major ship on display on the waterfront moves us to a much more recent but very significant sector of San Francisco's maritime past. The *Jeremiah O'Brien* is a Liberty ship, one of the 2,751 vessels of this type built in World War II when the nation desperately needed cargo carriers to replace those sunk by enemy submarines. She survives as a memorial to the men and women who built, manned, and sometimes defended these humble but highly useful vessels.

Far from beautiful, and designed on standardized plans to be built at maximum speed, the Liberty ships were put together like automobiles on an assembly line. By July, 1943, the average time of building a complete vessel of almost 11,000 tons was only 53 days. Many Liberties were built right in San Francisco Bay, and a constant stream went out the Golden Gate carrying supplies to our combat forces on the far side of the Pacific.

The *O'Brien*, which served a good part of the war in the Pacific, is believed to be the only Liberty ship to survive essentially unaltered and in operating condition. Some were sunk by enemy action; after the war many others were scrapped, some sold abroad, some altered for special purposes. Others just rotted away awaiting the shipbreaker. This would have been the fate of the *O'Brien* if farsighted San Franciscans hadn't recognized that at least one of these humble vessels deserved to be preserved as a significant part of America's and San Francisco's maritime tradition. Volunteers, assisted by the donations of thousands of visitors, restored and now maintain the sturdy old workhorse. They have done their work well; *O'Brien* is handsomely maintained and there is much to be seen in a visit to her at her berth in the Fort Mason Center, which was the Army Port of Embarkation during World War II.

Not to be missed by the technologically minded—and reasonably agile—is the *O'Brien*'s engine room. Liberty ships were powered by triple-expansion condensing steam engines, once almost universally used for ship propulsion but now as much relegated to maritime history as the spritsail and the steering oar. The *O'Brien*'s triple-expansion engine, which turns out 2,500 hp to drive her—in a pinch—at 11 knots, is intact and may be inspected by visitors willing to climb down one steel ladder after another to the engine room. To demonstrate that she is still in vigorous condition, twice each May the *O'Brien* steams out for a five-hour cruise around the bay; in the third weekend of every other month her engines are operated at dockside.

Visitors to the *O'Brien* will be interested in the details that remind us that the liberties were no ordinary peacetime merchantmen, sitting ducks for enemy attack. She is armed with 5.7-inch guns in steel "tubs" designed to give some protection against shell fragments, mounted at the bow and stern. In World War II she carried a Navy gun crew ready to use her battery against low-flying enemy aircraft or any submarine that might surface to try to sink her by gunfire.

Throughout the ship is an elaborate alarm system to call the crew to general quarters—red bells on the bulkheads with the stern admonition: "When this bell rings, go to your stations." On the bridge you'll find the station bills (where each crew member is to go) with "abandon ship" and "fire" the major emergencies listed. Nearby, are the flag bins where the signalman was stationed, ready to hoist flag signals to communicate with other ships in the convoy without breaking radio silence.

That the risk was great is made very clear by the life rafts at the ready should her crew of 41 have to abandon ship. The two rafts forward and two aft are mounted on sliding racks so that if the ship were torpedoed and listed heavily it would be easy to slide them off into the sea. Hard experience had taught that all too often it was impossible to lift stacked life rafts off the canting decks of a sinking ship.

In the latter part of World War II, the Liberty ships were superseded by the larger, faster, and more sophisticated Victory ships, but by that time the Liberties had done their job.

The *O'Brien*, incidentally, is named for a hero of the Revolutionary War who led an attack on a British ship near Machiasport, Maine, in the early days of the Revolution. The full story of Jeremiah O'Brien is told in the little museum at Machiasport, three thousand miles away from where his namesake ship is on view today.

SS *Jeremiah O'Brien*, an operable Liberty ship, is berthed at Pier 3 at the Fort Mason Center, on San Francisco's bay front. Parking available. Open all year except December 24 and 25, December 31 through January 2, Easter Sunday, and Thanksgiving. Hours: 9 a.m. to 3 p.m. Admission: $2.00; seniors and children, $1.00; families, $5.00. Ship restoration by nonproft National Liberty Ship Memorial, Fort Mason Center, Building A, San Francisco, California 94123. Telephone (415) 441-3101.

Finally, there is yet another interesting vessel on display. At pier 45, on the Embarcadero on the San Francisco waterfront between the piers of *Thayer* and *Balclutha*, is the USS *Pampanito*, a 1,500-ton fleet submarine that served in World War II. She was built at Portsmouth, New Hampshire, in 1943 and sent out to the Pacific. One of her memorable achievements was scooping out of the sea 73 Australian and British prisoners of war after the unmarked Japanese prison ship in which they were being carried to Japan had been torpedoed and sunk.

The *Pampanito* has been declared a National Historic Landmark and has been accurately restored, although the U.S. Navy, which still owns her, has removed some of her armament. A taped recording provides a description of each section of the vessel as the visitor reaches it on a tour.

Submarine *Pampanito* is berthed at Pier 45 in the Fishermen's Wharf section of San Francisco's waterfront. Open October 30 to May 31, Monday through Thursday, 9 a.m. to 6 p.m.; Friday through Saturday, 9 a.m. to 9 p.m. June 1 to October 30, Monday-Thursday, 9 a.m. to 9 p.m.

Figure 59
SS *Jeremiah O'Brien*, preserved as a National Liberty Ship Memorial, is berthed on San Francisco waterfront where she is open to visitors. The *O'Brien* is believed to be the last operable Liberty ship that has survived unaltered.

Friday-Sunday, 9 a.m. to 10 p.m. Admission: $3.00; students 12 to 18, $2.00; seniors and children 6 to 11, $1.00. Mail address: National Maritime Museum Association, 330, 480 Beach Street, San Francisco, California 94109. Telephone (415) 673-0700.

Another, much smaller museum in the bay area is in a sense complementary to the National Maritime Museum. The Treasure Island Museum, located on an island in San Francisco Bay, is dedicated to the three armed services afloat: the U.S. Navy, Marine Corps, and Coast Guard.

Treasure Island is attached to Yerba Buena Island in the middle of San Francisco Bay between San Francisco and Oakland; it is reached from both cities by the Bay Bridge. Now occupied by a U.S. Navy base, the island was created by fill to provide a site for the 1939-40 Golden Gate International Exposition. The museum is housed in a handsome Art Deco building that was the administrative center of the exposition and the air terminal of the Pan American China Clippers when they began their pioneer commercial flights across the Pacific to Asia.

The exhibition gallery is one enormous room, three stories high, curving in a graceful arch. Great windows on the west side present a magnificent view of San Francisco and the Golden Gate across the bay. Exhibits focus on the activities of the armed forces afloat in the Pacific and the history of Treasure Island itself. Ship models, uniforms, personal weapons, memorabilia, prints and paintings, photographs, and dioramas all help to tell the story of the three sea services.

Here are three ship models that are particularly worth looking out for:

• The sloop of war USS *Marion*, part of the Navy during the transition period between sail and steam, a period that is often ignored by model makers.

- The USS *Texas*, the battleship that served in the Navy from 1912 to 1948 and the only battleship to see active duty in both World Wars; shown in a model made by an officer who served in her. (The *Texas* herself, of course, is on exhibition near Houston.)

- A four-stacker destroyer, an example of the ships that were the eyes of the U.S. fleet for several decades, particularly in World War I and the years immediately following it.

Other notable exhibits include original documents from Commodore Matthew Gailbraith Perry's historic expedition to Japan in 1854. The Coast Guard is represented by a French Fresnel lens from the Farallon Island light, off the entrance of the Golden Gate. Relics of campaigns in the Pacific include uniforms and photographs dating from the U.S. Marines' intervention in the Boxer Rebellion in China and uniforms and weapons from World War II. Treasure Islands' own history is recalled by souvenirs and photographs of the 1939 exposition and a huge model of the original China Clipper.

A new permanent gallery, "Pacific Panorama," highlights the history of the sea services' activities in the Pacific.

Treasure Island Museum: Navy/Marine Corps/Coast Guard is located in Building 1 on Treasure Island (Yerba Buena Island) in the middle of San Francisco Bay. Library. Gift shop. Admission free. Closed federal holidays, otherwise open every day 10 a.m. to 3:30 p.m. Treasure Island Museum, Building No. 1, Treasure Island, San Francisco, California 94130. Telephone (415) 765-6182.

Now let's head north—but first a little detour to Vallejo, close by the historic Mare Island Navy Yard (now the Mare Island Naval Shipyard and Naval Station.)

The United States Navy came to stay in San Francisco Bay almost as soon as the United States itself. In 1853, only a few years after the annexation, the Navy bought Mare Island at the far end of San Pablo Bay and the following year established there the first naval base in the American West. The first commandant was David Glasgow Farragut, later a Civil War hero and the U.S. Navy's first admiral.

The Mare Island Navy Yard launched over 500 naval vessels between the USS *Sagamore* in 1859, and the nuclear-powered submarine USS *Drum*, which took to the water in 1970. Mare Island is not building ships at the present time but the yard still employs 13,000 civilians and more than 6,000 sailors and marines are stationed there. The yard serves as the

major repair and overhaul base for the Pacific Fleet Submarine Force.

The yard itself is not open to individual visits but can be toured by bus groups in a trip that takes about one and three-quarter hours. However, in the city of Vallejo which grew up across the little Napa River from the yard, the Vallejo Naval and Historical Museum is devoted to interpreting the history of the area and the U.S. Navy's activities. The museum's three galleries display many artifacts, including a large number on loan from the Navy Yard. On the roof is a working submarine periscope with which the visitor can get a submariner's view of the surrounding area.

From Vallejo harbor it is possible to take a tour by boat (about one hour, twenty minutes).

The California Maritime Academy is located nearby in South Vallejo.

The Vallejo Naval and Historical Museum is in the one-time city hall of Vallejo, California, across the Napa River from the Mare Island Naval Shipyard and Naval Station. Research library open by appointment. Book store. Gift shop. Museum will arrange Mare Island visits for touring bus groups. Open all year: Tuesday-Friday, 10 a.m. to 4:30 p.m.; Saturday, 1 p.m. to 4:30 p.m. Admission: 60 cents; children 25 cents. Vallejo Naval and Historical Museum, 734 Marin Street, Vallejo, California 94590. Telephone (707) 643-0077.

Now back to the road north. Route 101 will take us to the only significant natural harbor in northern California, Humboldt Bay, and its port city, Eureka. (Route 37 connects Vallejo to 101.)

North of San Francisco Bay there are no more major deep-water harbors on the Pacific Coast until the Columbia River, 600 miles away. The mountains of the Coastal Ranges come down to the sea and only small rivers slip out between them to form little bays and estuaries. But this mountainous coast, still sparsely settled, has one great economic asset: marvelous forests.

Enterprising lumbermen were quick to take advantage of the burgeoning market around San Francisco Bay in the post-gold rush days. Schooners brought lumber south to the Golden Gate, and in some of the larger harbors modest shipyards appeared to meet the demand for bottoms.

Some of the so-called harbors were too small even for a dock; a shallow-draft lumber schooner would tie up next to the bank. The timber was sometimes carried down the steep hillside on an aerial tramway; sometimes the logs were slid down a wooden chute onto the decks of the vessel.

But northern California had one port that, although shallow, provided a broad sheltered harbor for the lumber carriers. Eureka, on Humboldt Bay, was settled in 1850. In the midst of the most magnificent redwood forests in the world, Eureka's pioneers set resolutely to work to cut them down, load them up on the lumber schooners in the bay, and ship them south to build the houses of San Francisco.

A taste of this oceangoing tradition is preserved in the Clark Memorial Museum, housed in a handsome former bank building in downtown Eureka. Although a general historical museum largely devoted to the city's history, the Clark has a small but interesting maritime section. Things to look for include ship models, particularly of local craft, photographs of the area's shipping, tools, and photographs of the shipyards of Humboldt Bay.

Of particular interest is an entire fleet of tiny models made by Michael Jones, the assistant curator, who lovingly cherishes every aspect of the maritime collection. The many unusual vessels portrayed were almost all involved in West Coast maritime history such as California steamships of the Gold Rush period and other side-wheelers used on the Columbia River.

The collection of photographs of wrecks, many at or near Humboldt Bay, has a grim fascination of its own. Most visitors will be flabbergasted by the pictures of the cruiser *Milwaukee* ashore, a total loss. This little known fiasco of the United States Navy resulted from an unsuccessful attempt to pull off a submarine that had managed to strand itself on the beach.

New Englanders will probably be especially interested in pictures of off-beach whaling, which con-tinued in this area as recently as 1910. This was the original type of whale hunt that began on Nantucket Island in the 17th century, but was abandoned there in favor of whaleships that could make voyages to search for whales all over the globe. At Eureka, as elsewhere along the Pacific Coast, the shore-based whale hunters attacked their prey as the whales migrated back and forth between Alaska and wintering places in the Gulf of California.

Visitors to the city may be interested to know that some miles outside Eureka on the sandy peninsula that separates Humboldt Bay from the Pacific Ocean is the Samoa Cook House, a restaurant where the food is served at long tables, "in the old logging cookhouse style." Eureka is incidentally a center for many artists and craftsmen of the region, whose work may be found in local shops.

Clark Memorial Museum is in Eureka, California on Humboldt Bay, 285 miles north of San Francisco. Open Tuesday-Saturday, 10 a.m. to 4 p.m. Closed national holidays. Donation requested. Clark Memorial Museum, Third and E Streets, Eureka, California 95501. Telephone (707) 443-1947.

Now north again along the rugged coast of Oregon. The mouth of the great Columbia River is our destination, but we'll stop for a look at the little museum at Newport, a fishing town on Oregon's Yaquina Bay.

XIII
THE PACIFIC NORTHWEST

*Along the Oregon Coast and Up the Columbia River
Lieutenant Puget's Sound—and Northward*

Along the Oregon Coast and Up the Columbia River

In December of 1887, a tragic event occurred when the *Yaquina City*, Oregon Pacific's majestic 200-foot steamship, lost her steering gear as she came into the Bay. She washed up on South Beach and though her passengers walked off the ship to safety she was broken up by waves and destroyed. The replacement, *Yaquina Bay*, piled up on the jetty, on her first trip out of the harbor . . . There were dark hints of bribery and sabotage.

Yaquina Bay, 1778-1978 (a local history of the area)

Salvaged from the wreck of his ship, the desk of the captain of the *Yaquina City* is now on display at the little museum of the Lincoln County Historical Society in Newport, Oregon, the town at the entrance to Yaquina Bay. In the photographic collection the hapless vessel can be seen piled up on the beach, a total loss.

From the perspective of a century later, the loss of the *Yaquina City* was just a minor incident in the wreck-strewn history of the Oregon coast, but in the maritime history of little Newport it was an economic disaster. Connected only two years earlier to the rich Willamette Valley by a railroad through the coastal mountain range, Newport had visions of becoming a prosperous port, shipping Willamette crops down the coast to the San Francisco market. Now the loss of its two key cargo ships under suspicious circumstances was a devastating blow; Newport's dream finally collapsed when the little railroad reverted to being a local lumber carrier.

Newport survived the loss even if it never got rich. The demand for lumber continued strong and the schooners kept coming. A little shore-resort business was built up (the town had been named Newport in hopeful emulation of Newport, Rhode Island). Fishing prospered: One year a million pounds of halibut was brought ashore.

Today, Newport is still a pleasant little port on Yaquina Bay, one bank filled with yachts, the other with fishing boats. A big jetty built out into the Pacific protects the entrance to the harbor. The town's maritime traditions are recalled in a small but interesting section of the Lincoln County Historical Museum. The emphasis is heavily on the wrecks that littered this stormy coast where volcanic outcroppings create hidden reefs offshore to trap the unwary mariner. Artifacts from wrecks and mementos of the lifesaving station that once rescued many a sailor share the little exhibit with photographs of wrecked ships sullenly awaiting destruction from the blows of endless combers.

Lincoln County Historical Museum is in Newport, Oregon, on Yaquina Bay. Open all year. Closed Mondays. Hours: June through September, 10 a.m. to 5 p.m.; October through May, 11 a.m. to 4 p.m. Donations welcome. Burrows House, Lincoln County Historical Society, 545 S.W. 9th Street, Newport, Oregon 97365. Telephone (503) 265-7509.

Now, we'll continue northward along the Oregon coast to Astoria, the historic town at the mouth of the mighty Columbia River.

332

[On May 12, 1792, sailing south along the rugged Pacific Northwest coast past Cape Disappointment, we] saw an appearance of a spacious harbour abreast the Ship, haul'd our wind for it, observ'd two sand bars making off, with a passage between them to a fine river. Out pinnace and sent her in ahead and followed with the Ship under short sail, carried in from 1/2 three to 7 fm. and when over the bar had 10 fm. water, quite fresh. The River extended to the NE. as far as eye cou'd reach, and water fit to drink as far down as the *Bars*, at the entrance. We directed our course up this noble *River* in search of a village.

John Boit, Jr., quoted in Samuel Eliot Morison's
Maritime History of Massachusetts

Thus the 17-year-old fifth mate of the Boston ship *Columbia*, Captain Robert Gray, Master, recorded the belated discovery of one of the great rivers of North America. Captain Gray named the river the Columbia after his ship. Long afterward, when the Columbia had been fully explored and measured it was found to be a giant among rivers: more than 1,200 miles long to its furthest source, and draining more than a quarter of a million square miles to pour anywhere from 90,000 to 300,000 cubic feet of fresh water—according to season—into the Pacific every second.

Today, it seems extraordinary that for 250 years after the first Spanish explorers sailed along the Northwest Coast, this great river—the only deep-water harbor between San Francisco and Juan de Fuca Strait—had remained unknown to Europeans. Extraordinary also that when the Columbia was finally found, the discovery was not made by a naval expedition sent by one of the great European maritime empires, always interested in unoccupied real estate, but by a Yankee trader, not looking for geographical discoveries but simply seeking a sheltered harbor where he could bargain with the local Indians for sea-otter pelts.

Actually, there were several reasons. For one thing, it appears that for a century and a half, from the end of the 16th to the middle of the 18th centuries, no Europeans explored the coast of the Pacific Northwest at all. Wars at home and more obvious opportunities for trade, exploitation, and colonization kept the great maritime powers busy elsewhere. And when eventually national rivalries—as well as the discovery of great profits to be made selling sea-otter furs in China—turned the attention of Spain, England, and Russia to the region, their expeditions found topography and climate combined to make close inshore exploration of the coast both difficult and dangerous. The shore was rocky, lined with cliffs, and rimmed with hidden reefs and shoals. Giant seas, built up in 6,000-miles of travel eastward across the Pacific, often sent breakers crashing high against the shoreline.

There were no apparent harbors to provide refuge from the gales that lashed the coast. Sudden squalls added to the danger.

Worst of all, the prevailing wind was (and is) from the west, on-shore, making the entire coast what every sailing ship seaman dreaded: a lee shore. Get in too close and you might not beat your way out again against the headwind—and then find your ship driven inexorably against the rocks. On top of everything else, frequent fogs shrouded the uncharted rocks offshore and the mysterious mainland behind them.

Then, too, the mouth of the Columbia was not easily detected, despite the fact it was five miles wide. A sandbar had formed across it, and when the swells built up the surf broke in a continuous line from one shore to the other, giving the river entrance the appearance of a shallow inlet.

The ultimate factor in the discovery of the Columbia River was luck. Two great English explorers, whose missions were to chart the coast, had missed the entrance to the mouth entirely. The famous Captain James Cook was on the coast in 1778 and sailed north offshore, but as a result of bad weather and haste saw nothing. The Royal Navy's Captain George Vancouver, almost equally famous, had actually been right at the Columbia in HMS *Discovery* less than two weeks before Gray entered, but on that day the seas were breaking all across the entrance and he recorded that the bay had "the appearance of an inlet or small river, the land behind not indicating it to be of any great extent nor did it seem accessible to vessels of our burthen." So he sailed on.

Vancouver had good reason to be daunted by the line of great seas crashing against the sandbar that had formed across the mouth of the Columbia. The entrance to the great river has remained extremely dangerous to the present day, despite great jetties built to encourage the outflow of fresh water to scour out a safe channel. Over the years more than 1,500 lives have been lost and nearly 2,000 vessels wrecked or badly damaged on or around the bar. As recently as January, 1961, three Coast Guard vessels and a commercial fishing boat were lost on the bar in a single day.

And 18 years before Gray's discovery, another naval officer, Bruno Heceta in the Spanish service, had actually recognized the mouth of the Columbia as a river. His ship, the *Santiago*, was unable to enter against the rush of the outgoing current, however, and his crew was seriously weakened by scurvy, so instead of waiting to make another attempt, he simply recorded that here was the mouth of a river and sailed on home to Mexico.

Captain Gray's courage, seamanship and luck may well have changed the course of history. The

Boston ship's entry into the Columbia was a key argument for the American claim to ownership of the Columbia River valley and the Oregon country—the only part of the North American continent that the United States claimed by right of discovery. Spain, Russia, and Britain all had competing claims to the region based on coastal exploration, and it was many years before national ownership was finally settled.

Meanwhile, there was no great rush to take advantage of Gray's discovery. Twenty years passed before the first settlement on the lower Columbia. It finally came as the result of the enterprise and imagination of a German immigrant to the United States, John Jacob Astor. Fascinated to learn of the immense profits to be made in the fur trade, Astor planned a far-flung trading network in the Rocky Mountains with a post at the mouth of the Columbia River where furs could be picked up by ship.

The new post was duly planted and named Astoria by men sent out by ship from the East Coast. Washington Irving wrote a book about it, *Astoria*, that includes a vivid account of the arrival of the ship, the *Tonquin*, at the mouth of the Columbia River. The captain first sent two boats in to find a channel though the surf across the entrance. Both boats disappeared in the breakers with their entire crews. Then, Irving goes on:

> The attention of those on board the ship was now called to their own safety. They were in shallow water; the vessel struck repeatedly, the waves broke over her, and there was danger of her foundering. At length she got into seven fathoms water, and the wind lulling, and the night coming on, cast anchor. With the darkness their anxieties increased. The wind whistled, the sea roared; the gloom was only broken by the ghastly glare of the foaming breakers, the minds of the seamen were full of dreary apprehensions, and some of them fancied they heard the cries of their lost comrades mingling with the uproar of the elements. For a time, too, the rapidly ebbing tide threatened to sweep them from their precarious anchorage. At length the reflux of the tide and the springing up of the wind enabled them to quit their dangerous situation and take shelter in a small bay within Cape Disappointment, where they rode in safety during the residue of a stormy night, and enjoyed a brief interval of refreshing sleep.
>
> With the light of day returned their cares and anxieties. They looked out from the masthead over a wild coast and wilder sea, but could discover no trace of the two boats and their crews that were missing. Several of the natives came on board with peltries, but there was no disposition to trade. They were interrogated by signs after the lost boats, but could not understand the inquiries.

Eventually, the *Tonquin* crossed the bar and the party landed. They built a small fur-trading post on the south bank of the river, which was named Astoria after John Jacob Astor. Two years later, during the War of 1812, Astor's company sold it to his British fur-trading rivals, the North West Company, just in time to keep the little post from being captured by a British ship of war. At the end of the war Astoria once again became American, but the post was operated by British fur traders.

For a long time, almost the only ships to brave the bar were the supply vessels of the Hudson's Bay Company, the North West Company's successor, which had established regional headquarters way upriver at Fort Vancouver. Only at the very end of the 1840s did other vessels begin to appear on the Columbia. As always, it was cargoes that brought them. When the California Gold Rush created a market for provisions and lumber at exorbitant prices, Oregon farmers and woodsmen were ready. The Pacific Mail Line started a regular semi-monthly steamer service from California to Astoria, where they picked up passengers and freight that had been brought down the Columbia on little river boats. By now, the Hudson's Bay Company had withdrawn from the region and Astoria became the base for the bar pilots and tugs who brought sailing ships in through the ever-dangerous Columbia River entrance. When Portland became a great wheat port in the 1870s and 80s, Astoria supplied the river tugs that took the grain ships—square-riggers—up to load. River steamers flourished carrying passengers and freight on the Columbia.

About the same time, little Astoria became home port for salmon fishermen. Canneries sprang up to process the catch and provided cargoes to be picked up by deep-sea carriers. Eventually, here as elsewhere, railroads began to cut in on the traffic carried by the river steamboats. Today, the bulk cargoes that move by water are carried by barges. A high bridge over the Columbia has replaced the ferries that used to run over to the Washington side of the river. A center for sports fishing, Astoria is no longer as busy a place as it once was, but it cherishes its maritime traditions and in the Columbia River Maritime Museum it possesses one of the leading marine museums on the Pacific coast.

Located at the eastern end of downtown Astoria, Oregon, the museum is right on the river bank between the principal highway and the Columbia River. The buildings, with their 37,000 square feet of exhibition space, are probably the most striking architecturally of any maritime museum; as one observer has put it, they resemble two great waves sinking in the troughs and curling up in the crests.

The museum is even more interesting within than without. There are fine collections of ship models, maritime paintings, prints, photographs and artifacts, including—a grim note—relics from some of the many, many wrecks that have occurred at the mouth of the Columbia and the rugged shores nearby.

At the entrance to the museum, the visitor is greeted by a handsome Fresnel lens that sweeps the exhibits with light as it slowly revolves. In the vast exhibition hall, 57 feet high, a flotilla of interesting small craft is berthed on the museum floor. Two motor lifeboats are the self-bailing and virtually unsinkable Coast Guard craft that have played such a vital role at the mouth of the Columbia, saving many lives in these dangerous waters. Here also are regional fishing boats, including three types of gillnetters, used in fishing for the famous Columbia River salmon. Engine enthusiasts won't want to miss the display of small engines from fishermen and yachts, also in this hall. (Before going on, the visitor should be sure to climb to the gallery for a magnificent view of the Columbia River and the mountains beyond to the north.)

Beyond the main hall you enter a labyrinth of galleries, each devoted to some aspect of the historic maritime activities of the Columbia region. Every display is interesting, but here are some special highlights to look for:

- In the Fisheries Gallery are models of local types of fishing craft.
- In the Exploration Gallery you'll find models of historic ships, mostly those concerned with the discovery of the Columbia River. Among them are the ship *Columbia* from Boston, in which Captain Gray dared the breakers across the entrance to discover the Columbia River. A lesser-known vessel modeled is HMS *Chatham*, the vessel that Vancouver sent back down the coast to the Columbia after he had heard of Gray's discovery, and which became the first ship to explore the river's lower reaches.
- In the Sailing Vessel Gallery a particularly nice seven-foot model of the five-masted schooner *Inca* stands out. The shadow-box model of a lumber schooner made by a sea captain has a great feeling of authenticity.
- An entire case is devoted to delicate miniature marine engines in the Motor Vessels Gallery.
- The replica of a stern-wheeler's pilothouse is set up in the On the River Gallery.
- In the Naval History Gallery are a navigator's bridge and pilothouse of the World War II destroyer *Knapp*. Saved when the vessel was scrapped these relics were moved to the

museum site, where a portion of the building was erected around them. In this gallery there are also a number of models of naval vessels, including the famous battleship *Oregon*, which played a major part in the Battle of Santiago during the Spanish-American War.

Tied up at the museum's dock in the Columbia River is Lightship No. 604, the *Columbia*, which is open to visitors. She served for many years off the mouth of the Columbia, a dangerous, stormy station close to busy ship traffic and the scene of many marine disasters. *604* is well worth a visit.

Columbia River Maritime Museum is in Astoria, Oregon. At riverbank dock, retired Lightship *Columbia*, No. 604, is moored; open to visitors. Ample parking. Lectures; films; library. Admission: $2.50; seniors, children, $1.50. May through September, open every day; October through April, open Tuesday-Sunday. Hours: 9:30 a.m. to 5:00 p.m. Columbia River Maritime Museum, 1792 Marine Drive, Astoria, Oregon 97103. Telephone (503) 325-2323.

Now, upriver to the great port of the Columbia River Valley: Portland. The locally favored auto route follows the river.

For many decades after the settlement of Astoria, the Columbia remained a wilderness river. Indeed, the whole Oregon country—what is now the states of Oregon and Washington—was wilderness. Other than the Native Americans, only trappers and traders inhabited the region, most of them employees of the great fur trading companies, the Hudson's Bay Company and the Northwest Company, which eventually merged. The only ships to come up the

Figure 60
A pulling boat once used by pilots on the treacherous Columbia River bar dominates the Navigation Gallery of the Columbia River Museum at Astoria, Oregon.

Columbia brought supplies to the Hudson's Bay Company's regional headquarters at Fort Vancouver on the north bank of the Columbia, 120 miles from the sea, opposite the point where the tributary Willamette River ran in from the south. The first steamship in the Pacific Northwest was the Hudson's Bay Company's *Beaver*, built in England. In 1836 she came out under sail with her steam engine packed away in her hold, sailed up the Columbia to Fort Vancouver where her power plant and paddle wheels were installed, and steamed down again to the Pacific.

And then in the early 1840s, a different kind of traveler began to come down the upper Columbia from the eastward—not trappers or traders, but whole families of settlers. Word had gone out that there was fertile land in the Northwest and wagon trains began to plod westward over the Oregon Trail. When they got as far down the Columbia as the mouth of the Willamette River most settlers turned south up the fertile valley of the tributary.

Soon the newcomers began to produce more crops than their little settlements could consume. Some of this surplus could be sold to Fort Vancouver to provision the far-flung Hudson's Bay Company's trading posts, but this was a limited market. A few trading ships began to come into the Columbia directly from the East Coast; more coastal vessels came up from California, but the demand remained weak.

The Gold Rush changed everything. As thousands of '49ers poured into California, demand drove the prices of provisions sky-high; Willamette farmers found a steady stream of ships entering the Columbia ready to pay top prices for everything they could raise. The Columbia River was at last coming into its maritime heritage.

But it was not Astoria, the 40-year-old village and trading post at the mouth of the Columbia, that was destined to become the great port of the Oregon country. Deep-draft vessels came up the Columbia to the Willamette River, where the produce of the valley came down the little river on flatboats and, later, on small, shallow-draft steamers.

The point where the cargo would be transferred obviously had tremendous economic potential. Several places were possibilities, but the small town of Portland on the west bank of the Willamette just upriver from where it runs into the Columbia, had the best combination of features: nearness to the crop-producing area, access to the Columbia, and deep water. The Portland waterfront became the point where wheat from the Willamette, and later also from the newly opened wheat land of the upper Columbia River, was transferred to oceangoing ships. At first, coastal vessels carried the wheat down to California where it was mixed with California grain for export.

Later, square-riggers—mostly English—carried Oregon wheat directly to Europe. Eventually, sailing ships were in turn superseded by tramp steamers and bulk carriers that carried the wheat to markets all over the world.

Meanwhile, side-wheelers and stern-wheelers quickly began to throng the rivers. The first steamship built on the Columbia was launched at Astoria in 1850 and soon new steamship construction boomed: side-wheelers and stern-wheelers, passenger ships and freight vessels. Steamships ran inland up the Columbia and the Willamette to the head of navigation and downriver to Astoria. Eventually, picturesque stern-wheelers and side-wheelers were replaced by less romantic but far more efficient barges, which were pushed by so-called towboats up and down the river. But Portland remains a major port, the third largest on the Pacific coast and the connecting link between the great inland empire of the Columbia and the oceans of the world.

In Portland, the maritime traditions and history of the Northwest are preserved and displayed in the Historic Ships of the Northwest Coast Gallery on the second floor of the Oregon Historical Society Museum and Library. There, in chronological order, are the highlights of the Euro-American explorations, from the early Spanish explorations along these shores to the Hudson's Bay Company's arrival in the early 19th century.

Particularly interesting are models of Gray's *Columbia* and—what is more unusual—of the companion ship, *Lady Washington*, which was Gray's first command when he came out to the Northwest coast from Boston on a trading expedition. Here also is a model of the *Santiago*, the Spanish government's exploration ship that arrived at the mouth of the Columbia River in 1775. Her commander, Lieutenant Bruno Heceta, suspected there was a river there but because his crew was weakened by scurvy did not venture the dangerous crossing of the bar. Other models include HMS *Discovery*, Vancouver's ship; and, of course, the famous Hudson's Bay Company vessel *Beaver*, the sturdy little auxiliary steamship that spent some 50 years in the Northwest visiting her company's trading posts and surveying the coast for the British Admiralty, until she was finally wrecked at the entrance to Vancouver, British Columbia. The models are accompanied by paintings of the famous navigators and captains who commanded these vessels, along with artifacts from each period.

On the stairway of the museum is the beautiful figurehead of the bark *Forest Belle*, a vessel built in Maine for Portland owners. The vessel was wrecked near Formosa in 1877, but the figurehead was salvaged and sent back to Portland.

Oregon Historical Society Museum. Large research library on Oregon history. Bookstore. No admission charge. Open year round, Monday-Saturday, 10 a.m. to 4:45 p.m. Oregon Historical Society, 1230 S.W. Park Avenue, Portland, Oregon 97205. Telephone (503) 222-1741.

Here we'll detour for a look at a river craft that once made Portland her home but is now berthed on a tributary of the Columbia, hundreds of miles to the eastward.

When gold was discovered in Idaho in the 1860s, treasure hunters rushed inland from the Pacific Coast. The easiest way to get to the strike was by steamboat, first up the Columbia River to the point where it turned north, and then eastward up the river's rough and tumble tributary, the Snake. Freight was so profitable that a steamboat, the *Colonel Wright,* was built upriver, above the Columbia River rapids; she did yeoman service carrying gold miners and their baggage further up to Lewiston, the little village that was the base for the gold seekers striking out from the Snake River into the mountains. The steamer charged $120 a ton. As a ton was estimated by cubic feet rather than by weight, light and bulky cargoes paid as much as heavy ones. One steamboat is said to have collected $18,000 on a single upriver run.

The Lewiston gold rush has long since been forgotten, although Idaho is still a mining state. In recent years, however, the memory of steamboats on the Snake River has been revived by the passage up to Lewiston of one of the last remaining steamboats on the Columbia, the *Jean.* This twin stern-wheel steam tug for many years handled heavy barges in Portland harbor. Now, her tugboating days over, the *Jean* is moored at the spot on the Snake River where the wagon trains were ferried over from Washington to Idaho during the gold rush times. There the old-timer

(built in 1938) is being carefully but slowly restored by volunteers who are working to bring her back to as good as new after years of neglect. She is owned by the Idaho Historical Society and leased to a volunteer organization called the Friends of *Jean.*

The *Jean* is 168 feet overall but, designed for shallow river work, draws only 5 1/2 feet. Her hull is welded steel, very unusual for a steamboat. Even more unusual are the two paddle wheels fitted into the stern of the vessel side by side and driven by her 1200-hp stern engine. The two wheels can be operated separately so that by turning them in opposite directions at the same time, the *Jean* could spin around practically in her own length. Maneuverability is a tremendous advantage in a tug.

Jean, or at least portions of her, is already open to inspection by visitors. As the restoration work continues (progress depends on the availability of funds, which are raised by everything from cake sales to shows) more and more of the vessel will be available. While the *Jean* has no traditional connection with the Snake or with Lewiston, the fact that she is almost the last river steamer left of the many which once swarmed in the Columbia and its tributaries gives her considerable historical importance. And the loving care she is receiving in Lewiston—plus the significance of steamers in Lewiston's past—make it appropriate that her final mooring should be there.

SS *Jean*, twin stern-wheel river steamer, is moored in the Snake River at the Hell's Gate State Park at Lewiston, Idaho. Open year round for guided tours, Saturdays, Sundays, and holidays. April through October, 2 p.m. to 5 p.m.; November through March, 1 p.m. to 4 p.m. No admission charge but donations welcomed. Friends of the Jean, Mrs. Marguerite Cline, President, 3112 Seventh Street, Lewiston, Idaho 83501. Telephone (208) 743-2344.

Lieutenant Puget's Sound—and Northward

Few naval lieutenants have had their names so magnificently perpetuated as Peter Puget of HMS *Discovery.* In the late spring of 1792, Captain George Vancouver had brought the *Discovery* in through the Strait of Juan de Fuca; at the eastern end he found further passages leading off through islands both to the south and to the north. He turned south and eventually anchored off a point in a passage between two islands, west of the future site of Seattle. Lieutenant Puget was ordered to take a survey party in the ship's boats to explore the waterway that led further south and make sure it

wasn't the entrance to a passage through the North American continent. Puget did a thorough, workmanlike job in just two weeks and his reward is his name printed on every map and chart of the area he surveyed: Puget Sound, the great fjord surrounded by mountains, which penetrates deep into what is now the state of Washington. (Lieutenant Puget deserved his reward. Later surveys found his work, carried out by taking compass bearings of prominent landmarks, remarkably accurate.)

Puget Sound is really a continuation of the Willamette Valley in Oregon, which was scoured out by glaciers and then filled by the Pacific Ocean as the

Northwest Coast subsided. As Lieutenant Puget and his survey party found, the sound stretched about 100 miles between rugged mountains and its 2,000-square-mile area was cluttered with islands and rimmed with many miles of deep-water shoreline, heavily forested. The sound offered no water route through North America to the Atlantic, but did provide a number of large, safe anchorages.

None of these offered more advantages than the bay at the mouth of the Duwamish River. Sheltered on the south by a point of land, the harbor was the closest on the mainland to the Juan de Fuca Strait, the passage westward to the open Pacific. But despite these advantages, the site was left to the Indians for 60 years after Lieutenant Puget's explorations. Finally, in November 1851, four couples, 12 children, and a few single men were put ashore on the point by the schooner *Exact*, Nantucket built and commanded, now on her way to deliver would-be gold miners to a reported strike on an island further north.

The gold strike came to nothing. The *Exact*'s passengers, on the other hand, who had crossed to the Pacific coast from Illinois by wagon train, became the nucleus of one of America's great cities and ports, Seattle.

Named in honor of a friendly Indian nearby, Chief Sealth, or Seattle, the little settlement really got started when ships began to enter Puget Sound seeking lumber for the growing California market, where the demand was fed by the Gold Rush. A steam sawmill was set up, and by 1853 ships were carrying Puget Sound lumber not only down to California but out to China, Singapore, and soon even to Australia. Small settlements sprang up along the shore of the sound and soon steamboats were providing local passenger service. The United States Navy took an interest in the protected waters of Puget Sound and when an Indian attack threatened Seattle in the 1850s, the sloop of war *Decatur* came to the settlement's assistance.

In time, Seattle and Tacoma, the sister Puget Sound port a few miles to the south, became bustling cities. The great circle route made them—together with Portland on the Columbia River—the American ports closest to Asia and they proudly claimed to be the gateways to the Orient. Eventually, they were connected to the East by transcontinental railways. When the Alaskan gold rush came in the last years of the 19th century, Seattle became the outfitting base and departure point for thousands of would-be gold miners who crowded every kind of vessel in their efforts to get north to seek their fortunes.

Today, Seattle remains the major port for Alaskan shipping. What is more important, it is also the major port though which Washington state exports its fish, dairy products, wheat, and fruit to countries all over the world. The city is also the base for a big fishing fleet, and a yachting center. Not surprisingly, no city is more conscious than Seattle of its maritime heritage with 40 miles of salt waterfront plus more than a 100 miles of shoreline on freshwater Lake Union in the heart of the city and Lake Washington, to the east. With three marine museums, a historic ship in the process of restoration, and a unique center for the study, preservation, and recreation of the region's distinctive types of small craft, much is here for the maritime-minded visitor to discover and explore.

A good place to start exploring Seattle's maritime heritage is the Museum of History and Industry, located in the city's east side between Lake Washington and the edge of the University of Washington campus. The museum has devoted a large gallery to maritime history with exhibits from the Historical Society of Seattle and the Puget Sound Maritime Historical Society. Some special highlights to look for include:

- the racing hydroplane Slo-Mo IV that competed in the speedboat races on Seattle's Lake Washington;
- a model of a big tug used for towing log rafts, a major maritime activity in Puget Sound;
- a model of the Hudson's Bay Company ship *Beaver*, the first steamship on the Northwest Pacific Coast;
- some beautiful figureheads, including a delightful black-coated Victorian gentleman who had his beard removed when the four-masted bark to which he was attached was sold and renamed for a new owner who had only a moustache.

The more than 100 ship models in the collection include some fine specimens of elaborate owners' models of noted trans-Pacific passenger liners as well as a miniature of Captain Vancouver's famous ship, *Discovery*, in which he explored the north Pacific coast.

Plans are in the making for an ambitious revision of the gallery some time in the not too distant future with a new wall of exhibits showing the maritime history of Puget Sound chronologically from the age of exploration to the recent past. These would be housed in a two-thirds-scale mock-up of waterfront buildings along a Seattle dock. The other side of the hall, according to the plan, is for rotating special exhibits, some drawn from the museum's collections, others borrowed from other sources.

Many of the exhibits now to be seen in the gallery will undoubtedly be featured in the new revised display.

Other elements in the museum's maritime collection include a large variety of ships' artifacts: bells, whistles, name boards, cabin fittings, machinery, navigational instruments, shipbuilding tools, and so forth. The museum is also the proud possessor of nearly 100,000 marine photographs, largely local, and several thousand volumes of marine history.

Museum of History and Industry is close to Lake Washington and adjacent to the University of Washington campus in eastern Seattle. Large maritime-history library. Open year round except New Year's, Memorial Day, Thanksgiving, December 24, 25, and 31. Monday-Saturday, 10 a.m. to 5 p.m.; Sundays, noon to 5 p.m. Admission: $1.50, seniors and children 6 to 12, 50 cents; free on Tuesdays. Museum of History and Industry, 2700 24th Avenue, Seattle, Washington 98112. Telephone (206) 324-1125.

Now let's look at a very different kind of place: Seattle's Center for Wooden Boats has its own unique approach to preserving the maritime traditions of the area. According to its self-description, the Center is a "living museum . . . where the exhibits aren't locked up in glass cases but floating free where they can be touched, boarded . . . and used." Some people wouldn't call it a museum at all, but a small-craft restoration shop, or a teaching center, or a special kind of boat livery; actually it is all these things. Above all the Center is obviously an interesting place for anyone concerned with our maritime past, particularly in the evolution of the distinctive small craft of the Pacific Northwest, and Puget Sound in particular.

The Center is located at the southern end of Lake Union, right in the middle of the north end of Seattle; it is housed in a houseboat afloat in the lake with finger piers for assorted small craft. Visitors will not only find there the major types of regional small craft but if they demonstrate a reasonable skill in boat handling they can take the boats out and try them for themselves. "Classic boating by the hour" is one of the Center's offerings—actually some rentals have lasted up to six days. All the boats at the Center are small and made of

Figure 61
At the Center for Wooden Boats in Seattle, Washington, the visitor not only finds many historic types of small craft but also gets a chance to learn how they handle by taking them out on the waters of Lake Union.

wood but they come in many shapes: canoes, wherries, catboats, sloop boats, sharpies, dories, whitehalls, singles, doubles, boats big enough for the whole family.

But hands-on demonstrations of classic small craft are only one facet of the Center's activities: The houseboat headquarters also serve as both a workshop and a lecture hall. Here you can take a practical course on how to build a boat, or attend lectures on the types of small craft distinctive to the region. Dick Wagner, the founder and guiding spirit of this unique establishment, has hopes for an even broader and more ambitious program. Some day he would like to see the Center not only restore and display regional boats but also research their origins, their construction, and the ways they were used. Wagner sees a need for more research about the boatbuilders and the homegrown designers of Puget Sound. The Center has already published monographs of some of its more unusual types, such as the Poulsbo boat and the Davis skiff.

Maritime-minded travelers who are tired of just looking, no matter how fascinating the exhibits, and want to get back on the water will find the Center a particularly attractive and interesting place.

Center for Wooden Boats is at the south end of Lake Union in Seattle. Open all year, May through September, Monday-Friday, noon to 7 p.m.; Saturday and Sunday, 10 a.m. to 8 p.m.; October through April, daily 10 a.m. to 6 p.m. Admission: free. Center for Wooden Boats, 1010 Valley Street, Seattle, Washington 98109. Telephone (206) 382-BOAT.

Right next door to the Center for Wooden Boats—a cable's length away as the old sea dogs would have put it—is Northwest Seaport, which at the moment is devoting all its efforts to the restoration of the old lumber and fishing schooner *Wawona*. This 165-footer is reputed to be the largest three-masted schooner built on the West Coast; she was launched at Fairhaven, California, in 1897.

The *Wawona* suffered a major setback a few years ago; during an exceptionally heavy rainy season, she sank at her dock in Lake Union. Now once again afloat, the schooner is being gradually rehabilitated but is usually open to visitors on weekends.

The *Wawona*'s story is a segment of the economic history of the Northwest. Until 1913, she was in the lumber trade, carrying thousands of board feet each voyage from Puget Sound ports to distant Chile, Fiji, and Australia. From 1914 to 1941, *Wawona* became a cod-fisherman in the Bering Sea off Alaska. Every spring, her deck stacked with dories, she carried a crew of hardy fishermen north to the banks, where they spent the summer hand-lining for cod, then returned in the fall. During World War II, she was seized by the Army and spent four years as a mastless lumber barge.

After the war, she went back to fishing for a couple of years, but the day of sail was over even in the fishing fleet, and *Wawona* narrowly escaped being scrapped before she was eventually rescued for preservation.

The Northwest Seaport owns three other interesting vessels, which it has been unable to display at their Lake Union base for lack of room. One is the tug *Arthur Foss*, a husky 120-footer, which participated in the Alaskan gold rush and later was the star of the movie *Tugboat Annie*. Another is the lightship *Relief*, which served at danger points off both San Francisco and the mouth of the Columbia River. The third is the *San Mateo*, long a San Francisco Bay ferryboat but which came north to serve as a Washington State ferry in Puget Sound until her retirement in 1970.

Northwest Seaport hopes that eventually part of the Lake Union shore next to *Wawona*'s berth will become a lakeside park that will provide additional space making it possible to display all of the vessels.

Northwest Seaport is at 1060 Valley Street, next door to Center for Wooden Boats at south end of Seattle's Lake Union. Recently focused on restoration of lumber schooner *Wawona*. Tug *Arthur Foss* and lightship *Relief* are currently moored in Lake Washington. The *Foss* is open Saturdays, no charge; the *Relief* may be viewed by appointment. Ferry *San Mateo* is undergoing repairs to upper works and is not open to visitors; will be on Seattle waterfront upon completion; check status and location of these vessels by telephone. Northwest Seaport, P.O. Box 2865, Seattle, Washington 98111. Telephone (206) 447-9800.

In addition to the vessels listed above, several other ships of the past have been preserved in and around Seattle and are sometimes open to visitors. Since locations, schedules, and charges vary, it is best to check directly with the sponsoring organizations. Here are three:

Duwamish is most unusual: a 1909 fireboat, rebuilt to have the largest pumping capacity west of the Mississippi. Telephone (206) 682-5275.

Adventuress, 127-foot, two-masted schooner, built in 1913 for Arctic whaling, later became a San Francisco pilotboat. Now she is a youth-sail training vessel. Telephone (206) 232-4024.

Virginia V, 125-foot, is said to be the last steam-powered American-flag passenger vessel west of the Mississippi. She is operated by the Virginia V. Foundation. Telephone (206) 624-9119.　•

Just how the *Wawona* looked in her prime can be seen by the visitor to the Museum of the Sea and Ships. The *Wawona* is one of a large number of models displayed at the museum, which is located on the second floor of a waterfront building down on the Puget Sound side of Seattle.

Of special interest at the Museum of the Sea and Ships is a model of the steam turbine-driven *Turbina*. In 1894 this little vessel made maritime history by steaming 35 knots on her sea trials propelled by a steam turbine instead of the conventional reciprocating steam engine universally used at that time. The model is a fine big one and the informative notes that accompany it tell how the turbine was invented and developed and its significance in the development of marine propulsion. Well into the 20th century the reciprocating engine was standard, but eventually the more efficient turbine replaced it, only to be replaced in turn by marine diesels.

Another model at the Sea and Ships Museum—a 19th-century English revenue cutter—has something of a literary background: It once belonged to C.S. Forester who, as every maritime enthusiast knows, wrote about that wonderful, if mythical, British naval hero, Commander Hornblower R.N. Other models of interest portray the great steel square-rigger *Moshulu* (the original ship herself is now preserved in Philadelphia); the Confederate commerce raider *Alabama*; and a Victory ship, the turn-them-out-by-the-yard freighter that helped to win World War II.

The Sea and Ships Museum collection comprises much more than models, of course. Exhibits include many prints and paintings of maritime subjects, artifacts, and instruments. A curiosity is an armchair made entirely of whalebone by the carpenter of a whaling ship. Memorabilia include an interesting case of relics from famous liners, including a number from the ill-fated *Lusitania* and *Titanic*. An unusual find, particularly in an American museum, is the battle ensign of HMS *Sheffield*, the British cruiser that took part in the chase and sinking of the German battleship *Bismarck* in World War II. On Royal Navy ships, the battle ensign is hoisted going into action and remains flying until return to port.

The Museum of Sea and Ships is upstairs from the Seattle Aquarium on the mezzanine level of Pier 59. Gift shop. Open all year. Memorial Day through Labor Day, 10 a.m. to 7 p.m.; winter, 10 a.m. to 5 p.m. Admission: $2.00; seniors and students 13 to 18, $1.50; children 6 to 12, $1.00. The personal collection of Ken and Francine Zmuda. Museum of Sea and Ships, Pier 59, Waterfront Park, Seattle, Washington 98101. Telephone (206) 628-0860.

Seattle has one maritime museum, the Coast Guard Museum Northwest, devoted entirely to the activities of the United States Coast Guard and its predecessors, the Lighthouse Service, the Life-Saving Service, and the United States Revenue Service. The Pacific Northwest is a most appropriate region for such a museum: On these coasts, marked by reefs and shoals and strewn with wrecks, the Coast Guard has

had to carry out some of its most dangerous lifesaving operations. The museum is in a white two-story building at the entrance to the Coast Guard Support Center, located toward the southern end of the Seattle waterfront.

A major exhibit is a fine model of the Revenue Cutter *Bear*, the auxiliary steam vessel famous for her many years of service in the Arctic. Other models show the evolution of the cutters of the Coast Guard and the early U.S. Revenue Service from the age of sail right up to the most modern vessels of today.

Coast Guard uniforms and weapons, as well as drawings, prints, paintings, and photographs comprise other exhibits. Nineteenth-century drawings show early lighthouses on the Northwest Coast operated by the Lighthouse Service. The museum also displays the great lens from the New Dungeness light in the Strait of Juan de Fuca.

Incidentally, at the adjacent Coast Guard Support Center are based the two largest United States icebreakers, the *Polar Star* and the *Polar Sea*, and also several of the most modern Coast Guard cutters. The latter are usually open to visitors on weekends when they are in port.

Coast Guard Museum/Northwest is at the south end of the Seattle waterfront, just outside entrance to Coast Guard Support Center, Pier 366. Parking. Library. Open all year. Monday, Wednesday, and Friday, 9:30 a.m. to 4 p.m.; Saturday-Sunday, 1 to 5 p.m. Admission: free. Operated by nonprofit, nongovernmental corporation. Coast Guard Museum of the Northwest, 1519 Alaskan Way South, Seattle, Washington 98134. Telephone (206) 442-5019.
At the adjacent **Coast Guard Support Center** two of the largest polar icebreakers and two High Endurance Cutters are usually open to visitors on weekends when in port, 8 a.m. to 4 p.m.

An hour's pleasant ferry ride directly westward across Puget Sound from Seattle is Bremerton, on the shore of a long peninsula stretching northward from the lower end of Puget Sound. This little town was the site chosen by the United States Navy when, in the latter part of the 19th century, the service recognized that the growing importance of Pacific Northwest shipping made it desirable to have a base in the region. Over the years, the Puget Sound Naval Shipyard, built on the banks of a deep inlet, became one of the most important naval establishments on the Pacific Coast. Just how farmland was transformed into an industrial complex can be seen in a fine series of oversized photographs on the walls of the Bremerton Naval Shipyard Museum.

As its name suggests, the museum, housed on the second floor of the Bremerton terminal building of the Seattle ferry, is focused on the nearby shipyard. The museum suffers from lack of space and the exhibits are rather crowded in, so the visitor must search out its treasures. Among them he will find a fine collection of models of United States naval vessels, such as the cruiser *Richmond* and the aircraft carrier *Hancock*. Some are pretty unusual: for example, a completely transparent plexiglas model reveals the construction of the aircraft carrier *Midway* with bulkheads, decks, and all interior arrangements. The hull shape of one of the Navy's early submarines, the *O-2*, is recorded in a builder's pattern carved of wood, rather like a shoemaker's last. *O-2*, launched in 1918, was the first vessel built at the Puget Sound Naval Shipyard.

Some idea of the scope of the Naval Shipyard's activities at the height of World War II is shown in a handsome diorama in the museum. Other exhibits include, in addition to many photographs and drawings of shipyard activities, a beautiful miniature launch built to scale by apprentices in the yard, a model of the Japanese battleship *Nagato*, marine instruments and engines, and a whole series of photographs showing ships named for places in the state of Washington. Among the more unusual exhibits is a Korean wooden cannon dating back to the 14th century.

The museum has recently taken over additional space, so the visitor will find more exhibits have been put on display. Sponsored by the Kitsap County Historical Society, the museum owes its existence and continued excellence to one enthusiastic person, Lee Tennison, a former president of the society and retired shipyard employee. Mr. Tennison, long the director of the museum, has now retired but the museum is still staffed by volunteers, now under the direction of the Kitsap County Visitor and Convention Bureau.

The Puget Sound Naval Shipyard was for many years the retirement home of the historic USS *Missouri*, the battleship that was the scene of the final surrender of the Japanese forces at the end of World War II. Formerly open to visitors, the *Missouri* is going back on active duty and has now left the shipyard for modernization elsewhere.

Bremerton Naval Shipyard Museum is located on the second floor of the Bremerton Passenger Terminal of the Seattle ferry, adjacent to Puget Sound Naval Shipyard. Open all year, every day, 9 a.m. to 5 p.m. No admission charge; donations appreciated. Sponsored by Kitsap County Historical Society. Naval Shipyard Museum, Washington State Ferry Terminal Building, Bremerton, Washington 98310. Telephone (206) 479-7447. For information write/phone Kitsap County Visitor and Convention Bureau, P.O. Box 836, Bremerton, Washington 98310. Telephone (206) 479-3558.

Another bit of our maritime past that is being preserved largely through the energy and enthusiasm of one man, is at the Edmonds Museum in Edmonds, Washington, on the east shore of Puget Sound about 30 miles north of Seattle. There, Douglas Eagan, a retired shipping executive fascinated by our maritime tradition, has seen to it that a small but substantial collection of models, photographs, and artifacts relating to the region's maritime past has been preserved.

Like most towns on what were once the heavily forested shores of Puget Sound, Edmonds was formerly a bustling lumber port, and this is reflected in the Edmonds Museum's collection. One of the most striking exhibits—on the main floor of the museum—is a diorama of the Edmonds waterfront at the turn of the century when it was dominated by lumber and shingle mills. The cutaway of a shingle mill next to the diorama is animated so that you can actually see machinery turn.

In the Marine Room, on the lower floor, photographs show the evolution of the ferry vessels that traveled across Puget Sound from Edmonds to the little town of Kingston on the west side. A nice model portrays the ferry *San Mateo*, the last steam ferry on the Pacific Coast.

Other models show the Coast Guard cutter *Snohomish*, built in 1908, and the ship *Benjamin F. Packard*. One particularly nice little model, built by a ship's carpenter, portrays a typical windjammer of its period. There is also a fine model of J.P. Morgan's yacht *Corsair*, which later served as a survey ship.

This small maritime collection, well-arranged, displayed, and explained, is well worth stopping off at for a visit. The museum, housed in the city's former Carnegie Library, is operated by the Edmonds-South Snohomish County Historical Society. The Marine Room in the basement is in what was formerly the little town's police station.

Edmonds Museum is at 118 Fifth Avenue North in downtown Edmonds, Washington. Gift shop. Library. Open Tuesday, Thursday, Sunday; 1 p.m. to 4 p.m. Admission: free. Sponsored by Edmonds-South Snohomish County Historical Society. Edmonds Museum, P.O. Box 52, Edmonds, Washington 98020. Telephone (206) 774-0900.

At Bellingham, Washington, another timber port 90 miles north of Seattle, the Whatcom Museum of History and Art occasionally has exhibits on various aspects of the maritime traditions of the Northwest. Travelers visiting the area might find it worthwhile to check with the museum.

The museum is also the proud possessor of a notable treasure of maritime history: the H.C. Hanson Naval Architecture collection. Covering the period from 1914 to 1970, the collection includes 11,000 blueprints of Hanson's designs for working small craft, tugs, fishing boats, vessels, and small commercial vessels. There are also 4,200 drawings of boats and boat details and 17 half models, as well as a number of ship fixtures, publications, and papers relating to Hanson and his ships. This collection is in the process of being catalogued. Not only will it be a great maritime research resource, but plans call for highlights of the collection to be put on display, tentatively in 1988—another reason for checking with the museum.

Whatcom Museum of History and Art is in Bellingham, Washington. Open all year, Tuesday-Sunday, noon to 5 p.m. Contributions welcome. Whatcom Museum of History and Art, 121 Prospect Street, Bellingham, Washington 98225. Telephone (206) 676-6981.

Affiliated with the Whatcom Museum is the Bellingham Maritime Heritage Center, which at present includes a Salmon Lifecycle Facility at the foot of lower Whatcom Falls and a "Citizens Dock" on the Bellingham waterfront. At the Salmon Facility there is a demonstration hatchery and visitors can fish nearby for steelhead and cutthroat trout. Sponsored by the city of Bellingham, the center has an extensive program of environmental education activities.

Bellingham Maritime Heritage Center, 210 Lottie Street, Bellingham, Washington 98225. Telephone (206) 676-6873.

A few miles north at Blaine, Washington, the Semiahmoo Park Interpretive Center has on display a 28-foot Bristol Bay catboat, a double-ender used for gillnet fishing in Alaska. Most of these small craft were converted to motor boats, but this survivor escaped and has been preserved complete with spars, rigging, and sails. The center's exhibits are focused on the salmon canning industry and include artifacts, photographs, and a motion picture of the Alaska Packers Association fleet of square-rigged sailing vessels, 1918 to 1934.

Semiahmoo Park Interpretive Center, Blaine, Washington, on the Strait of Georgia. Open all year except Christmas and New Year's weekends; June to September, Wednesday-Sunday, 1 to 5 p.m. No admission charge; donations welcomed. Semiahmoo Park and Interpretive Center, 8609 Semiahmoo Drive, Blaine, Washington 98230. Telephone (206) 332-4777.

XIV
CANADA ON THE PACIFIC

Vancouver
Victoria

Vancouver

On the same 1792 voyage in which his expedition explored Puget Sound, Captain George Vancouver turned north at the east end of the Strait of Juan de Fuca and sailed up into a narrow passage, dotted with islands. He named it the Strait of Georgia in honor of King George III of England. As Vancouver eventually discovered, the strait separated a large island on the west—now named Vancouver Island—from the mainland of North America.

Ever wary of shoals and reefs, Vancouver anchored his ships, the *Discovery* and the smaller *Chatham*, and continued his exploration northward in two boats, commanded by himself and, once again, by Lieutenant Peter Puget. Rowing and sailing, they proceeded along the mainland shore, making a wide detour around a great sandbar that stuck out in the strait. They passed two estuaries, the two mouths of the Fraser River, but as in the case of the Columbia, Vancouver once again failed to recognize the river, largely because the sandbar had kept him well offshore. Just a few miles north, the two boats came to a wide inlet that penetrated deep into the coast on the east; the explorers rowed in and followed it all the way to the head, some 20 miles. Vancouver named it Burrard Inlet, after a Royal Navy man, and went on.

At Burrard Inlet, Vancouver had discovered one of the finest harbors of the whole Pacific Coast, but for many decades its waters saw no ships. The land behind it was a wilderness, inhabited by Indians, trappers, and Hudson's Bay Company fur traders: There could be no ships without cargoes. Seventy-odd years after Vancouver's visit, the point of land next to the inlet was still occupied only by a sawmill and a small company village that had gradually grown up around it.

And then, slightly more than 20 years later, the lightning struck; almost overnight the village became a bustling town; the empty inlet, a ship-filled harbor. The Canadian Pacific Railway, which had been laying its tracks across Canada, finally reached the Pacific Coast at the edge of Burrard Inlet, and the brand new city of Vancouver was born. Connected by rail to central and eastern Canada, Vancouver became the nation's window on the Pacific and its gateway to Asia. Trans-Pacific steamship service began almost at once. Lumber and wheat made up most of the early outgoing cargoes but eventually Vancouver became a great international port. Today, it is also recognized as one of the most beautiful port cities in the world.

Vancouver may be the youngest of the great ports of the Pacific Coast but it possesses a center for the preservation of the maritime past that many of its older sisters must envy: the Vancouver Maritime Museum. Here, on the shores of English Bay, is not only a fine museum but a truly historic vessel carefully preserved ashore. In addition, at the museum's own artificial harbor a one-time pilot schooner is being restored and others of the few remaining veterans of the age of sail call from time to time and can be seen by appreciative visitors.

The museum's historic vessel is the *St. Roch*, the

first vessel to voyage through the Northwest Passage from west to east. She is housed in a great hall, which from the outside resembles nothing so much as a gigantic A-frame of glass, towering over the museum proper, a long, low building alongside. The museum's exhibits are focused on the maritime activities of the Canadian West Coast and particularly, of course, Vancouver.

The most notable of the gallery exhibits are the beautiful ship models, many portraying vessels of regional importance to British Columbia and its isolated coastal and island settlements. Here, for example, is a model of the SS *Princess Maquinna*, named for the daughter of an Indian chief, the largest steel vessel built in British Columbia. From 1914 to 1952, *Maquinna* was the lifeline of isolated coastal communities. The model of the SS *Cardena* portrays the vessel that connected Vancouver to the port of Prince Rupert in the north. Other models include coastal freighters, deep-sea tugs, government steamers and yachts, and the various Puget Sound and Georgia Straits passenger ferries that still tie together the little towns on the innumerable islands. The Canadian Pacific's famous "empress" passenger liners are represented by the *Empress of Japan* and the *Empress of Asia*.

Two models are of special interest for quite different reasons: The first, the sealing schooner *Vancouver Belle*, portrayed by a model made by her captain, became in 1887 the first vessel launched in Vancouver. Five years later she was seized by the Russian authorities, charged with poaching seals on closed grounds off Siberia. The crew was sent home; the schooner was retained by the Russians.

The second, a model of the motor vessel *Skeena* of London portrays an unusual type: The model is cutaway to show the complex of inner ramps that enabled the vessel to carry a fleet of loaded trucks.

One of a number of striking dioramas at the museum shows lumber being loaded onto barges at a British Columbia port, with tugs standing by off the docks. In another, ships are taking on bulk cargo, while a third portrays ships loading grain. Other notable exhibits include a mock-up of the wheelhouse of an ocean tug and huge owners' models of the famous transatlantic passenger liners *Majestic* and *Caronia*. There is also an interesting built-up model of the four-masted bark *White Wings*.

The navigational instrument display includes Captain George Vancouver's chronometer. Chronometers had been only recently introduced, and Vancouver's instrument was of tremendous assistance to him in fixing the exact longitude of points along the Pacific coast.

At intervals, a loud bell rings in the museum

announcing the beginning of a tour of the *St. Roch* in its adjacent exhibition hall. Visitors should be sure to take advantage of the opportunity to be guided by a Parks Canada expert primed to answer every conceivable question.

The *St. Roch* was a Royal Canadian Mounted Police patrol and supply vessel. In June 1940, she set out from Vancouver to attempt a passage through the Arctic ice around the northern shores of Canada to the East Coast. When she completed her voyage, two years and 110 days later (she had spent 21 months frozen into the ice pack), she had made maritime history. On her return over the same route she made the east-west passage from Halifax to Vancouver in only 115 days. Later the *St. Roch* went from one coast to the other through the Panama Canal, thereby becoming the first vessel in history to circumnavigate the North American continent.

Here are some things to look for during the *St. Roch* tour:

- The tent erected on the main hatch is where the expedition's Eskimo guide, his wife, and their children lived—with his dogs and two sleds alongside. When his dogs ran out of food, the guide went out on the ice and hunted seals and walruses. The dogs themselves are represented by stuffed huskies of the same breed; on the fo'c'sle is a walrus, the type that provided their meals.
- Peer up at the crow's nest. The captain spent a lot of time up there scanning the ice pack ahead for open passages.
- Notice the spare rudder carried on deck in case the original was damaged by ice: the ship would have been helpless without a rudder. Actually, the original rudder came through intact, but the provision of a spare is an example of the great care with which the expedition was prepared in order to survive disaster when out of reach of help.
- In the fo'c'sle, notice the crew's uniforms, toilet articles, and gear, laid out as if the men had just stepped out on deck. In the mess hall, a half-eaten meal and partly filled coffee cups are on the mess table. Listen for the sounds (taped) of the ship pushing her way through pack ice.
- The galley is crammed with food cans and boxes contemporary with the 1940s voyages.

The *St. Roch* is mounted as if she were in dry dock so that the visitor can walk around her bottom. Notice that her beamy hull, double sheathed in oak, is rounded and without a keel so that when she was squeezed in the ice the pressure pushed her upward rather than crushing in her sides. This must have made her hard to handle under sail. And before you leave the *St. Roch*, take a good look at the maps in the gallery alongside, which show her routes through the Arctic ice.

The third and newest element of the Vancouver Maritime Museum is the little artificial harbor on the adjacent shore. Here the museum's schooner, the *Thomas F. Bayard*, is being restored. The oldest vessel still afloat in Canada, the *Bayard* was built in 1880 as a Delaware Bay pilot schooner. Later she was sent out around Cape Horn to the Pacific Northwest where she carried miners and supplies during the Yukon gold rush. After that, *Bayard* became a sealer in the Bering Sea until pelagic sealing was forbidden. Finally she ended up as a lightship off the mouth of the Fraser River. Although her reconstruction is a major project, the *Bayard* is an interesting vessel and the museum is happy to have people take a look at her as the work is being done.

The other slips in the museum's little harbor are used by visiting small craft of historic interest; their owners open them to visitors from time to time. On one typical occasion, for example, the visitor would have found among the little vessels tied up there a Bristol Channel pilot cutter, a Nova Scotia fishing schooner, and a classic Danish folk boat.

Vancouver Maritime Museum, historic schooners *St. Roch* and *Thomas F. Bayard*, are at the foot of Cypress Street, on the south shore of English Bay, just west of Burrard Bridge over False Creek. Model workshop. Marine archives and library open by appointment. Bookstore/gift shop. Open all year daily from 10 a.m. to 5 p.m. Admission: $1.75; seniors, students and children, 75 cents. Vancouver Maritime Museum, 1905 Ogden Avenue, Vancouver, British Columbia, Canada V6J 1A3. Telephone (604) 736-4431.

Before leaving the area of the Vancouver Maritime Museum, the visitor might well walk over to the Vancouver Museum, just a short distance away in Vanier Park. Here, the displays of maritime interest include a Nootka Indian whaling exhibit, with an eight-man whaling canoe with gear and photographs of the Indians on a whaling hunt. The museum's Exploration and Settlement gallery displays a reproduction of part of the steerage quarters of a mid-19th-century immigrant ship. Here also is a model of Captain Cook's ship, HMS *Endeavor*, in which he explored the coast of British Columbia. MacMillan Planetarium is also nearby.

Victoria

To find another fine maritime museum, the traveler should take the ferry across to the little city of Victoria, the capital of British Columbia, on Vancouver Island. The island, like the city, is named for British navigator and explorer George Vancouver, who was one of the first to sail around it and demonstrate that its 235-mile length was not a mainland peninsula. Victoria, on the southeast corner, is the island's only city; small and handsome, it has a harbor facing the Strait of Juan de Fuca, next to the Canadian Naval base at Esquimault. Built on the site of a Hudson's Bay Company post, the city is the capital of British Columbia. Many visitors are drawn to the city by its mild climate and many points of interest. Not the least of these attractions is the Maritime Museum of British Columbia.

The Maritime Museum of British Columbia is in what was once the Provincial Courthouse, close to where the original Hudson's Bay Company fort was built in 1843. As the museum's announcement puts it, it is dedicated to "the display of artifacts, models, and pictures covering the history of maritime activity in the N.E. Pacific from the days of Cook and Quadra until the present." The large collection of models emphasizes vessels that have played important roles in the development of the province: ships of the explorers and the Hudson's Bay Company, for example; work vessels such as the tugs and coastal steamers; the passenger carriers that tied the coastal settlements together; Coast Guard vessels, so vitally important on this dangerous and wreck-strewn coast.

The collection is displayed in eight theme galleries. Highlights include:

- A gallery is devoted to early explorers, who are portrayed in a row of handsome portraits. HMS *Chatham*, the armed tender that took part in Vancouver's exploration is shown in a fine model.
- Captain James Cook, the most famous of the Pacific explorers, has a gallery of his own where world globes flank a model of his ship, HMS *Resolution*.
- The Royal Navy, the Canadian Navy, and the Canadian Coast Guard each has its own gallery. A model of HMCS *Rainbow*, described as Canada's first warship, is particularly

noteworthy, as is another of the Canadian Coast Guard ship *Estevan*, a 57-year veteran of British Columbia's coastal waters. An unusual naval model is HMS *Zealous*, of the 1870s, a period of naval transition between sail and steam.

• The whaling gallery exhibits such tools of the trade as the harpoon cannon.
• Galleries devoted to coastal ships and working craft have a number of fine models, such as the CPR coastal line's *Princess Marguerite*, the salvage tug *Sudbury II*, and a self-loading log barge.

As might be expected, the Hudson's Bay Company is well-represented with models and photographs of its ships, including the famous *Beaver*, the first steamship on the coast, and the little brigantine *Cadboro*. Special exhibits display the tools of those important maritime tradesmen, the shipwrights and sailmakers. In addition, there are two very unusual small craft on the floor of the museum. *Tilikum*, a famous converted Indian canoe, was sailed all the way from Victoria to England. The voyage took three years, from 1901 to 1904. The other is *Trekka*, a yawl a little more than 20 feet long overall. The man who built her in Victoria, in 1954, then proceeded to sail her completely around the globe.

The museum has its own model builder, a fine reference library, and photographic and documentary archives. But it is the handsome models, organized into attractive and informative exhibits, that will hold

Figure 62
The stern section of HMS *Discovery*, the ship in which Captain Vancouver carried out his historic exploration of coastal British Columbia, has been recreated in a gallery of the British Columbia Provincial Museum in Victoria. The visitor enters the ship from a representation of Nootka Sound on Vancouver Island's coast. Within he finds the captain's main cabin and senior officers' sleeping places. Leaving, he steps out on a wharf typical of 18th century England.

the attention of most visitors—and at the same time expand their appreciation of the maritime traditions of Canada's Pacific West.

Maritime Museum of British Columbia is in downtown Victoria on Vancouver Island. Reference library. Maritime document archives. Open daily; July and August, 10 a.m. to 6 p.m.; balance of year, 10 a.m. to 4 p.m. Admission: $2.00; seniors, $1; children, 50 cents. Maritime Museum of British Columbia, 28 Bastion Square, Victoria, British Columbia V8W 1N9. Telephone (604) 385-4222.

Visitors to Victoria will not want to overlook the magnificent British Columbia Provincial Museum, which is only a few blocks away from the Maritime Museum. Most of the British Columbia Provincial Museum is devoted to the natural history of the province, its native inhabitants, European settlement, and the conversion of the wilderness to one of the great productive areas of Canada. However, the museum has at least one fascinating maritime exhibit: a full-scale replica of the stern portion of Captain George Vancouver's ship, HMS *Discovery*. Presented as if tied up to a typical 18th-century English wharf, this contains the cabins of Vancouver and his senior officers, fitted out with the gear and furnishings of the period. For a moment, the visitor steps 200 years into the past and feels as though he—almost—met the Captain as he is preparing to sail for the Pacific on the voyage that was to lead to the exploration and charting of the coast of British Columbia.

British Columbia Provincial Museum is at Heritage Court in downtown Victoria, on Vancouver Island. Open every day except Christmas and New Year's; 10 a.m. to 5:30 p.m. Admission free. British Columbia Provincial Museum, 675 Belleville Street, Victoria, British Columbia, Canada V8V 1X4. Telephone (604) 387-3701.

XV
THE SANDWICH ISLANDS
(HAWAII)

Honolulu and Pearl Harbor

Honolulu and Pearl Harbor

The square-rigger *Falls of Clyde*, which spent much of her working life in the Pacific, was a frequent visitor to the Hawaiian Islands, and at one time briefly flew the flag of the independent kingdom of Hawaii. Today, restored, honored and beautiful, she has found a home on the Honolulu waterfront, a prized exhibit at the Hawaii Maritime Center.

A 266-foot, iron-hulled vessel of about 1,800 net tons, the *Falls of Clyde* was built in Glasgow in 1878 for the Calcutta trade. During the next 20 years she made more than 70 voyages carrying general cargo from Europe to India and the East Indies. And then, in 1907, she embarked on a new career as one of the first bulk oil carriers. Up until that time, oil and petroleum products had been carried in individual cans but the *Falls of Clyde* was fitted with big tanks (capacity 17,500 gallons), a first step toward the enormous supertankers of today.

For the next several years the *Falls* carried petroleum from California to the Hawaiian Islands; sometimes she brought back molasses in the same tanks, a change of cargo that must have required rigorous tank cleaning.

In 1921, now a veteran of 43 years at sea, the *Falls of Clyde* reached what seemed to be the end of her active seagoing career; her masts were taken out and she became an oil barge at Ketchikan, Alaska. There, she spent the next 35 years as a floating service station, but then came a stroke of luck; someone familiar with old sailing ships admired her beautiful lines and took the first steps that eventually led to her salvage and restoration. Karl Kortum, Director of the National Maritime Museum in San Francisco, played a major role in finding the *Falls* a home in Honolulu. The search for support took so long, however, that the old ship had a narrow escape from becoming part of a breakwater in Vancouver.

Falls of Clyde has now been restored to her original rig as a four-masted ship, making her the only one of the type still afloat. She is also the only remaining sail-driven oil tanker. Both her fourth mast with its square yards and her big oil tanks are distinctive aspects of the vessel, adding interest to a visit to her at her berth alongside Honolulu's Pier 7.

Here are some other things to watch for:

- the original wheel, cabins, and deckhouse, which survived the vicissitudes of her life as a barge;
- the oil pumps, which date from her career as a tanker;
- the crew's quarters.

There are few more appropriate places than Honolulu for an elderly windjammer to find a retirement home. Despite the clash between Europeans and islanders that led to the killing of Captain James Cook in 1778, the Hawaiians were generally friendly to visitors all through the 19th century. Honolulu, which is one of only two good harbors in the islands (neighboring Pearl Harbor is the other), became a port of call for ships of many nations crossing or cruising the Pacific. Whaleships, naval vessels, cargo carriers, island traders, missionary schooners, all found a welcome, as well as fresh water, supplies, repairs if necessary, and an opportunity to give the crews a run ashore. After sugar cultivation began, there were also cargoes to deliver and pick up and Honolulu began its evolution from a remote island harbor into a great world port.

But actually Hawaii's maritime past stretches far further back in time than the European ships of the 19th and 20th century. Polynesians are believed to have discovered, and settled, the then uninhabited Hawaiian Islands around 500 A.D. To do it, these daring explorers and skilled seamen sailed north from islands far to the southward, crossing two or three thousand miles of open ocean in double-hull voyaging canoes lashed together with coconut sennit. Using no instruments, these ancient navigators set their course

by observing the stars and planets, the direction of trade winds and ocean swells, the flight paths of birds, and other natural phenomena.

The magnificent maritime heritage of Hawaiians and their Polynesian ancestors is commemorated by the vessel berthed next to the *Falls* at Pier 7. The *Hokule'a* is a full-sized replica of a double-hulled Polynesian canoe. Built in 1976, she has already made voyages from Hawaii to Tahiti without the aid of instruments. *Hokule'a*, now also a part of the Hawaii Maritime Center, operates as a floating classroom and will continue experimental voyages.

Both the Polynesian and European elements in Hawaii's maritime past will be explored, described, and displayed in the third part of the Hawaii Maritime Center in the Aloha Tower and a new shoreside facility on Pier 7. The Tower, for more than 50 years a landmark on the Honolulu waterfront, has been converted into a maritime museum. Currently a modest ninth-floor exhibit focuses on historic ships and the history of Honolulu Harbor; displays include ship models, artifacts, photographs, and documents. The Maritime Center plans to cover virtually every aspect of Hawaii's unique and colorful maritime past, starting with the canoe voyages that long preceded any contact with Europeans. Other exhibits will include such topics as early European exploration, whaling, merchant sail, U.S. Navy activities, and travel in the Pacific.

The Hawaii Maritime Center and restored windjammer *Falls of Clyde* are on Honolulu waterfront, close to Bishop Street and Nimitz Highway. Parking nearby. Center museum is in ninth floor of Aloha Tower, scheduled to expand throughout building by 1987. At same pier: *Hokule'a*, full-scale replica of Polynesian canoe (may be away on cruises). Open all year, daily 9:30 a.m. to 4 p.m. (Museum closed on Sunday.) Admission to museum free. Admission to ship: $3.00; children, $1.50. Hawaii Maritime Center, Pier 7, Honolulu Harbor, Honolulu, Hawaii 96813. Telephone (808) 523-6373.

Figure 63
Archival photograph shows the four-masted square rigger *Falls of Clyde* many years ago under sail, probably off the California coast. After many vicissitudes, the old ship (built 1878) has found restoration and a retirement berth at the Hawaii Maritime Center in Honolulu. (National Maritime Museum photograph)

Now to Pearl Harbor, and a memorial to those who died in a tragic moment in American Naval history.

At 7:35 on the morning of December 7, 1941, "Pearl Harbor was still asleep in the morning mist. It was calm and serene inside the harbor." So recalled the commander of the first formation of enemy planes to arrive at the American naval base. At 7:55, the Japanese planes were diving to the attack. At 7:56, the battleship *West Virginia* was hit by a torpedo, the first of five or six she took, and the battleship *Oklahoma* had taken three torpedoes and begun to capsize. At 8:10 the battleship *Arizona* was hit by an armor-piercing bomb in her forward magazine and exploded. By 8:19

Arizona had sunk in 38 feet of water, carrying with her more than 1,100 of her crew.

About 1,000 of them are aboard her still, their final resting place the ship they died defending. As their memorial, a gleaming white structure has been built over the sunken battleship, resting on piles so that it straddles the sunken hull. The elongated building, 184 feet long, 27 to 36 feet wide, "sags in the center but stands strong and vigorous at the ends," according to architect, Alred Preis, in order to express "initial defeat and ultimate victory." His description continues, "Wide openings in walls and roof permit a flooding by sunlight and a close view of the sunken battleship eight feet below, both fore and aft. At low tide, as the sun shines upon the hull, the barnacles which encrust it shimmer like gold jewels . . . a beautiful sarcophagus."

Within the USS *Arizona* Memorial is a shrine room where the names of the 1,177 Navy men and U.S. Marines killed in the *Arizona* are inscribed on a marble wall. Beside the Memorial the American flag flies every day from a staff mounted on a part of the battleship that is still above water.

The *Arizona* Memorial, which is now managed by the National Park Service, is reached from the Visitors Center ashore by Navy shuttle boats. On arrival at the center visitors receive a numbered ticket (no advance reservations are possible). When the number of a group is called, the visitors first go to the small theater in the center to hear an informative talk by a Park Ranger and see a documentary film on the Pearl Harbor attack; then are taken out to the memorial by a shuttle boat.

BIBLIOGRAPHY

Part One: Where It All Began: Atlantic and Gulf Coasts

I. *New England (and Its Stepchild, Long Island)*

The most important source of information for this section of this guide was *New England and the Sea* by Robert G. Albion, William A. Baker, and Benjamin W. Labaree (Mystic, Connecticut: Mystic Seaport Museum, 1972). The work is broad in scope and filled with interesting detail.

Throughout much of this section, Samuel Eliot Morison's classic *Maritime History of Massachusetts* was also essential. It is directly quoted in the section on Salem and briefly in reference to Nantucket. Any reader unfamiliar with this fine book is urged to hasten to enjoy it.

A yachtsman's view of New England's little harbors is presented in *A Cruising Guide to the New England Coast* by Roger R. Duncan and John P. Ware (New York: Dodd, Mead, 1972). *Salt Rivers of the Massachusetts Shore* by Henry Howe (New York: Rinehart, 1951) is particularly helpful in providing geographical and ecological background, as well as local maritime history.

Portrait of a Port—Boston 1852-1952 by W. H. Bunting (Cambridge, Massachusetts: Harvard University Press, 1971) is a wonderful collection of photographs, some very rare, with an extremely helpful text illuminating the changes in the port. "Old Ironsides," Oliver Wendell Holmes's stirring poem can, of course, be found in many anthologies. Two pamphlets, *The Constitution's Gun Deck* and *The Constitution's Fighting Top*, both by John C. Reilly, Jr. and both published by the Naval Historical Center, Washington, D.C., are filled with helpful information.

The background of the Tea Party ships is supplied in *Catalyst for Revolution: The Boston Tea Party, 1774* by Benjamin W. Labaree (Boston, Massachusetts: no publisher or date).

In the description of the area north of Boston, the quotation about ship models and art galleries is from "A Note on the Collection" by the editor, John Ratte, in *Models of American Sailing Ships* (Andover, Massachusetts: Addison Gallery of American Art, Philipps Academy, 1961), a "handbook" of the gallery's collection. With a picture of each model and an explanatory text, the little book is both handsome and useful.

Salem and its Peabody Museum are well described in "When Salem Ruled the Waves" (no author) in the November-December issue of *Contact* (Vol. IX, No. 2).

The Portsmouth Athenaeum by Lawrence R. Craig and James L. Garvin (Portsmouth, New Hampshire: The Portsmouth Athenaeum, 1966) fills in the history of that venerable institution. The poem quoted about Pulpit Rock was written by James Kennard, Jr. in the early nineteenth century. It is quoted in *The Piscataqua Gundalow, Workhorse for a Tidal Basin Empire* (Portsmouth, New Hampshire: Portsmouth Marine Society, 1983) by Edward E. Winslow III. His valuable book discusses both the original vessel and the full-scale reproduction that has been built at Portsmouth.

Shipping in York by Laurie Carpenter (York, Maine: Society for the Preservation of Historic Landmarks in York County, 1972) recounts the maritime history of the little Maine port that has preserved the John Hancock warehouse. The winning entry in a student essay contest, it is skillfully written and filled with interesting facts.

Steamboating on Moosehead Lake is the subject of articles by Walter E. Macdougal and others in *Maine Lakes Steamboat Album*, (Camden, Maine: Down East Enterprise, Inc., 1976). Well illustrated, the articles help to fill in the background of this region and of little ships.

For material about the area south of Boston there is Henry David Thoreau's *Cape Cod*, which continues, of course, to be reprinted in a number of editions as is Herman Melville's *Moby Dick*, also quoted several times. The little port of Duxbury's maritime past is recalled in *Tall Ships of Duxbury*, a pamphlet by Frederick T. Potter (Duxbury, Massachusetts: Duxbury Rural and Historical Society, 1982).

The story of what may be the oldest vessel to survive in New England—even as remains—is told in *Sparrow-Hawk—A Seventeenth Century Vessel in Twentieth Century New England* by H. H. Holly. The pamphlet is published by the Pilgrim Society (Plymouth, Massachusetts, 1969) whose museum displays the skeleton of the wrecked ship.

Mayflower II, the recreation of the Pilgrims' ship now gracing the Plymouth waterfront, was the design of William Avery Baker. Baker, the noted marine architect of historic vessels, described the intensive research involved in developing her plans and rig in *The New Mayflower, Her Design and Construction* (Barre, Massachusetts: Barre Gazette, 1958). This is a book of great interest to anyone interested in sailing ships of the past.

The background of Nantucket is filled in by *Rambling Through the Streets of Nantucket* by Edward A. Stackpole (Nantucket, Massachusetts: published by the author, 1981). The illuminating details about the old town, its houses, and the people who lived in them gradually builds a picture of the shore side of the island's maritime traditions.

Various issues of the *Dukes County Intelligenser*, published periodically by the Dukes County Historical Society, help to do the same thing for the sister island, Martha's Vineyard.

"Battle of Stonington" and "Battle in Retrospect," two articles by Captain Frank C. Lynch, U.S.N. (Ret.) in *Historical Footnotes*, help us to understand the amphibious attack on the little town. They were in the August 1969 issue of that periodical, which is published by the Stonington Historical Society.

Exploring visitors will find helpful *Built by the Whalers: A Tour of Historic Sag Harbor* by Nancy Boyd Willey (Sag Harbor, New York: Old Sagg Harbour Committee, 1945). From the same east end of Long Island comes the useful *Suffolk Maritime Folklife* (Sayville, New York: Office of Cultural Affairs, 1981).

II. *New York and Its Inland Empire*

In addition to the New York Work Projects Administration guide, like all such guides an invaluable publication, another publication is a helpful reference: *A Maritime History of the Port of New York*, compiled by The New York City WPA Writers' Project (Garden City, New York: Doubleday, Doran, 1941).

Alan Villier's *Way of a Ship* (New York: Scribners, 1953) will multiply many times over a visitor's appreciation of *Peking* at the South Street Seaport—and is also very much worth reading for its own sake. The Seaport has a number of leaflets and other small publications of its own that are very helpful, as are issues of the South Street's magazine,

Seaport. Maritime New York in Nineteenth Century Photographs by Harry Johnson and Frederick S. Lightfoot (New York: Dover Publications, 1980) is an attractive book that shows South Street at its prime.

The story of the Hudson River and the inception of the Erie Canal is told in the fascinating book *The Hudson* by Carl Carmer (New York: Farrar and Rinehart, 1939). The quoted poem on the opening of the Erie Canal is from Carmer's book, one of the best of the *Rivers of America* series.

The prototypes of the sloop *Clearwater* are ably described in *The Sloops of the Hudson* by William E. Verplanck and Moses W. Collyer (Port Washington, New York: Ira J. Friedman, Inc., 1968). The periodical, *Clearwater Navigator* (Poughkeepsie, New York: Vol. XIV, September/October 1983) is a good fill-in on today's sloop.

Old Towpaths: The Story of the American Canal Era by Alvin Harlow (Port Washington, New York: Kennikat Press, 1926) is a very useful history of the Erie and other American canals. Pamphlets published by the various canal museums are also helpful. Samuel Eliot Morison in his *Samuel de Champlain* (Boston, Massachusetts: Atlantic Monthly Press, 1972) gives a vivid account of the great explorer's warlike arrival at the lake that bears his name. *The War of the American Revolution* by Christopher Ward (New York: Macmillan, 1952) gives a fine account of events on Lake Champlain in that conflict; *The Birth of the United States Navy*, a pamphlet by Doris Begar Morton (Whitehall, New York: Whitehall Times, 1982) explains Whitehall's claim to be the birthplace.

Alfred Thayer Mahan gives a full account of the Battle of Plattsburgh on Lake Champlain in his *Sea Power in Relation to the War of 1812* (Boston, Massachusetts: Little, Brown, 1905). The USS *Ticonderoga*, the veteran of that battle, has been raised and exhibited and is the subject of exhaustive study in *The History and Construction of the Schooner Ticonderoga* by Kevin James Grisman (Alexandria, Virginia: Eyrie Publications, 1983). Another angle is presented by the pamphlet *Battle of Plattsburgh Bay—The British Navy's View* by Oscar Bredenberg (Plattsburgh, New York: Chester County Historical Association, 1926).

Interesting color on the Champlain Canal is provided in *My Canaling Days* by Martha Robbins Juckett (Whitehall, New York: Historical Society of Whitehall, 1985).

III. *The Road to Canada*

Two of America's most masterful historians have dealt with the early maritime history of the St. Lawrence. Samuel Eliot Morison discusses the early explorers in both his *European Discovery of America: The*

Northern Voyages—1492-1616 (New York: Oxford University Press, 1971) and in his biography, *Samuel de Champlain*. Francis Parkman's great history centers on New France. *Pioneers of France in the New World, Count Frontenac and New France under Louis XIV*, and *The Old Regime in Canada* are particularly concerned with events along the St. Lawrence. (Boston, Massachusetts: Little Brown, 1901.)

Montreal by Stephen Leacock (Garden City, New York: Doubleday, Doran, 1942) recounts the history of the city in an interesting fashion, although with rather less maritime information than one would hope for. The *St. Lawrence* by Henry Beston (New York: Rinehart) in the *Rivers of America* series naturally puts the river center stage.

More specific maritime information—perhaps not quite as popularized—is preserved in *From Sail to Steam—Ships and Shipbuilding in the Region of Quebec and Montreal*. Written by Diana Dutton and a number of others, this well-illustrated volume is a companion to a 1982 special exhibition at the Marsil Musuem of Saint Lambert, in Quebec Province, and was published by the museum. What is almost a companion volume is the *Saint Lawrence, 1900-1960* by Alain Franck. Dealing with a later period, it also focuses on ships and shipbuilding, as well as the development of the river. (L'Islet-sur-Mer, Quebec: Musée Maritime Bernier.)

Finally, even those who read French with difficulty will enjoy the many fine illustrations in *Les goelettes à voiles du Saint-Laurent* also by Alain Franck (L'Islet-sur-Mer, Quebec: 1984). *Goelette* means schooner while *voiles* are sails. The book is a full discussion of regional coasting craft especially designed for the little St. Lawrence harbors where vessels were left sitting on the bottom when the tide went out.

IV. *Canada's Atlantic Provinces*

Here, as in so many sections, Samuel Eliot Morison's *European Discovery of America—The Northern Voyages* is invaluable for the early explorations and also makes wonderful reading.

The Atlantic Provinces—Emergence of Colonial Society by W. S. McNutt (Toronto: McClelland and Stewart, 1965) gives a broad view of the early period that is most helpful.

The quoted Bliss Carmen verses about Saint John, New Brunswick are from the "Ships of Saint John" in Bliss Carmen's *Poems* (New York: Dodd, Mead, 1931). The description of the New Brunswick Museum in Saint John is in a communication to the writer from Robert S. Elliot, assistant curator, Department of Canadian History at the museum.

In *Canada's Smallest Province—A History of Prince Edward Island*, edited by Francis W. P. Bolger (Prince Edward Island: Centennial Commission, 1973), various specialists cover many aspects of the island's history. Their articles are most useful in understanding the background.

The vivid anecdote about dory fishing by a Prince Edward man, John Hemphill, are from the P.E.I. magazine *The Island* (Number 11, Spring-Summer, 1982) as is the account of the island's fisheries in 1803, written by Edward Walsh, a medical officer in the British Army. Stopping over on his way to Quebec, he recorded in his diary all he learned about the island.

Nova Scotia, the oldest of the three Maritimes, has been well covered. *Samuel de Champlain* by Samuel Eliot Morison deals with the early French exploration and settlement. Francis Parkman also writes about the period before the final British conquest in two volumes of his landmark work on New France: *Pioneers of France in the New World* and *The Jesuits in North America in the Seventeenth Century*.

The quotation about fishing and farming by early Nova Scotians is from *Acadia—The Geography of Early Nova Scotia* by Andrew Hill Clark (Madison, Wisconsin: University of Wisconsin Press, 1968). This interesting work ties together the environment of the region and its political and economic history.

John B. Brebner's *New England's Outpost: Acadia Before the Conquest of Canada* (New York: Columbia University Press, 1927) is of great help in filling in the colonial background of Acadia/Nova Scotia. It will be of particular interest to New England readers, who are likely to be unfamiliar with this segment of history.

The maritime activities of the region during their peak period in the nineteenth and early twentieth centuries have been covered in a number of interesting volumes. One that is recommended to readers is *Masters of the Sail—The Era of Square-Rigged Vessels in the Maritime Provinces* by Stanley T. Spicer (Halifax: Petheric Press, Ltd., 1968).

Francis Silver: 1841-1920 (Halifax, Nova Scotia: The Art Gallery of Nova Scotia, 1982) tells the story of the self-taught primitive painter of Hantsport. Lavishly illustrated with pictures of Silver's work, the book was published in conjunction with a traveling exhibition.

The history of Halifax is told in interesting fashion in *Halifax, Warden of the North* by Thomas H. Raddall (New York: Doubleday, 1965). The economic base of her small but famous neighbor down the coast is explored in detail in *The History of the Lunenberg Fishing Industry* by B.A. Balcom (Lunenburg, Nova Scotia: Lunenburg Marine Museum Society, 1977). The reader will learn a good deal about deep-sea fishing vessels and techniques as well as about Lunenburg. A very different and non-maritime aspect of the town that fascinates every visitor is described, explained, and illustrated in *Understanding Lunenburg's Arhcitecture* by Bill Plaskell (Nova Scotia: Lunenburg Heritage Society, 1982).

The saga account of Leif the Lucky's visit to North America is from "The Vinland History of the Flat Island Book," translated by Arthur Middleton Reeves. Originally published in England in 1890, it appeared in New York in Reeves's *The Finding of Vinland the Good*, published by Burt Franklin (n.d.). It is probably more accessible to most readers in *The Northmen, Columbus and Cabot, 985-1503*, edited by E.G. Bowne (New York: Scribners, 1925). Later translations have been made by others. Readers will enjoy reading the entire saga, which gives us a vivid picture of a long-forgotten world.

Morison's *Northern Voyages* is particularly interesting in its discussion of Vinland and Leif's discoveries. Morison visited and photographed the settlement site at L'Anse aux Meadows, Newfoundland.

Morison also is a fine source for reading about the early voyages to Newfoundland by John Cabot and those who followed him in the early years.

V. *The Middle Atlantic Coast: Raritan Bay to the North Carolina Line*

For this section, the 1904 edition of the *United States Coast Pilot: Atlantic Coast Part V*, "New York to Cheseapeake Bay Entrance," (Washington, D.C.: Government Printing Office) was particularly evocative of the nation's maritime past. Any vessel approaching the coast in clear weather "will be apprised of her approach to the land by the number of sail sighted."
Early maritime activities along the Jersey shore, a remote and little-known area, are recounted in *Smugglers Woods* by A.D. Pierce (New Brunswick, New Jersey: Rutgers University Press, 1960). The quotation about the Pennsylvania authorities' attitudes toward pirates is from this book, which emphasizes the area's long involvement in smuggling, privateering, and—eventually—rum-running as convenient sources of income.

For the ports in the Middle Atlantic colonies, as for others, a useful source of information is *Ports of Call* by Robert Carse (New York: Scribners, 1967).

The great bay south and west of New Jersey is vividly pictured and described in *The Bay and River Delaware: A Pictorial History* by David Budlong Tyler (Cambridge, Maryland: Cornell Maritime Press, 1955). The early days of the great port on the river are compellingly described in *Philadelphia, Port of History, 1609-1837* (Philadelphia, Pennsylvania: Philadelphia Maritime Museum, 1976). Of the several pieces,

"Maritime Philadelphia" by Marion Brewington, which is quoted in this portion of the guide, is particularly interesting.

Anyone visiting the ship *Moshulu* on the Philadelphia riverfront will be interested in reading *Windjammer* by Eric Newby. The author shipped aboard the *Moshulu* many years ago and the core of his book is a wonderful set of pictures of the vessel at sea. The background of another ship exhibited nearby, the famous protected cruiser *Olympia*, are explored in "Olympian Legacy" by Cdr. John D. Alden U.S.N.R. (Ret.). The account originally appeared in a 1976 issue of the United States Naval Institute's *Proceedings* and has been reprinted in *Penn's Landing: Crossroads of the Past*.

The other great bay and its rivers and ports have been the subjects of many interesting books. *This Was Chesapeake Bay* by Robert M. Burgess (Centreville, Maryland: Tidewater Publishers, 1982) is a collection of articles about various aspects of the bay by the retired curator of the Mariners Museum in Newport News. Brought together and nicely illustrated, they provide a wide range of information. The various distinctive Chesapeake small craft, including skipjacks, are published by the Chesapeake Bay Maritime Museum in St. Michael's, Maryland. The description of Chesapeake bugeyes in this section of the guide is from one of these museum pamphlets: *The Edna E. Lockwood* by Charles E. Kepner (1979).

The great port on the upper Chesapeake is the subject of *Baltimore Harbor—A Picture History* by Robert C. Keith (Baltimore, Maryland: Ocean World Publishing, 1985). *Baltimore on the Chesapeake* by Hamilton Owen (New York: Doubleday, Doran, 1941) is a useful volume in the *Seaport* series.

Readers who want to know more about the ill-fated *Pride of Baltimore* will be interested in the heavily illustrated little book with that title by Evelyn Chisolm (Baltimore, Maryland: Baltimore Operation Sail, Ltd., 1977). The *Constellation's* career is fully described in a pamphlet, *The Constellation, Yankee Racehorse*, by Sanford Steinlicht and Edwin M. Jameson (Cockeysville, Maryland: Liberty Publishing Company, 1981). The personal side of the ship is told in a booklet: *Yankee Tar: The Life of a Seaman Aboard the Constellation* by Michael Morgan (published by the author, 1980). The somewhat technical controversy between experts about the rebuilding and/or repair of the *Constellation* in the mid-nineteenth century is represented in *The Constellation Question* by Howard I. Chapelle and Leon D. Poland. There is enough here to keep maritime history buffs arguing for many a long winter night.

The recreated seventeenth-century vessel berthed at St. Mary's City is handsomely pictured in

The Maryland Dove by Burt Kammerow (St. Mary's City, Maryland: St. Mary's City Commission, n.d.). The description of the departure from England of the expedition in which the original *Dove* took part is from *A Briefe Relation of the Voyage Unto Maryland*, by Father Andrew White (1634). The quotation is made more accessible in "Andrew White, Apostle to Maryland, 1633-1645" by Robert Emmet Curran, S.J. in *The Pious and Noble Purpose* (Washington, D.C.: Paul VI Institute of the Arts) in which various writers discuss aspects of the St. Mary's settlement.

The Potomac by Frederick Gutheim (New York: Rinehart, 1949) is one of the *Rivers of America* series. *This was Potomac River* by Frederick Tilp (Alexandria, Virginia: published by the author, 1979) is loosely organized but crammed with detail. This book is written by a man who obviously loves the river and its history and has spent many years exploring both. In the National Museum of American History section, the Mahan quotation is from *The Major Operations of the Navies in the War of American Independence* (London: Sampson Low, Marsten and Co., 1913). Accounts of Jamestown and John Smith are found in many places. The quotation by an eyewitness to the siege of Yorktown is from *A Military Journal During the American Revolutionary War, from 1775-1783* by James Thatcher, M.D. (Boston, Massachusetts: Cottons and Barnard, 1827). Most people are more likely to find it quoted in *The Spirit of Seventy Six* (New York: Harper and Row, 1967), a wonderful collection of original materials about the American Revolution, edited by Henry Steele Commager and Richard B. Morris. The importance of the Battle of the Capes is made clear in Alfred Thayer Mahan's *Major Operations of the Navies in the War of American Independence*.

The relatively brief but very interesting history of the port of Newport News is recounted in *Endless Harbor—The Story of Newport News* by Park Rose, Jr. (Newport News, Virginia: Newport News Historical Committee, 1969). The long past of the other major Hampton Roads port is recounted in *Norfolk, Historic Southern Port* by Thomas J. Wertenbaker (Durham, North Carolina: Duke University Press, 1931).

VI. *The South Facing the Atlantic*

Early explorations of this coast are included in Samuel Eliot Morison's *European Discovery of America—The Northern Voyages*. Here also the reader will find the tragic story of Raleigh's Lost Colony.

The story of Cape Hatteras and its people is told in *The Hatterasman* by Ben Dixon MacNeill (Winston-Salem, North Carolina: John F. Blair, pub., 1958). The source of, among other things, the anecdote about the relative aesthetics of wives and ships, MacNeill's book is most interesting and highly recommended. A look at Cape Hatteras today is presented in *The Ouoter Banks* by Patrick D. Crosland (Arlington, Virginia: Interpretive Publications, n.d.) and another is included in *Atlantic Beaches* by Jonathan T. Leonard (New York: Time-Life Books, 1972). Both are heavily illustrated with striking photographs.

The background of Beaufort is filled in with interesting historical details by *The Old Port Town—Beaufort, North Carolina* by a local resident, Jean Bruyere Kell (Beaufort, North Carolina: published by the author, 1980). The quotations about the town as a Civil War liberty port are from *Three Years* by I.E. Vail and others, originally published in 1902 (New York: Abbey Press), but more accessible in an article on the blockade, "Men, Monotony, and Mouldy Beans," by James M. Merril, in the January 1936 *American Neptune*, or in *Thirty Years of the American Neptune* (Cambridge, Massachusetts: Harvard University Press, 1972) where it is reprinted.

The fine fearsome description of Cape Fear has been quoted many times; it is said to have originally appeared in the *Atlantic Monthly* in the 1870s. The Cape Fear River is the subject of Malcolm Ross' *The Cape Fear* (New York: Holt, Rinehart, and Winston, 1965), one of the *Rivers of America* series, which covers the early river ports.

The quotation about blockade running into the Cape Fear River is from *Never Caught, the Story of a Blockade Runner*, a first-person account written under the pseudonym of "Captain Roberts" (Carolina Beach, North Carolina: Blockade Runner Museum, 1967). This is a fascinating picture, written from first-hand experience, originally published shortly after the Civil War.

The design of the recreated seventeenth-century ship at Charles Towne Landing is discussed by its creator, William A. Baker, in *The Carolina and Adventure* (Charleston, South Carolina: Charles Towne Landing, n.d.). A running account of the Confederate submarine *Hunley* is included in *The Civil War in Charleston* by Arthur M. Wilcox and Warren Ripley (Charleston, South Carolina: News and Courier, 1983). The book is heavily illustrated with contemporary engravings and photographs.

As noted in the text, J. Bryan's *Aircraft Carrier* gives a vivid picture of life aboard the carrier *Yorktown* during combat in World War II (New York: Ballantine Books, 1954). The book, now available as a paperback, is highly recommended.

The account of Savannah is based, in considerable part, on *The Savannah River* by Thomas L. Stokes, another of the *Rivers of America* series (New York: Rinehart and Company, 1951). Readers who desire to know more about the Civil War in a remote corner of the South, closely related to the building of the river gunboats at Columbus, Georgia, will find them described in "Naval Operations in the Apalachicola and Chattahoochee Rivers, 1861-1865" by Maxine Turner (*Alabama Historical Quarterly*: XXXVI, Fall-Winter, 1974-75).

VII. *The Gulf Coast*

The early Spanish exploration of the Gulf Coast is recounted in Samuel Eliot Morison's *The European Discovery of America: The Southern Voyages 1492-1616* (New York: Oxford University Press, 1974). From *Pirates to Pilots—A Political History of the Pensacola Navy, 1528 to Present*, edited by Shirley M. Deacon (Pensacola Engraving Company, 1975), is a rather informal, illustrated history of the port. Some ports along the Gulf are discussed in *American Cities in the Growth of the Nation* by Constance M. Green (1957).

Descriptions of Farragut's passage of Fort Morgan at Mobile Bay will be found in every Civil War history. Mobile, the port at the head of the bay, is the subject of a number of interesting books, among them *Mobile, Industrial Seaport and Trade Center* by Edward L. Ullman (Chicago, Illinois: The University of Chicago, 1943). A Ph.D. dissertation, Ullman's book is particularly thorough and valuable.

New Orleans is, of course, a magnet for writers, but few deal with its maritime activities. An exception is *The Port of New Orleans* by Harold Sinclair (New Orleans: Tulane University Press, 1968). The article "Gateway to the Americas" by James P. Baughman is also valuable. It will be found in the collection about New Orleans called *Past as Prelude: New Orleans 1718-1968*, edited by Hodding Carter (Gretna, Louisiana: Pelican, 1968).

The striking history of Galveston is recounted in *The Galveston Era* by Earle W. Fornell (Austin, Texas: University of Texas Press, 1961). Galveston's favorite ship, *Elissa*, gets a full take out in the Winter 1983 (No. 20) issue of *Sea History*, including an article on the tremendous problems faced in her restoration.

Equally broad coverage of a unique vessel, the battleship *Texas*, is to be found in the April 1985 issue (Vol. 43, No. 4) of *Texas Parks and Highways* in "USS Texas: The Ship and the Myth" by Walter H. Rybka. The quoted description of the hit suffered by the USS *Texas* off Cherbourg is contained in a personal communication from correspondent Wilmot Ragsdale to the writer. The battleship's predecessor namesakes are explored in "Texas on the High Seas" by Jim Steely in *Texas Highways*, November 1975. The same magazine ran an interesting article with a confusingly similar name but quite a different subject in February 1983: "Texans on the High Seas" by Bess Whitehead Scott. This one deals with the little-known activities of the Texas navy during the period of independence.

VIII. *The Ohio Country*

Western steamboats are well described in *Life on the River* by Norbury L. Wayman (New York: Crown, 1971).

The two lines by Carl Sandburg are from his *Collected Poems* (New York: Harcourt Brace, 1950). The critical remarks on canal boating by John Quincy Adams are quoted in *The Colorful Era of the Ohio Canal* by James S. and Margot Jackson (Cleveland: The Ohio Canal Sesquicentennial Commission, 1977). The former president made them in a letter to a friend in 1843. The canal song is quoted in *Canals of the Ohio 1825-1913* (Columbus, Ohio: Ohio Historical Society, n.d.).

There are articles on a wide variety of Ohio Canal topics in *Western Reserve Magazine*, July-August 1982—a major source of information.

More canal background is contained in two small booklets published by the Roscoe Village Fuondation, Coshocton, Ohio: *Introduction to Roscoe Village* by Nancy Lowe Lonsinger and *The Big Ditch—Small Stories of the Ohio Canals* by Jim Baker (1983).

A general history of the state is *The History of Ohio* by Eugene H. Roseboom (Columbus, Ohio: Ohio Historical Society, 1969), although it does not contain a great deal of information on lake or river vessels.

IX. *The Mississippi*

There are many editions of Mark Twain's wonderful *Life on the Mississippi*; the edition used for the quotation about the palatial steamships was published by James R. Osgood, Boston, in 1883.

Twain's book is, of course, the classic first-hand account of pre-Civil War Mississippi steamboating that should be read by everyone. Wayman's *Life on the River* has considerable specific information about hulls and engines and is also a fine source of information on the Missouri River. *Mississippi Steamboatin'* by Herbert and Edward Quick (New York: Holt, 1926) presents a more recent overview than Twain's.

The comments by the Keokuk newspaper *Gate City* on the arrival of the SS *Verity* are quoted in *The George M. Verity Story* by David Tschbiggfrie. (Keokuk, Iowa: Keokuk River Museum, n.d.)

The fall and rise—after a fashion—of the USS *Cairo* are treated in illuminating detail in *Hardluck Ironclad: The Sinking and Salvage of the Cairo* by Edwin

C. Bearss (Baton Rouge, Louisiana: University of Louisiana Press, 1986).

The submarine that has found a home in the Arkansas River is described in *The History of the USS Batfish—America's Killer Sub* (Washington, D.C.: Naval History Division, Navy Department, n.d.)

X. *"Those Grand Fresh-Water Seas of Ours"*

The maritime history and background of the Great Lakes, both individually and collectively, have been well covered. One of the most interesting is *Great Lakes Reader*, edited by Walter Havighurst (New York: Macmillan, 1978), a wide-ranging collection of original materials from many periods and people. Mary Palmer's account of the wreck of the *Walk-in-the-Water*, now in the archives of the Buffalo and Erie County Historical Society, quoted in the Lake Erie section of this guide, is in the Havighurst *Reader*. *Long Ships Passing: Ships of the Great Lakes* by Walter Buehr (New York: G.P. Putnam & Sons, 1956) is more sharply focused on maritime matters. The lake captain's prayer, quoted in the introductory passage of this section of the guide, is from this very readable work.

The early European—largely French—exploration of the Great Lakes, and the subsequent Anglo-French struggle to control them, are discussed in a number of Francis Parkman's volumes on French Canada. In particular, the lakes are the scene of much that takes place in *La Salle and the Discovery of the Great West* and *The Jesuits in the New World in the Seventeenth Century*. As mentioned elsewhere, Parkman was not only a great historian but a writer whose work holds the reader as tightly as any novel.

The special small craft used and developed for lakes and rivers are interestingly explored in "The North American Fur Trade" by Robert C. Wheeler in *A History of Seafaring Based on Underwater Archaelogy*, edited by George F. Bass (New York: Walker and Company, 1972). Howard C. Chapelle's *American Small Craft* also deals, rather technically, with special types.

The extensive naval operations on the lakes are thoroughly explained in Alfred T. Mahan's *Sea Power in Relation to the War of 1812*. The reader will find this episode and recent marine archaeological discoveries about it described and beautifully illustrated in "Ghost Ships of the War of 1812" by Daniel A. Nelson in the March 1983 issue of *National Geographic* (Vol. 163, No. 3). *The Fate of the Lakes, a Portrait of the Great Lakes* by James P. Barry (Toronto, Ontario: G.R. Welch, 1972) focuses on the St. Lawrence Seaway.

The description of an eighteenth-century lake schooner told in relation to an episode on Lake Huron is quoted from an interesting little brochure, *HMS Nancy and the War of 1812* (Ontario Ministry of Natural Resources, 1978).

Several quotations in this section are from the excellent *Great Lakes* series, a major source of information on this region. The striking description of Lake Erie's storms is from *Lake Erie* by Harlan Hatcher. Father Vimont's description of Nicolet's meeting with the Wisconsin Indians is quoted in *Lake Michigan* by Milo M. Quaife. The Merman testimony is reported in *Lake Superior* by Grace Lee Nute. Captain Alexander McDougall's account of his whaleback design, from his *Autobiography*, is also quoted in this work. All three of these books were published by Bobbs Merrill, Indianapolis—Erie in 1944, the others a year later.

The other two works in the series, *Lake Ontario* by Arthur Pound (New York: Bobbs Merrill, 1945) and *Lake Huron* by Paul Landon (New York: Russell and Russell, 1972), are equally valuable.

The Haida by William Sclater (Markham, Ontario: Paperjacks, Ltd., 1980), quoted in the Lake Ontario section, is still in print. The Canadian destroyers were in extensive and exciting action in World War II and the book is highly recommended. Navy-minded readers should also look for *20 Million Tons Under the Sea* by Rear Admiral Daniel V. Gallery (Chicago: Regnery, 1957) of which a portion is quoted in slightly condensed form in the Lake Michigan section of this guide.

The quotation about the loss of the *Alvin Clark*, also in the Lake Michigan section, is quoted from "Alvin Clark: An Unfinished Voyage" by C. T. McCutcheon, Jr. in the May-June 1983 issue of *Wooden Boat* (No. 52). This issue has other articles on the same subject and is particularly recommended to anyone interested in the problems of salvaging wooden vessels long underwater. Incidentally, a far more recent and deadlier sinking is reported in detail in *The Wreck of the Edmund Fitzgerald* by Frederick Stonehouse (Au Train, Michigan: Avery Color Studios, 1982). The battered lifeboats from this wreck, discussed in the Lake Superior section, can be seen at Sault Ste. Marie, Michigan.

XI. *To the North: Manitoba*

Much of the early history of the fur trade to the Great Lakes and northward is covered in Francis Parkman's *France and England in North America*, particularly volumes one and two of *A Half Century of Conflict* (Boston, Massachusetts: Little Brown, 1901).

The history of the Hudson's Bay Company is attractively presented—from the viewpoint of the company itself—by the bicentennial issue of *Beaver*, the H.B.C. magazine, in "The Hudson's Bay Company and the Fur Trade: 1690-1870," by Professor Glyndwr Williams. Beautifully illustrated, this tells a great deal in a small space.

The stories of the *Nonsuch*, the pioneer fur trade ship, and of its modern recreation are told in an interesting book, *The Nonsuch*, by Laird Rankin (Toronto, Ontario: Clarke, Irvin, and Co., Ltd., 1974). Activities in the early years are attractively presented in a small illustrated booklet, *York Boats and Buffalo Robes—The Fur Trade at Lower Fort Garry* (Parks Canada).

The history and background of this part of Canada are unfamiliar to many visitors from south of the border. Those who would like to explore aspects of early Manitoba beyond the activities on its lakes and rivers will find two books of interest: *The Metis—Canada's Forgotten People* by S. Bruce Sealey and Antoine S. Lussier (Winnipeg, Manitoba: Pemmican Publications, 1975) and *Cornerstone Colony, Selkirk's Contribution to the Canadian West*, by Grant MacEwan (Saskatoon, Saskatchewan, Canada: Western Producer Prairie Books, 1977).

Part Three: The Pacific Coast and Hawaii

XII. *California*

Here, as elsewhere, the WPA guide for the state was a useful general resource. Samuel Eliot Morison's *European Discovery of America: The Southern Voyages*, covers the early exploration of the coast in a thorough—and fascinating—account.

The classic *Two Years Before the Mast* by Richard Henry Dana, Jr., quoted repeatedly in this section for its illuminating comments on the California coast in the early nineteenth centruy, has, of course, been published in many editions. These quotations are from that published by World Publishing Co., New York, in 1946. Anyone who has missed this wonderful book should hasten to enoy it. Samuel Eliot Morison in his classic *Maritime History of Massachusetts* discusses the role of the New England traders in early nineteenth-century California. As ever, he is fascinating.

The early years of San Diego are described in the *Story of San Diego* by Walter Gifford Smith (San Diego, California: City Printing Co., 1892). Written before the city became a port of consequence, the account is of considerable interest. San Diego has been well covered; another book readers are likely to enoy is *Harbor in the Sun* by Max Miller.

The quotations about emigrant travel on the *Euterpe* are from *Star of India, Log of an Iron Ship* by Jerry MacMullen (San Diego, California: Maritime Museum Association of San Diego, 1982). Filled with

facts ably presented, the book adds a great deal to the visitor's appreciation of the ship.

The background of the early years of San Pedro's development of an open bay into a great port are described in an interesting little book of local history: *Sails into Rails* by John M. Houston (San Pedro, California: published by the author, 1979). The same subject is covered in massive detail with illustrations in the *Port of Los Angeles* by Charles F. Queenan (Los Angeles Harbor Department, 1983).

The report from Sebastiano Viscaino on Monterey harbor is quoted in *The Early Maritime History of Monterey* by Jonathan Spaulding (published by the author, 1984). Spaulding's book is itself an interesting account of what was once the capital of California.

Of books about San Francisco, there is no end: most readers will be happy with *San Francisco Bay: A Pictorial History* by J. H. Kemble (New York: Bonanza Books, 1957).

XIII. *The Pacific Northwest*

Astoria, by Washington Irving, quoted in this section, has been published in many different editions. The book is of particular interest, not only because of Irving's professional skill, but becasue he knew personally some of the participants in the project.

The John Holt quotation is from Samuel Eliot Morison's *Maritime History of Massachusetts*, which also has a most interesting description of the Yankee role in the Northwest fur trade. The Yaquina Bay account is from *Yaquina Bay 1778-1978* by Darlene Castle and others, an illustrated local history written for the anniversary (Newport, Oregon: Lincoln County Historical Society, 1979).

The development of the Columbia River basin is ably described in *Empire of the Columbia, a History of the Pacific Northwest* by Dorothy O. Johansen and C. M. Gates, (New York: Harper and Row, 1967). Also consulted and found of value were *A History of the Pacific Northwest* by George W. Fuller (New York: Knopf, 1966) and the heavily illustrated *The Northwest Coast* by Richard L. Williams (New York: Time-Life Books, 1973). *Sternwheelers up the Columbia* by Randall V. Mills (Lincoln, Nebraska: University of Nebraska Press) recounts the great days of steam navigation on the river.

Puget's Sound by Murray Morgan (Seattle, Washington: University of Washington Press, 1979) gives a most interesting account of the early exploration of the Sound and the development of the competing cities of Tacoma and Seattle. *Northwest Gateway, the Story of the Port of Seattle* by Archie Binns (New York:

Doubleday, Doran, 1941) concentrates on the winner of the contest.

For the disaster-minded (most of us?), *Shipwrecks of the Pacific Coast* by James A. Gibbs (Portland, Oregon: Binford and Most, 1981) will supply an ample number—reminding us that this is one of the most dangerous coasts in the world.

XIV. *Canada on the Pacific*

Oceans of Destiny—A Concise History of the North Pacific 1500-1978 by J. Arthur Lower gives a very broad view of this important region from a strong Canadian perspective (Vancouver, British Columbia: University of British Columbia Press, 1978). "The Hudson's Bay Company and the Fur Trade: 1670-1870," a special issue of the H.B.C. magazine, *The Beaver* (Winnipeg, Manitoba: Hudson's Bay Company, Autumn, 1983), covers the important activities of the company in the Pacific Northwest as well as elsewhere. The account, heavily illustrated, makes very interesting reading—of course, emphasizing the outlook of the company itself. The H.B.C.'s famous ship, *The Beaver*, is given a full biography in *SS Beaver, The Ship That Saved the West* by Derek Pethick (Vancouver, British Columbia: Mitchell Press, 1970). Three guesses as to whom/what the West was saved from.

An overview of the province's maritime activities is provided in *The Ports of British Columbia* by Agnes Rothery (Garden City, New York: Doubleday, Doran, 1943). A graphic demonstration of the dangers of this coast is contained in *A Guide to the Shipwrecks Along the West Coast Trail* by R.E. Wells (Sooka, British Columbia: 1982). The 'trail' runs only 41 miles along the outer shore of Vancouver Island, but along it the hiker will find the remains of no less than 24 ships that have been identified.

XV. *The Sandwich Islands (Hawaii)*

The quotation from a Japanese pilot is from an information sheet supplied by the National Park Service entitled "It began on a battleship in Pearl Harbor . . . and ended on a battleship in Tokyo Bay." It was written by Commander Edward Peary Stafford, U.S.N. (Ret.) and gives a succinct account of the Pearl Harbor disaster.

Readers interested in the remarkable navigational achievements of the native Hawaiians will enjoy *Polynesian Seafaring* by Edward Dodd (New York: Dodd, Mead, 1972).

A full account of the history of the ship *Falls of Clyde* will be found in *Historic Ships of the World* by William C. Heine (New York: G.P. Putnam & Sons, 1977).

Permission to quote from the following copyrighted work is received and appreciated.
Quotation on: —

Page 10   from "A Note on the Collection" by John Ratte, editor; *Models of American Sailing Ships;* copyright 1961 by Addison Gallery of American Art, Andover, Massachusetts.

Page 37   from *A Maritime History of Massachusetts* by Samuel Eliot Morison, copyright renewed 1969 by Samuel Eliot Morison. Copyright 1921, 1941, 1949, 1961 by Samuel Eliot Morison. Reprinted by permission of Houghton Mifflin Company.

Page 88   By permission from *The Hudson* by Carl Carmer, published by Holt, Rinehart and Winston.

Page 110   from "The Ships of Saint John: by Bliss Carmen, reprinted by permission of Dodd, Mead & Company, Inc. from *Bliss Carmen's Poems.*

Page 115   from "Some of My Experiences at Sea, Part I" by John Hemphill, *The Island Magazine*, No. 11, published by the Prince Edward Island Museum and Heritage Foundation.

Page 120   from *Samuel de Champlain* by Samuel Eliot Morison, published by Little, Brown and Company.

Page 120   from *Acadia—The Geography of Early Nova Scotia* by Andrew Hill Clark, published by the University of Wisconsin Press.

Page 142   from "Maritime Philadelphia" by Marion V. Brewington, in *Philadelphia Port of History, 1609-1837*, courtesy of the Philadelphia Maritime Museum.

Page 196   from *Never Caught, The Story of a Blockade Runner* by Captain Roberts (C. Augustas Hobart-Hampton), published by The Blockade Runner Museum, Inc.

Page 203   from *Aircraft Carrier* by J. Bryan III. Reprinted with permission of the author.

Page 227   from "Whiffs of the Ohio River at Cincinnati" in *Good Morning America* by Carl

Sandburg, published by Harcourt Brace Jovanovich, Inc.

Page 251 from *Long Ships Passing* by Walter Havighurst. Copyright 1940 by Macmillan Publishing Company, renewed 1970 by Walter Havighurst. Reprinted with permission of the publisher.

Page 257 from the book *Haida* by William Sclater, published by Paperjacks Ltd., 330 Steelcase Rd. E. Markham, Ontario.

Page 260 from the narrative of Mrs. Mary A. Palmer, courtesy of Buffalo and Erie County Historical Society.

Page 260 from *Lake Erie* by Harlan Hatcher; copyright 1945 by Macmillan Publishing Company, renewed 1973 by Harlan Hatcher.

Page 281 from *Lake Michigan* by Milo M. Quaife; copyright 1944 by Macmillan Publishing Company, renewed 1972 by Helen Bowden, Dorothy Martin, and Mary Louise Tuttle.

Page 286 from *Twenty Million Tons under the Sea* by Rear Admiral Daniel V. Gallery, U.S.N. Copyright by estate of D.V. Gallery.

Page 290 from "An Unfinished Voyage" by C.T. McCutcheon, Jr., published in *Wooden Boat* No. 52, May/June 1983. Reprinted with permission of the author.

Page 292 from *Lake Superior* by Grace Lee Nute; copyright 1944 by Macmillan Publishing Company, renewed 1972 by Grace Lee Nute.

Page 294 from *Lake Superior* by Grace Lee Nute; copyright 1944 by Macmillan Publishing Company, renewed 1972 by Grace Lee Nute.

Page 314 Material quoted from *Star of India* by Jerry MacMullen. Copyright 1979 by Maritime Museum Association of San Diego; all rights reserved.

Page 320 quoted in *The Early Maritime History of Monterey* by Jonathan Spaulding, published by Allen Knight Maritime Museum, Monterey, 1984.

Page 333 John Boit quoted in *A Maritime History of Massachusetts* by Samuel Eliot Morison, copyright renewed 1969 by Samuel Eliot Morison. Copyright 1921, 1941, 1961 by Samuel Eliot Morison. Reprinted by permission of Houghton Mifflin Company.

INDEX

PHOTO CREDITS

Figure 1   Courtesy of U.S.S. Constitution Museum Foundation

Figure 2   Photo by Ulrike Welsch from Boston Tea Party Ship Museum

Figure 3   Peabody Museum of Salem, Photo by Mark Sexton

Figure 4   Gloucester Fishermen's Museum, Gloucester, MA

Figure 5   Maine Maritime Museum

Figure 6   The Kendall Whaling Museum

Figure 7   Copyright Pilgrim Society All Rights Reserved

Figure 8   Photo courtesy of Nantucket Historical Society

Figure 9   Old Dartmouth Historical Society Whaling Museum

Figure 10   Marine Museum at Fall River, Inc.

Figure 11   Claire White Peterson Photo, Mystic Seaport, Mystic, CT

Figure 12   The Connecticut River Foundation

Figure 13   Sag Harbor Whaling and Historical Museum

Figure 14   Photograph copyright Mitch Carucci: 1985, All Rights Reserved by the Photographer; Suffolk, Marine Museum, West Sayville, L.I.

Figure 15   Photo by Joel Greenberg, South Street Seaport

Figure 16   Intrepid Sea-Air-Space Museum

Figure 17   Paterson Museum, Paterson, NJ

Figure 18   American Merchant Marine Museum

Figure 19   F.D.R. Library, Hyde Park, NY

Figure 20   Hudson River Maritime Center, Kingston, NY 12401

Figure 21   Photo by Dick Blume, courtesy of the Erie Canal Museum

Figure 22   Courtesy of Shelburne Museum, Shelburne, VT

Figure 23   Environment Canada Parks, Cartier-Brebeuf National Historic Park, Quebec Park

Figure 24   New Brunswick Museum Photo

Figure 25   Maritime Museum of the Atlantic, Halifax, Nova Scotia

Figure 26   Yarmouth County Museum

Figure 27   Courtesy of New Jersey Department of Environmental Protection, Division of Parks & Forestry

Figure 28   The Mohawk Corporation, Wilmington, DE

Figure 29   Chesapeake Bay Maritime Museum

Figure 30   U.S. Naval Academy Museum, Annapolis, MD 21402

Figure 31   Baltimore Museum of Industry

Figure 32   U.S. Navy Memorial Museum, Washington, D.C. Navy Yard

Figure 33   National Museum of American History, Smithsonian Institution; Washington, D.C.

Figure 34   St. Mary's City Commission, P.O. Box 39, St. Mary's City, MD 20686

Figure 35   Jamestown-Yorktown Foundation Photo

Figure 36   Courtesy of The Mariners Museum, Newport News, VA

Figure 37   Elizabeth II State Historic Site

Figure 38   William Russ, Division of Travel and Tourism

Figure 39   Courtesy of the New Hanover County Museum, Wilmington, NC

Figure 44   Ohio Historical Society

Figure 45   Lin Caufield Photographers, Louisville, KY

Figure 46   Photo: Wolfgang Weber

Figure 47   Courtesy of Nebraska State Historical Society

Figure 48   Buffalo and Erie County Naval & Servicemen's Park, Buffalo, NY

Figure 50   Mackinac Island State Park Commission, Mackinaw City, MI

Figure 51   Collingwood Museum, Collingwood, Ontario

Figure 52   Museum of Science and Industry, Chicago, IL

Figure 53   Manitowoc Maritime Museum, 809 South 8th St., Manitowoc, WI 54220

Figure 54   Canal Park Marine Museum

Figure 56   Manitoba Museum of Man and Nature, 190 Rupert Avenue, Winnipeg, Manitoba R3B 0N2

Figure 57   Ken Clark, San Diego, CA

Figure 58   Official Navy Photograph Sea Bee Museum, Port Hueneme, CA

Figure 59   Photo: Joanie Morgan

Figure 60   Columbia River Maritime Museum, Astoria, OR

Figure 61   Center for Wooden Boats; Seattle, WA, Photo by Marty Loken

Figure 62   Photo courtesy of British Columbia Provincial Museum

Figure 63   National Maritime Museum Photo